STUDIES IN ECONOMICS AND POLITICAL SCIENCE

Edited by

THE DIRECTOR OF THE LONDON SCHOOL OF ECONOMICS AND
POLITICAL SCIENCE

No. 103 in the series of Monographs by writers connected with
the London School of Economics and Political Science.

THE ECONOMIC DEVELOPMENT

OF THE

BRITISH OVERSEAS EMPIRE

VOLUME TWO

Lilian C A Knowles

The
Economic Development
of the
British Overseas Empire

By the late

L. C. A. KNOWLES

M.A., LL.M. (Cantab.), Litt.D., Trinity College, Dublin
Professor of Economic History in the University of London
Author of " The Industrial and Commercial Revolutions in Great Britain
during the Nineteenth Century "

and

C. M. KNOWLES, LL.B.

Of the Middle Temple, Barrister-at-Law.

VOLUME TWO

COMPARATIVE VIEW OF DOMINION PROBLEMS
CANADA

LONDON
GEORGE ROUTLEDGE & SONS, LTD.
BROADWAY HOUSE : 68–74 CARTER LANE, E.C.
1930

The third and final volume will be devoted to the Economic Development of Australasia and South Africa.

PRINTED IN GREAT BRITAIN
BY STEPHEN AUSTIN & SONS, LTD., HERTFORD.

PREFACE

A T the time of her quite unexpected death in 1926 my
wife had published the first volume of the economic
history of the British Empire which she had planned and
had completed a substantial part of the manuscript of the
second. Knowing how great her desire would have been
that her work should be completed, and there being
abundant evidence of the interest with which the
appearance of the remaining volumes was awaited, I
accepted it as a duty to do what I could to carry to a
conclusion the task which she had undertaken, and to do
it so far as possible in accordance with her own plans.

Of the present volume, Part I, which embodies a comparative view of Dominion problems, is hers, with the
exception of Chapter VII, which was written by Dr Allan
McPhee. She also left the manuscript of the first six
chapters of Part II. Those chapters bring the economic
history of Canada down to 1867, the year of confederation.
It was at that point that I took up the story, and
accordingly I have to accept responsibility for the account
of what my wife called the National Period in Canada's
economic history, with the exception of Chapter XIII,
and the important section in Chapter XVII dealing with
wheat, which have been contributed by Dr McPhee.

I have followed the plan indicated by my wife in her
Preface to the first volume in that I have quoted freely
from articles, speeches, reports and other documents which
are not commonly accessible. I have been able to do this
mainly by making free use of the Dominions Office and
Colonial Office Library, with its wealth of Dominion
official reports, Parliamentary debates and other
primary authorities. In my search there for original
authorities the assistance of the Librarian, Mr E. E.
Wilkinson, M.B.E., and his staff has been invaluable.
Invariably they have been willing to take any amount of
trouble for the purpose of discovering and making available
the information sought.

Dr Allan McPhee assisted my wife in her researches from
the beginning, and I know how warmly she would have

wished to acknowledge that early and heavy work. In addition to the contributions to the body of the volume mentioned above, Dr McPhee compiled the two Bibliographies which are included in the present volume, and also the Index. I am glad to have the opportunity of acknowledging how much the volume owes to his knowledge of sources, his powers of research and his unfailing accuracy and industry.

The third and concluding volume will include the economic history of Australasia and South Africa. My wife's lecture notes on the subject are in existence, and I hope to be able to use them as the basis of the remainder of the work.

C. M. KNOWLES.

PROFESSOR LILIAN KNOWLES
1870–1926

The Law Tripos, Part I, of 1894 excited an unusual degree of interest far beyond the bounds of Cambridge, the reason being that for the first time a woman was in Class I and was placed " equal to 2 ". The interest was heightened, and it was felt that the movement for wider educational opportunities for women—then a struggling cause—had achieved a real triumph when it was found that the same woman had the previous year won a First Class in the Historical Tripos (she was, in fact, first in the First Class) and that " Tomn, L. C. A., Girton " was a Double First. The name that alone was above Miss Lilian Tomn in the Law Tripos was dismissed with but scant notice by the Press : " Mr. Jan Christian Smuts, Scholar of Christ's College, who heads the tripos and takes the George Long Prize, is a Dutchman from the Cape ".[1] On the other hand, the portrait of the Girtonian who was " equal to 2 " was published in scores of newspapers and periodicals together with such details of her twenty-three years of life as could be gleaned. Those who knew her will understand the hilarity with which she saw herself exhibited in a religious organ between portraits of M. Stambouloff and Prince Ferdinand of Bulgaria. The portraits of her may well have helped to destroy the hoary superstition that women with intellectual interests were blessed with few other attractions. In the course of his speech at the capping ceremony at the University of Otago, New Zealand, the Chancellor, according to *The Otago Daily Times*, called attention to " the latest triumph of woman " and continued : " I daresay you have seen in the English papers pictures and a description of this lady, a Miss Tomn. The pictures show that she is exceptionally good-looking and the descriptions of her which have appeared in the papers announce that she is very particular about her frocks."

The story of her early life was easily ascertained and was capable of quite brief statement. Lilian Charlotte Anne Tomn came of a Cornish family of the smaller landowning class, so as a matter of

---

[1] The two Firsts met again in sufficiently dramatic circumstances nearly a quarter of a century later. Hearing of his companion in the 1894 Law Tripos through a mutual friend, the head of that list invited " equal to 2 " to dinner at his headquarters in London. He was then General the Rt. Hon. Jan Christian Smuts, and a member of the Imperial War Cabinet. An anticipated air raid gave additional zest to the dinner.

course she became an excellent horsewoman and a keen rider to hounds. She received her early education at Truro High School and there her outstanding intellectual capacity became quickly apparent. " I can see her now," wrote a friend of her mother's, " called up time after time with renewed clapping to take nearly all the First Prizes."

The volumes she received as prizes bear evidence that she actually read them and her childhood's books which still survive indicate a developed taste for reading at a very early age. But she was no sentimental Miss. Her taste in poetry inclined in favour of the more full-blooded passages in Macaulay's *Horatius*. Novels which conjured up visions of the past appealed to her always. A duly inscribed copy of one of Ainsworth's novels presented to her by her nurse on her thirteenth birthday was, it is pretty safe to surmise, the choice of the donee herself ; and in after years many a student was sent back to the older novelists with renewed zest when she pointed out how *Quentin Durward* served to illustrate town life in the Middle Ages, and *Romola* the brilliance of Florence ; how *Ivanhoe* helped to visualize a little of the Manorial System, *Westward Ho!* the age of discovery, and Mrs. Gaskell's *Lois the Witch* the conditions of the early Colonies ; how *Bleak House* served very well to picture the insanitary condition of the nineteenth century towns, as also did *Martin Chuzzlewit*, while *Oliver Twist* was excellent for the Poor Law ; and how Mrs. Gaskell's *North and South* or Charlotte Bronte's *Shirley* helped with the effects of the coming of machinery.

Here, as in many other characteristics, it is possible to see that the child was mother of the woman. Her early preference for stories of action rather than of sentiment is paralleled in later life by her fondness for Kipling's books and her inability to read what she styled " problemy " novels. She found in her early life in the country plenty to stimulate her natural intellectual curiosity. She became a competent botanist and her love of gardening and her instinct for understanding plants and their ways remained with her throughout her life, so that whenever she returned to Cornwall for brief vacations she was always able to discuss crops with farmers and to give directions to gardeners with the authority that came from knowledge. She acquired a good deal of natural history by direct observation rather than from natural history books. Animals she loved and understood, and they loved her ; and if animal survival after death is really a fact, certain it is that she and her wire-haired terrier " Susan ", who had a place in her funeral procession, will meet on the other side.

Her lively letters, her inexhaustible stream of racy conversation, her wit and her fund of anecdote are also remembered as part of the make-up of her vivid personality in her schooldays as well as at Girton and later in her London years.

A schoolgirl epistle of hers describes how she was one of a school cricket team that " went to play Plymouth "—presumably a rather free description of the match. " We had lunch in the middle of the match, cold salmon and raspberry-and-currant tart which I appreciated so thoroughly that the captain of our side sent down a message to say : ' Someone please remind that wretched little Tomn girl that she has got to play and field after lunch and that there will be tea before she goes home.' I made top score after lunch."

She was persuaded to take a Sunday School class while still a girl in Truro. The results of her teaching must have been unusual, for, according to one of the members of the class, " Miss Tomn had taught them everything that there was in the Bible and most about everything out of it ".

When first she came to London she went for an evening a week to an East End Board School where the purpose of the organization that enlisted her services seems to have been to organize recreation for the children. All that remains on record of that experience is the story of the boy whom she was instructing in the manipulation of coloured crayons. The subject of their joint efforts is unknown, but it was described by the pupil as, "Beautiful, like a lady in a bar ".

Occasionally she imported a little unaccustomed liveliness into the rather staid pages of the *Truro High School News Letter*. Here, for example, are some of the episodes in her description of the Jubilee of 1897 : " Nobody in England ' did ' that Jubilee harder than I. I say it with admiration and satisfaction. . . . I was in London in June, 1897, and I determined to see all that was to be seen. . . . On Sunday I decided to go to Westminster Abbey, where the House of Lords were going in state to return thanks. I tried to get in by the canons' entrance, but the man at the door said only peeresses by this way and peeresses with *tickets*. . . . I got in from the side somehow and a stalwart policeman grabbed hold of me and shoved me in head foremost. . . . All the seats were filled with the aristocracy, which made me feel almost an anarchist. . . . I was wedged next a curate. I could not find the psalms for the 20th of June in my prayer-book, so he obligingly shared his book with me. The choir, however, came to an end before we did. I thought it odd. Then the curate apologized humbly and said he was afraid he had been misleading me, we had been singing the evening psalms by mistake. . . . I heard a bustle outside, so I went out to get a little air and saw the House of Commons coming in state, four in a row, to go to church at St. Margaret's, next door to Westminster. A burly policeman said to me, ' You must move on, lady.' I pretended not to hear. He looked dubious, and I smiled at him and he let me alone. The square was guarded by volunteers, and no one was allowed inside except the Members, some policemen, and me. . . . I was up by 4.30 next morning to attend the Jubilee Rehearsal at St. Paul's. Another lady in our house said she would like to come too. So she stayed awake all night in order to be ready in time. All the servants went with us on the strength of my information that there was going to be a rehearsal at 6. Well, we waited till 7 in the morning and nothing happened. Then I asked a policeman. He said that such a thing as a rehearsal at 6 in the morning had never been contemplated, it was 6 in the evening. So we went home— cross. . . . I thought that as I did not feel like settling down to anything I might as well go and see the Queen arrive at Paddington. So I made my way there and found an enterprising man by the Station letting out standing room on a small box, 1s. each. I paid my shilling and got up. There were already several on the box. Then the man disappeared. The police said that we were obstructing and must get down. . . . Then I went home and went to bed to rise at 5 next morning to go to my seat in the Borough betimes— there were such awful tales afloat of the blocks and crowds to be expected. . . . I carried a ticket in my pocket with my address on it, and the directions, ' If maimed, please take to nearest hospital, and send word to . . . my address—if dead, please wire Mrs. Tomn, Killagorden.' So I was prepared for any emergency."

On her father's death her mother took her and her sister on a three years' leisurely tour through Germany, France, and Italy, which enabled her to acquire that mastery of the three languages, and in particular German, which was to stand her in such good stead in her later researches in economic history. The family returned to their Cornish home and she persuaded her mother to let her go into residence at Girton in 1890, a step which was a distinct breakaway in the family history.

In after years Girton was to her " a memory of good times and dear friends and hard work ". The fame of her hats will apparently live as long as the memory of her Double First. She had her moments of depression. At one time she seems even to have had thoughts of " chucking the Examination ". Her tutor had no misgivings. It was true, he said, that she was wanting in style and finish, but that could not keep her out of the First Class if she worked steadily to the end. Of her capacity for work he had no fear, and she " needed more curb than spur ".

After Girton there seems to have been a period of indecision before she found her true course. She had visions of breaking down the barriers which excluded women from a legal career. Probably she was the first woman to read in Chambers and to follow up that experience by six months in the office of a firm of solicitors. Sir Frederick Pollock, with whom she arranged to read, regarded it as " rather a novel experiment ", but agreed to put a room in his set of chambers at her disposal " and with my wife's help, make it a little more habitable than the ordinary pupil room ". To him it was " refreshing to find someone interested in law for its own sake ". But she was a quarter of a century too soon, and she saw that she must give up any hope of being able to pursue the practice of the law.

Then came the golden opportunity that decided her career. She was invited to assist " that stimulating scholar and noble man, William Cunningham " (the quotation is from a letter written by another distinguished economic historian) in his *Western Civilisation in its Economic Aspects (Mediaeval and Modern Times)*, and in the preparation of the third edition of his *Growth of English Industry and Commerce in Modern Times* which had been out of print some years. In the Preface to the latter work, which was published in 1903, Dr. Cunningham paid generous tribute to Miss Lilian Tomn's " unwearied assistance " and to " her unrivalled knowledge of the sources of English Economic History ". The acquaintanceship begun at the outset of her Girton career ripened into a great friendship during their co-operation in the production of the new edition of his *magnum opus*. Her bump of reverence was not largely developed, but so far as she was capable of reverencing any man she reverenced Dr. Cunningham, and certain it is that to no other man would she accord the title " my Master ". Nor was her admiration for him based merely on his scholarship. She understood his character as few did. She knew how well he practised what he preached in his *Gospel of Work*, a book she was never tired of commending to any she saw hesitating on the threshold of their careers ; and she knew that as well as Cunningham the distinguished economic historian there was Cunningham the humble Christian and devoted parish priest.

Her work on Dr. Cunningham's books introduced her to her career as an economic historian. At her death she was busy on her own book in which the story of the economic development of the British Empire was to be told. In the period between was built up her reputation as (in the words of her chief) " a teacher and a great teacher " and as the author of books which broke new ground in economic history.

Her first experience as a lecturer in Economic History came to her as the result of an experiment for which that notable headmaster, J. L. Paton, of University College School, was responsible. He invited her to give two lectures a week in Economic History to a picked class of intelligent boys, and he later estimated her success in words which show that she speedily developed those characteristics which made her a great teacher : " She has from the first secured and held the interest of her class in a subject which is new to schools and which might seem at first to be unpromising from its connection with ' the dismal science '. She has got excellent work out of her classes and, what is more to the purpose, has got them into the way of working out a subject for themselves, of going to first-hand authorities and knowing how they should be used, of how to think out a question, and how to put their thoughts on paper ; in a word she has been successful in communicating to her class the spirit of research." She made the acquaintance of classes of students of maturer years as occasional deputy for Mr. W. A. S. Hewins, first Director of the London School of Economics, and when he left the School and Mr. (now Sir Halford) Mackinder becamed Director she was selected to take over the late Director's teaching work. Accordingly, in 1904, the Senate of London University appointed Miss Lilian Tomn to the Teachership in Modern Economic History at the London School of Economics and Political Science for a period of three years, at the end of which period it was to be " freely reconsidered ". In October, 1907, as Mrs. Lilian Knowles, she was re-appointed " with the status of appointed Teacher ". Believing, presumably, that example teaches better than precept, she constituted herself an illustration of the doctrine which she steadily upheld, that the mere fact of marriage ought not to disqualify a woman from pursuing any career for which she is otherwise fitted. It must be admitted that she carried the position with some degree of characteristic audacity. She regarded her marriage as nobody's concern but her own, and she merely intimated her change of personal status in order that her change of name might be noted for the purpose of the University records and the School of Economics syllabuses. Certainly she had no cause to complain of any narrowness of view on the part of the authorities. Two months later she was given the title of Reader in Economic History in the University of London. In 1919 she was co-opted a Governor of the London School of Economics with its incidental financial liability which was, however, " limited to £1 sterling " as she was duly informed. In July, 1921, she attained the summit of her ambition and received the title of Professor of Economic History in the University of London. A former chief of hers reported the event in slightly unacademic but quite accurate terms : " Dr. Knowles has been made a Professor and is much bucked up ". During the period 1920–4 she was Dean of the Faculty of Economics, and so, still pioneering, became the first woman Dean of a Faculty in the University. There had been women Senators, Professors, Readers, Chairmen of Boards and so forth, but hitherto no woman Dean. In 1925 she was elected to the Council of the Royal Historical Society. She had already been for several years a member of the Council of the Royal Economic Society.

She had to wait for the revolution in the status of women which was one of the results of the Great War before she received from Cambridge University the M.A. and LL.M. degrees she had fairly won many years before, but in 1905 she took advantage of Dublin's more liberal policy and applied for and was given the degree of *Doctor in Litteris* in that University.

She thoroughly enjoyed her academic appointments and distinctions, partly for the reason that she was vindicating the claims of women to equal opportunities with men, but mainly for their own sake, for she was an enthusiast in the cause of education. " I would rather be commemorated by a beautiful schoolroom than by a dozen glass windows in a church," she once announced to a mixed and startled audience of parents and scholars.

Her opinion, gained from reading many ancient Blue Books and much contemporary literature, was that all last century our ancestors were far too much afraid of the effects of education. The moral evils, the economic insubordination, the revolutionary tendencies, the desertion of the home which they foresaw had not eventuated nor had any of their fears been justified.

Her views on the nature and purpose of education were her own and they were not altogether acceptable to those who wanted what she termed " a merely bread and butter training " for their children. She found, as she told an audience less than six months before her death, " the most extraordinary belief abroad that the teacher could work miracles with any child in eight or nine years." The school was expected to do all that the Church was formerly expected to do. It was supposed to instil good morals which should last a man or woman for life and make him or her suitable for this world and the next. The school was also expected to provide such instruction that the boy or girl on leaving school would be able to earn a good living and moreover would be turned out a civilized human being with good manners. But the schoolmaster and the teacher had a wider vision. The aim of the modern school was to teach boys and girls to live, not to make a living ; that is to say, the schoolmaster was trying to train for wise and happy living. Education to the teacher was a thing of the spirit. The teacher, whether at the school or the University, was in many ways the priest of to-day. A lot of the civilizing, humanizing work that the Church used to do had been taken over by the schools. "The utmost the teacher can do is to give you a key with which to unlock the door of life yourself. From Geography you get a sense of space ; from History a sense of time ; from Science a sense of power, of the control of man over nature ; from Literature a sense of pleasure in good writing ; but these things do not last unless you tend them yourself in after life."

In both the manner and the matter of her lectures she was original. "Her lectures . . . were quite unlike anyone else's, and as a rule far more memorable. Her handling of students individually and in class was as effective as it was vigorous : she at once dominated and bullied them and gave herself up wholly to their service in a way that there was no withstanding." [1] And again : "She was a born teacher and her style in lecturing was all her own, vigorous, violent, full of asides upon every subject under the sun, but with an unerring power to seize the point of a thing, to see trends of development as a whole, to pick out what was important and ram it home, and never to lose the wood in the trees. Disdaining second-hand information herself, for she had to build up her subject when there were as yet no books upon it, she always made her students work on original materials, and in those second and third year discussion classes, which no one who attended them ever forgot, she could make a Blue Book as lively as a detective story." [2] In steam power and the control which it gave man over nature she found as much poetry as in the skylark or the rathe primrose, and in the history of the manufacture of the clothes people wear, that is to say, the history of the textile industry, as much romance as in the struggles of parties or the decapitation of Kings.

Having shown that Economic History could be made interesting, that indeed it was full of romance and colour and that it was no mere accumulation of facts but was capable of yielding ideas and of throwing up generalizations, she proceeded to expand its boundaries. Hereon let her speak in her own words : "When I first began to teach Economic History at the London School of Economics, it was held by such great authorities as Dr. Cunningham and Mr. L. L. Price that English economic history could not be taught after 1846. No one in England at that time taught the foreign economic history of the nineteenth or any other century. I have therefore had to break ground for the nineteenth century

---

[1] Sir William Beveridge, K.C.B., Director of the London School of Economics, in *Economica*, June, 1926.
[2] E.E.P. in the *Girton Review*, May, 1926.

with scarcely any books to help out other than Webb's *History of Trade Unionism*. The result was that what was usually taught at other places as far as recent Economic History was concerned was Labour, and that only one side of Labour, viz., Trade Unionism. I have endeavoured in my teaching to stress the overwhelming importance of transport, colonial development and agriculture, while allotting the social and labour side a very important place. It has, however, meant a great deal of pioneer work, especially in connection with the course on foreign economic development, which I have endeavoured to treat comparatively. I think my students realize that English Economic History by itself is one-sided, and that England must be treated as part of a great Western civilization acting on others Powers and being reacted on in turn by them."

The results of this " great deal of pioneer work " were exhibited in the courses of lectures she compiled and delivered on the Economic Development, first, of the Great Powers, and then of the British Overseas Empire. In her obituary of Dr. Cunningham, she wrote : " He used to say to me when we were labouring at the *Growth of English Industry and Commerce*, ' If I can only get this finished, my subject will never die. Seeley's subject tended to lapse with his death because he never left a text-book. This book will be altered and re-written, but I have sketched out the scheme and laid the foundations. Economic history teaching will always go on.' " [1] She had sketched out a scheme and laid the foundations of the wider Economic History, and she also determined that she would write text-books so that there should be a solid foundation on which others could build. She had nearly completed a book on *The Economic Development of France, Germany, Russia and the United States in the Nineteenth Century*, when she suddenly turned aside to write *The Economic Development of the British Overseas Empire*. She brought the first volume to a triumphant conclusion. According to one who speaks with authority,[2] the book " dealt mainly with the unexplored field of the British Tropics " and " will remain as a permanent addition to economic science ".

The book on the Empire had been preceded by her *Industrial and Commercial Revolutions in Great Britain during the Nineteenth Century*, "the best account that we have of the economic changes that followed the great inventions of the eighteenth and nineteenth centuries." [3] The matter of the volume, " four hundred pages of

---

[1] *Economic Journal*, xxix, pp. 390–3.
[2] Sir William Beveridge, K.C.B., in *Economica*, June, 1926.
[3] *Times Literary Supplement*, 13th Nov., 1924. She had many years before edited an English edition of Deploige's *Referendum in Switzerland,*

sound learning." [1] was original work, but the subject was pioneer work to a less degree than the subsequent book. The two works were however not unconnected. The later volume " takes the territories of the British Empire as a whole and the tropical Dependencies in particular, and traces their development under the stimulus of contact with the new economic civilization which was the subject of the earlier study ".[2] Both books exhibited characteristics not often found together : " the gift of happy generalization and the gift of faithful presentment of details ".[3]

If it was not until the later years of her life that she found time to write books of her own, so that although it was outstanding in quality her own literary output was comparatively small in quantity, it has to be remembered that she scattered ideas with a lavish hand and patiently assisted others out of the fullness of her own knowledge to produce books on a diversity of subjects. The earlier books published by students working under her included such a variety of subjects as *English Apprenticeship and Child Labour*, *Emigration from the United Kingdom to North America*, *The Commercial Relations between England and Scotland in the Seventeenth Century*, *The History of Bradford*, *The Working Life of Women in the Seventeenth Century*, *Irish Land Legislation*, and *The Development of Agriculture in Egypt after* 1870. At one time a dozen works on various aspects of economic history were approaching completion under her supervision, so that she would be criticising the manuscript of *The Economic History of London* one hour ; listening to a chapter on *The History of the Engineering Trade* the next, and helping to adorn the tale of *The Industrial Revolution in Scotland* the third. Another day she would be giving advice how to follow out the economic development of some part of Africa, or struggling to reduce to passable English the effort of a foreign student to present some aspect of the economic history of his own country.

Her training, her special knowledge, and her powers of speech seemed pre-eminently to qualify her to be one of the earliest of the women members of the House of Commons. Rather unexpectedly, however, she never had any ambition to enter politics. A political campaign conducted by her would have been a memorable event, but although hers was a combative nature, and although, in the words of one of her colleagues, " she went out to fight like an Elizabethan galleon under full sail, with all her guns firing and all

the translator being Mr. C. P. (now Sir Charles) Trevelyan. Her growing interest in economic history, however, soon thrust political science into the background.

[1] Professor Clapham, in *Economic Journal*, June, 1921.
[2] Ibid.
[3] Professor Egerton, in *Economic Journal*, March, 1925.

her trumpets sounding," she had no liking for the conditions of political warfare. She had perhaps a rather exaggerated view of the jealousies, the pettinesses and the insincerities of political life. Her one political ambition was to bring about a wise, sensible and unprejudiced understanding of what the British Empire means, and she felt that she could better accomplish that purpose through her writings and in the classroom than from the political platform.

She was, however, given the opportunity, which she valued very highly, of public service of a kind more congenial to her temperament than party politics. She was a member of the Committee appointed in March, 1918, by the Chancellor of the Exchequer, Mr. Bonar Law, " to enquire into and report upon (i) the actual increase since June, 1914, in the cost of living to the working classes and (ii) any counterbalancing factors (apart from increase of wages) which may have arisen under War conditions." Lord Sumner was Chairman and among her colleagues were Professor Sir W. J. Ashley, Professor Bowley, and Mrs. Pember Reeves.

In the following year the Royal Commission on the Income Tax was appointed, and to her great satisfaction " Our Trusty and Well-beloved Lilian Charlotte Anne Knowles, Doctor of Letters, Reader in Economic History, University of London ", was " appointed to be one of Our Commissioners for the purpose of the Inquiry into the Income Tax in all its aspects ". She was the only woman member of a Royal Commission of twenty-three.

She devoted her attention in particular to the position by which husband and wife were regarded as one unit for Income Tax purposes, the income of a married woman living with her husband being for this purpose deemed to be the income of the husband, with the consequence that Income Tax was levied on the joint income at a rate higher than that which would be applicable were the incomes assessed separately. The Commission was unable to recommend a change which would have cost the Exchequer a sum variously calculated at £20,000,000 and £45,000,000 a year, and concluded that the aggregation of the incomes of wife and husband should continue to be the rule. To this particular recommendation the one woman member prepared and signed a trenchant and elaborate reservation. To the official view that the income of husband and wife were aggregated in accordance with the outstanding principle of " ability to pay " which governed all questions of taxation, she retorted that the doctrine of " ability to pay " had " become a catchword to squeeze £20,000,000 per annum out of persons who, having been married, cannot separate, and do not usually wish to do so. They are therefore made to suffer because of their fundamental decency and respectability. I agree with my colleagues in thinking that persons are not likely to live together without being married merely to escape Income Tax. Human nature is too fine for that and the relationship of marriage too sacred. It seems, however, to me quite intolerable that the Crown should take advantage of that fact in order to single out these persons for special taxation when they both happen to possess money, and that on the ground that the tie is so close that the woman usually contributes towards the household. ' This is a beautiful relationship, let us tax it extra ' is the result." The conclusion of the whole matter was that she could not concur in a recommendation " by which the State would make it cheaper for certain persons to live together in irregular unions rather than in the honourable estate of matrimony ".

A well-known and distinguished weekly journal, which is given to commenting on affairs of the moment in rather uncompromising terms, fairly let itself go at the expense of the Commission and their Report.

" How many women," it was asked, " have the faintest notion of the meaning of taxes, indirect or direct ? How many of them understand what a contract is, or even what a cheque is, though they have learned to draw them fast enough ? Curiously enough, one of the three members of the Royal Commission on Income Tax who take broad and sane views of taxation is Mrs. Lilian Knowles, Reader in Economic History in London University. But women of this scope of intellect are extremely rare, not one in a million. . . . The Report of the Royal Commission on Income Tax is a very discreditable document. . . . It is evident that the Commissioners were cowed by the stream of Socialist evidence . . . and by the officials of the Treasury and the Inland Revenue. . . . The Commissioners who seem to have kept their wits are Mrs. Knowles, Mr. Geoffrey Marks and Mr. Walter Clark, and significantly enough they are unconnected with politics."

This was a sufficiently flattering testimonial to the woman member of the Commission, but, characteristically enough, she herself resented it. For she was intensely loyal by nature, loyal to her friends, loyal to her University, loyal to her sex, and no amount of flattery had any charm for her when it took the form of holding her up as the exception among women who proved the rule of their general inferiority and so made her the instrument of an attack on her own sex.

Indeed, her loyalty is one of her colleagues' most treasured remembrances of her. One of them, to whose political opinions she was strenuously opposed, has told, by way of illustration, how " when the editor of a London evening paper, who was disposed to make a " stunt " attack on the politics of myself and some other members of the School staff (and who had, perhaps, heard of the violent denunciations with which she sometimes enlivened the old lecturers' common room) sent a female reporter to her to gather matter for publication, the female reporter went out into Clare Market with a singing in her ears."

Intentionally or unintentionally, it seemed to be her lot to be constantly breaking down barriers. One experience of the sort she used to relate with particular gusto, that is to say, how she, a woman, dined at a notable and exclusive West End Club, a Club moreover which was by no means given to dangerous innovations, but, as was pointed out in the Press, when it got hold of the incident, was " a little old-fashioned ".

The chairman of the Income Tax Commission hospitably invited his fellow members to celebrate the completion of their work in a dinner at the Club referred to. Then it was realized that the inclusion of a woman might raise difficulties. She herself suggested that she should stand aside, but the host would not hear of it. Instead, he went to the committee of the Club and a special resolution was passed.

In the words of one evening newspaper, when describing the exploit under the picturesque heading " Revolution at a Club " : " Thus it came to pass, that a *woman* was smuggled into a side entrance of the Club and thence to a private room, where she dined with her fellow members of the Income Tax Commission ; dined, wined, and chatted and chaffed as if she were not the first woman to dine in a man's club. She was Mrs. Lilian Knowles, D.Litt., Reader in Economic History, University of London."

It is perhaps permissible to add that the Chancellor of the Exchequer, who was a distinguished guest at the dinner, had expressed the hope that by some means or other the " one woman member " should be there to meet him, and that she replied to the toast of " The Lady Member of the Commission " in a speech which, it is understood, was by no means the least entertaining item of the evening's programme.

Enough has been said to make it clear that hers was a full and a strenuous life. She was firmly convinced that only a busy life could be a happy life and that much unhappiness was the result merely of aimlessness and idleness. In the course of her address at a prize-giving at a School in Cornwall—and by a strange coincidence it turned out to be her farewell address—she told the audience of her own people who had crowded to hear her : " Life is not worth living if you do not work and work hard. You get no fun out of playing, and no fun out of leisure if you do not work. Your work may be dull, but unless you have the discipline of work there is no fun in life at all. The women who do nothing get so tired of playing and trying to find others to play with them, and they are the most miserable creatures in existence as well as the most useless." But it must be real and useful work, not mere fussiness. She had no sympathy with the woman who " makes an occasional erratic dash at doing something for the poor, and calls it social work ". A social worker dealt with social diseases just as a doctor dealt with physical illnesses, and just as a doctor had to undergo a long preliminary training, so " if you are going to help the poor and the downtrodden and the unfortunate you must understand the right way to do it ; you must train ".

Furthermore, she had no toleration for the woman who worked merely for pocket money and so undercut the labour market. In her own words, once addressed to a meeting of her own sex : " Whatever work women take up they must be careful, if it is paid work, not to take less than the market rate because they happen to be well off. It is not fair for the girl belonging to nine families out of ten to have to compete with the girl from the tenth family who works for pocket money. If you take work at all take it only on condition that the pay is such that a woman can live on it without being subsidized out of the home. The viciousness of so much of women's work to-day is due to the fact that she will accept low pay in a genteel occupation because her father is willing to keep her, or somebody provides her with clothes. Better unpaid work than inadequately paid work." She herself lived up to her convictions and consistently throughout her career refused to take less than a man's pay because she happened to be a woman.

In the records of her which were written after her death the picturesque side of her nature was so emphasized that there was a danger that the profounder aspects of her character would be unduly obscured. Much that was written would have amused her vastly. Thus in one paper which devotes itself to the affairs of her own sex it was written : " There was much about her to suggest that she was the reincarnation of some turbulent Phoenician princess who landed centuries ago on the rocky coast of Cornwall, whose spirit somehow eluded the patterns and conventions of later civilization, to blossom again in an academic world which had something to gain from its elemental values and roughhewn vigour."

Elsewhere she was portrayed as " a dynamic and tempestuous person who spoke her mind freely, sometimes too freely ; a woman with staunchest prejudices, a strong Imperialist, yet withal a stern servant of truth, and not to advantage her most cherished predilections would she swerve a hair's breadth from it. She dominated her company, and her memory is a living thing ".

That she exhibited all these aspects in a greater or less degree is perfectly true, but those who knew her best were aware that beneath these attractive coruscations of her rich nature there was a fundamental sanity of outlook and an entire fairness of judgment. An ardent supporter of any movement that made for equality of opportunity as between women and men, she marched in no suffragette processions, still less did she intend to go to gaol for her principles, although she would cheerfully have done both had she thought any good purpose would have been served thereby. But she held she was doing more good to the cause by showing that she, a woman, could do a man's job as well as any male creature and better than most. She had no sympathy with sex war. Comparing, in the light of experience, the brain capacity of men and women as University students : " She did not find any fundamental differences between them. Boys had different capacities within the masculine group and girls had different capacities within the feminine group, and it was difficult to say that one capacity was masculine and another feminine." [1] Nor could she discover any difference in the responsiveness of men and women students. In a memorandum prepared for an educational body she said : " I have had girls during the past year coming from Slough, Catford, Reading and Sidcup to attend lectures at 6 and 7.15 for four or five evenings a week and that after a day's teaching or office work. The same is true of the men. To miss a lecture or personal interview is something bitterly regretted (this was not so in my time at Cambridge), and with such an audience it is impossible to say that one sex is more responsive than the other. They are both a sheer delight to teach. The men work quite as well and conscientiously as the girls and are quite as diffuse and ungrammatical in their essays." And in the course of an address on University Education for Women, she told her audience : " There is the marriage where two people suit each other like a box and its lid, where they are companions in every sense of the word—the ideal marriage. This I hold is the best of all for any woman if she gets it—the marriage of perfect companionship and sympathy." Without doubt " a strong Imperialist ", her lectures, like her books, were apt to sparkle, but they were pure scholarship and in them economic history was presented undefiled by party polemics. Like all strong characters, she had her prejudices and did not try to hide them, and she had no doubt about the inherent superiority of the British race and in particular the Cornish section of it. Nevertheless, " no differences of political opinion, of race, of colour, or of religion . . . stood for one

---

[1] Address to Edinburgh Association of British Federation of University Women, February, 1925.

moment in the way when it was a question of helping them in their work or in their careers. A strong character herself, she was an admirable judge of character in others. She could weigh, accurately and fairly, temperaments and intellects with which, emotionally, she had nothing in common." [1] One of the most touching and striking of the multitude of messages of condolence that her death called forth was a telegram from Jaffa, signed by ten of her old students whose signatures bore witness that these representatives of the two races there were at one in their sorrow at the passing of " revered Professor Knowles ".

It was this essential sanity of outlook and this fairness of judgment which enabled her in her lectures and in her books to approach thorny questions with what a fellow worker in the same field characterized as " her detached philosophic attitude ". [2] By her gift of happy generalization her work became illuminating. Her capacity for concentrated work on original authorities gave it authority. Her vivacious method of presentation and her sense of the dramatic gave it life and attractiveness.

She was in the full tide of life and looking forward to many years of happy work when, suddenly and unexpectedly, the call came. In the consoling words of a friend, uttered at a time when consolation was difficult to find, " she was wanted for work elsewhere."

C. M. K.

---

[1] *The Economic Journal*, June, 1926, p. 319.
[2] Professor Egerton, in *Economic Journal*, March, 1925.

CONTENTS

xxiii

PART I

COMPARATIVE VIEW OF DOMINION PROBLEMS

CHAPTER I

ECONOMIC PROBLEMS OF TEMPERATE DOMINIONS COMPARED WITH PROBLEMS OF TROPICS AND OF EUROPEAN COUNTRIES

Problems of temperate Dominions and of Tropics compared.
>   Similarity in early dependence of all colonies on agriculture.
>   Dissimilarity seen in primary importance in Tropics of such problems as
>>   Health ;
>>   Personal freedom ;
>   and in easy transition in temperate colonies to
>>   Money economy ;
>>   Financial and political independence.

Trade development—
>   In temperate colonies (i) in hands of colonists themselves ; (ii) rapid because imports essential from beginning.
>   In Tropics (i) in hands of outside traders ; (ii) slow because natives largely self-sufficing.

Industrial development
>   In temperate colonies an early tendency.
>   In Tropics still only beginning in India.
>   Paternal attitude of Government in early days of all colonies, but problems to be dealt with different in nature in temperate and tropical areas.
>   Religious and race problems belong mostly to Tropics.

Dominion and European problems compared.
>   Similar effects of emancipation of serfs in Europe and abolition of slavery in colonies.
>   Problem of relative merits of large and small scale farming in Europe has its counterpart in colonial problem of large plantations or small native holdings : of great sheep or cattle runs or small homesteads.
>   State-directed agricultural research in new countries even more important than in old.
>   The Industrial Revolution has no counterpart in colonies.
>   Great importance of transport in Europe, but importance greater still in new countries.
>   Emigration and immigration.

THE economic development of the areas peopled predominantly by the British race has gone through two stages—one a period of colonial dependence and the other a period of colonial nationalism. Before the colonies

3

attained responsible government,[1] it was the Colonial Office and the British Parliament that decided such fundamental questions as emigration, commercial policy, finance, and taxation. A British free trade Parliament dealt with the preferences and Navigation Acts of the old colonial system by abolishing both without consulting the colonies. Thus the policy of colonies was assimilated to that of the mother country under the impression that what was good for England was good for mankind. When a colony attained to self-governing status it decided its economic questions for itself.

Problems of Temperate Dominions and of Tropics Compared

While the problems which confronted the settlers in the temperate regions necessarily differed in many respects from those which faced the governors and the Colonial or India Office in the Tropics, yet there were many similarities. Economic evolution goes through much the same stages whether it be a question of Europe, America, India, or Africa. The Tropics with coloured backward races and the temperate regions peopled by whites resembled each other in the fact that their very existence rested on agriculture ; they were alike in the urgent need of finding markets for agricultural products and in the supreme importance of cheap transport by land and water ; and they resembled each other in the large part played by the Government in their economic development. On the other hand, the health movement has not been nearly so important in the temperate colonies as in the Tropics. This is partly due to climate, partly also to the fact that the British colonists inherited and brought with them many of the sanitary ideas of the home country, whereas Tropical medicine did not develop till the twentieth century.

Nor did the question of personal freedom involve anything like the same reconstruction of economic life in Canada, Australia, or New Zealand as it did in the West Indies or Africa. The transition from human beings as barter commodities and from services as payments to payment in money for goods and services was a difficult period of

---

[1] Responsible government was conceded to Canada in 1848, to New Zealand in 1852, to New South Wales, South Australia, Newfoundland, Tasmania, and Victoria in 1855, to Queensland in 1859, to the Cape in 1872, Western Australia in 1890, and to Natal in 1893.

evolution in the Tropics. But in the temperate colonies the British emigrants had been used to a money economy at home, and if they did have to use barter at first, or card money in Canada, or reckon in rum in Australia, they already thought in terms of money and took to coin readily when it became available. They did not have to be taught and coaxed to use it as in the Tropics. They were accustomed to regular taxation and not to occasional bursts of extortion. The colonists of the nineteenth century inherited a developed financial mechanism such as banks, budgets, and national debts. Then, being part of a nation at home and reared in a protectionist system till the 'forties, they had a sense of common economic policy for the whole region. They developed in consequence protectionist tariffs to help their own industries—after all had not the England they left grown great under protection—federated into larger areas and were able with the financial knowledge they had inherited to adjust the difficult questions of the financial relations between the central government and local provinces. While colonial governors in the Tropics could amalgamate Northern and Southern Nigeria, the peoples themselves were incapable of dealing with these questions, and taxation, as we have seen, had to be organized very carefully as it affected the whole social fabric and a people unused to taxation are apt to make trouble when asked to pay a hut tax for the first time or a camel tax, as in Somaliland. An alien ruler has to tread delicately in the matter of taxation.

With the development of protection there arose the further question as to what should be the commercial relations between a free trade mother country and protectionist colonies and between the various parts of the Empire dependent and independent. The result was the reintroduction of inter-imperial preference by the colonies after the mother country had abandoned it.

The first problem of the self-governing colonies in their colonial and dependent stage was to get something to exchange or sell. This had somehow or other to be conjured out of an empty country. In the Tropics primitive natives could and did lead a self-sufficing existence. They only slowly developed a taste for luxuries in the way of beads, scented soap, tinned salmon, bicycles, and gin. But civilized peoples began in new countries with developed wants. Tea, sugar, and tobacco had become necessaries to British colonists by the eighteenth century ; axes to fell trees, mills to grind flour, clothing and utensils were the essentials of existence. Without something to sell, a civilized life could not be carried on and a fresh population attracted. Fish in Newfoundland, furs in Canada, wool, and later on gold, did much for the beginnings of Australia and South Africa. Even pickled heads and whales helped to make New Zealand known. It was outside traders who first developed the possibilities of tropical dependencies. Planters failed to produce those staples in organized and large quantities. At a later date the Imperial Institute, founded after Queen Victoria's Jubilee in 1887, was a place to which colonial governors could send tropical products with a view to examination of their commercial possibilities. The practice grew up of certain tropical regions like Malaya, the Sudan, and the West Indies having their own agencies in London like the self-governing colonies. Planters also formed associations for pushing their own products.

When the colonies entered the national stage there emerged the ambition to be an industrial and not merely an agricultural country. A desire to use their own raw materials instead of exporting them thousands of miles and fetching them back as finished articles became as strong in the self-governing colonies as it had been in the England of Elizabeth or all the past century in the United States. Canada wished to make paper out of her own timber and flour out of her wheat, and Australia cloth out of her own wool and boots out of her hides. These colonies wished to diversify their national life, to show that they were really grown up and that they could make as good things as anyone else if they tried. Iron and steel works, coal mines, engineering shops, electrical works, and textile factories became the height of Dominion ambition. Subsidies were given to industries in every colony and annual censuses were taken to prove their advance in industrial production. The tropical regions are not yet in the stage to yearn after industrial development. India, however, is the exception. There are emerging, as we have seen, the beginnings of an industrial development in the jute mills of Calcutta, in the cotton mills of Bombay, and the iron works of Bengal. Her educated minority, reinforced by the manufacturers, has developed a national feeling and has demanded a protective tariff against Manchester cotton goods, a demand which was granted in 1917.

All the British colonies at first leaned on the mother country for defence and finance. This attitude of looking for help to the Government continued when the colonies became self-governing, only it was to the colonial government and not to England that they turned for help. It was found that the State could raise capital cheaper than individuals, hence the State began to pledge its credit for public works and above all for railways. The energies of the individuals of the new countries are so absorbed in making good in a wrestle with nature that the Government alone can command the brains to carry out schemes. In addition to this, the Government has to take account of the future. The State has to think of generations yet unborn and to plan ahead, whereas the individual colonist is occupied with his own immediate welfare from day to day.

The general opinion that it is " up to " the Government to make the colony prosperous finds expression in many ways. There is the feeling that it is the duty of the Government to build railways and run them cheaply, subsidize industrial undertakings, find markets, grade produce, conserve national resources, dispose of land, provide irrigation, recruit and assist emigrants who are healthy, energetic, young, and intelligent, start and encourage scientific agriculture, furnish agricultural as well as other types of education, fight insect pests and cattle diseases, develop new staples, evolve an ideal system of land tenure to suit every kind of condition, remedy old abuses in land tenures, break up large farms, encourage the small holder, and lend him money or seed. The Government is expected to advertise widely in order to get men, capital, transport, industries, and above all cheap loans from England. Labour laws, the settlement of labour disputes, and in Australasia the fixing of wages are simply casual extras. It is pre-eminently the function of colonial governments to make the colonies pay. As in the Tropics, their governments are fundamentally commercial and paternal, though they are more in the nature of a joint stock company in which the Government constitutes the directorate.

Whereas in the Tropics the economic problems could be summed up as those of transport, the protection of the native, the settlement of land tenures, the encouragement of scientific agriculture and marketing, the evolution of a satisfactory system of taxation and currency, and the development of health measures, the problems of the larger self-governing Dominions have been concerned with the creation and working of federal areas, the development and control of transport, the procuring of population, the disposal of vacant land, the encouragement of agriculture, the subsidizing of industrial development, and the attempted settlement of labour problems. They have claimed and gained the right to settle their own tariffs, to adopt free trade or protection, and to make their own treaties. They have developed a new preference system to cement imperial economic ties, and they have joined in the new responsibility for the Tropics.

There is in all the self-governing Dominions an essential similarity of problems as well as essential differences in their economic outlook and development. They represent Western civilization in a new and less crowded environment, but their economic evolution is proceeding along much the same road as the West has already trod. Religion and Race, the incalculable factors in the Tropics, are almost absent as factors in the Dominions, except in the Union of South Africa and Rhodesia where the numbers of the negro races complicate the problem.

Dominion and European Problems Compared

It is interesting to see how the great economic problems of Europe are, in the nineteenth century, reproduced in both the Crown Colonies and self-governing Dominions. Starting afresh in new and almost empty lands, the same questions have nevertheless had to be faced.

Perhaps the fundamental problem of Europe in the nineteenth century was connected with the reconstruction of agriculture after the emancipation of the serfs and the establishment of personal freedom. In the colonies, after the abolition of slavery, many of the same difficulties recur as had to be faced after the emancipation of the serfs. The labour supply in both Europe and the colonies was disorganized by the emancipation and a new agriculture, based on personal freedom and wages, had to be initiated to take the place of the old methods of production.

The problem to be solved in Quebec was the abolition of seignorial tenures in French Canada. The feudalism of old France had to be recast in a modern mould and the status of serfdom abolished. With the exception of South Australia, which never admitted convicts, the other five Australian colonies had to lay down regulations for the treatment of emancipated convicts and to provide for a labour supply after the abolition of transportation. New Zealand had never been a convict settlement, but she had her own problem in her relations with the Maoris. In tropical Queensland, where Kanakas or Pacific Islanders were imported under indenture, a process known as " black-birding ", a very acute question arose. Should tropical Australia be sacrificed to the White Australia policy by the exclusion of all forms of coloured labour, including Kanakas ? Even in so new a country as Australia, founded only in 1788, all the questions of convicts versus free men and white labour versus coloured have been at the root of economic development.

One of the great questions of Europe centred round the relative values of the large and small farmer, the former being the more technically efficient, the latter socially desirable. In the same way in the Tropics we have encountered two types, the large plantation with European supervision of working natives producing for a market, and the little holding of the native himself with a very small surplus for sale. Which type is it the more desirable to encourage ? Again, in the self-governing Dominions, is the desirable type of cultivation that of the great sheep or cattle run of Australia, reckoned in square miles, or the 160 acre homestead of Canada ?

In Europe the State had to intervene to protect the small farmer and to train him. It had also to promote scientific agriculture and agricultural education. In the colonies the function of the State has been even more important, as in new countries the pests are so much more difficult to eradicate and call for that drastic regulation and scientific exploration which, especially there, only the State is rich enough to undertake. The colonies are primarily great agricultural producers and their agricultural development occupies the leading place in their economic history.

The Industrial Revolution which vitally affected England and France in the first half of the nineteenth century, and Germany, Russia, and the United States chiefly after 1870, cannot be said as yet to have radically affected the overseas Empire. In Canada the transition to mechanical pro-duction is only now beginning and only the beginnings of a labour movement are emerging. A large proportion of the Australian population is gathered in towns, and this concentration favours a certain amount of industrial production, and combined action by the labour party is strong enough to secure at times a Labour Government. Elsewhere the scattered nature of settlement tells against strong trade unionism.

A commercial revolution due to the spread of mechanical transport followed the Industrial Revolution in Europe. Mechanical transport and cold storage enabled raw materials and perishable goods to be moved as they had never been moved before. All this reacted on those units of the Empire which held great possibilities as providers of food and raw materials. In fact the whole development of the modern Empire has hinged on mechanical transport. Almost every question of colonial development is intimately bound up with transport problems. The Dominions produce chiefly bulky and perishable goods. How can these be moved cheaply enough to be sold in Europe at a price that the European can pay ? Important as transport is in Europe, it holds a place of still greater importance in new countries whose whole existence rests on transport facilities which attract capital and population, cause emigration to be something less than exile, and enable these regions to buy and sell and keep in touch with England.

In Europe there has been a growing tendency to discard *laissez faire* and the economic functions of the State have been ever widening ; but in both temperate and tropical parts of the Overseas Empire the State has, as we have seen, assumed a still greater prominence.

The racial expansion of Europe has been one of the great characteristics of the nineteenth century. There, however, it has chiefly been a question of assisting, regulating, or retarding emigration ; of acquiring or defending tropical and semi-tropical areas ; or of sending out to the Tropics a few white administrators, planters, soldiers, merchants, missionaries, or engineers. But problems of emigration and immigration have in the past been a question of the very existence of colonies. The Dominions have had to devise a means of attracting to a manless land those emigrants that the mother country is willing to let go, and in some cases of importing coloured labour when white labour did not suffice, as in Queensland, or where the native population would not do the work required, as in Natal and the West Indies.

CHAPTER 2

The Economic Beginnings of the Idea of Nationality in Colonial Development, and the Economic Foundations of Federation

Turning point :

In Canada : completion of the C.P. Railway in 1886 resulting in opening up of prairies, immigration, and wheat export on grand scale.

In Australasia : discovery of gold 1851, resulting in stimulus to development of transport, agriculture and high finance, influx of new class of population and protectionist movement.

In South Africa : discovery of diamonds 1867–70 and of gold 1886, resulting in railway extension, a new immigration, capitalist enterprise and inland penetration.

Economic conditions making for unity :

(1) Breaking down of internal tariff barriers in Canada 1867, Australia 1901, South Africa 1910.

(2) Railway through traffic in Canada and South Africa.

(3) In Canada, resistance to pressure of United States. In Australasia, opposition to Asiatic immigration. In South Africa, the native question.

(4) Commerical organization.

THE economic history of the self-governing Dominions goes through three stages. There is the start ; then a period of slow development that almost amounted to stagnation, with consequent dependence on England ; and then a period of rapid expansion. When a colony became wealthy enough to stand on its own feet it demanded and was given self-governing status and settled its own economic policy. In all the racial colonies there is a distinct development point which marks the end of the colonial and the beginning of the national period in their economic history.

The turning point in the economic development of Canada came when the Canadian Pacific Railway opened up the great prairie belt and it became feasible for her to make her returns to England in wheat. It was then possible to advertise for immigrants with success and to offer the great bait of 160 acres of land free. As the

11

advertising was conducted with great skill and the fares were cheap, there was a rapid emigration of people into Canada from England, the continent of Europe, and the United States of America. She differs from the other Dominions in that the great impulse to settlement sprang from agriculture. Canada was late in starting effectively owing to lack of capital, and it was not till after 1897 that she enjoyed real prosperity. The United States of America had accumulated capital in the colonial period, emigrants poured in, and the capitalists could use them as wage labour. There was in the early nineteenth century no capitalist class in Canada. The French Canadians held land on the manorial system, that is to say, for services and payments in kind ; the English settlers got land easily ; and there was no one who could be employed as a wage-earner, no convicts as in Australia, no black slaves as in Africa ; there was no product like raw cotton that could form a basis of exchange as in the South of the United States of America. The Canadians caught animals for fur, felled a certain amount of lumber, burnt timber for potash, and ground flour from wheat bought chiefly in the United States. As Canada could not export products she had to export men, and the result was that Canadians had to go over the border and work in the United States, and that country, by reason of its proximity, sold its manufactures in Canada. Partly to protect themselves from Americanization, partly to develop their own industry in order to lead their own national economic life, Canada initiated the " national policy " with a protective tariff in 1878. But the real economic turning point in the history of Canada came in 1886 when the Canadian Pacific Railway was finished and the export of wheat developed on the grand scale.

The turning point came earlier in Australasia. In 1851 gold was discovered in Ballarat, and that meant the rapid development of both Australia and New Zealand. So short of food was Australia after the gold discoveries that it drew on New Zealand and provided a market for that struggling colony. In 1861 gold was discovered in New Zealand itself, in Otago, and New Zealand too felt the great impetus which a gold boom provides.

It is not merely the gold that attracts people and creates the impulse to emigrate ; the need of supplies for a mining camp is so urgent that their provision is a profitable business. Anyone may go prospecting for minerals, labour

becomes scarce, local prices rise rapidly, and further supplies
have to be brought from a distance.   More people are
attracted by the prospect of profitable farming and agriculture develops.   Mining needs increased transport for
the carriage of supplies, mining gear, and ore.   Railways
come into existence, and, in their turn, further assist
agricultural settlement.   Financiers are also attracted by
the prospects held out by mining ; they begin working
on the grand scale ; the stage of the small prospector soon
passes and wealthy companies with elaborate machinery
and chemical treatment of the ore succeed the domestic
miner and his primitive appliances.

The discovery of gold not merely meant settlement, it
altered the whole type of the Australian population.   New
people flocked in who swamped the convict element.   Wool
had started Australia, but it needed very few hands.   There
were only 400,000 people there before 1851.   It was mining
that attracted the people to a place so remote.   Moreover,
when the mines were worked out the people went to the
towns and started small industries or took to agriculture,
and they began to resent the squatter and the large estate.
Railways were promoted, the revenue had to be put on
a new basis, and the protectionist movement to encourage
industrial development was commenced.   As soon as the
gold discoveries were made in Australia, labour became so
scarce that the Pacific peoples began to enter in increasing
numbers to eke out the scanty supply.   The cry for a
" white Australia " was heard in the land, and the demand
for the exclusion of the Asiatic was re-echoed in New
Zealand.

Australia had from the beginning a valuable raw material,
wool, with which to build up a trade, and good quality
merino wool such as Australia supplied was wanted badly
in England.   This led to the accumulation of capital ;
Canada had only furs and lumber, so that her economic
development was in comparison slow till the grain trade
provided her with something to exchange.   South Africa
had nothing of importance to sell until diamonds and gold
were discovered, and she had to live on her Kaffir wars.
There has been a capitalist element in Australia from the
first, which perhaps accounts for the fact that there is more
Socialism in Australia than elsewhere in the Empire.   It
had been a settlement of the capitalist plantation type with
" hands ".

The finding of gold at so many points and in so many different places was a circumstance that vitally affected the history of Australia. The gold mines of Queensland, of Victoria, of New South Wales, and of West Australia all provided new points of departure from the Australian coast-line, while tin at Mount Bishop proved to be the point of attraction in Tasmania. In New Zealand gold was found in both North and South Island and in the East as well as the West. This again made for settlement at many different points, as farmers tend to congregate in the neigh-bourhood of their best market—in this case the mines. In Canada traffic and settlement entered at one mouth and spread itself out along the alimentary canal of the river, lakes and railways, not, as in Australia, proceeding inland from a number of different points.

The finding of diamonds in Griqualand West (Kimberley) in 1867–1870 and of gold in Johannesburg in 1886 was the turning point in the history of South Africa, leading as in Australia, to railway extension, a new immigration, capitalist enterprise, and inland penetration. In South Africa the fact that the gold and diamond fields were situated so far inland led to the development of towns in the interior and the extension of British rule far beyond the limits originally contemplated. The whole of South Africa began to hinge on the Rand ; the revenue was largely derived from the customs on goods imported for Johannesburg ; the railways earned their profits for the various States through carrying goods and passengers to and from the gold and diamond mines ; the ports struggled with each other and with Delagoa Bay to obtain the handling of the traffic for the Rand. As the gold on the Rand is only obtained from rock which requires crushing and chemical treatment and then is obtained only in small quantities, there has been no room for the individual miner, and the domestic stage of mining was omitted. The extraction of the ore required large scale management, machinery, and elaborate plant from the first. In the diamond mines, however, the stage of the small man was only gradually superseded by the large company, the small men being bought up by the rival companies of Rhodes or Barnato and finally consolidated into "De Beers". The hope of finding another Rand tempted financiers and others into Matabeleland and Mashonaland, so that Kimberley and Johannesburg proved to be the jumping-off grounds of a new inland expansion. The capitalist element has been all important in the development of South Africa, but the Boer farmer was still driving his flocks from the high veld to the low, according to the seasons, when this highly developed capitalist industry was grafted on to his isolated pastoral, almost nomadic, existence, and there was acute friction, followed by the Boer War.

The continental colonies begin, like Germany, with being a number of disunited States with their own tariff barriers against their various neighbours. Then comes the abolition of those tariff barriers and a united federated region emerges, a stage attained by Canada in 1867, Australia in 1901, and South Africa in 1910. In each case there has been one outstanding portion more difficult to bring in than the others. British Columbia on the Pacific only joined the Canadian Union in 1871 on condition of a transcontinental railway being built. Special financial terms had to be given to Western Australia and Tasmania, as in the case of Hesse and Hanover in the German Customs Union, to induce them to come in. In the Union of South Africa, Natal was the difficulty, but was eventually incorporated. The question of the inclusion of Rhodesia was decided by a referendum in 1922 in favour of self-government.

In two of the Dominions, Canada and South Africa, the great physical uniting link was the railway, as it was in Russia and Germany, but this is not so in Australia, as there the different States have different gauges which prevent through traffic. Both Australia and Canada have islands on their outskirts, New Zealand and Newfoundland, which have not yet come into the federation and which may never come in. New Zealand is, however, 1,200 miles away from Australia while Newfoundland is quite near to Canada, and the absorption of the former is therefore more difficult than the latter. Two other islands, Prince Edward Island and Tasmania, have, however, come into their respective federations.

The tendency of the continental colonies to start from separate points and then coalesce into a union has been a marked feature in the development of each of them, and is comparable to the impulse which formed the German Zollverein or a United Italy. It is a movement to a larger unit. In the Dominions the chief motives of union have been economic, as they were in Germany before 1870.

The United States, angry at the sympathy Canada was supposed to have shown to the South, and becoming increasingly protectionist after 1866, refused to renew the Reciprocity Treaty which gave free access to Canadian products in the United States in return for fishing rights and other concessions. This had the effect of making Canada feel that she must be big enough to carry out an economic policy of her own ; the tariff barriers between the Canadas and the Maritime Provinces were thrown down, British Columbia was enticed in, and there was free trade throughout the Dominion. The desire to put up a united front against Asiatic immigration was the dominant factor in forcing the Australian colonies into a union against the growing power of Japan and the migration of Chinese. The Union of South Africa was almost entirely due to economic causes. The necessity of adjusting railway rates and the desirability of a united front against shipping companies were strong motives resulting from the transport situation. The difficulties of internal trade with all the internal tariff barriers between the Cape, Natal, and the Transvaal were further causes of union, while another, and probably the greatest, was the necessity for a common policy in regard to the black inhabitants in a country where they enormously outnumber the white and are the principal source of the labour supply.[1]

The self-governing Dominions have not merely become great federations. Each has tried to realize a national economic existence of its own ; each has evolved a high tariff, partly for revenue, partly with a view to developing its own native industries. There is in all the self-governing Dominions a movement towards nationalism which aims at developing its own economic life apart from England. There is nothing they resent more than any suspicion of " centralization ". They resented so strongly the very name of " colony " that the official title was changed to " Dominion ". Two of them, Canada and Australia,[2] aimed at having their own mercantile marine, and have appointed their own Trade Commissioners. The Dominions make their own trade arrangements with each other on a

---

[1] The same tendency to abolish internal tariffs is also seen in the abolition of the tariff between Northern and Southern Nigeria in 1914 and between Kenya and Uganda in 1922, showing how all continental areas, whether self-governing or paternally governed, are actuated by the urge to form a bigger unit.

[2] Australia sold its shipping in April, 1928.

preferential basis ; since 1907 they make treaties with foreign countries, and Canada has her own Minister at Washington.

But the Dominions are bound to England by the fact that their great market is in this country. The United States, as well as Canada, supplies wheat, therefore Canada must depend on England as the market in which to sell her principal product, Australian wool is affected by the United States tariff, so Australia and New Zealand look to England to sell their wool, meat, and dairy products. South Africa had for years lived on provisioning the English wars with Kaffirs and providing the necessary transport by land, then on the gold mines ; but now that her agriculture is developing she also looks to England for her market for wool, fruit, and meat. The self-governing Dominions are economically focussed upon Great Britain, and their prosperity depends on her purchasing power.

A Dominion is a great commercial firm. As it does not pay rival firms to compete beyond a certain point, so that they form a combination, so the various units of each of the federations have also combined for marketing. Wheat pools, wool pools, meat pools, and butter pools are characteristic of the organized attempt to keep up prices. State marketing and State guarantee of quality by inspection are important unifying instruments in all these great selling regions.

CHAPTER 3

TRANSPORT

The revolution wrought by railways and their outstanding importance in colonial economic development.

Special features :

In Canada: limitations of water transport so that railways made winter transport possible ; vast new wheat region opened up.

In South Africa : importance of railways emphasized by absence of waterways and by the difficulties of transport by means of draught animals.

In Australia : population being assembled in towns and along coast, comparatively little railway penetration inland ; railways built for local needs ; begin at different points and have different gauges ; each State has its separate system converging on capital ; construction costly.

Railways mainly built by private enterprise in Canada and by the State in Australia and South Africa.

Sea communications : Canada the most favourably situated. Australasia handicapped by distance from Europe. South Africa's grievance is high freights due to the nature of the return cargo. State lines as antidote to shipping rings.

IN the period of rapid colonial expansion, the railway and the steamship were the essential factors. They revolutionized the continental colonies so fundamentally that it is almost essential to consider the effects of mechanical transport first in order to accentuate its overwhelming importance. It is the vital problem which affects self-governing and Crown colonies alike. Railways and more railways are needed to move bulky goods, to open up lands for immigrants, and to supply them with manufactures, implements, building materials, and markets. Railways and settlers are interchangeable terms. Shipping and cold storage enable the goods they produce in exchange to reach the town populations of Europe in good condition.

Inhabited Canada up to Winnipeg is a clearing made by men. Once the canals were made along the St. Lawrence to avoid the rapids and the falls, there existed a magnificent system of 2,000 miles of uninterrupted water transit right into the heart of the continent, but it is closed for four to five months of the year by ice and then communication depends upon the railways, and with few exceptions the canals can only take vessels drawing 14 feet of water. The railways therefore mean winter trade, winter movement, and a winter outlet. Except for the lakes, Canada has had to rely wholly for its development upon the railway which opened up the treeless prairie lands and made a new wheat region available for settlers. The Canadian Pacific Railway has been described as a " narrow band drawn by indomitable pluck from the Atlantic to the Pacific gate ". But there has been hitherto one great handicap : that the goods traffic is seasonal—wheat—and it all goes one way, from West to East, and pours through one funnel with a narrow neck at Winnipeg with consequent congestion. The railway has meant more to Canada in the West than can possibly be conceived, especially when one realizes the great scarcity of material for road-making. In addition to the federating or uniting effect of the railway, the Canadian Pacific made Canada the commercial high road of the Empire, the great link between the Atlantic and Pacific for the British Empire.

In South Africa the railway is even more important than in Canada or Australia, the former having the lakes and the St. Lawrence, and Australia a long coast-line with good harbours. But South Africa is very inaccessible ; there is no St. Lawrence Gulf leading right into the heart of the country and no harbour such as Sydney possesses. The coast does not invite trade or settlement. It was known in the sixteenth century as the Cape of Storms and was merely a port of call for water or for refitting on the way to India. The ranges of terraced mountains are serious natural barriers and there are no natural waterways into the interior, not even one fine navigable river. Horse sickness periodically destroyed the horses, and bullock wagons were the chief means of transport, but coast fever and other epidemics took terrible toll of the draught oxen. Moreover, in large parts of Africa the tsetse fly has always made any draught animals impossible, and the only alternative used to be native porters, for which there was great competition in the fly-belt, and the rates of pay were correspondingly high.[1] Lord Milner, when reconstructing

[1] The following account will give some idea of the difficulties of proceeding inland from Cape Town : " The Cape Peninsula, which includes Cape Town and Simon's Town, had been, during the Dutch occupation and continued for many years after its cession to the British Government, cut off from free communication with the interior of the Colony by a belt or line of drifting white sand, extending across the isthmus between

the Transvaal and Orange Free State after the Boer War, experienced the hampering effects of lack of transport, especially as there was a great scarcity of transport animals due to the wholesale destruction of farming stock. He wrote : " The absurdity of the conditions which cause a country like South Africa to import meat and grain from America and Australia has become almost a common-place. Something is due to defective farming ; but more to defective means of transport. The country adjacent to the existing lines of railway, not being closely cultivated, does not produce nearly enough to supply the towns. . . . To take a glaring instance, mealies, the stock food of the Kaffir, can be grown in abundance and almost without expense in Basutoland and the south-eastern parts of the Orange River Colony. Yet because wagon transport is too dear and too slow, Johannesburg and the Rand rely to a great extent on mealies imported from America and brought up from Durban. Similarly, while fruit can be, and is, grown in profusion in the Rustenburg district, the centres of population in the Transvaal are supplied with it mainly from the coast. Railways traversing these districts will bring up their products and while leading to a great agricultural development will incidentally relieve the through lines by taking away the necessity of importing all the staple products of the land from abroad." [1]

In reading Hyatt's *Old Transport Road* one begins to realize what railways must have meant to Africa. The book pictures wagons sticking in mud-holes and held up

False Bay and Table Bay, from the Atlantic on the one side to the Indian Ocean on the other. This sand was continually set in motion by the prevailing trade winds, which still blow in summer from the south-east and in winter from the north-west, oftentimes with great violence. These opposing forces caused the sand to shift from one end to the other, and to continue in a state of active mobility for a couple of miles and more in breadth, and with a depth of several feet, across the only road track to the country beyond Cape Town . . . The wagons conveying produce to, and returning with goods from, Cape Town, were generally drawn by oxen ; and though a span or team of twelve oxen sufficed for the country roads, twice that number of animals were needed to draw these wagons through this belt of sand, whilst men and cattle were further subjected to the uncomfortable infliction of harassing showers of drifting sand, not unlike in appearance to a blizzard." ("The Railway System of South Africa," in *Proceedings of the Royal Colonial Institute*, December, 1897, vol. xxix, p. 4, Sir D. Tennnat, Agent-General for Cape of Good Hope.) Road-making, which began in 1844, and for which special taxation was imposed, was helped by depositing town refuse on this belt of sand and fixing it by trees.

[1] Worsfold: *Reconstruction of the New Colonies under Lord Milner*, vol. i, pp. 129–30.

for weeks by the sudden risings of rivers. " Of course transport work during the summer was a risky business, financially. With reasonable luck you did extremely well, for rates were always high and loads plentiful ; but if a river held you up for a long time you might easily find a month's profits gone ; whilst if you struck exceptionally bad mud you might tire your oxen so greatly that you had to give them a protracted rest. Naturally, we never agreed to deliver loads within any specified time." [1] The Rinderpest and the African coast fever wiped out the bulk of the cattle in 1896 and then the railway, as almost the sole means of transport, became synonymous with civilization.

When the pioneer expedition of the Chartered Company into Mashonaland was organized in 1890, it took from 6th May to 11th September to get from Kimberley to Salisbury, and that was under very favourable circumstances, when the whole country was dry and the rivers at their lowest. " When I drew a mental picture of what the route would be like for four months during the rains . . . and for four months after the rains—first, impassable torrents and then a waterlogged country. . . Supplies and agricultural and mining machinery could not be brought up at any reasonable cost—for a great part of the year could not be brought up at all—by the road they had come. The new country must find a new way or perish." [2] The roads were made and the Beira railway was built.

A railway which will penetrate inland, past sand deserts, over mud-holes, over rivers in spate, through malaria belts, and which defies the tsetse fly makes a new world of all Africa. It promotes settlement, intercourse, education, and political and social security. The great contrast between Canada and both South Africa and Australia is that in Canada the railways were built mainly by private enterprise with the help of great land grants and subsidies, and in Australia and South Africa by the State. In Canada, during the war, part of the railway system became bankrupt, and as a consequence the State has taken over all the principal lines outside the Canadian Pacific, this State-owned system comprising more than half the railway mileage of the country.

In Australia, where, again, the river system is poor and

[1] Hyatt : *The Old Transport Road*, p. 255.
[2] Colvin : *Life of Jameson*, vol. i, p. 149.

the water an uncertain quantity for navigation owing to drought, the railway is the chief inland means of transport. The Murray and Darling are only navigable in times of average rainfall for six months of the year, being only a series of water-holes at times, though they may be valuable for irrigation purposes. On the other hand, as such a large proportion of the population of Australia is collected in towns and on the coast, the railways are not the vital factor that they are in the other two countries with a very small coast-line. The systems begin at many points ; they have different gauges. The lines were primarily built to serve the existing traffic of the mines or the wool industry. " The route taken by the New South Wales lines was determined by the needs of the wool growers, who alone at the time could supply freight enough to make the lines pay ; the Victorian lines connected the gold-fields with Melbourne and sought out the best patches of farming land ; in Queensland the southern lines were built to carry wool to the ports, the northern to carry sugar or to connect mining districts with the coast. Consequently the later developments of new farming industries have found the existing railway systems inconvenient in many ways ; and one of the problems . . . is how to adapt the old systems—catering for the wool traffic and centred on the State capitals—to the new conditions, which demand quick transit for many kinds of produce to the nearest possible port." [1]

Each Australian State, having its own railway, feeds its own capital, and this does not make for dispersal of population. Railways have been expensive to construct in Australia owing to scarcity of labour and also owing to the fact that the mining districts are mainly in mountainous districts so that the cost of constructing the railways leading to them was high. Individuals could not make railways pay and the State had to build the lines. Australia is a country with " a garland of verdure " round the coast ; there inland penetration has not been up to now so necessary as elsewhere, and so her railways tend to encircle the coast with branch lines leading inland.

The railways are largely responsible for the loans which make Australian indebtedness per head so very heavy. It is always said that the borrowing is for productive undertakings, but they have to pay considerable sums to

[1] A. W. Jose : *History of Australia*, p. 252.

Great Britain for interest, and as politics have entered very largely into their construction, it is doubtful if some of the lines will be remunerative. This is in marked contrast with South Africa, where the State railways before the war paid well.

Thus the provision and management of their railways have become one of the great features of colonial governments. When a government owns railways it becomes a partner in every industrial and agricultural enterprise. Transport is the vital question in a new country, and the railway is the pioneer of all progress.

The South African Government even owns the ports as well as the railways ; as also in some cases do the Australian governments. Probably the convict system made for a tradition of State action in Australia and the military government of the Cape and the Kaffir wars would have the same tendency. On the other hand, the individualist tradition of the United States of America possibly made for the fact that the emigrants into Canada, the United Empire Loyalists, left their railway building mainly to private enterprise ; and conceivably their proximity to England enabled Canadians to get their capital more easily. With the money made out of wool, Australians might have been expected to have been able to build their own railways, but to the man on the spot there are so many more profitable investments and, after all, sheep would walk. So railway building was left to the State. South Africa was poor, and again only the Government could provide the capital. The first railway was commenced in 1859, but not till the development of the diamond and gold mining was it worth while to extend the railway net far inland. The Boer was pastoral and flocks and herds use their own legs. Military reasons and famines helped to develop the railway net of India, but such considerations were almost absent in Canada, Australia, and South Africa.

Sea communications are vital for two reasons, export of goods and import of men. The sheer difference in the cost of the emigrant's passage led to the more rapid settling of Canada than Australia and South Africa. Geographically Canada abuts on two oceans. Her Atlantic ports give her nearer touch with the concentrated markets of the world than any other British Dominion. She has natural sea connexions with the United Kingdom and South Africa by the Atlantic and by the Pacific with India and Australia.

The English liners which did such an immense business with the United States of America serve Canada as a sideline, but as they were apt to enter into rings to control freights, a strong feeling grew up as to the necessity of developing communications outside the rings. It is therefore not surprising that the Canadian Pacific should run its own steamers and that the Canadian Government should own steamers and subsidize steamship lines to the West Indies and South Africa. The State lines in both Canada and Australia [1] were set up as an antidote to the shipping trusts.

In Australia and New Zealand the shipping question is a serious one. They are so far away. Barred out from the United States of America by a high tariff, they are inevitably focussed upon Europe. Of all England's customers and purveyors New Zealand is the furthest off, and distance makes for dear money, for slowness in the growth of population, and general isolation. Therefore swift and cheap communications by sea or air are the great needs of the Dominions in the Southern Hemisphere. Ironically enough, much of Australia's trade is necessarily carried on with India, in spite of the White Australia prepossession. There is, accordingly, in both Australia and New Zealand, the greatest desire to stimulate cheaper shipping and the greatest objection to shipping rings. Communication with the great free trade market, with her great market for loans, is all important.

South African interests have also been much bound up with shipping for another reason. She has had so little to send back. The heavy cargoes of wool, wheat, dairy produce and meat need more shipping for export than import, but, in the case of South Africa, gold, diamonds, and ostrich feathers do not take up much room, and so there is the problem of the return cargo or else the imports must bear a large proportion of the whole of the freight both ways. So keenly does South Africa feel about the high freights, which she attributed largely to shipping rings, that she has refused to give the mails to lines in the ring.

Other countries are protectionist, England is the great trading centre of the world ; and cheap connexions with England have been absolutely essential to her Dominions.

[1] The Federal Government sold its shipping to private interests in April, 1928.

CHAPTER 4

LAND AND AGRICULTURE

No " enclosure " in new countries.

> Canada : Method of land appropriation is free grant. The country of the small farmer. Agricultural development partly the subject of private enterprise, e.g. the C.P. Railway and irrigation; and partly a government matter, e.g. State subsidies to co-operative societies, agricultural research (Marquis wheat), agricultural credits.

> Australia : Drought makes farming a gamble ; this and labour shortage make farming unsuitable for the small settler. Attempts of State to effect closer settlement on smaller farms. Tendency to change from sheep and cattle to dairying and wheat farming. Hence importance of irrigation.

> South Africa : Little free grant of land. Lord Milner and State encouragement of scientific agriculture and war against insect pests. Popularity of agricultural education. Irrigation schemes.

Systems of agriculture :

> The stump-jumping plough and the stripper harvester in Australia.
> The fenced-off block of Australia impossible in Canada, where cattle and sheep must be free to move before the storm.
> The elevator in Canada.
> The marketing of Australian wool.

IN the self-governing Dominions the question of " enclosure ", that is to say, of uniting small scattered strips of land into a compact farm, has not arisen. The land was surveyed and occupied in compact areas from the first. In India enclosure or restripping is a very important question, as under the Hindu law of inheritance, fragmentation has proceeded to such an extent that uneconomic holdings are common and the strips lie scattered over such large areas that it is difficult to cultivate them efficiently. In Russia the strips were so dispersed that they sometimes lay two day's journey away from a man's home, and the problems of that country with its droughts, ignorant peasantry, and famines have great parallels with India. In Egypt the typical holding would not provide a living were it not for the fact that cotton is such a valuable crop that tiny morsels of land will produce a certain amount of revenue ; but there, too, a large number of the holdings are uneconomic.

In the unoccupied countries the land question is largely a question of the terms on which land shall be appropriated.

Shall it be sold or given away ?   Shall it be disposed of in
large blocks or in small ?   What attitude should the State
take up with regard to intensive cultivation or irrigation ?
To what extent should it grant loans to settlers or subsidize
co-operative societies for credit, production, or sale ?   To
what extent should it assist agricultural education ?   To
what extent should it clear the land or build houses ?

In Canada the whole basis of settlement has been on the
footing of giving the vacant land away in small farms. The
United States Government was offering " free homes to
free men " only just across the border. If Canada wished
to attract immigrants she could not hope to sell her land if
people could get it for nothing next door. The settlements
of new France in Canada had been effected like those of old
France in Europe, that is to say, there was a lord of a manor
with a peasantry under him settled on small holdings to
cultivate the lord's land and help to furnish part of the
fighting force when required. The new settlers from the
United States after 1783, the United Empire Loyalists,
took up land in small portions, a necessity when every acre
had to be cleared of timber. With the opening of the West,
the American unit of the quarter section of 160 acres was
adopted, and land was again given away free. The settlement
of Canada was typically that of the self-sufficing non-
capitalist type. It is true that the Canada Company in 1825
got a grant of a million acres of land, and the Canadian
Pacific Railway 25 million acres more than half a century
later. But the Canadian Pacific grants were in alternate
blocks and only recently were the directors allowed to
coalesce the blocks in certain dry areas in Alberta so that
they might carry out a large scheme of irrigation.

It is typical of the Dominion of Canada that she has none
of the large programmes for agricultural development and
improvement that characterize South Africa and Australia.
Even her irrigation has been carried out by a railway and
other private companies. The power that controls the water
controls the means of life in dry areas and irrigation schemes
nearly always imply autocratic control of economic life.
This is so in India and Egypt and will probably prove to
be the case in Australia and South Africa. But in Canada
irrigation is so far not a State affair. As Canada is the land
of the small farmer, it is interesting to find that the
Provincial Governments are going the same way as Europe
in subsidizing co-operative societies. When the cheap grain

from the Prairie Provinces and from the Middle West of the United States threatened to ruin the grain farmers of Ontario, Quebec, and the Maritime Provinces, dairying with cold storage had to be developed to take the place of grain growing. A great deal was done by the Provincial Governments to assist the organization of cheese factories and co-operative creameries in the Eastern Provinces and Ontario. A similar movement is now to be observed in the West. Like South Africa and Australia, the Canadian Government undertakes the support of institutions for scientific agricultural research. It has had an outstanding success in the discovery of the Marquis variety of wheat, which is prolific, and ripens earlier, thus avoiding the early autumn frosts, and yet possessing all the commercial qualities. Canada has set up a Conservation Commission, but even here there is great tenderness for private rights.[1]

The special problem confronting a new colony which aims at attracting small settlers is that of financing them over their first few years.

The settler gets land free, but he has to live for a year till his harvest is reaped ; he is forced, if he has little capital, to mortgage his land for a plough and a wagon and for food until his first crop is ready. He has to build a house and get some necessaries in the way of clothes. The result is that he goes to a bank or a money-lender and often runs hopelessly in debt. In almost every province of Canada the Provincial Governments have passed legislation enabling them to grant loans to farmers or to credit societies to obviate this difficulty of making a start, and the same is done by the various Australian Governments.

---

[1] " A word now as to Government control. Canadian industrial expansion has proceeded chiefly along lines of private initiative and enterprise. The stimulus of individual profit remains in almost every field the most potent force in our development. Every motive of honour and of interest enjoins that that stimulus be not blighted or destroyed. . . . Such of our resources as from time to time pass from public ownership into private hands are thereafter subjected to control only that waste and locking up for selfish and speculative ends may be avoided and by no means that their legitimate earning power may be checked. The dictates of our policy have suggested that our invaluable water powers—an asset of a clearly distinctive character—should be to the utmost possible extent not only State owned and controlled but State developed and operated. . . . The long years that are required in the production of a forest crop render forest management also a proper sphere of Government activity. But private enterprise has and will have in Canada abundant opportunity." (" Canada's Natural Resources and their State Control," A. Meighen, Minister of the Interior, in the *Geographical Journal*, August, 1918, vol. 52, pp. 77–8.)

The question of the small holding is also largely one of good soil. The soil of Canada in the Prairie Provinces consists of rich black earth. The frosts prevent the nitrogenous food being washed out by the rains. It needs little manure and the yields are high. The railway companies, by providing elevators, enable the settler to dispense with barns, and the machines cut and stook as they go. In Australia it is a question of rainfall, and much of the land is quite unsuitable for the small settler. Indeed, the periodic droughts make all farming there a gamble against the weather, and in this gamble the small man is apt to go to the wall. Western Australia, which copied the 160 acre unit of Canada, found that with the poorer soil 160 acres was not enough for the settler. In South Africa the soil is deficient in chemical constituents and therefore needs scientific treatment and artificial manures, and much of it is in consequence unsuitable for small settlers. When it comes to scientific treatment of the land, the large man with capital and a good education produces the best results, and in South Africa black labour can be got for farm work as it cannot in Canada or Australia. The agricultural economy of the two latter countries has been planned to obviate the labour shortage as much as possible. In Canada a man cultivates a unit that he and his family can handle with occasional help at harvest time, as much aid from machinery being made use of as possible. In Australia he adopts the great ranch for cattle or sheep, which requires very little labour except at shearing time. The climate and the soil in both South Africa and Australia make for the large farm.

In South Australia, Victoria, and New South Wales, the vacant lands have been sold to bring out emigrants, as the six months' journey was so expensive that most people could not afford to come by themselves. When land is granted away to railway companies like the Canadian Pacific, the companies, of course, sell to would-be settlers the land now made valuable by the railway.

The recent policy of Australia and New Zealand has been to try to break up the large stations, resume the land, and promote closer settlement in smaller farms, a very interesting social experiment, but so far the large unit holds its own and shows little appreciable diminution in size.

In South Africa there is very little vacant Crown land to be either sold or given away ; it can only be purchased from some previous owner, generally a land company.

In this region perhaps more is done to encourage scientific agriculture than in any of the self-governing Dominions. The interesting thing is that this stimulus to agriculture is largely the outcome of the Boer War. Lord Milner had to settle repatriated Boers on the land. He was anxious to settle Englishmen on the land as well, so as to mix the races. Previously the English had lived in the towns and the Boers in the country. Above all he wished to introduce better agriculture under the new conditions. After the war, the Government was for a time that of the Crown Colony type in the Transvaal and Orange River State, and so he had a freer hand for reconstruction than he would have had with a Parliament.[1] South Africa was an agricultural country, but its agriculture was primitive in the extreme ; a large part of the food was imported and even farmers lived on tinned milk. Lord Milner started the Transvaal Board of Agriculture and got scientists from all over the world, but mainly from the United States, to help him to deal scientifically with African agricultural problems. Science is needed more in Africa than almost anywhere by reason of the insect pests, and because the soil, not being naturally rich, needs chemical treatment if it is to yield well. Much of the country is very dry. The general results of these organized efforts to check noxious ticks, locusts, flies, and mosquitos and to preach scientific agriculture were little short of a miracle. The combined effect of the education of the farmer, the starting of land banks and the popularization of*scientific research has been to turn South Africa from a pastoral, almost nomadic type of agriculture, importing the bulk of its food, into a self-sufficing country exporting hides, great quantities of wool, together with meat and maize.

The fusion of the four colonies in the Union in 1910 enabled the mobilization of the agricultural experts in a single department, with great advantage to agricultural research. The veterinary department has helped to discover and fight the diseases of cattle and has rendered it possible to keep good stock. South Africa was particularly prolific in animal diseases. After describing how there is horse sickness for horses, glanders for donkeys, scab for sheep and goats, a special complaint for poultry, dog sickness and

---

[1] It is interesting to notice that two Englishmen have had great opportunities to reconstruct parts of Africa after a devastating war, Lord Kitchener in the Sudan and Lord Milner in the Boer Republics.

cat sickness, lung sickness, gall sickness, and spleen sickness for cattle, the author of *The Old Transport Road* goes on to talk of the rinderpest and the African coast fever.

" Rinderpest spared about ten per cent of the cattle and these latter, being salted, at once increased enormously in value. The Coast Fever spared practically none. I myself had one beast left out of hundreds. . . . Out of a thousand Australian cows belonging to Cecil Rhodes, all except three had died within a few days. . . . It appeared that, along the sea-coast, all cattle were born with this ' African Coast Fever ' in their systems. So long as they remained near the sea the poison never affected them, but the moment they were moved to the high country they died from it. Cecil Rhodes' Australian cows were landed at Beira, and were allowed to mix with the local cattle. In a few days every one was infected, the infection being carried by the ordinary tick. When they reached Umtali the disease came out. They died quickly enough ; but they left hundreds of thousands of infected ticks behind them," and these infected all the other cattle. The Rinderpest had killed all the buffalo in the fly belt, and the tsetse fly had died out with the buffalo, as they bred in the animal's dung. It was, therefore, possible to take cattle from the coast into the interior, as there was now no tsetse fly to kill the animals en route. The Rinderpest destroyed the fly, incidentally, and the result was that Coast Fever could spread with the animals into the fly country.

" Our cattle died. We lost everything we owned in material wealth ; yet the latter was but a small part of it all. We might make fresh fortunes, but there were the things we could not replace, the things which had gone from us for ever—our youth and our enthusiasms and our illusions. These we had buried for ever in that dreary South African veld, as so many thousands of other men have done. Africa takes all and gives nothing in return—except a grave, and even that the hyænas do not respect." [1]

It was just that sort of epidemic and ruin that the new departments of agriculture were designed to prevent. The Union possesses one of the largest and best equipped institutions in the world for investigating the diseases of animals peculiar to warm countries, and it has achieved great results in eradicating contagious diseases or keeping them under control in various ways, one of which is a system

[1] Hyatt : *The Old Transport Road*, pp. 294–300.

of chemical dips, of which there are 2,000, into which the cattle are driven at intervals and the ticks eliminated. The value of its work is estimated at millions of pounds per annum. The Division of Entomology had for a time the almost complete annihilation of the locust to its credit—an incredible scourge which used to eat the country bare. The swarms were traced to their breeding-places and the young locusts were sprinkled with a mixture of arsenic and molasses. When killed themselves they poisoned the others who fed on their corpses. The Division of Botany has introduced new crops and valuable grasses such as teff from Abyssinia, which is invaluable for hay crops.[1] There are few, if any, countries in the world in which agriculture has made such strides in the last eighteen years, except perhaps in Germany, also the land of autocracy and scientific farming. In the interior of South Africa farming has been transformed from what was little more than nomadic grazing into an organized industry.[2]

This very success is raising in an acute form the question of the native and his land. He is impeding the white man's expansion, and he is not a good farmer. To what extent shall he be allowed with his thriftless farming to hold lands outside his reserves which can now be turned to good account ?

While Canada has been primarily the land of the small farmer, and South Africa, since the Boer War, the land of Government development by science, Australia has had to face the great problem of irrigation. She is also changing her type of cultivation from sheep or cattle farming to dairying and wheat, and both these latter developments afford the possibility of settling the small man satisfactorily on the land. The Labour Party is very anxious to do this, partly because its members dislike the capitalist squatter, " the squattocracy," partly because they feel that in Australia the town congestion is a real menace and that people should have facilities to get out and settle in the country. Nearly three out of the six and a quarter millions of people in Australia are gathered in five towns on the coast.

[1] 260,000 acres were grown in 1920–1.

[2] In the discussion on Mr. F. B. Smith's paper on " South African Agriculture and its Development," Major Struben said: " The settler required was not the kind of man suitable for Canada or Australia. The farmer in South Africa should be a scientist, or, at any rate, farm on scientific lines and he should be equipped, besides knowledge, with a certain amount of capital enabling him to tide over the first few trying years." *United Empire*, July 1921, p. 513.

For the first sixty years of her existence Australia's economic life hinged on sheep. The country to the east of a line drawn from Adelaide to Brisbane was a vast sheep run. The average land allowed was one sheep to the acre, and great runs as large as English counties were not uncommon. Runs actually ranged from 1,000 to 9,000 square miles in area.[1] It has been the aim of both Australia and New Zealand to break up these huge runs. As the rainfall is, however, deficient or uncertain over large parts of Australia, irrigation is absolutely necessary if a small man is to settle and cultivate intensively. In Australia it is said one pays for water not for land. The efforts of the Government of Australia have of recent years been devoted either to digging artesian bores for watering stock—the water is alkali, and not suited for plants, though cattle can generally drink it— or to making available some of the river and storm water for wheat and fruit growing. The governments have devoted themselves actively to repurchasing estates and breaking them up into wheat farms. And yet in times of depression or drought small farmers go under and farms coalesce into bigger units which weather the uncertainties of the climate with a larger amount of success. In their desire to have more small farmers, Australia and New Zealand have been greatly helped by cold storage, which made dairy farming a financial success and enabled a big export trade in Australian and New Zealand butter to develop. Equally striking has been the development of Australian wheat for export since 1890, but the yields per acre are poor and the agricultural methods are as yet by no means scientific.

The area under wheat in Australia increased from 3,500,000 acres in 1895 to 12,484,512 in 1915–16, figures which show that wheat was encroaching on cattle and sheep. The bushels produced increased from 48·35 millions in 1900–1 to an average of 118·5 millions during the period 1917–27, and the exports from 20·26 million bushels in 1901 to an average of 87·1 millions in 1922–7.[2]

Thus, from merely pastoral countries both South Africa and Australia are changing to agricultural countries. Australia, too, finances small settlers and advances money to farmers to tide them over bad drought years. New Zealand also pursues much the same policy. Like Canada, Australia has taken to machinery, her great specialities being the

---

[1] J. Collier : *Pastoral Age in Australasia*, p. 71.
[2] *Commonwealth Year Book*, 1928, pp. 671, 675.

stump-jumping plough, which evades the tree-roots, and the stripper harvester, which picks the grain, threshes it, and puts it in bags all at the same time. This is possible because the dryness of the climate dries the grain sufficiently in the ear. In Canada the grain has to dry off before threshing. Canada has been helped in her wheat production by the flat treeless prairie land and the absence of stones. Australia has had to ring-bark the eucalyptus trees and let them die, so the stump-jumping plough helps her over the special obstacles of roots and stumps which do not occur in the Canadian West. In Australia, in order to avoid the great expense of shepherds, huge areas or paddocks are fenced and the animals are left to look after themselves. The typical Australian worker of the back block is the boundary rider who simply repairs fences. He does not tend sheep. Australia with its artesian bores and its great fenced areas is being taken as the model for the development of German South-West Africa now mandated to the Union Government.

In Western Canada this system of ranching is impossible by reason of the climate. The sheep or cattle would move before a blizzard till they came to a fence, where they would be snowed under. They must be free to move in front of the storm. An absence of fences with branding and a round-up is therefore typical of Canadian cattle-rearing in the prairies or at the foothills of the Rockies.

Both South Africa and Australia provide facilities for agricultural education, but in South Africa they are appreciated and in Australia they are not. The Australian stock farmer is a scientific breeder of sheep and cattle who is second to none, but labour is too short to permit the Australian agriculturist who is a small farmer to send his son to an agricultural college for a couple of years. In Africa the presence of negro labour obviates this difficulty, and no less than a thousand students have taken a one or two years' course at the agricultural schools since the Union, while 3,500 have attended shorter courses.[1]

Australia has no monopoly of irrigation projects. South Africa, too, has its deserts, and the Union in 1912 passed an Irrigation Act, by which seventy irrigation districts were laid out, loans of many millions were to be forthcoming, and an irrigation rate levied to repay the advances. The

---

[1] F. B. Smith : " South African Agriculture and its Development," in *United Empire*, July, 1921, p. 510.

production of crops under irrigation demands much more skill than production under rainfall only. Sometimes irrigation brings out the brack or salt in the soil and makes it useless. Different quantities of water are required for different crops : for cereals four waterings, for lucerne three. Moreover, the land needs to be levelled so that the water can be supplied evenly. An uneven distribution of the water means an uneven crop. It is, therefore, obvious that the country that undertakes irrigation on a large scale will have to undertake agricultural education as well.[1]

At present the great cereal of South Africa is maize, which is used, as in the United States, for producing meat by fattening cattle ; the chief cereal of Canada is wheat, and then oats; but comparatively little attention has been paid hitherto to meat production for export, though dairying is developing in both East and West. Cattle ranches are to be found in Alberta at the foot of the Rocky Mountains, but here distance from the British markets is the great obstacle. It was only when Klondyke provided a great market that the alternative to wheat had a chance to develop. Indeed, the great problem of Canada is to get not only its cattle but the grain to market at a cost that will surmount the great disadvantages of the enormous land distance it has to travel. The handling of wheat in elevators by the steamers on the lakes and by the railways is all highly organized, and a Government Board of Grain Commissioners appointed in 1912 samples and grades the wheat. Much Canadian grain has to be held over the winter either at the

---

[1] That irrigation needs great skill and is not always uniformly successful may be seen from the following quotation from a former Director of Agriculture in the Bombay Presidency :

"Wet cultivation requires far more capital than dry cultivation. For effective work the land must be levelled and in many cases drained, tillage is more exacting and the handling of the valuable crops more costly. Few of the land-holders have the necessary capital for the purpose and few have the requisite skill or business capacity to grow the more valuable crops successfully ; and their efforts to grow sugar cane are often lamentable. There is a small number of really skilled cultivators who grow good crops of about 50 tons of cane to the acre and make large profits. . . .

"The present situation of the canal areas may be roughly described as follows : The land is seldom levelled or laid off for irrigation in the manner essential to effective production and the economical use of water. The fields are greatly subdivided into sizes and shapes which make proper irrigation almost impossible. . . . On the Godavari Canals, which have been opened up only ten years, 6,300 acres have been totally or partially ruined up to date by water-logging and the salt efflorescence that results from it. This water-logging is no doubt largely due to waste of water on the part of the cultivators." (Keatinge : *Agricultural Progress in Western India*, pp. 81–3.)

farms or in the elevators, as freight is too expensive to send it on by rail when the lakes freeze. The small farmers experience great difficulty in finding time in the spring when there is open water to do the haulage to the railway, as that is just the time they ought to be sowing the new crop. Hence there is an autumn rush to get the wheat out before the lakes close up. Should it prove profitable to send wheat out by Vancouver and round by the Panama Canal, the terrible disadvantage of the winter hold-up on the lakes would be obviated, and a much needed alternative route to the Winnipeg neck would be provided, but there is the long expensive haul over the Rocky Mountains, the absence of elevator accommodation at Vancouver, and the heavy dues to be paid on going through the Canal, to say nothing of the special precautions needed to prevent grain in bulk from heating when going through the Tropics. Moreover, the ships to fetch the grain would probably have to go out in ballast to Vancouver and would have to pay the Canal dues for going out as well as returning. But if China should take to eating wheat instead of rice, then Vancouver would certainly become a great outlet for the export of wheat.

In Australia, the highly organized market is in wool. Banks have grown up which buy and sell the wool as part of their business. Commission houses exist which sell the wool on commission and finance the grower. So famous has Australian wool become that a large portion of it, about 90 per cent, was sold in Australia itself before the war, buyers coming from all over the world to the sales. On the other hand, there is no big organization in Australia for the marketing of the wheat, though since the war New South Wales has been building a few silos or elevators. The wheat is brought to the sheds at the railway stations in bags, where it lies for some time, and while there it is often destroyed by weevils, or the bags are eaten through by mice or rats, so that the wheat runs out and transport becomes a great problem. Two years' harvest during the war were destroyed by plagues of mice and weevil. The wheat is taken on in a more or less dilatory fashion to the capital, and there sold for what it will fetch. It is one of the most expensive wheat crops in the world to handle, but as all the machinery is designed for bagging and not for elevators by which grain is taken mechanically out of cars and poured again into the holds of cars or steamers, the method of handling is unlikely to be radically changed in the near future, to say nothing of the difficulty of preventing the wheat from heating when taken in bulk through the Tropics.[1] The bags allow the air to get through, so preventing the wheat from swelling. The Australian wheat export is not yet large enough to build specialized steamers with divided compartments for the traffic.

On all these factors depends the bulk of England's imported food supply. Whether or not there is closer settlement in Australia may make all the difference to the English butter and meat supply, and to the clothing industry of Yorkshire. Small farmers are not likely to grow merino sheep for wool and may not grow cattle in numbers for frozen meat, but they will probably produce more dairy produce. If Africa can conquer its insect pests, the South may take the place of Australia as the great source of the English wool and meat supply. In the last respect Nigeria, Northern Rhodesia, and possibly the Sudan will be, with improved methods of stock breeding and cold storage, one of the great meat supply areas of the future. At present the quality of meat grown in the Tropics is inferior, as the animals do not put on fat. From both South Africa and the Tropics increasing quantities of fruit may be expected with more irrigation and scientific culture. The railway rates of Canada or an early winter, closing the great lakes, may make all the difference to the price of the English loaf.

If China with her millions takes to eating wheat, instead of rice, and Canada can ship there in quantities the price of the English loaf will surely rise.

Nevertheless, if these countries can sell they will buy, and the great workshops of Northern Europe will hum to supply both the regions near the Arctic and those of the Antipodes. The British Empire is at present a vast agricultural Empire, focussed on Great Britain for markets and loans. Outside the British Empire is the great British financial colony of Argentina. Canada, South Africa, and Australasia have to sell in competition with each other and with Argentina in the British market, the greatest market for food and raw materials in the world. On Great Britain's prosperity the prosperity of her Dominions and Dependencies must in the long run hinge. If she cannot

---

[1] Elevators have been built in New South Wales, but it has been found more expensive to handle the wheat in this way than in bags (*D.O.T. Report*, 1923, pp. 55–6).

sell manufactures she does not require raw materials, and there is a slump in rubber, cotton, and minerals all over the Empire. If she cannot sell she has to cut down her food bill, the food-producing regions suffer, and there is a slump in tea in Assam, in cocoa in West Africa, in sugar, in mutton, and wheat. All the Tropics and the temperate regions are affected by the depression " at home ". If Great Britain cannot sell she cannot accumulate capital and the whole of the future development of the Empire is checked. As Lord Islington, speaking in the House of Lords [1] said : " Thinking imperially without thinking inter-imperially will lead under our modern conditions to grave trouble if not to disaster."

[1] *Hansard*, 14th July, 1920, p. 129.

CHAPTER 5

INDUSTRIAL DEVELOPMENT AND LABOUR PROBLEMS

So far, nothing in the Dominions corresponding to the Industrial Revolution.

Canada : Cold storage.
        Water power and electricity.
        Poor coal.
        Iron imports from U.S.
        Small scale industry; possibility of development of large scale industry via U.S.

Australia : Industrial development still in incipient stage and bounty-fed.
        Agricultural implements' manufacture.
        High freight on imports owing to distance a stimulus to manufacturing development.

South Africa : Scattered population and high cost of distribution discourage industrial development.

Town Development : In Canada due not to factories but to necessity of having centres of exchange for the farming interest.
        In Australia due to demand for labour at ports, to disposition of shearers and others to look to town for diversion after isolation of country.

Labour Movement : In Canada only slightly developed.
        An echo of the labour movement in U.S.
        Hostility to immigration.
        In Australia a strong labour movement. Social experiment.
        " Socialisme sans doctrines."
        Hostility to immigration.
        Labour unrest.

IF by the term " Industrial Revolution " is meant large scale engineering works and textile factories, the Industrial Revolution has as yet scarcely touched any of the self-governing Dominions. The beginnings of industrial development are, however, apparent.

The railways are always the great stimulus to industrialization in new countries. They necessitate repairing sheds and if the colony possesses iron and coal a certain amount of rail-making is likely to follow, though locomotives are usually imported.[1] The principal industries are, however, usually of an agricultural nature or connected with extractive processes. Thus flour-milling follows naturally on the Canadian wheat supply, pulp factories arise out of her timber supply and are followed by the development of

---

[1] Australia and India are the two best customers for British locomotives.

paper factories. Cold storage is an industrial development following on an available supply of carcases ; butter and cheese factories are reckoned in Canada as industrial undertakings. It was almost inevitable that Canada should take to ship-building on the Lakes ; and with iron in Newfoundland and coal in Novia Scotia there are ship-building possibilities on the Atlantic coast. The future of Canada, however, seems to be bound up with electricity, although her water-power is hampered by the severity of the winter, when much of it freezes and dams to conserve and equalize the supply have great difficulties with block ice. Frazil ice also interferes with the working of the turbines. The Great War enormously stimulated the industrial development of Canada and the exploitation of her hydraulic resources. Coal is found in Canada in the Maritime Provinces and in Alberta, that is, East and West. Much of it in Alberta is lignite or brown coal with a low heating and power capacity. For the central region coal is imported from the United States, and this region would be very badly off for power were it not for the great electrical development centred round Niagara and lesser waterfalls. Electricity seems specially adapted for certain types of chemical and iron production, and to these a great stimulus was given by the War. The difficulty in Canada is that no iron of good quality has yet been found either near the coal or near the waterfalls and she has to import the bulk of her iron ore from the United States. Although bounties were given by the Canadian Government to 1911 on the production of iron, the engineering trades, the basis of a great industrial development, have always been unduly hampered. She has, however, a considerable industry in agricultural machinery. In Canada industry is carried on by men with small capital working on a small scale. The recent tendency is for firms in the United States to set up branch factories in Canada, and it is from these that the stimulus to large scale industry seems to be coming.

In Australia there is little industrial development of the large factory type. Although she is passionately anxious to work up her own wool, only some 7 per cent or so is retained in the country in spite of bounties on wool-combing and a high tariff on cloth. There has been only a slight development in the manufacture of iron and steel, though the Broken Hill Proprietary Company made arrangements for bringing the ore round by sea from Iron Knob in South Australia to Newcastle, New South Wales, where there is a vast coalfield situated on the coast.[1] Bounties are given in Australia as formerly in Canada on the production of iron and steel. With the Australian specialities of the stripper-harvester and the stump-jumping plough, there is naturally an important industry of agricultural implement making. Indeed, the enormous distance from Europe should stimulate an attempt to be self-sufficing in manufactured goods. Canada's wants can so easily be satisfied either from England or from the United States next door ; but Australia has to pay a freightage so high as to be equivalent to an additional tariff. In all colonies there are necessarily industries connected with heat, light and power, such as gas-works, electric light and waterworks ; and the building trades and some furniture making necessarily exist ; but the general stage of evolution is that, apart from the engineering works stimulated by railways, the first developments come in treating the raw materials of the district.

The average number employed in factories in the Commonwealth in 1926–7 was 467,247. In that year 17,259 establishments had 20 hands and under ; 3,587 factories had from 21 to 100 hands and 733 over 100 hands. It is obvious, therefore, that Australia is still in the stage of small scale industrial establishments.

In South Africa the white population is so small and scattered that large scale industrial development seems unlikely in the near future, though bounties on iron and steel [2] and a protectionist tariff have both been resorted to since the end of 1918. The cost of transporting manufactured articles over the long distances of South Africa is at present an almost impassable obstacle to a successful industrial development and the population is too small to provide a big enough market in any one spot. It is the cost of distribution rather than the cost of manufacture that is the difficulty.

Town life, which is usually an outcome of the industrial revolution, has developed in both Australia and Canada for quite other reasons than those connected with factories. In Canada, the type of settlement is in homesteads and the " whole of the groups practising commercial farming may be said to be devoting themselves to the production

[1] In 1927 the output of pig iron was 416,533 tons and of steel ingots 387,929 tons. (*Commonwealth Year Book*, 1928, p. 773.)
[2] Iron and Steel Industry Encouragement Act, 1922 (Act No. 41 of 1922).

of wheat for sale. They are thus under the necessity of purchasing what they consume and of buying all the implements and materials they use. For the service of this class the towns have grown up. Through the towns there pass on the one hand the products of the commercial farmer and on the other nearly all the commodities he consumes." [1]

In Australia the development of towns is abnormal, being due partly to the fact that little labour is required for sheep-rearing in the back blocks and that a great deal is required for handling the products at the ports. The biggest class of labourers is the shearers and they are migratory and seasonal. The railways, leading as they did to the capital, increased the town congestion and the Australian idea of having a good time and not being a " wowser " inclines him to the social amenities of a town rather than to the isolation of the farming life.

In Canada the labour movement is but slightly developed. The labour required on the farms is seasonal, and in the winter, unless a man can get work in the lumber camps, he drifts into the towns. These people lower the wages of the artisans in the towns, being a reserve of labour that can be drawn upon. On the other hand, it is easy to migrate into the United States, and this again makes for a migratory international class who do not support strong labour unions. At the same time such control as there is in the labour movement comes from the United States, as the Canadian workmen are in American Unions and thus Canadian employers have to submit to American control of their labour. The labour movement in Canada is merely an echo of the movement in the United States. On the whole the labour movement in Canada, such as it is, is hostile to immigration, as the newcomers either stay in the towns and bring down wages or go on the land and form a winter problem of unemployment with the further chance of lowering wages.

In Australia, where immigration is nothing like so easy owing to much higher fares, the community is far more self-contained, and there is perhaps the strongest labour movement in the world. The failure of several strikes in the 'nineties caused it to turn its energies in the direction of getting control of the Government, and Australia was

[1] J. Mavor : " Economic Survey," in *Oxford Survey of the Empire*, vol. iv, p. 157.

the first country in which a Labour Party has really been in power. In New Zealand Labour and Liberals combined. There has been a great deal of social experiment in both Dominions in consequence. Minimum wages have been fixed by law, and compulsory arbitration boards have been set up to prevent strikes, in which object, however, they have failed.[1] The Labour Party when in power carried out the attack on the big estates and attempted all sorts of public works and State businesses. The various States and New Zealand have even started State insurance offices. A State fishing fleet was worked by New South Wales until 1923 and the Government had fourteen State retail fish depôts in Sydney and six elsewhere. It has built large refrigerating works at Newcastle, Clarence River, and Port Stephens. The Commonwealth has great freezing works at Port Darwin, which were erected at the cost of £750,000. Many other remarkable experiments have been undertaken in Queensland. It is no wonder that a Frenchman, Siegfried, writing on Australasia, characterized its peoples as practising " Socialisme sans doctrines ".

The labour party in both Australia and New Zealand is hostile to the immigration of white artisans for fear they should lower the standard of comfort the workers have attained. They are ardent supporters of the "White Australia" policy for fear Asiatics should undercut wages. Yet the high standard of wages has not brought industrial peace. Probably in no country is there so much labour unrest.[2]

[1] Between 1916–19 there were 1,710 strikes and 12,500,000 working days lost.   H. Heaton : " Basic Wage Principle in Australian Wage Regulation," in *Economic Journal*, 1921, vol. xxxi, p. 309 n.

[2] " In spite of the Federal and State Arbitration Courts and other industrial tribunals, there were 624 strikes in Australia in 1921 involving a loss of £750,000 in wages. In the last nine years there have been 3,791 strikes, with a loss in wages of £11,000,000. The Broken Hill strike of miners and smelters caused a loss of £2,500,000 in wages besides the loss to the companies." (*Times*, quoting its Melbourne Correspondent, 23rd August, 1922.)

CHAPTER 6

TENDENCY TO PATERNAL GOVERNMENT IN NEW COUNTRIES AND FACTORS SHAPING POLICIES

In new countries the State has to finance enterprises which in old countries would be financed privately.

Assistance to immigrants.

Inherited influences predisposing to State action :

In South Africa : Early military importance ; native questions; reconstruction under Milner.

In Australia : Administration of convict Settlements.

In New Zealand : Maori wars.

In Canada : Less reliance on the State than in other Dominions.

Generally : Sanitation, public health and scientific agriculture; railway questions.

Divergency of interests between different regions of same Dominion as factors in Dominion politics

Canada : Industrial East versus agricultural West.

Australia : Tropical North versus temperate South.

South Africa : Agriculture versus mining.

General tendency towards protection, but to abolition of tariff barriers internally.

Stimulus from local fears as factors in shaping policy :

Canada : Effects of proximity of United States.

Australasia : Chinese and Japanese immigration.

South Africa : Native questions.

THE importance of State activities in new countries has already been emphasized. State action is further urgent in a struggling community in that the State alone seems able to secure money and credit, the prime necessity of the immigrant. Even if he brings a certain amount of capital with him, the actual expenses of the settlement are generally so heavy that he usually has to borrow. He must build a house and sink a well ; to cultivate the land he must have a plough and a horse or two ; he must buy seed and must also be able to tide over at least the first year until the crops are harvested and the returns come in. Manufacturers who start new businesses in a new country must usually obtain credit or borrow the capital. The shopkeeper generally buys his stock on credit and sells on credit and has to wait till the customers' crops are grown to get his payment. In other words, there must be adequate banking and credit facilities if the country is to go ahead. While private banks have usually been the pioneers in this respect, the government has had to find a great deal of money which in the older countries would have been found through the banks or through joint stock companies. In New Zealand the Government actually does a money-lending business. Again, in their early days all colonial governments, whether federal, provincial, or municipal, have been obliged to raise large loans for public works and railways which could not be undertaken by private enterprise, and as the domestic accumulation of capital ready for investment is small, such borrowing is usually effected abroad.

Immigrants have to be helped by grants of money or seed or by advances to tide over droughts. Subsidies, a guarantee of a minimum price, bounties on production and the marketing of the produce have all formed part of State activities in the newly settled countries. Indeed, the functions of the Government in such countries seem only to be limited by their capacity to borrow and to pay interest on their debts.

Certain inherited influences, however, predispose the overseas States to widen or restrict their functions apart from the ease or difficulty of obtaining loans. Cape Colony was a military settlement, and Cape Town was a port the chief object of which was to guard the sea route to India and provision the ships going to India. The Kaffir wars increased the military element and led men to look to the Government for protection against the incursion of savages. A ruling race always on the *qui vive* against Kaffir invasions or native risings necessarily develops a military and autocratic outlook, and this was intensified by the fact that the officials lived in the towns and the Boers in the country, and the towns were the dictators on questions of policy. The Boers, being a Dutch Puritan stock reinforced by Huguenots, would be naturally individualistic and self-dependent, but the native danger counteracted their inherent dislike of government in much the same way as the Prussian military tradition operated in Germany when the threat from Poles, Russians, and French was pressing. The tendency to State control in South Africa was continued with the abolition of slave-owning and the necessity of supervising the proper treatment of native races.   This State tradition was intensified after the Boer War, when Lord Milner reconstructed the whole economic fabric of the Transvaal and the Orange Free State.

In New South Wales, which at first included what is now Victoria, Queensland, and Tasmania, the convict foundation also had its influence in favour of State action.   Not merely was the whole life of the convicts in the hands of the Government, but the military sent out to guard them also introduced the autocratic element.   The Government had to provide the clothing and the food for both convicts and soldiers, and often for the settlers as well.   It assigned convicts to settlers and was responsible in this way for the labour supply, and therefore for the development of the estates.   It disposed of vacant land either by gift, sale, or lease, and bought the produce of the land to feed the convicts.   It had thus in the early years of the colony almost the whole of the economic interests of Australia in its hands, and was at once the chief source of the labour supply, the principal market, and the universal provider.   In the 'thirties the State land sales provided a fund for emigrants who were brought out at State expense.   It was the State every step of the way.

Although there was no military element in the foundation of New Zealand, the wars with the Maoris soon led to its introduction.   According to the Treaty of Waitangi of 1840, no land could be acquired from the Maoris except through the Government, and this tended to accentuate the principle of State control.

In Canada the French military tradition and the feudal system of Quebec naturally exalted the Government, but this was so strongly counteracted by the immigrants of Puritan origin from the United States and by later Scotch and English settlers and also by the *laissez faire* tradition of the flourishing republic next door that Canada has been far more individualistic in her policy than either Australia, New Zealand, or South Africa.

The activities of all Governments were increased with the growing knowledge of the principles of sanitation and public health and the advent of scientific agriculture.   In the destruction of insect pests, mosquitoes, ticks, locusts, and plant parasites, the Government alone can afford the co-ordinated research necessary and is the only power able to insist on the necessary steps for carrying preventive measures into effect.

All Colonial government is intimately bound up with railway questions. In the self-governing Dominions a burning question has been whether the railways shall be run by private companies controlled by Parliament or by a Commission acting for the State. In this latter case a further conflict has arisen as to whether the Commissions shall be directly dependent on Parliament or rendered independent of parliamentary influence and changes in government. The Australian railways are State railways, and after a somewhat hectic career were put " out of politics ". The Commissions which managed them were made independent, being appointed for a term of years, but as the State Parliaments still decide as to the building of new railways, they control to that extent the growth of the railway system. New Zealand tried an independent Commission and went back to Parliamentary interference. In South Africa the railways are also State railways, but were carefully put " out of politics " on the creation of the Union in 1910, the history of the Australian railways having proved a salutary warning. Contrary to the usual experience of State railways, they were, up to 1914, a considerable financial success.

The Canadian railways, on the contrary, were in the main left to private initiative, but the Intercolonial Railway connecting the Atlantic provinces with the St. Lawrence was a State railway from the first, as there seemed to be no chance of its being a paying proposition and it was politically necessary as a connecting-link between the Provinces in winter. Its management gave rise to some scandals, as did also the initial Government efforts in connexion with the Canadian Pacific Railway, which was at one time planned as a State undertaking but was completed as a privately managed railway with the aid of large land grants from the Government. After 1900, railway development in Canada was very rapid, fostered as it was by State subsidies and the mileage built was in excess of the requirements of the country. The Grand Trunk, with its offshoot the Grand Trunk Pacific, and the Canadian Northern ceased to pay during the war, and a Royal Commission—the Drayton-Acworth Commission—was appointed to make recommendations as to their fate. They reported that the railways would have under the circumstances to be taken over by the Government and they recommended that they should be managed for the Government by a

Committee quite independent of the Legislature,[1] for : "It is only when the management is protected from the pressure of special interests that a railway can be managed in the interest of the public as a whole ; that it can be expected that alterations and improvements will be made, even though they injuriously affect certain individuals, because they are justified by greater benefits to the people at large. To take one example. We are satisfied that there are many cases where in the interest of economy duplicate services should be abolished and duplicate stations closed. Any such change must injure somebody. Supposing that it results in a saving of $1,000 a year to the taxpayer while the injury can be measured by a loss of $25 a head to three or four people, clearly the change ought to be made. But if the three or four men can get their grievances voiced in Parliament while the taxpayer is an abstract entity with no one to speak for him probably the change will never be made."

Unwilling as Parliaments are to surrender power to a bureaucracy, nevertheless the Canadian Government, in obedience to this recommendation, handed the Canadian Government Railways over to an independent Board of Management.

Thus the tendency of State policy is towards State railways. It is a policy which affects the life of a new country at every stage and makes the State a partner in all trade and development.

In the State politics of every European country there is as a rule considerable divergency of interests between different regions. There was, for instance, the hostility of the manufacturing Catholic Rhineland to the agricultural Junker of Germany east of the Elbe, and the opposition of Prussia and Bavaria. In the United States there are great divergencies between North and South, East and West. In Canada the great dividing line is East and West. The Western grain growers complain of the middleman and the elevator companies, and resent the preponderance of the industrial East. So strong are they that they have formed a Farmers' Party in politics and a great wheat pool for marketing wheat. All agricultural exporting interests favour low duties. They want to extend their own markets and buy their manufactures

---

[1] Report of the Royal Commission on Railways in Canada, Sessional Paper 20g (1917).

cheap. They are therefore free trade while young industries are protectionist. In Australia the opposition is between North and South. In the North is found the palm tree ; the hills are clad with cedar ; there is luxuriant vegetation and tropical jungle. There are great tracts of sugar cane, pineapples, rice fields, and banana groves. Further south come the temperate climates with fruit orchards and dairy farming. The Country Party clashes with the Labour Party in the towns. Agricultural Cape Colony resents the dominion of the mining magnates, while they in their turn, before the Union, resented the policy of high freights which the Union railways charged by way of making the mines pay for the railway system.

All young countries, being intensely national, want industries, they regard it as part of the equipment of a nation that it should have a diversified economic life. Canada resents " wheat mining " ; Australia the squatters and the concentration on wool ; and South Africa the gold and diamonds. They are earnestly desirous of having more varied opportunities available. Hence they all have protective tariffs, whereas the tariffs of the Crown Colonies are merely revenue tariffs. Canada especially wants protection from the more developed American industries. Australia wishes to defend herself against goods made by the " pauper labour " of Europe. And yet all the time there has gone on a widening of the internal free market by federations and the abolition of internal tariff barriers. Therefore from end to end inside Canada, Australia, and South Africa since 1867, 1901, and 1910 respectively, goods pass free where previously they were taxed, and New Zealand abolished her Provinces in 1875.

In the economic development of the nations within the Empire the influence of Great Britain can be traced all through ; nevertheless, outside influences have had a good deal to do with shaping the policy of each Dominion. There have been certain stimuli and certain fears which have had much to do with the evolution of the British colonies.

In the history of Canada, jealousy and fear of the United States have been constant factors. Canadians are very anxious to preserve their British nationality and to avoid Americanization. This motive has been the determining factor in their protectionist policy and has influenced a good deal of the railway policy. The Intercolonial Railway goes a long way round rather than take the short cut through Maine. Canadians are afraid of their industries being swamped by those of the United States ; they are afraid of the power of American trusts ; and they have been incensed by the way in which the United States Government has refused to grant reciprocity since 1866 ; they are even now afraid that the hordes of American immigrants who are taking up land in the West may divert the West from its allegiance to the East and try to promote annexation to the big neighbour. On the other hand, there is no denying that such watchful jealousy is a great spur to effort and that in rivalry Canadians have learnt a great deal from Americans. Nor has the growing power of Japan been without its influence.

Australasia is haunted by the nightmare of Chinese and Japanese immigration. Australia knows that a large part of its land is in the Tropics, that it is unlikely that the white man will be able to develop the Northern Territories, and that empty lands are a standing invitation to the over-populated peoples of Asia. China is computed to have four hundred million people and Japan sixty-three million.[1] Can Australia with only six millions arrogate to herself any moral right of exclusion ? She is mortally afraid of having a colour question like that of the United States, her Labour Party have a horror of cheap Asiatic labour, and she regards the Chinese and Indians as unfit for a share in democratic government.

South Africa once had the fear of the Germans before her eyes, and although this is now removed, a mere handful of whites always has to fear a native rising. Hence she has to try and deal constructively with the problem of black and white.

The policy of Canada then is to handle wheat cheaply, develop if possible native industries on the basis of her great water resources, and keep free of the United States. The problem of Australia is that of distance from her markets and shipping freights are her principal concern. Her State policy is dictated by a wish to maintain a high standard of comfort for her people. She also wishes to develop industries so as to be self-sufficing as her imports have to bear such a large burden for freightage. South Africa aims at replacing a great mining with a great agricultural industry. Meanwhile with her centralized position she

[1] *Statesman's Year Book*, 1928, p. 1059.

is destined to become more and more of an entrepôt for
ships that are too large to go through the Suez Canal. We
know that the old Empire was kept together in the eighteenth
century by the fear of the French. The defeat of Russia
by Japan in 1904–5 roused a new fear for the colonies
bordering on the Pacific ; while Germany's proximity
exercised a potent influence on both South Africa and
Australia. But these great dreads have also been great
incentives. The awakening and striving in South Africa
after the Germans established themselves there in the
'eighties is no less remarkable than the effort in Canada
in 1866 and later after reciprocity was turned down by
the United States. The Germans and the Japanese
in the Pacific have done more than anything else to make
Australia conscious of world politics and to create for her
larger horizons. In all the discussions about unifying
the railway gauges in Australia so as to make it possible
to have through traffic from State to State, the military
argument of the greater facility of moving troops is always
urged. If the fear of Japanese invasion accomplishes
the unification of the diverse railway systems it will have
done a great service to Australia.

CHAPTER 7

COMMERCIAL RELATIONS WITHIN THE EMPIRE

Historical Divisions.

The Old Colonial System (to 1776).

Decline and Fall of the System (1776–1846).

Achievement of Fiscal Freedom (1846–1897).

The New Imperial System (1897 onwards).

The Flow of Capital.

Organization and Research.

Linking up.

Diplomatic Relations.

THE commercial relations between the Mother Country and other parts of the Empire have at all times reflected the varying economic and political relations existing within the Empire. Till 1846–9 the Colonies were in a position of political and economic tutelage and also of commercial subordination to the Mother Country. The Empire was then strongly centralized in London, whence issued political laws and also a compendious code of commercial regulations, together ordering colonial life in all departments. The commercial code aimed at two things : an open door policy within the Empire and a bolted door policy to all countries outside the Empire. This meant that all trade between the Empire and the outside world had to flow through the Mother Country, which acted as the sole entrance and exit for the Empire. The trade and shipping of the Empire were Imperial monopolies, both focussed on England. While considerable relaxations were permitted in this rigid system after 1776, the system as a whole was not overthrown until 1846–9.

After 1846–9 the Mother Country attempted to throw off almost all responsibility for the Empire. Economy was the order of the day, and the greatest economy possible was to disband the Empire, for that would bring to an end what James Mill had stigmatized as the " system of outdoor relief to the Colonies "—those substantial grants-in-aid from the Imperial Exchequer to enable the Colonies to balance their Budgets.   Responsible government was almost thrust upon the Colonies in North America, in Australasia, and in South Africa, and with responsible government went sooner or later autonomy in commercial relations.   As a result the Empire was no longer centralized, but came to consist, it might almost be said, of " a congeries of warring atoms ", a number of semi-independent units with extremely independent views on commercial regulations and economic policy.   In no case, however, did economic independence, or any degree of economic self-sufficiency, accompany this political and commercial emancipation.   There was, therefore, a danger of the Colonies falling to some wealthy, industrially developed country which would act as foster-mother in lieu of their own step-mother country and supply the capital and directive ability that were lacking.   The danger was only theoretical in the cases of Australia, New Zealand, and South Africa, for there was no country at hand that could mother them.   In the cases of British North America and the British West Indies, however, the danger was quite real that the United States would mother the Colonies and finally annex them.   Mercantile opinion in Canada after the events of 1846–9 called out for annexation to the United States, American politicians spoke loudly of Canada's " manifest destiny " to become part of the Republic, and a prominent Englishman like Colonel Perronet Thompson exclaimed in the House of Commons : " If we could but lose Canada. . .."

The danger only passed entirely when the Dominions acquired a sense of Colonial nationalism and achieved economic strength, when they felt strong enough to stand on their own legs and to dispense with mothering.   The daughter nations of the Empire had then come of age. This took place for most of the Dominions towards the end of the nineteenth century.   Thereafter with waxing strength and with an increasing sense of the value of the Imperial connexion, the Dominions have developed their twin and somewhat contradictory policies of Protectionism and Imperial Preferences, which to-day have attained the tangled complexity of jungle undergrowth.   The Old Colonial System, with its subordination of the Colonies and its centralization in the Mother Country, has been succeeded by the New Imperial System, with its community of equal nations and its diversity of development and policies.   Between lies half a century of Imperial anarchy (so far as a harmonious Imperial policy is concerned), when the Old System was in the melting-pot and the New System was being laboriously forged.

Historical Divisions

A study of the commercial relations of the Empire naturally falls into four divisions. There is, first of all, the period before 1776 when the Old Colonial System was flourishing in its entirety. Secondly, there is the period between 1776 and 1846, which witnesses the decline and fall of the Old System. Then there follows the period from 1846 to 1897, when commercial and fiscal autonomy was being achieved. Finally there comes the period after 1897 when the New Imperial System (if something so unsystematic can be called a " System ") was established.

Old Colonial System (till 1776).—In the early days Colonies were the " Possessions " of the Mother Country and existed for its benefit.[1] This was not unreasonable since they were costly to the Mother Country in man-power and in the expenses of defence and administration. The return for part of the outlay was generally in the form of various commercial and industrial advantages which the Mother Country enjoyed in the Colonies.

The Old Colonial System may be summarized briefly as follows : (*a*) The Colonies had to import English commodities, being encouraged thereto either by prohibitions or heavy duties on foreign commodities. (*b*) The Colonies had to refrain from certain manufactures which conflicted with the interests of English manufacturers, especially in iron and wool and hats. (*c*) The Colonies had to export their products to England, so that England would have first claim on them (especially in the matter of naval stores) and would also be the great entrepôt in international trade, for such things as tobacco and dye-woods. (*d*) The Colonies had to use English and Colonial shipping both in the import and export trade.

The system, however, was not so rigid and unfair as it sounds and as it is often regarded. Apart from the laxity of administration,[2] certain exceptions were permitted that eased the situation. " Non-enumerated " articles could be

---

[1] Knowles : *Industrial and Commercial Revolutions*, pp. 316–17 ; and G. B. Hertz : *The Old Colonial System*, pp. 37–69.
[2] *Report on Colonial Tariff Policies, United States Tariff Commission* (hereafter known as " C.T.P."), p. 631.

exported more freely than " enumerated " commodities, and the export trade to ports south of Cape Finisterre was gradually relaxed. In addition, certain countervailing prohibitions were laid on the Mother Country in favour of the Colonies. Even as late as 1782 a Yorkshire farmer was fined £36,000 for growing tobacco (a monopoly of the revolting Colonies), and the Justices were empowered to root up all tobacco plants.[1] Moreover, bounties were granted on certain Colonial products, such as tar, hemp, and masts. Finally, it can be argued quite convincingly that the bulk of the Colonial trade would have flowed in those channels, quite apart from regulations,[2] and that the Old Colonial System has been quite unfairly decried.

To enforce the system, it was essential that all vital power should be in the hands of the Mother Country. Nor was this situation unnatural when it is considered that throughout the period the Mother Country heavily subsidized the Colonies. "Legislation of a fiscal and commercial character . . . was supplementary to the fiscal legislation enacted at Westminster for the Empire at large. All laws enacted . . . were not only supplementary to the fiscal legislation of Parliament : they were subordinate to the Acts of the Imperial Parliament. Every Act of a legislature of a colony concerning customs duties had embodied in it the statement that it was effective only in so far as it did not contravene any Act passed by Parliament at Westminster."[3] Till long after 1776 the Mother Country fixed the colonial tariffs and the Colonies could only levy further duties for revenue purposes, which even then might be disallowed by England. Such was the Old Colonial System, not altogether unbeneficial and almost inevitable.

Decline and Fall of the System (1776–1846).—The American Revolt was the beginning of the end, though the end was seventy years in coming. In 1779–80 Ireland demanded and under menaces extorted commercial concessions which for twenty years trenched on the Old

---

[1] W. Page : *Commerce and Industry*, i, p. 27.

[2] " Moreover it was soon evident that the greater part of American foreign commerce continued to be with England, as it had been before the war, this despite the fact that the former colonies were now foreign to the Empire and free, supposedly, from the effect of the Navigation Laws " (S. F. Bemis, *Jay's Treaty*, p. 22).

[3] E Porritt : *Fiscal and Diplomatic Freedom of the British Overseas Dominions*, pp. 82–3.

Colonial System.[1] Further, to conciliate Colonial opinion the Declaratory Act of 1778 was passed.[2] This Act decreed that the proceeds of British-imposed tariffs in the Colonies should accrue to the Colonies but still left the dominant power of imposition with the Mother Country. " On 8th September, 1842, the Governor-General of Canada, in the speech from the throne, announced that the Imperial Parliament had framed a tariff for the British Possessions in North America, which, it was anticipated, would promote essentially their financial and commercial interests. This was the last Canadian tariff made in England." [3]

By the Peace of 1783 England was left a greatly shrunken colonial power, inferior to Spain so far as Colonies were concerned. The British West Indies and British North America were the chief possessions left. India was still in the hands of the East India Company ; South Africa (or the Cape) was still Dutch ; and Australia and New Zealand were as yet unclaimed. From the Empire that was left the United States was rigidly cut off from trading, although its commerce with England, conducted on favoured terms, increased rapidly. This rigid exclusion was gradually, but only slightly, broken down by Executive Proclamations and Orders-in-Council to meet emergencies. The general rule in the case of the British West Indies was that only tobacco, provisions, and naval stores could be exported from the United States to the Islands, and those only in British vessels, while in the case of Canada trade was restricted to British ships and no American goods could be imported.[4] As a result of the emergency measures, the situation was somewhat anomalous : " American vessels were *generally* excluded from all the British colonial possessions, but were *occasionally* received there . . . whenever the interest or necessities of the colonies required supplies from the United States." [5] Even inland trade between Canada and the United States was at first forbidden, but between 1787 and 1793 tobacco, potash, pig iron, and wampum were allowed to enter Canada overland, and in 1788 " all ordinary goods, the product of the

---

[1] W. E. H. Lecky : *Ireland in the Eighteenth Century*, vol. ii, pp. 242–3.
[2] 18 Geo. III, c. 12.
[3] O. D. Skelton : *Canada and the Most Favoured Nation Treaties*, 1912, p. 6.
[4] S. F. Bemis : *Jay's Treaty*, p. 23.
[5] L. W. Tazewell : *Review of the Negotiations between the United States of America and Great Britain respecting Commerce*, p. 3.

province ", could be exported.[1] Jay's Treaty did not alter the situation as much as is commonly thought. It was proposed to permit American vessels up to 70 tons' burden to trade with the British West Indies (rather an empty concession), but this was indignantly rejected by the United States Senate, and trade between the United States and the British West Indies continued as before. As to the inland trade between Canada and the United States, St. Johns on the Richelieu was designated as " the sole port of entry for all goods coming from the United States by land or inland navigation ", and the rates of duties on both sides were determined. No American ship was permitted to enter a British North American seaport, but the islands in Passamaquoddy Bay, a kind of No Man's Land, were found useful exchange centres for merchants of the United States and the Maritime Provinces.[2] These brittle ties were all snapped by the outbreak of the war of 1812.

The wars of 1793–1815 led to further developments in the Colonial System, almost all in favour of the Colonies. By an Act of 1805 free ports were established in the West Indies, and by a further Act of 1809 the system was extended to British North America, and direct trade was permitted between these ports and European ports south of Cape Finisterre.[3] In 1809 and 1810, in addition, a very substantial preference was awarded on colonial timber, which was still further increased in 1813. This was a heavy tax on the Mother Country, but an undoubted benefit to British North America, whose export of timber and commercial prosperity thereafter grew rapidly. In its origin the preference was given so as to guarantee an adequate supply of timber, when the ordinary source of supply from the Baltic was threatened by Napoleon's Continental Policy. Its maintenance after the threat was removed was unalloyed gain to the Colonies.[4]

After the Peace of 1815, the Old Colonial System steadily declined. At first it was attacked piecemeal, but finally it was assailed in its entirety and collapsed in 1846–9. After the war of 1812 was over, the United States demanded access to the Colonies. On England's refusal, the United

[1] *Canada and Its Provinces*, vol. iv, pp. 534–5, 545–6.
[2] Ibid., vol. iv, pp. 547, 554.
[3] Porritt, pp. 6, 12.
[4] J. R. McCulloch : *Dictionary of Commerce*, 1882, p. 1387–92.

States retaliated in 1818 by forbidding ships from the Colonies to enter American ports, and would not even be mollified by the eleventh hour creation of Halifax and St. John as free ports for American ships " carrying certain specified goods which were essential as West Indian supplies ".[1] A precarious peace was patched up in 1823. In 1822 further breaches were made in the Navigation Laws. By an Act of that year England offered to admit other nations into the colonial trade if they would grant reciprocity. By another Act direct trade was permitted between the Colonies and countries north of Cape Finisterre, but only in British vessels. In 1825 Huskisson offered a further relaxation of the Colonial system on a reciprocal basis, but the United States refused the offer, while many other countries gladly accepted it. Then in 1826 the Imperial Government issued an Order-in-Council excluding United States vessels from the ports of the British West Indies and imposing heavy duties on United States vessels frequenting the British North American ports. This led to a paralysis of the trade between the United States and British North America. At last in 1830 the United States and the Imperial Government came to an understanding, and trade was resumed on fairly free terms.[2] No further changes were made, and till 1849 inter-Imperial trade remained a monopoly for Imperial shipping.[3]

Apart from the Navigation Laws, the whole system of preferences and prohibitions came up for overhaul in the 'twenties before its final crash in the 'forties. Between 1822 and 1825 Robinson and Huskisson abolished practically all the prohibitions on importation of foreign goods and substituted comparatively light duties for the onerous existing ones, while in 1824 Huskisson sponsored an Act repealing prohibitions on exportation, such as the export of partly finished material for manufacture in the Colonies, the export of machinery used in manufacturing industries and the emigration of skilled workers.[4] Despite this vigorous pruning, the Old System was still flourishing in the 'forties. In 1840 preferences were given on eighty-two items, and, when Sir Robert Peel extended the list in 1842, they amounted to 375 separate items out of a total of 1,825 items

---

[1] *Canada and Its Provinces*, vol. iv, pp. 567–8.
[2] Ibid., pp. 570, 571, 573, 584, 586.
[3] *C.T.P.*, p. 632.
[4] Porritt, pp. 12–13.

listed, and covered, besides tropical produce, such things as oats, barley, wheat, lumber, fish, and naval materials.[1]

In addition to the reduction of restrictive duties and the abolition of prohibitions, there was also a whittling down of the colonial preferences. Of these the most important was the preference on lumber, which almost prohibited the importation of any but colonial growth. This meant high prices for lumber in England, and high prices in the time of distress prevailing after 1815 meant discontent. In 1820 a House of Lords Committee recommended a reduction in the timber duties and the timber preference. Thereupon the preference was reduced from £3 5s. a load to £2 5s., without damaging the Colonies. In 1835 another Committee recommended further reductions, but in vain. In 1843, however, the preference was reduced to 24s. a load on timber and 30s. on deals. Further reductions followed in 1847 and 1851. Finally Gladstone put an end to the preference in 1860 by equalizing the duties on foreign and colonial timber and in 1866 he abolished the duties themselves.[2]

While the timber preference died away gradually and steadily, the wheat and flour preference flickered into brief and brilliant life in 1843 and as suddenly flickered out in 1846-9. Slight wheat preferences to the Colonies can be traced as far back as 1766. In that year wheat was admitted from the Colonies duty-free for a short time, while foreign wheat was subject to the very high duty of 22s. per quarter. In 1791 colonial wheat was admitted on paying 6d. a quarter when the price rose above 52s., whereas foreign wheat had to wait till the price was 54s. In 1804 the entrance prices for colonial and foreign wheat were 56s. and 66s. respectively.[3] By the Corn Law of 1815 colonial wheat could enter duty-free if the price rose to 67s. per quarter and foreign wheat if the price rose to 80s. In 1822 the entrance prices were altered to 59s. and 70s. respectively, with a sliding scale of duties in the latter case above 70s. In 1825 wheat from British North America was allowed to enter, whatever the price, on the payment of a flat rate of 5s. per quarter, but this permission was only for one year. In 1828 the duty on colonial wheat was fixed at 6d. a quarter when the price was above 65s., and 5s. a quarter when the price was below that. On the whole,

[1] C.T.P., p. 632.
[2] J. R. McCulloch : Dictionary of Commerce, 1882, pp. 1389-91.
[3] J. S. Nicholson : History of the English Corn Laws, pp. 135-6.

these preferences meant little to the Colonies, because they were slight in amount and because until the 'forties the Colonies had little wheat to export. Then in 1843 Lord Stanley conceded a generous preference on wheat and flour from British North America, admitting the wheat at a fixed duty of 1s. a quarter and the flour at a proportionate rate. This was a great boon to colonial farmers and especially to colonial millers, since American wheat ground into flour in Canada counted as Canadian flour. This short burst of prosperity was brought to an end in 1846–9 by the repeal of the Corn Laws, which abolished all duties in wheat and thus all preferences.[1]

The only remaining preference of importance was that on sugar. Till 1826 the duty on colonial sugar was 30s. per cwt. irrespective of origin, with a superimposed sliding scale according to prices in the English market, while foreign sugar was subject to a prohibitive duty. In that year the duty on West Indian and Mauritius sugar was reduced to 27s., while in 1830 it was further reduced to 24s. All this time there was preference given to one part of the Empire at the expense of another, but that was stopped in 1836, when the duty on East Indian sugar was reduced to 24s. also. Meantime there was a prohibitive duty of 63s. per cwt. on foreign sugar, which was costing English consumers almost £3,500,000 per annum in higher prices. In 1844 and 1845 the duties on colonial and foreign free labour sugar were considerably reduced and the preference was thereby greatly lessened. In 1846 foreign sugar, whether free grown or slave produced, was admitted on the same terms. Finally, in 1854 the Imperial Preference of 9s. 4d. per cwt. was abolished and the duty on all sugars equalized.[2]

Achievement of Fiscal Freedom (1846–1897).—The collapse of the Old Colonial System was brought about by the ascendancy of the *laissez-faire* philosophy, which combined belief in the benevolence of natural laws with disbelief in the beneficence of human laws. All legal restrictions on trade were bad, and whether they were monopolies or colonial preferences they had to go.[3] In 1850 Lord John Russell declared in Parliament : " By the repeal, last year,

---

[1] McCulloch, pp. 432–4.
[2] Ibid., pp. 1339–43.
[3] Josiah Tucker, an eminent eighteenth century economist and divine, was praised on his tombstone for being an enemy of all " monopolies and colonial preferences ".

of the navigation law I conceive we have entirely put an end to the whole system of commercial monopoly in our colonies. We have plainly declared that, on the one hand, if we require productions similar to those which our colonies produce we shall be ready to take them from other parts of the world ; and, on the other hand, we have left our colonies free to provide themselves with the products of other countries than our own and to impose upon the manufactures of Great Britain equal duties with those imposed on foreign manufactures ".[1] Inter-Imperial commerce was to give place to international commerce, and England instead of being the Mother Country of an Empire was to become the metropolis of the world.

The Old System passed away by the following stages between 1846 and 1849. First, there was the almost total abolition of all colonial preferences especially on wheat and flour. Secondly, there was the passing of the Enabling Act of 1846, which permitted the Colonies to abolish all differential duties protecting the goods of the Mother Country and penalizing foreign goods on their entry into the Colonies. Thirdly, there was the repeal of the Navigation Laws, which threw the inter-Imperial carrying trade open to the ships of all nations and flags. Finally, the prohibition of certain manufactures as inimical to the interests of the Mother Country had long been winked at. In the case of the Enabling Act, where corresponding action was necessary on the part of the Colonies the response was not slow in coming. The Mother Country had repudiated all her former favours to the Colonies : by 1855 the Colonies had withdrawn from England all the favours formerly enjoyed in the colonial market and had enacted tariffs of their own.[2]

Fiscal freedom was thus conferred in theory on the Colonies. In reality it was only freedom for the Colonies to do what the Imperial Government wanted them to do, and that was to adopt free trade.[3] A long fight had to be fought under a continuous free trade bombardment from the Colonial Office before real fiscal freedom was achieved. Here, as usual, Canada, the oldest, biggest and richest of the Colonies, bore the brunt of the struggle. There were really two objectives in the struggle :   the

---

[1] *Parliamentary Debates*, III, cviii, 541.
[2] *C.T.P.*, p. 634.
[3] A. B. Keith : *Responsible Government in the Dominions*, 1927, ii, p. 928.

right to impose differential duties and the right to pursue a policy of Protectionism.

Now the imposition of differential duties, the favouring of one nation at the expense of another, was a distinct contravention of the free trade policy of an open door to all nations and of a tariff for revenue purposes only. At the same time it is obvious that differential duties are inevitably bound up with any policy of selective preference or reciprocity. As early as 1843 a circular despatch had forbidden the imposition of differential duties by the colonies, and thereafter until 1878 the instructions to Governors always contained a clause ordering them to reserve any such Bills.[1] In 1850, however, Canada won the right of imposing differential duties, although Earl Grey protested against it and the Colonial Office continued to protest against each fresh instance of differential duties until 1870.[2] And yet it was only by means of this right that the British North American Colonies were able to arrange for reciprocity amongst themselves and with the United States in the famous Elgin-Marcy Treaty of 1854. Thwarted in that direction, Earl Grey, then Colonial Secretary, sought to prevent the same thing happening in the Australian Colonies by forbidding categorically the imposition of differential duties in their charter of government conferred in 1850. Characteristically enough, New Zealand, which obtained its charter of government in 1852 from a Tory Government, was given a free hand as to differential duties. Yet New Zealand's freedom availed it little, for the Australian Colonies were the only possible parties to a reciprocity deal and their lack of freedom tied its hands. After a series of " rasping interchanges " extending over six years, the Australian Colonies in 1873 obtained authorization from the Imperial Government to impose differential duties.[3] Nothing, however, was done in the way of reciprocity or preference as the freedom conferred upon the Colonies was not quite complete. In 1895 their freedom in this respect was completed, and the door stood wide open for Imperial preferences. Even then Lord Ripon, the Colonial Secretary, signified emphatically his personal antagonism to inter-Imperial preference on the ground that discrimination amongst the Colonies in their own favour

[1] Porritt, p. 223, and Keith, ii, p. 928.
[2] Ibid., pp. 154–5.
[3] Ibid., pp. 77–8, 94–5, 96–7, 100, 111.

was bound to mean discrimination against the Mother Country.[1]

Analogous to the fight for the right to impose differential duties was the conflict over protectionism. Here Canada again led the van. From 1846 onwards Canada had been gradually heightening its customs duties until by 1858 under the Cayley Tariff they practically meant protection for certain Canadian industries. No alarm was felt in England until 1859, when the Galt Tariff was imposed. Cayley had raised the tariff from 15 to 20 per cent on many manufactured articles, and charged 15 per cent on the residue of the imports. Now Galt raised some articles to 25 per cent, and the bulk of the imports to 20 per cent.[2] Immediately protests arose in England, especially in Sheffield, where the steel manufacturers feared a blow to their trade and strongly petitioned the Colonial Office against the tariff. Thereupon the Duke of Newcastle, the Colonial Secretary of the time, forwarded the petition to Galt, with a covering despatch which rebuked him for his tariff. This elicited from Galt the famous reply, which was to rank as the Colonial Magna Carta for fiscal freedom and the right to adopt protectionism. Galt declared: " Self-government would be utterly annihilated if the views of the Imperial Government were to be preferred to those of the people of Canada. It is therefore the duty of the present Government distinctly to affirm the right of the Canadian legislature to adjust the taxation of the people in the way they deem best, even if it should unfortunately happen to meet the disapproval of the Imperial Ministry. Her Majesty cannot be advised to disallow such acts unless her advisers are prepared to assume the administration of the affairs of the colony irrespective of the views of the inhabitants." [3] Thereafter Canada was permitted to pursue its own fiscal pathway unmolested, and the other Colonies, sheltering behind Canadian precedent, were able to follow the same policy. About 1850 a Bill offering bounties on industry in one of the Maritime Provinces had been disallowed by the Imperial Government, despite the fact that earlier Bills offering bounties had not been even reserved.[4]

---

[1] C.T.P., p. 643.

[2] O. D. Skelton : Life and Times of Sir A. T. Galt, p. 268.

[3] Correspondence on the Removal or Reduction of the Duties charged on British Goods entering Canada, in Parliamentary Papers, 1864, xli, p. 88.

[4] Porritt, pp. 98–9, 87–90.

After 1846, however, was the time of unadulterated free trade, when the hunting of protectionist heresies was the order of the day. By 1859 the Colonial Office had withdrawn its veto on the granting of bounties by the Maritime Provinces, but it still protested. In 1867 Victoria adopted protectionism under the preaching of David Syme ; New Zealand followed, and the Colonial Office was dumb. While. Canada protected its stock raisers, grain growers, tanners, shoemakers, saddlers, cabinet makers, tailors, and soap manufacturers, New Zealand began by protecting its brewers.[1] Protectionism then spread throughout the Empire, with the exception of Newfoundland, which remained faithful to Free Trade. In 1879 the Macdonald Government in Canada inaugurated the National Policy, which aimed at all-round industrial development by means of protective tariffs, and led to the granting of bounties on iron and steel in 1883. High protectionism was in the saddle, and the only real cleavage of political opinion since has been between the respective merits of high tariff and low tariff policies.

Protectionism is universally accepted in the Empire and the reasons are obvious. The example of the United States has been of primary importance. The circumstances of the United States were very similar to those of the Colonies. It was a new country, full of potentialities but lacking population and inherited wealth, and yet desirous of rapid and full-blooded development to a strong, opulent and advanced state. The Mother Country was old and already full of population and inherited wealth, and almost deeming itself to have reached its zenith of development. Thus the Colonies, as new countries, looked to the United States, and seeing its speedy progress in population and wealth and all-round economic development, they began to frame their policies, tariff and otherwise, on that model. Canada, as a neighbour of the United States, was first and most obviously affected, but the influence of the United States spread quickly through Canada and even apart from Canada throughout the Empire. Many of the colonial arguments as to the protection of infant industries, the protection of highly paid labour, the importance of economic self-sufficiency, were drawn from the American armoury. Colonial protectionists were not necessarily of opinion that England itself should revert to protection, for England had

---

[1] Ibid., pp. 114, 124.

perhaps outgrown it, but they certainly believed that England's greatness in the past had been built up by protection. Very often the colonial apostles of protection were men who had emigrated from a protectionist England before 1846, and they therefore saw nothing inherently absurd in a protectionist policy. The root of the matter .was, of course, that the Colonies wanted to speed up their industrial development, to pass from a mere pastoral or agricultural and extractive economy and achieve a greater measure of economic self-sufficiency by means of manufactures, and to that end they adopted protectionism as (in their opinion) the most effective means.

Parallel with the growth of fiscal freedom was the development of diplomatic freedom, so far as commercial treaties were concerned. In 1848 W. H. Merritt, on behalf of Canada, had considerable powers for bargaining with the United States for reciprocity. When reciprocity actually came in 1854, it was " floated through on champagne ", and that was the work of Lord Elgin, the Governor-General of Canada. Still, though the negotiations were carried through by the representative of the Imperial Government, the treaty itself was for British North America alone and not for the whole of the Empire, and as such was the thin edge of the wedge driving towards diplomatic freedom in commercial matters. The Quebec Conference of 1865 resulted in Galt and three other delegates going south in 1866 to assist the British Minister at Washington in an attempt to arrange for a continuation of reciprocity, which failed. Canadian delegates also visited Spain in an advisory capacity with a view to a commercial treaty affecting trade with Spain's American colonies, but nothing was accomplished.[1] Then in 1871 Sir John Macdonald was appointed one of the British plenipotentiaries for the negotiation of the Treaty of Washington, but as somewhat subordinate to other members of the Mission. The Hon. George Brown, again, had powers in 1874, for negotiating another Reciprocity Treaty at Washington, and in 1879 Sir A. T. Galt was in Madrid attempting along with the British Ambassador to arrange for reciprocity between Spain and Canada, but in a very subordinate position, being merely a commercial commissioner.[2] Thus even in the 'seventies Canada had made little headway in achieving diplomatic freedom, and it

---

[1] Porritt, pp. 177–8, 184–5.
[2] Ibid., pp. 187–8.

could be said that " in the field of foreign policy and international relations Canada was then all but voiceless ". [1]

Still some advance was made in another direction in the 'seventies. In early treaties the Empire bargained as one unit, and thereby the Mother Country bound all the Colonies, whether they wished to be so or not. Thus the whole Empire was involved in the two famous treaties arranged with Belgium in 1862 and Germany in 1865, the latter of which was to form a *cause célèbre* in the 'nineties. At last, in 1877, " the Imperial Government agreed that the Colonies should no longer automatically be bound, but should be given the right to adhere within two years."[2] This provision was only prospective, and the Colonies remained bound by treaties negotiated before that date.

After the 'seventies rapid progress was made in accomplishing Canada's diplomatic freedom. In 1884 during further negotiations with Spain, Sir Charles Tupper held an equal, if not superior position to the British Ambassador.[3] This happened again in the negotiations with the United States in 1888, with France in 1893, and with the United States once more in 1898. At last, in 1907, Canadian plenipotentiaries by themselves negotiated a new Canadian-French reciprocity, and thus Canada achieved independent treaty-making powers.[4] An earlier instance of more or less independent negotiating powers was afforded by the formation of the South African Customs Union in 1889. However, in that case there were special local circumstances which made the instance almost valueless as a precedent and, in fact, placed the negotiations on quite a different footing from those conducted by Canada.

In 1877 the Colonies were given the right of adhering within two years to any future commercial treaty arranged by the Mother Country. In 1899 and 1900 another step was taken, when Colonies were given the right of separate withdrawal on a six or twelve months' notice. Since 1911 all commercial treaties have conformed with this provision. " The rule accordingly is now absolute that in any negotiation for concluding a treaty an effort is made to secure for the Dominions and India the privilege of separate adherence and separate withdrawal . . . But with minor

[1] W. S. Wallace : " Growth of Canadian National Feeling," in *Canadian Historical Review*, 1920, p. 157.
[2] Keith, ii, p. 848.
[3] Porritt, p. 191 and note.
[4] Ibid., pp. 192, 193, 200, 201–2.

exceptions the position now is clear that the Dominions are bound by no treaties from which they cannot retire, and with the lapsing of the older treaties through the War and other causes are bound by very few treaties to which they have not fully subscribed." [1]

The New Imperial System (1897 *onwards*).—The new system, which is marked by Imperial preferences and inter-Imperial reciprocity springs from the nationhood of the Dominions and their newly acquired fiscal and diplomatic freedom. At the same time, it reveals the strength of the Imperial links. This system would have arisen before it did if it had not been for the doctrinaire free trade attitude of the Mother Country. The Mother Country more or less forbade any movement towards reciprocity within the Empire. It certainly permitted reciprocity between Canada and the United States in 1854, but it prohibited reciprocity in the following year between Canada and the West Indies. [2] The Old Colonial System and the new Imperial system had certain strong kindred features. There was this great difference, however, between the earlier system and the network of Imperial preferences and inter-Imperial reciprocity that grew up after 1897. The Old Colonial System was compulsory and complete, and dictated from above by the Mother Country, whereas the new Imperial system was voluntary and piecemeal and either granted freely or arranged by negotiation between the Dominions and the Mother Country and Dependencies.

Although 1897 was the birth year of the new Imperial system, tentative steps were taken or suggested in that direction even before that date. In 1870 Sir John Macdonald on behalf of Canada gave a preference on salt imported from England. [3] Then, at the first Colonial Conference in 1887, Hofmeyr, of South Africa, proposed a small uniform duty of 2 per cent on all foreign goods entering any part of the Empire, so as to encourage Imperial trade and to find funds for Imperial defence, but nothing came of it. [4] In 1894 came the Ottawa Conference, when the Dominions themselves met together apart from the Mother Country and strongly recommended Imperial preferences and inter-Imperial reciprocity. Before such a system could be established, it was necessary for the Mother Country to denounce certain existing Favoured Nations Treaties, which impeded any

---

[1] Keith, ii, p. 849.   [2] Porritt, p. 453.
[3] C.T.P., p. 662.   [4] Ibid., p. 639.

attempt at selective preferences or reciprocity within the Empire by extending any advantage England received to certain foreign countries. As these treaties, especially those with Belgium and Germany, brought great gain to England, Lord Ripon, the Colonial Secretary, refused to consider the matter, pointing out that the trade with the said foreign countries was worth much more than the trade with the Dominions.[1] Earlier, in 1881, 1890, and 1891, England had refused similar requests.[2] The cause of Imperial preferences and inter-Imperial reciprocity seemed hopeless.

Then came the turning point, in 1897, when Canada gave the Mother Country preference without asking for anything in return. This was called in Canada " Jug-handled Preference ", that is, one-sided preference. Fielding, the Finance Minister, in introducing the preference, said : " But why should we wait for England to take action ? England has dealt generously with us in the past. She has given us liberty to tax her wares even when she admits our goods free, and we have taxed them to an enormous degree."[3] And Sir Wilfrid Laurier, the Premier, declared : " There will be no more pilgrimages to Washington. We are turning our hopes to the old motherland." [4] Between 1865 and 1898 there had been eleven distinct overtures from Ottawa to Washington, all without result,[5] but now this period of " Exodus to Lamentations " was to come to an end. Canada was becoming conscious of its own strength and of the advantages of the Imperial connexion.

Although Canada had conferred preference freely on the Mother Country, it was still essential that England should denounce the obnoxious treaties which insisted that any benefit or favour conferred on England must be transferred also to the countries in treaty relations. This denunciation was achieved in 1898 by Lord Salisbury, who brought to an end the treaties with Belgium and Germany. An immediate result of this action was resentment on the part of Germany, who objected to the Imperial preference, and a Tariff War between Germany and Canada which raged between 1897 and 1910 and ended in peace without victory

---

[1] *C.T.P.*, pp. 642–3.
[2] O. D. Skelton : *Canada and the Most Favoured Nation Treaties*, p. 13.
[3] *C.T.P.*, p. 666.
[4] *Report on Reciprocity and Commercial Treaties, United States Tariff Commission*, p. 100.
[5] *Canada and its Provinces*, vol. ix, table opposite p. 126.

for Germany.[1] Since then the Dominions have claimed that Imperial preferences are a domestic concern with which foreign countries have nothing to do.[2] Foreign countries are, however, very loath to accept this ruling.

Canada's example was speedily followed by others of the Dominions and some of the Dependencies, and a network of inter-Imperial preferences has sprung up.[3] New Zealand and South Africa granted preference to the Mother Country in 1903, Australia in 1907, the British West Indies in 1913, Trinidad in 1917, Cyprus in 1920, and Fiji in 1922. Newfoundland alone can give no preference to the Mother Country, for its tariff aims merely at producing revenue, though at the Imperial Conference in 1926 the Prime Minister spoke of attempting to give the Mother Country preference.[4]

In addition to granting preference freely to the Mother Country, the Dominions generally and some of the Dependencies began to arrange preferences amongst themselves. In certain cases the preference was granted freely to the whole Empire. This was the line of action pursued by New Zealand in 1903, Trinidad in 1917, Cyprus in 1920, and Fiji in 1922. Generally, however, it was the result of negotiations and based distinctly on the principle of reciprocity. In 1904 Canada gave New Zealand preference in return for its general Imperial preference, and in the same year negotiated the first inter-Imperial preference agreement with South Africa. In 1906 South Africa and Australia negotiated an inter-Imperial preference agreement, which after some modifications was rescinded in 1926, when both Dominions relapsed to non-preferential terms.[5] In 1906–7 South Africa and New Zealand also arranged for reciprocal inter-Imperial preferences. Still later, in 1922, Australia and New Zealand agreed to mutual preferences, and in 1925 Australia and Canada reached an agreement. Apart from inter-Dominion preferences, inter-Imperial preferences were arranged between Dominions, on the one hand, and Dependencies on the other. The most important instance of this was between Canada and the British West Indies. Canada began in 1898 by granting

---

[1] Porritt : *Evolution of the Dominion of Canada*, pp. 444–6.
[2] T. E. Gregory : *Tariffs*, pp. 269–70.
[3] C.T.P., pp. 53–4.
[4] Imperial Conference : Appendices, Cmd. 2769, p. 95.
[5] *South African Year Book*, 1910–25, pp. 579 n., and *Commonwealth Year Book*, 1927, p. 211.

preference freely to the British West Indies, as to the Mother Country. Then in 1912–13 Canada and the British West Indies negotiated a mutual preferential agreement, which was renewed in 1920–1 and in 1925–6. On the last occasion the agreement was to run for twelve years, and amongst other things Canada was to improve the steamship service to the Islands.[1]

The reason for the development of the new Imperial system after 1897 is undoubtedly connected with the growth of Imperial sentiment in the 'eighties onwards. Imperialism had its prophets, poets, and propagandists, like Froude and Kipling and Seeley. In addition it had a solid materialistic basis. Improved communications by rail, steamship and air, by postage and cable, were binding the Empire as a whole into unity. Further, the increasing flow of capital from the Mother Country to the rest of the Empire made the Empire realize the benefit of close contact with London, the Money Market of the world. Then the value of the Dependent Empire in the Tropics was just beginning to be realized, as it was being opened up by the Mother Country and as the value of its products became known, such as rubber and cocoa and fruit.[2] To be part of the same Empire was something, for it gave especially good

---

[1] Text in *West Indies and South America Pamphlets* (Dominions Office and Colonial Office Library), vol. ix, No. 402.

[2] " There is no doubt whatever as to the importance of the British Tropics in the economy of the world to-day. In an age which travels on rubber tyres and walks on rubber heels, which is largely dependent for its supplies of soaps, candles, margarine, paints and lubricants on palm oil, copra and tropical oil seeds ; which consumes cocoa in increasing quantities, either as a drink ' grateful and comforting ', or in enormous quantities as chocolates ; in which much of our wheat reaches us in gunny bags made from jute ; in which our linoleum and some of our carpets and rugs are also packed with or made of jute ; in which sugar and tobacco are in increasing demand all over the world ; in which binder twine, used wherever agricultural machinery is employed, is made from sisal hemp ; in which there is a threatened famine in raw cotton ; and in which tropical and sub-tropical fruits and such universal stimulants as tea and coffee come from the tropics or sub-tropics, there can be no two opinions as to the overwhelming importance of the study of tropical economic problems. The Tropics are, however, not merely important as yielding indispensable commodities, but if they can sell they can buy, and they afford growing markets for engineering and textile production of all kinds. Railway equipment, harbour equipment, drains and water pipes are all part of the return payment Great Britain makes for tropical products. As the native inhabitants of the Tropics increase in wealth they demand more cloth, scented soap, bicycles and even motor cars. I have little doubt that the nation which controls the Tropics will in the twentieth century control the most important raw materials and the growing markets of the world." Letter of L. C. A. Knowles, in *Journal of the Royal Society of Arts*, 1924–5, vol. lxxiii, p. 333.

opportunity for mutually beneficial agreements.   Even on
the side of England, the advantages of the Empire became
apparent, as foreign countries built up higher and ever
higher tariff walls round their own markets, whereas the
Dominions were actually lowering their tariff wall for the
Mother Country's benefit.   Thus the growing feeling of
nationhood in the Dominions and the growing desire to
promote industrial development dictated protectionism,
but the growing sense of Imperial unity, especially
with the Mother Country, worked towards Imperial
preferences.

The war marked a change in the attitude of the Imperial
Government towards Imperial preferences.   Hitherto
preferences to the Mother Country had been one-sided
(" Jug-handled "), but as a result of the recommendation
of the Balfour of Burleigh Committee,[1] and the declaration
of the Imperial War Cabinet endorsing the recommendation,
preference was reciprocated on certain Dominion commodities in the Budget of 1919.   In order to avoid offending
Free Trade susceptibilities, the Chancellor of the Exchequer
inaugurated preference by reducing the duties on colonial
goods and not by raising the duties on foreign goods.   Thus
in England preference smacks of tendencies towards Free
Trade rather than of protectionism.   The duties on tea,
coffee, chicory, cocoa, sugar, dried fruits, tobacco, and
motor-spirit were reduced by one-sixth if they hailed from
within the Empire, and the McKenna duties on cinema
films, clocks, and watches, motor-cars and cycles, and
musical instruments by one-third, and the duties on wine
from the Empire by amounts varying from 30 to 40 per
cent.[2]   In 1923 the Imperial Government attempted to
put into force a recommendation of the Imperial Economic
Committee by proposing some new duties in order to make the
preference granted more effective.   The attempt was
defeated, and instead the Imperial Government promised
an annual grant of £1,000,000 to aid the marketing of Empire
produce.   In 1925 the preferences in existence were
guaranteed for ten years, and were increased where possible.
As a result of the preferences the importation from Imperial
sources of raisins has risen from $2\frac{1}{2}$ per cent before the War

---

[1] Appointed in July, 1916, " to consider the commercial and industrial
policy to be adopted after the War."   See *Final Report of the Committee*,
1918, Cd .9035, pp. 44, 48.
[2] *Times*, 1st May, 1919.

to 36½ per cent in 1925–6, of sugar from 6–7 per cent to 22½ per cent, of tobacco from 1½ per cent to 11 per cent, and of wine by one-third.[1]

The amount of preference conceded by the Mother Country is so small that the Dominions are always asking for preference that is really reciprocal. Mr. Havenga said that in 1924 South African preferences meant £890,000 to the Mother Country but the Mother Country's preferences to South Africa were worth only £12,000.[2] The total value of the preferences enjoyed by England in the Dominions as a whole was about £12,000,000 per annum, while the Dominions enjoyed preferences of less than £1,000,000.[3] Of course, this kind of reckoning leaves out of account all sort of invisible preferences conferred by the Mother Country upon the Dominions. Apart from the expense the Dominions have been to the Mother Country in the past, there are present benefits rendered in the way of cheap capital and of Imperial Defence. Thus the estimated Imperial Expenditure in 1925–6 on Imperial Defence, that is to say on Navy, Army, Air Service, War Debt Service, and War Pensions, was :—

	Total.	Per head.
Great Britain and Northern Ireland	£546,673,407	£12 8 3
Australia	33,094,248	6 1 9
Canada	29,536,746	3 7 2
New Zealand	6,538,190	5 1 9
South Africa	3,021,806	1 19 3 [4]

No doubt much of the £546,673,407 was spent locally on the local needs of Great Britain and Northern Ireland. Still there was enough spent on Imperial Defence in general by the Mother Country to balance the preference accounts quite easily.

Inter-Imperial preferences are generally accomplished by means of the Three-Decker Tariff, which Canada introduced in 1907. There are three scales of duties : (a) General or maximum rates, which apply to the goods

---

[1] *Appendices to the Imperial Economic Conference*, 1926, Cmd. 2769, p. 38.
[2] *Times*, 26th April, 1928.
[3] *Round Table*, March, 1926, p. 246. The figures for 1925 were:

Australia	£7,800,000
Canada	2,470,000
New Zealand	2,860,000
South Africa	375,000

Times, 15/3/28.

[4] Ibid., p. 255.

of countries that have not entered into treaty relations with the Dominions ; (b) intermediate or favoured nation rates which apply to the goods of countries that have entered into treaty relations with the Dominions ; and (c) preferential or British Empire rates, which apply to the goods of the Mother Country and of such Dominions as have achieved or received preferences.[1]

The following estimates have been made as to relative amounts of preference : " Upon a relatively small number of items, rarely dutiable at more than 10 per cent, the differential reduction takes the form of free admission. Generally, however, the base rates run from 20 to 50 per cent, and the preference is a minor fraction of the rate, usually from one-fourth to one-half, and amounts to from 5 to 20 per cent *ad valorem* ".[2] The Balfour Committee on Industry and Trade [3] in their Interim Report, entitled "Survey of Overseas Markets ", drew attention to " the remarkable fact that the main increases of tariff rates on British exports have been within the British Empire, where the average *ad valorem* incidence has risen by nearly two-thirds, while in foreign countries, despite the great increase in the United States tariff, the average *ad valorem* incidence has decreased by one-fifth ".[4] Nevertheless so generous is the scale of preferences to the Mother Country and so severe is the discrimination against foreign countries, that the higher tariffs with their higher percentages of preference have actually produced a situation more favourable than before to British manufacturers in competition with foreign manufacturers, although, of course, the handicap in competition with colonial producers has become greater.

Apart from the Imperial interest of preferences, there is the local interest of protectionism, which concerns particular parts of the Empire and varies from Dominion to Dominion. By 1897 the Dominions, as then known, had fully achieved the power of adopting protection, and since 1897 a leading feature has been the development of the embryonic protectionism in force before that date. Tariffs have been raised all round, and bounties and bonuses have been granted towards various ends. In South Africa, Parliament offered a bounty of 15s. per ton of pig iron and 15s. per ton

[1] T. E. Gregory : *Tariffs*, pp. 71–2.
[2] *C.T.P.*, p. 39.
[3] Appointed in July, 1924, " to inquire into the conditions and prospects of British industry and trade, with special reference to the export trade."
[4] Quoted by *Round Table*, September, 1926, p. 696.

of steel produced in the Union from native ores by a concern capable of turning out 50,000 tons per annum. When this offer failed the Government planned a nationalized steel undertaking with a capital of £5,000,000, which so far has not come into fruition.[1]

Another leading feature since 1897 has been the rise of India to fiscal freedom and the consequent adoption of a protectionist policy. In March, 1917, a small beginning was made by granting very slight protection to the Indian cotton industry. The import duty was increased from $3\frac{1}{2}$ per cent to $7\frac{1}{2}$ per cent without the excise tax being raised, and thus Indian cotton received protection to the extent of 4 per cent.[2] Since then the development of the Indian tariff has been on scientific lines, the motto being " a policy of discriminating protection ". On the recommendation of the Fiscal Commission a Tariff Board was established in June, 1923. It was to consider applications for protection from Indian industries, and its guiding rules were to be : " (a) that the industry possesses natural advantages ; (b) that without the help of protection it is not likely to develop at all, or not so rapidly as is desirable ; and (c) that it will eventually be able to face world competition without protection." Furthermore, the protection was to be " adequate but not excessive ". Since 1923 the Board has conducted investigations into the following industries : steel, coal, cotton yarn and textiles, paper, cement, printers' ink, ply wood, galvanized hardware and enamelled hollow-ware, and matches. The tariff schedule now covers nearly fifty items, mostly connected with steel. In the case of steel, after the duties had run for three years and the output had been greatly increased (from 125,871 tons in 1921 to 380,000 in 1926–7) and the costs diminished, the Tariff Board in 1927 courageously awarded a considerable reduction in the protective rates.[3]

The Flow of Capital.

Amongst the invisible preferences conferred by the Mother Country upon the rest of the Empire, one of the most important is the supply of cheap capital. Intimate connexion with the London Money Market is, and has always

[1] *Round Table*, September, 1927, pp. 834–6.
[2] *C.T.P.*, pp. 333–4. See also *Report of Indian Fiscal Commission*.
[3] Sir D. T. Chadwick : " Work of the Indian Tariff Board," in *Journal of the Royal Society of Arts*, 1928, vol. lxxvi, pp. 195–205.

been, an inestimable boon to the whole of the Empire, Without capital there could be no railways, no public utilities, no irrigation schemes, no scientific farming, no large scale industry and mining—in short, no development, no modern civilization.

Till 1900 England was the chief source for the supply of capital, not only to the Empire but to the world at large. Between 1860 and 1876 London loans to foreign Governments totalled £320,700,000, to the Colonies and India £159,900,000, and to foreign and colonial Companies £232,000,000 : altogether a grand total of £712,600,000, averaging yearly almost £42,000,000.[1] By 1900–4 the average annual export of capital from England was calculated at £65,600,000, and it was rising steadily.[2]

After 1900 France, Germany and the United States began to supply capital on a large scale to the world, but England easily remained the foremost supplier, expanding its annual exports rapidly. By 1913 the amount exported by England had risen to the colossal figure of £181,000,000,[3] and the total of its debts held abroad was estimated at £4,000,000,000.[4] Of this sum about one half was invested within the Empire,[5] where, with the possible exception of Canada, the Mother Country had almost a monopoly of investment. The following figures give the English investments overseas in 1910 in millions of pounds [6]:

	£	£
India and Ceylon	430	
Australasia	395	
Africa	391	
Canada	365	
Other British Possessions	71	
		1,652
United States	610	
Argentine	292	
Europe	151	
Brazil	105	
Other Foreign Countries	462	
		1,620
Total		3,272

[1] L. H. Jenks : *Migration of British Capital to* 1875, p. 425.
[2] E. Crammond : " British Investments Abroad," in *Quarterly Review,* 1911, vol. 215, p. 50.
[3] Balfour Committee : *Survey of Overseas Markets,* 1925, p. 665.
[4] Jenks, p. 6.
[5] Throughout the period it would appear that British capital invested abroad was divided almost equally between the Empire and foreign countries. E. Crammond : " British Investments Abroad," in *Quarterly Review,* 1907, vol. 207, pp. 265–6.
[6] E. Crammond in *Quarterly Review,* vol. 215, p. 45. The estimates here given are lower than those of other calculators.

In the case of Canada, due to the proximity of the United States and to the spread of American industries across the frontier, the United States was estimated to have invested £150,000,000 in Canada by 1914, but against that the Mother Country had invested an estimated sum of £540,000,000.[1]

After 1914 great changes were wrought in the financial world and the New York Money Market came to the front. Before 1914 the United States exportation of capital was more or less balanced by its importation of capital. After 1914 it had an ever-expanding net surplus for export. By 1923 the total United States investments in Canada were estimated at about £500,000,000, while the total amount of British investments remained about £540,000,000, sales amounting to £40,000,000 being offset by corresponding fresh investments.[2] Since 1923 British investments in Canada have increased somewhat, but the United States investments have gone up by leaps and bounds, totalling in 1927 between £600,000,000 and £800,000,000.[3] Taken all over it was calculated in 1926 that the United States was sending abroad yearly £200,000,000 as against England's £100,000,000.[4] While the United States has gone from strength to strength, England's balance of income available for overseas investment has fluctuated severely [5] :

	£
1920 . . .	252,000,000
1922 . . .	154,000,000
1923 . . .	102,000,000
1924 . . .	29,000,000
1925 . . .	54,000,000
1926 . . .	— 7,000,000
1927 . . .	96,000,000

This has handicapped England in its competition with the United States for the Canadian market. In 1900 Canada's industrial capital was £90,000,000. In 1920 it was £680,000,000, of which the United States held 24·5 per cent, or almost £170,000,000, and England only 9·6 per cent.[6] In 1923 it was thought that the United States

---

[1] H. E. Fisk : "Flow of Capital—Canada," in *Social and Economic Conditions in the Dominion of Canada*, 1923, edited by W. P. M. Kennedy, p. 173.
[2] H. E. Fisk, p. 175.
[3] *Round Table*, September, 1927, pp. 803–4.
[4] Ibid., September, 1926, p. 702.
[5] *Balfour Committee*, p. 665, and the *Board of Trade Journal*, 2nd February, 1928, p. 135.
[6] *Round Table*, September, 1926, p. 701.

holding of industrial capital in Canada would be about £250,000,000, or about half its total investments in that country. There were also said to be over 700 branch factories in Canada belonging to Americans, and others seeking suitable locations. The two great incentives in this movement were the advantage of being inside Canada's tariff walls so as to supply the Canadian market and the advantage of being inside the Empire so as to enjoy the Imperial preference in the English market. In 1923 United States capital comprised 40 per cent of the electrical apparatus, meat-packing, rubber, paint and varnish, brass and copper, condensed milk and refined petroleum industries, 61 per cent of the motor car industry, 80 per cent of the pulp and paper industry, and practically 100 per cent of the motor car accessory, proprietary medicine and artificial abrasions industries.[1] In addition to the United States supplying Canada with capital, Canada has taken to supplying itself with capital more extensively than ever before. To-day Canadians hold £400,000,000, or over 80 per cent of their Dominion Debt, while between 1925 and 1926 they purchased some £85,000,000 of their own municipal securities ("a form of investment practically unknown before the war"), and they also supplied money for loans on mortgage "on a scale hitherto unknown".[2]

If Canada is becoming more independent of the London Money Market due to American investments and to its own developing supplies of capital, the rest of the Empire still hangs on the Mother Country almost entirely. The solitary exception is Australia, which has floated a loan in the New York Money Market. Even then its London holdings are much more important than its American holdings. At the end of 1926 £15,411,487 of the Commonwealth was payable in New York, while £155,194,832 was payable in London.[3] Apart from that, Australia does not appear to possess the same internal borrowing power as Canada. The other Dominions and the Colonies especially look to the London Money Market alone.

Before 1900, England, except where the Imperial Government made or guaranteed the loans,[4] supplied money to the Empire through the ordinary competitive channels of

---

[1] H. E. Fisk, pp. 175–6.
[2] *Round Table,* September, 1927, pp. 799–800.
[3] *D.O.T. Report on Australia,* 1927, p. 11.
[4] The Colonial Loans Act of 1899 (62 and 63 Vict., c. 36) empowered the Treasury to give loans to Crown Colonies repayable within fifty years.

finance. In 1900 the Colonial Stock Act [1] was passed, which placed Colonial Stocks in the category of Trustee Stocks and enabled the Colonies to borrow money for productive purposes more cheaply than before. Home Stocks depreciated, but the rest of the Empire gained. In 1911 Sir Edgar Speyer calculated that the annual saving of interest on the Colonial loans, raised under the Colonial Stock Act and totalling £650,000,000, amounted to at least £10,000,000, " a very handsome preference by the Mother Country." [2] To-day the total amount loaned under the Colonial Stock Act is just under £800,000,000,[3] which at the same rate as above means an annual saving of about £12,000,000, a still more handsome preference.

Another encouragement to the investment of money in the Overseas Empire was given by the provision contained in Clause 28 of the Finance Act of 1920, following a recommendation of the Royal Commission on Income Tax. The provision affords relief against double taxation of income accruing within the Empire. Double taxation would occur where money earned on an investment in a Dominion with Income Tax was paid out, in the Mother Country, and was thus liable to the Dominion Income Tax and the British Income Tax. While the effect of this provision cannot be estimated statistically, it is bound to operate in favour of investment within the Empire in so far as other countries adopt the Income Tax, for in these cases British investments will be mulcted in a double tax.

Still further financial assistance has been offered by the Imperial Government under the Trade Facilities Act of 1924. By Clause 2 the Imperial Government promised to contribute three-quarters of the interest over the first five years on loans for public utility undertakings within the Empire, provided the bulk of the loan was disbursed in England. So far the applications for aid under this scheme have not been numerous. In addition, considerable aid has been granted directly to British firms which have works in the Dominions and Colonies. Thus, apart perhaps from Canada, the whole Empire may be said to be centred financially on London, as it is focussed commercially on England.

---

[1] 63 and 64 Vict., c. 62.
[2] *Times*, 25th May, 1911, referred to by L. C. A. Knowles : *Industrial and Commercial Revolutions*, p. 334.
[3] *Stock Exchange Year Book*, 1928, pp. 62–76.

Organization and Research

On the economic side attempts have been made to secure joint action and to pool knowledge for the common good throughout the Empire, largely as an outcome of the Colonial and Imperial Conferences held since 1887. Imperial Trade Commissioners were appointed as a result of the 1907 Conference to act as inter-Imperial Consuls for the promotion of trade within the Empire.[1] The Imperial Shipping Committee was established in June, 1920, on the recommendation of the Imperial War Cabinet to inquire into and seek to remedy shipping complaints within the Empire and to inquire into and report on maritime facilities and shipping factors, also within the Empire. Under the independent chairmanship of Sir Halford Mackinder, the Committee has issued reports dealing with such subjects as Deferred Rebates, Law referring to Bills of Lading, Speed of Vessels in Australian trade, Transshipment of Canadian cattle and Facilities of Mombasa (Kilindini) Harbour.[2] A later creation was the Imperial Economic Committee, which, founded in March, 1925, sprang out of the 1923 Conference. It seeks to deal with those economic problems that are outside the sphere of the Imperial Shipping Committee. Under the chairmanship again of Sir Halford Mackinder it has investigated and reported on the marketing and preparing for market of Empire meat, fruit, fish, dairy produce, poultry and eggs, honey within the Empire, chiefly in England.[3] Inquiries into tobacco, pig products, timber, hides and skins, rubber goods and agricultural machinery will follow.[4] Then out of the annual grant of £1,000,000 by the Imperial Government to further the sale of Empire goods within England has sprung up the Empire Marketing Board which is not an inter-Imperial body but is a creation of the Imperial Government. This Board supervises the annual spending of the £1,000,000 in three directions : (a) Scientific research into better methods, better breeds and better species, (b) Economic investigation of problems affecting marketing, and (c) Publicity by means of posters, pamphlets

[1] Sir H. L. Smith : *The Board of Trade*, pp. 76–8.

[2] Report on the Work of the Imperial Shipping Committee, 1920–2, *Cmd*. 1872. Report on the Work of the Imperial Shipping Committee, 1923–6, *Cmd*. 2706.

[3] Report on Functions and Work of the Imperial Economic Committee, 1928, *Cmd*. 3018.

[4] Ibid., p. 10.

and newspaper advertisements.[1] Again this £1,000,000 is to be considered as another invisible preference conceded to the Empire, for although the order of importance is home producers, colonial producers, foreign producers,[2] yet colonial producers are bound to benefit. Finally there is a miscellaneous group of Departments, Boards, Commissions, Committees, Institutes and Colleges all working to the same end. The Department of Overseas Trade, founded in 1917, issues reports of trade possibilities, tariff rates, and public contracts in the Dominions and Dependencies as well as in foreign countries.[3] The Dominions Commission set up on the suggestion of the 1911 Conference, issued a number of bulky reports on the economic resources and trade facilities within the Empire in Alliance.[4] The Empire Cotton Growing Corporation seeks to promote the cultivation of cotton within the Empire, and the Imperial Bureaux of Entomology and Mycology, the Imperial College of Tropical Agriculture in Trinidad, and the Imperial Institute seek to improve agriculture generally.[5] The Crown Agents transact business for the Dependencies.

Linking up

Another link of Empire before the War was the Imperial Penny Postage, which owed as much to the preaching of Sir John Henniker Heaton as the original Penny Postage did to the assiduity of Rowland Hill.[6] Originally proposed at the Colonial Conference of 1887, it did not find favour with the Colonies and they vetoed it.[7] At last after strenuous propaganda the Imperial Penny Postage was agreed upon in 1898 with the exception of Australia which did not come in until 1905–11, and till the War the system held good, binding the whole Empire into a postal unity.[8] The War led to great changes in postal rates, and the former Imperial unity was broken up. To-day Canada charges 2 cents for letters within Canada and to the United States, but 3 cents to Great Britain and the rest of the Empire.[9] Similarly

[1] Empire Marketing Board : *A Year's Progress*, June, 1927, p. 7.
[2] Mr. Ormsby Gore in the *West India Committee Circular*, 1927, p. 166.
[3] Sir H. L. Smith : *The Board of Trade*, pp. 82–6.
[4] Final Report, 1917, *Cmd.* 8462.
[5] Imperial Conference, 1926, Summary of Proceedings, *Cmd.* 2768, p. 50. Also Appendices, *Cmd.* 2769, pp. 49–50, 314–16.
[6] Sir John Henniker Heaton in *Dictionary of National Biography*.
[7] Keith, ii, pp. 1176–7, also *D.N.B.* under " Heaton ".
[8] Ibid., p. 1179.
[9] *Canada Year Book*, 1926, p. 664.

South Africa charges a penny for letters within South Africa, 2 pence for letters within the Empire, and 3 pence for foreign countries.[1] Nor is there any talk of a return to an Imperial Penny Postage or even to a uniform system throughout the Empire, except for newspaper and magazine postage by the Empire Press Union.[2]

Of increasing importance of recent years have been the cable and the wireless. The " All-Red " cable, linking all the Empire together without impinging on foreign soil, was long the dream of Imperialists. The first " All-Red " Cable was laid to Canada, and then the West Indies were linked up in the same way.[3] In 1902 the Pacific Cable from Canada to Australia and New Zealand began to operate, being owned in conjunction by the Governments of Great Britain, New Zealand, Australia and Canada as the Pacific Cable Board.[4] The Pacific cable had just been doubled between New Zealand and Fiji in 1923, when the wireless sprang upon an astonished world as a commercial rival. The cheap Beam method of transmission was widely adopted, and receiving and transmitting stations were built in different parts of England to hold converse with Canada, Australia, South Africa and India.[5] The cheapness and speediness of the message which can " girdle the globe in the seventh of a second ", took away a great deal of business from the cable, and immediately there were proposals for a beneficial pooling of interests between the cable and the wireless,[6] which have resulted in a merger. The possibilities of wireless in binding the Empire into still greater unity have not yet been fully explored. A means of communication that makes it as easy to speak from England to Canada or to Australia as from one part of London to another is bound to have great repercussions. No longer will the Empire be held apart by distance and months of delay, those fertile breeders of misunderstanding and discontent, but the whole Empire will be able to take counsel together and to act together with the briefest of delays. Moreover, wireless is being supported by air-travel, and even now it is proposed to make the journey to Canada in two and a half days, India

---

[1] *South Africa Year Book.*
[2] *Cmd.* 2769, pp. 262–3.
[3] Ibid., p. 119. The lines to the West Indies are controlled now by the Pacific Cable Board.
[4] *Canada Year Book*, 1926, p. 656.
[5] Sir Robert Donald, *Cmd.* 2769, pp. 251–2.
[6] *The Times*, 22nd May, 1928.

in five days, Cape Town in six days, Australia in eleven days and New Zealand in thirteen.[1] With such a speeding-up of transportation, Imperial Conferences could be held each year without difficulty. In Canada aircraft have been put to all sorts of uses. Aerial survey and photography have paved the way for timber exploitation and mining development, as well as for the investigation of rust diseases in wheat, the protection of fisheries, the prevention of smuggling, and the detection of forest fires.[2]

Diplomatic Relations

The Inter-Imperial Relations Committee propounded to the Imperial Conference of 1926 the following formula as summarizing the status of the Dominions : " They are autonomous communities within the British Empire, equal in status, in no way subordinate one to another in any aspect of their domestic or external affairs, though united by a common allegiance to the Crown and freely associated as members of the British Commonwealth of Nations ".[3] This formula has been, and is being, worked out in the diplomatic world, and the end is not yet. Speaking at Liverpool, on January 18th, 1928, the Right. Hon. W. Ormsby-Gore observed : " The declaration of equality in external affairs as well as domestic affairs has led to the appointment of direct diplomatic representatives to foreign Governments. Canada and the Irish Free State both have Ministers at Washington. Canada has just announced the creation of the post of Canadian Minister in Paris and a French Minister at Ottawa. . . . Doubtless, the practice of this exchange of diplomatic representatives between Dominions and foreign Governments will be steadily extended ".[4] Thus at last the Dominions are achieving complete freedom, not only in the fiscal sphere, but also in the diplomatic sphere—the full status of autonomous nations. The Old Colonial System has given place to the New Imperial System.

[1] Sir Samuel Hoare, *Cmd.* 2769, p. 194.
[2] Mr. Mackenzie King in *Cmd.* 2769, pp. 202–3.
[3] *Cmd.* 2768, p. 14.
[4] " Inter-Imperial Relations " in *United Empire*, 1928, p. 89.

CHAPTER 8

The Obtaining of People

Factors to be considered :

Incentive to emigrate.
Organization to encourage emigration.
Possibility of employment on arrival.

Difficulties and hardships of life in a raw country.

Why United States preferred to Canada.

Assisted emigration versus colonization.

Scottish emigration.

1831. Organized emigration begins. Conditions on emigrant ships. The Wakefield System.

1855. Colonies begin to claim to control and restrict emigration.

1873. Beginning of period of organization of emigration as remedy for distress in Great Britain coupled with realization by Colonies of need for immigrants, but of special types.

New worlds in the making.

PERHAPS one of the most important things the self-governing Dominions have to undertake is to recruit a population ; and the attraction of a good type of emigrant, together with the exclusion of undesirables, has become one of the most important functions of their governments. To obtain a population ready-made not merely involves advertising and giving assisted or free passages, but often land settlement, loans and other forms of State assistance such as the inspection of immigrants, the care for the welfare of orphan children planted out on farms, the attraction of equal numbers of both sexes and the decision as to the amount of capital to be owned by the emigrant before admitting him.

There are three factors for consideration in the great migration of the British peoples. Circumstances at home must make them willing to leave ; there must be some mechanism for getting indigent persons over to the other side ; and there must be something for them to do when they get there. We have already seen [1] that the industrial and agricultural revolutions in England made people willing

[1] Vol. I, p. 91.

to go, and that the Government, scared by the unemployment and depression after the French wars, was only
too willing to let them go. The mechanism of transference
was partly provided by assisted passages. Land companies
bulked largely as agents for taking people out to Australia,
New Zealand and Canada and at a later date to South Africa
and Rhodesia. But the chief difficulty in the first half of
the nineteenth century lay in the fact that there was so
little for emigrants to do on the other side. The general
result all through the past century was that the bulk of the
British emigrants went to the United States and not to
the British Colonies.

Life is apt to be very hard at the start for the inexperienced
emigrant. The pioneer's life is deprived of all the amenities,
and crops were often unsaleable through lack of transport.
The following account by a colonist in 1869, describing
his own youthful recollections of Natal, discloses some of
the difficulties of making a new start.[1] " At that time the
old-fashioned slow-sailing tubs which frequented that part
of the world had not been superseded by the fast clippers
of the present day ; and a voyage which now is done in an
average of 70 days took 90, and often 100 days in the
performance. Passengers were often detained at the outer
anchorage in all the enjoyment of ground swells and with
the promised land in full view for several days at a time.
At last they would be sent on land in large flat-bottomed
surf boats, a good drenching being their first introduction
to the African coast. After scrambling ashore they would
find themselves and such baggage as they had with them
left helpless on a deep sandy shore where the naked forms
of savage men speaking in a wild uncouth tongue, a strange
dark-leaved vegetation and a hot sun overhead were all
tokens that the regions of barbarism had been reached.
In those days such rarities as European labourers were
unknown, and the natives were scarcely available to people
utterly ignorant of their language and rather in dread of
such fierce-looking barbarians. Between the little town
and the landing-place a distance of two miles of sandy
soil, winding through a thick leafy jungle, intervened, and
this was traversed by emigrants as best might be, either
in wagons drawn by teams of fourteen oxen, where people
were rich enough or fortunate enough to get hold of them,

[1] J. Robinson, " Social Aspects of Colonization," *Proceedings of Royal
Colonial Institute*, vol. i, 1869, pp. 142–7.

or on foot. Many such a group have I seen toiling painfully along through the heavy sands, the fathers laden with weary infants and the panting mothers having tired children clinging to their skirts. . . . In the days of which I speak the common necessaries of daily life were not always to be had. Pure water was not unfrequently a luxury seldom seen. Supplies of flour would often run so short that none but the wealthiest would dare to use it. . . . Butcher's meat was not at all times purchaseable ; while the commonest grocer's wares were in too many cases out of the reach of the mass of emigrants. . . . To the respectable tradesman unused to rural life and untrained to the ruder arts of domestic economy, the sudden need of self-help in everything is most perplexing and baffling. . . . What is now the best cultivated and most productive district of the colony was then a bushy wilderness with scarce a homestead on it, with not a road through it, with not one of its many rivers bridged and without any experience yet obtained of its industrial capabilities. Although their allotments might not be more than thirty miles distant, the journey thither would be both tedious and perilous. African rivers are beset by dangers of flood, quicksands, ond alligators. African roads, as they were then, consisted af mere tracks taken heedlessly over hills and down valleys and through thick bushy jungle. Wagons would often stick fast in morasses or mud-holes or break down in the ascent or descent of stony hills ; oxen would fall sick or get lost, or rain would come and cause days' detention before the settler could land his party at their destination or before he could take what little produce he might have to a remunerative market."

After building a hut made out of straw fastened over poles and bent twigs, and having grown his crop, the settler had to dispose of it, and here fresh difficulties arose. " It costs something to transport by such a tedious process as that I have described a load of produce to any distant point, and when it gets there prices may be so low as to be scarcely if at all remunerative. I speak now, it must be remembered, of the early times of a settlement, before regular markets are established, before a proper shipping trade has developed, before buyers on a large scale have appeared, and when the openings to producers are, in the main, measured by the scanty needs of the small and impoverished community. Schools at first there are none. For some time such teaching as children will get will be imparted to them by their parents or their elder brothers and sisters. Churches are also a memory of the past. . . . In course of time these needs are little by little supplied. The parents' place as teacher is taken by a badly paid country schoolmistress or schoolmaster. . . . When I first went to Natal there were but two posts a week between the capital and the seaport of the colony, and country posts were next to unknown. Rural settlers had to send in as often as they could native messengers to one or other of the two towns if they desired to get news of men, of friends or of events in the outer world. . . . The isolation of a colonist's life is in one respect a serious drawback. Man or men, when confined to some one spot of the earth's surface, seeing few of their race but themselves, knowing nought by personal observation of other men and other places, having little traffic with communities outside their own, run the risk of becoming narrow, selfish, illiberal, cramped, intensely localized and fatally self-complacent. Seclusion is the bane of colonial life." Under these circumstances it is not surprising that people who wished to leave England went if possible to the American Republic, whither others followed because their friends were already there. In the United States of America land was surveyed, towns existed, capital had been accumulated, and there was plenty of employment for skilled men. The Irish, with their fierce dislike of England, went naturally to the United States if they could, and there they made good and ran the saloons and politics of their adopted country. Therefore, to get people to go to the British colonies at all was a task of some difficulty. The British Government was anxious to get an English element into Canada, partly to strengthen it against the United States, partly to increase the English element as against the French. As the fares were lower to Canada than to any other British Dominion, parishes, philanthropic societies, and land companies naturally threw their energies into taking people to Canada. The bulk of the people who settled there went, however, on their own account, or were helped out by remittances from friends.

The difficulty in Canada was that there was so little employment unless the emigrant had capital enough to make a clearing and wait for the returns, and that involved quite £500 for a family of five.[1] The writer of the letters

---

[1] Magrath, *Authentic Letters from Upper Canada*, 1833, pp. 21, 24.

referred to warns people that wages are not excessive. At the Government works on the canals it was only 2s. 4d. a day, and at Toronto 2s. 6d., and the labourers had to work from light to dark in winter and from 6 o'clock to dusk in summer. Therefore many of the British emigrants went over the border to the United States, even when they had been assisted out to Canada.

If a passage to Canada was expensive, to Australia it was far more so, and Australia had the additional disadvantage of having been a convict colony at the start. Transportation and emigration seemed to be synonymous terms. The only possible chance in this case seemed to be the assisted passage. The Government, which was losing heavily on its convicts, did not see the force of assisting other types of emigrants till the change of policy in 1834.

South Africa had the great disadvantage of continuous Kaffir unrest and a black population already able to do the bulk of the manual work. But the Government, wishing to create an English element in the colony, did finance the Albany settlement at a cost of £50,000, and was instrumental in transferring 5,000 emigrants, who constituted a British nucleus further up the coast as an offset to the Dutch settlement at the Cape.

Of the 983,227 emigrants who left the United Kingdom for all destinations prior to 1840, 499,899 went to British North America, 417,765 went to the United States, and 58,449 to Australia and New Zealand.[1]

There are, as a matter of fact, two different methods of peopling an unoccupied country. People can be given an assisted passage, when they find their own jobs on arrival, or they can be taken out and settled on a piece of land— this is usually called colonization as distinct from emigration. Practically every attempt at colonization has failed, as the people do not stay on the land provided. Assisted emigration alone has been successful.

Scottish emigration is such an important factor in the history of the Empire, and especially of Canada, that it is necessary to find out the reasons for such a transference of population as really altered the character of one Dominion and affected the land policy of two others.[2]

---

[1] S. C. Johnson, *History of Emigration from the United Kingdom to North America*, 1763–1912, p. 16.

[2] On the whole subject see Miss M. I. Adam, *Scottish Historical Review*, xvi, " Highland Emigration of 1770 ; xvii, " Highland Emigrations of 1783–1803 ; xix, " Highland Landlords and the Poverty Problem."

The outstanding fact is the great increase in population in the Highlands in the eighteenth century. The land was poor and incapable of supporting an increasing population. Adam Smith said in 1776 that " a half-starved Highland woman frequently bears more than twenty children ", but that it was " not uncommon, I have been frequently told, in the Highlands of Scotland for a mother who has borne twenty children not to have two alive ".[1] This began to alter after 1780. The decline of mortality from smallpox and the cessation of clan fighting no doubt were contributory causes of the great increase in population which took place, but undoubtedly one of the most important causes was the prevalence of potato growing about 1780. Potatoes gave a cheap food supply, and above all stopped the scurvy which was one of the great causes of infant mortality.

Sir G. Stuart Mackenzie, in his *Survey of the Agriculture of Ross and Cromarty in* 1813, said [2] :—

" About forty years ago a basket of potatoes was esteemed a valuable present. By degrees their value increased, and the cultivation of them is now carried on in the most approved manner, seaweed being principally used as manure. This addition to the means of subsistence has had a wonderful effect on the amount of the population. The Rev. Mr. Downie has stated to me as a fact (and a very important one it is, for the consideration of those who seem alarmed for the decrease of the population), ' That within the last sixty years, *nothwithstanding the drains by emigration to America,* and for the supply of our armies, the population of all the parishes within this district (i.e. Western Ross) and generally along the coast, *has more than doubled.*' "

Famines were not infrequent in the Highlands, and that of 1782–3 was so severe that a special report was sent to the House of Commons. All intelligent travellers, including Pennant, remark on the numbers of idle able-bodied adults in the Highlands and their poverty-stricken condition.

Anderson, writing in 1785, said : " There is no doubt that one-tenth of the present inhabitants (of the Highlands) would be sufficient to perform all operations there were their industry properly exerted." [3] Alexander Irvine, Minister of Rannock, wrote in the *Scots Magazine* in 1803 (February) : " In some valleys the population is so excessive that it is

[1] *The Wealth of Nations*, Cannan's edition, i, p. 81.
[2] p. 249.   [3] *Scottish Historial Review*, vol. xvii, p. 87.

a question with many discerning people how one-half of the inhabitants could subsist though they should have the land for nothing. Those who would be tenants are so numerous, and the land fit for cultivation so scanty, that all cannot be satisfied. The disappointed person, feeling himself injured, condemns the landlord and seeks a happy relief in America." [1]

The whole economy of the Highlands was, in fact, altering. The value of a man to the chief had been that of the fighting unit, and for the land he received he was expected to join his chief when required. The rent was not calculated on the basis of an economic rent, but on that of a hanger-on whose living and loyalty depended on protecting his overlord.

After the rising of 1745 and the building of the roads, the chiefs had little chance of raiding each other or the Lowlands. The roads opened out new markets for cattle, and it was now worth while to farm for a market. Moreover, as the chief could not longer earn a living by depredations, he had to make his land keep him. The result was a large enclosure movement, which, varying in different parts of the Highlands, yet had the effect of making farms more difficult to obtain just at the time when the population was increasing rapidly and more farms were needed. Small farmers who owned their land sub-divided it amongst their sons so that the portions became too small to afford a living. Meanwhile, this superfluous population was too haughty and too proud to work as agricultural labourers, and there was actually an excess of population and a shortage of day labourers. Highlanders preferred to emigrate rather than work at such a menial occupation where they were known. The emigration went on in well-marked phases.

The first phase was represented by the tacksmen or middlemen, who had sublet land received from the chief. When rents had to become economic, many of these middlemen dropped out. They disliked the loss of prestige when they were no longer leaders, and complained, according to an article in the *Edinburgh Advertiser* in 1772,[2] that " the rents are risen above what the land will bear ". These men boasted, so the same writer said, that they would be revenged by " spiriting the lower class of people to

---

[1] Ibid., pp. 88-9.
[2] *Scottish Historical Review*, vol. xvi, " Highland Emigration of 1770," p. 292.

emigrate ", and " we shall carry a class to America and when they are there they must work for us or starve ".

This early migration went to the United States, but many of the men, as United Empire Loyalists, moved to the Maritime Provinces or Upper Canada, and formed a centre of attraction to other Highlanders who wished to emigrate later.

The second phase of emigration began from below ; the earlier had been an emigration from above. The Highlanders very often went first to Glasgow and even to Manchester, and got employment in the cotton factories. The Irish came across, however, and undercut them in many ways, and then the Scotch took a timber ship from Glasgow to their friends. Others came out straight from the Highlands under leaders like McNab or Lord Selkirk.

This emigration was marked at the end of the eighteenth century, and continued throughout the nineteenth. While the increase of population already referred to created the real difficulty, it was also a period when many by-employments dropped, making all the difference between just holding on and starvation. Kelp gathering had been an important by-employment, but at the beginning of the nineteenth century, it was superseded by the imported product barilla and by salt, from which the duties had been removed in 1817.[1] The fishing bounties had been stopped in 1830.[2] The roads and canals were finished, and so there was less employment for navvies. The drovers who began to take to the roads with their cattle, learned to move south. Many Highland regiments had been settled out in Canada after both 1783 and 1815, and they wrote home to friends and acquaintances, inviting them to come out. It was not a plunge into the unknown.

Meanwhile the competition for farms increased, but the sheep farmer could afford to give three times the normal rent. In 1760 three small farms were let to nine tenants at a total rent of £9, i.e. £1 a head, the farms including a hundred acres of meadow and rough pasture. Rents were raised to £30 and some of the tenants gave up their holdings. By 1813 the farms had been made into a sheep run, and the rent was £100 a year.[3] It is a curious fact, however, that the

[1] *Parliamentary Papers*, 1841, vi, 167.

[2] J. R. McCulloch, *Dictionary of Commerce*, 1882, p. 700.

[3] *Scottish Historical Review*, vol. xvii, p. 79, quoting Mackenzie's " Agricultural Report of Ross and Cromarty ".

numbers of the population increased even in the sheep farming areas, because sheep occupied much land hitherto vacant.' Sheep merely accentuated the problem, they did not create it, and the effect of the enclosures has been much exaggerated. Had there been no sheep, the problem could only have been solved by emigration or by an increase of infant mortality.

These Scots were badly housed and poorly fed. A large proportion of men and beasts perished every winter from want. Winter food for the cattle was non-existent. In Glenorchy 510 cattle died in one winter.[1] The standard of living of the Highlanders was so low that they did not complain about the terrible hardships of a new country, and they held on and throve when Englishmen migrated to the United States. But the idea that it was sheep that had led to their ousting persisted, and was at the back of a great deal of the agitation led by Scotchmen in both New Zealand and Australia against the large sheep run, to which may be traced many of the Australasian experiments, the purpose of which was to create small farms and closer settlement.

From 1815 to 1831 the Government was overwhelmed with the fear of over-population and heartily approved of emigration as a remedy,[2] but, except for the Albany settlement and the transportation of convicts, they did little to assist it.

From 1831 to 1855 systematic emigration was tried. Edward Gibbon Wakefield had written in 1829 advocating the sale of colonial lands. He claimed that the free gift of land prevented men from being labourers, therefore capital would not come to the colonies as there was no labour, and so the colonies were kept poor. Land, he claimed, should be sold. Men would then have to work to obtain it, and would supply a reserve labour force. The proceeds of the land sales should be used to bring out fresh emigrants,

---

[1] *Scottish Historical Review*, vol. xix, p. 164.

[2] The Bishop of Limerick, who appeared before the 1826 Select Committee on Emigration, said, " The evil is pressing and immediate. It therefore calls for an immediate remedy. Take any system of home relief, it must be gradual in its operation ; before it can be brought to bear, the present sufferers will have died off, but not without a dreadful course of intermediate horrors. Now, emigration is an instantaneous relief, it is what bleeding would be to an apoplectic patient. The sufferers are at once taken away ; and, be it observed, from a country where they are a nuisance and a pest to a country where they will be a benefit and a blessing." (First Report of the Committee, 1826, p. 142, quoted by S. C. Johnson, op. cit., p. 17).

who would thus swamp the convict element in Australia and make it a respectable and attractive place. His arguments seemed so convincing that land was ordered to be sold in New South Wales in 1831. An Emigration Agent was appointed in 1837 to select the emigrants and he was absorbed in 1840 by a body called the Colonial Land and Emigration Board who sold land and sent out emigrants.[1] It was also the duty of these men to see to the enforcement of the Passenger Acts and the coolie traffic. The disposal of waste lands in Australia was regulated and systematized by the Waste Lands Act of 1842, which adhered to the principle of the sale of unoccupied lands.

The conditions on board the emigrant ships were a scandal, as the following account of the Canadian passage will show :

" Before the emigrant has been a week at sea he is an altered man. How can it be otherwise ? Hundreds of poor people, men, women and children of all ages, from the drivelling idiot of ninety to the babe just born, huddled together without light, without air, wallowing in filth, and breathing a fetid atmosphere, sick in body, dispirited in heart, the fever patients lying between the sound in sleeping places so narrow as almost to deny them the power of indulging by a change of position the natural restlessness of the disease ; by their ravings disturbing those around, and predisposing them, through the effects of the imagination, to imbibe the contagion ; living without food or medicine except as administered by the hand of casual charity, dying without the voice of spiritual consolation and buried in the deep without the rites of the Church. The food is generally ill-selected and seldom sufficiently cooked in consequence of the insufficiency and bad construction of the cooking places." The passengers had to do their own cooking. " The supply of water, hardly enough for cooking and drinking, does not allow washing. In many ships the filthy beds, teeming with all abominations, are never required to be brought on deck and aired ; the narrow space between the sleeping berths and the piles of boxes is never washed or scraped, but breathes up a damp and fetid stench until the day before arrival at quarantine, when all hands are required to

---

[1] Between 1847 and 1869 they sent off 339,338 emigrants at a cost of £4,864,000. Of this £532,000 was provided by emigrants. These went mostly to Australia (Johnson, *Emigration to North America*, p. 26). " Between 1840 and 1873 the Board granted free or reduced passages to over 325,000 settlers." (Report of Overseas Settlement Committee for 1928, *Cmd.* 3308, p. 7.)

'scrub up' and put on a fair face for the doctor and government inspector. No moral restraint is attempted, the voice of prayer is never heard, drunkenness with its consequent train of ruffianly debasement is not discouraged because it is profitable to the Captain who traffics in the grog.

"In this ship, which brought me out from London last April, the passengers were found in provisions by the owners, according to a contract and a furnished scale of dietary.

"The meat was of the worst quality. The supply of water shipped on board was abundant, but the quantity served out to the passengers was so scanty that they were frequently obliged to throw overboard their salt provisions and rice, a most important article of their food, because they had not water enough both for the necessary cooking and the satisfying of their raging thirst afterwards. They could not afford water for washing by withdrawing it from the cooking of their food. I have known persons to remain for days together in their dark close berths because they thus suffered less from hunger, though compelled at the same time for want of water to heave overboard their salt provisions and rice.

"No cleanliness was enforced and the beds were never aired." Food given out was often falsely measured. "Once or twice a week ardent spirits were sold indiscriminately to the passengers, producing scenes of unchecked blackguardism beyond description." The writer states that he has reason to know from other emigrants "that this ship was better regulated and more comfortable than many that reached Canada". The result was not merely disease and death, but "the utter demoralization of the passengers" after two or three months so passed.

"The emigrant, enfeebled in body and degraded in mind, even though he should have the physical power, has not the heart, has not the will to exert himself. He has lost his self-respect, his elasticity of spirit, he no longer stands erect; he throws himself listlessly upon the daily dole of Government."

The transport into the interior was equally bad. "I have seen small, incommodious and ill-ventilated steamers arriving at the quay in Toronto after a forty-eight hours' passage from Montreal, freighted with fetid cargoes of 1,100 or 1,200 government emigrants of all ages and sexes, the healthy who had just arrived from Europe mixed with the half-recovered convalescents of the hospital unable during that time to lie down or even to sit. In almost every boat were clearly marked cases of actual fever, in some were deaths ; the dead and the living huddled together. Sometimes the crowds were stowed in open barges and towed after the steamer standing like pigs upon the deck of a Cork or Bristol packet. A poor woman died in hospital here in consequence of having been trodden down, when weak and fainting, in one of these barges. I have myself, when accompanying the emigration agent on the arrival of the ship, seen him stagger back like one struck when first meeting the current of fetid infection exhaled from between her decks. It is the unhesitating opinion of every man I have spoken to, including government officers and medical men, that a large proportion of the fever throughout the country has been actually generated in the river steamers." [1]

The Wakefield system was never really tried in Canada, although lands were ordered to be sold and not given away in Upper and Lower Canada after 1831.[2] But with the United States offering such a favourable field next door, it was not possible to sell lands " at a sufficient price ", which was one of the principles of the Wakefield system. People seemed only too anxious not to come to Canada, or to leave it if they did. It was futile to make the acquisition of land difficult.

Cape Colony with its droughts and cattle diseases has never been a small man's country. There was no question there of selling land and bringing out emigrants, but this was done to a small extent in Natal.

It was in Australia and New Zealand that Wakefield's system was partially tried. Two chartered companies were founded to carry out Wakefield's schemes. The South Australian Company started in a new area of Australia in 1834.[3] There were no convicts here. Land was sold and a new population recruited. In 1840 another Wakefield company made the beginning of the prosperous settlement of the South Island of New Zealand ; and its two offshoots, the Canterbury Company and the Otago Company, settled

[1] Letter written to T. F. Elliot, of the Land and Emigration Commission, 30th November, 1849, by Mr. Vere, who travelled steerage to Canada, the voyage then occupying two to three months.

[2] F. Bradshaw, *Self-Government in Canada*, p. 311.

[3] It was proposed at a shareholders' meeting in June, 1923, to wind up the Company finally and distribute the assets. *Times*, 28th June, 1923.

the regions known by their name. At a later date another company, the Falkland Islands Company, formed in 1851, developed this outlying part into a vast sheep run.

In 1855 another phase began. The Australian colonies, dissatisfied with the way the emigration was managed from England, demanded the right to sell their own lands and bring out their own emigrants. The lands were ceded to them and they began to work emigration from the colonial side. Sometimes the fare was paid, sometimes it was restricted to a " nominated passage ", that is to say, the person had to be nominated by someone already in the colony to bring out a relative or wife. The gold discoveries did a great deal to stimulate emigration, as they stimulated shipping and offered prospect of employment and even wealth on the other side. In most of the colonies, as they became settled, a movement grew up to restrict emigration. The Labour Party began to be a political power, and its members were afraid of under-cutting by emigrants. The desire to get emigrants was therefore succeeded by a general tendency to discourage immigration and the subsidized passages were suspended. The occupation of the Colonial Land and Emigration Board was gone when the colonies began to manage their own lands and emigration, and it ceased to exist in 1878. The task of supervising the conditions of the passage then developed upon the Board of Trade and the Colonial Office. It was by no means easy to get the right kind of emigrant to go then any more than it is now. The Colonial Land and Emigration Board, in their report of 1852, say that : " Many of the applicants were unfit and few who were eligible were willing to go. The class of emigrant to which our selections are almost confined as the only one entirely satisfactory to the colonists is more limited than at first sight would be imagined. Paupers, as they are called, are below the required class, mechanics are generally above it, old people are useless, young children inconvenient, idlers are mischievous in a colony, active people can generally get on at home. Single men are not desired in excess of single women and respectable single women are not generally anxious to try the risks of a new country." [1]

There ensued between 1873 and 1886 a great depression in England. Changes in the methods of manufacture led

[1] Twelfth Report of the Land and Emigration Commissioners, *Parliamentary Papers*, 1852, xviii, p. 182.

to unemployment ; changes in food imports produced an agricultural depression ; and changes in transport produced a new competition among nations. All these factors combined to produce an economic dislocation. As in 1815, emigration then began to be advocated again in England as a remedy for unemployment. This coincided with a new desire on the part of the Canadians to obtain emigrants when the Canadian Pacific Railway, opened in 1886, made the unoccupied prairies of the West available. On the English side the Emigrants' Information Office was founded in 1886 as a result of the depression and unemployment. It was a voluntary committee, with lay experts on it, and it existed to give advice and spread information about the possibilities in the colonies, to prevent fraudulent recruiting by agencies, and to direct the stream of emigration to the British possessions if possible.[1] The Government was too laissez-faire still to subsidize emigration, but a whole host of emigration societies were started to relieve specially distressed classes. No less than thirty-eight were enumerated in the Emigrants' Information Handbook. On the Canadian side a vigorous policy of advertisement for emigrants was undertaken and 160 acres of land were offered free to the settler. The Canadian Pacific Railway Company also began a great campaign to attract settlers and traffic.

Between 1891 and 1900 only 28 per cent of those emigrating from the United Kingdom went to the British colonies. In the twentieth century this was changed, partly in consequence of the advertised possibilities of Canada and partly because the Boer War and Milner's land settlement schemes had attracted numbers of Englishmen to South Africa. The result was that between 1901–12 no less than 63 per cent of the emigrants from the United Kingdom went to places within the Empire, and in 1913 no less than 78 per cent.[2] Canada was successful in diverting a stream of British emigrants from the United States to

---

[1] The name was changed to Oversea Settlement Committee after the Committee of the Emigrants' Information Office, a voluntary body, resigned in December, 1918. The retiring Committee " welcomed the decision of the Government to exercise closer supervision over emigration on the lines recommended by the Dominions Royal Commission ". (Report of the Oversea Settlement Committee for 1919, Cmd. 573, p. 2.)

[2] Dominions Royal Commission, Final Report, 1917 [Cd. 8462], p. 85. This Commission was appointed in April, 1912, to inquire into the natural resources of the Dominions and their development and how far the trade of the Dominions with the United Kingdom might be improved and extended.

the Dominion. She also attracted a great many foreigners, but has not been anything like so successful in assimilating them as the United States. Her French Canadians have never been absorbed like the French population in Louisiana. Her Doukhobors are really independent Slav communities, speaking a different language and having an economic organization totally alien to that of Canada, and are quite as unassimilated as the French *habitants*. Australia, scared by coloured immigration and realizing that she needs more people for defence and development, has shown signs, since the Union of 1900, of wishing to attract white emigrants, but the Labour Party is the obstacle. The difficulty is that both Canada and Australia really want the type of people England most needs herself, the domestic servant and the agricultural labourer. Australia especially wants male youths between 16 and 24, and does not require women except as domestic servants. She does not want married couples without capital. Nor does Canada require married couples. On the farms there is no accommodation for them, and a man cannot earn enough in summer to keep a wife in the town, to say nothing of the difficulty of keeping a wife in the winter, when he is probably out of work or in a lumber camp. People who are wanted are single persons in the prime of life with capital, and to such there is no great incentive to emigrate. The Dominions do not require the skilled man in any numbers, nor the town type, who suffers horribly from the loneliness of the prairie or back blocks, nor do they want the specialized or the professional teacher, the nurse or the typist—those they can supply themselves. Nor was there in England before the War a great surplus of single women who could be induced to face the hardships of life in a raw new country. The surplus female population were elderly women whom it was useless to help to emigrate, as they were too old to be adaptable. It was calculated by the Dominions Royal Commission in 1917 that there were then only 346,000 women in the United Kingdom between 15 and 45 who had no statistical prospect of marriage. There was therefore not much surplus for emigration.[1]

Although the development of the Dominions has been slow, chiefly owing to their lack of attractive possibilities to a town-bred people like the British there has, nevertheless, been quite sufficient emigration to give an English cast to their population. This is especially true of Australia.

[1] Final Report [*Cd*. 8462], p. 96.

While some persons have been enthusiastically in favour of emigration as tending to relieve over-population and to create new markets, others are opposed to it. In the Rider Haggard Commission, appointed in 1906 to inquire into the advisability of financing land settlement in the British Colonies by the British Government, a dissentient report said : " If it were right and if it were practicable to send elsewhere the idle, the drunken, the weak-minded, and the feeble-bodied among the poorer classes, our own community would obviously gain by the transfer. But this is proposed by no one. The emigrants are to be men and women in the prime of life, healthy, sober, honest, industrious, and enterprising. I cannot agree to the doctrine that any national benefit is to be found in sending such persons out of the country. . . . . If, however, emigration is to be the relief which should be freely offered to men physically and morally fit, who are for a time unemployed, then a valuable part of the population would be removed in periods of bad trade, and when good times returned it would be found that the labour force of the nation was insufficient for its needs. To propose emigration as a cure for temporary distress is— to use Swift's illustration—like a man cutting off his feet because he has no shoes." [1] While the population in England and Wales has steadily increased, the population of Ireland has been halved by the departure of the Irish, most of whom went to the United States. This was a relief for an over-populated country, but a large proportion of the very young and old were left behind. It was the young and vigorous who departed.

In Scotland, between 1901 and 1911, the emigration exceeded half the natural increase, and in 1912 and 1913 exceeded the whole natural increase, and the number of persons between 18 and 30 who emigrated from both Scotland and Ireland was double the natural increase.[2]

The Unemployed Workmen Act of 1905 [3] permitted the Distress Committees to subsidize emigration, which was another step away from *laissez-faire* in this question.

After the end of the Great War, another great depression set in, and the usual remedy was suggested—emigration. This time, however, the British Government went further,

---

[1] Sir H. Samuel, in the Report on Agricultural Settlements in British Colonies, 1906, vol. i [*Cd.* 2978], p. 23.
[2] Dominions Royal Commission, Final Report [*Cd.* 8462], p. 87.
[3] 5 Edw. 7, c. 18.

and was willing to advance sums up to £3,000,000 on condition that the Dominion Governments provided a similar amount.[1] Australia was no longer so strongly dominated by the Labour Party ; she could not be uninfluenced by the prosperity of Canada, and its larger population, although a considerable proportion of Canadian immigrants had come from the United States and continental Europe. She began to realize that only by getting people could she create a sufficiently large market for industrial development ; that only by attracting population could she hope to fill her land, as her natural increase was slow. To be really a " white Australia ", and not merely an empty colonizable area in the Pacific which was to be a standing invitation to Asiatics, she began to exhibit less hostility to emigrants.

South Africa, with her great problem of the " poor whites ", had no opening for the labouring classes, but tried to attract the man with at least £2,000 of capital. Only by attracting more white people could the preponderance of white over black be maintained.

In these various ways, by the emigration of loyalists from the United States of America after 1783, by a convict system, by companies, by Government-assisted passages, by land sales, by philanthropic societies, by the giving of information, by remittances from friends, by advertisement, by the recruiting carried on by railway and steamship companies, by individual enterprise, a white population has been induced to dribble out here and there from the United Kingdom and has created a new racial expansion.

Colonial development by the English race may not be as rapid in the near future as in the past. The natural increase in the Dominions is slow ; there is considerable emigration from the Dominions themselves. The unemployed town labourer of England is of little use on the prairies or in the lumber camps of Canada and the skilled labourer is not wanted by the Labour Party in either Australia or the Dominion of Canada. " They must go on the land," is the cry, and that is just what the Englishman does not want to do when he knows of the appalling loneliness of the back

---

[1] The British Government took the necessary powers enabling it to carry out its part of the scheme in the Empire Settlement Act, 1922. The policy embodied in the Act "is to distribute the white population of the British Commonwealth as effectively as possible between all its parts ". It was not intended as a mere temporary expedient for dealing with depressed industrial conditions. (Report of Oversea Settlement Committee for 1928, *Cmd.* 3308, p. 10.)

blocks of Australia and the isolation of the Canadian winter.
Nevertheless, this gradual transference of people to create
great English-speaking communities in new lands has been
one of the most striking developments of the past century,
a century of personal mobility to an unparalleled degree.

The same rapid progress is noticeable in the self-governing
Dominions as in the Tropics. Nothing is more striking than
their boundless optimism. Everything is possible of accomplishment, everything open to remedy. If the centre of
Australia is a desert, are not such things as 5,000 feet bores
possible to reach a vast basin of artesian water ? If the
north of Canada is in the Arctic regions, is it not possible
to push settlement and cultivation further north than was
ever imagined and has not a railway been built to Hudson's
Bay ? Is South Africa afflicted with insect pests ? Why,
surely science can scotch them, and is it not the finest
climate in the world ? The Dominions are always looking
to the wonderful possibilities of the future. Is not Australia
as big as the United States ? Is it not the same shape as
the United States turned upside-down ? Then why should
it not equal the United States ? The great handicap of
Australia, namely its distance from anywhere, can be
annihilated by aeroplanes. Surely Canada can be
refashioned by electricity with her wonderful water power
resources ; and is not British Columbia, situated where she
is on the Pacific, destined to be the future centre of the
world's trade, and Vancouver, with her coal supplies, to
be the Liverpool of America ? Will not South Africa, too,
become a great industrial centre with her wonderful coal
resources ? There is an extraordinary stimulus from the
perpetual attitude of expectation.

The development of the North-West of Canada after 1886
is, like Africa, another of the miracles of our generation.
It is a commonplace now to talk of a new nation in the
West. The most extraordinary refashioning of a quarter
of the earth is going on, and going on at so great a pace
that to forecast the future is impossible. It was prophesied
by a great colonial authority in 1893–4 that the north of
Australia would be aristocratic and that it would be a region
of great plantations with coloured labour. In the south
would be found the democratic development with closer
settlement, co-operative societies and small farms. In the
north the Kanakas or coloured labourers have been
repatriated, and the sugar plantations are being worked

with white labour or broken up into small sugar farms worked by white farmers. It had been previously maintained that the white man could not do manual labour in the Tropics, but sugar cultivation still goes on manned by whites and Australia may yet prove that the white man can and will live and work in the Tropics. To sugar cane, successful cotton-growing has been added, and Australia may yet become one of the great cotton countries of the world.

South Africa has become unrecognizable since the reconstruction by Lord Milner after the Boer War. It has become united ; it has developed scientific agriculture ; and the Boers and English are no longer segregated in country and town respectively. In less than three years after peace Lord Milner had reconstructed the entire political and economic fabric of the Transvaal and Orange Free State on a wider and more enlightened basis. " In so doing he had vastly increased the material resources of their inhabitants, created a civil service at once pure and efficient, doubled the railways, built schools and public buildings, and brought the joint finances of the two colonies to a point which secured the early provision of the funds necessary to complete their equipment as civilized and progressive States." Is not the geographical situation of Cape Town such that it is destined to be the centre of the Empire ?

Constructive statesmanship, good order, railways, and sanitation are remaking the Tropics ; and modern transport and English capital are helping to fill up parts of three self-governing continents. Here are the colonial administrators of tropical colonies, aided by the scientists, training the native, fighting the insect pests and altering the cultures and trade of the world ; there are colonial Parliaments, with their " national policies ", constantly trying new experiments in State control, in tariffs, and in the settlement of the vacant spaces of the earth.

The impress of England in the nineteenth century is to be found on all the world. She has had great opportunities and she has used them to refashion a large part of the earth. The story of British overseas development since the nineteenth century is the fascinating tale of new worlds in the making.

PRINTED MATTER

Please send me particulars
of any new books you publish
on the subjects ticked (✔) on
the other side of this card.

Name.......................................
(Mr., Mrs., Rev., etc.)

Messrs.....................................

....

....

MESSRS.

GEORGE ROUTLEDGE & SONS, LTD.,

AND

KEGAN PAUL, TRENCH, TRUBNER & CO.,
LTD.,

68-74 CARTER LANE,

LONDON,

E.C.4.

ARCHÆOLOGY.
ARCHITECTURE.
ART, AND EDITIONS-DE-LUXE.
BELLES LETTRES ; DRAMA ; ETC.
CHEMISTRY AND PHYSICS.
CLASSICS.
COMMERCIAL.
COOKERY.
ECONOMICS.
EDUCATION.
ETHNOLOGY.
FURNITURE.
GARDENING; AGRICULTURE; ETC.
HISTORY.
JEWISH.
LAW.
MEDICINE.
MODERN LANGUAGES.
MUSIC.

NATURAL HISTORY.
OCCULTISM ; THEOSOPHY.
ORIENTAL.
PHILOLOGY.
PHILOSOPHY.
POETRY.
PSYCHIC RESEARCH.
PSYCHOLOGY.
REFERENCE BOOKS.
ROMAN CATHOLICISM.
SCIENCE.
SPORT.
TECHNOLOGY.
THEOLOGY.
TRAVEL.

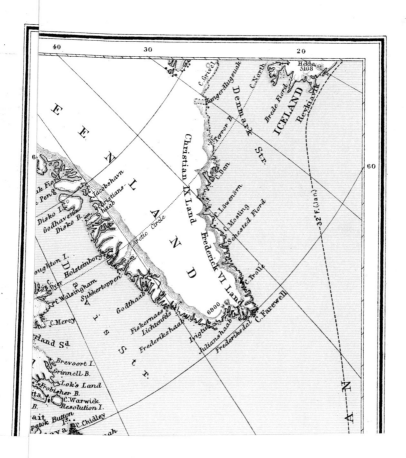

PART II

ECONOMIC DEVELOPMENT OF CANADA

CHAPTER I

Dominating Factors in Canada's Economic Development

Geographical and climatic characteristics.
    Five regions : Maritime Provinces ; Quebec (Lower Canada) ; Ontario (Upper Canada) ; Prairie Provinces ; British Columbia.
    The Ice-free outlets.
    The Forest.
    The open Prairie.
    The St. Lawrence Waterway ; the Rapids and the Canals.
    The Winter Freeze : Seasonal occupations : Lumber and Fur.
    The Laurentian Plateau.
    Waterfalls and Electric Power.
Slow Development.
    A Gambling Basis : Fur, Lumber, Fish.
    Poor Communications.
    Railways.
    Prosperity of the 'nineties.
Immigration and Race Problems.
    The French :
        Rivalry between British and French Settlers.
        Difference in Economic Outlook.
    The Pull to the United States :
        Exchange of Settlers.
        Convenience to Canada of United States Ports.
        Adoption of American Methods.
        Factors making for Canadian independent Development.
    The Scottish Element :
        Causes of Early Emigration from Scotland.
        The Great Scottish Pioneers.
The Six Starting Points :
    The Eastern Shores.
    Quebec.
    Hudson Bay Company's Forts.
    Pacific Coast.
    Ontario.
    Red River Settlement.

CANADA is to-day the most important of the Dominions, if one judges by population, trade figures, and the general industrial and commercial development. If an Englishman had been asked in the decade 1850–1860 which was the least obnoxious colony of the Empire— which is the form the question would probably have taken at that time—he would almost certainly have fixed on

Australia. From there England obtained the valuable merino wool for her looms and the newly discovered gold mines were beginning to attract emigrants and were creating an excellent market for British goods. Few people would at that period have regarded Canada, with its long hard winters, its forests which made settlement so difficult, its two divergent races and its small farmers, as a great Imperial asset. A large number of the subsidized English and Irish emigrants did not stay to build up Canada but went across the border to the United States and helped to develop the former English possession and possible rival. There was, in fact, nothing spectacular about Canadian economic development. Canada did not have the great sheep stations stretching over many square miles of territory, nor the long controversy over the benefits and disadvantages of the transportation of convicts that advertised Australia. Nor was the country made known by a heated campaign against slavery, nor did it attract the great Protestant missionary effort that did so much to make Africa familiar to every church and chapel-goer in Great Britain. The fine exploring work of Mackenzie and others roused little attention compared with that of Livingstone, because the latter sought souls and the former furs and the Western sea-outlet.

In order to understand the general economic evolution of Canada, certain facts must be borne in mind. The first are the special geographical and climatic features which have influenced its agricultural and commercial development. Secondly, it is a story of the slow evolution of an agricultural country where minerals, except in British Columbia, played no part in its development till the end of the nineteenth century, but in which railways were all important. Partly because Canada is a country of small sea-board and long land distances, partly because of the winter closing of the rivers and lakes, and partly because of their unifying influence, railways have in the last half century dominated both the political and economic history of Canada. On the railway question Governments have risen and fallen ; the railways have complicated finance by the subsidies granted them and later by their deficits ; they have influenced the land policy ; and on their freight rates, their elevators and methods of conveying grain the prosperity of the Western farmer and the largest single export of Canada have to a great extent hinged.

The third feature of Canadian economic history lies in the effort to fill up the empty spaces with a population. The character of these immigrants influenced all Canadian development. It was only natural that many English-speaking emigrants should come from the United States, and throughout Canadian history there is a continuous attraction to the United States, partly on account of geography—there being only an artificial political boundary between the two countries—and partly because of the absence of the barrier of race and language. On the other hand, there is equally a pull towards Britain, stronger at one time than another, and this was due in no small measure to the large Scottish emigration, especially from the Highlands.

There were four possibilities, namely, that Canada might become the " fourteenth colony " of the United States ; that it might become French by the sheer increase of the French families ; that it might remain essentially a British colony with a segregated French element ; that it might develop a Canadian nationality of its own, in which all the different races would be absorbed and make something different from either Britain or the United States. In other words, the question was would Canada become French, American, a British colony, or just Canada—a region *sui generis* ?

Fourthly, Canadian economic history has been shaped by the fact that modern Canada started at six different points, namely Quebec, the Maritime regions, Ontario, the Red River Settlement (now Manitoba), British Columbia, and Hudson Bay, each separated from the others by barren stretches of land, or formidable geographical features. Five of these centres originated in connexion with the fur trade : the sixth, Nova Scotia, owed its origin to fishing. The economic history of Canada is largely bound up with the question of linking these areas together, and with the policy which attracted the emigrants to fill the gaps in between the penetration and settlement points.

One cannot withhold one's admiration for such a successful triumph of art over nature as is the Dominion of Canada. It is a tale of individual enterprise and initiative succeeding against great odds and in its development Governments have played but a small part. Companies, railways, and individual emigrants have been the making of Canada.

Contrasted with Australia and the Union of South Africa, Canada is the land of individualism.

Although there is nothing spectacular, and although economically it is pre-eminently a story of struggle, to those who can visualize it, it is an interesting struggle. To watch the small man of Nova Scotia or New Brunswick, half-farmer and half-fisherman, fetching the lobsters left behind in the pools in cartloads to manure his fields, gives one an idea of the potential wealth of the fisheries.[1] To read of the general indignation against the lumbermen who would insist on having white bread and white flour although other people had to put up with inferior breadstuffs, enables one to realize the low standard of comfort in general. It is almost tragic to watch the difficulties of hacking out a home in the forest, seeing that the expensive work of cutting down the trees and clearing them out of the way had to be undertaken before a cart could bring goods to the homestead. The deaths through the trees falling on inexperienced settlers who were unskilled in the art of felling ; the unsightliness of the rotting tree-stumps everywhere ; the bargaining for furs at lonely stations ; the drink with which those furs were largely bought ; the almost squalid misery and the loneliness of people who went out to find a new home on the prairies ; their indignation with the Government and the railways who did so little to help when these great powers might, as it was imagined, have done so much— all these things are part of the picture of the economic state of early Canada. The almost passionate longing for some boom—oil, gold, iron—which should give a lift to a struggling land that always felt the full blast of an agricultural depression is very striking, as is also the initiative and pluck shown in fighting the hardship involved in the change over in the East from wheat to dairy farming, when wheat fell to slaughter prices owing to the rapid development of wheat-growing in the United States and the North-West. Indeed, the very uncertainty of wheat-growing in Canada, owing to the weather, makes the pursuit akin to mining in its risks. " The vast majority of the farming population are dependent for a living on the success or failure of the wheat crop. If it is a success they may enjoy a trip to California or Europe ; if it fails, they may have a visit from the sheriff. And the wheat crop has many

[1] Shortt and Doughty, *Canada and its Provinces* (hereafter cited as C.P.), vol. xiv, p. 583.

vicissitudes to surmount : late frosts in May, drought in June and July, excessive rain and absence of sun in August, and early frost in September . . on the weather depends the health of the wheat crop, and on its health hangs the fate of the whole business community." [1] The early struggles with the forest of the Loyalists from America or the disbanded soldiers from England are paralleled by the struggles of the wheat farmers when the prairies were opened.

The adventurers or philanthropists like Talbot, Galt, and Lord Selkirk, who successfully planted out men in uninhabited and remote regions, the labourers and weavers from Sussex or Devon, the Irish from Ulster, the Highlanders, the men from the Orkneys who were the backbone of the great Hudson's Bay Company—these are the real makers of Canada as a British Dominion, though the history books usually punctuate time by Carleton, Lord Durham, and Sir John Macdonald. After all, forms of government only exist to make economic life function more easily and to enable people to live a social life. But first people must eat, if they are to vote, obey orders, or become intelligent citizens. In the case of the Australians, crowded in their urban areas, and the Union of South Africa revolving round its gold and diamond mines, it is more correct to write economic history, so to speak, from above. In their case the Government and the great capitalists were the important factors which determined economic development. Canadian economic history is to a far greater extent the history of small men in close contact with the soil, and it is history from below. Though the fur lords of Canada offset the wool lords of Australia or the gold and diamond magnates of South Africa, and while Lord Selkirk, creating Manitoba, has his counterpart in Cecil Rhodes in Rhodesia, yet Canada on its economic side is essentially the tale of ordinary folk.

It is, then, striking to find that by 1921 the population of the Dominion was 8,788,483 persons, and that they were spread out over a land stretching from the Atlantic to the Pacific, a distance of 3,494 miles.[2] The value of the exports for the year 1926 was 1,315 million dollars, with an import trade for the same period valued at 927 millions. The steam railways had, in 1926, 40,353 miles in operation. Montreal,

---

[1] " Grain Growers in Western Canada," *Round Table*, vol. iii, June 1913, p. 459.

[2] The distance from Vancouver to Halifax.

in spite of the frozen river which isolates it from water traffic for four and a half months of the year, is one of the great ports of the world. In 1926 the Canadian export of wheat was of a value of 364 million dollars ; its cheese exports totalled 33 million dollars, and its bacon and hams 28 million dollars. Its exports of wood pulp in the year 1926 were valued at 52 million dollars, and its exports of paper products at 121 million dollars ; while no less than 2,700 sawmills dealt with lumber in 1925, the total selling value of which at the mills was 134 million dollars. In 1926 the total value of mineral productions was 240 million dollars. Canneries have been set up for lobsters on the Atlantic and for salmon on the Pacific coasts. The total of manufacturing investment in 1925 was 3,808 million dollars. In 1926 over 756 million dollars was invested in the electric power industry and of the total output of current 95 per cent was produced by water power.[1] These figures are boring if one does not remember that they represent solid achievements of men who, with nothing in the way of a mining boom to assist them, and with no sort of valuable natural or cultivated monopoly like cotton, wool, indigo, jute, or tea to make traders seek them out, yet created a great country and a great trade out of the furs, the forest, and the empty prairies, with the constant enemies, ice and snow, to hold them back.

Geographical features and their influence on Economic Development

Of the five economic regions into which Canada is divided, two of them are mountainous, fishing and lumbering areas on two oceans, the Atlantic and the Pacific. Both have fertile valleys suitable for cereal cultivation and orchards. The Atlantic or Maritime Provinces consist of the mainland strip of Nova Scotia and New Brunswick and of Cape Breton and Prince Edward Islands. These regions are so separated from the interior of Canada by rocky, hilly, and in places mountainous forest country that they virtually turn their back on Quebec and Ontario and look out towards the Atlantic, while their natural market for fish and lumber lies to the south, in the United States.

[1] For these and other statistics see the *Canada Year Book* for the respective years.

They are, however, the only regions in Canada east of the Rockies which have ice-free ports, St. John and Halifax being the only Canadian entrances on the east to Canada in winter. As the only winter outlet on the Atlantic, they are of supreme strategic importance for any country that does not wish to become dependent on the United States during the winter for its external trade.

The other fishing and lumber coastal region is British Columbia, with the great island of Vancouver. Here, too, the province is separated from the interior by the Rocky and Selkirk ranges, a more formidable barrier before the days of the railways than the rocky heights on the east. British Columbia has some excellent ice-free harbours, but the trading centre of the world is England, and to reach that country ships have either to go round Cape Horn or through the Panama or Suez Canals. Goods by this western route from the interior of Canada have to stand the expensive rates for carriage over the Rocky Mountains as well as the dues through either of the Canals added to the costliness of a long sea journey. Here, too, the main market for fish and lumber has hitherto been in the United States, i.e. in Oregon and San Francisco to the south.

Sandwiched between these two outlets come the industrial, dairying east and the prairie grain-growing west. Both these are situated far inland from the coast, and they have to solve the problem of getting goods and men in and out cheaply. The industrial east has its best market in the west, but it also has to solve the problem of bridging the great distances between the east and west by cheap transport. Edmonton is 2,163 miles and Calgary 2,190 miles from Montreal, and even then a steamer takes two days to get out of the River and Gulf of St. Lawrence into the open sea. Although Edmonton is only 769 miles from Vancouver City, there are the Rocky Mountains to surmount. That central Canada under these circumstances can enter so largely into world commerce is a triumph of man over space. Obviously, too, the best market for central Canada would lie just across the border in the United States, where there are no natural obstacles to prevent free exchange. This, however, is prevented by the tariff policy on either side, and by the fact that both have similar products so that no necessity is felt for exchange.

Alongside the enterprising, go-ahead, industrial Ontario, comes the agricultural French-speaking province of Quebec, with its great port of Montreal on an island situated in a lake made by the junction of the Ottawa and the St. Lawrence rivers. The Province of Quebec is a little world in itself of quite another civilization—New France— that is now older than France in Europe in its ways and habits of thought.

Up to Winnipeg, which stands at the edge of another world, Canada is a region of primeval forest, out of which the axe has hacked every acre all the way ; it has a hilly rocky surface, interspersed with lakes and streams in which there is very little flat ground, a wooded wilderness stretching up to the north, the great danger of which is forest fires. It is possible to go long distances in Canada by water with only short portages from one lake or river to the other. In Quebec towards the mouth of the St. Lawrence and in Ontario north of Lake Superior are two stretches of inhospitable country, useless even when the forest is cleared, by reason of its rocky nature. Nova Scotia and New Brunswick are only fertile in parts. The forest, which is the dominant factor throughout eastern Canada, consists of " woods of dense, tangled growth springing out of the rotting wreckage of fallen trees, or scattered more thinly over the rough surface of barren rocks. The hills and even the mountains, where such they be, are covered to their summits with timber of some kind. You move for ever as if with a hood over your head. The only smooth and open places are the surfaces of the many lakes and rivers, while through all the summer months mosquitoes and other pestilent insects hold unchecked sway. Even the cleared, civilized, and populous areas show at once that they have been cut in no very remote times out of the all-pervading primeval forest—heavy and thick in this case, for the land was fertile in varying degree, and it was an arduous task. . . . The close fencing, for farms and consequently fields are everywhere small, is mainly of lumber rails . . . The whole inhabited rural country of every province of Eastern Canada consists either of forest or of railed-in fields under cultivation . . . for the manœuvring of cavalry, even on a small scale, there is not a single natural arena between the prairies and the Atlantic." [1]

After 1,500 miles of forest wilderness, with but this narrow fringe of prosperous civilization to the south about a hundred miles wide, the country changes completely.

[1] A. G. Bradley, *Canada*, Home University Library, pp. 13–15.

Almost everything in the prairies is the reverse of the eastern country. " The woodland is in mere patches and of small stature, upon an otherwise open landscape, or it grips the sides and summits of low hills and nearly always grows thick along the water-courses. Here, too, practically the whole country is of smooth surface, without rocks or stones. The streams and rivers are fairly numerous, but they have cut deep hollows through the down-like prairie country and slide smoothly along with muddy current between soft, woody banks. . . . The enclosures here are larger than in eastern Canada, and are of wire fencing, which scarcely detracts at all from the wide open look of the landscape." [1]

The rainfall decreases towards the Rocky Mountains, the foot hills of which are a ranch country for cattle. In Southern Alberta irrigation is necessary. The treeless nature of the prairie is creating an excellent market for lumber from British Columbia in the regions where building has proceeded so rapidly.

The other outstanding geographical fact about Canada is the water access to the interior by the St. Lawrence and the series of Great Lakes. The natural obstacle in the St. Lawrence occurs in a series of rapids above Montreal, separating Montreal from Lake Ontario, and it was not until the river was improved up to Montreal that it was possible for large steamers to get even there. In 1835 timber had to be floated down to Quebec for shipment. [2]

As vessels floated up with the tide to Quebec, and as it was easy to float down the river, the ocean-going traffic centred in Quebec. Steamers were, of course, independent of the tide and could reach Montreal, but they had to pass through Lake St. Peter, which only had 11 feet at low water, so that until dredging operations cut a canal through the lake in 1851 only small steamers could reach the port. [3]

As a port the position of Montreal was revolutionized by steam shipping, which could steam against the current, and the deepening of the channel enabled larger and larger vessels to get up stream. The export of grain from Ontario and the American grain which came by the lakes all con-

---

[1] A. G. Bradley, *Canada*, Home University Series, pp. 16–18.

[2] Report of Select Committee on Timber Duties, *Parliamentary Papers*, 1835, xix, S. Revans, Q. 2584.

[3] In 1851 it was dredged to 14 ft. of water ; in 1853 to 16 ft. 2 in. ; in 1865 to 20 ft. ; and in 1888 to 27 ft. 6 in. (*Encycl. Britannica*, 11th edn., article " Montreal ").

tributed to make Montreal an important port. The Canadian railways, when built, diverted traffic from the Erie Canal and the American railways to the water route by the St. Lawrence, and, once joined up with Portland by railway in the 'fifties, Montreal had an ice-free port all the year round. The winter paralysis of the freeze was thus obviated. With the opening out of the West by railways in the 'eighties, Montreal gained enormously as a great grain transfer port and began to reap the reward of that exploration undertaken by its fur company into the West, which had blazed the trail from Montreal to Vancouver.[1]

Between Lake Ontario and Lake Erie there is another obstacle in the Niagara Falls, and between Lakes Huron and Superior there are the Sault Rapids.

In the days of birch-bark canoes, which were easily conveyed overland round the obstructions, it was possible for explorers and fur-traders to penetrate two thousand miles into the interior by the water route and the very ease of penetration made the French scatter themselves over huge distances. The English, on the other hand, settled and concentrated on the coastline for purposes of trade with the West Indies or England. It was useless to go inland when home-grown products had to be exchanged as transport costs were prohibitive. So the English formed solid colonies and strong bases for future expansion. To the Frenchman each fresh stretch of water was an invitation to explore and get furs, and the consequent dispersion proved the weakness of much of French racial expansion in the New World.

On the other hand, when the English took over Canada, the great waterway gave the fur trade very largely into their hands. The Americans, who would have liked to have

[1] Growth of Population :—

	Quebec.	Montreal.
1739	4,603	4,210
1765	8,967	
1790	14,000	
1815		15,000
1825	22,101	
1826		22,357
1831		27,297
1844		44,591
1846	46,000	
1851	42,052	57,715
1861	51,109	90,323
1871	59,699	107,225
1881	62,446	140,747

S. Drapeau, *Canada : le guide du Colon français, belge, etc.*, 1887, pp. 50, 58.

absorbed the furs after 1783, were unable to compete because the goods they offered in exchange were so much more expensive than the English goods owing to land portage as against lake and river transport, and the return carriage of the furs was also much more expensive by land than by water. It was this ease of communication that made the St. Lawrence valley, the Ottawa River, and the Lakes so much more important in the fur trade than even the Hudson's Bay Company's sea route.

But for goods that were not suitable for light canoes and which could not be borne on men's shoulders past rapids and falls there was a barrier between Montreal and the Lakes. Not till a series of canals was made to avoid the rapids and Niagara could the regular transport of such goods as wheat take place. Thus, before the days of the railway the canals were the principal public works that were undertaken, the result of which was uninterrupted access by water into the interior. This great waterway, however, is closed by ice for from four to five months of the year. Water traffic is accordingly suspended for part of the year, and generally speaking Canada is a country which has to make her money in seven months in order to live for twelve. It is necessarily a land of seasonal occupations, except in British Columbia. The stopping of the fisheries by ice on the east does, however, set a natural close time for fish during the spawning season and this accounts partly for the extraordinary fertility of the eastern fishing grounds. David Stevenson, writing in 1838,[1] said : " The rigour of a Canadian winter, covering the face of the country with snow and congealing every river, lake, and harbour, produces a stagnation in trade which cannot fail to have a bad effect on the commerce of the country and the habits of the people, who are compelled to complete their whole business transactions during the summer and autumn months, and remain in a state of comparative indolence during the remainder of the year." The climate militates too, against mining in such places as Klondyke, where the ground had to be thawed before it could be worked or where the hydraulic sluicing had to be done by hot steam to melt the frozen ground.

The other great geographical feature is the Laurentian Plateau, otherwise the Canadian Shield, a vast V-shaped wedge of pre-Cambrian rock, about two and a half million

---

[1] *Sketch of Civil Engineering of North America*, p. 69.

square miles in extent covering more than one-half of the Dominion. This plateau cuts Canada in two on the north side of Lake Superior and extends to the Atlantic, leaving only a narrow margin of one to two hundred miles in width at the lakes and river. It approaches the river's edge after Quebec. The plateau is not suitable for cultivation except in favoured spots, but being pre-Cambrian rock it is rich in minerals, which are as yet, however, largely undeveloped. There is, therefore, a region of barren lands to the north and also between Quebec and the Gulf of St. Lawrence, and again between east and west on the north side of Lake Superior. This last has made railway construction between the east and the prairies very expensive as so much of the line had to be taken over rocky ground, entailing expensive engineering in a region where it was unlikely that freight would be ever produced which would pay for the expenses of construction. "Here it is a swamp whose viscous, treacherous mass stretches for mile after mile to all points of the compass, until it attains an area sufficiently large to absorb an English county. There it is a litter of jagged rock as if Nature had been at play with the mountains, and after pulverizing their solid masses had tossed the debris promiscuously on every hand. Covered with slippery, decaying vegetation their surfaces are as dangerous as orange peel on an asphalt pavement, and a slight slip may result easily in an ugly contusion or a badly broken limb. Could one survey the scene of solemn grandeur presented by the vegetation from a coign of vantage, nothing could be seen of the maze of fallen tree trunks, levelled by wind, water, and fire, piled up beneath the trees to a height of ten, fifteen, and twenty feet in an inextricable mass, and over which one has to make one's way with infinite labour, menaced with danger to life and limb." [1]

This stretch north of Lake Superior and the stretch of line over the Rockies are dead strips as far as the railways are concerned, and the other regions have to pay for them in extra rates. There is also another dead strip for the Intercolonial Railway between New Brunswick to the south of the St. Lawrence and Montreal. The prairies, on the contrary, are composed of a rich humus soil in which the yields of grain per acre are remarkably high for unmanured soil. The rates for grain by the steamers and the lakes

[1] F. A. Talbot, *The Making of a Great Canadian Railway*, p. 46.

have been in the past cheaper than the railway rates, and the rush to get the grain out before the winter freeze of the lakes has been one of the great features of the Canadian wheat trade. Wheat is now being sent out in increasing quantities during the winter by the ice-free port of Vancouver City, either to find its market in China or Japan or through the Panama Canal to Great Britain.

As the rivers have to flow out over the Canadian Shield there are many waterfalls and rapids. These, together with the rapids of the St. Lawrence and the Niagara Falls, make Canada a country specially suitable for the generation of electricity by hydraulic power. The fortunate thing is that this water power is abundant in that region, Ontario, which has no coal and in which the railway rates are too high owing to distance to bring the coal from the coal-bearing regions of Alberta or Nova Scotia. Electricity makes the Province less dependent on coal supplies from the United States. In winter the capacity of the railways is seriously taxed to bring in fuel for domestic purposes alone.

The outlets to the sea on either side of Canada are in the hands of a people predominantly of English or Scottish descent and sandwiched in between are a French people of Roman Catholic faith in Quebec, a Protestant and British group in Ontario, and then a mixed group of English, Americans, and non-English speaking peoples in the Prairies. Thus two non-English or semi-English groups are situated alternately between three predominantly British groups. To the south, without any perceptible dividing line, comes the American Republic ; and Canada is the only British Dominion that has any important foreign neighbour to consider. The pull to England and the pull to the United States have been two of the leading features of Canadian economic history.

Slow Development

The striking thing about Canada is the late arrival of real prosperity. Not till 1900 can the country be said to have made rapid progress. Although there were important political happenings such as the advent of self-government and the federation of the Provinces in 1867, economically speaking it was a long-drawn-out struggle against climate, forests, and the superior attractions of a more developed nation across the border, with occasional booms in war years like 1812–15, the Crimean War of 1854, and the American Civil War 1861–5, when timber and grain were in special request. Canada, though old constitutionally speaking, is young in all that represents economic development of the modern type. Nothing strikes the economic historian more than the long persistence of barter and the absence of coin, except in such centres as Montreal or Quebec. One gains the impression that barter and payment in kind were quite usual up to the end of the first half of last century. Under those circumstances there could not be much accumulation of capital, and there was little chance for the settlers to attain the luxuries or refinements of European civilization. On the one hand, there were the staples of fur, lumber, and fish, all three risky, seasonal, and somewhat of a gamble. Neither the lumber men nor the fur traders provided the solid nucleus of a settled society, since they were always moving further afield. The fisherman's business made him stick to the coast and from him no inland penetration could be expected. On the other hand, in Ontario there were the farmers slowly hacking little clearings out of the forest and selling the burnt ashes for potash, and gradually from these clearings producing a surplus of wheat. Fish, sold on account of proximity to the United States, or in a dried and salted form in the West Indies ; lumber, which, near the coast, would be in request for ship-building and which would necessarily slump when iron steamships came in ; timber for the houses of the new towns and for the new railways ; furs which were a monopoly of two great companies which afterwards united in 1821 ; potash ; and wheat—these were the staples with which the Canadians could hope to buy manufactured articles, tea, and tobacco.[1] As, however, the United States also produced wheat and lumber, Canada was almost exclusively centred on Great Britain for her markets and purchasing power. Great Britain made up the deficits in the Civil List and paid for the Army stationed in Canada, which had the effect of introducing a body of men usable for police purposes and some coin with which to pay them. Great Britain subsidized the building of the canals which made the St. Lawrence navigable as far as the Lakes ; and the United Kingdom after 1815 provided fresh batches of emigrants, of which the Scottish were a most valuable element, as they did not suffer so much from the climate

[1] Sugar was partly obtainable from the maple tree.

as southern English. A great object of Canadian policy at one period was to attract American goods, especially wheat, and to use the natural highway of the Lakes and St. Lawrence, and the Mother Country assisted this by giving a tariff preference on wheat and flour, which also extended to the American wheat and flour coming by the Lakes and the River. As England gradually went over to free trade the preferences were whittled down and then abolished, that on wheat going in 1846 with the Repeal of the Corn Laws. This was a considerable blow to a struggling country.

The slow development of Canada was due to the difficulty of finding markets for lumber and wheat, and this in its turn was partly due to deficient communications. Wheat and potatoes which could not be sold were converted into the spirits which were so cheap and abundant that the most appalling drunkenness resulted. When roads were developed this evil largely ceased. Travellers in the 'thirties and 'forties of last century wax eloquent on the awful state of the roads. Mrs. Jameson, writing of Canada in 1838, says : " A wheel here and there or a broken shaft lying by the wayside told of former wrecks and disasters. In some places they had in desperation flung huge boughs of oak into the mud abyss and covered them with clay and sod, the rich green foliage projecting on either side. This sort of illusive contrivance would sometimes give way and we were nearly precipitated into the midst. By the time we arrived at Blandford, my hands were swelled and blistered by continually grasping with all my strength an iron bar in front of my vehicle to prevent myself from being flung out, and my limbs ached woefully. I never beheld or imagined such roads. The settlers around are too much engrossed by the necessary toil for a daily subsistence to give a moment of their time to road-making without compulsion or good payment. . . . Specie, never very plentiful in these parts, is not to be had at present, and the £500,000 voted during the last session of the Provincial Parliament for the repair of the roads is not even raised, I believe. Nor is this all : the vile state of the roads, the very little communication between places not far distant from each other leave it in the power of ill-disposed persons to sow mischief among the ignorant, isolated people." She took 9 hours to travel 25 miles. Walking, she said, was impossible as there was only wild tangled untrodden thicket on either side impervious to the

foot. Again she writes : " The roads were throughout so
execrably bad that no words can give you an idea of them.
We often sank into mud holes above the axle tree ; then over
trunks of trees laid across swamps, called here corduroy
roads, were my poor bones dislocated." She describes in
another district the " deep holes and pools of rotted vegetable
matter mixed with water, black, bottomless sloughs of
despond " which dotted the so-called highways.[1]

Shirreff, writing in 1835, describes much the same experience. " At Brantford we engaged a wagon in preference to horses, under an idea of its being an easier mode of
conveyance, but I am now satisfied our opinion was
erroneous, as horseback would have been more expeditious
and less fatiguing than our wagon over such roads as we
travelled. The roads formed by the Canada Company in
the Huron Tract have been styled good by the backwoods-
men, and so puffed off in every British newspaper that
Englishmen may be apt to imagine they are macadamized.
They are simply straight lines, formed by felling trees,
the branches and trunks of which have been burnt, or
formed into corduroy, and the stumps, from two or three
feet in height, left standing. I have already alluded to the
extent of corduroy, a description of roads which most
travellers speak of with horror, and, without meaning to
praise it, I must say it was by far the best and smoothest
portions of the Goderich roads. The roots projecting from
the stumps in a slanting direction kept the wheels and
axles of our wagon moving up and down with the regularity
of the beam of a steam-engine, and were alike annoying to
us and fatiguing to the horses, and more especially when
travelling between Van Egmont's tavern and London." [2]

" In the then condition of the roads it would have been
almost impossible to have brought members to a Common
House of Assembly except in seasons of the year when
their presence was indispensable at home," said a Canadian
writer when speaking of the Constitutional Act of 1791.
In other words, long distance travel was only possible in
summer and that was just the time when people were
wanted on the farms. If it was difficult to move people
connected with the business of government it was far more

---

[1] *Winter Studies and Summer Rambles in Canada*, vol. 2, pp. 119–20,
121–2.

[2] *Tour through North America*, p. 180. Corduroy roads have been
described as tree trunks laid transversely and nailed to longitudinal side
pieces so as to afford a stable surface for vehicles and animals.

difficult to move ordinary people and low grade bulky goods like wheat and lumber. The coming of winter and the closing of the waterways by ice kept even different sections of the same Province remote from one another, not merely in the exchange of goods but in the exchange of ideas. This does not mean that there was no communication by sleighs in the winter when the snow became packed. The great highways were then as now, the frozen rivers with the ice surface covered with snow. But the number of people in Canada who could in the early days afford to hire horses and sleighs for a day's journey or more was limited. A trip to town or to a neighbour might be easy in winter on frequented tracks, but in the forests and the isolated clearing of early days communications during that season were simply at a standstill. Before the river was sufficiently frozen to stand the snow and the traffic and again when the ice was breaking up, there was a hold-up of all transport. Water transport, when possible, was cheap and easy, but its cessation checked the flow of economic life in the country. This would not apply to the fur trappers and the lumbermen, whose chief occupation would be in the winter. The fur-bearing animals have thicker coats in the winter and therefore are in prime condition. The lumbermen need the frozen skidways to slide the logs to the streams, thence to be floated out to the world by the spring freshets. But the winter stoppage especially affected what one might term the settled, as apart from the roving, type of occupation.

The difficulty of moving any heavy goods through the forests was the great obstacle to the development of the interior of Canada. All settlement had to be on waterways with easy rapids as all freight traffic apart from short hauls was practically impossible on the highways, which at best were made of logs which were heaved out by the frosts while the melting mud of spring turned them into impassable morasses. This made it very difficult to dispose of any surplus produce. Even the existence of a corduroy road with all its deficiencies as a highway raised the value of farms by 50 per cent. The dependence of such an important centre as Montreal on open water was such that as late as 1851 the cost of fuel and food was doubled when the ice was forming.[1]

Thus of necessity Canadian settlers of British origin who

[1] *C.P.*, vol. x, p. 363.

lived in upper Canada were much like the French habitants, in that theirs was necessarily a self-contained existence for a large part of the year. The stagnation of the isolated inhabitants was remarked on by intelligent travellers like Howison and Mrs. Jameson.

" The first view of a new settlement excites pleasing emotions. It is delightful to see forests vanishing away before the industry of man ; to behold the solitude of the wilderness changed into a theatre of animation and activity ; and to anticipate the blessings which a bountiful soil will lavish upon those who have first ventured to inhabit its bosom. A new field seems to be opened for human happiness ; and the more so as those who people it are supposed, by the casual observer, to have been the victims of poverty and misfortune while in their native land. But a deliberate inspection will destroy all those Arcadian ideas and agreeable impressions. He who examines a new settlement in detail will find most of its inhabitants sunk low in degradation, ignorance, and profligacy, and altogether insensible of the advantages which distinguish their condition. A lawless and unprincipled rabble, consisting of the refuse of mankind, recently emancipated from the subordination that existed in an advanced state of society, and all equal in point of right and possession, compose, of course, a democracy of the most revolting kind. No individual possesses more influence than another ; and were any one whose qualifications and pretensions entitled him to take the lead to assume a superiority, or make any attempt at improvement, he would be strenuously opposed by all the others. Thus, the whole inhabitants of a new settlement march sluggishly forward at the same pace, and if one advances in the least degree before the others, he is immediately pulled back to the ranks." [1]

" A deliberate inspection of a new settlement cannot fail to sink mankind lower in the estimation of the observer than, perhaps, they ever were before. Human beings are there seen in a state of natural and inexcusable depravity that can neither be palliated nor accounted for in any way except by referring its origin to those evil propensities which appear to be inherent in all men and which can be destroyed or counteracted only by the influence of reason, religion, and education. The apologists of the human race vainly tell us that men are rendered vicious by artificial means,

[1] Howison, *Sketches of Upper Canada*, pp. 169–70.

and that they are excited to evil by those miseries, disappointments and oppressions which are inseparable from an advanced and cultivated state of society. If we examine the wilds of North America, we will find men placed beyond the reach of want, enjoying unbounded liberty, all equal in power and property, and independent of each other. Such a combination of happy circumstances would seem well adapted to extinguish and repress evil habits and vicious propensities ; but it has no effect of the kind whatever, for the inhabitants of the bountiful wilderness are as depraved in their morals, and as degraded in their ideas, as the refuse population of a large city. It will be found that the lower classes are never either virtuous, happy, or respectable, unless they live in a state of subordination and depend in some degree upon their superiors for occupation and subsistence." [1]

The coming of the railways first made centralized government, functioning at all times of the year, into a workable system. The abandonment of self-sufficiency, the exchange of products and general expansion were all a result of the railways. The economic history of Canada after 1871 is really the history of the railways. They linked up province with province, created towns in the prairies, necessitated great repair workshops, stimulated engineering and joined up Canada with the United States. Capital flowed into the country from England to construct the lines and build the western towns. Coin took the place of barter. Politicians began to frame a national policy of protectionist tariffs and the encouragement of industries, especially iron and steel. Still, performance lagged behind hopes and enthusiasm until the 'nineties, then, with the possibility of cultivating the prairies, the campaign to attract immigrants carried on by both the Canadian Pacific Railway and the Government was successful in attracting a population, and the mass export of wheat began to develop. The east felt the reaction of the west in the demand for manufacturers, and this did much to stimulate its industrial development. The organization of wheat handling and selling had to be brought to the highest pitch of economy before the wheat could be advantageously sold over all those thousands of miles of land and ocean in the world's greatest market, England. This took some time to develop. The United States grew enough wheat for herself and exported the

[1] Howison, *Sketches of Upper Canada*, pp. 175-6.

surplus ; the Pacific peoples mainly consumed rice ; and so Canada became once again focussed on England as she had been before the repeal of the Corn Laws and the preferences in 1846. England in her turn found large amounts of capital for Canadian development and railway building.

In the earlier period of railway construction the settlers went ahead of the railways and blazed their own trail inland from the rivers. In the later period the railway preceded the emigrant and created the economic environment which enabled him to prosper. Thus the earlier period was a slow advance, the later a rapid advance.

While the end of the 'nineties saw the real beginnings of prosperity based on wheat and railways, the new economic developments, in particular the new discoveries of minerals, the making of paper from timber and the utilization of the water power for electricity had a cumulative effect in making the twentieth century an era of rapid advance.

It must be remembered that Canada, like, for instance, Malaya, is essentially a trading country. She has to import cotton, rubber, sugar, wool, tobacco, petroleum and southern fruits. Her population is not big enough and may never be big enough to consume the surplus grain and her geographical situation makes it inevitable that she should exchange northern products for those of the tropical and sub-tropical regions. It is no mere accident of history that she has special trade connexions with the West Indies. Her limitations on the one hand and her abundance of forest and cereal products on the other, make her an important part of the world's economy. Transport facilities are, however, absolutely vital to enable her to effect this exchange.

Also Canada is a commodity country. Wheat and pulp will not convey themselves like animals in a pastoral country such as Australia, and so the railway and the steamers on the lakes and rivers have meant more to her than to any other part of the self-governing Empire, except perhaps Rhodesia.

The railways and steamers conveyed goods across a continent and an ocean at rates which enabled Canada to reach in Europe the great wheat markets of the world. They enabled her to overcome the limitations imposed on trade by her climate and the winter stoppage. Geographically Canada belongs to the United States ;

the railway and the steamer counteracted the north and south tendency and, diverting the traffic east and west, made Canada part of the British Empire economically as well as politically.

French, American and Scottish Influences on Canadian Development.

When Great Britain took over Canada in 1763 it was a French province of 65,000 people.[1] The French, divorced from France, clung to their church, and from this time onwards their religion, their parishes, and their French nationality became inextricably interwoven. Their general attitude was one of defence against Anglicization.

Ontario, with its three or four thousand families, was in 1791 but the outpost of a province, yet nevertheless struggle after struggle took place for economic predominance between this handful of new settlers and the older inhabitants. It was thought that the French with their large families would dominate the English element in Canada as it could not be reinforced from England till the end of the Napoleonic wars.

The English Government, regarding themselves as administering a French province, accorded toleration to the Roman Catholic religion and confirmed the French land and legal systems. The colonists hailing from America were not, however, content to remain under French law, which they held was feudal and unsuited to a progressive region. Accordingly, the two regions had to be separated, and in 1791 Upper Canada and Lower Canada were placed under different legislatures and legal systems by the Constitutional Act, English law holding good in Upper Canada.

The next struggle took place over the fact that French Canada blocked the outlet and ingress of the inland and more progressive colonists since goods had to come and go by the St. Lawrence, of which the Province of Quebec held the key. Moreover there was friction over the customs and general finances. The outcome was that Lower Canada, mainly French, and Upper Canada, mainly English, were re-united by the Union Act in 1840, Lord Durham hoping

[1] See R. M. Martin, *Statistics of the Colonies of the British Empire*, 1839, p. 153.

that, once united, the English element would dominate the French.

The French also resented all attempts of the English-speaking colonists to settle in western Quebec and in the eastern townships in that part of Quebec south of the St. Lawrence river, for fear of being submerged, just as it was always feared in Ontario that the French-speaking population might obtain a large proportion of the land there, especially along the Ottawa River.

The economic policy of the English element in Canada was liberal and progressive ; that of the French was conservative and stationary. The British wished to develop communications with England and foreign countries ; the French wished to lead a self-sufficing existence, and to them the English were enterprising middlemen keeping the French in a sort of economic helotry. Hence there was friction between the races. Gradually, however, the English-speaking race proved itself economically superior and the French, as far as trade, wealth, power and influence were concerned, dropped behind in the economic struggle.

An acute French observer ascribed this falling behind to the influence of the Church. After stating that the parish and the priest formed the rallying point of the French when their own country abandoned them, he says : " It is the country *curé* who by dint of daily instruction has kept alive in them those modes of thought and manners and customs that characterize the French Canadian race. . . . The protection of the Church is precious, but the price paid for it is exorbitant. Its influence has made the French Canadians serious, virtuous and industrious as well as prolific. Their domestic qualities are the admiration of all ; their health and strength show no signs of diminution. But, on the other hand, are not the intellectual bondage in which the Church would keep them, the narrow authority she exercises, the antiquated doctrines she persists in inculcating all calculated to hinder the evolution of the race and to handicap it in its rivalry with the Anglo-Saxons long since freed from the out-worn shackles of the past ? " [1]

But after 1763 it was not merely a question as to whether the English speaking element was to become subordinate to the French, it was a question whether Canada was to become the fourteenth member of the United States. When that danger passed, owing to the hostile attitude of Canada

---

[1] A. Siegfried, *Race Question in Canada*, pp. 50–1.

itself in 1812, it was a question whether the country would not of itself fall naturally into the lap of the United States from sheer economic inter-dependence.

The contiguity of the United States is a factor which has constantly to be borne in mind when considering Canadian economic history in whatever aspect.

The pull to the United States arose partly from the fact that so much of Canada was colonized by the British or their descendants who had first settled in the American Colonies. The European colonization of Nova Scotia was begun by the French from the Loire district, but when the colony was transferred to England and the French settlers made difficulties about taking the oath of allegiance to King George, forty years after the transfer, there was a partial clearance, and emigrants from New England took their place. The Loyalists came from the United States to Nova Scotia and New Brunswick in 1784 and still further Anglicized the region into which German and Scottish colonists had previously been successfully introduced. Other Loyalists were settled in Ontario and to them came further settlers from across the border called the " Late Loyalists ". In British Columbia, too, many of the settlers came from the United States, first of all for fur, then they penetrated up from California for mining and salmon canning. With the development of the prairies, American farmers came across the border and settled in all three Provinces ; with their experience of prairie conditions they were a valuable asset, but they tended to Americanize the region.

On the other hand, there has been a constant emigration from both French and English Canada to the United States, especially in times of agricultural depression.

Then, too, it must be remembered that the St. Lawrence and the Lakes are frozen from the beginning of December to the end of April and that the main outlet during that period for Canadian goods that would reach an ice-free port is to be found in such harbours as Boston and Portland, while at all times it is a shorter route by rail from the Lakes to the United States ports than the all rail route to the ice-free ports of St. John or Halifax. In 1913, according to the Dominions Royal Commision, two-thirds of the Canadian export of wheat was shipped through ports in the United States.[1]

Again, the pull to the United States, as far as the Maritime

[1] Fifth Interim Report [*Cd.* 8457], p. 22.

Provinces were concerned, arose from the fact that it was easier to import their food stuffs from the United States than from Canada, owing to the sea access and the non-frost bound harbours. From the United States they also drew much of their supplies for the West Indian trade. On the other hand, one of the principal markets for their fish was to be found in the United States. Until recently fish from Nova Scotia was even sold in Boston and re-exported by rail into Ontario, a state of things which the Canadian Government tried to prevent by fixing specially low rates for fish from the Maritime Provinces inland.

America takes the bulk of the Canadian exports of lumber and pulp. Americans have invested much capital in Canadian industrial enterprises. Canadians have copied the American elevator and the American methods of handling wheat ; they have copied in the prairies the 160 acre homestead policy and the system of land survey obtaining in the Middle West and West of the United States.

Ontario, the industrial area, has no coal, and, although she utilizes electricity from her water power, she imports her coal for heating, cooking, and to some extent for her manufactures, from the Republic, as well as iron ore from the Lake Superior fields. Both American and Canadian steamers compete for traffic, and the carriage of Canadian grain on the Great Lakes and the return cargoes of American coal to Fort William which the grain steamers can obtain, while lowering the freights on grain, tend to encourage the steamers to unload the grain at American Lake ports where they can get the return coal cargo.

The cheese factory and creamery, the steam plough and other agricultural machinery were also adopted from the United States. Newspapers, fashions, commercial methods and even the decimal coinage and the dollar show how much Canadians have been influenced by the America next door. The film and wireless broadcasting are also powerful factors tending to form public opinion in Canada according to American ideas. The desire for reciprocity or free trade with the United States has led to frequent " pilgrimages to Washington ".

The influence of the United States on Canada has, however, come mainly from the eastern or English part of the United States. The middle west and the west of that Republic may speak English and recite the Declaration of Independence, but that is a foreign country which it is the task of the east to absorb and in which it has to create its own standard of civilization. While the eastern part of the United States is similar in habits of thought and standards of civilization to Eastern Canada, a large part of the west, owing to the immigration of Italians, Poles, Jugo-Slavs and other Central and Eastern European races, is alien to the essential Britishness of Canada. Thus, although Americans have declared on many occasions that it is the " manifest destiny " of Canada to be part of the United States, the dislike of the French Canadian for the Americans, the hatred of the United Empire Loyalists transmitted to their descendants for the rebel country that persecuted them, and the growing foreign-ness of America itself towards the West tend to make Canada a nation to itself. Moreover, Canadians know that America assimilates her people. She aims at uniformity, not diversity among her citizens, and Canadians are repelled by the idea of such assimilation, although economic and geographical factors make so strongly in that direction.

In studying the economic history of Canada it is impossible to over-estimate the importance of the large Scottish element there found. The Highlanders began to migrate to the Maritime Provinces partly as a result of the breaking-up of the clan system after 1745 and partly from sheer over-population in a country too poor to support the increasing numbers. This movement was reinforced by the spread of enclosure for sheep-farming, the decline of the kelp industry and the cessation of military road-making. Owing to changes in diet and increased medical knowledge, babies lived when previously they died, and numbers increased in the Highlands at the same time as the chances of employment tended to decrease. The holdings became subdivided and could not support the people. Many Highlanders came first into Glasgow and found work in the new factories until they were undercut by the Irish with an even lower standard of living, and so Scotsmen left for the Maritime Provinces and the Canadas. As they settled in clan groups they helped each other and on the whole made good, and as their standard of living was already low, they did not readily succumb to the hardships of the life.

One of the most successful settlements in Canada was that of the Canada Company, which was organized by John Galt, who hailed from Ayrshire. The British American Land Co., organized by his son, A. T. Galt, " doubled the revenues of the province (of Quebec) and provided funds for much needed development. His scheme of emigration brought to Canada some of the best stock that has ever gone to its making." [1]

The Hudson's Bay Company, according to the Select Committee of 1857, recruited its men almost wholly from the Orkneys. Sir Alexander Mackenzie, who discovered the land route to the Pacific and who was also a power in the North West Fur Company, hailed from Inverness. Fraser who, like Mackenzie, gave his name to a river, was also a Highlander. William McGillivray, after whom Fort William is named, is another Scotsman who has left a geographical landmark.

Lord Selkirk, who started Manitoba and brought out large numbers of Scotsmen to both Prince Edward Island and the Red River Settlement in 1812, was a Douglas. Indeed, it has been said that a casual observer would take Winnipeg to be American unless he were there on a Sunday, when he would recognise its essential Scottishness. The Canadian Pacific Railway, on which so much of the prosperity of Canada has hinged, was completed and made into a success by two Scotsmen afterwards Lord Strathcona and Lord Mount Stephen.

While Scots have played a large and important part in the development of the British Empire generally, whether in the Tropics or in the temperate regions, it is the Dominion of Canada that is the colony of Scotland *par excellence*, and there the strong Scottish element has hitherto successfully counteracted both Frenchification and Americanization.

Nevertheless, it must always be remembered that the capital for the promotion of trade and industry in British North America was, up to the first half of last century, supplied by English merchants, especially by London houses.[2] The Hudson's Bay Company is one outstanding example. Many English merchants settled for a time in British North America to establish their businesses ; in other cases English houses set up branches under the control of junior partners or agents.[3] These agents were usually

---

[1] O. D. Skelton, *Life and Times of Sir A. T. Galt*, p. 28.

[2] *C.P.*, vol. 15, pp. 121, 134–5. Also Report of Select Committee on Timber Duties, *Parliamentary Papers*, 1835, xix, *passim*.

[3] The grandfather of Edward Ellice was a merchant in New York. His father removed to Montreal after the American Rebellion and supplied a large part of the capital for the fur trade. The St. Lawrence fur trade,

Scotsmen who launched out later on their own account and became Canadian capitalists. They, too, usually obtained their working capital in England. Not till the last half of the nineteenth century did a class of Canadian capitalists arise. The capital for the Grand Trunk Railway was supplied by England and its management was in England, while the canals were financed by the British Government.

The Starting Points

The Dominion of Canada started from six different points. Her growth has not been brought about by pushing back a land frontier, as in the United States ; it has been a process of coalescence of different starting points by the filling in of the intermediate spaces. With fish and furs as the original bases on which the Colony rested for a century and a half, the economic story is one of different groups of settlers who super-imposed upon those bases the new economic values to be obtained from lumber, wheat and dairying. Settlers turned what was once regarded as a bleak, inhospitable land of ice and snow, given over to fur-bearing animals and extending over 3,500 miles east and west, into a successful expansion of European civilization in the New World.

The Eastern shore, settled primarily for fishing and naval purposes, the French province of Quebec based on the fur trade, and the forts of the Hudson's Bay Company founded in 1670 were the three points touched by European trade and civilization before 1763. After the English conquest and retention of French Canada, another point of penetration was initiated by Captain Cook, who, exploring the Pacific in 1778 for a North-West passage, obtained a cargo of furs from the neighbourhood of Nootka Sound and advertised in his book the value of the coast for the fur trade. This immediately attracted other fur traders from England and the coast began to be frequented by Americans, Spaniards, Russians and English, and out of this a fourth point of settlement, namely, British Columbia, emerged. In 1784 the United Empire Loyalists had been settled in Ontario, and this formed a fifth point and the starting point of the

therefore, was worked on capital supplied by the English firm of Ellice. (*Dict. Nat. Biography* under " Ellice, E.") The system of business in the timber trade is described clearly and in detail by J. Rankin, *A History of our Firm, being Some Account of the Firm of Pollock, Gilmour and Co., and its offshoots and connections*, 1804–1920.

K

sixth. When French rule was surrendered, many isolated individuals were carrying on the fur trade, and these formed themselves into the North West Company in 1783. They blazed into the interior trails which at first followed the French trails, but eventually went beyond their limits to the North and the West, so that Mackenzie, one of their number, discovered in 1789 the river named after him, and by 1793 he had reached the Pacific by land. He was followed by Fraser in 1806, also on behalf of the North West Fur Company, and posts and forts were established throughout the interior and on the Pacific. The Hudson's Bay Company began to come further inland and in self protection planted new trading forts, for the North West Company was cutting its communications with Athabaska, the richest fur-producing region. Previously the Company had largely clung to the coast and waited for the natives to bring furs, now it penetrated the Continent to the Pacific. The two Companies united in 1821. The difficulty of an extension of settlement from Ontario lay in the stretch of barren country to the north of Lake Superior and as the Company had to buy from Great Britain the bulk of the food for its forts and of the flour for the Indians it was not unwilling to listen to the project of Lord Selkirk for settling a colony in the middle of the continent just where the barren country ends and the fertile lands begin. This was the famous Red River Settlement of 1812, which afterwards became the province of Manitoba, the sixth point of settlement.

Perhaps some idea of the enormous distances that separated each of these points from the rest, and therefore the magnitude of the task of filling in the gaps, may be grasped when one realizes that from Halifax in Nova Scotia to Toronto it is 1,040 miles, while Winnipeg (Red River Settlement) and Halifax are separated by 2,029 miles; and that from Winnipeg to Vancouver it is 1,465 miles, while Toronto and Winnipeg are separated by 1,232 miles. It is even 419 miles from Winnipeg to Fort William at the head of the great Lakes.

Between Quebec and the Maritime Provinces lay a barren inhospitable stretch of mountain, forest and bleak shore; the Provinces of Upper and Lower Canada were separated by the rapids between Montreal and Lake Ontario; and Lake Ontario was separated from Lake Erie by the Niagara Falls. Again, all along the north of Lake Superior is another barren stretch. Between the prairies and British Columbia stands the mountain barrier of the Rockies. Thus each point of penetration was geographically and economically isolated. It is the engineering feat of the bridging of the gaps by canals and railways ; the financial feat of finding the money to pay for it ; and the economic feat of colonization that constitute the triumph of the Dominion and unity over Nature and separation.

CHAPTER 2

The Main Periods in Canada's Economic History

The Colonial Period 1763–1867.

1763–1815. A Period of Readjustment.

1815–1846. A Period of British Influence.

> Emigration, Land Companies, Canals, Stagnation and Rebellion, Lord Durham's Report, Loss of Preferences in the British Market and Growth of American Influence.

1846–1867. A period of American Influence.

> Reciprocity Treaty.
> Wars bring Prosperity.
> Failure to Renew Reciprocity Treaty in 1866.
> Movement towards Federation.

The National Period, 1867, *to Present Day*.

1867–1897. A Period of National Policy.
> Railways and Prairie Settlement.

1897–1914. Canada as a World Factor.

> The Tariff and the In-flow of Capital.
> Railway Enterprise.
> Wood Pulp.
> Gold and other Mineral Discoveries.
> Penetration of the Laurentian Plateau.
> East versus West.
> Hydro-electric Power.

THE big line of division in the modern economic history of Canada is to be found between 1867 and 1871 when Confederation became an accomplished fact and the Dominion stretched from sea to sea. Provinces like Quebec and Ontario, however important they may be, count for little in a world of big units. They do not get the yield of revenue that large States can command. They cannot afford to pay first-rate minds in administration and they do not tend to attract them because there is little prestige in serving in a small State. They have not the same facilities for raising loans for public works and are powerless to carry out a policy of development of large unoccupied areas because their resources are too small. Not till Canada was federated could she undertake the big task of developing the prairie West or building the trans-continental railway.

132

The century between 1763 and 1867 was a period when the Provinces were distinctly Colonies, and so this may be termed the Colonial Period. It is true they obtained self-government in 1848, but they did not even then pay their own way and it was a period of alternate economic dependence on England and the United States.

From 1867 to the present day may be termed the National Period so far as economic matters are concerned. There was a national economic policy for the whole Dominion, which included a protectionist tariff and the development of the prairies where the land was national land and not provincial. A new policy of development by railways was initiated and a policy of conserving national resources was outlined.

The Colonial Period, 1763–1867

In the first period there is a break at 1815 and the period itself may be termed the period of readjustment and colonization from the United States. The chief economic events between 1763 and the end of the Napoleonic Wars were the retention of the French customs and law under the Quebec Act of 1774, and the introduction in 1784 of a new English element into Ontario where the settlers claimed and obtained the right to be under English Law. Thus two systems of law, the one adapted to a feudal state and the other to modern conditions of trade exchange and individual enterprise existed side by side. To these Loyalists came other Americans in considerable numbers to increase the English-speaking element. The discovery of the land route to the Pacific, the formation of the North West Fur Company and its rivalry with the Hudson's Bay Company, all resulting in further knowledge of the prairies and the Western coast, and the establishment of the Red River Settlement in 1812 were the leading economic events of this period.

The War with the United States in 1812 and the repulse of the Americans did a great deal to influence subsequent Canadian economic history, besides creating a temporary boom. The Napoleonic Wars in Europe also created a brisk demand for lumber and grain in Canada and stimulated the Maritime Provinces and their ship-building, as Halifax was the base of many of the naval operations against the French and later against the Americans in the war of 1812. From 1815 to 1846 was the period of settlement from Great

Britain and the period when British policy was all important to the economic development of Canada. It may be termed the Period of British Influence.

Before 1815 there had been but little English emigration; there was too much employment at home; but when the wars ceased, a period of unemployment set in, and English, Irish and Scottish emigration began to be directed to Canada, and the subsequent years witnessed the formation of various land companies and more rapid land settlement. The British element increased; soldiers were garrisoned in Canada to prevent any more incursions by the United States as in 1812; and the canals were built to avoid the rapids of the St. Lawrence, partly with the object of moving troops by water quickly and at a safe distance from the American frontier. These canals provided a much needed source of employment for emigrants who had no capital, enabling them to go on the land, and the waterways when completed were a great stimulus to trade. So greatly did they facilitate transport that American grain began to use this route for export purposes.

In 1791 the two Provinces of Upper Canada and Lower Canada were created, each with a separate Legislature, but there was continual friction between French and British over the customs and between the Colonists and the Government about the alienation of land and the areas reserved by the Government to pay the clergy and to provide a revenue. The general characteristic of the two Provinces in the 'thirties was stagnation and the general discontent resulted in the rebellion of 1837. Lord Durham went out and reported that the two Canadas should be under one Legislature and that the Colony should have responsible government. The two Canadas were re-united in 1840 and responsible government was attained by both the Maritime Provinces and Canada by 1848. The repeal by England of the Corn Laws in 1846, involving as it did the abolition of the Canadian preference on wheat in the British market, stimulated the desire for responsible Government. The preference had been so substantial an advantage that its disappearance brought about a great dislocation of trade and roused much ill-feeling against the Mother Country. The timber preferences were successively lowered in 1843, 1847 and 1851, and finally abolished in 1860 as preferences, though the small duties on all timber, foreign or colonial, were retained till 1866.

The Navigation Acts were repealed in 1849 partly to enable the people of British North America to trade freely in any direction they chose and in any ship they liked to charter, foreign or national.

The action of the Free Trade party in England in the matter of timber and corn references was so much resented that Canada turned to the United States and in 1854 concluded a reciprocity treaty with her neighbour and for eleven years, between 1855 and 1866, enjoyed practically a free trade market in that country. Hence the period from 1846 to 1867 is the period of American influence.

Reciprocity with the United States, coinciding as it did with the Crimean War of 1854 and the American Civil War 1861–5, in each of which food and timber were required by belligerents, produced an era of comparative prosperity for Canada. As it proved impossible to renew the Reciprocity Treaty in 1866, Canadians turned to the plan of federating their own Provinces. Cut off first from preferences in England and then from reciprocity with the United States, they had to stand on their own feet, and the advantages of constituting themselves as large a political unit as possible became at once apparent. In 1867 the Maritime Provinces and Upper and Lower Canada were united, Manitoba was added in 1870, and in 1871 British Columbia agreed to come in on the condition that a railway should be built to connect her with the East. As the prairies, formerly a monopoly of the Hudson's Bay Company, had been acquired in 1869, there was no obstacle save distance to the expansion of Canada from sea to sea. The railways, by abolishing distance as a barrier, made it physically possible to work a common government for a large trans-continental area.

The commencement of the railway net in 1850 and the development of steamer traffic both on the Great Lakes and between England and Canada, lifted the burden of barter and introduced cash payments ; and the abolition of the feudal land tenures in Quebec in 1853 gave Lower Canada a modernized land system.

The expiration of the Reciprocity Treaty with the United States in 1866 was, however, only one of many causes which combined to bring about federation. Hitherto neighbouring Provinces had raised tariff barriers against each other as readily as against Europe or the United States. There was now a growing desire to break down the tariff barriers as between themselves and throw open to all a combined market of four millions of people. The desire to undertake a colonization policy which should develop the prairies, an undertaking only to be faced by a government with considerable resources, was also a powerful economic motive in a movement which was in itself an expression of nationality.   The purchase in 1869 of the lands of the Hudson's Bay Company, with which the old North West Company was merged, was the first official step in the expansion of the Canadas to the west.   There were in addition political motives such as the desire to let the French and English peoples lead their own lives as separate provincial entities while enabling them to form part of one whole in a federation.

Already, as has been seen, the railways in the East had made a centralized government possible and the guarantee of three million pounds by the United Kingdom for the Intercolonial Railway to connect the Maritime Provinces and the Canadas helped to smooth the physical difficulties in the way of a central Legislature.   The railway not merely made for a closer union of the four older Provinces but opened up new possibilities of connecting them up as the outlets of the hitherto remote prairie lands.

Meanwhile the Pacific region, which had been more and more frequented to obtain furs, had been the scene of continual boundary disputes between England and America. This was settled in 1846 by the Oregon Boundary Treaty, so that what is now Vancouver Island and British Columbia went to England and Washington, Oregon and Idaho to the United States.   The Hudson's Bay Company was entrusted with the government of the mainland, to which the Island of Vancouver was added in 1848, but again the matter got too big for a Company when gold was discovered in 1858 on the banks of the Fraser River and miners came up from California.   British Columbia was made a Crown Colony in the same year and Vancouver Island, in which coal was already being worked, was united with it in 1866.   This region agreed in 1871 to come into the Federation if a railway were built to connect it with the East.   Thus federation pre-supposed the development of the prairies and the creation of a great trans-continental railway, which in themselves were going to alter all Canadian economic values. No longer were men going to hack down the forest and laboriously stub up stumps to clear land when they could farm the open prairie, but a market had first to be provided and this rested on railway and steamer development and the economic handling of grain and elevators.

The National Period, 1867 to present day

This era divides itself into a period of depression and slow advance up to 1897, and then a period of extraordinarily rapid expansion.

The years between 1867 and 1897 may be termed the period of national policy, since the chief economic features were the inception of a protectionist tariff and a policy of conscious national development by railways. The three Prairie Provinces were colonies of Eastern Canada and a new colonial policy had to be inaugurated involving a campaign to get population and assistance to railway development by means of land grants and subsidies. Moreover loans had to be raised to carry out this great work of colonization. The Canadian Pacific Railway was opened in 1886. Opposed to the protectionist party was a party always striving for reciprocity with the United States and therefore advocates of a lower tariff. The world depression of 1873–1886 hit Eastern Canada very hard, as agricultural countries felt the depression most and the competition of the United States made it difficult for her to get a remunerative price for her wheat, with the result that she took up dairying.

Meanwhile a new plan of settling the prairies by giving away 160 acres of land free had been adopted and lent itself to advertisement. Both the Government and the railway began an active campaign for settlers and, as the United States was getting filled up, migration was diverted to the Canadian West. Germans, Swedes, Russians, French Canadians, the sons of Ontario farmers, men from the Maritime Provinces, men from the United States joined British settlers in the cultivation of the Western prairies.

The Liberals came into power in 1896. They were pledged to a lower tariff, but, as the United States had refused reciprocity, they tried to lower the tariff by granting a preference to the United Kingdom in 1897. This still further advertised Canada in Great Britain and led to large advances of British capital. In 1900 two new trans-continental railways were projected and they were completed before 1914. Their building created new towns and attracted a large population of skilled artisans. Population increased rapidly, the exports and the imports grew, and the period after 1897 may be termed the period of Canada as a world factor.

At the beginning of the 'nineties wood pulp was needed for the manufacture of newspapers and, the American supplies being in process of exhaustion, the attention of American manufacturers was diverted to Canada. For paper-making the spruce or balsam were preferred, types of wood not in great demand by lumbermen. The demand for wood pulp has also been increased since the War by its use in artificial silk. This led to penetration further into the interior of Canada on to the Laurentian Shield, this being the area of the spruce. Places were also chosen to pulp the wood on the spot, while in other cases the timber was floated down the rivers to convenient spots where large vessels could load the pulp in quantities, as on the Saguenay River.

In 1896 the gold deposits of Klondyke were discovered and a new impetus was felt on the Pacific coast. British Columbia also profited from the new market for timber for building purposes in the prairie as she also profited from the provision of food-stuffs for Klondyke. A new market was also found on the Yukon for the meat from the Canadian ranches in the foothills of the Rockies. Gold was also found in Ontario at Porcupine. Copper and nickel were developed at Sudbury and silver and cobalt in the same Province. These mineral discoveries led to penetration into the hitherto useless and uncultivatable parts of Canada, just as had happened in the case of pulp. Miners require food-stuffs ; patches of clay land were discovered on which produce could be grown for this market. Thus Canada's potentialities were no longer confined to a narrow strip about a hundred miles broad. A considerable expansion North was taking place in the prairies for cultivation at the same time as a considerable penetration was taking place on to the Laurentian Plateau for minerals and timber.

Meanwhile the prairie West began to feel that it was being exploited by the East. " The West feeds the cow, the East milks it," was the expression. The West felt they were being " done " by railway companies and elevator companies. A protectionist tariff did not suit them ; they wanted to sell in the United States, where much of their grain was already milled at Minneapolis, and they wanted to buy manufactures from the United States or England at a cheap rate. They saw no point in paying a toll to the East in the shape of a high protectionist tariff. Hence the West began to organize, firstly in Co-operative Societies to run their own elevators and effect their own sales, and then to form a definite Farmers' Party in politics to insist on low railway rates and reciprocity with the United States. Thus two areas with two distinct economic interests arose. The East did not want the competition of the United States. The West wanted an easier market for grain and cheaper goods and so turned to the neighbour across the purely artificial boundary.

At the end of the 'nineties Canada began to use her great water powers for electricity and this developed the paper pulp industry and stimulated manufacturing generally by providing cheap power. Wheat was supplemented by paper, engineering and minerals, with the result that Canada became a power in world commerce.

As the Dominion became a better market, American capital was increasingly invested in industrial and mineral enterprises, a movement which was encouraged by proximity and the ease of telephoning and directing branch businesses from the United States.

CHAPTER 3

The Economic Development of the Maritime Provinces (Nova Scotia, New Brunswick, and Prince Edward Island) in the Colonial Period

Early Settlers : French Acadians—Scottish Highlanders.

Settlement of the Loyalists from America.

Creation of New Brunswick, 1784.

Immigration from Scottish Highlands and Ireland.

Prince Edward Island.

The Timber, Shipbuilding, and Carrying Trades.

The War of 1812 : prosperity and depression.

Emigration after 1815.

Agricultural Conditions.

Barter Economy.

Growth of the Mercantile Marine.

The Lumber Trade and its Social and Economic Effects.

The Decline of the Maritime Provinces.

IN no British settlement does one get such an impression of overwhelming difficulties in the way of creating a prosperous community as in Canada. The stifling effect of the forest, the difficulty of letting in light and air on more than a small fraction of land in a life-time, the apathy and stagnation engendered, the long prevalence of barter due to the absence of coinage and the corresponding inability to save capital, the bondage to the store-keeper, the loneliness, the discontent and home-sickness, especially of the women, the dependence of Canadian trade on English politics, which had preferences to give or withhold which might make all the difference to struggling Provinces, the ague and fever which struck down the working force of the family, the destruction of life and property from forest fires, the universal prevalence of drunkenness, the absence of communications and the intense isolation—all these are the impressions conveyed by the records of travellers in British North America in the first half of the nineteenth century.

" I know it has been laid as a principle that the more and the closer men are congregated together the more prevalent is vice of every kind : and that an isolated or scattered population is favourable to virtue and simplicity. It may be so, if you are satisfied with negative virtues and the simplicity of ignorance. But here, where a small population is scattered over a wide extent of fruitful country, where there is not a village or a hamlet for twenty, or thirty, or forty miles together—where there are no manufactories—where there is almost entirely equality of condition—where the means of subsistence are abundant—where there is no landed aristocracy—no poor laws, nor poor rates, to grind the souls and the substance of the people between them, till nothing remains but chaff—to what shall we attribute the gross vices, the profligacy, the stupidity and basely vulgar habits of a great part of the people, who know not even how to enjoy or turn to profit the inestimable advantages around them ? And alas for them ! There seems to be no one as yet to take an interest about them, or at least infuse a new spirit into the next generation. In one log-hut in the very heart of the wilderness, where I might well have expected primitive manners and simplicity, I found vulgar finery, vanity, affectation, under the most absurd and disgusting forms, combined with a want of the commonest physical comforts of life and the total absence of even elementary knowledge. In another I have seen drunkenness, profligacy, stolid indifference to all religion ; and in another the most senseless fanaticism. There are people, I know, who think—who fear, that the advancement of knowledge and civilization must be the increase of vice and insubordination ; who deem that a scattered agricultural population, where there is sufficiency of daily food for the body ; where no schoolmaster interferes to infuse ambition and discontent into the abject, self-satisfied mind ; where the labourer reads not, writes not, thinks not—only loves, hates, prays, and toils—that such a state must be a sort of Arcadia. Let them come here ! —there is no march of intellect here !—there is no ' schoolmaster abroad ' here ! And what are the consequences ? Not the most agreeable to contemplate, believe me." [1]

It is a history of little men and multitudinous failures, great stagnation, some successes, endless struggle and a slow advance until the railways lifted men above the

[1] Mrs. Jameson, *Sketches in Canada*, 1838 (1852 edition), pp. 115–16.

supreme difficulty of inland communications. The railways brought in capital and currency, they created new employments and above all gave access to the prairies where there was not this heart-breaking pitting of the cultivator against the forest.

Various factors were at work in the century and a half before 1763 when Lower Canada became an English colony, which modified subsequent economic development. The influence of the English colonists in America, the influence of the Newfoundland fishing industry, the influence of the original French settlers both in Acadie and Quebec, and the influence of the Fur Company in the North laid the economic foundations of the present Dominion. While the English colonists, the French traders, and the Hudson's Bay Company were all engaged in a struggle to get furs from the Indians, the region known as the Maritime Provinces (Nova Scotia, New Brunswick, and Prince Edward Island) had an economic history peculiarly its own. The English had frequented Newfoundland for cod fish ever since 1498, and on the discoveries made by Cabot, sailing from Bristol under a commission from Henry VII in 1497, they had based a claim to Acadie, the coastal area now New Brunswick and Nova Scotia, and the whole of Canada. The fishermen grew to know the coast and the gulf and New England colonists in the seventeenth century pushed up and joined in the cod fishing. Dried and salted cod was an article in universal demand. It was taken to the West Indies, from which the rum for the fishermen was obtained and the slave trade pursued. Salt cod fish was sold throughout the Mediterranean for the Catholic fast days and was a welcome addition to the diet of any country till the agricultural revolution of the eighteenth century introduced a more varied supply of fresh food. Hence France and England struggled for this trade and its profits. The fishing trade was regarded as the " nursery of seamen " for the Navy and so governments encouraged it.

French settlers from the Loire had come to the Bay of Fundy and settled on the marshlands on its Western coast. They did not reproduce, as in Quebec, the feudal régime with its seigniors ; it was essentially a colonization by small farmers. French fishermen also settled in Cape Breton Island. In 1713, at the Peace of Utrecht, Acadie was transferred to England by the French and was renamed Nova Scotia. At the same time the rights of the Hudson's Bay

Company to trade in the North were confirmed. Cape Breton was, however, reserved by France and here the important fort of Louisburg was set up as a military base against England. Here, too, the New England colonists found a market for food-stuffs. In opposition to this great fort, the port of Halifax on the eastern side of Nova Scotia was established by the English Government in 1749, and four to five thousand immigrants were brought there, who in their turn attracted others—Germans, Swiss and British. The French Acadians, who numbered about ten thousand, were always on the side of their compatriots and were joined by the Indians. In 1755, on the outbreak of war, the Acadians were required to take the oath of allegiance to King George. They refused, and about six thousand were in consequence deported. Others escaped into the woods but later wandered back and some took the oath and remained. The general effect, however, was the swamping of the French element by the English, though there are still many descendants of the Acadians in Nova Scotia and New Brunswick. Louisburg was captured by a British force in 1758, so that Cape Breton Island was also ready for a permeation of British influence.

A great many Scottish Highlanders began to move in after the pacification and opening out of the Highlands after 1745, and many of them settled in Cape Breton Island. The Scottish chiefs, after the subjugation of the Highlands, had no further use for crowds of men as a warlike following. When lowland raids were no longer possible and when instead of levying tribute the Highland chief had to make his land pay on an agricultural or pastoral basis, so many unproductive mouths were of little use. The Scottish crofters with uneconomic holdings were in a very miserable condition as cultivators, and in many cases the landlord himself assisted the emigration. Lord Selkirk in the early nineteenth century took a ship-load of Highlanders to Prince Edward Island, but throughout the second half of the eighteenth century they poured into the Maritime Provinces to the tune of about 25,000. No less than 6,000 are said to answer to the name of Macdonald in Prince Edward Island alone. In the eighteenth century, with the development of coal-mining, iron founding, enclosing, road and canal making, and the growth of the cotton industry, England was actually short of hands and was importing Irish, while many Highlanders also reinforced the industries round

Glasgow. The French Wars, too, created employment, and men were needed for the Navy and the Army. There was accordingly little question of any considerable English emigration till the after-war depression set in in 1816. Thus at first only the Scotch were available for Canada. The population of the Maritime Provinces and the Islands consisted of people who were half fishermen and half farmers, or half fishermen and half lumbermen, or of men who combined felling timber with agriculture, in addition to which the naval station at Halifax attracted ship-builders, while a certain retired naval element settled in or near the port. It is no accident that Samuel Cunard, the founder of the famous line of steamers, should have hailed from this region with its naval, seafaring and fishing traditions.

The rebellion in the thirteen colonies of the United States found no echo in Nova Scotia or Quebec.

As far as the Nova Scotian peninsula was concerned, it was inaccessible to attack by land, and to reach it the rebels would have had to take to the sea and the sea was controlled by British cruisers. Nova Scotia suffered nevertheless from the War of Independence, as she was cut off from her supplies of bread stuffs, which she had previously obtained from the New England Colonies, and that also meant that she had no longer a market there for her goods. Wages, however, rose in Nova Scotia, as there was a great demand for timber for ship-building for naval purposes and this stimulated the handling and sale of lumber. The fact that Halifax became of increasing importance as a naval base against the rebels also set money circulating in the country, and privateering, as in the subsequent war of 1812, put money into the pockets of the inhabitants.

Many of the recent emigrants to America before 1776 had been Highlanders from Scotland, and these and other colonists constituted a considerable body of Loyalists who sympathized with or fought on the English side. After the Peace it was found impossible for these and their Indian supporters to return to their homes. England had, it is true, stipulated at the Peace that the States of the Union were to be recommended to repeal their Confiscation Acts and that there were to be no future confiscations nor prosecutions of any sort against any person because of the part taken in the late War. The Loyalists knew, however, that these stipulations would not be observed, and they left the countryside in their thousands and congregated in the town

still held by the English, New York. In some cases the
Loyalists who tried to return were tarred and feathered
or tied up and whipped. Town meetings were held
threatening vengeance on those who did return, a movement
probably engineered by those who had got possession of
Loyalist properties. The town of Boston declared that
these " ingrates " should be excluded " from having lot
or portion among us ". Delaware, after describing them as
" worse than robbers or even common murderers ", passed
a resolution that they would stand by each other in expelling
those who had supported Great Britain.[1] Some plan had,
therefore, to be devised for helping these Loyalists who had
lost everything. Moreover, there were various regiments
which had been fighting on the English side that had to be
disbanded at the end of the war. The British Government
determined to convey them to Nova Scotia, which was
accessible and defensible by sea. An outpost of the attack
on the Colonists and part of the defence of Canada had been
based on Lake Ontario. This region and its possibilities
had become known to the authorities and a settlement
of refugees had been made during the War at Niagara,
and to this region some few of the Loyalists betook themselves while others at their own expense went to the West
Indies. The bulk of them went, however, to Nova Scotia,
which did not at that date consist merely of the peninsula
but included a great tract of the uninhabited mainland
and Prince Edward Island as well.

Colonists cannot, however, go into the wilderness unprepared. Surveys have to be made and lands located,
and a supply of axes, clothing, food and tools is necessary
for some years, to say nothing of such necessities as mills
for grinding corn. It was no light task to take people having
for the most part a standard of comfort appropriate to a
prosperous settled people into an untrodden forest wilderness, nor was it a prospect to be lightly faced by the
emigrants. But the choice was said to be " Hell or
Halifax ".

The majority of the colonists were transferred to the
neighbourhood of the St. John River, where an industry
of cutting white pine masts for the Navy had developed
since 1779, and here the city of St. John was founded by the
Loyalists. " At the time of the arrival of its founders its
site was a dense wilderness. Masses of barren rock were

[1] *C.P.*, vol. xiii, pp. 141–2.

interspersed with cedar swamps and there seemed little good soil anywhere." [1]

Each Loyalist received 500 feet of boards and an allowance of bricks and shingles to build a house.[2] They were given land according to their rank, 100 acres to each private soldier, 200 to non-commissioned officers, while other officers received grants the size of which varied according to degree.

The difficultes were enormous. The lands were not properly surveyed, the regiments when landed did not know in what direction to proceed or where their lands were situated. Many persons were not landed till October, at the beginning of winter, when it was hopeless for them to do anything, even if they reached their locations in that bitter season. Some who did were snowed in. The winter, therefore, had to be passed by most in rude tents or huts on the coast. " There were days when strong proud men cried like children and, exhausted by cold and famine, lay down in their snow-bound tents to die." [3]

The original idea had been to plant out men by regiments, but it did not succeed except in a very few cases because of the difficulty of communication. Men were not willing to settle 150 miles from the sea, where they could not exchange their products and were in danger from Indians.

The Government at Halifax seemed so far away that a new colony called New Brunswick was carved out of the original Nova Scotia in 1784.

The great difficulty was, however, communications, and as late as 1803 it was reported that ten miles of road fit for any wheeled vehicle were not to be found in the Colony except on the east bank of the St. John River. For twenty-five years the rivers were the main routes of travel, and the settlements and the administrative divisions were determined by them.[4]

Many of the Loyalists gave up their lands. This happens in every pioneer settlement, but at any rate some land had been cleared and a breach made in the wilderness into which others could follow later. Some of those who gave up their lands moved on to the northern shore to take up the fishing industry, which they greatly developed [5] ; some joined

---

[1] C.P., vol. xiii, p. 145.
[2] In the course of a year Major Studholme issued 1,731,289 feet of boards and 1,553,919 shingles and 7,400 clap-boards. Ib., p. 145.
[3] C.P., vol. xiii, p. 151.   [4] Ib., p. 169.
[5] C.P., vol. xiv, p. 566.

their fellow exiles in Ontario ; others, as the feeling against them subsided, went back to the United States. British Colonies had hitherto been founded by companies or proprietors, and Ontario and New Brunswick are remarkable for the fact that they were the first Colonies founded by the British Government from which the settlers received rations.

It must be remembered, too, that during the years from 1783 to 1790 (while the Commission of Inquiry into Loyalist Losses was sitting), the British Government was doing a great deal for the Loyalists in other ways. Many of the better class received offices under the Crown. All who wished it received a grant of land. And in addition to all this, the British Government clothed and fed and housed the Loyalists until they were able to provide for themselves. Including the cost of surveys, official salaries, the building of saw-mills and grist-mills, and such things, the figures must have run up to several millions of pounds. The claims allowed by the Royal Commission amounted to £3,112,455, while the total outlay on the part of Great Britain, both during and after the war, on account of the Loyalists, must have amounted to not less than £6,000,000, exclusive of the value of the lands assigned.[1]

Nor did the British Government take the treatment of its Loyalists by the United States lying down. When the demand was made for the delivery of the eight frontier posts on the American side of the boundary which were held by the English, the British Minister replied that they were held because of the failure of the States to restore the property of the Loyalists. For thirteen years, until after Jay's Treaty of 1794, the posts remained under the flag of Great Britain, a fact which some American writers consider secured the fur trade for Canada.[2] Geographical reasons, however, namely the control of the water-way, probably determined that the fur trade should remain in British hands.

The Loyalists who came to Halifax were in many cases destitute of clothes and provisions. The voyage sometimes meant tossing on the wintry sea for weeks. So bad was the climate deemed to be by the Americans that the nickname " Blue-nose " was given to those who lived in

---

[1] W. S. Wallace, *United Empire Loyalists*, pp. 117–19.
[2] J. B. McMaster, *Camb. Modern History*, vol. vii, p. 308.

Nova Scotia.[1] Shelter could not be provided for them all and provisions rose to famine prices.

"If men remembered their comrades drowning, after all their battles, almost within sight of port, the hopeless misery between decks of the crowded transports through long weeks at sea, the sickness that lacked every comfort and alleviation and ended in shrouded corpses committed to the deep, their half-fed wives and little ones shivering in huts or tents through the driving snows and icy rains and hard frosts of the northern winter ; if they remembered all they had left behind, their attempts to begin life anew as pioneers in the wilderness, and, after all their sacrifices and bitter toil, to have their hopes blighted ; if they recalled all this and handed on the tale of suffering and persecution and loyalty to their children's children and left them a legacy of hatred and prejudice, the fault lies with those who in the hour of triumph did not remember mercy." [2] This accounts for the dislike of the Americans felt in Ontario and the Maritime Provinces which was noticed by travellers and partly explains why British North America resisted any attempt to become the Fourteenth State of the Union.[3]

---

[1] "But the increase of population in Nova Scotia from immigration during the years immediately following 1783 was partly counterbalanced by the defections from the province. Many of the refugees quailed before the prospect of carving out a home in the wilderness. "It is, I think, the roughest land I ever saw " ; " I am totally discouraged " ; " I am sick of this Province " ; such expressions as these abound in the journals and diaries of the settlers. There were complaints that deception had been practised. " All our golden promises," wrote a Long Island Loyalist, " are vanished in smoke. We were taught to believe this place was not barren and foggy as had been represented, but we find it ten times worse. We have nothing but his Majesty's rotten pork and unbaked flour to subsist on. . . It is the most inhospitable clime that ever mortal set foot on." At first there was great distress among the refugees. The immigration of 1783 had at one stroke trebled the population of Nova Scotia ; and the resources of the province were inadequate to meet the demand on them. " Nova Scarcity " was the nickname for the province invented by a New England wit. Under these circumstances it is not surprising that some who had set their hand to the plough turned back." W. S. Wallace, *United Empire Loyalists*, pp. 61–2.

[2] *C.P.*, vol. xiii, p. 240. The following poem gives some idea of the way in which this region was regarded :—

> "Of all the vile countries that ever were known
> In the frigid or torrid or temperate zone,
> From accounts I have heard there is not such another,
> It neither belongs to this world or the other."

[3] "I found many of the Canadians filled with inveterate prejudice against the inhabitants of the United States, whom they regarded as a band of cheating and lying democrats. Some excuse might have been found for this feeling had it alone existed amongst the first settlers who suffered during the late war ; but the greatest degree of inveteracy

A town, Shelburne, was founded in Nova Scotia by the Loyalists and flourished for a time, but its ice-bound harbour prevented its development. Nevertheless, the Loyalists formed an important element in Nova Scotia and the Province advanced rapidly in prosperity partly owing to the vigour and capacity of its new population. Its trade with the United States was, however, cut off and a new orientation of trade with the West Indies and Great Britain had to be built up. The Loyalists brought with them such bitter memories of their treatment that it was not likely that their relations with the original Colonies would be cordial.

To these Loyalists came a large migration of Highlanders. The famine of 1782–3 was so severe in the Highlands that a special report was sent to the House of Commons on the subject. In consequence of the famine a Nova Scotia correspondent writing from Halifax described the arrival of thousands of emigrants.[1]

The Highlands generally were greatly over-populated. More people were being kept alive owing to the introduction of potatoes, which checked one of the great causes of infantile mortality—the scurvy. This resulted in the sub-division of farms to an uneconomic level. Sheep and cattle farming promised better returns to the landowners, but they needed less labour, and any way the Highlander was too proud to work at home as an agricultural labourer. Hence he was willing to migrate to America. The Loyalists, being partly Scottish, formed a nucleus of attraction to other Scotsmen and, generally speaking, the standard of living of the Highlanders was already so low that they were not overwhelmed by the hardships. As the timber trade with Great Britain developed, they got a cheaper passage out in the empty ships which had unloaded their timber in the United Kingdom. Hence the ease of getting to the Maritime Provinces made them the most attractive spot for emigrants.[2]

was evinced by persons lately from Britain, whose conduct, in the intercourse of the world, had not been altogether blameless at home. The prosperity of the people of the United States seems to excite the envy of the Canadians. The same feeling does not exist in the State of New York towards the Canadians, who are there considered indolent and dissipated." P. Shirreff, *Tour Through North America*, p. 390.

[1] Miss M. I. Adam, "Highland Emigrations of 1783–1803," *Scottish Historical Review*, vol. xvii, p. 77.

[2] In 1801 and 1802 Highland emigrants to the Maritime Provinces numbered 1,137, or including others whose destination was not specified, 2,037. Those going direct to Upper Canada numbered 473, while 550

To settle in Upper Canada meant not merely the long voyage up the St. Lawrence, but transhipping at Quebec, the end of tide-water, to get into a smaller vessel to go up to Montreal, and then a further transhipment into flat-bottomed boats to be poled through the rapids. This meant not merely an increase in the length and expense of the voyage, but the endurance of further hardships in the open river boats. In the Maritime Provinces emigrants could settle down at some coast port or they could easily transfer themselves, as they did later in large numbers, to the United States. Hence the Maritime Provinces were up to about 1820 the most important parts of British North America. After that the canals gave easier access to Upper Canada and more powerful steamboats were built which could get up stream better, and, with this minimizing of transport difficulties, the inland regions tended to attract emigrants rather than the older seaboard provinces. The Irish came in large numbers after 1815, partly owing to the great over-population of their country, but also because the place to which they were to go was largely determined by the low cost of the outward voyage on the empty lumber ships and by the chances of employment on arrival. In 1835, 30s. was the outward fare from Ireland to Quebec on the timber ships, and another 30s. would cover the cost of their food on the voyage, that is to say, the oatmeal and potatoes provided by themselves.[1] The fare from England or Scotland was twice that from Ireland, hence the large emigration from the latter country. The reason for the low fares from Ireland was that the timber ships were calling more and more at Irish ports because of the lower range of duties prevailing on timber imported into Ireland than existed for timber imported into Great Britain and because of the demand that was springing up in Ireland for staves in connexion with the export of Irish provisions.[2] The lumber vessels going out in ballast were described as a " cheap bridge " for the passage of emigrants,[3] and another writer

others were " to land at Quebec to go on to Upper Canada as they could," and 250 were bound simply for " Canada " unspecified. Incidentally, some 730 set sail for the United States. In 1802 the passengers took out of the country more than £100,000 in cash, including freight money." Report on the Survey of the Coast of Scotland, etc., relating to Emigration, in *Parliamentary Papers*, 1802–03, vol. iv, pp. 40–1.

[1] Report of Select Committee on Timber Duties, *Parly. Papers*, 1835, XIX (referred to hereafter as *C.T.D.*), J. Neilson, Qq. 1976–77.

[2] *C.T.D.*, J. Dowie, Qq. 3803–7.

[3] N. Gould, *Sketches of the trade of British America*, 1833, p. 10.

said : " The timber trade has been the handmaid of emigrations." [1]

Regiments were stationed in New Brunswick [2] and Nova Scotia and time-expired soldiers were settled on the land, especially on the border between the United States and British America, as part of the frontier defence scheme, but except for these and retired naval officers and their families, the English element was confined to the merchants who came out to engage in the shipping of lumber. The Loyalists and this middle-class English element gave an English tone to a population largely recruited from the Highlands or Ireland.

It must .be clearly borne in mind that the Maritime Provinces, with their fishing, ship-building, lumber and West Indian trade, seemed to Englishmen during the first thirty years of the nineteenth century to be the most important part of British America. Only slowly did the Province of Ontario dwarf the importance of the Atlantic seaboard. [3]

Prince Edward Island, originally the Isle St. Jean, was transferred from French rule to that of Nova Scotia in 1763. The English sent out to survey it in 1764 and land was light-heartedly granted away with certain reservations by putting a list of persons who applied into a bag to be drawn " by some indifferent person ". The proprietors who emerged from the lucky bag were to pay a rent of 2s. to 6s. per 100 acres. They were to place a European Protestant on every two hundred acres of land. This, however, was not fulfilled. [4] A sparse population was reinforced by 120 families from Scotland in 1770 and one, Macdonald of Glenaladale, sent

---

[1] A. Gesner, *New Brunswick*, 1847, p. 300.

[2] William Cobbett was a sergeant-major in one of them.

[3] " With respect to what part of North America I would recommend, my answer is, every part, you cannot go amiss in the Colonies : yet in this, as in all other things, there is a choice, and I must acknowledge, if I have a predilection, it is in favour of New Brunswick, my reasons for which are as follows : first, that it is as yet thinner (*sic*) inhabited, and consequently more eligible situations are vacant ; secondly, its commerce, which is great both in timber and fish, affords a choice of occupation of the emigrant ; and lastly, the circumstance of St. John (its principal port) . . . having an open harbour during winter, bids fair for its becoming the emporium of the North American Colonies. Some parts of the Canadas, however, it must be admitted, have a warmer climate, and are more productive, yet they are less healthy, and further from market, which operates as an offset to their other advantages " (*The Advantages of Emigrating to the British Colonies of New Brunswick, Nova Scotia, etc., etc.*, by a Resident of St. John's, New Brunswick, 1832, pp. 13–14.)

[4] *C.P.*, vol. xiii, p. 337.

out a large emigration in 1772.[1] In 1783 the proprietors, anxious to get settlers, offered asylum to the Loyalists, and as the Loyalists were stranded at Shelburne about 605 arrived on the island. The real development of the island began when Lord Selkirk brought out about 800 immigrants from Scotland in 1803. According to the census of 1901 the number of persons of Scottish descent numbered 41,573.

Lord Selkirk seems to have employed a remarkably enterprising agent to recruit the Highlanders. " He persuaded them that tea . . . could be gathered in the swamps ; that the maple tree yielded a copious stream of sweetness that with little trouble could be transformed into whisky ; and that the Indians who had been converted to Christianity by Catholic missionaries . . . were anxious only for an opportunity to join the Church of Scotland." [2]

Apart from the continued emigration of the Highlanders and the Irish, the main economic interest of the Maritime Provinces rested on the development of the timber trade, ship-building and the trade with the West Indies. Ships from the Atlantic Provinces took out fish to the West Indies and brought back rum and molasses. The former was considered one of the necessaries of life. Indeed, the main source of the revenue of New Brunswick came at first from the penny per gallon charged as customs duties on rum, which was an article of universal consumption.[3]

" As early as 1774 a cargo of squared timber was shipped to Britain from Pictou Harbour." [4] During the Napoleonic wars the Baltic was closed in 1807 and in 1808 there was a great shortage of timber, both for ships and for the mining industry. The price of Memel timber, which had been 78s. a load in 1802, rose in 1809 to 320s. a load. In order to ensure a supply from the Colonies very heavy duties were put on European timber and a substantial preference given to Colonial timbers, whether from the Canadas or the Maritime Provinces. In 1803 no fewer than 50 vessels loaded timber at Pictou alone and in twenty years, 1800–1820, the average

---

[1] By 1841 there were 4,500 persons of the name of Macdonald on the island. *C.P.*, vol. xiii, p. 358.

[2] Ibid., pp. 355–6.

[3] " When the House of Assembly met for the second time, the quantity reported as having been imported in ten months and a half was 97,990 gallons. As the population was less than 20,000, the quantity of rum consumed on an average was nearly half a pint daily for every male over 16 years of age " (Ibid., p. 170).

[4] Ibid., p. 254.

annual value of the timber from this one port, which was typical of the impetus given to the whole Province, was no less than £100,000.[1] Indeed, the whole seaboard was stimulated by the preferences.[2]

A large ship-building industry grew up in the wake of the lumber trade. The timber of the Maritime Provinces provided excellent masts and spars for ships and a second-class timber suitable for houses. In general the timber was said to be " not equal in quality to the best timber brought from Norway," except the red pine. It seems to have been liable to dry rot.[3]

The ship-building and lumbering seem to have been carried on in these Provinces on a sort of family system, in sharp contrast with Lower Canada, where large amounts of capital seem to have been employed. That there were large capitalists operating in the Maritime Provinces is brought out by the Committee on Timber Duties in 1835, but it does not seem to have been a typical condition. Professor Johnston, writing in 1851, says : " A farmer on the South mountains will cut down lumber on his farm and will convey it with his own horses to the shores of the bay. With or without the aid of a carpenter he will lay down the lines of a ship. He will build it himself with the help of his sons ; he will even do the smith's work with his own hands. He will mortgage his farm to buy the materials and will rig it himself. He will then load it with fire wood from his own farm and himself sell the cargo or ship or both in Boston, or he will take freight thence to the West Indies if he can get it." [4]

---

[1] *C.P.*, vol. xiii, pp. 254–5.

[2] In 1832 it was said that as a result of the preferences upwards of one million sterling was invested in saw-mills, wharfs, etc. (Cooney, *Compendious History of New Brunswick*, 1839, p. 59.)

[3] Report of the House of Lords Committee on Timber Trade, *Parly. Papers*, 1820, iii, p. 435 : " In minor buildings of every description none but inferior timber is used ; it is also used in second-rate houses ; for other common purposes it is equally applicable. Of the deals consumed in this country, about one-third is by box-makers for packing-cases, and for these purposes inferior timber, whether from the Baltic, from Norway or North America, has always been used. There are many purposes for which the American timber is preferred, and which also constitute a large feature in the consumption : as in the manufacture of musical instruments, picture frames, window blinds and toys . . . to these might be added the press boards used in the cotton manufactures, and for other purposes where a large surface is required. For these purposes the American timber is preferred, because it is what is technically called cleaner, that is, free from knots, and larger." Ibid., p. 426.

[4] *Notes on North America*, p. 31. " Often the same men felled the trees, squared the timber, hauled or rafted it to the shipyard, returned to their farms to sow their crops, then built the ship, manned and sailed her to her

When the War broke out between England and the United States in 1812, Halifax became the great naval base. Very successful privateering was carried out by the inhabitants and the Halifax papers reported almost daily captures of ships. No less than twenty-three enemy vessels were sold on 17th March, 1813, by a Halifax auctioneer.[1] The Loyalists were getting a bit of their own back. Money was said to be extraordinarily abundant, and " a stick of timber will pay for this " was the excuse for any extravagance. The War of 1812 also gave an important stimulus to internal communications between Ontario, Quebec and the Maritime Provinces, as the former were cut off from the sea outlet by way of Boston and New York. The result was to bring up the question of uniting the interior and the Atlantic regions by a road.

After the war, depression set in, both in Great Britain and in the Maritime Provinces. The royal dockyard was moved from Halifax to Bermuda, creating much unemployment. There was a continued emigration from Scotland, where it was said that none but the bed-ridden would be left behind, due to the old cause, over-population ; and this was reinforced by a large emigration from Ireland.[2]

Regiments were also settled out in New Brunswick after the Peace, and the soldiers were employed on making the military road to the Canadas. The emigration went on steadily but increased greatly in the 'forties with the failure of the potato crop in Ireland. No less than a hundred thousand people are said to have landed in New Brunswick

destination " (C.P., vol. xiii, p. 255). The ship would be loaded with timber, and both the ship and the cargo would be sold for cash in the United Kingdom.

[1] C.P., vol. xiii, p. 257.

[2] " With a slight exception . . . the emigrants who came to me were all Irish ; and there is this difficulty about this description of persons, that they will often apply for and receive aid when they are in possession of sufficient funds of their own ; and it is almost impossible to determine between cases of real poverty and affected want. The Scotch seldom or never beg ; and I do not recollect an instance of a person of that nation applying for charitable relief under ordinary circumstances On their arrival they generally penetrate into the country and procure employment ; but the Irish will hang about towns while a farthing remains in their pockets and then, when necessity compels them to resort to the country, will demand wages far beyond what they can earn, or farmers can afford to give. I feel much gratified, however, in stating that the Irish emigrants who have arrived out during the last two years in particular were remarkable for sobriety ; and I never saw an instance of inebriety, either among those who applied at my office or in the street " (Edmond Ward, Assistant Emigration Agent, in Papers relating to Emigration (New Brunswick), in Parly. Papers, 1843, vol. xxxiv, p. 37).

in the fifteen years ending in 1848, many of whom went on to the United States.[1]   The economic possibilities of lumbering, ship-building, fishing and the trade with the West Indies made this region the most attractive part of British America.   The trade of these regions became so important that a bank was started in 1825 with a capital of £50,000.   It was called the Halifax Banking Company, now the Bank of Commerce.   It was said to have made such large profits that a second bank, the Bank of Nova Scotia, was started in 1832.[2]   Nova Scotia was much more advanced in its agriculture than New Brunswick because of the interest which a Scotsman named Young had aroused in the subject.   He had written a series of letters under the pseudonym Agricola, pointing out that the prevailing system of husbandry was wretched in the extreme and the calling of a farmer despised.[3]   The result was the formation of agricultural societies and a loan by the Government to farmers of £10,000.[4]   The difficulty was that other things were so profitable.   Nova Scotia " does not raise her own bread, but while one barrel of her mackerel will purchase two barrels of flour she can always afford to buy what she requires," was the report in 1852.[5]   The farming of New Brunswick was, however, very backward and culminated in a crop failure over four successive years, 1844–7, owing to rot among the potatoes and the ravages of the weevil in the wheat.   The result of the failure of the potato crop was not merely a partial famine with great suffering, but it caused a large emigration from New Brunswick to the United States.   It was necessary to do something, and Professor Johnston was invited in 1849 to examine and report on the state of agriculture in the Province with a view to its improvement.[6]   In his *Notes on North America*, published in 1851,[7] he speaks of the way in which people

[1] *C.P.*, vol. xiii, p. 191.   [2] Ibid., p. 270.
[3] " The social status of the cultivators of the soil was such as would be regarded incredible were it not vouched for by so respectable an authority as Agricola, who says that ' the cultivation of the earth, that prime fountain of national wealth and the first and most essential of arts, was accounted so despicable and vile as to be the fit employment only of the unlettered and vulgar herd—the keeper of a tavern, or tippling house, the retailer of rum, sugar and tea, the travelling chapman, the constable of the district, were far more important personages, whether in their own estimation or that of the public, than the farmer who cultivated his own lands '." (D. Campbell, *Nova Scotia*, 1872, pp. 221–2.)
[4] *C.P.*, vol. xiv, p. 664.
[5] Despatch of Sir J. G. Le Marchant to the Duke of Newcastle covering the Blue Book of Nova Scotia for 1852. *Parly. Papers*, 1852–3, lxii, p. 32.
[6] *C.P.*, vol. xiv, p. 664.   [7] p. 411.

still thought it degrading to be a farmer in Nova Scotia and New Brunswick. He observes the lumberers as an unsteady, unthrifty race, but says that lumber overshadowed and lowered the social conditions of every other occupation. " The lumberer, fond as the Indian of the free air and un-trammelled life of the woods, receiving high wages, living on the finest flour and enjoying long seasons of holiday, looked down upon the slavish agricultural drudge who toiled the year long on his few acres of land." [1]

The farmers who engaged in lumbering mortgaged their land to the merchants who furnished supplies for the life in the woods. The farm was then neglected because wood had to be floated in the spring when the crops ought to have been put in. In bad years the farmer could not pay and was sold up.[2] The young men became demoralized and trained to extravagant habits and were indisposed to continuous farm work.

" And lastly while living in the woods both employer and employed live on the most expensive food. They scorn anything but the fattest pork from the United States and the finest Genesee flour. The more homely food, therefore, which their own farms produce becomes distasteful to them and thus expensive and sometimes immoral habits are introduced into their families which cause more frequent demands upon the merchants and a consequent yearly increase of unpaid bills." [3] Johnston also emphasized the dangers and desolation wrought by forest fires.[4] This

---

[1] This opinion had also been expressed earlier : " As the country [round the settlement at Wallace in Cumberland County] was well stocked with timber, they [sc. the Loyalist settlers] entered largely into the lumber trade, which as in every other part of Nova Scotia where it has formed the chief occupation of the inhabitants, has retarded the cultivation of the land and impoverished the people . . . It is to be hoped that the experience of the delusive nature of this trade will ultimately induce them to abandon it and to direct their efforts to the improvement of their farms " (T. C. Haliburton, *Nova Scotia*, 1829, vol. ii, p. 67).

[2] " Farmers and many others who engaged extensively in the timber trade have been dispossessed of their property or hold it encumbered with mortgages " (*C.T.D.*, J. Macgregor, Q. 1780). It was also remarked that there had been a great many sales of lands " under those burdens " in the previous eight years. (Ibid.)

" . . . with the exception of one or two men on the Miramichi I know of none who have entered largely into the timber trade who have any property whatever left not encumbered to the amount of more than its value . . . I have taken occasion to notice, where there are no timber shipping ports at all, in one or two colonies, that the inhabitants are perfectly free from debt, and that they are in good circumstances " (Ibid., Qq. 1786, 1802).   [3] Johnston, op. cit., p. 98.

[4] An appalling fire in 1825 spread over 6,000 square miles of woods. " In a country like this one gets to look on trees in a new light. Not only

traveller considered that the lowering of the timber preferences was a positive advantage to this region in that it focussed the attention of the inhabitants more on farming. Though " the merchants exclaim loudly against the timber duties at home and have even put the cry of Annexation into the mouths of many ", the failure of the lumber trade " is really leading to the most permanently beneficial results. . . . The steady settled farmer is worth to the future welfare and prosperity of the colony a dozen unsettled lumberers . . . who if they remained in the colony would continue an unsteady unthrifty race." [1] An agricultural society was founded in New Brunswick in 1851, the work of which was taken over by a Board of Agriculture in 1855.[2]

The scarcity of money which was so notable in the Canadas was also experienced in both Nova Scotia and New Brunswick, which is rather remarkable seeing how a good deal of coin must have come in by way of the West Indian and British lines of trade.

It is not until one reads the description of the virtual serfdom engendered by the system of barter in British North America and the stagnation consequent on the absence of coinage, that one can grasp the reason for the slow progress and discontent in the British North America Colonies. A man who had no cash could not move. How could he pay for moving ? A man who was bound to the store-keeper had to deliver his goods to that store-keeper at the store-keeper's prices and the store-keeper often had a glut that he could not dispose of owing to the winter freeze or other causes. He naturally took no risks. Under these circumstances capital could not accumulate and was brought in from outside by English merchants who regarded British North America as if it were the East or West Indies, where the objective was to make their pile and get out and live at " home ".

The extraordinary confusion of the coinage and the effect of barter in discouraging agriculture is brought out by two contemporaries.

Moorsom, in his *Letters from Nova Scotia*, in 1830, says :—

" The settler in a young country, although he be *dives equum* is never *dives auri* : the small quantity of hard

are they an obstacle to cultivation, which must be cut down and burnt, but so long as natural roads are near it is dangerous to leave any about the dwelling place for shelter or ornament ", on account of forest fires (Johnston, ibid., p. 97).

[1] Ibid., p. 411.   [2] *C.P.*, vol. xiv, p. 664.

cash that passes through his hands from one year's end to the other is scarcely credible by those who inhabit an old country overflowing with capital . . . The state of trade between the province and other countries is such that every hard dollar which may have been realized in the fisheries or mines eventually finds its way to the States or England in payment of flour or manufactured goods. The coins current in various parts of the province are doubloons and their fractions, chiefly of the South American republics ; and in Halifax, occasionally a British sovereign ; Spanish and American dollars and their fractions, and British silver ; and, in the eastern parts, every description of English and Irish tokens, and French silver, passes at a higher nominal rate than that at which it is received elsewhere. Paper from the Provincial Bank is in circulation to the amount of nearly forty thousand pounds at present, and is limited by statute. Old British and Colonial copper coins complete this medley ; which, as long as we remain within the province, offers little inconvenience ; but, when we go beyond its limits, we find this piece will not pass here ; that piece is only of such a value there ; and the Bank paper must be changed at a discount, to the annoyance of all unprepared travellers. The Imperial Government has, at different times, sent out British silver to facilitate the payment of the troops ; but this silver performs a march of circulation no farther than from the commissaries' chest to the troops (with whom its halt is marvellously short), thence to the retail merchant in Halifax, and back again to the commissary, in lieu of bills of exchange for mercantile remittances to England. The effects of this scarcity of cash are not apparent in the capital, or in those parts of the country frequented by persons of property ; but go into the country towns, which serve as so many *nuclei* for the settlers in the wilderness around, and you will there find the most extraordinary systems of barter and exchange : regular scales established for the different modifications of mixed payment in cash and goods ; while the person who produces the former without delay or subterfuge is looked upon as a prodigy of affluence and generosity. In this state of affairs, the bringing up arrears of quit or any other rent, is a very difficult, not to say impracticable, measure for those on whom the weight will chiefly fall." [1]

[1] Pp. 86–8. " The rate of exchange between Nova Scotia and Great Britain is one-ninth in favour of the latter. The premium on bills is variable

" About Windsor (which perhaps affords the readiest market out of the immediate vortex of Halifax) although a farmer can always sell, he can very seldom get payment. When a farmer wishes to dispose of any considerable quantity of produce, he usually advertises the same at auction, and will thus obtain fair prices by giving six months' credit, but even then his payment will probably be partly in kind owing to the general scarcity of ready cash."

" During the last American war, a few successful priva-teering cruises made Spanish dollars roll along the streets crying ' Come, pick me up ' [i.e. in Liverpool, on the east coast of Nova Scotia]. Such a thing as hard cash is now seldom met with. Two scales of value, the ' cash price ' and ' goods price ', are established, and the various grada-tions thereof distinctly marked in all transactions between employers and labourers. In the summer of 1828, the wages of a coloured man as labourer—on the wharfs, for instance—were three shillings per diem cash, or four shillings in goods, his keep, i.e. two meals, and half a pint of rum." [1]

Johnston, writing twenty years later, is equally emphatic as to the depressing influence of the barter system on agricultural development.[2]

" The custom of paying in kind, or the want of cash markets, is much complained of in the remoter districts, and especially among the smaller farmers. This is no doubt an inconvenience, and in some respects an evil, but it is almost inseparable from the still youthful condition of things in most parts of the Province. The produce of the farmer must ultimately be converted into the wares of the merchant. Whether this is done by means of one or two transactions—by first selling to one for money, and then with this money buying from another, is of no consequence to the farmer, provided he obtains as much tea, sugar, and other merchandize for his produce, by the one way as the other. In places where the traffic is small, the merchant is unable to obtain money from his customers, and is obliged to take grain or other farm produce, and with this again to pay his own debts to the wholesale merchant. But he buys his goods at a fixed price, and has to pay for them in

---

but a bill on England drawn at Halifax, in colonial currency, usually produces an addition of one-fourth upon the pound sterling " (Ibid., p. 88 note).

[1] Moorsom, pp. 209, 291–2.
[2] *Report on the Agricultural Possibilities of New Brunswick*, 1850, p. 140.

articles, the price of which varies very much in different seasons of the year. He is thus compelled in self-defence to take the farmer's productions at a very low rate, so as to avoid the risk of loss when he sends them to the varying market. Thus the farmer often has just reason to complain that his market is bad, and prices too low, while the merchant is only doing what prudence dictates, and what, to avoid the risk of bankruptcy, he is bound to do. At the same time it is in the power of the merchant often to take undue advantage of the power, and this no doubt is frequently done." [1]

It is reported officially in 1852 that for the first time there were parts of the Colony in which the timber trade was conducted on ready money principles. [2]

Johnston chronicles also a good deal of farming on shares, by which a man who had nothing received a farm, stock, implements and seed and provided the labour and gave half the produce to the man who provided the capital. [3]

A company, the New Brunswick and Nova Scotia Land Co., was formed in 1831 to colonize the country. It purchased a tract of 589,000 acres in the county of York at 3s. an acre. The Company, like most colonization companies, did not pay its promoters, but it was the means of founding twenty prosperous communities, including Stanley. The Company sold its land, but as the Provincial

---

[1] He refers to this practice again in his *Notes on North America*, 1851, i, p. 353, referring to Quebec, which shows the prevalence of the barter trade : " The extra produce in grain, etc.," of the Lower St. Lawrence, "is shipped to Quebec, from whence all necessary supplies are obtained in return. A merchant located at Metis, and with whom I took up my quarters, serves as the medium of communication between the farmers of the district and the importers of Quebec. In autumn he gathers in his debts, in the form of produce, from his neighbours ; and in return for these he obtains his winter's supply of tea, coffee, and clothing from the capital of the province. " These supplies during the winter and spring he again sells, chiefly on credit, and waits for his payment till harvest comes. The system is worse for the farmer than the merchant, whose profits are large."

[2] " As a working lumberer said to me a few weeks ago, ' It is the first year since I've lumbered that a man was even asked what he'd take for his lumber.' His meaning was that the increased demand and consequent competition on the part of the buyers had broken up the old system by which particular houses were accustomed to secure the timber of the working men, who were dependent on those houses for their advance of stores and provisions. Your Grace will not understand me as imputing any blame to the parties who acted so. They did but trade upon the local conditions which the nature of the market made necessary at the time ; but a more healthy condition of that market is undoubtedly denoted by the altered system." Report on the Blue Book of New Brunswick for 1852, in *Parly. Papers*, 1852–53, vol. lxii, p .36.

[3] Op. cit., pp. 47–8.

Government virtually gave it away, exacting only a small quit rent, which was never paid, very naturally the Company was not a financial success.[1]

So far as the development of the country is concerned, one pictures from the descriptions a constantly moving population. One group would fail to make good and would push on or pull out to the fisheries, another would come in on the half-cleared land and make good or shift to the United States. Generally speaking, the lines of settlement were along the coast and the river banks.[2] The roads when made ran along the back doors, the fronts faced the rivers. The French inhabitants were the most fixed part of the population.

When the American Colonies became independent they became at the same time a foreign country and ceased to be able to trade with the British Colonies ; in other words, they were automatically cut off from exchange with either Canada or the British West Indies. The restrictions were relaxed for the Canadas in 1794 (Jay's Treaty) as it was obviously impossible to maintain the prohibition between neighbouring land areas, especially seeing that the route by Lake Champlain and the Richelieu River was the natural outlet of the State of Vermont. American vessels were not, however, allowed to frequent the seaports of either the Maritime Provinces or the West Indies. It was thought that Great Britain would do the trade which the United States had previously done with the West Indies, but geographical proximity operated in favour of the American continent. The Nova Scotians frequenting Passamaquoddy Bay, which was neutral, as the islands were not apportioned as between Great Britain and the United States until the Ashburton Treaty of 1842, got food stuffs from American vessels and took them on to the West Indies.

To the Caribbean the Maritime Provinces took fish and lumber of their own production, and pork, wheat, flour, oats, bread, butter, and cheese, much of which came from the United States. Onions and herrings as well as English manufactures also constituted part of the cargoes and the ships returned with the inevitable rum, as well as sugar, coffee, cocoa, tobacco and cigars. The sailors from the Atlantic seaboard even took their dried fish as far as Brazil and Italy.

[1] *C.P.*, vol. xiii, p. 202.
[2] See map, *C.P.*, vol. xiii, p. 192.

M

A proposal to relax the Navigation Acts in favour of American vessels was nullified by the War of 1812–15, during which the Maritime Provinces continued to trade with the West Indies, so that the Atlantic Provinces became a sort of entrepôt for the West Indian Trade.

In 1818 both St. John and Halifax were made into free ports, which enabled American vessels to bring the cargoes of flour and pork there direct. In 1830 the prohibition with regard to American vessels in the West Indian trade was taken off, but it took a decade for a direct trade to develop and then the competition for the Atlantic Provinces became serious. It was interrupted again in the Civil War 1861–5, which again gave a great impetus to the shipping trade of the Northern Provinces. The repeal of the Navigation Acts in 1849 seems to have had little or no effect on the shipping of Nova Scotia, which continued to flourish. Montgomery Martin, quoting a report by Sir John Harvey, speaks of the great growth of the foreign trade of Nova Scotia since 1824 [1] : " With every relaxation yielded by the Imperial Parliament, the foreign commerce of the colonies had attained a further development, and Nova Scotia vessels, besides their traffic with the neighbouring States, Canada and the West Indies, now trade to the Baltic, the Mediterranean, China, the Mauritius, the East Indies, the Brazils, the Havannah . . ."

In 1852 Sir J. G. Le Marchant described " the very extraordinary growth " of the mercantile marine of Nova Scotia : " In 1846 Nova Scotia owned 2,583 vessels, Canada but 604, New Brunswick but 730, Newfoundland but 937, Prince Edward Island 265. The tonnage of all those colonies collectively was in that year 252,832 tons, while that of Nova Scotia alone reached as high as 141,093 tons. . . . At the close of the last year, 1852, the number of vessels registered in this province and actually employed in conducting its fishery, commerce and carrying trade, had increased to 2,943 with a tonnage of 189,083." He concludes : " That Nova Scotia is destined at no distant day to be one of the largest ship-owning countries in the world, is apparent from the status already achieved. She owns now nearly one-third as much tonnage as France." [2]

---

[1] *British Colonies*, vol. i, p. 197.
[2] Despatch to the Duke of Newcastle, covering the Blue Book of Nova Scotia for 1852, in *Parly. Papers*, 1852–3, vol. xlii, pp. 30–1.
Despatch from Sir E. Head to the Duke of Newcastle covering the Blue

Only gradually did the iron steamer alter the situation between 1860 and 1880. The peak year for shipbuilding for the Maritime Provinces was 1874 ; after that the decline set in.[1]

The trade between the West Indies and Canada continued to be an important trade all through the last century. In the twentieth century the activity of the United Fruit Company, with its widespread net of vessels, and the growth of the tourist traffic from America to the West Indies, have developed important connexions between the two regions. This has been countered by the Canadian and West Indies agreements in 1912, 1920 and 1925, making for preferential trade relations.

It must be noticed how impossible it was to dissociate the trade of Canada from that of the United States, since the latter were so often the bridge between the Canadas and the Atlantic Provinces. Even before the days of the railway, the Nova Scotians often bought from the United States flour which had been grown in Upper Canada, and the oil and fish which were brought by Quebec and Ontario from the United States came there originally from Nova Scotia and went on to the Lake region.

As salted cod bulked so large as an article of commerce, and as salt was needed to preserve the barrels of pork and other meat sent up to the lumbermen, salt was a very important article. It was imported from England in the ships designed to load timber on the return voyage. The amount required was said in 1835 to be 45,000 to 50,000 tons per annum.[2] Much of the flour was obtained from the

Book of New Brunswick for 1852, in *Parly. Papers*, 1852–3, vol. lxii, p. 37 :

" The average tonnage of the vessels built continues to increase. In fact, the reputation of our ships has been greatly improved by the voyages of the *Marco Polo* and one or two other vessels which our enterprising ship builders have lately turned out. . . . At the present moment, our ship-yards are in full activity, and the wages of the ship carpenters and workmen employed in them are such as to show the great demand for skilled labour of this description and the reliance of the master shipwright on a profitable market."

Despatch from the Earl of Mulgrave to the Duke of Newcastle covering the Blue Book of Nova Scotia for 1861, in *Parly. Papers*, 1863, vol. xxxix, p. 117 :

" . . . during 1862 shipbuilding has been again prosecuted with greater enterprise than ever."

Colonization Circular, No. 28, 1869, p. 21 : R. Shives reported of New Brunswick : " There has been a falling off in ship-building, but all other branches of industry are in a healthy state."

[1] F. W. Wallace, *Wooden Ships and Iron Men*, p. 192.
[2] *C.T.D.*, J. Dowie, Q. 3879.

United States, but oats were grown in the colony to satisfy the desire of the Scotch settlers for oatmeal porridge.

The timber trade had developed out of the preferences given by Great Britain in 1809 to secure an Imperial supply when the Baltic was shut owing to Napoleon's Continental System. The preferences had been very advantageous both to the Maritime Provinces and to Lower Canada in developing a staple which could be exchanged for manufactures.[1] It was in request not only for shipbuilding but for houses for the rapidly increasing towns and for furniture ; the perennial difficulty was to find something to sell that was in general request and something that could be transported at a price that made it buyable in the markets to which it was sent.

Timber had the additional advantage that emigrants could earn their living in the woods or at the wharfs at once, and this proved the special attraction which drew emigrants to New Brunswick. On the other hand, as we have seen, it tended to deflect men from agriculture.[2]

---

[1] The rise in the imports into the United Kingdom of colonial timber after the preferences are illustrated by the figures given to the Timber Duties Committee :—

	Loads.		%	
	Baltic.	Colonial.	Foreign.	Colonial.
1788–1792	219,396	2,660	99	1
1803–1807	232,477	16,533	94	6
1808–1812	73,718	120,537	38	62
1819–1823	116,600	335,556	26	74
1824–1828	191,890	410,903	32	68
1829–1833	122,783	412,682	24	76

C.T.D., J. D. Hume, Q. 11.

The preferences even in 1842 were considerable :

	Foreign.			Colonial.
Deals per load 50 cu. ft. . .	£1	12	0	2s.
Staves, per load . . .	£1	8	0	2s.
Lathwood, per fathom . .	£2	0	0	1s.
Spars, per 120 . .	£2	0	0	1s.
Handspikes, per 120 . .	£1	0	0	6d.
Knees, per 120 . . .	£2	0	0	1s.

E. Porritt, *Fiscal and Diplomatic Freedom of the British Overseas Dominions*, p. 47.

[2] The reason why people prefer lumbering to agriculture is that " those who engage in the timber trade get something immediately ", while those who till the soil without means suffer much before achieving self-sufficiency (*C.T.D.*, J. Macgregor, Q. 1851). Lumbering was said to give immediate returns but no prospects, while agriculture gave slow returns but an assured prospect. Ibid., J. Macgregor, Qq. 1790 and 1803.

" The timber trade furnishes employment to a numerous body, but less so in Nova Scotia than in the neighbouring provinces ; which as far as my observation goes, the former has no cause to regret. That trade may rather be termed a necessary evil than a benefit to a young country. The settler who arrives in summer from Europe without a shilling in his

Timber had the quality of transportability from two areas, the Maritime Provinces and Quebec. Only those tributaries which led into the Ottawa River made it possible to export lumber from Upper Canada.[1] The trees were cut in winter and floated down in great rafts when the melting snow made the streamlets into rivers. The development of the lumber industry had, however, quite a different effect in the Maritime Provinces and in Quebec. In the Maritime Provinces it led to a neglect of agriculture because the import of food-stuffs from U.S.A. was so easy. In Quebec and along the right bank of the Ottawa it created a market because the import of food was so difficult. The lumber camps in the Canadas were said in 1827–8 to have actually attracted settlers because of the market the camps provided for local produce. The timber trade meant saw mills and booms, ponds, warehouses and wharfs, and a good deal of money was sunk in these works, bringing a general increase of trade and employment in their wake.[2]

pocket finds he is too late to raise any crop, and that he can only provide for the winter by constructing his log hut and cutting a few staves and shingles, which meet with an immediate sale ; so far, so good : if he then devote himself steadily to agriculture, he will in all human probability become eventually independent ; but he is more frequently tempted by his first little gains to engage in ' lumbering ' or cutting timber. He lives a severe and laborious life in the forests ; he flatters himself with the prospect of realizing a considerable sum in a very few years : the timber market falls in England : he finds himself overwhelmed with debt, and has to work his way again from his first potato plot." W. S. Moorsom, *Letters from Nova Scotia*, 1830, pp. 51–2.

Also, *Advantages of Emigrating to the British Colonies of New Brunswick, Nova Scotia, etc., etc.*, by a Resident of St. John's, New Brunswick, 1832, p. 18.

[1] " The Committee are aware that scarcely any timber can be brought down from any part of Upper Canada except by the Grand River, the Rapids of the St. Lawrence increasing very much the risk of bringing lumber down by that navigation from Upper Canada and, of course, the expense of it." Oak timber and staves, it was added, being more valuable, might stand the cost of transport. *Parly. Papers*, 1820, iii, p. 433.

[2] The variety in the type of wood produced may be seen from the following list of exports in 1835, quoted H. Murray, *Historical and Descriptive Account of British America*, vol. ii, p. 22, as follows :

Oak	.	.	.	.	tons	19,798
Ash	.	.	.	.	,,	3,319
Elm	.	.	.	.	,,	16,054
Pine	.	.	.	.	,,	303,340
Birch	.	.	.	.	,,	1,517
Masts	.	.	.	.	pieces	508
Spars	.	.	.	.	,,	2,633
Staves	.	.	.	.	,,	1,969,536
Puncheons	.	.	.			3,559,184
Pipes	.	.	.	.		545,998
Barrels	.	.	.	.		350,471

In New Brunswick, according to the evidence given before the Timber Duties Committee in 1835, there were 229 mills, the value of which was said to be £232,030. In 1831 there were 737 sawmills in Lower Canada, 670 in Upper Canada and 29 in Prince Edward Island. The capital was, however, found in England, and when the lumber merchants made their fortunes they left the country as they did in both the East and West Indies.

The earliest lumbermen were Americans, then the French Canadians took up the trade, and finally Irishmen proved themselves to be expert axemen.[1]

The lumberer's life was a hard one. The men rarely lived, so it was said, beyond the age of forty. Bonnycastle thus describes the water-carriage of the timber [2]:

"A raft a quarter of a mile long—I hope I do not exaggerate, for it may be half a mile, never having measured one but by the eye—with its little huts of boards, its apologies for flags and streamers, its numerous little masts and sails, its cooking caboose, and its contrivances for anchoring and catching the wind by slanting boards, with the men who appear on its surface as if they were walking on the lake, is curious enough ; but to see it in *drams*, or detached portions, sent down foaming and darting along the timber slides of the Ottawa or the restless and rapid Trent, is still more so. . . . Numberless accidents happen, the *drams* are torn to pieces by the violence of the stream ; the rafts are broken by storm and tempest ; the men get drunk and fall over ; and altogether it appears extraordinary that a raft put together at the Trent village for its final voyage to Quebec should ever reach its destination, the transport being at least 450 miles and many go much further."

Deals				pieces	2,123,853
Deal Ends				,,	101,581
Boards				,,	8,821
Battens				,,	27,196
Batten Ends				,,	65
Oars					16,471
Handspikes					28,618
Hoops					23,000
Trenails					3,011
Knees					120
Lathwood				cords	2,452
Shooks				packs	2,282
Shingles				bundles	25,500

It also shows that a large number of men would be required for the various processes of preparing timber.

[1] *C.T.D.*, S. Revans, Q. 2493.
[2] *Canada and the Canadians in* 1846, vol. i, pp. 70–1.

Logs were not shipped at Montreal but were floated down to tide water at Quebec, as timber vessels could not get up so far. Bonnycastle already in 1846 speaks of " a new trade " of shipping the logs in steamers.[1]

The trade introduced an immense spirit of gambling into the early colonies. There was the great loss of timber. On the lake below Montreal, fourteeen of these great rafts of timber were wrecked in a single storm.[2] Forest fires were most destructive. The booms burst and the timber was lost or the rivers did not rise sufficiently to float the wood. The lumberers were notoriously lively when they arrived with the rafts.[3] One witness in 1835 considered that a concentrated population was more amenable to law and order than a population which was as scattered as were the lumbermen, though the Irish employed in making the canals, who were aggregated workers, seem to have been particularly turbulent. A witness in 1820 said that persons cutting timber were a race apart and " the worst part of the population of Canada ",[4] but this was denied by others.

The merchants of Quebec, who were always afraid of a repeal of the preferences, in one of their petitions in favour of their continuance stated in 1831 [5] that they had invested £1,250,000 in wharfs and mills in the Province and that the sudden withdrawal of the preferences would be a " dreadful visitation " to the young colony and " spread overwhelming ruin and misery ". They stated that agricultural work was suspended from November to May, that lumbering gave winter employment, that it was the means of retaining a vast body of emigrants who would otherwise be driven to get their living in the United States, that the lumber ships provided cheap transport for emigrants on their outward voyage,[6] that the lumber trade provided employment for shipping and enabled the settlers to get the much needed salt cheaply for their winter provisions or for the fishing industry.[7] So important were the preferences considered

[1] *Canada and the Canadians in* 1846, vol. i, pp. 71–2.
[2] *C.T.D.*, S. Revans, Q. 2444.
[3] " The lumberer's life is truly an unhappy one, for, when he reaches the end of the raft's voyage, whatever money he may have made goes to the fiddle, the female, or the fire-water." Bonnycastle, *Canada and the Canadians in* 1846, vol. i, p. 70.
[4] E. Ellice, *Parly. Papers*, 1820, iii, p. 434.
[5] *Parly. Papers*, 1830–1, x, p. 481.   [6] Ibid., pp. 482–3.
[7] One witness before the Committee on Timber Duties in 1835 said that five-sixths of the whole trade of New Brunswick, one-half of that of Lower Canada, one-quarter of that of Nova Scotia and Prince Edward Island was bound up with the lumber trade. *C.T.D.*, H. Bliss, Q. 2284.

that when the news of the defeat of one of the many proposals for reducing them arrived there were illuminations and oxen were roasted whole in the streets.

But in England there was a great deal of opposition to the timber preferences. It was said that Englishmen thereby had to pay dearer for an article of " the very first necessity", an article " without which, in fact, scarcely any other manufacture could be carried on ".[1] Moreover, " It will be found that the loss to the public at large, through adherence to the present system, amounted to nearly or quite one million and a half of money " in 1833, and the loss was greater in subsequent years.[2] Now in the decade 1830–1840 England was not flourishing. There were deficits in her revenue in 1830, 1832, 1834, 1835, 1839, 1840, as also in 1841, 1842, 1843, 1848 and 1849, and it is scarcely to be expected that she would continue the system for long. It was only the interests of the shipowners that caused the diminishing preferences to be retained till 1860.

The vessels employed in the trade were loaded up to the decks and of the 309 wrecks between 1832 and 1838 no less than 252 were lost on the voyage between British North American ports and the United Kingdom.[3]

The loaded timber vessels did not sink as easily as other vessels, so very old ships were employed.[4] The scandal was so great that stowing cargo on the decks was prohibited by two Acts, of 1839 and 1842. On an average the timber ships made one voyage a year between Nova Scotia or New Brunswick and the United Kingdom. Lumber was also taken to the United States and the West Indies. A great deal of American timber was imported into the Maritime Provinces and sent on as colonial to get the preference, and vessels from the Baltic actually crossed to Canada to get a certificate of colonial origin so that they might sell their timber as colonial when they recrossed the Atlantic with their cargo.[5]

The lumber trade has been much condemned as socially harmful to Canada. The lumber merchants who provided the capital did not, up to the 'thirties at least, make their homes in Canada. The lives the men led in the woods, the dangers and the exposure, the standing in icy cold water

---

[1] Porter, *Progress of the Nation*, 1847, p. 381.   [2] Ibid., p. 382.
[3] *Parly. Debates*, 1839, iii, xlix, 421, quoted by Porritt, *Fiscal and Diplomatic Freedom of the British Overseas Dominions*, p. 24.
[4] *Parly. Debates*, iii, xlix, 421–2, quoted Porritt, pp. 23–4.
[5] Earl Russell, *Recollections and Suggestions*, quoted by Porritt, p. 25.

up to their waists, the appalling conditions of the sailors on the timber ships, and the conditions of the emigrants on the outward passage are almost as overshadowing as the difficulty of making a clearance in the woods. Yet these very lumbermen did help to make clearances, though it was often on land too poor for cultivation.[1]

While it did introduce a speculative gambling element into the colonies and was to a certain extent unfavourable to steady progress, nevertheless the very large investment of capital in the trade did help struggling backward regions. Lumbering assisted emigrants both by cheap passages and by providing employment ready to hand at once in the saw mills, wharves and ship-yards or in connexion with the felling camps, and enabled them, if they were thrifty, to earn enough capital to buy land. Without this trade it is difficult to see how New Brunswick could have absorbed many emigrants.

Moreover, it caused in Lower Canada a demand for food supplied from Upper Canada and for horses and oxen to drag the logs to the waterside, and in consequence had an important reaction on farming. Also it helped men out through the winter and thus again assisted struggling colonists when farm work was shut down. But for the lumber trade, it is difficult to see how the colonists with developed wants could in the first half century after 1763 have got their clothing, food and tools. Furs, fish and potash were not sufficient to balance the imports required.

The causes of the decline in the importance of the Maritime Provinces are a little obscure. The chief symptoms are the stationary population and the fall in the number of immigrants. The natural increase of population seems itself to have emigrated to the prairies or the United States. In the 'twenties the population of the Maritime Provinces exceeded that of Upper Canada, whereas by 1851 the population of Upper Canada was more than double that of the Maritime Provinces :

Nova Scotia	(1817)	81,351	(1851)	276,854
New Brunswick	(1824)	74,176	(1851)	193,800
Upper Canada	(1824)	150,069	(1851)	952,004 [2]

Then again, after 1830, the Americans were allowed to

---

[1] " Any land on which pine timber trees grow is the very worst land that can be found in the colonies ; the fertile land is always known by the hard wood growing upon it." *C.T.D.*, J. Macgregor, Q. 1938.

[2] " The Social and Economic Conditions in the Dominion of Canada," edited by W. P. M. Kennedy, in *Annals of the American Academy of Political and Social Science*, vol. cvii, May, 1923, pp. 1, 3.

trade with the West Indies and in about a decade they seem to have got a good deal of the West Indian trade into their hands, to lose it again during the Civil War.

The timber preferences to which the trade was originally due, were reduced in 1842 (to take effect in 1843) and again in 1847 and 1851, and were finally abolished in 1860 [1] ; but the Colonies, other than New Brunswick, where timber was all important, do not seem to have been much affected, although they have regarded it as a dire disaster. Lower Canada still went on with its export trade of lumber and its ship-building. The report of Israel Andrews to the American Treasury in 1852 on the trade and commerce of British North America, says that the repeal of the timber preferences caused Baltic timber to be used more extensively and created a larger demand for colonial timber to be used with it, " while the change in the navigation laws has so reduced freights that the producer of timber and deals in the North American Colonies now receives more for his articles than he ever did before the reduction of the duties." [2]   The demand for sleepers for railways in England and in the United States created a new demand for timber in all the lumber regions to which there was only a temporary set-back when the railway mania collapsed in 1846.

Both New Brunswick and Nova Scotia experienced a boom in ship-building with the Californian and Australian gold rushes of 1849 and 1851, which caused a shortage of shipping and raised the price of ships. This was followed by the Crimean War with a further demand for ships for the transport services. This offset any depression from the repeal of the Navigation Acts in 1849 which threw open the trade of British colonies to all ships, whether national or foreign. The ship-owners, fearing the competition of American vessels, lowered freights to meet it, and the export of timber from Nova Scotia and New Brunswick was thereby stimulated. It would seem as if the profit of the preference had previously gone into the pockets of the ship-owners.[3]

---

[1] By the Tariff Act of 1842 the duties on foreign timber were reduced from 55s. to 25s. and 32s. on deals per load and the duties on Colonial timber from 10s. to 1s. In 1847 the 25s. was reduced to 15s., and in 1851 to 7s. 6d. In 1860 they were reduced to 1s., thus abolishing the preference, and in 1866 importation was free. J. R. McCulloch, *Dictionary of Commerce*, 1882, p. 1391.

[2] Report on the Trade and Commerce of the British North American Colonies, 1853, 1st Session, *Senate Document*, No. 112, pp. 616–17.

[3] Despatch from Sir E. Head to Earl Grey covering the Blue Book of New Brunswick for 1849, in *Parly. Papers*, 1850, vol. xxxvi., p. 192.

The reason for the cessation of emigration to the Maritime Provinces seems to have lain in the fact that the United States and Upper Canada proved to be more attractive fields. Once the canals were deepened and steamers plied regularly the difficulty of getting as far as Ontario was largely removed, and once there it had a better climate and a large market for its lumber in the development of the Middle West. The development of railways on a large scale in Ontario provided constant employment after 1850, which attracted emigrants, whereas railway building in the Maritime regions was on a small scale and spasmodic. The industrial development in the United States also tended to attract adults both from Quebec and the Maritime Provinces.[1]

On the other hand, the Reciprocity Treaty with the United States, which established a state of free trade from 1855 to 1866, gave the Maritime Provinces a good market close at hand for both fish and lumber. This enabled the Maritime regions to maintain their position.

" . . . a remarkable diminution has taken place in the cost of transport of our timber to Great Britain. As a consequence of this, timber which was previously unsaleable at remunerating prices has been shipped, and although a loss of profit has no doubt been felt by the shipowners, some relief must have been experienced by the owners of lumber in the colony . . . The trade with the Pacific has been a new feature in the commerce here, as elsewhere." For 1850, see *Parly. Papers*, 1851, vol. xxxiv, pp. 126-7.

[1] " Probably not more than one-tenth of the emigrants that arrived during the past year have remained in this colony, there being no employment immediately remunerative to induce them to stay . . . As no extensive works of a public or private nature are either in progress or about to be commenced in this Province, there is not the least prospect of a demand either for ordinary, or skilled labour, the resident population being quite sufficient to meet present requirements.

" The emigration from the Province has continued during the past year, but has been much more limited in extent than in 1848. Many families have departed from the northern part of the Province, and others from lumbering districts on the River St. John and its tributaries. More than 200 young females, natives of the Province, were induced to leave the country by agents for the cotton factories in the New England States. . . . These young persons have been followed by many of their friends and relatives, who have found employment in the manufacturing villages of Maine and Massachusetts, and are not likely to return."
Immigrants into New Brunswick in 1848 numbered 4,141.
  ,,   ,,   ,,   ,,   1849   ,,   2,671.
  ,,   ,,   ,,   ,,   1850   ,,   1,507.
Report for 1849 by M. H. Perley, Emigration Officer of New Brunswick, in Papers relative to Emigration, *Parly. Papers*, 1851, volume xl, p. 342.
" . . . The greater number of the immigrants into New Brunswick by the timber ships depart for the United States. . . . A great number of the immigrants into Canada during several past years have found employment on public works. . . . In New Brunswick there are no public works that require such labour. . . . And when there is any check applied to the timber trade, emigration from the Province proceeds rapidly." A. Gesner, *New Brunswick*, 1847, p. 373.

Indeed, Israel Andrews in 1852 speaks of the improvement of the character of colonial vessels and says : " They are selling very readily in England at remunerative prices, and are found to be as good vessels as are built in the world. The St. John and Quebec ships take the lead in colonial shipping." [1] The Civil War from 1861–5 opened up new chances to shipowners in running the blockade for raw cotton and in carrying provisions and other stores to both belligerents. Thus the 'sixties were still prosperous times.

The real blow came from the development of iron ship-building, which began to make itself felt after 1870,[2] and from the changes in the trade routes, which began to be felt about 1880. Direct lines of steamers began to ply between England, the West Indies and the Pacific, and the ' liners ' carried on a regular traffic between England and the United States. With the greater cheapness and efficiency of steam shipping, the main bulk of the entrepôt trade shifted to England, to the detriment of Nova Scotia. With the rapid development of the United States, English vessels found that they could get a full cargo out to Portland or Boston when there was nothing offering for such relatively small places as the ports of the Atlantic Provinces. Having arrived at Portland, they picked up the grain or other exports brought by the railways, such as the Grand Trunk, which found that the easiest route to the seaboard lay through the State of Maine to Portland. Canadian exports from the interior, therefore, tended to take the American route rather than that by Halifax or St. John. There were more ships offering in American ports, freights were cheaper with this competition, and insurance rates were more favourable. Hence they tended to become the outlet for Upper Canada. The sheer development of the United States which reacted favourably on Ontario, giving her a large wheat and other traffic by the Lakes, tended to draw away population and trade from New Brunswick and Nova Scotia. In this way the continental expansion in both America and Ontario checked the expansion of the Maritime Provinces. It was, however, a relative and not an actual decline.

---

[1] Op. cit., p. 628. Also F. W. Wallace, *Wooden Ships and Iron Men*, pp. 42–88.

[2] *C.P.*, vol. x, pp. 574, 579–580, 582, 586.

CHAPTER 4

LOWER CANADA (QUEBEC)

THE second point of penetration, Quebec, resulted from the same desire for fish that had brought the English to Newfoundland and the English colonists in New England up to Nova Scotia. The Breton and Norman fishermen, who frequented the Gulf and the St. Lawrence, soon, however, realized that there was another source of wealth, and they began to trade their brandy with the Indians for furs, a valuable article in universal demand for wearing apparel and head coverings such as beaver hats. In this way a regular trade in furs sprang up between the Saguenay River and St. Malo.

The Dutch in New Amsterdam and the New Englanders also began to carry on the fur trade ; in their case rum, which was brought in for the fishing trade, was the counterblast to the excellence and cheapness of French brandy. At a later date, when the priests of the Catholic Church tried to stop the French exchange of brandy for furs, they were told that the choice lay between the Indians coming to get the brandy where they could be influenced by the Catholic Church, or going to the English settlement for rum, where they could be reached by the Protestant Church. In other words, it was brandy and possible salvation, or rum and certain damnation.

The French then proceeded from these mere speculative ventures to found a racial settlement, and the usual mechanism of expansion of that time—a trading company with a monopoly—was the result. Someone must be responsible for the recruiting and conveyance of emigrants, someone must be responsible for parcelling out and allotting land, someone must be responsible for the defence against Indians and for religious observances. The commonest solution in the English and French settlements was to delegate these tasks to a Company with a charter from the Government, who gave a monopoly of trade as a reward for the capital invested and the pains taken. But whereas an English Company had primarily the idea of profit, much as had the English Company trading to Hudson's Bay, the French Government had an ambition to further the expansion of the race in New France. This was due partly to the fact that the territory was colonizable. The movement from the first depended far too much on Government support, and the rule of the Companies was fitful and evanescent owing to the financial loss involved in each attempt. Herein lay the weakness of French colonization. It did not pay. The "Company of Adventurers of England trading into Hudson's Bay", which merely traded and did not attempt settlement, made large profits out of the fur trade. This again was due largely to the fact that the territory was quite uncolonizable.

From the first there were two distinct aims in the French colony. The Companies seeking some reward for their outlay devoted themselves to the fur trade. This meant pushing inland, but it did not mean settlement. The French Government wanted to establish settlers who would cultivate land and supply the French West Indies with grain. The Companies did not want to undertake settlement, especially as the forest would have to be cleared and there was the ever-present danger from hostile Indians, which meant a great outlay on defensive measures.

The Company of Rouen, under the leadership of Champlain, established the first colony of settlers in Quebec in 1608. It had the usual difficulty of early settlers with the food supply, but in this case it was intensified by the fact that the English captured the first fleet of vessels sent out with stores. By 1629 so little impression had been made in racial expansion that only five families of twenty-five persons were settled in the Colony, occupying twenty acres of land.

In 1632 another Company, the Company of the Hundred Associates, or the Company of New France, again took up the task of settlement and a hundred colonists were brought out in three vessels. The colony still did not flourish, although fur trading and fishing still went on. In 1642 a sub-company was created which settled in Montreal to carry on the fur trade and further exploration. As in England, there were attacks on the monopoly of the Company, and its trade was thrown open in 1645 about the same time as the English " free trade " movement was successful, namely the abolition of the monopoly of the Companies under Cromwell's régime.[1] As in England, too, the monopoly was again re-established and another Company, this time composed of a few Canadian merchants, continued to carry on the fur trade. All the time they encountered considerable competition from the Dutch and the English. The French had a great asset in their cheap brandy as a medium of exchange, but the English gave a better price for furs. The Indian danger made farming in Canada almost impossible and incidentally barred the Lake route so that the French traded via the Ottawa River. The Iroquois, in whom the chief danger lay, were hostile to the French and friendly to the English.

Thus Companies in New France succeeded one another, the economic attraction being furs, and therefore little impression in the direction of racial expansion was made. Whatever Company was in power, the trade monopoly was so strict that the colonists were prevented from dealing with Indians or with each other. They could only sell furs of their own trapping to the Company at the Company's prices and if they wished to buy anything, they bought it from the Company at the Company's prices. The Company itself was the sole medium for exchange with the Indians. There was, under these circumstances, no room for a middle class and the bulk of the colonists were therefore employees of the Company. The cod and whale fishing alone was free to all.

[1] Cunningham, *Growth of English Industry*, vol. ii, p. 189.

Colbert, who was in power from 1660 to 1680, was a great believer in racial expansion. He wound up the old Company of New France in 1663. At that date the Colony contained 2,500 people, of which 800 were in Quebec. So little was cultivation undertaken that the Colony imported from France most of its provisions.

A West India Company was formed in 1664 to work the whole of the French possessions in the West. Thus the French West Indies, needing fish and grain, were to be brought in touch with Canada, which was to be developed so as to supply these things, while the Colony would furnish France with furs.

An energetic period of colonization now began. The French Government agreed to send out troops to protect the colonists from the Indians, for only so could agricultural settlement prosper while the colonists were too few to organize themselves. Emigrants from France were despatched ; potential wives were duly provided and housed in care of the nuns until they were selected to found their own homes ; and a certain amount of compulsion was exercised so that the male portion of the colony should seize the opportunity and settle down quickly. The regiments were settled at the expiry of their term of service along the river bank until they resembled one long continuous village. Officers, merchants or other persons of sufficient pecuniary or social standing were given seigniories, or, as the English would have said, manors, with a river frontage, since the river was the great highway for defence mobilization against the English or the Indians. The seigniors were supposed to bring out emigrants and settle them on these grants. The bulk of the present inhabitants of the Province of Quebec whose ancestors came from Normandy are descended from those who came out under the Colbert régime.

The France from which these men came was a feudal State where serfdom or the remnants of serf obligations were still prevalent ; where industry was elaborately controlled by ordinances promulgated by the Crown ; where taxation was of a threefold nature consisting of dues paid to the King, the seignior or overlord, and the Church ; and where men looked to the authority of the King or the overlord to arrange everything for them in this world and to the Church to arrange everything for them in the next. Of the great Protestant revolt against authority in both

Church and State which was finally successful in England when Charles I lost his head, no reverberation was felt in New France, to which even the Huguenots were not allowed to penetrate as settlers. There therefore lay to the South an energetic race of dissenters who came from a country where since the sixteenth century both guilds and serfdom had ceased to hinder industrial or agriculture movement and change, who acknowledged no authority but the Bible and their own consciences, who believed that it was the Lord's will that they should get on in the world and prosper, and who fiercely resented any restraint as to where they should or should not buy or sell. On the other side of the border was a French community regulated in every condition of its life and trade, accustomed to give so many days' work a week to their feudal lords, accustomed to the stipulation that they must only trade with a Company or the Crown, accustomed to the fixing of prices and primarily mobilized along its river frontages and its settlements for defence and therefore still further encased in a military organization. Minute regulations hemmed them in on every side—feudal or royal or ecclesiastical—and the basis of their tradition was military and not commercial. Many adventurous spirits broke loose from this and took to the woods and traded with the Indians, and as they were then proclaimed outlaws they often traded with the English. These *coureurs de bois* married Indians and often became savages, although occasionally an amnesty was proclaimed so that they might return and settle, which they rarely did for any length of time. Even when pardoned, they usually took to the woods again and were again proscribed.

The settled peasants, afterwards known as *habitants*, rendered the seignior in New France the usual feudal dues that they would have paid in old France, i.e. so many days' work a week, a payment on the transfer of their land (*lods et ventes*) and a small annual payment known as *cens*. In addition they had to take their corn to be ground at the seignior's mill, for which he took his toll in grain.

The West India Company was bankrupt in 1667 and the company system was given up, Canada becoming, like its neighbour across the border, a royal Province, and the political and economic life was henceforth directed by Intendants or governors.

From the economic point of view it is a long tale of corruption by which officials in high and low places obtained furs

N

for their own profit and manipulated trade for their own benefit. No consistent policy was pursued in France with regard to the economic development of the Colony, and this was all the more disastrous since the colonists were trained to be regulated from above, as is usual in a military régime. The habitants looked to the lord and the priest and mobilized when required. They lived a self-contained existence with their grain and their fish and no middle class developed. A certain amount of money came in with the French garrisons. There were no open markets for the produce of the Colony—this could hardly be expected when the grain traffic was so carefully regulated in France itself. The agents of the Government collected the food supply and paid for it in worthless card money or other depreciated paper. Enterprise was stifled. "The people . . . looked . . . to the government to take the lead, to clear the path for them, to direct and protect their every effort and to ensure the promised results. There were passed, and presumably enforced, more than enough minute and conflicting regulations to have destroyed any industry no matter how prosperous at the beginning."[1] It was obvious that when English merchants and middlemen came in to take the place of the officials there would be trouble, and that the supposed or actual exploitation of the French by the English settlers would intensify the difficulties of the two races, two religions, and two economic traditions.

Nevertheless, the French had done magnificent exploration work during the eighteenth century. They had penetrated to the end of the great Lakes, had crossed the prairies and had reached the Lake of the Woods and Lake Winnipeg. They had penetrated up the Saskatchewan and down South to the Mississippi. They had discovered Lakes Manitoba and Winnipegosis, and La Vérendrye and his sons had come within sight of the Rocky Mountains. In this great work of geographical discovery they were explorers and not fur traders. Such exploration as was to be done under the English was done by the fur traders, and its main object was to get new fur areas, which again is characteristic of the different outlooks of the French and the British races. But both had to their credit a great geographical record.

At the close of the Seven Years' War (1763) the English

---

[1] *C.P.*, vol. ii, pp. 477–8.

had to arrange for the government of four new areas—
Quebec, West and East Florida, and Grenada. Labrador, the
Island of Anticosti, and the Magdalen Islands were attached
to Newfoundland.[1] Quebec then comprised the valley of the
St. Lawrence from the western end of Anticosti to the forty-
fifth parallel and Lake Nipissing. The English made
regulations for the only paying thing, the fur trade, and
sent out letters to the Governor to see if in the new
Province of Quebec there was any prospect of obtaining
hemp and flax, raw materials of which the English stood
in great need.

They had taken over in Quebec an isolated Province of
French Catholics of about 65,000 persons, half farmers, half
fishermen, left without any Government of their own. It
proved a considerable financial burden. Large sums were
spent to conciliate the Indians and to assist the fur trade.
The English Government spent 35 million dollars on the
fortress of Quebec alone.[2] The British set out to win the
loyalty of their new French subjects by preserving their
religion and their customs as far as possible intact. In
1774, under the Quebec Act, the seigniorial system was
retained although previous grants of land between 1763
and 1773 had been made in freehold. The Church was
confirmed in its privileges ; the tithe was made obligatory ;
and the commerce of Canada, such as it was, was brought
under the ancient French Law or Custom of Paris—long
obsolete in France itself. This was due to the intense opposition of the clergy and noblesse to English Laws. As Canada
was a French Province, true to the prevailing idea of toleration, it was French Law and Custom that received the
British *imprimatur*. As there was then no prospect of the
future development of the Province of Ontario, the prevailing
notion was that French Law and Custom would apply
generally to all the St. Lawrence region. This aroused great
friction later, as English settlers objected to live under what
they regarded as so backward a legal system. Nor would
they accept the French system of land tenure with its serf
implications and obligations to the seignior.

The economic life of the French Province which England
took over was composed of two distinct elements. There
were firstly the *coureurs de bois*, or Indianized Frenchmen,

[1] Labrador was restored to Quebec in 1774.
[2] Castell Hopkins, *French Canada and the St. Lawrence*, p. 342, cited
J. C. Bracq, *Evolution of French Canada*, p. 44.

who went far and wide and knew no law. Secondly, there were, within the settled area, the habitants, living rigidly according to rule on fixed lines in fixed places and guided by the priest and the seignior.[1]   As French Canadian life was organized for defence, little agriculture was undertaken because the men might be called up at any time for fighting, and they therefore relied to a large extent on hunting and fishing. Peltries were the main export. The habitants had been settled in groups in seigniories where they could be mobilized early as a local military force against Indians or the British American colonists.

The climate does not in any case allow of continuous cultivation of the soil. " Thus in a fair season the farmers from Gaspé to Rimouski may count upon nearly five months for agricultural work, from Rimouski to Three Rivers upon nearly six months, and from Three Rivers to Soulanges County upon seven months." [2]

When tillage was undertaken the habitant ploughed half his land and took a crop of hay without seeding from the other half. At the end of three years he ploughed the grass land and sowed grain and let the other half go back to grass. Very few animals were kept and consequently the ground was not manured. Such manure as there was they collected and dumped into the St. Lawrence. The implements were primitive, being made at home in the winter evenings out of wood. To make a clearing the trees were cut and burnt and the seeding was done in between the standing stumps.

The French Canadians depended but little on imports. Theirs was a self-contained existence. Their chief need was caps and blankets because sheep did not thrive, but they could and did use fur for clothing. They produced a small amount of flax which was woven into coarse linen for home consumption. This was a line which England was very anxious to develop as an export, since she was so short of flax for linen, which then had many uses for which cotton and jute are now employed.

Iron was necessary for arms and for cooking pots, and was worked at Three Rivers by forced labour. Wood for the furnaces was supplied by feudal requisition.

Canada was a country of undeveloped wants. The priest and the seignior were the two prominent external features

---

[1] Lucas, *Introduction to Lord Durham's Report*, vol. i, p. 25.
[2] *C.P.*, vol. xvi, p. 512.

of the life of the habitant, and according to the report of Murray in 1762, of the eight million acres of land held by the French, two million were in the hands of the Church.

The normal grant of land had a frontage on the river of 768 feet and a depth of about 1½ miles. The house was built on the river. " On the St. Lawrence they (the villages) form practically a continuous line between Quebec and Montreal, the Parish Church being in the centre of each village and the houses extending on either side of it. On the tributary rivers the villages present the same aspect. Fish traps stand opposite almost every house and from the beginning of colonization until the present time the habitant is as dependent upon the fish which *le bon Dieu* sends into his trap as he is upon the produce of his farm. . . . The absence of shops in the villages, though not in the small towns, discloses the predominantly self-contained character of village life." [1]

The household was organized on the French patriarchal system by which the sons, their wives and children lived in the family home, the property was common property, and the whole family shared in the common labour. On death the property was subdivided, and as each of the heirs must equally have a river frontage, the result is a series of long narrow strips of land.

Into this settled life of feudal France came, after the taking of Quebec, the traders from New York and Massachusetts. They bought up and organized the supplies of grain for the troops and also took over much of the fur trade. Many of the Indians, however, when the French left, found no customers and went short of supplies and so took their wares to the Hudson's Bay Company. A fishing company was also established in 1764 by a family called Robin, from Jersey, and they and their descendants controlled the cod fisheries of the Gulf of the St. Lawrence for over a century and exported great quantities of dried cod to Brazil, Hayti and Spain. [2]

At the Peace, all the French officials left, as also did many of the fur traders, a quarter of the priests, and many of the seigniors, whose place was taken by English colonists, who bought up the land. In 1774 Sir James Marriott asserted in Parliament that Englishmen held the principal

---

[1] J. Mavor, " Economic Survey " in *Oxford Survey of the Empire*, vol. iv ; *America*, p. 118.
[2] J. M. Clarke, *The Heart of Gaspé*, p. 176.

seigniories of the day.[1] Even in Lord Durham's time, fully half of the most valuable were held by men of British descent and almost all were bought at panic prices from Frenchmen leaving the country.[2] The habitants were, therefore, left dependent on their priests for guidance unless they wished to mix with the alien. These, disgusted with the treatment of their Church during the French Revolution, tended to isolate their flock both from France and England overseas.

The English colonial contractors, coming in mainly by way of the old Colonies, were, from the very beginning, middlemen who, by organizing the collection of grain and military supplies, not merely got the wholesale trade of Canada into their hands but were the financial powers operating with the bills drawn on England to pay for supplies.

The British Government had obtained from France an indemnity of 560,000 dollars in bonds and 120,000 dollars in money for Canadians, but a large part went to the new British Canadians who had previously redeemed much of the French paper money at pawnbrokers' figures.[3]

The French, with their isolated self-contained existence into which money scarcely entered, had neither the tradition nor training for commercial enterprise and the colonial traders took the place of the French officials as the organizers of the disposal of the economic surplus. It was to their vigour and enterprise that much of the recovery of Canada at this time was due. Even in 1775, Chief Justice Hey, of Quebec, said business " depends upon the English merchants with whom almost the whole trade of the country lies and which without them was, and without them will continue, except for a very few articles, and these of no extent, a country of no trade at all ".[4]

The respective economic conditions of the two races was the result of their respective political traditions and histories.

" French colonization was born of the State, it was reared by the State, it was controlled by the State. Its essence was feudalism imported from the old world to the new, which was not, however, as in the old world, a growth, but

---

[1] Sir H. Cavendish, *Debates in House of Commons*, 1774, p. 319, cited by J. C. Bracq, *Evolution of French Canada*, p. 37.
[2] De Gaspé, *Les Anciens Canadiens*, p. 159, cited Bracq, p. 38.
[3] Heriot, *Travels through the Canadas*, pp. 227, 98, cited Bracq, p. 36.
[4] *C.P.*, vol. iv, p. 530.

the creation of the Crown. In New France the authority of the Crown and of the Church was absolute."

" The British colonies, which were the neighbours and rivals of Canada, were largely the product of antagonism to the State. The typical New Englanders were men or the descendants of men who had gone out to America to live their lives as they wished and not as the King or the Home Government wished. They were cradled in freedom, political and religious, and self-government in one form or another was of the essence of their being." [1]

What was true of the political was equally true of the economic life ; and just as when the English colonists in Canada were sufficiently numerous they intended to refuse to continue under French law, so they were going to demand freedom to control their own tariff, the direction of their own foreign trade, and to regulate the disposal of their own lands as they chose.

The French, accustomed to levies of goods and to be exploited by officials, were inferior in business methods and in acquiring and creating wealth. They were therefore liable to exploitation by clever middlemen of English race, and this apart from the friction created by a different religion and nationality, was bound to give rise to trouble from the very feeling of inferiority in economic matters.

The relative positions of the two races is strikingly illustrated by the organization of the timber trade which was carried on in Lower Canada by quite different methods from those of the Maritime Provinces already described. In the latter it was, as we have seen, of the nature of a domestic industry and the exporting merchant advanced to the little family groups tools, provisions, tobacco, molasses and the indispensable rum. The merchants also owned or provided the capital for the saw mills. In Lower Canada, French Canadians, who were rapidly increasing in numbers with their high birth-rate, supplied the labour. As a race they were accustomed to regimentation, and they readily lent themselves to the discipline of the lumber gang under capitalist supervision. Moreover in Lower Canada it required a larger outlay of capital in shoots and other forms of transport, as the rapids made it more difficult to deliver the timber than in the Atlantic provinces. Hence the trade was carried on by English merchants who invested their money while

Lucas, Introduction, pp. 24, 26.

local men organized the gangs and delivered the timber.[1]
As many as 500 horses would be employed by large operators
in Lower Canada.[2]   The head-quarters of the trade were,
therefore, in London and Glasgow.   By 1839, however,
Canadians were also carrying on the timber business themselves.   The result was said to be very beneficial to the
Colony.   Whereas the Englishman or his agents when they
retired went back to England, just as the official did from the
East Indies, the native Canadian remained in Canada and
invested his money in banking or insurance or canals.[3]

It was only the commercial communities of Quebec and
Montreal that were vitally affected by the timber trade.
In French Canada the timber trade did not supersede
agriculture, which was carried on in the usual traditional
fashion by the settled habitants   It was only their superfluous
sons who went off and earned wages, and there is evidence
that these had to compete with the Irish as a labour supply.[4]

Again, it was a native of Britain who in 1767 established
an industry allied to the lumber trade.   He set up a potash

---

[1] " Our house in Canada generally contracts with respectable head men,
who are to deliver certain quantities of timber and deals at Quebec in the
course of the year ; these head men take all risks in bringing it down.
We do not pay in full for the timber ; except some advance in money
and in goods, we do not settle for the timber until it is delivered into our
waters at Quebec."   C.T.D., J. Dowie, Q. 3741.
In Canada the export merchants purchase the timber from the lumbermen, whereas in New Brunswick they made advances to the lumbermen
who are paid the current price for the timber at the time of shipment.
C.T.D., A. Gilmour and W. Allan, Qq. 3523–3525.

[2] "Canada and the North West", Quarterly Review, 1861, vol. 109,
p. 18.

[3] " In the early periods of most of our colonies, commerce properly
so called remains in the hands of the Mother Country, or is supported by
capital drawn from thence.   In such circumstances the settlers confined
themselves to the retail trade and it is not until they have advanced
in wealth and intelligence that they aspire to the character of merchants.
Ten years ago, the former state of things prevailed in Canada ; of late,
however, a great alteration has taken place, and at this moment some of the
most extensive houses in Montreal consist of native partners, who are
not inferior to those of the British establishments either in respect of
funds or of professional knowledge."   H. Murray, Historical and Descriptive Account of British America, 1839, vol. ii, p. 51.

[4] It was suggested by a member of the Committee that the lumber
trade chiefly carried on by Irishmen and not by settlers.   C.T.D.,
Q. 2122. "We have a letter from one house in Canada in which
they speak of competition going on between the Canadians and the Irish
emigrants about bringing down the rafts ; the Irish emigrants have got
much of the labour, and they wish to take the whole. ' We fear the red
pine will not be down early, in consequence of the conduct of the Irish
in the red pine timber country, who are attempting to drive the Canadians
away, taking possession of the portages and narrows, and disputing the
passage of rafts manned by Canadians.' "   Ibid., J. Dowie, Q. 3825.

and pearl-ash business in Quebec and by 1770 was shipping fifty tons of good potash. This was made from the ashes of the hard wood timber and was used in the English bleaching industry. The trade in potash grew and was very valuable to the pioneer, as he could cut and burn his timber and the ashes when treated would bring him in a certain amount of money or goods, a most valuable help in the first year when no crop was grown and all was outlay. In addition, trade in oak staves was begun in 1771 and in the same year 188,000 bushels of grain were shipped from the St. Lawrence.[1]

A certain impetus was given to the energetic Puritan race that were striving to organize trade by the American Rebellion of 1775, which had the effect of creating a market for French Canadian produce, in that the troops defending Canada from the colonial rebels had to be fed.

As Lower Canada was liable to invasion by the American rebels to whose country it was to be added as " the four-teenth State ", preparation for defence was necessary. To guard against invasion down the St. Lawrence, defensive works were established at the fur posts of Niagara, Detroit, and Deer Island. Vessels were also built for patrolling the lakes.

The fur trade took the route by the Ottawa River and Georgian Bay, Lakes Erie and Ontario being almost unknown. The importance of the war was that men learned how to get up the rapids with large quantities of stores, and secondly they began to learn the possibilities of this region to which Loyalists were afterwards introduced, leading to the founding of the province of Upper Canada.[2]

Another effect of the American Rebellion was to bring a great batch of new emigrants into Canada, thus intensifying the friction between the French and the English settlers. The trade routes were also altered, since under the old colonial system no foreign country—and the United States was after 1783 a foreign country—could trade with a British colony. And this was important when the two land frontiers marched and the Great Lakes, the Richelieu River and Lake Champlain were obvious highways from one country to another.

On the other hand, there was opened out to Lower Canada the possibility of supplying the West Indies (now cut off

[1] *C.P.*, vol. iv, pp. 528-9.
[2] *C.P.*, vol. iv, p. 532.

from the United States) with bread-stuffs and timber ; and it became the outlet and inlet for the new Loyalist settlement in Ontario.

As the French population increased after the River frontages became fully occupied, there was bound to be colonization of the lands behind or emigration elsewhere. Both things happened.

One of the most striking events in the economic development of rural Quebec was the beginning of the colonization of the backlands of the Province. The British Government had surveyed some of the vacant lands on the Upper Ottawa and had divided them into townships of 5,400 to 6,000 acres each. These were called the Western Townships. To the south, between the St. Lawrence and the American border, was another extensive undeveloped territory which was surveyed and labelled the Eastern Townships. The French, as we have seen, had settled along the St. Lawrence in one " continuous white cottaged street ", but ten miles behind this line the land was unbroken. To the south of the St. Lawrence it was a hilly, densely wooded country with swamps. The usual reservation of one-seventh of the surveyed land for Crown reserves and one-seventh for clergy reserves was made. The other land had been disposed of to soldiers and others, but land jobbers and speculators had got large quantities of it into their hands and made no use of it.

The British American Land Company was formed in 1833 to purchase and develop 251,336 acres of Crown reserves, and an unsurveyed area of 596,325 acres between the Richelieu and Chaudière Rivers, as the Canada Company was doing in the Huron tract. For this they were to pay the Crown £120,000 in ten annual instalments, one-half of which might be used locally for roads and bridges. Further purchases were made of clergy reserves from private owners amounting to 400,000 acres, and altogether the Company were prepared to deal with almost 1,250,000 acres in the Eastern Townships. The French population objected strongly as they feared that the French element would be swamped by hosts of English-speaking settlers. In 1835 a capital of £300,000 was raised, of which 15 per cent was at once called up. The Company planned several towns, of which Sherbrooke was one, and intended erecting wharves, grist mills, saw mills, and asheries in their grant. It was very unfortunate at the start because the rebellion of 1837 scared off emigrants and the depression which followed had the same effect. The majority of the early settlers failed, as pioneer settlers generally seem to have done, and they left the country deep in the Company's debt.

Alexander Galt (the son of John Galt, of the Canada Company) was appointed in 1840 to supervise the Company's affairs and he reported that sales had ceased, pauper emigrants were of no use, and the roads were falling into ruin so that on some of them bushes four feet high were growing. The " town " of Victoria held one family, the " town " of Robinson four, including the agent, and emigrants from the United Kingdom would not go to the Eastern Townships as they liked living among an English-speaking population as in Montreal or Upper Canada, and thought that the Eastern Townships were French. Galt recommended that colonization should be attempted with French Canadians and Americans, who could at least wield an axe.

At the same time in French-speaking Canada there was considerable anxiety about the prevailing wholesale emigration of farmers' sons to the United States. This emigration was particularly marked after the troubles of 1837 and the depression which followed. The priests objected to the French Canadian getting away from the supervision of his religious advisers because he often lapsed into Protestantism or nothing. There was, therefore, considerable support for Galt when he wished to attract French Canadians as settlers, and an Association for establishing French Canadians in the Eastern Townships was formed.

The new settlers were allowed to make their payments in the form of grain or cattle and Galt said that he carried on for the Company the most extensive system of barter in the Western world. The annual sales of land on long deferred payment rates soon rose from 1,500 acres a year to 12,000, and in 1851 the Company paid its first dividend, which practice, however, was not long continued.

The region became more prosperous when the railway began to be built between Portland and Montreal in the years 1851–2, as it passed through Sherbrooke and opened up the territory of the Company. It brought in capital, gave employment to and therefore attracted emigrants and others to supply the wants of the railway builders. By his policy Galt, so the Directors declared in 1856, had " changed the position of the Company from one of almost hopeless insolvency to that of a valuable and remunerative under-taking ".[1]   He also did a most important piece of coloniza-tion backed by British capital.

A picture of the everyday life of the people who lived in the Eastern townships about the year 1850 has been left on record by one who passed his early years there.[2] The population was made up of representatives of every race.   There were the descendants of the early Dutch settlers and numbers of Irish and Scotch emigrants had found their way into these parts.   " The Habitants, whose ancestors had settled along the valley of the St. Lawrence more than two hundred years previously, still clung to the home of their childhood and were less in evidence in the townships fifty years ago than they are to-day.   It is true many of them found temporary employment in the lumbering operations and about the saw mills of the settlers of that time . . . but their abiding place—their home—was in the " French country " away off towards *la belle Rivière*. . . .

" Villages and habitations that are now in an open country and discernible as far as the range of vision can reach were then mostly but a few little log cabins hidden by a dense forest growth of mighty pines, hemlocks, cedars, tamarack, beech, birch, maple, and other indigenous trees.   The few acres comparatively of arable land reclaimed from the wilderness in their day could only by courtesy or by a stretch of language be dignified by the name of farms, while to-day they would see teeming acres limited only by the extent of country, and the extensive and forbidding forests of their time entirely blotted out. . . .The newcomer, often accompanied by his trusting, hopeful, helpful wife, and a few small children, with little or no money, and all their worldly belongings in a crude box, carpet bag, or tied in a bundle—strangers among strangers—alighted from a rude stage at the post office, or possibly having made the journey on foot from the place of disembarkation, carrying all their belongings, and sought for a shelter for the night. They were usually given a warm welcome at the first log cabin large enough to accommodate them, as its occupants, prompted by a fellow feeling, recall a similar favour extended to themselves not long since, and the best the cabin affords

[1] Skelton, *Life and Times of Sir Alexander Galt*, p. 55.
[2] Dr. George McAleer, *Reminiscent and otherwise* : *Life in the Eastern Townships of Quebec Fifty Years Ago*, Worcester, Mass., 1901 (Canada Pamphlets (Dominions Office and Colonial Office Library), vol. v, No. 146.

is cheerfully shared with the latest accession to the neighbourhood. Land is taken up and the toil begins of carving
out a home from untoward surroundings. An axe is bought
at the only store for miles around and which also serves
as a post office ; trees are felled and soon a log cabin takes
their place above a hole dug in the ground which becomes an
apology for a cellar.

" The spaces between the logs are filled with mud or
moss or a combination of both, logs are hewn for a floor and
cedar is rifted for a covering for the roof.

" An apology for a door is provided, which swings upon
wooden hinges, and its hardwood latch is operated from
without by a latch-string which is withdrawn at night so
the door cannot be opened from the outside. A crude fire-
place is fashioned of rough stones in one end of the cabin,
the family moves in, and life is begun in the new home. . . .

"There was then in Canada not a single mile of railway; and
turnpike roads were well-nigh impassable, especially during
the spring and fall when nearly all travel was practically
at a standstill, and when distant journeys would be more
readily undertaken on horseback or on foot than with a team.
At such times when it became necessary to go to the grist
mill the grain was bound upon the horse's back and the owner
trudged alongside leading the animal. In many cases the
roads were but the sinuous ways improvised through the
forests by lumbermen for hauling out timber logs and wood,
and which by continued use and improvement have become
the public highways of the country.

" The territory being substantially a forest it was perfectly
natural that lumbering operations, peeling hemlock bark,
shaving shingles, and the like, would be the principal
occupation of the people for many years succeeding the
earliest settlements. While large quantities of lumber
were cut and exported to the United States the price paid
therefor was so low that only the most valuable and easily
obtained was thus utilized. . . .

" During the dryest portion of the year fires were started
in the choppings of the previous winter and they were
encouraged to extend into and devour the uncut forest and
consume what to-day would be most valuable timber. . . .
In many places the hardwood ashes were gathered up by
the more enterprising, the lye extracted by very crude
appliances and boiled into potash in great iron kettles and
an honest dollar well earned thereby. . . .

" Old and young of the households found abundant work, when other labours permitted, in clearing up the land, piling up and burning the logs and odds and ends which escaped the first burning, repiling and firing the embers, chinking up and around and urging up the devouring element to consume the huge pine and other stumps. . . . Mowing machines, harvesters, and horserakes had not then been invented ; but had they been in existence they would have been as useless as a smokestack upon a wheelbarrow, as the land was too rough to permit their use, and the people for the most part were too poor to buy them. All hay and grain was cut with the scythe and sickle—a large part of the grain and the timothy grass for hayseed with the latter implement. No threshing machines were then in existence and many weary days were spent wielding the hand flail to thresh the grain and hayseed. . . .

" In early spring time sap troughs were made of basswood, poplar, ash, and similar wood and scorched over an open brush fire to prevent checking later by the sun when put into use. The maple trees were tapped with a gouge chisel, the spouts were rifted from cedar with the same gouge so as to fit, and a great score or notch cut into the tree with an axe above the spout to increase the flow of sap. . . . Many tons of sugar were so made and families of several generations supplied therewith before the refined white sugar of the cane was ever seen in these parts."

The Eastern Townships were not, then, wholly French. There was a considerable further interpenetration of English and Americans with railway building and, as has been seen, there were still some of the original settlers scattered about. As long as the migration to the Eastern Townships meant a mixing of the races and religions, the priests opposed it for the French Canadian. It was only when the settlement could be carried out in groups and in the lands where the English had not penetrated that they approved. But English capital and organization had to step in to carry the undertaking to success and the French Canadians stand indebted to British capital in the matter of their spread into the Eastern Townships.

Other colonization schemes for the backlands of Quebec were tried, but none was so successful. Colonization societies were formed in parishes or groups of parishes from which it was not so easy to move to the United States. The movement was under the leadership of the Church. In

1847 and afterwards, priests began to organize colonization parties into the backlands.[1] The Saguenay was one of the chosen regions.

The movement for settling the French Canadians in the backlands of Canada had become a national one in Quebec. The big religious element was one factor but there was also the political jealousy of the success of the English in Upper Canada in settling their backlands, and joined to this was the overwhelming fear of an English predominance unless Lower Canada could retain her own French population.[2]

The success of settlement in the backlands away from the river, which after all was frozen for six months, depended upon roads being made. This was stressed in the Report of the Special Committee on Emigration.[3]

The causes of emigration from Lower Canada to the States, to which reference has been made, are described as first and foremost, " The want of roads and bridges as a means of communication between the old settlements and the unconceded lands of the Crown. The unanimous opinion of all the persons consulted by your Committee on this subject assigns this as the main cause. A considerable number of the sons of farmers, at this time unprovided with land, would be ready to settle on the lands of the Crown if access to them were made easy. How is it to be expected by young people or fathers of families, all, or nearly all, of whom have but scanty means, perhaps none, that they can resolve to plunge into the recesses of a boundless forest, made aware as they are by the experience of those who have gone before, that they must give up all hope of intercourse in their new locations with their relatives and friends, otherwise than on the hard condition of traversing miles of trackless swamps and mountains, intersected by rivers and streamlets, and a thousand obstacles which defy human courage and energy to surmount them ? " To arrest emigration, " Your Committee can find no better terms to express their opinion on this head than the words used by Mr. Marquis : ' Without roads no colonization is profitable. The most magnificent speeches of distinguished orators at Montreal and Quebec and the pompous reports of meetings at which active

---

[1] *Report of Special Committee on Emigration in Canadian Assembly Journals*, vol. xv, 1857, Appendix, vol. viii.

[2] Attempts were even made in the 'seventies and 'eighties to attract emigrants from France and Belgium. S. Drapeau, *Canada : le guide du Colon français, belge, etc.*, 1887. This was a failure.

[3] *Canadian Assembly Journals*, vol. xv, 1857, Appendix, vol. viii.

Presidents, Honorary Presidents, Vice-Presidents . . . are appointed, are buried out of sight in the first mud hole which the settlers falls in with on his way. All the finest words in the language of eloquence are then of less importance to him than one poor acre of corduroy road.' "

Small sums were occasionally doled out by Parliament from 1854 to build roads to the settlements and to encourage others. Most of the settlements seemed, however, to stand still after the initial stimulus died away, the Eastern Townships with its railway being the only progressive area.

In the 'sixties larger organizations were promoted. The societies varied in their objects. Some were formed to help relations and friends to settle in the backwoods, others to help new settlers to build missions and chapels. Two settlements, one in the Gatineau Valley and one far up on the Ottawa River—the Timiskaming Settlement—were promoted by the Church. In the late 'eighties and 'nineties the railways did more than anything else to fill up the backlands and revolutionized the conditions in the Saguenay region, the St. Maurice, the Gatineau and Timiskaming.

In Gaspé there has been little backland settlement. The men of Gaspé were fishermen and the merchants did their utmost to prevent these fishermen wandering from the water or diverting their attention to the land.[1] After the break-up of the merchants' power over the fishermen and with the fall in the price of fish, the tendency was to turn to agriculture.

Emigration to the United States still went on, but the colonizing movement described above had the effect of extending the borders of Lower Canada.

The French Canadians are now settled in three strata.[2] The riverine region is fertile and has water communication, the intermediate region consists of clay of medium fertility and the mountains are covered with coarse poor soil. The French settled in the patriarchal family groups with sons and daughters, their wives and children living in the family house. This seems to be breaking up in the riverine areas.

In the mountain area the family cannot hold together, the soil is too poor to make a living for the group. Its sons go to the lumber camps or to the New England factories. In the intermediate group patriarchalism still survives. In this intermediate region the habitants supply many of

---

[1] Abbé Ferland, quoted by J. M. Clarke, *The Heart of Gaspé*, p. 186.
[2] J. Mavor, " Economic Survey " in *Oxford Survey of the Empire*, vol. iv, " America," pp. 118–20.

their domestic needs and are good shoemakers and carpenters. On the river the French Canadian is richer as he can reach a market. Illiteracy was $6\frac{1}{2}$ per cent in the riverine area, 10 per cent in the intermediate, and 24 per cent in the mountains, and the religious faith varies from the intense faith of the mountains to formality in the intermediate and a state bordering on indifference in the river region.

The general characteristic of the agriculture of Quebec was its poverty up to 1850 when special Committees were appointed to consider the state of agriculture in Lower Canada. These reports led to the creation of a Board of Agriculture in 1853 and to the establishment of agricultural schools, the first of which was opened in 1859.[1] In 1854 the repressive and obsolete feudal or seignorial tenure was abolished and a freehold system instituted.

There has been since that date a considerable improvement. Agricultural societies encouraged the breeding of good animals and the use of better implements. One of the most interesting societies—the Agricultural Missionaries—was formed in 1894 by the Catholic bishops of the ecclesiastical province of Quebec. This Society consists of parish priests selected in each diocese by the bishop, whose business it is to act as agricultural missionaries and combat idleness, want of method, the drink habit and luxury, and encourage better agriculture generally.[2]

The organization of butter and cheese factories also began in 1865 in the Province and there were in 1881 no less than 162 butter and cheese factories and 3,040 in 1911. A dairy school was started in 1881. The development of the butter and cheese industry has revolutionized farming in Quebec.

A great deal of the agriculture is still largely self-contained and only the surplus is sold. There is little purchasing and little selling. According to a French observer in 1906[3] the British element possess the wealth and control the economic life of the Dominion. " Even in most French districts the Dominion is thoroughly under Anglo-Saxon domination. . . . With some notable exceptions, which are now growing in number, our people have remained outside the great economic current. The principal banks, the leading railway companies, the great industrial, commercial, and shipping concerns belong to their rivals ; English is the

---

[1] *C.P.*, vol. xvi, pp. 522–3.
[2] Ibid., pp. 524–5.
[3] A. Siegfried, *The Race Question in Canada*, 1907, pp. 249, 250.

language of business ; Montreal is a satellite of London or New York—an Anglo-Saxon centre *par excellence*, in which the presence of more than a hundred thousand Frenchmen is a factor of secondary importance."

The French Canadians do not want to join in any movement of British Imperialism, and they are utterly opposed to absorption in the United States, where they would lose their individuality and their position as a French community. It has been said that in a war between Canada and the United States, the French Canadians would be found in the last ditch. Nor does Quebec look to France. The Catholic Church, shocked at the religious vagaries of France ever since the Revolution of 1789, has shepherded the French Canadian away from possible religious contamination.

CHAPTER 5

THE WESTWARD SETTLEMENTS OF THE FUR TRADERS AND THEIR FOUNDATION OF BRITISH COLUMBIA AND THE RED RIVER SETTLEMENT.

Outstanding importance of the Fur Trade.

The Company of the Hundred Associates.

The Hudson's Bay Company.

The North-West Company of Fur Traders:
Montreal as the centre.

The North-West Company's Organization.

The Fur Trade Explorers in the West.

The Beginnings of British Columbia.

Struggle between the Hudson's Bay and the North-West Companies.

Selkirk's Colonists and the Foundation of the Red River Settlement.

Amalgamation of the two Companies.

Struggle for supremacy in British Columbia between the Hudson's Bay Company and American Traders.

THERE are features in the economic development of Lower Canada which resemble those of South Africa. In both cases there was a non-British population, self-sufficing and carrying on a primitive agriculture, on whose primitive economic life was engrafted by an alien race another type of economic exploitation of the resources of the country, the capital for which was found by that alien race. Thus there existed, side by side, two strongly contrasting economic civilizations. The pastoral Boer in the Transvaal saw the great capitalistic gold mining industry started in his midst. The French Canadian saw the development of capitalistic lumbering in Quebec ; and although the fur and lumber trades as organized by the British played an important part in the development of the Province, they were excrescences on the peasant agriculture of French Canada. The diamond mines of Kimberley proved to be the jumping-off ground for a new extension into Rhodesia. The fur trade as organized from Montreal after 1763 became the jumping-off ground for fresh exploration and settlement in the Prairies and on the Pacific coast.

In a new country the difficulty is to find something to sell in exchange for things with which to satisfy the wants of the pioneers. Even the humblest need seed, an axe, a kettle and generally clothing, tobacco and tea.

Fish and furs were the two staples that had helped to supply the wants of the early French settlers, and the English merchants, after the conquest of Canada, turned at once to the fur trade as the only substantial source of profit.

Among the furs, beaver stood out pre-eminent, for the beaver top hat was an article of universal wear among " the gentry and nobility ". Even to-day the beaver is the national emblem of Canada. The most valuable of the furs was the pelt of the sea otter (now extinct), which was caught off the Pacific coast and sold in China or Russia to royalties or very wealthy persons at prices varying from £30 to £40 a piece. The great value of this fur led to the frequenting and settlement of the Pacific coast. Marten, muskrat, mink, fox, bear, squirrel, racoon, and wolverine were the other valuable furs which, with the decline of the beaver and otter, came to assume a prominent place in the trade. Sables and ermine are obtained from Asiatic Russia. So important was the beaver that in 1650 at Tadoussac, in Quebec Province, no less than a hundred canoes laden with beaver skins came in the year to the post.

The fur trade was a monopoly for the Company of the Hundred Associates, founded by Richelieu in 1627, and, after its disappearance in 1663, of the French Government. This monopoly was the subject of attack both from the north and south, by adventurers pushing up from New Amsterdam, later New York, and by an English Company operating on Hudson Bay.

Two French traders, Radisson and Des Groseilliers, had been in the service of the Company of the Hundred Associates and had also traded on their own account They seem to have worked the territory between Lake Superior and Hudson Bay, and it is said that they were the first to round Lake Superior. They came down to Montreal accompanied by three hundred Indians and in possession of sixty fur-laden canoes. They were fined for illicit trading and, being Huguenots, found no support for their suggestions for extending the fur trade to the north. After trying in Boston, they came over to England to offer their services to the rival nation. They were fortunate in interesting

Prince Rupert, and in 1668 Des Groseilliers is credited with having guided the *Nonsuch,* an English vessel, into Hudson Bay to the mouth of the Rupert River, from which the ship returned laden with furs. The result was the formation of a chartered company in 1670 entitled " The Governor and Company of Adventurers of England trading into Hudson's Bay "—the name the Company still bears. Prince Rupert was the first Governor. The two Frenchmen were not faithful and tried to bring the trade under French control, but without success. Radisson became a stock holder in the Hudson's Bay Company and was pensioned in 1710.

The charter of the Hudson's Bay Company included all the lands draining into Hudson Bay, but the right of the Company to trade was disputed by the French and there was a taking and re-taking of forts until the Treaty of Utrecht in 1713 definitely decided the struggle by ceding Hudson Bay to the British. There was still friction between the two owing to disputes about the boundary. The difficulty lay in the fact that ships could only reach the Bay during three months of the year and the forts had to be provisioned and stocked for twelve months and had to be able to withstand attack when no help could reach them. From the first the Company supplied the Indians with weapons, and, once used to firearms for obtaining furs or food, they became dependent on the factories from which they could obtain powder and shot. The St. Lawrence route possessed by the French was the more favourable one and the French seem to have obtained the larger share of the fur trade. They were subject, however to two disabilities. The English held the command of the sea and the French had some difficulty about transshipping the furs. They bought the merchandize exchanged for furs in the American Colonies, and when the Governor of New York prohibited the sale of these goods the French were considerably hampered.

The Hudson's Bay Company seems to have thriven and an inquiry in 1749 shows that they were making 40 per cent profit. The capital with which they started was originally £10,500, but in 1720, what with the ships they owned and their factories, the actual value of their possessions was estimated at £94,500.

There was great opposition to the Company in London as it was said they showed little initiative, and London hatters complained that they could not get sufficient beaver, owing to the supineness of the Company, while their French rivals were well supplied and could sell beaver hats more cheaply.[1]

There were actually three centres of the American fur trade, Hudson Bay, Montreal and New York. Montreal had become a centre of the trade because the usual route was to follow the Ottawa River, Lake Nipissing, the French River, and so get into Georgian Bay. The avoidance of hostile Indians was one reason for taking this route, which also cut out Lakes Ontario, Erie, Huron, the Rapids and Niagara— a long detour with many portages. It actually took nine days to get from Lachine (Montreal) to Kingston (Lake Ontario) in 1789.[2] There were also many portages to pass the rapids on the Ottawa, but it was quicker and a less hazardous route and continued to be used, even when the danger from hostile Indians passed away.[3] After the surrender of Montreal (1760) the French monopoly *ipso facto* terminated, and at the end of the Seven Years' War with the cession of Canada (1763), the fur trade was open to every British subject on payment of a licence fee.

Numbers of private traders began to prosecute the fur trade from Montreal, many of them coming in from the older Colonies and New York. There was keen competition, and, in their endeavours to cut each other out, they explored further afield and opened out new districts. The competition was so cutthroat that in 1779 the traders amalgamated for a year, the combination was reconstituted in 1780, and finally in 1783-4 they combined into the North West Company of Fur Traders, the bulk of the capital being found in England by the firm of Ellice.[4]

Until the British preference started the lumber trade in 1809, the fur trade was the only way of producing an exchangeable staple to satisfy wants. When giving evidence before the Hudson's Bay Committee of 1857 Ellice, a son of the above-mentioned firm, said that "in 1803 . . . the whole of the Canadian society, every person of eminence and of consequence there, was engaged in the fur trade, it being the only trade of importance in the country".[5] The lumber trade was largely in the hands of British merchants, but the

---

[1] As to the Hudson's Bay Company generally, see Beckles Willson, *The Great Company*.

[2] Davidson, *North West Company*, p. 212, n. 56.

[3] Davidson, op. cit., p. 213.

[4] E. Ellice, Q. 5776, in Evidence before the Select Committee on Hudson's Bay Company, *Parly. Papers*, 1857 (Sess. 2), xv.

[5] Ibid., Q. 5775.

fur trade from Montreal was managed by men who lived in the country and it had more the aspect of a Canadian enterprise, though many of them retired to England in the end. The Hudson's Bay Company, on the other hand, hardly touched Canada or Canadian life as they did not move in from the coast until the rivalry with the North West Company became acute.

But the economic effects of the fur trade included far more than the obtaining and marketing of an exchange product. The rivalry between the various companies led to the exploration of Canada and the settlement of British Columbia. It led to the founding of the Red River Colony and the start of the Province of Manitoba. It brought a good deal of capital into Canada and focussed attention on the country. There were dramatic incidents about forts and furs, the fur lords and Red Indians, bears and wolves, the canoes and the frozen North that the more prosaic settler, wearily hacking down trees for a clearance and letting light and air into dank dark woods, does not seem to have provided.

There were really four companies to be considered, all engaged in the struggle for furs—the Hudson's Bay, the North West and an offshoot and rival of this, the X.Y., and the Pacific Fur Company. The latter was an American venture founded in 1810 by J. J. Astor, who had been engaged in the fur trade in New York as early as 1784. All these were at one time or another bitter rivals, and their rivalry led to the finding of new routes, the establishment of new ports and the alteration of national boundaries. The two protagonists were, however, the Hudson's Bay Company and the North West Company of Fur Traders.

The organization of the North West Company was that of a partnership and its success lay in the way in which it promoted its subordinates and gave them a share in the profits according to their efficiency. Promotion and remuneration depended on their actual success in getting furs and no questions were asked as to methods. The Hudson's Bay Company, on the other hand, was a joint stock company, paying its employees a yearly fixed salary and distributing the profits in England to its shareholders.

"For hard, keen, shrewd efficiency, the North West Company was perhaps the most terribly effective organization that had ever arisen in the New World," is the verdict of a recent writer.[1]

The North West Company had its " agents " at Montreal.[2] They supplied the goods for the Indian trade and marketed the furs. Below them came the " wintering partners " who dealt with the Indians in the interior. Once a year some of the agents from Montreal would meet the wintering partners at Grand Portage,[3] or later at Fort William on Lake Superior, and would take charge of the year's furs. Below the partners came the clerks and apprentices, who might reasonably hope in their turn to become partners and agents. Then came the guides and the canoe-men, who were the great bulk of the employees and were generally French Canadians. While it was the usual arrangement that there should be a share in the profits, it was open to the Company to punish its clerks by only giving them a fixed salary. In the case of the opening out of new regions, the chief traders were awarded a commission. The incentive supplied by this method of organization was so great that the Hudson's Bay factors were regarded by their rivals as a lot of old women.

The main articles of exchange varied from time to time and according to the tribes dealt with. Mirrors, chisels, guns, gunpowder, blankets, buttons, beads, bells, kettles, knives, hatchets, tobacco, nails and paint were standard articles. Drink was not sold but was given away to clinch a bargain. To the Pacific coast a ship was usually sent containing these articles, but a speciality of this trade was an iron collar weighing seven pounds, which found great favour with Indian belles, and it was not unprofitable as the price was three otter skins—£120.[4]

It was stated in 1811 in a pamphlet that the North West Company spent annually £50,000 in Canada in salaries, wages and colonial produce,[5] and that £30,000 worth of goods were purchased in England for the trade of the North West.

---

[1] Chester Martin, *Lord Selkirk's Work in Canada*, Oxford Historical and Literary Studies, p. 31.

[2] On this whole subject, see Davidson, *North West Company*, University of California Publications, vol. vii.

[3] Grand Portage was on the north side of Lake Superior to the South of Fort William and was used until 1802 when the United States began to tax the furs going by that route when the main fur route took the line of Fort William and the Kaministikwia River in British territory. *Ibid.*, p. 105.

[4] *Canadian Handbook for British Association*, 1924, p. 296.

[5] *Origin and Progress of the Fur Trade*, p. 15, cited by Davidson, p. 233.

According to a memorandum on the trade in 1780, the Province of Quebec was said to ship each year on an average £200,000 worth of furs, of which one-half came from the region around Lake Huron and beyond, one-fourth from Niagara and Detroit, and one-fourth from the ports below Montreal.[1] The value of the furs shipped in 1788 from Quebec was, according to the Collector of Customs at that place, £258,970, which figure rose to £371,139 in 1801.[2] Furs from a British Colony became an " enumerated article " in the reign of George III, and so were obliged under the Navigation Acts to come to London, and with the increasing activities of the fur companies in Canada, London became the great fur market of the world. Among the list of the average number of peltries cleared from the Quebec custom house for nine years, 1793–1801, there were said to be 137,548 beaver skins, 38,638 martens, 169,811 deer, 144,439 racoons, 57,151 muskrats, 19,286 bears, 11,329 minks, 18,349 otters, 10,141 foxes, 6,885 wolves, 1,978 seals, on which the duties payable were £16,071 15s. 4d.[3]

The capital employed in the trade was necessarily large, as Mackenzie showed in his pamphlet on the Fur Trade in 1801 that it took nearly four years to complete a transaction in furs.

" The orders for the goods are sent to this country 25th October, 1796.

" They are shipped from London, March, 1797.

" They arrive in Montreal, June, 1797.

" They are made up in the course of that summer and winter.

" They are sent from Montreal, May, 1798.

" They arrive in the Indian country and are exchanged for furs the following winter, 1798–9.

" Which furs come to Montreal, September, 1799.

" And are shipped for London, where they are sold in March and April and paid for in May or June, 1800."[4]

The disadvantage under which the North West Company laboured was the distance of its operations from the base of its supplies and the necessary expenses incidental to a system which spread over such a vast continent. A small army of over a thousand men was required to manage the ports and transport the provisions, goods and peltries.

[1] Davidson, op. cit., pp. 18–19.
[2] Ibid., pp. 270, 283.   [3] Ibid., p. 282.
[4] Mackenzie, *General History of the Fur Trade*, 1801, p. xxiv.

On the Ottawa alone no less than 540 men were employed, of whom 400 went on to Lake Superior for furs. It was said that there were no less than 1,200 to 1,400 men wintering in the interior in connexion with the Company.[1] When Mackenzie wrote there were 50 clerks, 71 interpreters, 35 guides, and 1,120 canoe-men or voyageurs.

The Montreal " agents " had to import the necessary goods for the trade, store them at their own expense, get them made up, pack and forward them, supplying cash to the outfit. Each canoe was manned by eight or ten men. It carried their baggage and 65 packages of goods, 6 cwt. of biscuit, 2 cwt. pork and 3 bushels of peas, and two oilcloths to cover the goods, a sail, an axe, a towing-line, a kettle and some materials for repairs. The actual cost of transport by the Ottawa route added 20 per cent to the goods.[2] At times goods went by the Lakes and Niagara, but this was by no means usual. Around the forts some provisions were grown, especially potatoes. There were cows at Grand Portage. Other food supplies were obtained from the Plains Indians, the staple foods being pemmican from the buffalo and fish. The Indians who brought in the furs were often supplied with clothing and other things in advance and subordinate officials travelled round and collected furs from them. The standard price was reckoned in beaver. One beaver equalled three martens or eight muskrats or one lynx or one wolverine skin.[3] A silver fox was equivalent to two beavers and a large black bear or black fox to four beavers. A woollen blanket was equivalent to eight skins and a fowling piece to fifteen. The employees ran accounts at the stores and were often deeply indebted to the Company.

The North West Company obtained a much larger share of the fur trade than its rival. Thus in 1795 a North West partner, writing from Athabaska, estimated that the North West Company got about eleven-fourteenths of the trade, the Hudson's Bay Company two-fourteenths, and the various other interests one-fourteenth.[4]

The three events of pre-eminent economic importance in the history of the fur trade in Canada are the settling of the Pacific coast ; the rivalry between the North West Company and the Hudson's Bay Company, one incident of which was the founding of the Red River Colony; and the amalgamation of the two companies in 1821.

---

[1] Davidson, 229. See also n. 131.   [2] Ibid., 210–12.
[3] Ibid., 242.   [4] Ibid., 72, n. 19.

The French had a chain of fur posts from Montreal towards the Rockies, but these were abandoned after the British conquest, and the Indians carried their furs to Hudson Bay. A number of traders, Henry, Pond, Frobisher, were also explorers. Alexander Mackenzie spent a year in Athabaska with Pond in 1789 and explored the Great Slave Lake and discovered the river named after him. In 1793 he crossed the Continent westwards by way of the Peace River to the Bella Coola River. The North West Company was extremely anxious to have a charter in the Pacific region, which should give them a monopoly, and its agents were encouraged to make further explorations in the West so as to have a good ground for their claim. Hence there were a whole series of expeditions between 1797 and 1808 when the Fraser River was explored. The roll of names of the fur-trader-explorers is a long one.[1]

After the Pacific had been reached, the great market in furs lay in China, but the difficulty here was the fact that all British trade with China was a monopoly in the hands of the East India Company, and if tea were taken in return for furs it infringed the East India Company's monopoly. An American Company would, however, have no such difficulties. In 1810 Astor had organized the Pacific Fur Company and engaged men who were North West Company's men. He founded Astoria on the Columbia River in 1811. When the war of 1812 broke out, the British were in a superior position, as they were expecting a vessel, the *Isaac Todd*, and to avoid capture Astoria was sold in 1813 to the North West Company. In 1814, at the end of the war, it was returned to the United States, and in 1818 the U.S.A. flag was hoisted again. It was on the ground of this prior settlement and other later immigrations from America that the boundary was settled in 1846 giving the lower part of the Columbia River to the United States. After the amalgamation with its rival the Hudson's Bay Company continued to be the government as well as the economic power in the region, and when the East India Company's monopoly was abrogated in 1833 they carried on a trade with China. The sales of furs in China were £101,155 in 1815 and in that year £15,300 worth of goods were imported by sea from England, rising to £28,500 in 1818.[2]

In 1798 some partners broke off from the North West

[1] See Davidson, chaps. 3 and 5.   [2] Davidson, pp. 166–7.

Company and formed another Company. It was joined by Sir Alexander Mackenzie, the explorer, and was called the X.Y. Company. This led to the reorganization of the North West Company with the promotion of many clerks to be partners to keep them loyal. In 1804, after a bitter competition, when the amount of liquor consumed seems to have risen from 10,098 gallons in 1800 to 21,299 gallons in 1803 (the North West Company using 16,299 and the opposing traders 5,000), the two companies amalgamated to turn to face another foe—the Hudson's Bay Company.

The effect of the formation of the North West Company had been to give a great stimulus to the old Company, making it advance into the interior to meet the furs halfway. Previously the furs had been brought by the Indians to the forts around the Bay. Cumberland House had already been established in 1774 but was now followed up by Fort Osnaburgh in 1786 and a penetration into Assiniboia and Athabaska.

In 1815 Robertson and Clarke left the service of the North West Company and transferred themselves, as so often happened, to the rival concern and pioneered the penetration into Athabaska for the Hudson's Bay Company. Owing to the hostility of the North West Company, eighteen of the party were starved to death and fifty others, being kept without food for two or three days to make them submissive, took an oath that they would not return to the region. The loss to the Hudson's Bay Company was forty to fifty thousand pounds.[1] They returned again in 1818. Reprisals followed, and there were duels, arrests, drownings, and other cheerful incidents.[2]

Lord Selkirk, in his *Sketch of the British Fur Trade*, 1816,[3] talks of " the ferocious spirit which had been fostered among the clerks and servants of the two Companies by six years of continual violence " ; and of the " torrent of aggression " and the " lawless violence " of the struggle. The Indian tribes were demoralized by the attempts of one Company to take furs which they were pledged to deliver to the other Company and for which they had already received an advance, and by the bounteous supply of liquor.

---

[1] Davidson, p. 157.   [2] Ibid., pp. 158–63.
[3] Earl of Selkirk, *Sketch of the British Fur Trade in North America with Observations relative to the North-West Company of Montreal*, pp. 68. 78 n. The two Companies referred to are the North-West and the X.Y., which amalgamated and then concentrated their fury on the Hudson's Bay Company.

Another move in the struggle was the establishment of the Red River Colony. Lord Selkirk, who was deeply interested in emigration, especially of superfluous Scottish Highlanders [1] and who had a great tradition of public service, conceived the idea of founding a colony in the prairies. He had already made a successful attempt at settlement in Prince Edward Island and an unsuccessful one in Ontario. To found the Colony he had to obtain land from the Hudson's Bay Company. The plan had the advantage of providing a place in the interior from which the Company might get grain, which otherwise had to be brought by ship from England. The proposed settlement, however, lay right across the main route of the North West Company to Athabaska and the Pacific.

It is impossible to realize the strategic importance of the settlement without realizing the importance of the river and lake communication at this point. A hostile settlement at Red River could obstruct canoes which wanted to take the line of the Red River and Lake Winnipeg and proceed west to the Pacific or north to the Arctic or northeast to Hudson Bay or south to the Gulf of Mexico.

The Pacific could be reached by following the north or south branch of the Saskatchewan River and portaging to the Columbia River ; or it could be reached by following the Athabaska River, Lake Athabaska, the Peace River, and striking the head waters of the Fraser. The Arctic could also be reached by following the Athabaska, Lake Athabaska, the Slave River and the Great Slave Lake into the Mackenzie River.

Hudson Bay was reached from Lake Winnipeg by following the Hayes River. It was also easy to portage from the Red River to the Mississippi and so down to the Gulf.

The Red River Colony could, therefore, if the Hudson's Bay Company chose, block all the main water routes. Hence it is not wonderful that Simon McGillivray should write to the North West "partners" in 1812: "The Committee of the Hudson's Bay Company is at present a mere machine in the hands of Lord Selkirk, who appears to be so much wedded to his schemes of colonization in the interior of North America that it will require some time and I fear cause much expense to us, as well as to himself, before

---

[1] *Observations upon the Present State of the Highlands of Scotland with a View of of the Causes and Probable Consequences of Emigration*, 1805, B.M., 982, c. 11.

he is driven to abandon the project, and yet *he must `be* driven to abandon it for his success would strike at the very existence of our trade."[1]

Lord Selkirk bought up the larger part of the Hudson's Bay Company's shares and so acquired such a degree of control as to obtain a grant of 116,000 acres of land.[2] The North West Company disputed the claim that the Hudson's Bay Charter extended so far. They claimed to be themselves the heirs of the old French fur traders and that this carried a prior claim which excluded the Hudson's Bay Company's right to dispose of the land at all.

The settlement was established at the junction of the Red and Assiniboine Rivers in 1812, Selkirk paying for the transport, settlement and government of the emigrants. The farms were laid out in long narrow strips fronting the river after the manner of the French-Canadian farms of Quebec. In 1813 the settlers who had come out by Hudson Bay numbered nearly a hundred. The wheat harvest of that year and 1814 were total failures, but that of 1815 was more fortunate. There was not a plough in the whole colony, and only one harrow, and this could not be used owing to defective parts, so that the breaking up of the prairie had to be done with the hoe. The birds took devastating toll of the harvest.

The North West Company resented the settlement not only because it cut across their lines of communication, but also because they were afraid it might destroy their supplies of pemmican from the buffalo by too indiscriminate slaughter ; because they thought that settlement would drive back the fur-bearing animals ; and because they feared it might control the Athabaska beaver trade.

In 1815 the North Westers and their half-breed adherents trampled on the settlers' crops, stole their horses and burnt Fort Douglas. Most of the settlers were driven away but were induced to return later. A new Governor, Robert Semple, came out. In the spring of 1816 wheat and barley were sowed but not reaped because in June an armed combat took place at Seven Oaks, and Semple and twenty of his men were killed and no colonist was permitted to remain to reap the crops which they had sown. In 1817 a force sent by Lord Selkirk re-took Fort Douglas and the

---

[1] Chester Martin, p. 171, note 1.
[2] Cf. Cecil Rhodes and his control of diamond shares to get a fund to go North. Basil Williams, *Life*, pp. 102–3.

settlers returned, to have their crops ruined again by a hurricane.

In 1818 the locusts came and covered the ground to the depth of several inches, and formed for three years a sickening and destructive plague ; and there were floods in 1826 which buried the settlement under several feet of ice and water. After that the settlement relapsed for half a century into an obscure frontier colony, thrifty, primitive and self-reliant, trading mainly with the United States and selling the buffalo skins there. In 1857 no less than 1,200 Red River carts plied between the colony and the U.S.A. border. In 1871 Winnipeg was a village of 241 persons.

Lord Selkirk and his heirs spent £114,000 on the different settlements, and he died, a disappointed man, in 1820, his estate encumbered with debts to the amount of £160,000.[1] The Red River Colony was re-purchased from his family by the Hudson's Bay Company in 1834.[2] But had it not been for the Red River settlement the history of Columbia in 1846 might have been repeated and the Americans might have claimed the country in virtue of prior settlement as in the case of Astoria.

" Founded by an individual proprietor, twice destroyed by men of kindred race, overwhelmed during its early years by almost unparalleled disaster, developed for two decades under the protection of a private family, relapsing into the ownership of a monopolistic trading Company which was accused by its enemies, justly or unjustly, of having ' locked the door upon the settlement and put the key in its pocket ' ; and finally, after an ignoble insurrection in 1869 taking its place as one of the most promising provinces of the Dominion " [3]—that was the result of Lord Selkirk's work in pegging out a claim in the most important strategic point of the prairies. The Red River Settlement was the anchor of British rule in the West and the one vested interest which kept intact the territory north of the 49th degree of latitude until the Canadas were ready to colonize. The desire to colonize the North-West and so carry on the work of the fur companies and Lord Selkirk was one of the reasons for federation in 1867.

Meanwhile the fur lords of Montreal had made large fortunes. Simon McTavish's fortune when he died was estimated

---

[1] Chester Martin, p. 191. Nevertheless seed wheat to the value of £1,000 was sent out by the executors of the Selkirk estate (ibid., p. 173).
[2] Ibid., p. 223.　　　　　　　[3] Ibid., p. 179.

at £126,000.[1] Mackenzie not merely got a knighthood for his exploration but was able to purchase an estate in Ross-shire. William McGillivray purchased an estate in Argyllshire for £20,000. The entertaining at Montreal seems to have been lavish and one meal lasted from four o'clock in the afternoon to four in the morning and 120 bottles of wine were said to have been consumed by the dozen or so participants.[2]

In 1821 the Hudson's Bay Company and the North West Company united under the name of the former Company. It was obviously better business to put an end to the rivalry and no doubt the North West Company was influenced by the fact that the Red River Settlement might be used by the rival Company in such a way as to obstruct their traffic. The details seem to have been arranged in England, where feeling did not run so high. The violent spirit engendered in the struggles of the rival fur traders made it impossible to look for an impartial or reasonable outlook in Canada. It was a conflict between the aims of settlement and the interests of fur and in Montreal fur was king. The new Company bound itself to limit the supply of liquor to Indians. The general result was that all furs and trade began to take the Hudson Bay route and that Montreal ceased to be the great fur port until the development of steam shipping and improved overland communications restored some of its former importance as a fur centre. Profits after 1821 drained off to London. Less was spent in the country and Lower Canada lost by the transference.

The British North American Act, 1867, authorized the admission of Rupert's Land into the Union, and the Rupert's Land Act, 1868, enabled that provision to be carried out by authorizing the acceptance by Her Majesty of the surrender of the " lands, privileges and rights " of the Hudson's Bay Company, the Company only retaining the right to continue to carry on trade and commerce in that territory. The terms embodied in the deed of surrender which was signed in 1869 included the payment of £300,000 to the Hudson's Bay Company by the Government of Canada and the retention by the Company of all their posts and stations. It was not, however, until the following year,

[1] Borthwick, *History of Montreal*, pp. 213–14; cited by G. Myers, *History of Canadian Wealth*, vol. i, p. 62.
[2] Landmann, *Adventures and Recollections*, vol. i, pp. 233–8, quoted Davidson, pp. 243–4.

when the Manitoba Act was passed, that the long struggle between settlement and the fur trade finally died down.

Perhaps the most important incident in the development of the fur trade after the amalgamation of the Companies was the duel between the new Hudson's Bay Company and the Americans on the Pacific coast.

Before 1811 there was no permanent settlement on the Pacific coast in connexion with the fur trade. The coast was, however, frequented by traders from Boston. Although the North Westers established their first station in the Rockies in 1807 and David Thompson wintered there then, and, although Spokane House was founded as another post in 1810, these was no coastal settlement. The Pacific was simply the land's end and communications were solely overland.[1]

The Americans and their ships dominated the coast, but Astoria, purchased in 1813, gave the Company their first permanent station on the Pacific itself and vessels were sent out from England to carry on trade in those waters, the *Isaac Todd* being one.

The East India Company, which had a monopoly of the trade between Cape Horn and the Cape of Good Hope, objected to its monopoly being infringed, and so the North West Company simply employed Boston ships to do their trans-Pacific trade for them. In this way they shipped their furs to China.

The trade was not always profitable, however.[2] When the Companies amalgamated, the Hudson's Bay Company put forth its strength, now no longer absorbed by the rivalry at home, to meet the rivalry of the Americans, and the Company was eventually successful in eliminating the Americans as traders.[3] In 1837 the Hudson's Bay Company was said to have fully occupied the country between the Rocky Mountains and the Pacific with six permanent stations on the coast and sixteen in the interior.[4] The territory now

---

[1] T. C. Elliott, "Fur Trade in Columbia River Basin prior to 1811," *Washington Hist. Quarterly*, 1915, vol. 6, pp. 5, 9.

[2] So unprofitable was it in the years 1818–22 and so difficult of management that several of the leading and most intelligent persons in the country strongly recommended that the Company should abandon it altogether. Statement of Hudson's Bay Company laid before Parliament 8th August, 1842, cited R. M. Martin, *Hudson Bay Territories and Vancouver Island*, 1849, pp. 53–4. Statements of the Company need some verification as they did not wish to invite rivalry and were anxious to accentuate their great services.

[3] Martin, op. cit., p. 54. [4] Ibid., p. 57.

known as Oregon, Washington and Idaho was claimed by the United States, but a series of ten year treaties left the question of ownership unsettled till 1846.[1]

The Hudson's Bay Company was also so successful in eliminating Russian competition that it had practically ceased by 1840. The Indians apparently preferred to trade with the Hudson's Bay Company and the Hudson's Bay blanket was the standard all along the coast in the Indian trade.[2]

The Company had a " steam vessel heavily armed which runs along the coast, and among its bays and inlets, for the twofold purpose of trading with the natives in places where they have no post and of outbidding and out-selling any American vessel that attempts to trade in those seas. They likewise have sailing vessels measuring from 100 to 500 tons burthen and armed with cannon, muskets, cutlasses, etc. These are employed a part of the year in various kinds of trade about the coast and the islands of the North Pacific and the remainder of the time in bringing goods from London and bearing back the furs for which they are exchanged." [3]

The Pacific Coast was known as the Columbia Department and at one time there was exported from there a quarter of the Company's beaver skins. By the end of the 'thirties, in the Southern areas the beaver and other furs seem to have worked out and a move north was made to the wilder and colder sections. It was the deliberate policy of the Company apparently to have a fur-less border so as to offer no inducements to other traders.[4]

As the Oregon region lost its value for furs the Company promoted agriculture, lumbering and salmon fisheries. It was said that they " had laid out farms on the most extensive scale, erected mills, established manufactures, entered into the fisheries, employed vessels for the purposes of commerce." [5]

---

[1] C. O. Ermatinger, " Columbia River under Hudson's Bay Co. Rule," *Wash. Hist. Quarterly*, 1914, vol. v, p. 195.

[2] C. L. Andrews, " Alaska under the Russians," *Wash. Hist. Quarterly*, 1916, vol. 7, p. 290.

[3] Wilkes, *History of Oregon*, 1845, reprinted *Wash. Hist. Quarterly*, 1907, vol. 2, p. 65.

[4] " In certain parts of the country it is the Company's policy to destroy them (the fur-bearing animals) all along the whole frontier ; and our general instructions recommend that every effort be made to lay waste the country, so as to offer no inducement to petty traders to encroach on the Company's limits." J. McLean, *Notes of Twenty-five Years Service in Hudson's Bay Territory*, 1849, vol. i, p. 262.

[5] Wilkes, *History of Oregon*, 1845, p. 87.

At the rearrangement of 1846, land south of the forty-ninth parallel was delivered over to America, and that meant that the cultivatable land, or what looked like it, was given to the United States. The rest was rocky, inhospitable country north of forty-nine, which was suitable enough for fur traders but not for settlers, and only slowly did the valleys and pockets of cultivation become known and timber assert its importance. Vancouver Island as a whole was given to Great Britain, and it was granted to the Company in 1848. On the whole this region remained an unknown outpost of British trade. The Company stated before the Committee of 1857 that they had spent £80,000 in sending out settlers and miners to work the coal mines of Vancouver Island but colonization had made little impression. When gold was discovered in 1856, and miners began to flock in and order had to be kept, it was the natural thing that the factor of the Hudson's Bay Company should become the Governor who administered the region for England.

CHAPTER 6

UPPER CANADA (ONTARIO)

THE planting of the Loyalists in Ontario was an epoch-making event, although not more than about 10,000 of them went to Upper Canada, while approximately 35,000 [1] went to the Maritime Provinces. As soon as settlement was undertaken so far inland with the barrier of the rapids and the Niagara Falls between the new Colony and the outside world, a new colonial policy was initiated. The sea tradition was given up, since no vessel could penetrate above Montreal. Emigrants and goods had to be transferred to that type of flat-bottomed boat known as *bateaux* in order to navigate the rapids. Therefore when it came to settling Upper Canada the Mother Country had to begin to think in terms of land development rather than in terms of the carrying trade and the necessary naval protect-tion. A policy of inner colonization was initiated and a continental instead of a coastal policy was the outcome.

It was the growth of population in Ontario that began

---

[1] W. Stewart Wallace, *The United Empire Loyalists*, pp. 62–3.

the Anglicization of Canada. Originally only a few isolated settlements, a mere apology for a colony, this region, by reason of its fertility, its situation and its climate, began to attract British, German and American emigrants so that it outstripped in importance the old French colony of Quebec. The Maritime Provinces were isolated from the rest of the continent. Ontario was a plantation of English interests right in the middle of American interests, and its economic development so prospered that, with neither the fisheries nor the lumber trade of New Brunswick or Quebec, nor the coal of Nova Scotia, as an economic background, it became the most important part, economically speaking, of the whole. That Canada is now British with a French Province, and not French with English settlements like raisins in a pudding, is due to the settlement and subsequent economic history of Ontario, originally known as Upper Canada.

The leading fact about the development of Upper Canada was the succession of rapids and falls which divided the Lakes from the St. Lawrence. These made transport too costly for anything but the most valuable oak and pine timber until the canals were made, and the Province had to adopt a self-sufficing basis instead of resting on exchange. Quebec, with the Saguenay, St. Maurice and Ottawa Rivers all giving access to the St. Lawrence at points where ocean-going vessels could reach the lumber or from where it could be easily floated to Quebec for shipment, became the great lumber Province after the grant of preferences by England.[1] She also had an important fishing industry. This was not so in Upper Canada, where the only things to exchange were potash and furs, and as settlement proceeded, furs became scarcer. The cost of transporting wheat even to Lower Canada was so high that until the canals were developed it prevented a wheat export except at famine prices. This had a determining influence on the whole development of the Province. If hired labour had to be employed to raise wheat, the cost of wheat production became too heavy for export and this made large scale farming for an overseas market impossible. Hence Upper Canada was necessarily a Province of small farms with family labour, and it depended on the restricted local market afforded by the garrisons, the canal workers and the

---

[1] Cf. Petition of Quebec Merchants in 1830 against any reduction of the Timber Preferences, printed in *Parly. Papers*, 1830–1, x, pp. 481–4.

Ottawa lumber camps. Nor, apart from the difficulty of transport, was it at first a country for the lumberman. The lumberman only wanted the big trees. He left the undergrowth and small stuff. The small farmer wants a clearance of all timber, not selected logs. Hence he chopped and burnt and made the potash from the ashes with which he bought flour and supplies.

A certain amount of valuable timber was cut in the neighbourhood of the Trent and floated down to the Bay of Quinte and on to Quebec. But it was a trade carried on under grave disadvantages.

Montreal and Quebec, the one the depôt of merchandise and the other the centre of the lumber trade, were far away and could then only be reached by a navigation which, on account of its rapids, was difficult and dangerous.

" There was but little money and business was conducted on an understood basis of exchange or barter. During the winter months the farmer threshed his grain and brought it, with his pork and potash, to the merchant, who gave him goods for his family in return. The merchant was usually a lumberman as well, and he busied himself in the winter time in getting out timber and hauling it to the Bay of Quinte, where it was rafted and made ready for moving early in the spring. As soon as navigation was open, barges and *bateaux* were loaded with potash and produce, and he set sail with these and his rafts down the river. It was always a voyage of hardship and danger. If good fortune attended him he would in the course of three or four weeks make Montreal, and Quebec with his raft two or three weeks later. Then commenced the labour of disposing of his stuff, settling up the year's accounts and purchasing more goods with which his boats were loaded and despatched for home. . . . By the time he got home two or three months had been consumed." [1]

While chloride of lime and soda began to cheapen potash at the end of the 'thirties, it was still an important export in the 'fifties, and by the time it was ousted by chemicals an agricultural development and a wheat export had grown up in its place. Potash is made by burning the hardwood trees like oak, not soft wood like pine. These, unlike the pine, only grow on good soil. Thus it was an export of Upper and not Lower Canada. It was a valuable help to

[1] C. Haight, *Life in Canada Fifty Years Ago*, 1885, pp. 241–3.

the early settlers because the good soil bearing hardwood trees was just the type of land that they would want to clear and the ashes from the trees they felled and then burnt gave them almost at once an exchangeable commodity.

It was not till 1860 that timber assumed a great importance in Upper Canada. The railways first opened an internal market for lumber both for sleepers, stations and houses, and assisted to transport timber from places off the river routes. In 1827, only $360 came to the Treasury from licences to cut timber ; by 1867 the revenue was still only $150,000, enough however to manifest the development of the demand due to the railways. But between 1900 and 1910, the licence revenue averaged $1,750,000 per annum and the cut was said to be worth $30,000,000.[1] Ontario had become the great lumber Province and continued so until displaced about 1912 by British Columbia.

Apart from the returns for the furs and potash sold, the Colony was dependent to a large extent on the market created by the British garrison quartered there to defend the country from the United States and on the demands of the Ottawa lumber camps. The Colony had the greatest difficulty in paying for its imports of tea, sugar, axes, saws, and clothing materials, and was continually exporting the coin which came in for the payment of the garrisons or which was brought in by emigrants to pay the balance. There was a great shortage of coinage and barter or payment in kind was general.

Bonnycastle, writing in 1846,[2] speaks of the saw mills at Seymour being " ready to saw whatever timber the farmer has left into boards and planks for him, receiving so many feet of timber, and giving so many feet of lumber " in return. " The flour mills at Percy proceed upon the same principle ; a farmer brings sacks of grain and receives sacks of flour in exchange, said exchange being of course three to one, or more, against him. Throughout Canada is this truck or barter system pursued, and very little money finds its way either into or out of the back townships, unless it be the receipts of the lumber-merchants from Quebec or the lakes."

Another writer says : " The skins of the cattle, calves and sheep that were slaughtered for the wants of the family were taken to the tanners, who dressed them and returned

[1] *C.P.*, vol. xviii, pp. 585–6.
[2] *Canada and the Canadians*, vol. ii, pp. 253–4.

half of each hide. The currency of the day was flour, pork and potash. The first two were in demand for the lumber-men's shanties and the last went to Montreal for export. . . . Vegetables were unsaleable and so were many other things for which the farmer now finds a ready market." [1]

Struggling poverty was the most salient characteristic of Upper Canada, and, just as the diminution of the British timber preference roused the merchants of Montreal to fury, so the disappearance of the wheat preferences when the Corn Laws were repealed reacted unfavourably on Upper Canada, on the American transit trade in wheat, and on Montreal, which handled the wheat and which, though situated in Quebec Province, was an outpost of Upper Canada.

Another circumstance which threw Upper Canada to a large extent on its own resources was the fact that all its exports and imports had to pass by way of the French Province, which levied customs duties on the goods. The only successful type of settlement where the difficulties of reaching or being reached by the outside world were so great would be group settlement on a self-sufficing basis. And the early history of Ontario is the history of groups under military authorities, or a leader, or a company which could organize economic life. This explains the large land grants to such men as Talbot or to associations like the Canada Company. Only capitalists with resources enabling them to plan things on a considerable scale could undertake the expensive task of surveying for roads, building flour and saw mills, and furnishing provisions for at least a year and so make a successful start in settling Upper Canada. Then others would join them. It was quite useless to send out a mass of unattached emigrants to Upper Canada hoping that they would find their feet somehow. In the Maritime Provinces and Quebec there was the demand for labour connected with lumber. In Ontario there was only land from which the forest had to be cleared (hence the saying, " Canada is a clearing "), and this necessitated a long wait before a living could be made. The bulk of the fur trade went by the Ottawa River and had little influence on the development of Ontario.

The first task was to obtain a population that would tackle the great enemy, the forest. After that there ensued a long period of struggle somewhat lightened by the

[1] C. Haight, *Life in Canada Fifty Years Ago*, pp. 105–6.

construction of the canals to avoid the rapids. This canal building brought money into the country, provided employment for emigrants and a market for food-stuffs. With the canals it was possible to develop a wheat trade, and a considerable impetus was given to Ontario by the steamers which made all communications easier and brought more emigrants to the Western parts of Canada. But even then the Erie Canal, and later the construction of the American railways, deprived Upper Canada of a great deal of the transport trade that it hoped to gain from the Canadian canal system. Early Canada was unfortunate in its deferred hopes and blighted prospects. First, it was just capturing the carrying trade in connexion with the Great Lakes via the St. Lawrence, when the Erie Canal was constructed and drew the carrying trade back into American channels. Secondly, it had just completed its own canals as a counterblast to the Erie Canal at great cost and was drawing to itself the carrying trade again when the advent of railways in the United States drew back trade once more into American channels.

Not till the 'fifties was there a real and striking advance in Upper Canada and that was due to the railways. A self-sufficing, struggling existence was the leading feature of its early economic life.

The Province of Ontario is about three and a half times the size of the British Isles, but most of it is in the Laurentian plateau and consists of forest or ice-bound fur lands. The Ontario that counts from an economic point of view is the axe head and coastal strip along Lakes Ontario, Erie, and Huron, some five hundred miles long and about a hundred miles in depth. It is about the size of England.

On the disbanding of the Loyalist regiments, some of them were settled in Ontario, which had already become known as playing a part in the scheme for the defence of Lower Canada which was partly based on the Lakes. Land was bought from the Indians, surveys were made and a scheme instituted for allotting land. The Loyalists were conveyed by boat up the St. Lawrence and with each party were sent tents, clothing, provisions and tools. The first regiment (Royal Regiment of New York or Royal Greens) was taken to what is now Cornwall and the land was drawn for by lots. Many of these men were Scottish Highlanders and German Palatinates. Tools were given out as well as rations and *bateaux* were provided for each township. Saw

mills and flour mills were established along the streams.   The
amount of land allotted was a hundred acres to the head
of a family and fifty more for each person in that family.
A non-commissioned officer got 200 acres, a private 100,
their family 50 apiece.   Every field officer was entitled to
1,000 acres, a captain to 700 and a subaltern to 500.   Land
Boards and Courts organized in each district continued
to grant lands to those " late loyalists " who came in during
the rest of the century.   An extra 200 acres was granted
in 1787 to those who had improved their lands. The
organization of settlement and the distribution of rations
was done by officers.

Land was also purchased in the tracts between Lakes
Ontario, Erie and Huron for the settlement of the Mohawks
and such others of the Six Nations as had supported the
British cause.

Many Americans in the depression after the Revolutionary
War came to Canada and settled along the shores of Lakes
Erie and Ontario.   They, too, took the oath of allegiance
and received land grants.   Indeed a great advertising
campaign was carried on in the United States to get
immigrants, as the wars prevented their arrival from Great
Britain.

It was difficult at first to get immigrants from the United
States as Canada was under French Law, as was formally
recognized in 1774, and that, being largely feudal, was
considered a hampering system by an enterprising go-ahead
people.   They desired to live under the Law they had been
accustomed to, English Law, which protected the rights
of property and of contract in a way which they understood.
In 1791, accordingly, the two Provinces of Upper Canada
(Ontario) and Lower Canada (Quebec) were constituted
each with its own Legislative Council and Assembly [1] so
that Upper Canada was definitely placed under the English
system of laws.   This encouraged emigration from across
the border to Upper Canada rather than to Quebec.

In 1793, to encourage the more influential people of Upper
Canada to bring in settlers, very large areas were granted
to these undertakers.   Many of these new American settlers
were convinced republicans and had no hesitation about
proclaiming their doctrines.   The war of 1812 showed the
danger of granting land recklessly to persons holding these
far from loyal views and caused a re-action in favour of

[1] The Constitutional Act, 1791 (31 Geo. III, cap. xxxi).

securing settlers from the United Kingdom. Many of the settlers were not of British extraction. Quakers from Pennsylvania and New Jersey, who had been non-combatants during the war of 1776, found the disorder in America more than they could bear and emigrated to the flag where law and order still existed. Mennonites (i.e. descendants of Menno Simons brought over by Penn) and Dunkers of Dutch and German origin also came and were joined by others from Germany. These settled in the Niagara district and the counties of York and Waterloo. People did not just wander in by themselves; emigration was organized by officers of the Crown or by various enterprising persons who hoped to make their land grants valuable and at the same time assist poverty-stricken persons. In very few cases were these plans successful. The emigrants usually turned against the promoters, who had spent considerable sums of money in bringing them into the country and could not recover the advances. Berczy, who said he had lost £30,000 on German emigrants,[1] and de Puisaye, who also failed with French emigrés after the French Revolution, were but precursors of Lord Selkirk, McNab, and others. On the other hand, Colonel Talbot, who was on the staff of Governor Simcoe, obtained a grant of 5,000 acres and founded a very successful settlement on the north shore of Lake Erie which is commemorated in the name of Port Talbot. He obtained further grants of land of 65,000 acres on condition of securing colonists, and altogether the area of his lands amounted to 540,443 acres, which he began to settle in 1809 with men from Pennsylvania, Highlanders, Quakers, and some Irish. His settlement suffered in the war of 1812, but further Scots arrived in 1819 from Argyllshire and settled at Aldborough. Other settlers followed. Talbot was successful because he made roads, but he was not unduly lenient with his people and saw that he was paid what he was owed.[2] He was naturally not particularly popular. He claimed that he had placed 20,000 persons on lands without any cost to the Government but at a cost of £20,000 to himself. He stands out as one of the few successful individual organisers. Companies would naturally have a stronger financial backing. By 1831 the settlers he had been influential in locating were

---

[1] *C.P.*, vol. xvii, p. 51.
[2] J. H. Coyne, *Talbot Papers*, p. 54.

estimated at 40,000. Mrs. Jameson in 1838 speaks of the good roads in the Talbot settlement and gives the following description of Talbot and his methods.[1]

" For sixteen years he saw scarce a human being except the few boors and blacks employed in clearing and logging his land. He himself assumed the blanket coat and axe, slept on the bare earth, cooked three meals a day for twenty woodsmen, cleaned his own boots, washed his own linen, milked his cows, churned the butter and made and baked the bread."

He granted the usual 200 acres, 50 gratis and 150 at $3 per acre. Each settler had to clear and sow 10 acres, build a log hut and construct one chain of road in three years or forfeit the land.

Howison [2] described the settlement in 1821 as follows :—

" Few of the farms in the more improved parts of the Province retain their original owners, who have generally been bought out by people of similar habits, but greater wealth ; and new settlements have hitherto almost invariably changed their inhabitants within ten or twelve years after their commencement. It is to be hoped that this will be the fate of the Talbot Settlement, and that its present occupants will henceforth gradually disappear and be succeeded by a population of a superior kind. That this will be the case seems highly probable, for emigrants of some capital now begin to make their appearance in the Province, and most of them will of course rather purchase partially improved farms at a moderate rate than expose themselves to the hardships and difficulties that attend the clearing and cultivation of waste land. The advantages which the Talbot Settlement presents will induce many persons of this description to take up their residence in it, more especially as a large number of the farms will soon be offered for sale, at a low price, by their present possessors.

" The Talbot Settlement exhibits more visibly than any other part of the Province these advantages and that amelioration of circumstances which Upper Canada affords to the peasantry who emigrate from Europe. Nine-tenths of the inhabitants were extremely poor when they commenced their labours, but a few years' toil and perseverance has placed them beyond the reach of want. All of them have rude houses and barns, also cows and oxen,

---

[1] *Sketches in Canada*, p. 103.
[2] *Sketches of Upper Canada*, pp. 170–3.

and innumerable hogs. Some of the wealthier settlers feed sheep, but on most lots the quantity of cleared land is so small that they cannot afford to lay much of it out on pasture. Most of the settlers might live much more comfortably than they do at present if they exerted themselves, or had any ideas of neatness and propriety; but they follow the habits and customs of the peasantry of the United States, and of Scotland, and consequently are offensively dirty, gross, and indolent in all their domestic arrangements. However, these, it is to be hoped, are temporary evils, and do not at all affect the conclusions that a view of this settlement must force upon every unprejudiced mind. It is evident that the advantages to be derived from emigration to Upper Canada are not altogether chimerical, as has been too generally supposed; but that, in so far as concerns the lower classes of Europeans, they are equally numerous and important, as some of our most sanguine speculators have represented them to be. No person, indeed, will pretend to say that the settlers, whose condition I have described, are in a way to grow rich; but most of them even now enjoy abundant means of subsistence, with the earnest of increasing comforts; and what state of things can be more alluring and desirable than this to the unhappy peasantry of Europe?

" Great numbers of emigrants, from the Highlands of Scotland, have lately taken lands in the upper part of the Talbot Settlement. These people, with the *clannishness* so peculiar to them, keep together as much as possible; and at one time, they actually proposed, among themselves, to petition the governor to set apart a township into which none but Scotch were to be admitted. Were this arrangement to take place, it would be difficult to say which party was the gainer, the habits of both being equally uncouth and obnoxious. However, the Scotch, notwithstanding their dislike to an American and Canadian neighbourhood, do not fail to acquire some of those ideas and principles that are indigenous to this side of the Atlantic. They soon begin to attain some conception of the advantages of equality, to consider themselves as gentlemen, and become independent; which, in North America, means to sit at meals with one's hat on; never to submit to be treated as an inferior; and to use the same kind of manners towards all men."

Other Scottish Highlanders continued to come to reinforce

the Loyalists in Ontario. In 1786 five hundred settlers from Glengarry arrived and were joined by more Highlanders in 1792 and 1803. This settlement provided no less than two regiments at the beginning of the war of 1812. Lord Selkirk also settled 111 Highlanders at Baldoon in Ontario in 1804, but was not successful in making a permanent colony, partly on account of the swampy situation of the land, partly because the settlement was raided in 1812 and again in 1813, and the thousand merino sheep provided by Lord Selkirk were driven off to Detroit.

The war of 1812 advertised Upper Canada and for a time the settlers were exceedingly prosperous in supplying the troops, and many of them obtained much-needed gold as compensation for losses. After that there was a great depression. The general effect was summarized by a contemporary British traveller as follows :—

" The last war was productive of most injurious consequences to the colony, and these have not been counterbalanced by a single advantage, except that the militia now feel a confidence in the efficiency of their arms, which may induce them to take the field with boldness and alacrity should hostilities again commence. Before the declaration of war took place, Upper Canada was in a state of progressive though slow improvement, and her inhabitants prudently attempted such exertions only as were proportioned to their means. Agriculture was pursued by all classes, and few thought of enriching themselves by any other occupation. But militia duty obliged them to abandon their farms, which were of course neglected—the lands became waste, the cattle were carried away, and the buildings perhaps burnt by the enemy. However, the military establishments had brought such an influx of money into the country, that everyone forgot his distresses, and thought himself on the high road to wealth, when he found he could sell anything he possessed for double its real value, and have his pockets stuffed with army bills, as a recompense for some trifling service done to government. At this time, the abundance of circulating medium, and the liberality with which it was expended, induced many people to bring large quantities of goods from Montreal, and retail stores soon became numerous in every part of the country. As the people continued to buy a great deal and to pay for a great deal, the merchants willingly allowed them unlimited credit, erroneously supposing that their customers would always be able to discharge their debts, and that the temporary wealth of the Province would continue. But when peace was restored, when the troops were withdrawn, and all military operations suspended, the people soon perceived that a sad reverse awaited them. They found that the circulation of money gradually decreased, that they could no longer revel upon the bounty of a profuse Government, and that they began to grow poorer every day ; while the prospect of returning to their ravaged and uncultivated farms afforded but little consolation, as the spirit of industry had been extinguished by the lavish manner in which most of them had lived during the war. As a large portion of the live stock which the country contained had been carried away by the enemy, or consumed by our own troops, the farmers were obliged to purchase cattle from the Americans, and thus the country was still further drained of much of the circulating specie, and in a way too that produced no commercial advantages.

" In course of time, the Montreal wholesale merchants began to urge their correspondents in the Upper Province for remittances, which many of the latter could not make ; for, on applying to those whom they had formerly trusted to a large amount, they found that, with a few exceptions, they were alike unable and unwilling to discharge their debts. The country thus fell into a state of embarrassment, which continues to increase : most of the merchants have very large outstanding debts, which, if collected by means of suits, would ruin two-thirds of the farmers in the Province ; and should the Montreal wholesale dealers have recourse to similar measures, many of their correspondents would become insolvent likewise. Both parties, therefore, judiciously temporize, being satisfied that it is, at present, the most advantageous policy they can pursue.

" The war has thus been the main cause of the present embarrassed and unpromising state of Upper Canada, and produced this effect in three different ways : first it was the means of withdrawing the minds of its inhabitants from their usual pursuits and occupations ; next it extinguished that steadiness and spirit of industry which had formerly characterized them ; and, lastly, it created a temporary wealth in the Province which induced the people to be lavish in every respect, and contract debts that were altogether disproportionate to their means of payment. Time has in some degree ameliorated the two first bad effects ;

but the merchants have been, and will be, the means of perpetuating the last."[1]

Canadians, however, received from one to one and a half million dollars compensation for the losses from the British Government, some of which went to Lower Canada.[2]

The victory, as a matter of fact, had the effect of giving the Canadian Provinces a belief in themselves and stimulated a growing nationality. From the point of view of land settlement, it had the effect of preventing any more land grants being given to Americans who were republicans and it turned men's attention to recruiting men of loyalty from the United Kingdom. After 1812 the question whether British influence would predominate in Canada was no longer in doubt.

The depression in Europe following the French wars, after 1815, gave a new impetus to emigration. Moreover, after the American War of 1812 it seemed desirable to people Canada with soldiers and Englishmen who could defend it against annexation. There was the usual problem of disbanding the army after 1816 and the idea grew up of settling the ex-soldiers along a route leading from the Ottawa to Kingston, which would avoid the St. Lawrence and so give an alternative route of communication in case of further war with the United States. The Rideau Canal was projected, the Ottawa River was to be improved and soldiers and loyal persons settled along the banks. Emigrants from Scotland were brought in, and, having started in May, were landed at Quebec in September,[3] which shows the time sometimes taken on the voyage. They settled at Perth and to them came the disbanded soldiers of the Glengarry Fencible Regiment and others from Scotland and Ulster. The military authorities granted them rations, clothes and tools. Each settler had a hundred acres and had to clear part of it and live on it to obtain the title. Here again rations and settlement were organized by officers.

Howison,[4] writing in 1821, thus describes the settlement :

" As our road lay through the Glengarry settlement, I had an opportunity next morning of seeing it, and was

---

[1] Howison, op. cit., pp. 79–82.
[2] James Stuart, *Three Years in North America*, p. 157, cited by Bracq, p. 44.
[3] *C.P.*, vol. xvii, p. 76.
[4] Op. cit., pp. 20–1.

rather disappointed, the improvements bearing no proportion to what I had anticipated. The majority of its inhabitants were indeed very poor when they commenced their labours, and had a variety of discouraging circumstances to contend with, the principal of which were, the peculiarities of the climate, the almost inaccessible situation of their farms, the badness of the roads, and the immense woods which encumbered the soil. They have, in some degree, surmounted the greater number of these difficulties ; but still the settlement is not in a very flourishing state, and its inhabitants seem too unambitious to profit by the advantages of their condition. A very great majority of the houses are built of logs, and contain only one apartment ; and the possessors display no inclination to improve their mode of life, being dirty, ignorant and obstinate. Few of the settlers have more than sixty or seventy acres cleared, and the generality only thirty or forty ; yet, how many comforts, and even luxuries, might persons of moderate industry derive from a domain of this extent !

" While they were preparing breakfast, at the tavern at which I had stopped, I strolled out for amusement. Diminutive log-houses, surrounded with a few acres of cleared land, presented themselves in various directions, and the feeble vestiges of civilization which these objects exhibited, seemed to be derided by the clumps of immense oaks that everywhere waved their colossal boughs as if threatening destruction to all below. A profusion of decayed and half-burnt timber lay around, and the serpentine roots of trees, blown down by tempests, stretched into the air in the most fantastic forms. In different places, piles of blazing timber sent forth columns of smoke, which enveloped the forests far and wide. . . ."

The county of Lanark was also peopled from Scotland on much the same terms, except that they received their fare to Quebec and were transported by the Government from Quebec to their settlement and were given £6 in cash. About 1,200 emigrants came out in this way.[1]

All over England, Scotland and Ireland emigration societies sprang up to help people out to Canada. The Hon. Peter Robinson was a man who brought out a large number of Irishmen and settled them near the present town of Peterborough in 1825, having first made a road to convey his people inland from the lake, and so effected a penetration

---

[1] *C.P.*, vol. xvii, p. 77.

into the uplands. Rations were provided by the Government for a year and a half. Each family was provided with a cow, an axe, an auger, a handsaw, a hundred nails, two gimlets, three hoes, one kettle, one frying-pan, one iron pot, five bushels of seed potatoes and eight quarts of Indian corn.[1] These people suffered terribly from dysentery, plague and ague. The town after the advent of the railways became a great timber centre and is now an important manufacturing town with electric power derived from its water power.

The MacNab, a Scottish Highland chief flying from his creditor, the Earl of Breadalbane, came to Canada and obtained in 1823 the grant of 80,000 acres on the Ottawa in the county of Renfrew and named it MacNab. He was to have 1,200 acres for himself and to bring over settlers. His friends and relations advanced money to bring out twenty-one Scottish families (eighty-four persons). They arrived at the settlement from Montreal in twenty-eight days and were followed by further families, all of whom were to reimburse the passage money and other expenses and to pay for their land. The usual difficulty of making a living in uncleared forest occurred, the payments were not made and the immigrants blamed the chief, who was accused of holding them in feudal vassalage. After a time the township prospered, but The MacNab was bought out by the Government for $16,000.

It would seem as if the original planner of a settlement, like the first settler, could never make a success of it. Very different, however, was the course of the Canada Company.

The Canada Company was perhaps the most successful of all the colonizing companies. It owed its inception to the fact that a Scotsman, John Galt, was appointed agent in England to press the claims of those in Canada who were entitled to compensation for the destruction of their property by the Americans in the war of 1812. There were all sorts of difficulties in the way of compensation. Galt proposed to found a Company which should take over some of the vacant public lands, the money paid for their purchase to be used to compensate his clients.

Under Imperial legislation, one-seventh of the land in each township had been reserved for the Crown as a future source of profit and one-seventh was allotted for the maintenance of the Protestant clergy. These were known

[1] Ibid., p. 86.

as the Crown Reserves and the Clergy Reserves. They were very unpopular. Nothing that the British Government did in Canada ever went uncriticized—that was the tradition inherited from the United States—and these islands of undeveloped land provided a first-class grievance. It was said that these Reserves prevented roads being made and that they were " wild beast reserves " or " wolf reserves ". Any increase in their value would, so it was said, be due to the enterprise of the farmers on adjoining lands. As Great Britain had constantly to make up deficits in the Civil List, there seemed on the face of it no reason why the Crown should not make some profit out of some portion of the land it was granting so freely. But the Reserves were a useful scapegoat. Then it was said that these detached islands of waste prevented closer settlement. But it need not have been so if purchasers had been forthcoming, the Government being only too anxious to turn the land into money. Galt's proposal was that a Company—the Canada Company—should purchase these Reserves from the Crown. This would remove the grievance because the Company would have to promote settlement. Accordingly an agreement was reached by which the Company was to purchase 1,384,413 acres of Crown Reserves and 829,430 acres of Clergy Reserves. As the Anglican Church was opposed to the sale of the Clergy Reserves the Company was given instead a solid block of unexplored, unsurveyed land of 1,100,000 acres known as the Huron Tract on the shores of the lake.[1] The Clergy Reserves remained the subject of sectarian jealousy and strife until 1854, when a complete measure of disestablishment and disendowment decreed separation of Church and State and the payment of a commuted sum to existing incumbents, the balance of lands and funds being divided among the municipalities. The Company obtained its charter in August, 1826. Galt was placed in charge of the operations, and he determined to make road building precede settlement. Like many of these leaders of pioneer settlements, he encountered endless difficulties not only with the settlers but with the Colonial Office and the local government, and he retired in 1829. The Company was, however, a great success as far as colonization was concerned, and brought out some of the best settlers to Canada.[2]

[1] See S. C. Johnson, *A History of Emigration from the United Kingdom to North America*, 1763–1912, pp. 216–17.

[2] Some of their difficulties of persuading emigrants are described in a

Apart from road-making, the Company concentrated on developing large blocks at a time, thus avoiding isolated settlement. Guelph, Goderich, Stratford, and St. Mary's are all prosperous towns on their lands, and the Huron tract is one of the most flourishing sections of the Province.

The importance of the work of the Canada Company lies in the fact that it initiated the settlement of the Midland and Western areas. Previously, except for Talbot's settlement, the bulk of the people had congregated round Kingston, as that was the easiest point to reach. The Rideau and Ottawa Canal system also helped settlement in the Eastern portion of the Province. But the Canada Company initiated a corresponding development of the Western region and contributed to the growth of Toronto by providing it with a central hinterland of settlers with whom it could trade.

An account of the Company and its methods of attracting emigrants is contained in a pamphlet of 1844 entitled *Lands in Canada West to be disposed of by the Canada Company*. It speaks of there being 11,000 persons on their Huron Tract in 1843, and above 70,000 acres of land disposed of within the year and describes the twelve grist mills and twenty saw mills of the district. "Seventeen of the townships are bounded on one side by the great roads traversing the tract in two directions for about a 100 miles in extent and six of them are bounded by the Lake on the other side." The price of land varied from 8s. to 17s. 6d. an acre ; one-fifth of the purchase money to be paid down, the balance in five equal annual instalments. The Company was also willing to lease with the option of converting into freehold.

The Company furnished some figures for the report on

pamphlet : "Hints and Observations on the Disadvantages of Emigration to British North America" by an Emigrant, 1833 :

" During the voyage it was not a little amusing to listen to the conversations of some of our sanguine fellow-passengers with regard to their future prospects. Many already imagined themselves in possession of large farms, well stocked, and promising all the abundance which fertility and labour could elicit ; whilst others, on the contrary, began to bewail their precipitancy, and to believe that they had been woefully misled by the Canada Company's agent at Great Yarmouth, who had caused large bills to be posted up in the villages, with the figure of a vessel in full sail gliding, apparently motionless, through the ' ocean stream '. ' For,' said they, ' had we known that the ship would have rocked and tossed about thus we would never have ventured on board.' The fact was, that nine-tenths of the passengers had never even seen the ocean, as the following anecdote will testify : Several families from the inland villages, on arriving at Yarmouth, refused to emigrate because they positively believed that they should have been able *to see America in the distance !* "

Highland Destitution in 1841 referring to its operations in the previous years. Of 724 settlers in 38 townships 327 had originally no property and were computed to be worth £116,228 9s. 6d., or on an average £334 17s. 9d. Another class consisting of 89 settlers originally possessing less than £20 had collectively £38,213 10s. 6d., an average of £429 7s. 4d. a head. A third class consisting of 298 persons who, when they arrived, had an average of £111 19s. 10d., were collectively in possession of £169,304 1s. 9d., being an average of £568 2s. per head, showing how the settlers prospered in proportion to the capital they brought.

The Company also stated that between 1844 and 1850 they had remitted no less than £77,661 on behalf of their settlers to persons in Britain.[1]

The Company was, and still is, a great financial success, for its methods, although criticized, were business-like. To its efforts Upper Canada owes a great deal. The Company realized that the better the class of immigrants they brought to the country, the more prosperous would be the settlement and the larger the returns. Accordingly they laid themselves out to attract and assist settlers of the better type.

Nevertheless, the very first settlers did not remain on the land, so confirming the general impression gathered from all writers that it is the second comers on partially cleared land who made good, rarely the first. Shirreff wrote thus :—

" I found the Canada Company very unpopular at Goderich, although Dr. Dunlop is a favourite amongst the settlers, who are of the poorest class, and seemingly without industry or energy of any kind. Indeed, when men despair of overcoming their pecuniary difficulties, which must have been the case with most of the first settlers, they are apt to become both indolent and dissipated. The Canada Company charges 7s. 6d. per acre for land, payable, with interest, by instalments ; and when a specified extent is taken, part of the settler's travelling expenses are allowed him out of the second instalment. This is a most disadvantageous regulation for emigrants, being a premium to purchase beyond their means of paying, and an unprofitable locking up, or perhaps rather transfer of capital, which cannot by possibility fail of ending in ruin, as it hath been proved by the whole history of American wood settlers, that they find it difficult,

---

[1] These figures and facts are taken from J. Cassell, *The Emigrants' Handbook*, 1852.

for the first three years with the utmost industry, to do more than maintain their families. In this case, the interest on the unpaid instalments is more than the cleared part of the farm will yield of profit at the end of five or six years, where a person trusts alone to his personal labour for improving. When all the instalments are duly paid, the price of the forest land, which seldom yields a blade of grass, and is totally unproductive, remains an overwhelming burden on what is cleared. Dr. Dunlop told me that only one of the original settlers continued to hold his land at the time of my visit to Goderich, and alluded to a cause for their removal, which I did not think likely to have produced the effect. The first settlers at Goderich were people of limited means, the majority of them paupers, and they soon became so involved to the Company as to induce them to leave the district. Many of the recent purchasers, perhaps forty or fifty of them, were working on the Company's road while I was present, which the Doctor told me was the only means by which they could render payment." [1]

The following account of the different nationalities settled on the Canada Company's lands is interesting as showing the different types and their characteristics as settlers :—

" From pretty close observation during the past eight years, I have come to the conclusion that the *Scotch* are the best and most successful of all emigrants. Come they with or without money, come they with great working sons, or with only little useless girls, it is all the same ; the Scotchman is sure to better his condition, and this very silently, and almost without a complaint. Of all the sons poor Scotchmen bring out with them, scarcely any become servants. I observe they work with and for their parents till the latter are well stocked in and securely provided for, when these young men betake themselves to land on their own account. This is worthy of notice, and should be imitated by others, as the greatest advantages are derived from the family having a head in good circumstances, and ready with its assistance in times of need. The industry, frugality, and sobriety of the Scotch mainly contribute to their success, and such habits are absolutely necessary to be rigidly followed by poor settlers on first entering the ' Bush '. I have carefully watched the progress and result of the Scotch, Irish, and English emigrants in the race to the goal desired by all, viz. to obtain a deed for their land, and

[1] Op. cit., p. 175.

find that, where all have appeared to me to be equally well mounted, and precisely the same course to go over and the same hills of difficulty to ascend, the Scotchman is generally first in at the winning-post. Next to the Scotch, I am of opinion the *Englishman* comes in for his meed of praise ; but it is infinitely more difficult to speak of him than of his *Scotch* or *Irish* neighbours, as every shade and grade of character, conduct, and success is to be found amongst the English in this place and its neighbouring townships ; suffice it to say, that were it not for a considerable number of good men from Yorkshire and Nottinghamshire, who are prospering in this part of Canada, I must have left my own countrymen to be noticed last. Generally speaking, English families do not hold together long enough to ensure success ; the sons of poor English emigrants leave their parents, and become servants at the usual high wages, and instead of saving money to purchase land, the same is squandered away in fine clothes and at the numerous country balls, etc. This course is followed up by taking a wife, becoming a common labourer, and hiring a smart house *in the town*, where he is determined his wife shall wear as rich a silk dress on a Sunday as any lady in the place. The lowest characters we have in Guelph, and pests they are, turn out to be English drunkards. I do not intend to make any attempt to deprive our *Irishmen* of their well-earned and well-known forte in making occasionally more noise than any other men when a little *high* ; but in common I find them more at their farms or at their respective callings than the English are. . . .

"I have now to speak of the Irish settlers, and what I have just said of English *gentlemen* will apply to the same class of Irish ; the only fault I find in some of them is a too frequent boiling over of their ardent opinions and feelings of loyalty upon unnecessary occasions, and a too frequent indulgence in invectives against sound constitutionalists, who do not, they think, come fully up to their idea of patriotic perfection. We have here a good many of the ' middle men ' of Ireland, who succeed well and make excellent settlers, adding to the wealth and strength of the province. In times of commotion these men show their loyalty, and were amongst the foremost of volunteers to defend the province against enemies within and without it. There is here a very remarkable difference between the educated and uneducated Irish ; nearly every man of the *former* does well for himself and family, and while he pays a cheerful deference to his superiors, comforts, supports and consoles himself with an assurance that he is a worthy descendant of some highly respected ancestors of universal renown, and in duty bound so to demean himself as not to bring disgrace upon the family escutcheon !

" A very large portion of *Irish* settlers hereabouts are composed of the *lower orders* of that country, and *because of their numbers* spoil the Irish sample of settlers. This class go upon land as soon as they arrive here, and being without means, make very slow progress . . ." [1]

Another Company was formed in London in 1861, The Canadian Land and Emigration Company, which purchased ten townships from the Crown Lands Department. The Company, however, came to an end in two years, but the towns it founded, Haliburton and Minden, prospered.

The difficulty about all emigration to Upper Canada was the way in which the emigrants drifted across to the United States and reinforced the Western expansion there. Artisans from Britain found the United States a much more attractive field. There was capital in the country made from the great cotton export and shipping ; there was town life, roads and much better opportunities. Only the poorer settlers and persons without a trade would go to Canada, such as the Irish, the Highlanders and some of the agricultural population of the South of England, especially the emigrants from Kent, Surrey, and Buckinghamshire. Many of these were despatched so as to relieve the parishes from the burden of keeping them out of the rates. The rebellion in Canada in 1837 did not tend to encourage the better class of emigrant, especially as it was followed by a depression in Canada itself.

The best type of emigrants were to be found among the small farmers, who found it impossible to hold on in England with war prices gone and war taxation remaining. This class usually had a little capital from the sale of their land. They were reinforced by many handloom weavers who were half farmers and who had been crowded out partly by the power loom and partly by the Irish who undercut them as handloom weavers.

---

[1] Letter of Dr. Alling, of Guelph, quoted in *A Statement of the Satisfactory Results which have attended Emigration to Upper Canada from the Establishment of the Canada Company until the Present Period*, 1841, pp. 14–15, 17–18.

Some of the emigrants were quite well-to-do and Bonny-castle says that in one year alone, 1832, forty thousand arrived in Upper Canada and brought half a million in sterling with them. "The new settlers of substance," he says, "were chiefly to be found in the Western districts. . . . The wild lands to the rear of Lake Ontario and the fertile district of Newcastle with the townships . . . in the Home district were rapidly settled by the poorer classes."[1]

The pauper type seems to have been universally condemned, but the pauper who is a failure makes himself obvious, whereas the pauper who becomes a success does not mention his antecedents. Many of the successful settlers in Upper Canada in the 'thirties had apparently come from the United States,[2] and were a counterweight to the English who migrated there.

As we have seen, one type of emigrant came out in the empty timber ships, others were conveyed out by the Canada Company or by leaders who hoped to make their lands profitable. But there was a third class who paid for themselves and were above the type of Irish immigrant who would get work in the lumber camps or on the quays.

It is rather surprising to see how much it cost to transfer an ordinary family to Canada. A labouring man, married, with three children, was said to need £107 10s. as capital in hand, to which had to be added the fare to Canada, the transshipment at Quebec for Montreal, then a further change into *bateaux* and the cost of landing and moving into the bush. £130 was said to be the lowest sum on which an emigrant could get on comfortably.

---

[1] Sir R. Bonnycastle, *Canada as it was and may be,* vol. i, pp. 122–3.

[2] "At the time of my visit nine-tenths of the hotel-keepers and stage-drivers, and most of the active business people, had originally come from the United States. Every horse and ox of size or fatness could be traced to have come from the same territory, and the Canadians appear to me to be much indebted to the people of the United States for any activity and refinement that is to be met with in the province.

"The first settlers, the people of business, and almost all travellers for pleasure or health, having come from the United States, their manners and customs have been impressed on the inhabitants of Upper Canada, and I do not think the large influx of British emigrants which has taken place of late years will efface them. I found much less refinement than in the lower province or in the United States, while the coarse manners of the people, and their habits of intemperance, were so prominent, that I heard more oaths and witnessed more drunk people the first few days I was in Canada than I had met with during my previous wanderings in the States. I must do Upper Canada, however, the justice to say that such characters appeared to be late importations from Britain and Ireland, and I was sorry to observe intoxication was by no means confined to the lowest class of emigrants." Shirreff, *Tour in British North America,* p. 389.

A more ambitious man would need far more.   Shirreff, as quoted by Murray, gives the following estimate :—

		£
Purchase of 200 acres		180
Loghouse and furniture, barn, cowhouse and yoke of oxen		100
Clearing, fencing and sowing 100 acres .		400
Subsistence of 1½ years		75
		£755 [1]

The land was usually bought on instalments and the Government could rarely collect the instalments as " the collecting of small arrears is a task extremely ill-suited to a government," and you cannot eject a whole community.[2]

The expense of moving into the bush was very great. To get to the clearing a yoke of oxen and a sleigh had to be hired. The master and his men started before the oxen and prepared a bush road, which was done by felling and drawing aside all trees under five inches in diameter and by cutting a pass through any fallen timber, thus leaving the great trees standing around.

Magrath in 1833 [3] gives the cost of taking possession of a farm of 200 acres distant only 30 miles from York (Toronto), in which there was an open road for 20 miles, as follows :—

	£	s.	d.
Coach hire, 15 miles on public road		5	0
Wagon hire to farm house, 5 miles . . .		12	6
Guide to lots—3 days		15	0
Coach and wagon hire returning		17	6
Removing family	3	0	0
Transport of luggage and provisions . . .	4	10	0
Lodging for family of six at farm, 20 days . .	2	0	0
Provisions	5	0	0
Hire of 5 men for building loghouse and making road, 20 days	12	10	0
Provisions for them	6	5	0
Hire of oxen		10	0
Iron work frames for doors	8	0	0
Clearing and fencing 10 acres at £3 5s. per acre .	32	10	0
Taking family from farm house to log house . .	1	5	0
Purchase of 200 acres at 10s. per acre . . .	100	0	0
Total . . .	£178	0	0

It cost the Magrath family of husband, wife, servant and six children £50 for their passage to Montreal and then they brought their own provisions and consumed them on board ship. They were 2 cwt. of corned beef in a tub, 1 cwt. of

[1] *Historical and Descriptive Account of British America*, vol. iii, p. 123.
[2] Ibid., p. 126.
[3] T. W. Magrath, *Authentic Letters from Upper Canada*, 1833, pp. 42–3.

biscuit, 1 cwt. of flour, the same of oatmeal, half a dozen hams, half a dozen tongues, live fowls, two dozen wine, two gallons of rum, potatoes and other vegetables, 10s. bread, and some fresh beef and mutton.[1] The water was said to be so disgusting that its taste could not be disguised and the intending emigrant was advised to bring bottled ale or porter.[2]

Cabin passage from Liverpool to Quebec varied from £15 to £20, but from Leith, Greenock or Aberdeen it was only £10 or £12 when Murray wrote.[3] By New York the passage was shorter but dearer, owing to the want of accommodation for the timber on the homeward voyage. Steerage to New York was said to be £3 10s. to £4, without provisions, and cabin £20–£25.

It is easy to enumerate settlements ; it is not easy to give an idea of the terrible difficulties of effecting a clearing and making a living. Agues, fevers, biting flies in myriads, the untidy depressing effect of the clearings and the rotting stumps, the almost annual fires burning the wooden houses, the impossibility of meeting the payments due on purchase, the falling behind, the selling out and leaving partially cleared land to others, these were the usual incidents of pioneer settlements. Shirreff, a farmer from Mungoswells in East Lothian, went to Upper Canada to see about a farm there for his brother, and he had no hesitation in recommending settlers to go to Illinois in the United States instead. Writing in 1835 in his *Tour in British North America*, he says :—

" The settler of Upper Canada has to struggle with the forest before he obtains a site for his house. If he ventures to keep a cow, she must browse on weeds and leaves of trees in summer, and in winter on the boughs of felled trees ; the milk and butter which she yields is of the worst quality, and scarcely repays the trouble of roaming after her in the woods. A pig and poultry cannot be maintained at first, and many years must pass away before the farm can furnish mutton and wool for family use. Trees must be cut down, chopped into logs, and burned before even a garden can be formed. The first crops suffer both from the effects of frost and the want of a circulation of air. The plough cannot be profitably used until eight years after the forest is cut

---

[1] Magrath, pp. 20–1.
[2] Ib., p. 65.
[3] III, p. 155.

down ; during the greater part of this period the harrow and scythe move amongst blackened stumps, and there is difficulty in growing sufficient food for a family." [1]

An anonymous writer who styles himself an emigrant also gave a most discouraging picture of the difficulties confronting the new settler.

" The labour required to clear a forest of gigantic trees is appalling to a man who has nothing to depend on but the physical strength of his own body ; and if its powers have been impaired by low living arising from want of employment previous to the period of his emigration, and if he have a wife and large family depending on him for support, that labour must be exercised at the outset to a painful degree. All the shelter he can expect in the first winter of his sojourn is in a house of trees piled together, and his wooden furniture must consist of the rudest construction, blocked out of the timber which he himself has cut down. Though the air is clear and bracing, the intensity of the cold in winter is far beyond what he can conceive, and the heat in summer is so great for a short period as to blister the skin, if left exposed to the influence of the sun's rays. . . . Mosquitoes swarm on every new settlement, and annoy everyone by their stinging and raising inflamed spots over the body. They dwell chiefly in the woods and in the vicinity of swamps, and come out in hot weather. A small black fly annoys also very much by settling among the hair in the morning and evening. Sleep is completely driven away when they make an attack, and they produce the most uneasy sensation.

" The state of the roads prevents a constant or rapid communication between places ; and in a new country, where coin as the circulating medium is scarce, and barter exists as the medium of exchange, difficulties are often encountered in disposing of the surplus stock of agricultural produce. The intrusion of wild animals is an evil which ought not to be overlooked as affecting a new settler. If the cattle and sheep are not penned up at night, they may be partly destroyed by the ferocity of the bears. Squirrels and racoons, of which there are plenty, may destroy the corn crops materially, particularly in any season that is unfavourable to the formation of beech mast and nuts. Mice and rats eat the seed of the Indian corn after it is in

[1] Op. cit., pp. 458-9.

the ground, so that two or three successive sowings are sometimes necessary."[1]

The life of the average woman in the backwoods was very hard, with everything to do, no conveniences, the long winter, the constant need for fuel, the ice which had to be melted to obtain water, and the difficulty of washing, to say nothing of the uncertainty of the food supplies added to the prevalent drunkenness and the want of the necessaries and the decencies of life. No wonder Mrs. Jameson wrote : " I never met with so many repining and discontented women as in Canada. I never met with *one* woman recently settled here who considered herself happy in her new home and country. . . . For those who have recently emigrated, and are settled more in the interior, there is absolutely no social intercourse whatever ; it is quite out of the question. They seem to me perishing of *ennui* . . . they may be said to live in a perpetual state of inward passive discord and fretful endurance."[2]

Physicians, schoolmasters, and clergymen were not to be obtained by inland settlers. Speaking of the lack of apothecaries in 1832, Magrath says : " Ignorant persons act in that capacity who scarcely know the drugs they sell. At Niagara that most necessary branch is solely conducted by a female, who compounds medicines and puddings with equal confidence, but not with equal skill."[3]

Socially there would be the struggling settlers in the backwoods, then one or two wealthier persons who could afford to build a saw or flour mill and would take planks and wheat in return for sawing and grinding. They would usually act as storekeepers and advance provisions to their customers in return for future wheat and ashes.

In the towns there would be the exporting and importing merchants, fur agents connected with the North West Company, whose headquarters were at Montreal, and the professional classes.

Barter or " natural economy " was the dominating factor of economic life, and the general indebtedness to the storekeeper, and the hopelessness of ever being free from bondage inevitably produced listlessness, apathy and paralysis in a struggling colony. The producers were tied

---

[1] *Hints and Observations on the Disadvantages of Emigration to British North America,* by an Emigrant, 1833, pp. 15–16.

[2] Op. cit., pp. 82 and 87.

[3] Op. cit., p. 109.

to the storekeepers, with whom they exchanged goods, as the absence of roads prevented exchange elsewhere.

" In remote parts of the country, the traffic is carried on chiefly in barter, and many tradesmen in such situations almost never finger money.

" The merchants and storekeepers are said to be the most wealthy and influential people in the province, and owe the position they have attained to the situation and character of the inhabitants. The settlers, being thinly scattered over an immense and almost inaccessible territory, are necessarily unacquainted with traffic and the price of commodities. Their limited produce does not spur them into active exertion to dispose of it ; and the state of the roads only admitting of transport for a part of the year, confines the time of sale to the winter months. During this season, the St. Lawrence, which is the only channel of trade, being closed by ice, limits the number of merchants, and drives all out of the market but capitalists. The necessities of farmers do not enable them to hold produce from year to year, and they appear to be at the mercy of the merchants, who obtain thousands and tens of thousands of bushels of wheat, at the head of Lake Ontario, in exchange for shoes and other necessaries, without a fraction of cash being paid on either side. The inland storekeeper has still greater advantages over the farmer, and their profits are said to be excessive ; 300 per cent on dry goods having been currently obtained at one time. The merchant and storekeeper is, however, distant from the markets of Britain, which regulate the price of Canadian wheat ; and the navigation of the St. Lawrence, and transport of goods, are so expensive, that profits may not be so great as is reported. Of their influence in the country, there is, however, no doubt ; and that it arises from the pecuniary difficulties of landowners is universally admitted, who, in numerous instances, are irretrievably burdened with debt.

" The first settlers, at the close of the war with the colonies, being at too great a distance to admit of much intercourse with each other, and having no outlet for their produce, soon sunk into listless inactivity. Many Germans and Dutch afterwards followed, who commonly settled near each other, and although quiet and industrious people were altogether without enterprise. The greater portion of British emigrants, who first settled in the province, having little capital or education, and obtaining grants of forest in isolated situations, made small progress in a mode of farming so new to them. Having been nurtured in poverty, they had few wants and were not ambitious to improve their condition. From a people so situated, and composed of such materials, little could be expected. Individuals connected with Government seem to have been more solicitous about their own than the people's welfare, and little was done to call forth the resources of the country, or to rouse the slumbering energies of the inhabitants. The people, however, formed good subjects for active traders, who still gather a plentiful harvest. How long this state of things may last with traders will depend on competition. Their profits will fall with the opening of communication throughout the country, but capital employed in trade is likely to yield a good return, so long as the necessities of the agricultural population continue urgent." [1]

The paralysis engendered by this state of affairs was more acute than in the Atlantic Provinces, where after all there was the sea and ice-free ports with traffic all the year round ; and, as has been seen, there was a considerable shipping and distributing trade. In Ontario development was blocked not merely by the absence of land communications but by the difficulty of getting goods to tide water at Quebec owing to the rapids. Hence the release from bondage once the canals were made and steamer traffic developed. In any case, however, the St. Lawrence was closed by ice for several months.

Competing merchants, wider markets, and payment in coin began to transform conditions between 1840 and 1850 and when in the decade 1850 to 1860 the railways began to do for land traffic what the new accessibility and steamers were doing for water traffic, the paralysing effects of barter and natural economy began to wear away.

While many enterprising individuals did well on their land, one gains the impression of a very sordid existence between 1815 and 1840.

Contemporary writers dispel the idea held by the followers of Rousseau, that when a man got close to nature his faults would disappear. They make it clear that this was not the case in Upper Canada and also bring out the appalling task confronting settlers in a new country in the first thirty years of the nineteenth century.

[1] Shirreff, op. cit., pp. 387–8.

Shirreff, who, being a farmer himself, was competent to judge agricultural conditions, thus describes the general stagnation to be found in Ontario.

" For eight or nine miles the shores of Lake Erie resembled the beach of the sea. The country at some distance was wet and partly newly cleared. . . . Houses were mean ; the inhabitants ragged and dirty. Cattle were small and lean. Many pigs were pictures of starvation . . . First crops on small clearings were half suffocated for want of air." [1]

" Knowing that a great deal of moral worth, physical energy, and capital have lately flowed into Canada, I have no doubt of time producing an important change in the state of the country and people. Indeed, hewing down the forest may be termed mortgaging labour to nature, whose generous returns accumulate like compound interest, and I look on Upper Canada as the germ of a numerously inhabited and wealthy state. Nothing but misgovernment can prevent such a consummation. A number of human beings have, however, been most improperly seduced into the province of late years, and at present I regard Upper Canada as a wretched, an immoral, and a misgoverned country." [2]

Shirreff seemed to think that it required two entirely different sets of people to make a successful settlement, the one to open up the land and the other to cultivate it, the latter requiring more capital and a higher degree of knowledge than pioneers generally possess. " In several instances I saw families of first settlers possessing a considerable extent of excellent cleared land, without the knowledge or means of rendering it productive, and they certainly would benefit themselves by disposing of their properties, and adopting another mode of life. Living almost in idleness, they cultivated, in the most negligent manner, only so much wheat and potatoes as was judged sufficient for home consumption, relying on the hay crop for procuring what necessaries they did not themselves produce, and appeared so encrusted with sloth, that they were likely only to fire a gun with the view of obtaining food, and to cut down a tree for the purpose of cooking it." [3]

---

[1] *Tour*, pp. 99, 101.

[2] Ibid., pp. 389–90. Shirreff is confirmed by Howison, writing in 1821, and Mrs. Jameson in 1838.

[3] Op. cit., p. 132. In another place he emphasizes this : " The old settlers are evidently the least enterprising class. Having come to the country uncultivated themselves, and ever since living without inter-

Howison testifies early to the same fact, viz. that the first settlers rarely remained on the land and made good ; and Dr. Dunlop, who managed the Canada Company, told Shirreff that only one of the original settlers in the Company's great territory was still to be found on his land after ten years.[1] Indeed, the amounts of partially cleared land that could be bought very cheaply [2] show how difficult it must have been for the pioneer. Shirreff said that it took four years to clear thirty acres, which with fences and roads would give a man twenty acres to cultivate. About forty acres was the limit of clearance in a life-time.[3] In other words, a farmer had to invest an enormous amount of time and labour in clearing the forest. It took six or seven years, so Shirreff said, before a farm could pay. The settler could not produce his own food till he had cleared the land and was forced to live for a time on flour and salt provisions supplied by the store-keeper. He constantly speaks of the bad effect of the barter system and the general system of bondage to the store-keeper and is especially critical of the methods of paying for land by instalments.

Shirreff considered that many of the difficulties of the farming population were due to the purchase of land on credit.

" Paying the purchase-money by instalments induces people without capital to become purchasers, who, for the interest of themselves and the community, ought to have assisted others in clearing and cultivating land, until they had accumulated sufficient capital, by saving, to purchase without credit. To the system of disposing of land by credit, much of the wretchedness and poverty of the present Candian landholders may be justly attributed. The experience of the United States Government demonstrated this, and a law was passed to abolish credit on the price of land. How difficult it seems to be for Britain to adopt legislation to the existing age of the world !

" The Canada Company possess immense tracts of country, and sell land on terms similar to Government, giving credit and drawbacks to induce people to purchase. The price of the company's land at Goderich is 7s. 6d. per acre, and equal to the price of Crown lands in other parts.

course with the world, they seem content with the necessaries of life, which are easily obtained. Their descendants imbibe the same sentiments and habits ; and before the first settled portions of Upper Canada can be farther improved, the present farmers must either sell to others of more enterprise, or another generation arise with new opinions." Ibid., p. 95.

[1] p. 175.   [2] Magrath, pp. 44–8.   [3] Shirreff, p. 364.

R

" Much land is held by absentee proprietors, or the members of the party who sway the councils of the province. It is commonly in the hands of agents empowered to sell. The prices are generally higher than Crown lands and credit unlimited.

" The greater portion of British emigrants, arriving in Canada without funds and the most exalted ideas of the value and productiveness of land, purchase extensively on credit, and take up their abode in the midst of the forest, with the proudest feelings of independence, and in the confident hope of meeting their engagements, and becoming fine gentlemen at the end of a few years. Everything goes on well for a short time. A log-house is erected with the assistance of old settlers, and the clearing of forests is commenced. Credit is obtained at a neighbouring store, and at length it is found necessary to work a day or two in the week for hire to obtain food for the family. The few garden stuffs and field crops, grown the first year, produce little for want of a free circulation of air, and the imperfect manner in which they had been sown. Should fever and ague now visit the emigrant, which is frequently the case, the situation of himself and family, enfeebled by disease, is truly wretched. Hope is, however, still bright, and he struggles through the second year with better crops and prospects than the preceding one. The third year brings him good crops, which furnish a supply of food for his establishment. During this period he has led a life of toil and privation, being poorly fed and most uncomfortably lodged. But the thoughts of owning so many fair acres have been a never-failing source of joy and sweetener of life. On arrival of the fourth harvest, he is reminded by the storekeeper to pay his account with cash, or discharge part of it with his disposable produce, for which he gets a very small price. He is also informed that the purchase-money of the land has been accumulating with interest. The phantom of prosperity, conjured up by his imagination, is now dispelled, and, on calmly looking into his affairs, he finds himself poorer than when he commenced operations. Disappointment preys on his spirits, and the aid of whisky is perhaps sought to raise them. The hopelessness of his situation renders him indolent and immoral. The land ultimately reverts to the former proprietor, or a new purchaser is found.

" To render the situation of an emigrant purchasing

without capital more evident, his case shall be illustrated
by figures. Suppose 200 acres, which is the common size
of lots purchased, at 15s., and that the emigrant has the
means of maintaining himself without working for hire,
and continues in good health. The first three crops being
required to feed the family and obtain necessaries, he may
be supposed to have nearly thirty acres in crop the fourth
year, if he has been very industrious, but making allowance
for stumps, fences, and roads, the actual surface in crop
will not exceed twenty acres. At this time, near the end
of the fifth year, when the fourth crop is reaped, the purchase-
money, and interest on it, will amount to about £200.
The interest on this sum at the rate of the country is £12,
and a burden on the land in crop of more than 10s. an acre,
which it cannot meet. In this estimate there is no return
made for forest land, which is generally as unproductive
of grass as the surface of the sea. It is the quantity of land
purchased which operates so unfavourably on the settler.
If, in the case chosen for illustration, 50 had been purchased
instead of 200 acres, the result would have been very
different. It is seldom a person depending on his labour
clears and cultivates more than 40 acres in the course of
his life. Therefore 50 acres is a sufficient extent for such
a character to buy, and under no circumstances ought he
to exceed 100 acres." [1]

On the other hand, Howson considered that the
indebtedness was due to the " absurd and monstrous
vanity " of the settlers who wanted to rise above their
condition in life.

" The number of merchants that Upper Canada contains,
and the mode in which they carry on business, are circumstances equally destructive to the interests of the colony.
Extensive credit is almost universally given to the farmers,
one-tenth of whom have neither inclination nor prudence
enough to adapt their expenditure to their means ; and,
as they generally pay and contract debts in an inverse
ratio, their difficulties increase every year, and often at
last terminate in the sale of their property, which sometimes
takes place with the consent of the owner, but oftener in
consequence of a suit. If the merchants desisted entirely
from selling on credit, it would be equally advantageous
for themselves and their customers. The latter might

---

[1] Op. cit., pp. 362–4.

indeed be sometimes put to a little inconvenience, if they wanted to purchase anything, and had not produce or money to pay for it at the time ; but this would teach them a habit of economy, which they never acquire while the present facility of supplying their wants exists, or as long as their absurd and monstrous vanity remains unchecked, and urges them to indulge in luxuries and finery to which their condition in life does not entitle them. Had the farmers of Upper Canada been prevented from getting into debt, and had they remained satisfied with *homespun*, they would now enjoy, in its fullest extent, that independence which they profess to value so highly, but the substantial part of which they have wholly lost, as there is hardly an individual among them who is not liable to have an execution served against him when it suits the interest of those to whom he is indebted " [1]

Most of the writers and travellers bring out the difficulties inherent in a system of natural economy such as prevailed in Upper Canada.

As Upper Canada was obliged to live to such a large extent on its own resources, there was little growth of town life such as existed in Quebec and Montreal.

Up to 1830 Kingston (Cataraqui) was the only important town in Upper Canada as the emigrants had settled far more quickly in that region than anywhere else, because it was the first point reached after the rapids and had a shorter communication with the outside world by the St. Lawrence route. The site of York (afterwards called Toronto) was cleared by the regiment known as the Queen's Rangers in 1794. It had an excellent harbourage or port, but from its low-lying position it was known as Muddy Little York. It was made into the seat of Government, but the land to the West and behind it was too unsettled for it to be anything but a village for many years. In 1801 it only contained 336 inhabitants and 1,200 in 1817. By 1830, however, there were 2,860 persons. " Toronto was even after 1818 the most Western town in Upper Canada ; between the city and Amherstburg, a distance of 325 miles, few villages, and these altogether diminutive in size, were to be met with." [2]

The lands round York (or Toronto) were unsettled and there was little trade. Mrs. Jameson remarked in 1838,

---

[1] Op. cit., 82–3.
[2] A. Lillie, *Canada*, 1855, pp. 160, 162.

" Ten years ago Toronto was a village, with one brick house and four or five hundred inhabitants ; five years ago it became a city, containing about five thousand inhabitants . . . now it is Toronto, with an increasing trade, and a population of ten thousand people." [1]

This improvement was due to the Canada Company and the development of the Western districts. Moreover, a road leading inland from the town to Lake Simcoe for forty miles facilitated settlement and, with a hinterland and the general increase in population, Toronto became a marketing centre and a pivotal point of the transport of the lake steamer traffic.

Nevertheless Captain Sibbald remarked in 1842, " There is so little specie in the country that payments in full at the time of purchase are scarcely known. Wheat is considered as cash in Toronto in paying your grocer and your linen-draper." [2]

The crying need of Upper Canada was capital. There could be little saving with so much payment in kind and it was only when public works such as canals were promoted, the wheat trade started, and above all when the railways came, that it was possible to get sufficient capital on which either the province of Ontario or the town of Toronto could begin to make an appreciable advance. The famine in coin and the famine in capital left Upper Canada in a backward condition for over half a century.

The want of money was undoubtedly one of the greatest drawbacks of the country. " Storekeepers constitute the most wealthy and powerful class in the community, land-owners and workmen being generally indebted to them, hence enormous profits. The common percentage on retailing provisions at Kingston being stated at 70 per cent, dry goods 100. Potash sells at Montreal for £24 a ton, the farmer at Kingston gets £17 store pay, equal to £12 cash." [3]

There seems to have been little change since 1821 when Howison wrote : " From what I have stated, it will be seen that the necessaries of life can be obtained at a small expense in Upper Canada ; but that labour is very high, and quite out of proportion to most other things. This circumstance arises from the scarcity of labourers, and from their wages

[1] *Sketches in Canada*, p. 1.
[2] " A few Days in the United States and Canada," p. 31, *Review of Historical Publications relating to Canada*, vol. 22, p. 104.
[3] Shirreff, op. cit., p. 128.

being in a great measure *nominal*. Money is so difficult to procure that almost all the farmers are obliged to pay those they hire with grain of some kind, which being unsaleable, those who receive it are obliged to barter it away with loss for anything else they may require. He who has a little money at command in Upper Canada will possess many advantages. He will get his work done at a cheaper rate than other people who have none ; and, in making purchases, will often obtain a large discount from the seller. A third cause of the high wages of labourers is the exorbitant rate at which all merchandize of British manufacture is sold in Upper Canada, the retail prices of such being, on an average, one hundred and fifty per cent higher than they are in Britain. The different articles of wearing apparel cost nearly twice as much as they do on the other side of the Atlantic, and are of very inferior quality." [1]

It needed a capital of £1,000 as a minimum to set up a small store. The large profits were obtained by numerous transactions with embarrassed individuals and were not realised " without difficulty and under disagreeable circumstances." [2]

Wages were, as a matter of fact, quoted in two ways, either as credit on the store or as cash. Speaking of Kingston, Shirreff says : " We learned that masons employed at the fort got $1 a day without finding or board and in town considerably more, when store pay is given . . . and a workman said he would prefer $9 cash to $12 store pay." [3]

This is not surprising, as goods at the stores paid out in this way were charged 20 to 30 per cent above their real value. From being seldom paid in money, Shirreff says the labourer " sees the hopelessness of raising himself by purchasing land and the disappointment often leads to drunkenness." [4] It is not surprising that many of this class, and small farmers, too, emigrated to the United States where there was not the labour of clearing the forest and the prairie was remunerative after a year's work.

Even the professional classes seem to have encountered the same difficulty. Bonnycastle, in 1852, writing of Upper Canada in the 'thirties, says : " Such was the scarcity of ready money, that fuel, beef, pork, flour, and even ashes, were taken in liquidation of newspaper debts, and the editors of many journals lived really by barter." [5]

---

[1] Op. cit., p. 237.   [2] Murray, *British America*, vol. iii, p. 134.
[3] Op. cit., p. 128.   [4] Op. cit., p. 384.
[5] Sir R. Bonnycastle, *Canada : As it was, and as it may be*, 1852, vol. i,

The currency difficulties and the general backwardness and depression created such an economic and racial malaise that the small and abortive rebellion of 1837 resulted. The rising was largely due to economic causes in each of the two Canadas, but a contributory cause lay in the fact that Ontario provided so much of the revenue in the shape of customs duties on the imported articles that that Province felt a grievance over the division of the proceeds. The English element, whether in Montreal or in Ontario, felt that they were the all-important element in Canada. The French, backward in their agriculture and employed mainly as servitors by the English, felt that they were being exploited and resented their economic subordination. Moreover, they wished to get some proportionate reward out of their favourable geographical situation by taxing exports and imports. Lord Durham found " two nations warring in the bosom of a single state . . . a struggle not of principles but of races," and ascribed most of the economic evils to the maladministration of the empty lands. He sought a political rather than an economic solution ; his practical remedy was to tie the two Colonies together as one so that the French might be swamped by the English. Accordingly the year 1840 saw the two Canadas united, and self-government was recommended even though the Provinces could not pay their way. England, wishing to abolish the preferences on both timber and wheat which had done so much for Lower and Upper Canada respectively, was willing to face the prospect of letting them govern themselves, even at the risk of having to pay the price of their possible mistakes and consequent deficits, and self-government was conceded.

The two Canadas, however, were far from happy in their union and were anxious soon to separate again. As England had, so it was thought, repudiated the Colonies by going over to free trade, and as the United States had also turned them down by refusing reciprocity, while the railways made a union physically workable even in winter, the general result was that the two Colonies separated again to form, in the end, two constituents of a federation.

p. 139. Cf. also, " The man who drove me . . . was baker general for a large neighbourhood, rarely receiving money in pay but wheat and other farm produce ". Mrs. Jameson, *Sketches in Canada*, 1838, 1852, edition, p. 81. Murray in 1839, says : " Cash indeed is scarcely ever seen in the remoter parts," iii, p. 105.

CHAPTER 7

Position at Time of Confederation.

Early doubts as to advantages of union.
The pull to the United States.
Canada in 1867 (British North America Act).
American thrust between eastern and western Provinces.
Linking-up by railways.

THE British North America Act, 1867, was but the first overt act in the era of Canadian nationalism. The work of preparation before Canada could enter fully upon the development of her resources was arduous and prolonged. The Confederation had come into existence, but it was not yet upheld by a unanimous people. There was still a strong minority who regarded union with the United States as Canada's natural destiny. The Confederation which was called into existence in 1867 was but the Eastern corner of the present Dominion. It was necessary for the British North America Act to provide for railway communication between the Maritime Provinces and the Provinces of Canada—henceforth Quebec and Ontario.

The Quebec Resolutions, which became the British North America Act, were opposed by a substantial minority in the Canadian Legislature. After the British North America Act was on the Statute Book, Nova Scotia started an agitation for its repeal: "and men openly spoke of exchanging British for American allegiance".[1] At the first Dominion General Election, out of nineteen members returned in Nova Scotia only one was a supporter of the Union. Neither the minority that favoured independence nor the school which regarded Canada's inevitable destiny as union with the United States were ever plants of vigorous growth, but it was twenty years or so before they drooped and died. In the mother country Cobden felt called upon to write in such terms as these: "Then I cannot see what substantial interest the British people have in the connexion to compensate them for guaranteeing three or four millions

---

[1] H. E. Egerton, *Historical Geography of Canada*, part ii, p. 245.

of North Americans living in Canada against another community of Americans living in their neighbourhood. . . . In my opinion it is for the interests of both that we should, as speedily as possible, sever the political thread by which we are as communities connected and leave the individuals on both sides to cultivate the relations of commerce and friendly intercourse as with other nations." [1] Lord Blachford, the Permanent Under Secretary for the Colonies, when the Canadian delegates came to England for the negotiations that preceded confederation "was no imperialist, and believed that the ultimate destiny of Canada was separation." [2] It was not until the hopelessness of looking for a renewal of reciprocity with the United States in matters of trade was fully realized that Canadians became united in their conception of nationality. [3]

The British North America Act, 1867, called the Dominion of Canada into existence, but it was little more than the legislative framework of the Dominion as we now know it. The actual Dominion as constituted by the Act consisted only of four Provinces, namely, the two Canadas (now Ontario and Quebec), Nova Scotia and New Brunswick. But provision was made by which Newfoundland, Prince Edward Island, British Columbia, Rupert's Land, and the North Western Territory might subsequently be admitted into the Union. The Province of British Columbia joined the Union in 1871 and Prince Edward Island came in in 1873. When we reflect that between these two Provinces there stretches three thousand miles of territory, we realize what a wonderful achievement it was that knitted such widely separated regions into a common political organization and how essential it was that the vast territories which lay between Ontario and British Columbia should become part of the organization of the Confederation.

The farmers of the Confederation saw quite clearly that, if Canada was to remain a country separate from the United States, the latter country must not be allowed to intercept the route to the Pacific. The danger of annexation of the

---

[1] J. Morley, *Life of Cobden*, chap. 37.

[2] H. E. Egerton, *Historical Geography of Canada*, pt. ii, p. 239.

[3] Professor James Mavor expresses the opinion that the movement in Ontario towards the end of the 'eighties in favour of annexation to the United States had its origin in the trade depression through which the Province was then passing. " Symptoms of returning trade activity had by 1892 caused the movement to lose impetus, and the crisis in the United States in 1893 for the time being gave it the *coup de grâce*." *My Windows on the Street of the World*, vol. i, p. 326.

Red River Settlement by America was very present to the minds of those who looked forward to the appropriation of the North West for Canada and the Empire and they could not forget the object lesson of the Oregon Territory. All that territory which originally included what are now the American States of Oregon, Washington, and Idaho, as well as British Columbia, was thought to be safely under British dominion, but the rapid settlement of the territory by Americans in the 'forties, brought the two countries to the verge of war until the Washington Treaty of 1846 fixed the 49th Parallel as the boundary. The American settlements on the Red River were seen to promise to be a parallel case. The Hudson's Bay Company had brought its supplies to that region from York Factory on Hudson Bay, but had to yield to the wishes of the settlers for a more convenient route from the South by way of the Red River. The result of this linking up of the Red River Settlement with Minnesota was a movement for the inclusion of, at any rate, that part of the North West Territory within the Union. The Red River Rebellion in 1869–70 brought the movement to the surface : " Among the American settlers there was an open movement for annexation to the United States, a movement fostered partly by American Fenian influences and quite in accord with the well-known ambition of Minnesota's political leaders, to add the British North West to the territory of the United States." [1]

In 1870 the Red River Settlement became permanently a part of the Confederation as the Province of Manitoba ; but much of the map still remained vacant, and it was not until 1905, when Alberta and Saskatchewan were given full provincial status, that the Confederation of Canada could be said to be a continuous chain of Provinces stretching from the Atlantic to the Pacific.

The consolidation of public opinion in favour of Nationalism and the organization of Canada into one political entity were the first essentials if her resources were to be developed on national lines. To bind the Provinces together by a transcontinental railway into a single economic unit was equally necessary.

At Confederation there were only 2,278 miles of railway in the Dominion. The provisions of the British North America Act, as we have just seen, only organized a small

[1] R. G. Trotter, *Canadian Federation*, p. 290.

portion of Canada politically. The provision made by the Act on the economic side for its equipment with a railway was equally restricted. It was declared to be the duty of the Government of Canada " To provide for the commencement within six months after the Union of a Railway connecting the River St. Lawrence with the City of Halifax in Nova Scotia ", that being " essential to the consolidation of the Union of British North America ". The Intercolonial Railway was duly constructed but was not opened until 1876, and it was not until 1885 that the line which was " essential to the consolidation of the Union of British North America ", as we now know it, was completed and the Pacific coast joined to the Atlantic by the Canadian Pacific Railway, so giving to the Dominion the right to inscribe upon its coat of arms the proud motto : " *A Mari usque ad Mare.*"

CHAPTER 8

Inland Communications

Waterways

THE story of Canadian internal communications is probably the most romantic and interesting in the world. Even to-day in picturesque contrast are seen on the one hand the men of the Hudson's Bay Company carrying the mail and distributing hundreds of tons of supplies annually with dog sleighs as the means of transport, and on the other hand the transcontinental railways, the last word in luxurious travelling. Fleets of steamers are engaged in purely internal voyages, carrying cargoes from one port to another on the shores of Canada's inland seas : sometimes strings of vessels get frozen in on Canadian waterways.[1] Quite recently the capital city was seriously threatened by a tremendous log-jam, which banked up the waters of a tributary of the Ottawa River. Confederation itself

---

[1] Thus according to information sent by the Toronto correspondent of *The Times*, on 7th December, 1926 : " One hundred and sixty-five vessels are now blocked by the ice in the East and West Neebish Channel below Sault Ste Marie. The blockade extends south for 100 miles from Detour to White Fish Bay, through which all traffic between Lake Superior and the Lower Lake ports must pass. The lines of steamships, extending for miles, motionless and silent, with smoke floating from the funnels, suggest a closely built industrial district. A score of tramp steamers are also held up by ice in the St. Lawrence River below Montreal. There is, too, an icefield reaching out for 12 miles from Midland which effectively prevents the entry of 40 or 50 vessels which should reach that port before the close of navigation."

depended on bargains as to the construction of railways. Provinces have been on the verge of secession by reason of the central government's sin of omission in regard to the construction of some much desired line. Railway questions have wrecked Ministries : railways saved the greater part of Canada to the British Empire. Force of circumstances rather than political agitation has compelled the Canadian Government to take over and operate as a State-owned system the greater part of the country's railway lines.

Waterways

The earliest means of communication and transport in Canada were those provided by nature herself in the shape of the wonderful system of waterways consisting of the River St. Lawrence and its tributary, the Ottawa, and the Great Lakes. Nature also provided difficulties in the shape of the winter " freeze " ; and the frequent rapids, which could only be passed by " portages ", when the birch-bark canoes had to be unloaded and they and their contents carried overland. The first condition was a hopeless impediment in the way of the development of Canadian trade until the railways came. To avoid the rapids, lateral canals have been constructed with numerous locks to overcome the differences in level.

The earliest of the canals were constructed to accommodate vessels of but modest tonnage. The Lachine Canal, for instance, which goes round the Lachine Rapids, just above Montreal, and is the first of the series of canals belonging to the St. Lawrence system, was opened for traffic in 1824 to accommodate vessels of $4\frac{1}{2}$ feet draught. The last of the St. Lawrence system of canals, the Sault Ste Marie Canal, the purpose of which is to correct the difference in level of 19ft. between Lakes Superior and Huron, had a lift of 9 ft. when constructed. By successive enlargements, the series of canals constituting the St. Lawrence system, including the Welland Canal, which goes round Niagara, now enables vessels with a draught of 14 ft. to pass through from Lake Superior to Montreal and Quebec, while the Sault Ste Marie Canal has 19 ft. of water on the sills. This, it is claimed, is the finest system of fresh water navigation in the world, providing as it does through navigation with a minimum depth of 14 ft. for over two thousand miles. Nevertheless, the ambition of the Provinces is to enlarge the series of canals so as to provide 30 ft. of water on the sills and to make deep water navigation possible from the Atlantic to Lake Superior.

Another system of canals centres in Ottawa : one to make continuous navigation possible from Ottawa to Montreal, along the Ottawa River ; the other, the Rideau Canal, providing a continuous waterway along the Rideau River between Ottawa and Kingston, and so giving access to Lake Ontario. These are shallow draught canals, 9 ft. for the most part, but the Rideau Canal provides for 6 ft. only.

The Canal System is owned and worked by the Government. This is necessarily so, for so far from being a source of direct revenue, the canals have always been a heavy drain on the resources of the State. In support of this it is only necessary to state that since 1904 all canals have been free of toll to vessels using lock facilities, and that " the total cost of Canadian canals since their construction was begun is set at $175,812,316." [1]

It is deep waterways that help the development of business and industry, and, realizing this, the policy of the Canadian Government has been to carry out a programme for making their waterways deeper and deeper so that larger vessels may penetrate further and further into the heart of the continent : " The St. Lawrence up till 1858 was not navigable above Quebec for vessels drawing more than 11 ft. of water ". In 1900, " vessels drawing 27½ ft. can proceed to Montreal." [2] At the present time a channel 35 ft. is available for ocean steamers to Montreal.

An enterprise of outstanding importance was entered upon when the construction of the Welland Ship Canal was begun in 1913. Following in part of its course the route of the existing canal and in part an entirely new line, the canal when completed will be twenty-five miles in length and will have a depth of 30 ft. of water on the sills. The enterprise is a costly one. Up to 1926 over $62,000,000 has been spent on it, that is to say, one-third of all the expenditure hitherto incurred on Canadian canals. The return that is anticipated is a reduction in the freight rate of east-bound grain shipments and the diversion to the St. Lawrence route of a substantial proportion of the Canadian grain now shipped by way of Buffalo and New York.

---

[1] *Canada Year Book*, 1926, p. 635.
[2] Lord Strathcona, *The Dominion of Canada*, in British Empire Series, vol. iii, p. 13.

So far as the new Welland Ship Canal is an attempt to divert the grain traffic from the American to the Canadian route, it is but the most recent phase of a struggle which has been going on since the early part of the nineteenth century.

There are two natural outlets on the east ; one by way of Canada and the other through United States territory. The Canadian outlet is the St. Lawrence : the American is the Hudson River. These waterways have been made possible for through traffic by rival canals. The Erie Canal connects Buffalo, on Lake Erie, with New York, by way of Troy and the Hudson River. It was begun as a State enterprise in 1817 and opened to boats of 75 tons burden in 1825. It has since been successively deepened. By way of reply the Welland Ship Canal connecting Lakes Erie and Ontario was begun by private enterprise but had to be completed by the Provincial Government and was opened in 1829.

In their attempt by means of the Welland and St. Lawrence Canals to attract the traffic of the American West from the " petty barge canal " to their own splendid lake and river route, Canadians have met with successive disappointments, largely for reasons beyond their control. It was found that the question whether traffic should go by the St. Lawrence or the Erie Canal route was not determined merely by the normal factors in transport problems, namely, freight rates, quickness of transport and facilities for handling cargo. Factors which played a large part were the English duties on imports by the two respective routes. The repeal in 1848 of the differential duties in favour of the St. Lawrence route was also a damaging blow. Another factor was freight rates from the ports of the respective routes. Ocean freights from New York to Europe were lower than those from Quebec or Montreal by reason of the greater competition at the American port.[1]

That the burden undertaken by the Canadian Government in building a Welland Ship Canal is inevitable is apparent from the recent unfortunate experience of the Canadian Sault Ste Marie Canal.

Lakes Superior and Huron are joined by rival canals. There is a Canadian Sault Ste Marie and an American

---

[1] " In 1850, for example, the freight on a barrel of flour from New York to Liverpool was 1s. 3½d, while from Montreal it was 3s. 0½d. This was because the majority of vessels arriving at Montreal came in ballast." O. D. Skelton, *The Railway Builders*, pp. 84–5.

Sault Ste Marie Canal and each is available for vessels of either country. In 1814 United States troops destroyed the original canal constructed at the end of the eighteenth century on the Canadian side. The greater canal which has replaced it is in process of being reduced to a derelict state, also by the action of the United States Government, but this time using economic weapons.

High water mark in Canadian canal traffic was reached in 1913 when the total freight carried was 52 million tons. Of this 42 million tons went by the Canadian Sault Ste Marie Canal, nearly 90 per cent being of American origin. The principal traffic was in grain and iron ore. Since that year the decline of traffic on the Canadian canal has been rapid. In 1916 when the traffic on the Canadian canal had already fallen to 17 million tons it was explained to be due to " a diversion of both Canadian and American traffic to the American canal at Sault Ste Marie owing to the availability on the American side of a new and larger lock ".[1] By 1919 four modern locks had super-seded the old one.

A mid-nineteenth century writer,[2] in the course of an acute examination of the difficulties in the way of attracting paying traffic to Canadian canals, put on record the following striking prognosis :—" The St. Lawrence offers us access to the markets of the world since our canals have been constructed : but, from the lingering effect of commercial maltreatment, the superior facilities of wealthier and better supported routes, and some disadvantages on the score of winter shipments, our own limited commerce is insufficient to keep open this mighty highway.

" It is evident that this great highway cannot be " kept in repair " by our trade alone. It was never designed by nature for this selfish end : our canals were not built for Canada, but for the *valley of the St. Lawrence* : we ought therefore to " club together " with our neighbours on the opposite side in order to place this noble outlet in the most efficient state, by giving it as large a support as possible. . . . An exclusive policy will certainly recoil upon ourselves, for we are too poor in capital to purchase a tithe of what is needed to ' stock ' the St. Lawrence and control the business of the North and West."

---

[1] *Canada Year Book*, 1916–17, p. 455.
[2] T. C. Keefer, *The Canals of Canada* (1850), pp. 34–5.

Only after the lapse of three-quarters of a century has any attention been paid to this invocation of the spirit of international co-operation.

A scheme for deepening the St. Lawrence and constructing the necessary locks so as to make it an international waterway for ocean traffic between the Atlantic and the Great Lakes has in recent years been the subject of discussion between Canada and the United States. A Joint Commission reported favourably on the possibility of the scheme in 1921, but the Canadian and United States engineers failed to agree on methods, and the Atlantic Provinces, and in particular Quebec, have been consistently hostile to the whole project, with the unfortunate but perhaps inevitable result that the matter has become a political issue.

With the disappearance of iron ore as an important item in Canadian canal traffic, wheat, oats, and barley, soft coal, and pulpwood take the highest places in the statistics. This is just the heavy and slow traffic which according to European experience remains with waterways when railway competition has become effective. For competition with the railways the Canadian waterways are handicapped by the fact that the navigation season extends only from May to November [1] But Canadian waterways are exceptional in that to make a total length of 1594 miles available only 117 miles of canals had to be constructed. Nowhere else in the Empire is inland navigation of such importance. Especially valuable is the service they render in the " fall " months when they come to the assistance of the railways in their heavy task of moving the harvest. The waterways must continue to carry a large amount of traffic and, that being so, they render railways less absolutely necessary than in other countries, and this factor the Drayton-Acworth Commission felt bound to take into account when estimating the future of the Canadian railways.

[1] So, according to *The Times*, of 28th November, 1927 :—" Last week was regarded in the freight markets as marking practically the close of chartering for grain from Montreal before the end of navigation on the St. Lawrence this season. . . . and it is certain that very large quantities of grain will remain to be shipped through the United States ports during the winter months, or through Montreal after the reopening of navigation in the spring."

CHAPTER 9

Railways

The Canadian Pacific

THE domination by the railways of the economic history of Canada since Confederation has already been pointed out and the part they played in diverting the natural North and South tendency of traffic in an East and West direction has been indicated. While politically the national period in Canada's history dates from 1867, the national period in her economic history really begins at a date so recent as 1885 when the rails which had been gradually creeping inland from the Pacific and Atlantic sides of the continent at last met in the Eagle Pass and Donald Smith, later to become Lord Strathcona, performed the ceremony of driving in the last spike in the first of the transcontinental lines, the Canadian Pacific Railway. It was only then that the Dominion was equipped with the instrument with which to develop her untold natural resources on a national scale.

It had been thought that the completion of her canal system would secure to Canada a large share of the western trade. This might have come about but for the railways which had been constructed south of the international boundary. The trade of Western Canada itself began to drift from the St. Lawrence to the United States railways and it became evident that unless she could combine a railroad system with her system of water transport Canada's heavy outlay on canals must remain largely unproductive.

Confederation removed the purely local and provincial outlook which had kept Canada so far behind the United States in the organization of transport. The United States had been federated for a century and already their transport routes were on a national basis and on continental lines. But at Confederation the Dominion was merely the eastern side of the continent and the Intercolonial Railway was not a continental line. Then the Pacific Province and the North-West were brought into the Confederation and at once railway enterprise took on a continental aspect.

The first railway locomotive appeared in Canada in the year when Queen Victoria came to the throne. It replaced horses as the motive power on the 16 miles of railway in the Province of Quebec between St. Johns and La Prairie and this represented the total railway mileage of Canada at that time. At Confederation this had only increased to 2,278 miles, most of which was contributed by the Grand Trunk Railway system, the main purpose of which was to provide through communication between Canada and the United States rather than to link one Canadian Province with another. In 1925 there were 40,352 miles of steam railway in operation in the Dominion, seven-eighths of it organized in two great systems, the Canadian Pacific Railway and the Canadian National Railways, the latter an amalgamation of ninety-two constituent companies of which the chief are the six great lines : the Intercolonial, the Grand Trunk, the Grand Trunk Pacific, the National Transcontinental, the Canadian Northern, and the Hudson Bay Railway.[1] The Candian Pacific Railway alone among

[1] Unless and until it is brought into physical relationship with Canadian transcontinental lines—and that this might be done by a train-ferry service across the Gulf of St. Lawrence after the manner of the train ferries on the Great Lakes and elsewhere was suggested to the Dominions Royal Commission in 1914—the railway system of the Dominion of Newfoundland must remain of purely local interest.

That it must remain a self-contained Dominion, however small, seems to have been the view accepted by those concerned, for the Dominions Royal Commission found that its 800 miles of railway had been built on the 3ft. 6in. gauge throughout. The history of the lines which begins in 1880 is a somewhat chequered one, but the upshot is that " the contractors received a fixed sum per mile for construction (£3,250 for the original trunk line and £3,215 for the later extensions) and a land grant in fee simple of some thousands of acres per mile of track on account of operating expenses. The lines are leased to the Company for a term of 50 years from 1901. No rent is payable to the Government. . . . It thus appears that whilst the Government has provided the capital for the

the great systems of the Dominion retains its original name and separate history ; and whereas the other transcontinental lines were begun by private enterprise and are now part of a State system, the Canadian Pacific began as a Government enterprise and is now in private ownership. The Canadian Northern and the Grand Trunk Pacific both failed to make good. The Canadian Pacific is, in the words of the Drayton-Acworth Report, " to-day one of the wealthiest and financially strongest railway companies in the world."

The Canadian Pacific Railway

The romantic story of the Canadian Pacific begins with the Order in Council of 1871 by which British Columbia was admitted into the Dominion of Canada subject to the Terms of Union which became effective under the British North America Act. By Article XI the Government of the Dominion undertook " to secure the commencement simultanously, within two years from the date of the Union, of the construction of a railway from the Pacific towards the Rocky Mountains and from such point as may be selected east of the Rocky Mountains towards the Pacific to connect the seaboard of British Columbia with the railway system of Canada " and to complete the railway within ten years from the date of the Union.

A completed transcontinental railway meant over 2,500 miles of line. At the beginning of 1881 the length of line completed and in operation was only 264 miles.

Quite early all the spectres of contemporary Canadian politics seemed to emerge from their lairs to impede and harass the Dominion Government in its endeavours to carry out it bargain with British Columbia. The race rivalry between the British and French stocks of Ontario and Quebec became a factor in the problem. The Eastern Provinces asked why they should be taxed for the benefit of the West. The national resentment of any attempt on the part of United States capitalists or politicians to involve themselves in Canadian affairs boiled up. That the bonds which united the Provinces into a single organization might be snapped at any moment seemed possible.

The problem was not comparable with that involved

construction of the railway system (which will amount in all to some £3,000,000 when the present extensions are completed), it obtains no direct return for the amount expended ; nor will it do so during the currency of the existing lease." See Fourth Interim Report [Cd. 7711], p. 11–13, also Evidence [Cd. 7898], p. 19; Dominions Royal Commission.

in the construction of the other political railway, the Intercolonial. The road which had to be constructed as one of
the terms of union between Upper and Lower Canada was
only 500 miles long ; it ran through a favourable and
settled territory ; at most points along its course there
was ready access to the sea. The Canadian Pacific undertaking was concerned with a region as vast as that stretching
from France to the Ural Mountains ; great mountain
ranges barred the way on the west ; the 2,500 miles of
country to be traversed had a population of less than 20,000
and for the most part was entirely uninhabited. Moreover
the line had its full share of the special difficulties imposed
upon railway builders by reason of the exigencies of the
Canadian climate. The frost may penetrate the ground to
a depth of three or four feet, especially where the blanket
of snow has to be removed as from the railway track.
" Embankments, when newly formed, retain much of the
rain of autumn. During the ensuing winter this moisture
is converted into ice, and when the thaw of spring is felt,
the material, to the extent the frost has penetrated, is
frequently reduced to the consistency of paste. The material
has then a tendency to slide and to produce results exacting
considerable outlay to restore the soil to its original form. . .
There is but one remedy to meet this condition, thorough
drainage." [1] The contingency of destructive bush fires,
especially in a region of resinous forests, has also to be
provided against by a sufficiently wide clearing.

It was not that less formidable means of joining up
East and West were not available. It would have been easier
to connect the Eastern Provinces with the North-West by
making use of the railways already constructed south of
Lake Superior. They, however, were in United States
territory and the economic importance of a solution of
the problem independently of the United States had been
clearly seen in Canada as early as 1872, for in a memorandum
in which the Interoceanic Company explained their
objections to amalgamation with the Canada Pacific Company
it was urged, in opposition to the scheme of the latter, that
" If the scheme is carried out, our great national enterprise,
instead of being the successful rival of the American Company,
competing for the Asiatic trade, which is now in its infancy,
and building up the Dominion as no other undertaking
can, will simply be the Canadian branch of the Northern

---

[1] Sandford Fleming, *The Intercolonial, p.* 109.

Pacific Railroad, entirely under its control and dictated to by it relentlessly ".

Then many in Canada, among whom the Liberal Prime Minister, Alexander Mackenzie, was conspicuous, thought that a scheme more suited to the means of the Dominion at the time could be based on the utilization of water communications. To reach Red River would not be expensive, and thereafter water communication by Lakes Winnipegosis and Manitoba and the Saskatchewan River to the Rocky Mountains would be feasible, at any rate during the summer months. The obvious objection to any scheme based on water communications was of course its merely seasonal availability. Nevertheless, in spite of the discouraging nature of the enterprise, during the Session of 1872, rival companies thought it worth while to obtain Acts of Incorporation, the Canada Pacific Company, formed by Sir Hugh Allan, one of Canada's most prominent capitalists, in which the interests of Quebec predominated, and the Interoceanic Company, organized by Senator Macpherson, with predominating Ontario interests. To give the Charter to either Company would be to favour one Province as against the other, Quebec as against Ontario or *vice versa*, with consequent political disaster. The policy of Sir John Macdonald's government accordingly was to bring about the fusion of the competing companies, but the Interoceanic Company refused to consider amalgamation, alleging that the Canada Pacific Company and its President had the intention of co-operating with United States capitalists who were interested in the American Northern Pacific Railway. The Government promoted a new and independent company of which Sir Hugh Allan was made chairman, and thereupon a first-class political scandal developed. The charges against Sir John Macdonald's government in connection with the granting of the charter to Sir Hugh Allan and his associates for the construction of the line were crystallized by the Governor-General, Lord Dufferin, in the statement that his Ministers were charged " with no less a crime than that of having sold Canada's most precious interests to certain American speculators with a view to debauching the Canadian constituencies with the gold obtained as the price of their treachery." [1]

---

[1] *Parliamentary Papers* (*Great Britain*): *Accounts and papers*, vol. xlv, 1874, pp. 1–266, Correspondence relating to the Canadian Pacific Railway, [C. 911].

The allegations of corruption were referred for inquiry to a Commission of three Canadian Judges. They confined themselves to the collection of evidence and left to the Canadian Parliament the expression of the judgment upon the facts elicited. The papers were laid before the House on 23rd October, 1873 ; four days later a debate censuring the Government was begun, and in a little more than another week Sir John Macdonald, without waiting for the test of a vote of the House, handed to the Governor-General his resignation, and a Liberal Government under Alexander Mackenzie succeeded to the problem of uniting the Eastern Provinces with British Columbia by rail.

By the Canadian Pacific Railway Act, 1874, a railway was to be made from a point near Lake Nipissing " to some point in British Columbia ". Public lands along the line were to be appropriated and sold for the purposes of the railway ; the work was to be done under the general superintendence of the Government.

British Columbia remained dissatisfied. " In consequence of the course pursued by the Dominion, British Columbia is suffering great loss ; her trade has been damaged and unsettled : her general prosperity has been seriously affected : her people have become discontented : a feeling of depression has taken the place of the confident anticipation of commerical and political advantages to be derived from the speedy construction of a great railway uniting the Atlantic and Pacific shores." So spoke this Province with its white population of barely 10,000 in the petition which it addressed to the Queen complaining that the Dominion had broken faith.[1]

It was realized that only the intervention of some external authority could relieve the tension, and Lord Carnarvon, the Colonial Secretary, tendered his good offices as mediator. His intervention was accepted ; he considered the matter in all its aspects, and " the Carnarvon terms ", the central ideas of which were the speeding up of the construction of the railway and its completion in 1890, became a sort of slogan in British Columbia. In 1876 the Governor-General, Lord Dufferin, thought it his duty to pay a personal visit to the discontented Province for the purpose of making an attempt to bring home to the local malcontents the difficulties

---

[1] *Parliamentary Papers (Great Britain): Accounts and Papers*, **1875**, vol. lii, p. 44, Correspondence respecting the Canadian Pacific Railway Act, [C. 1217].

of a literal fulfilment of the bargain into which the Dominion had too hastily and prematurely entered. The acuteness of the feeling which the controversy had generated was brought home to Lord Dufferin when, in the course of his ceremonial entry into the British Columbia capital, he encountered a triumphal arch decorated with the minatory legend, " The Carnarvon terms or Separation."

Sir John Macdonald's name, as has been seen, is intimately associated with the perplexities of the early phases of the transcontinental railway problem. Returned to power in 1878 at the head of a party which was to enjoy eighteen years of office, he was destined to bring about its final solution.

That solution involved the abandonment of the attempt to prosecute the scheme as a Government enterprise and an agreement for the construction of the railway by a private syndicate. The wisdom of this course became abundantly evident when, in 1882, the report was published of the Royal Commission appointed two years previously to inquire into all facts connected with the conduct and prosecution of the Canadian Pacific Railway from the beginning. The Commissioners set in a strong light the difficulties and dangers encountered by a still young Government in a new country, with traditions still to be formed and experience still to be gained, and whose control over its agents is of necessity somewhat loose. The construction of the railway " was carried on as a public work at a sacrifice of money, time and efficiency ". They found that " numbers of persons were employed as Government officials who were not efficient in the positions to which they were appointed, having been selected on party grounds ". Progress had been delayed by " the necessity of staying operations from time to time until the necessary appropriations were made by Parliament ". There had been a general want of foresight, economy and business system.[1]

The contract, which was ratified by the Canadian Parliament early in 1881,[2] provided for a completed Canadian Pacific Railway extending from the east side of Lake Nipissing in Ontario to Port Moody in British Columbia.

[1] The Report was not reprinted in the Canadian Sessional Papers, but is summarized in the *Dominion Annual Register and Review for* 1882, edited by H. J. Morgan.

[2] The contract, which was signed on behalf of the Government by Sir Charles Tupper and on behalf of the Syndicate by George Stephen and six others, together with the Act of Incorporation, will be found set out in *Debates, House of Commons, Canada, Session* 1880–81, vol. i, pp. 28 ff.

To enable the system to be made truly transcontinental, the Charter of Incorporation empowered the Company to acquire certain railways east of Lake Nipissing. Under these powers the Canada Central Railway, running east from Lake Nipissing to Ottawa, was acquired, and in 1885 traffic in Eastern Canada was further secured by the leasing of the Ontario and Quebec Railway.

The Government granted a subsidy in cash of 25 million dollars and a subsidy in land of 25 million acres. From the economic point of view this latter item is perhaps the most important in the transaction, for thereby the Canadian Pacific Company became a great colonizing agent. The land was to be in alternate sections of 640 acres each, extending 24 miles deep on each side of the railway. The ultimate purpose of such land was indicated in the clause which provided that if any of such sections of land " consist in a material degree of land not fairly fit for settlement " the Company was to be at liberty to choose instead lands in the Fertile Belt, " that is to say, the land lying between parallels 49 and 57 degrees of north latitude." [1]   It was largely by the sale of this land and the issue of bonds secured thereon that the Company was about to weather its early financial difficulties and complete the line.

The land grants to the Canadian Pacific Railway were the subject of much criticism, but if precedents were wanted they were furnished abundantly by United States history. " A precedent was set on 2nd March, 1833, when Congress, desirous of assisting the Illinois Railroad Company in the

---

[1] The total amount of public assistance rendered to the Canadian Pacific Railway was ascertained by the Drayton-Acworth Commission in 1917, to have been 228,500,925 dollars, made up as follows :—

Cost of road made by Government and handed over to Company free of cost	$37,785,320
Cash aid by Dominion and Provincial Governments and Municipalities	66,905,481
Proceeds of lands and town-sites	123,810,124
	$228,500,925

In addition the contract provided for indirect public assistance in the form of exemption from taxation of the property of the Company (following the policy of the United States which regarded railways as created for the benefit and development of the whole country) ; and the admission of railway material free of duty.

According to evidence given before the Dominions Royal Commission in 1916, the total land grants, including Branch Line Grants had been 27,787,921 acres. Of this the area not disposed of was at that time 6,511,394 acres. *Dominions Royal Commission : Minutes of Evidence* [Cd. 8458] Q. 2718.

work of linking up Illinois with the Atlantic coast, made the Company a grant of 290,915 acres, part of which was absorbed in building the permanent way and part sold in small plots to immigrants. Ever since that date Congress has made a practice of voting extensive tracts of land to railroad concerns whose lines penetrated into undeveloped country. The Company is usually given the land required for building the permanent way, the stations, and the workshops, together with alternate farm sections on either side of the track. The remaining plots are held by the Government. These are eventually sold to settlers and as a rule secure good prices owing to the rail advantages which they enjoy."[1]

It has to be remembered that the Government had already entered upon the work of constructing a substantial portion of the line. Thus the Lake Superior section was under construction as also was the western section from Kamloops to Port Moody in British Columbia. These sections, amounting to 712 miles in length, the Government undertook to complete and to hand over to the Company. The eastern section from Lake Nipissing to Selkirk on the east of the Red River and the central section from Selkirk to Kamloop the Company were to construct.

The whole line was to be completed by 1st May, 1891, and when completed the whole of the undertaking, including the part constructed by the Government, was to become "the absolute property of the Company", and, to give it a chance to find its feet, no other line of railway was to be authorized for a period of twenty years between the line of the Canadian Pacific Railway and the boundary of the United States.[2]

Certainly, as a set-off to the delay which had occurred, the Government secured a settlement on much more favourable terms then earlier schemes would have exacted. The Allan Charter provided for a cash subsidy of 30 million dollars and a grant of 54,700,000 acres of land. The Mackenzie Act of 1874 proposed to make a land grant of 20,000 acres a mile and a cash subsidy of $10,000 a mile, also a further Government guarantee.

---

[1] S. C. Johnson, *A History of Emigration from the United Kingdom to North America*, p. 205.

[2] The "monopoly clause" was cancelled in 1888, the consideration being an agreement by the Government to guarantee the interest on a new issue of bonds secured on the Company's land grant.

Public opinion generally was favourable to the enterprise, but formidable interests had to be reckoned with. Ontario and Toronto feared the diversion of traffic to Montreal. The Grand Trunk Railway resented the invasion of its territory by the Canadian Pacific's threatened acquisition of lines and running powers. Nevertheless, the false starts and slow progress of the last ten years now gave place to a concentrated and feverish activity. The new order of things gave full scope to the furious energy of William Van Horne, the " Master Builder " of the line, and the opportunity for heroic enterprise to two of Canada's greatest sons, Donald Smith, afterwards Lord Strathcona and Mount Royal, long distinguished in the service of the Hudson's Bay Company, who ventured the whole of his fortune in the new work to which he had put his hand ; and his cousin, George Stephen, the head of the Canadian Pacific Syndicate, later to become Lord Mountstephen.

The earliest section of the railway to be available for traffic was that which ran through the territory between Red River and Lake Superior, " a waste of forest and rock and swamp, every mile of which had to be hewn, blasted or filled up." [1] It was on this section that the Government had been at work, and as early as 1882 the line was open from Thunder Bay on Lake Superior to Winnipeg and 500 miles further westwards. The stipulated date for the completion of the line was 1891. The first Canadian Pacific through train left Montreal on 28th June, 1886, and reached Port Moody on the Pacific coast, a few miles from Vancouver, with its seventy passengers, in the scheduled time. No longer could it be said that the only means of communication which British Columbia had with Ottawa was by way of the United States at a distance of more than 2,000 miles through foreign territory, in addition to a sea voyage of 800 miles. Canada now had a line of its own which tapped every Province except Prince Edward Island. And whereas Lord Dufferin had to make his pilgrimage from Ottawa to British Columbia in 1876 by way of Chicago and San Francisco and thence by ship to Esquimault, the representatives of British Columbia could now reach the legislative capital by a comfortable journey entirely through their own territory.

The persistent bullying to which a Province with a total white population no greater than that of a quite

---

[1] W. L. Griffith, *The Dominion of Canada*, The All Red Series, p. 314.

small English county town subjected the Dominion Government has its humorous side, and the material profits which might be expected from so great an enterprise with its infinite demands for labour and materials may not have been altogether absent from the minds of individuals : but the fact remains that by her initial bargain for a transcontinental railway and her insistence on its being carried through, British Columbia saved the Pacific seaboard for Canada and the British Empire.

At the end of 1925 the Canadian Pacific system had 13,667 miles of railway. Of this only 2,896 miles represents the main line from Montreal to Vancouver, through Winnipeg, Regina and Calgary, crossing the Rocky Mountains at Kicking Horse Pass, a point considerably south of Yellow Head Pass originally laid down in the contract as the point of entry into British Columbia. Nor is the system wholly situated in Canada. The 5,100 miles in the United States which the Canadian Pacific Railway controls through its holding of stocks includes such lines as the Minneapolis, St. Paul and Sault Ste. Marie Railway, itself over 4,000 miles in length. Nor again is it merely a railway. The vast grants of land the Company received made it a colonizing agent, and its steamers carry its traffic across the Atlantic and the Pacific. Of its 10 per cent dividend, 7 per cent arises from railway revenue proper, the other 3 per cent being derived from other sources, such as telegraphs, steamers and hotels.[1] In 1907 the President of the Company claimed that if to their employees and their families were added the men engaged in industrial establishments for the purposes of the Company, " one-fifteenth, if not one-twelfth of the people of this country, directly or indirectly, receive their income from the Company."

Incidentally the building of the first Canadian transcontinental railway called into existence a force that was subsequently to become " the pride of Canada and the envy of the world ", the North-West Mounted Police. Not only were there a zone of vast mountains and a vast plain of impenetrable emptiness to cross but " the plains, it was said, were sadly Indian-ridden, and prospective shareholders could scarcely be interested in laying rails across a desert where fifteen thousand redskins stood eager to pull them up again. Nor could surveyors be expected to work accurately

---

[1] In 1929, " the largest hotel in the British Empire " built by the C.P.R., was opened in Ottawa (*Times*, 12th June, 1929).

in an atmosphere of alarms and scalpings.   It was clear to
Sir John Macdonald that a sort of safety must be provided." [1]
So the famous force which was to be the Dominion's
stand-by on many a difficult occasion, came into existence.

Whether certain of the constituent Provinces of the
Dominion could much longer have withstood the pull of the
United States in the absence of a transcontinental railway
is very doubtful. We have seen that British Columbia openly
threatened secession unless the Dominion Government held
to its bargain to build such a railway. Sir Charles Tupper,
the Minister for Railways, who carried through the Canadian
Pacific Railway contract, has expressed his very clear view
on the matter : " What would have been the fate of British
Columbia if it had remained isolated from Eastern Canada
by an unexplored sea of mountains and vast uninhabited
prairies ?   There is no question that it would inevitably
have resulted in the absorption of the Crown Colony on the
Pacific coast by the United States.   Social and economic
forces were working in that direction from the date of the
discovery of gold in 1856.   Thousands of adventurous
American citizens flocked to British Columbia and between
the two countries there was a good deal of inter-communica-
tion by land and sea. . . . Under the existing circumstances
it had no means of advancement except by throwing in its
lot with the great nation to the south with which it had
constant communication both by land and sea." [2]

Then again railway lines running north and south brought
the territory that is now Manitoba into a much closer and
a much more sympathetic connexion with the neighbouring
States of the Union than with the sister Provinces of the
Dominion and the opinion was widely held that if the
Canadian Pacific Railway had not been built Manitoba
would inevitably have gravitated to the United States.
In 1870 Sir John Macdonald recorded the opinion that
" the United States Government are resolved to do all
they can short of war to get possession of the Western
territory " and that the way to counteract them was " to
show unmistakably our resolve to build the Pacific
Railway ". [3]   Americans indeed openly expressed their
anticipation of its " annexation ".   " The opening by us
first of a North Pacific Railroad seals the destiny of the

[1] T. Morris Longstreth, *The Silent Force.*
[2] Sir Charles Tupper, *Recollections of Sixty Years*, p. 124.
[3] Sir Joseph Pope, *Correspondence of Sir John Macdonald*, pp. 124-5.

British possessions west of the 91st meridian. They will become so Americanized in interests and feelings that they will be in effect severed from the new Dominion and the question of their annexation will be but a question of time." [1]

Other transcontinental lines were built later, but the Canadian Pacific Railway was the barrier that permanently dammed back United States political and economic penetration.

Another of the services rendered by the transcontinental line was thus referred to by Sir Charles Tupper : " We all know that the great barrier to the successful development of the North-West was that in the absence of a Canadian Pacific Railway our immigration was obliged to filter through the territories of the United States. The great efforts which have been made to secure immigration into the United States, and intercept those who were on their way to the North-West, have not been made by the Government of that country, or by the Legislatures of the States, but by the railway companies who have a personal interest in seducing these immigrants into their own territories." [2]

As an engineering feat the construction of the Canadian Pacific Railway was remarkable. " The finest day's journey in all the Empire is surely the ride from Calgary westward and up into the Canadian Rockies. The prairies, with their long line of wheat elevators stretched like a chain of forts, lie far behind. . . . And the train climbs mile after mile into the mountains, past Banff and its buffalo park, until the straining engine seems a noisy intruder in the cathedral silence of the snows. Then over the " Great Divide ", where you may see the waters run east and west, and a race down the other side into the rugged valley of the Fraser River. . . . The traveller . . . for an hour or more watched the rails ahead boring their way through tunnels, flashing over bridges, and winding down mountain-sides until thought began to wander from the grandeur of the scenery around and turned instead to the greatness of Strathcona and Van Horne and the men who built the line. [3]

And we admire the sporting instincts, or as some would prefer to put it, we reverence the faith of men who were ready to stake their all on a scheme for driving a railway

[1] Report of United States Senate Committee on Pacific Railroads (1869).
[2] *Dominions Debates* 1880–1, vol. i, p. 67.
[3] " The Empire by Rail," *Times*, 3rd March, 1928.

through two thousand miles of untamed and largely uninhabited country. Still the important thing is that their great gamble made available to the world the rich minerals north of Lake Superior, increased immeasurably the food supply of the world by the creation of the Prairie Provinces, and inaugurated a new route between Great Britain and Eastern Asia by way entirely of the ocean and British soil.

CHAPTER 10

THE CANADIAN NATIONAL RAILWAYS

THE principal constituent enterprises which have become the great system of the Canadian National Railways [1] are the Grand Trunk, serving the region between the St. Lawrence and Lake Huron, the earliest of the great Canadian railways ; the Intercolonial, constructed in pursuance of the British North America Act to unite the Maritime Provinces and the Canadas ; the Canadian

---

[1] " The Canadian National management was not handed a railway system : it was handed a conglomeration of various entities all over the Dominion of Canada, many of them having no connexion with any other part of the system . . . in this system there are more than one hundred different companies." Minister of Railways and Canals, *Dominion Debates*, 1925, vol. iii, p. 2,914.

Northern, begun in 1896 and completed ten years later, the second, and the Grand Trunk Pacific, the third of the transcontinental lines ; and there is the newest of them all, the Hudson Bay Railway.

The earliest of these systems, the Grand Trunk, became, in its late years the parent of the comparatively recent arrival, the Grand Trunk Pacific, and the older line is most conveniently considered at a later stage in association with the transcontinental systems rather than in strictly chronological order.

The Intercolonial

A railway connecting Quebec with a port on the Atlantic that would be open all the year was first projected at a time when it would have been possible to construct a line running due east and west between St. Andrews on the Bay of Fundy and Quebec without leaving British territory. The people of the United States were quick to see the commercial and military advantages which would accrue to British North America from such a railway and their government were determined to thwart it.[1] The Maine Boundary question provided the means. The boundary between the State of Maine and the British Province of New Brunswick had been in dispute ever since the Treaty of Paris, 1783, which purported to define it, but the question had more or less been allowed to remain in abeyance. It was now revived on the demand of Maine and settled in 1842 by the treaty which was negotiated by Lord Ashburton for Great Britain

---

[1] Their attitude was expressed in a New York journal in 1837 in such terms as these : " The plan which the Canadians and the New Brunswick people, under the auspices of the British Government, have projected, of a railroad from Quebec to St. Andrews in New Brunswick or the City of St. John, so as to make, it is said, St. Andrews a wharf and the Bay of Fundy a harbour for the St. Lawrence is . . . calculated to involve, ultimately, the most important political consequences. The idea was stolen from the Maine Legislature where the project originally started. . . . The difficult and dangerous navigation of the St. Lawrence is thus avoided. The British will also thus have a port where their produce can be sent to or from the West Indies. Military and commercial advantages prompt the British Government to expend $4,000,000, for with the harbour of Halifax, as it is near Europe, a cordon of British bayonets can be made to surround us in the shortest possible time, and the produce of the Canadas, now seeking a mart in New York in American ships, can thus be turned to St. Andrews or St. John in British bottoms. But, rely on it, there is no question when a foreign power now so vastly involving the future destinies of this country as the disputed boundary line with England." Quoted by Sandford Fleming in *The Intercolonial, a History*, p. 14.

and Daniel Webster for the United States. In the result some 5,000 miles of territory hitherto claimed as part of New Brunswick was ceded to the United States, so driving a great wedge between the Maritime Provinces and the St. Lawrence and rendering impossible the projected railway save by a wide detour. The hopes of St. Andrews of becoming the terminus of the Intercolonial railway were shattered once and for all and the whole scheme for a railway connecting the Maritime Provinces with the Canadas was indefinitely postponed and was only brought to life again as part of the great scheme for confederation.

Flowing out of the idea of confederation and the change in the direction of the trade of the Provinces that would result there arose the need for a readjustment of routes and trade channels between the Canadas and the Maritime Provinces. Hitherto the Canadas had communicated with the United States and England by means of the waterways and of the railways through the United States, and the Maritime Provinces with the United States and England by sea. Between the Canadas and the Maritime Provinces little traffic existed, except by the St. Lawrence in the summer-time and by the United States railways and the ocean in winter-time. With Confederation an all-the-year-round route within the bounds of British North America would be required, and that could only be effected by the building of such a railway as the Intercolonial.

Accordingly the British North America Act, 1867, which brought Confederation into being, made provision by Section 145 in the following terms :—

" Inasmuch as the Provinces of Canada, Nova Scotia and New Brunswick have joined in a declaration that the construction of the Intercolonial Railway is essential to the consolidation of the Union of British North America and to the assent thereto of Nova Scotia and New Brunswick, and have consequently agreed that provision should be made for its immediate construction by the Government of Canada : Therefore, in order to give effect to that agreement, it shall be the duty of the Government and Parliament of Canada to provide for the commencement, within six months after the Union, of a railway connecting the River St. Lawrence with the City of Halifax in Nova Scotia and for the construction thereof without intermission and the completion thereof with all practicable speed."

By a further Act, and largely on account of the military

importance of the railway, the Imperial Government guaranteed a loan for three millions.

Portions of a through railway had been constructed by the respective Provinces previous to confederation. These passed to the Dominion Government under the British North America Act, and it was the task of that Government to link them up so as to become the completed Intercolonial Railway. This was done and the railway was opened for traffic in 1876. Starting on the Atlantic seaboard at Halifax, the line was made to meander along northwards and westwards by the coast-line to the St. Lawrence and then to come south to join the Grand Trunk, again along the coast line, at Rivière du Loup. A branch comes south from Moncton in New Brunswick to St. John. But " the Inter-colonial is merely a local line terminating at Montreal, and with no direct connexion with the markets of Ontario and the West ; and the Maritime Provinces have suffered from this isolation ".[1]

Through having to avoid entering the State of Maine as enlarged after the Ashburton Treaty, the line had to follow a route which held out but a poor promise of remunerative traffic. This determination to keep the lines within the bounds of British territory at any cost was a triumph of national sentiment, later to be repeated when the Canadian Pacific declined to connect the Eastern Provinces with the West by utilizing American railways south of Lake Superior. Had a direct line east and west been possible, the distance between Montreal and Halifax would have been some 200 miles less, and the building of 250 miles of line unnecessary. " The direct line would have attracted certain branches of traffic which by the longer route must either be carried at a loss or be repelled." [2] The line has been a serious financial burden on the Dominion. " As much as one and a half dollars had to be expended in order to secure the return of one dollar." [3] The Drayton-Acworth Commission found that the capital cost of this railway had been over $106,000,000 and that " in the twenty-eight years from 1889–1916 there was an accumulated deficit on operation of $6,491,232 ", and moreover the line was exempt from the payment of local taxes, and " down to 1908 no charges were made against revenue for necessary renewals and replacements."

[1] *Drayton-Acworth Report*, p. lxvii.
[2] Sandford Fleming, op. cit., p. 78.   [3] *Annual Register*, 1881.

The truth, in the words of Sir Wilfred Laurier,[1] was that " the Intercolonial never was intended and never was conceived and never was built for transcontinental traffic. The Intercolonial was first conceived as a military road. It was built and located for political reasons and not from any commercial consideration ". The route followed by the line, the result of " the blunder which was made by British diplomacy in settling our boundary line by the Ashburton-Webster Treaty " make it impossible for the ports of St. John and Halifax to compete with the nearer ports of Portland and Boston in the United States. It became so urgent in the 'eighties that the state of things should be mended, that Sir Charles Tupper allowed the Canadian Pacific to build a direct line connecting Montreal with St. John through Maine. He was content if only the terminus were on Canadian soil and if St. John could really become a Canadian winter port.

The building of the Intercolonial was primarily a political measure. In the words of one speaker in the confederation debate it was " just as necessary to the proposed confederation as the spinal column to the human frame ". Economically the Maritime Provinces stood to gain more by obtaining access to the market of Ontario than did Ontario by getting access to the Maritime Provinces. Ontario looked to England for a market rather than to the Provinces in the east, and the outlet by way of the St. Lawrence and the United States railways served its purpose well enough. In New Brunswick especially a vast new territory was opened up, and in Nova Scotia the importance of Halifax as a port was bound to be enhanced. Ontario was not nearly so enthusiastic ; its interests turned in another direction. There emerged that divergence of aim and disparity of outlook between the Maritime Provinces and the Provinces west of the St. Lawrence which has persisted to the present day.

The result was that there was a good deal of friction as regards the relative importance of the Intercolonial and of communications with the North-West. Section 68 of the Quebec Resolutions declared that the Intercolonial Railway should be constructed " without delay ", while Section 69 affirmed that communications should be opened up with the North West " at the earliest possible period that the state of the finances will permit ". The Intercolonial thus obtained priority of treatment, but only on the understanding that

[1] *Dominion Debates*, 1903, vol. iv, col. 7660.

the interests of Ontario in the North West should not be neglected. Mr. McMaster on the occasion of the Confederation Debate said : " And I trust the promises made with reference to the widening and deepening of our canals, and the opening up of the North West Territory will be carried out in good faith. Indeed no Government can afford to treat with entire neglect works of so much importance to Upper Canada, and at the same time incur the large expenditure required for the Intercolonial Railroad." According to Mr. Joly, " Upper Canada objects, in general terms, to the construction of the Intercolonial Railroad. Its wish is to see the resources of the future Confederation applied to opening up the immense territory of the North-West, and to the enlargement of its canals. The Atlantic Provinces desire the Intercolonial Railroad ; but they hold in dread the expenditure which would be entailed by the opening up of the North-West territory and the enlargement of the canals." Finally Mr. McGiverin laid it down that " We must have these promises respecting the North-West and the canals fairly carried out, and not be placed in such a position that after the Intercolonial Roalroad shall have been constructed, there will be a combination of eastern interests to prevent the accomplishment of these other works and swamp the great North-West ".[1]

The Grand Trunk

The Grand Trunk Railway system and the Canadian Pacific Railway illustrate in the most striking way the fundamentally different conceptions which existed before and after the year 1867, as to the lines along which Canada should develop. The Canadian Pacific Railway, belonging to the national period, was in its essence a national line, undertaken to unite the eastern Canadian seaboard with the west. The Grand Trunk, organized as it was in the 'fifties, had for its main purpose the access of Canada to the Atlantic through the United States and the development of traffic between the two countries. It was essentially an international railway.

The early railway policy of the Canadian Government favoured private rather than public construction and management. The part played by the Government was accordingly to provide inducements for the attraction

---

[1] *Debates on Confederation, Canadian Provincial Parliament,* 1865.

of capital to railway enterprise in Canada by guaranteeing a proportion of the cost of the proposed lines or by offering a loan based on mileage. In 1853 Acts were passed laying down the broad lines of policy on which the Grand Trunk system was built up. Provision was made in that year for the amalgamation of various companies making up the main line ; power was given to construct the Victoria Bridge connecting the lines west of Montreal with those leading to the Atlantic ; and the lease of the United States line connecting the Canadian railways with the ocean at Portland was authorized. Even then the difficulties attendant upon the selection of a United States port as the winter terminus of a Canadian railway which were fully to emerge when nationalism was formulated as a principle of Canadian politics, were not altogether unrecognized. " Efforts have been repeatedly made as well by Canada as by New Brunswick and Nova Scotia, to induce the Imperial Government to promote the extension of the Grand Trunk Railway to some colonial winter port, but without success ; and it is as yet wholly beyond the power of the provinces, unaided, to construct a line which is more valuable on national rather than on commercial grounds." [1]

By 1860 the Grand Trunk had a main line running from Rivière du Loup on the east of the St. Lawrence north-east of Quebec through Quebec and Montreal to the United States boundary at Sarnia on Lake Huron ; the line from Portland, Maine, to the Canadian boundary had been leased ; and the Victoria Bridge over the St. Lawrence at Montreal, where the width of the river is nearly two miles, gave the company a through route from Portland to Sarnia. The Grand Trunk had also crossed the international boundary in another direction in 1859 when it leased the line between Detroit and Port Huron, the Lake Michigan port on the United States side opposite Sarnia.

The expansion effort of the system had by this time spent itself and during the 'sixties and the 'seventies the Company did little more than mark time. When extension was resumed in the 'eighties there was no change of policy. The system struck out for independent access to Chicago

---

[1] Galt, The Hon. A. T., " Canada 1849 to 1859 " (*Canada : Pamphlets*, vol. i, No. 3, in Dominions and Colonial Office Library). The charge to the Province on account of public aid to railway construction was already £250,000 per annum, and of the total public debt of £9,500,000 some £4,000,000 had been contracted by the Province in the prosecution of its railway policy. (Ibid.)

and in 1880 the southern points of Lakes Michigan and Huron were joined together by a line from Chicago to Port Huron. On the Canadian side development mainly took place in Ontario.

Finally in 1891 the Grand Trunk policy was consummated by the completion of " the link that binds two nations ", that is to say the two miles long St. Clair Tunnel, under the river of the same name, which joined the Ontario port of Sarnia with Port Huron in Michigan.

The system as it existed in 1922 extended from Portland, Maine, to Chicago, with 4,776 miles in operation, of which 3,612 were in Canada and 1,164 miles in the United States.

Of all the Canadian railways, the history of the Grand Trunk system most nearly resembles that of the development of railways in Great Britain with which it was contemporary. There is the same history of successive amalgamations. In its early stages it preceded confederation and the policy of wholesale government subsidies to railways, and so to a greater extent than any other Canadian railway had to rely on capital raised from private sources.[1] It had no land subsidies. Government help in some measure was, however, found necessary, and small as that assistance was in comparison with that given to later lines, it is important as initiating the application of the principle in Canada of extending Government aid to railway construction. The resemblance even extends to expensive mistakes. In England the Great Western Railway had to spend millions in the conversion of Brunel's 7 feet broad gauge to the 4 ft. 8½ in. which had been adopted by its rivals. Similarly the Grand Trunk was faced with the necessity of converting nearly 1,400 miles of railway from the 5 ft. 6 in. gauge on which it was originally constructed to the standard 4 ft. 8½ in. if there was to be free interchange of traffic with the United States, a work which was courageously carried out in 1873–4. The early railway builders have also been criticised on the ground that they built unnecessarily expensively. The Victoria Bridge, built by Robert Stevenson, at Montreal, for example, cost between six and seven million dollars. " A few miles up the river is the steel bridge built long after by the Canadian Pacific Railway, performing exactly the

---

[1] The *Drayton-Acworth Report* states the total Government aid to the Grand Trunk to have been $28,000,000, of which $13,000,000 were subsidies and $15,000,000 loans.

same office, which was built in a year and cost less than a million dollars." [1]

The Drayton-Acworth Report stated in 1917 that " the Grand Trunk had always met its obligations though over a series of years the return to its shareholders had been but small ". The common stock never paid a dividend in the seventy years of the separate existence of the Company.

The Canadian Northern

The two transcontinental railways to which the Canadian Government has succeeded, the Canadian Northern and the system of which half was the Grand Trunk Pacific and half the Transcontinental, were the outcome of the determination of the North-West to break the monopoly of the Canadian Pacific [2] They made the mistake of competing not only with the Canadian Pacific but with one another with results which, financially, have been disastrous. As was pointed out in the Drayton-Acworth Report [3] " The Canadian Pacific had . . . the advantage of gathering its own traffic for itself and of keeping it in its own hand throughout. The other two companies were in a different position. The Canadian Northern had to depend for westbound rail traffic on what the companies in the east, one of which was a rival, handed to it. On the traffic which it collected in the west, it lost the long haul to the east. It was not unnatural that the company should reach out to the east. For the same reason it was equally natural that the Grand Trunk Company should reach out to the west. And further sentiment, which felt that the growth of the country justified and required more than one transcontinental line, undoubtedly sympathized with the companies' ambitions. The natural solution of the question undoubtedly was that the Canadian Northern and the Grand Trunk should join forces and construct a line from North Bay, or its neighbourhood, to Port Arthur. Negotiations for the amalgamation of the two companies were, we understand, actually set on foot in 1903. Unfortunately they came to

[1] W. L. Griffith, *The Dominion of Canada* (The All Red Series), p. 59.
[2] The monopoly clause in the C.P.R. contract " nearly threatened the Dominion with secession on the part of Manitoba ". (M. Lemieux, *Dominion Debates*, 1903. vol. iv, col. 8786.)
[3] The Commission was appointed in 1916 to investigate the general problem of transportation and in particular the position and prospects of the three transcontinental systems. Their Report will be found in *Sessional Papers, Canada*, vol. 52, No. 12 (20 g.–1917).

nothing ; and each company set out independently to construct into the territory of the other." [1]

Two Scottish Highlanders carried the construction of the Canadian Pacific Railway to its successful conclusion. The names of two other Scots, Mackenzie and Mann, are indissolubly associated with the creation of the second of the transcontinental lines—the Canadian Northern.

Encouraged and assisted by the Government of Manitoba whose desire it was to create competition with the Canadian Pacific, the Canadian Northern has been built up by a process of radiation from the Winnipeg region. A beginning was made in 1896 when Mackenzie and Mann acquired the derelict charter of the Lake Manitoba Railway and Canal Company from Gladstone, which is west of Winnipeg, to Winnipegosis, 123 miles to the north. By 1902 they had a line connecting Winnipeg and Port Arthur on Lake Superior. By leases, by absorption and amalgamation and by construction, the system reached out east and west, following a course in one direction from Winnipeg along the north of Lake Superior to Nipigon, Lake Huron, and Quebec, and westerly to Prince Albert and Battleford in Saskatchewan, through Edmonton, across the Yellowhead Pass, when it dips south to Vancouver. So favourable was the gradient that when the " Inaugural Special " crossed the continent in October, 1915, one ordinary locomotive hauled the train of fifteen coaches successfully through to the Pacific coast. The Canadian Northern contributed a total length of 9,971 miles to the Canadian National system, of which total 9,361 miles were in operation in 1915.[2]

State aid to the Company has been generous. The aggregate to the Canadian Northern was greater than to any other company, but two-thirds of it was indirect aid in the form of guarantees. Direct aid in the shape of subsidies and land grants was much less than that accorded

---

[1] " The first proposition made to the Grand Trunk Railway . . . was for the Grand Trunk Pacific Railway to start at Gravenhurst or North Bay to connect with the Canadian Northern system at Port Arthur, to obtain control of the Canadian Northern system, and to build a line from its western terminus to the Pacific coast . . . Had that proposition been carried out, a train could have started from Halifax or St. John and reached the Pacific coast without running over a single mile of the Canadian Pacific Railway track and it would have been altogether in Canadian territory." *Dominion Debates* 1903, vol. iv, col. 9159 : Mr. A. E. Kemp.

[2] See Dominions Royal Commission, *Minutes of Evidence in* 1916 [Cd. 8458]. *Memorandum* by Mr. L. C. Fritch, General Manager of the C.N. Railway, p. 389.

to the Canadian Pacific. The Drayton-Acworth Commission found " $370,000,000 to be the maximum possible cost of the Canadian Northern system as at present existing ". Of this sum the " total public assistance, direct and indirect ", was $298,250,000. This sum included subsidies from the Dominion Government, the Provincial Governments and the Municipalities, and cash loans for which the Dominion Government received no interest. The method of extending Government aid to the Company most in favour was by way of public guarantee of its bonds. These figures are impressive. The Dominion Government guaranteed over 100 million dollars and the Provincial Governments between them a like amount. The Company was thereby enabled to raise money at rates of interest substantially lower than would have been exacted had it had to rely on its own credit. Furthermore the Company received land grants amounting to 6,555,000 acres.[1]

According to the Drayton-Acworth Commission " up to 1914 the Company apparently met its obligations from its own resources ". The Company had no Preference Stock and no dividend was ever paid on its $100,000,000 of Common Stock.

But the railway " had gone ahead too fast and had undertaken various expensive schemes which could not possibly carry themselves from the outset ", and doubtless the Great War contributed to its difficulties. Whatever the cause, the Drayton-Acworth Commission reported that in 1917 " the Company is living from hand to mouth, and is nominally borrowing from the Government to pay interest on the Government's own loans ". They summed up the position by the statement that " the Company is not at present able, and will not for some years to come be able, to meet its fixed charges ", and they recommended that, since the people of Canada had already found or assumed responsibility for the bulk of the capital, and must needs find any further capital needed and make up for some

[1] The *Drayton-Acworth Report* in 1917 thus summarized Government aid to the Canadian Northern :—

				$
Subsidies	.	.	.	38,874,148
Land Grants	.	.	.	34,379,809
Cash Loans	.	.	.	25,858,166
Securities Guaranteed	.		.	199,141,140
Total	.		.	$298,253,263

years to come considerable deficits in net earnings, " the people of Canada should assume control of the property."

The Grand Trunk Pacific

The Canadian Northern has been seen stretching out to the east in order to retain for the long haul the traffic it collected in the West and in order to end its dependence upon other railways for West-bound traffic. When Charles M. Hays took charge of the Grand Trunk, his mission as General Manager being to rescue the line from impending bankruptcy, he found a similar problem confronting him. He had to hand over his West-bound through traffic to a rival. Such traffic, collected in the West, as he carried, was that which other lines handed to his system. This was especially galling, since the West was at the time in a state of boom. He determined to provide the Grand Trunk with its own outlet to the West, and to this conception in the brain, this time not of a Scot but an American, the third of the great transcontinental lines, the Grand Trunk Pacific, owes its origin.

But the railway which has been constructed was not the scheme proposed by the original promoters when, in 1902, Hays first approached Sir Charles Rivers Wilson, the President of the Grand Trunk Railway. His proposal was to construct a line to connect the Ontario lines of the Grand Trunk with the North-West, and the petition to the Government asked for authority " to undertake the construction of such a line from North Bay, Ontario, or some other point north thereof to be defined, to the Pacific coast". Further, "to provide for connexion with the Atlantic seaboard all the year round and through an all-British territory route, your petitioners will be prepared to enter into an arrangement . . . for an interchange of traffic or other satisfactory agreement with the Intercolonial Railway at Montreal". Such a scheme " would have the advantage of all the eastern connexions in Ontario and Quebec of the Grand Trunk Railway " and there would be established " a complete system from ocean to ocean ".

But the country had not yet learned the lesson which it was later to be taught by bitter experience, that, to be successful, railway enterprise must be entirely divorced from political considerations. First Sir Wilfred Laurier and his Cabinet requested Hays to amend his Bill so as to provide for the construction of a line from North Bay to Quebec. Next the Maritime Provinces brought such pressure to bear that the Government removed the eastern terminus from Quebec to Moncton whence both Halifax and St. John could be reached over the Intercolonial.

The ostensible motives which induced the Government to give ear to the scheme were thus expressed in the speech from the throne on the opening of the Parliament which passed the National Transcontinental Railway Act, 1903 : " The great influx of population into our North-Western Territories and the very large additional areas of fertile land which are being brought under cultivation combine to further press upon us the need for increased transportation facilities for the forwarding of our grain and other products to the markets of the world through Canadian channels."

There had been difficulties in moving the grain grown in the North-West during the previous two years.[1] There had been complaints of hardship due to the scarcity of fuel and building materials arising from lack of transport facilities. Merchants reported that they had been out of certain lines of goods for weeks and months at a time because the railway could not get them in, although the goods had been promptly despatched by wholesalers in the east. It was pointed out that immediately south of the boundary of Manitoba were four or five of the best equipped railway systems in the world, and the question was asked whether it could be doubted that, unless something was done to relieve the condition of things by which grain was held up and traders left without goods for lack of transport facilities, the trade would go south to the United States. As put by Sir William Van Horne in 1902 : " Canada has been adding sides to her hopper for a long time but has neglected to enlarge the spout. She has for many years been spending millions generously in the development of the interior and her railways but has neglected her outlet at the Atlantic. Her crops and industries have grown and her hopper is full to overflowing and the outlet at Montreal is not large enough. Her exports take the easy routes by the Great Lakes and the Erie Canal to Boston and New York."[2]

[1] According to the *Mail and Empire* of 25th November, 1902, " Last year the crop was more than the Canadian Pacific Railway exerting all its great reserves could handle before the close of navigation." (Quoted by Hon. Clifford Sifton, *Dominions Debates*, Session 1903, vol. iv, col. 8652.)

[2] Quoted *Dominion Debates*, 1903, vol. iv, col. 9835.

Then " one of the great industries of the North-West Territories is grazing cattle as contrasted with raising cattle.
Last year we imported into the North-West Territories
no less than 50,000 head of what are called stockers, that is,
young cattle, bought by the ranchers for the purpose of
being finished and perfected for the English market. Where
did they get them ? They got 25,000 from Ontario . . .
Where did they get the rest ? They got them from Mexico.
Cannot the farmers of the Province of Quebec and the
Maritime Provinces raise cattle to supply the stock-grazier
on the North-Western plains . . . Here we have 25,000
stockers in one year coming from Mexico because we have
not the facilities to take them from Eastern Canada.[1]

The Canadian Pacific had done much, but not enough
to satisfy the North-West. There was a time when the
merchants of Quebec, Montreal and Toronto were obliged,
when winter closed navigation, to shut down business and
sit with folded arms until the spring. The railway era
made every day a possible working day whether in winter
or summer. In the regions of the North-West where no
railway as yet penetrated, the business of forwarding
produce was closed down in winter just as was business
in Eastern Canada many years previously. The Canadian
Pacific Railway could take a certain amount of grain out
of the West, but it was hoped that with another transcontinental line it would be possible for the farmers to ship
their grain all the year round.

Another question which played a great part in the conflict
which went on around the transport question was thus
referred to by Sir Wilfred Laurier :—

" From the early days of railway development in the
country we have been dependent upon American goodwill
for the transportation of our goods across American,
territory. From the early days of Canadian railway development we have been forced to make use of American territory
and harbours. The American Government granted us the
bonding privilege. They granted us the privilege of using
their harbours for our imports and exports without paying
them tolls and customs dues. But . . . the privilege had
always been held over our heads by the American authorities
as a sword of Damocles . . . the abrogation of this privilege
has been used again and again as a threat to obtain from us

---

[1] Hon. Clifford Sifton, Minister of the Interior, *Dominion Debates*,
Session, 1903, vol. iv, col. 8677.

concessions . . . If we have used American ports and the bonding privilege it was not because our harbours were ice-bound in winter, but simply because we had no railways to reach them." [1]

One occasion when the United States threatened to bring pressure to bear by the withdrawal of the bonding privilege was when they desired the abrogation of the Fisheries Convention of 1818 under which American fishermen were granted certain privileges in Canadian waters, not including, however, the privilege of buying bait or landing fish on Canadian territory. When the Canadian Government declined to concede these latter privileges except upon terms which were unacceptable to the United States, President Cleveland, in August, 1888, sent a message to Congress in which he said : " During the last six years the imports and exports of British Canadian provinces carried across our territory under the privileges granted by our laws, amounted in value to about 270 million dollars, nearly all of which were goods dutiable under our tariff laws, by far the larger part of the traffic consisting of exchanges of goods between Great Britain and her American provinces brought to and carried from our ports in their own vessels. . . . I recommend immediate legislative action conferring upon the Executive the power to suspend by proclamation the operation of all laws and regulations permitting the transit of goods in bond across or over the railways of the United States to or from Canada." [2]

Canadian Conservative politicians repudiated the notion that they were the bond slaves of the United States and expressed the view that the bonding privilege was as advantageous to the United States as to the Dominion. " It is undoubtedly a great benefit to this country to have the products of the United States come to our seaports for shipment ; but it is a greater benefit to the United States to have our products go to their ports. There were times when signs were not wanting that the American people might cancel the bonding privilege. But those days have long gone by." [3]

But the Laurier Government saw in the new railway a

---

[1] *Dominion Debates*, Session 1903, vol. iv, col. 7670.

[2] Quoted by Sir W. Laurier in *Dominion Debates*, 1903, vol. iv, col. 7673. He cited two further instances where the refusal of certain privileges demanded by American Railway Companies upon Canadian Territory were followed by a similar threat, the second by President Harrison.

[3] A. E. Kemp, *Dominion Debates*, Session 1903, vol. iv, col. 9166.

striking and effective manifestation of that nationalism which had become the dominating principle in the minds of a majority of Canadian electors. If, said the Prime Minister, the railway were built, " we shall have access from January to December to our harbours and be able to say to our American neighbours : ' Take off your bonding privilege whenever it suits you, we are commercially independent.' " [1]

Ardent nationalists found a further recommendation of the scheme in the location of the railway. The United States interests of the Grand Trunk Railway, and especially the fact that its eastern terminus was at Portland, gave rise to suspicion when it was known that this was the Company behind the Grand Trunk Pacific project. When the St. Lawrence route was closed during the winter months, of the railway routes from Winnipeg to the coast that via the Grand Trunk Railway to Portland was the shortest.[2]

The Maritime Provinces regarded the Grand Trunk as their enemy. As a line with one terminal in Chicago and another in Portland, its interests were not those of Halifax and the ports of New Brunswick. " The Grand Trunk cannot serve Portland and Halifax." It was pointed out that the route of the new Grand Trunk Pacific line would bring St. John as near as Portland.

It was urged in some quarters, but not very seriously, that the Government should own and operate the new railway. This the Liberal Government declined to consider, holding that the demands that would be made by politicians for the construction of branch lines, for the lowering of particular rates, and for concessions of every kind to particular districts would foredoom the line to failure.

Another ground of opposition to the Grand Trunk Pacific project was found by the Conservative Party in the fact that the Americans had improved the organization of lake traffic far ahead of the Canadians. The waterways were adequately lighted and buoyed so that navigation

[1] *Dominion Debates*, 1903, vol. iv, col. 7670.

[2]

		Miles.
Via C.P. Railway—		
Winnipeg to St. John, N.B. . . .		1,989
Winnipeg to Halifax, N.S. . . .		2,264
Via Intercolonial Railway—		
Winnipeg to St. John, N.B. . . .		2,248
Winnipeg to Halifax, N.S. . . .		2,346
Via Grand Trunk Railway—		
Winnipeg to Portland		1,805

—*Dominion Debates*, Session 1903 (Mr. Girard), col. 10,003.

by night was as safe as by day.   In all important inland
ports elevators had been erected.   In 1903 Duluth and West
Superior had 22 elevators with a capacity of 34 million
bushels.   Buffalo had 28 elevators with a capacity of 21
million bushels.   For all the grain could not be shipped in
two or three months : some must be stored.

As to rates : " The average rate on grain from Port
Arthur to Montreal by rail on the Canadian Pacific has
been about 12 cents a bushel ; whereas the average rate by
lake and rail has been about 7 cents a bushel "—5 cents
against the all-rail route.[1]

The Conservative opposition to the Grand Trunk Pacific
policy of the Laurier Government accordingly favoured
rival development, on the Canadian side, of the lake ports
and those of the St. Lawrence waterway.

The terms of the partnership between the Government
of Canada and the Grand Trunk Pacific Railway Company
for the purpose of the construction of the new transcontinental railway are set out in the agreement which is
scheduled to the National Transcontinental Railway Act,
1903,[2] whereby the agreement was ratified.

The gauge was to be 4 ft. $8\frac{1}{2}$ in.   There was to be competition in the West but in the East the Government made
the Grand Trunk system, with its long established connexions in Ontario and Quebec, the foundation of the
scheme.

The Eastern Division (the National Transcontinental)
from Moncton, New Brunswick, where connexion with the
Atlantic ports, St. John and Halifax, was available by the
Intercolonial through Quebec and Northern Ontario to
Winnipeg, the meeting place of East and West, was to be
constructed by the Government.   The Western Division
(the Grand Trunk Pacific) from Winnipeg to the Pacific
was to be built by the Company.   When completed the
Eastern Division was to be leased to and operated by the
Company for fifty years, the Company paying to the Government by way of rental after the first seven years a sum
equal to 3 per cent per annum on the cost of construction.
The Act which ratified the agreement provided that the

---

[1] *Dominion Debates*, 1903, vol. iv, col. 9742.

[2] *Statutes of Canada*, 3 Edw. VII, chap. lxxi.   There is a further Act
of 1904 (4 Edw. VII, chap. xxiv) amending the principal Act mainly in
financial details and enlarging the Grand Trunk Company's power of
co-operation.   The Company was incorporated by the Grand Trunk
Pacific Railway Act, 1903 (3 Edw. VII, chap. cxxii).

Government part of the line should be constructed and operated until completed and leased under the control of Commissioners to be appointed by the Governor in Council.

The finance provisions of the agreement included clauses by which the Government agreed to guarantee principal and interest on bonds to be issued by the Company for an amount equal to 75 per cent of the cost of construction of the Western Division ; and the Grand Trunk Railway, in addition to taking 25 million dollars of common stock, was to guarantee bonds for the balance required for the construction of the Western Division. The ratifying Act made Government aid conditional on the Grand Trunk so undertaking and agreeing. The only lands granted to the Company were such as were required for the construction and working of the railway. So long as the Government guarantee continued and during the term of the lease of the Eastern Division the Government was to have the right to appoint one Director of the Company.

The purely national purpose of the railway is insisted on throughout the agreement. The preamble recites how, " having regard to the growth of population and the rapid development of the production and trade of Manitoba and the North-West Territories, and to the great area of fertile and productive land in all the provinces and territories as yet without railway facilities, and to the rapidly expanding trade and commerce of the Dominion, it is in the interests of Canada that a line of railway designed to secure the most direct and economical interchange of traffic between Eastern Canada and the provinces and territories west of the Great Lakes, to open up and develop the northern zone of the Dominion, to promote the internal and foreign trade of Canada, and to develop commerce through Canadian ports, should be constructed and operated as a common railway highway across the Dominion, from ocean to ocean, and wholly within Canadian territory." Supplies and material so far as possible were to be purchased from Canadian producers. The Government aid provided for being granted " for the express purpose of encouraging the development of Canadian trade and the transportation of goods through Canadian channels ", freight was wherever possible to be routed entirely on Canadian territory or between Canadian inland ports.

At the outset it was decided that in several respects the construction of the Grand Trunk Pacific should depart from

U

the practice hitherto generally pursued in the construction
of American transcontinental lines. Hitherto speed of construction and cheapness has been regarded as indispensable
conditions. A rough track, initially cheap, but ultimately
very costly by reason of the need for constant repairs and
overhaul was the result. Moreover, on such a track the
passengers must be prepared to endure a degree of pitching
and rolling which brings home to them the knowledge
that car sickness can be as uncomfortable as sea sickness.
It was determined that the new line should follow the British
rather than the American practice and should be solidly
built at the outset.

The one calamity which occurred during the construction of the railway is strong enough testimony in favour of
the wisdom of this policy of Thorough.

The line had to get from one side of the St. Lawrence
to the other and the question was anxiously debated whether
it should be by way of a tunnel or a train ferry or a bridge.
The first was found financially impracticable ; the annual
freeze-up would make the second impossible for several
months during the year ; and in the end a bridge, on the
model of that which spans the Firth of Forth, was decided
on, for no impediment could be permitted in the river to
liners proceeding up to Montreal or to the vessels carrying
freight to the ports of the Great Lakes. So American
engineers were employed to build a bridge with the largest
cantilever span in the world, namely, 1,800 feet, carrying
trains 150 feet above the water. The work was pushed on
rapidly and some 800 feet of the main span had been placed
in position, and the attainment of the American engineers'
ambition to build a greater than the Forth Bridge seemed
to be in sight, when one day the whole mass collapsed into
the river under its own weight. British engineering opinion
had persistently regarded American bridge-building practice
with suspicion, and in particular the tendency to build too
light a structure. American engineers had regarded British
methods as unduly costly and unnecessarily solid. The
Quebec disaster vindicated British practice and the lesson
was taken to heart when the new bridge was designed.
In the result Quebec has a gigantic bridge with a total
length of 3,240 feet and a main span exceeding that of the
Forth Bridge by 90 feet.

Then again, the fundamental principle of sound railway
economics, that gradients should be low and curvatures

easy, were rigidly observed. Heavy gradients enormously increased the costs of operation. Steep gradients and too acute curves reduce speed. A normal minimum grade of 21·12 feet per mile, otherwise four-tenths of 1 per cent, was prescribed, this being regarded as the maximum grade that would enable grain to be brought from the North-West to the ports of the Maritime Provinces. It was found possible to adhere to this specification with but few exceptions. To cross the Rockies on such terms seemed an impossible task. After long search and laborious exploration the choice was reduced to three possible routes through the mountains, the Yellowhead Pass, the Peace River Pass, and the Wapiti Pass. The Yellowhead Pass, an old Indian highway, was finally chosen, and across it the Grand Trunk Pacific is carried at a level which is lower than that of any other North American transcontinental line and, more remarkable still, with a gradient which, for east-bound traffic, does not exceed the prescribed 21 feet per mile, and for west-bound traffic exceeds it by very little.[1]

The region north of the Great Lakes had always presented difficult problems to the Canadian Pacific Railway. The region itself was unproductive of traffic and, according to a statement of Sir William Van Horne in 1903, "The Canadian Pacific Railway shipped every carload of wheat that it was possible to ship by their steamship line on the great lakes from Fort William to Owen Sound and thence east by rail, or else by way of Buffalo and the Erie Canal." The reason why wheat could not be hauled around the north shore of Lake Superior was stated in the Canadian House of Commons to be that the Canadian Pacific Railway gradients in that region were too heavy.[2] Therefore the new line was located well to the north of the region in Quebec and Ontario traversed by the earlier railways, for further away from the shores of Lake Superior the country was not only less inhospitable[3] but its configuration and nature presented a

---

[1] The Canadian Northern was located to thread the same Pass but with a maximum grade of 52·8 per mile. The Canadian Pacific breasts the Kicking Horse Pass handicapped with a maximum gradient of 116 feet per mile.

[2] *Dominion Debates*, 1903, vol. iv. col. 9836.

[3] " The climate in going northward from the Height of Land towards James' Bay does not appear to get worse but rather better. This may be due to the constant diminution in the elevation more than counter-balancing the increasing latitude . . . the water of James' Bay may also exert a favourable influence the bulk of it being made up, in the summer time, of warm river water." Report of R. Bell, Civil Engineer, quoted in *Dominion Debates*, Session 1903, vol. iv, col. 9965.

much simpler problem than that which confronted the engineers of the Canadian Pacific.

Again, in keeping well to the north, the new line opened up vast new territories of very promising character. In Quebec Province, which the new road traversed for about 450 miles, the computation was that 6 million acres of land, mostly well timbered and fit for agriculture, would be opened up. For 1,000 miles the line was located to traverse the " clay belt " of Ontario, that is to say, assuming settlement for a depth of 15 miles either side the railway, from 15 to 20 million acres would be brought into use.

As on the east, so in the west, the Grand Trunk Pacific was designed to open up territory further north than any served by the existing transcontinental railways. Prince Rupert, the Pacific terminus, is 550 miles further to the north than Vancouver. A site where " the mountain sides were covered with towering trees and dense undergrowth reaching down to the water's edge while the soil comprised two feet or more of muskeg, damp and cold, covering the solid rock ".[1] was preferred before Port Simpson for the reason that in Tuck's Inlet—a homely name promptly abandoned in favour of that of the illustrious first governor of the Hudson's Bay Company—a magnificent natural harbour had been discovered where the warm chinook wind kept the climate more temperate than that of Dakota or Minnesota.

Prince Rupert is to all intents and purposes an instance of a seaport made to order. When the spot was fixed on by the President of the Railway Company, C. M. Hays, the nearest human habitations were an Indian missionary village several miles away. In 1908 " most of the existing edifices are rough shacks propped up on piles : tents are still used as business quarters and residences ; and wooden pathways have been constructed, sometimes at a considerable height above the peaty ground, which was covered by virgin forest three years ago and has not had time to dry . . . The stumps of the vanished trees still stick up in all directions like broken decayed teeth." [2] In 1921 it had a population of 6,393. Its claims to prospects of future prosperity are based on its natural advantages ; the circumstance that, as the port of the railway which offers the shortest

---

[1] Talbot, *The Making of a Great Canadian Railway*, p. 318.
[2] Osborn, " Canada's New Transcontinental Railway," *Proceedings Royal Colonial Institute*, 1908–9, p. 147.

route between Europe and Asia it is favourably situated for the Chinese and Japanese trade[1]; and its position as a centre for the development of the vast fishing, lumber and mining resources of the Province.

The Grand Trunk Pacific was officially in operation as a completed undertaking as from January, 1916. From Winnipeg to Prince Rupert the total distance is 1,748 miles.[2] It was clear that financially the position of the line was bound to be difficult for some considerable time. The cost of building it had been more than two and a half times the original estimate, and the Transcontinental especially ran through a country for which population still had to be procured. The Dominion Government and the Grand Trunk Company were both heavily involved. In 1917 the Drayton-Acworth Commission found that Government aid to the Grand Trunk Pacific had been as follows :—

	$
Subsidies (Provincial and Muncipal only) . .	726,320
Other Cash Aid (mostly Loans upon or Purchase of Securities) by Dominion Government . .	70,311,716
Guarantees of Bonds by Dominion Government .	43,432,848
	$114,470,884

On the same authority, the total commitment of the Grand Trunk Railway Company in respect of the Grand Trunk Pacific amounted to no less than $123,280,980, of which over $97,000,000 represented guarantees of debentures and bonds issued by and loans to the latter Company. The estimate was that in 1916–17 the liability of the Grand Trunk in respect of the Grand Trunk Pacific was considerably over $5,000,000 per annum.

Henceforth the fate of the old established Grand Trunk was inextricably bound up with that of the newest undertaking and in the end parent and progeny shared a common fate.

As already stated, the eastern division of the undertaking, the Transcontinental, was, when completed, to be leased to and operated by the Company, the Company paying to the Government by way of rental after the first seven

[1]

	Miles.
Prince Rupert to Yokohama . .	3,860
Vancouver to Yokohama . . .	4,283
San Francisco to Yokohama . .	4,470

—Osborn, op. cit.

[2] See Dominions Royal Commission, *Minutes of Evidence* 1916 [Cd. 8458]. Q. 5361.

years a sum equal to 3 per cent per annum on the cost of construction. But as " the cost of construction of the National Transcontinental, which had been estimated at $61,415,000 was permitted to reach $159,881,197, the Company objected to carrying out their bargain. And the Government, by accepting the Company's refusal and commencing to work the line themselves, have in effect released the Company unconditionally ".[1]

As to the obligations of the Grand Trunk to the Grand Trunk Pacific, in December, 1915, the President of the parent line informed the Prime Minister that it was " quite impossible for them to meet the extra liabilities arising from the Grand Trunk Pacific Company, " and that they proposed to retire altogether from the concern. Unless they were relieved from those liabilities there would be a receivership, with the consequent destruction of its own credit and the impairment of the credit of the Dominion itself.

The Grand Trunk Pacific Company ascribed their difficulties, first, to the fact that the Government " had by subsidies and guarantees enabled a rival (The Canadian Northern) to come into existence, and that this action of the Government was, in view of its position as partner with the Grand Trunk Pacific, tantamount to bad faith " ; and secondly, the fact that the simultaneous construction of the two lines in the same territory greatly enhanced the cost of labour.

The Drayton-Acworth Commission accepted the second contention as a fact, but regarded it as an ordinary business risk. As to the first they found that " on the evidence there is nothing whatever to justify any charge of lack of fairness or good faith on the part of the Government in its dealings with the Company." And they rejected without hesitation the claim that there was an obligation on the country to make good what they referred to as " the Grand Trunk's mistaken investment in the Grand Trunk Pacific."

The Commission came to the conclusion that the difficulties of the Grand Trunk had been largely due to its Board of Directors being 3,000 miles away in London and their recommendation was that the Company should be relieved of its obligations in respect of the Grand Trunk

---

[1] *Drayton-Acworth Report*, p. xxiii.

Pacific only on condition that " the control, not only of the Grand Trunk Pacific Company, but also of the Grand Trunk Company of Canada should be surrendered into the hands of the people of Canada ".

The Hudson Bay Railway

The Hudson Bay Railway, running mainly through Manitoba, and connecting Le Pas on the Saskatchewan River with Hudson Bay, which was completed in 1929, represents one of the many questions which have always been an issue between the eastern and the western Provinces of the Dominion. " Shut out absolutely from its natural outlet to the south ; its outlet to the east preyed upon by the bold bad barons of the " Big Sea waters " ; and its only outlet to the north too often made the sport of political caprice." In these words one of the members for the West summed up the grievances of his constituents ; and the disposition to take a provincial rather than a Dominion view is illustrated in the declaration of another member of the legislature that : " The people of Western Canada are not prepared to leave the project in abeyance . . . while we continue to spend millions of dollars annually on the Welland Canal." The main argument of the legislatures and the organized farmers of the three Prairie Provinces was that the project meant the short and therefore the cheap railway haul. Thus, from Winnipeg to the Bay is some 900 miles. From Winnipeg to Montreal is over 1,400 miles. From the terminal port grain will pass to the markets of the world by the Hudson Strait route, the route by which the Selkirk settlers from Scotland reached the Red River and the route by which British troops were sent in 1846 to assist the Hudson's Bay Company to guard the frontier regions of Manitoba against possible American aggression. But the navigation season during which the route can be used is a short one, for the Arctic stream of ice from Baffin's Bay closes the eastern entrance to the Strait from the middle of November to the middle of July.

The construction of a railway to Hudson Bay was begun by Sir Wilfred Laurier's Government in 1911. By reason of war conditions work was suspended in 1917 when a point 92 miles from Port Nelson, the terminus then intended, had been reached. When work was resumed it was necessary to recondition the line already built and, furthermore, to reconsider the question about which there had always been acute controversy, whether Nelson or Churchill should be the terminal port on Hudson Bay. Nelson was chosen in 1912 and its development as a harbour was actively pursued, so that up to 1926 over six million dollars had been expended on the Nelson terminals. Nevertheless, as a result of a new investigation of the problem by a special Committee of the Senate in 1920, the conclusion was reached that " sufficient care was not taken in the selection of Nelson as the terminus of the railway ", and the Government were recommended to incur no further expenditure on the port " without first making a new and thorough examination into the relative merits of Churchill and Nelson as a terminus for the railroad ". The engineer who carried out the new investigation of the problem reported strongly in favour of Churchill.[1] It was less exposed to storms than Nelson and there were splendid natural breakwaters. There was deeper water and less dredging would be necessary. The selection of Churchill rather than Nelson would involve the construction and maintenance of an extra 87 miles of railway, but on the other hand the initial cost of the port and ultimate expenditure for its maintenance would be less. Which port would be open to ocean-going vessels for the longer period only experience would show.

The Government accepted this advice, cut the six million dollar loss, and transferred development operations to Churchill.

In the summer of 1910 Earl Grey, the Governor-General, undertook a tour through the northern region of Canada " to explode the theory of the frozen north ". The route was that of the proposed Hudson Bay Railway and the grain route via Hudson's Strait to Europe. " The climatic conditions were found to be surprisingly favourable throughout. No wraps were required when sitting on deck at night and coffee was taken at 6 a.m. on deck in pyjamas. Summer sailing on the Mediterranean of Canada was found as pleasant as it would have been on the Mediterranean of the Old World " [2]

Up to 1925, capital expenditure on the line had been $14\frac{1}{2}$ million dollars, irrespective of the 6 million dollars

---

[1] *Report on the selection of a Terminal Port for the Hudson Bay Railway* (October, 1927), by F. Palmer, M.Inst.C.E., to be seen in Dominions and Colonial Office Library.

[2] *Annual Register*, 1910, p. 456.

spent on the first selected terminal at Port Nelson. The cost was specially provided for by the sale of pre-emptions in respect of certain lands in the West which were earmarked for the purpose by the Dominion Lands Act, 1908, so that the Western farmer claimed that this Western railway was paid for not by Canada as a whole, but by the sale of Western lands.

The opinion of the Drayton-Acworth Commission was that "unless considerable mineral wealth should be discovered in the territory which this line will open up, it must, we fear, continue to be almost indefinitely a burden upon the people of Canada ".

The Drayton-Acworth Commission

The great crisis in the history of the Canadian railways came in 1916. The increase in the cost of fuel, material and labour ; the decrease in remunerative traffic ; and the inability to market the securities which the Dominion and Provincial Governments had guaranteed as a means of public assistance to the two new transcontinental lines, all of them conditions resulting from the Great War, made it impossible for either the Canadian Northern or the Grand Trunk Pacific to pay its fixed charges or to carry on its undertaking. The Government was faced with the choice between continued subsidies of indefinite amount, and the assumption of control. The outcome was the appointment of the Drayton-Acworth Royal Commission to inquire into the whole problem of transportation in Canada and in particular the status of the three transcontinental railway systems, and whether they should be reorganized or acquired by the State. The Commission reported in 1917.[1]

The railway position in Canada, as found by the Commission, was as follows :—

The lengths of main track in operation was 37,434 miles and a further length of 3,150 miles was under construction. Taking the population at 7,500,000, Canada had only 185 inhabitants to each mile of railway.

[1] Report of Royal Commission to inquire into Railways and Transportation in Canada : Ottawa, 1917 (20g., 1917), *Sessional Papers, Canada* 1917, vol. xii. The Commissioners were : A. H. Smith, of New York (Chairman) ; Sir H. L. Drayton, of Ottawa ; and W. M. Acworth, of London. The two last signed the Report, the Chairman signing a Minority Report.

The railways then in the hands of the Dominion Government were :—

				Miles.
Intercolonial	.	.	.	1,514
Prince Edward Island		.	.	275
Transcontinental		.	.	1,810
				3,599

The privately owned and managed systems were :—

				Miles.
Canadian Pacific		.	.	12,900
Canadian Northern	.		.	9,648
Grand Trunk	.	.	.	3,556
Grand Trunk Pacific		.	.	1,964
				28,068

In addition there were 6,366 miles operated by other Companies and by Provincial Governments.

The extent to which public credit was involved is brought out in the following passage from the Report : " Not counting the loss of interest for many years upon the investment in roads operated by the Government, it appears that for the eight systems in which the public is most interested the people of Canada, through their Governments, have provided or guaranteed the payment of sums totalling 968,451,737 dollars.[1] This works out at at over 30,000 dollars per mile of road. But even this is not all. In addition, they have granted great areas of land as yet unsold and unpledged. They have undertaken the construction of other lines whose cost will be an important addition to this large outlay. Further, in the case of some of. the companies included above, to which they have given or lent large sums of money to meet pressing needs, unlike private lenders, who would naturally have demanded a security charged in front of all previous investment, they have voluntarily accepted a charge ranking after the bulk of the private capital already put in the undertaking."

From the point of view of the shareholders in the various companies the position was that while the Commission found the Canadian Pacific Railway " one of the wealthiest and financially strongest railway companies in the world ; fully able to raise on its own credit and on the most

---

[1] The sum was distributed as follows :—

				Dollars.
Subsidies	.	.	.	157,294,329
Proceeds of Lands Sold		.	.	158,189,933
Loans Outstanding or Investment	.		.	396,924,483
Guarantees Outstanding		.	.	256,042,992

favourable terms all the new capital which will be required to meet the demands for new development that the future will bring ", the Canadian Northern, the Grand Trunk and the Grand Trunk Pacific had all " broken down ".

Basing their position on the belief that " in normal circumstances, railway enterprise is a matter best left in private hands, subject to proper regulation by the Government ", inasmuch as " we know of no country in the world where a democratic State owns and operates its railways, in which politics have not injuriously affected the management of the railways and the railways have not had an injurious influence on politics ", the Commission come to the clear conclusion that it was " not in the interests of Canada that the operation of its railways should be in the hands of the Government ". Other considerations which forced them in the same direction were that inasmuch as the three great Canadian companies owned, leased or controlled 7,000 miles of railway in the United States " the Canadian Government would be ordered by the United States Interstate and State Commissions to alter its rates " and Canadian Government officials " would be required by United States law courts to explain their actions and justify their conduct ", a state of things which would hardly " conduce to international harmony ". Furthermore " if the State took over and undertook to operate the Grand Trunk, the Grand Trunk Pacific and the Canadian Northern, it would be morally bound to offer to purchase the Canadian Pacific also. . . . The Canadian Pacific is exposed throughout its whole territory to the competition of either one or both of the other systems. So long as that competition is in the hands of other organizations, also having to earn the interest on their bonds and striving to earn a dividend on their stocks, the Canadian Pacific Railway has no cause for complaint. But competition with railways operated by the Government stands on an entirely different footing. It would be at any time possible for the Government deliberately to adopt a policy of lowering rates, in some part or throughout the territory involved, below a commercial basis, and making up the deficiency out of general taxation. . . . The Canadian Pacific Railway would be absolutely forced to follow any rate reduction made by the Government railways on pain of losing its business entirely ".

Their recommendation being that " the three undertakings, the Canadian Northern, the Grand Trunk and the

Grand Trunk Pacific be united in one system ", and Government operation being barred, the next question was to whom the management should be entrusted.

The suggestion that the Canadian Pacific Company should be enabled to acquire control of these other roads and operate the whole as one system in partnership with the Government was rejected on the ground that a railway monopoly whether in the hands of a company or of the State was undesirable. What Canada wanted was " two great systems, both with substantially similar management, operating alongside in healthy rivalry from ocean to ocean ".

The formal recommendations were " (i) That a Board of Trustees be constituted by Act of Parliament and incorporated as ' The Dominion Railway Company ' ; (ii) That the ownership of the Canadian Northern, Grand Trunk and Grand Trunk Pacific Railways be vested in this Company ; (iii) That the Government assume responsibility to the Company for the interest on the existing securities of these undertakings ; (iv) That the Intercolonial (including the Prince Edward Island) and National Transcontinental Railways, be also handed over by the Government to the Company ; (v) That the whole of these railways . . . be operated by the Company as one united system ".

The State and the Railways

But events were shaping the destiny of the railways quite independently of the recommendations of any Commission, and the State ownership of over 20,000 miles of railway was brought about, not as the result of any programme of State socialism, but by the force of circumstances. Already the Intercolonial, the Prince Edward Island and the Transcontinental Railways were in the hands of the Dominion Government, the latter, as has already been seen, as a result of the refusal of the Grand Trunk Pacific to carry out its bargain to lease and operate the line. Also the Government had the new Hudson Bay Railway under construction. In 1916 the Canadian Northern Railway applied for further State aid, but was told that such assistance could only be forthcoming upon condition that the Government should acquire all the remaining stock of the Company at a price not exceeding $10,000,000. This was authorized by an Act of 1917.

Next, in 1919, the Grand Trunk Pacific notified the Government that it would cease to operate its line and thereupon the Government took the system over as receiver. Having taken over the Canadian Northern and the Grand Trunk Pacific, it was essential that the Grand Trunk should follow, inasmuch as otherwise the first two lines would lack connexions in the east and the Canadian Pacific would dominate the situation. Accordingly by an Act of 1919 the Government were empowered to acquire the capital stocks of the Grand Trunk Railway, the value to be determined by three arbitrators, of which W. H. Taft was one. The majority award declared that the first, second and third preference stock as well as the ordinary stock of the Company, representing altogether a total of 180 million dollars of stock at par, had no value.

At the end of 1921 the Government-owned railways were still being operated in two groups by two separate Boards, though with such co-ordination as was possible under separate management. Since 1918 there had been a Canadian National Railways Board to which the Government had handed over the railways one by one, and only the parent Grand Trunk system remained outside that Board's control.

A Canadian Grand Trunk Board appointed by the Government succeeded the English Directors in 1921, and then the way was clear for complete unification of all the Government-owned railways under a single management. This was accomplished at the beginning of 1923 when the Grand Trunk was united with the Canadian National Railway system, and an Englishman, Sir Henry Thornton, General Manager of the Great Eastern Railway, appointed President and Chairman of the new Board of Management.[1] When the appointment was announced, the Prime Minister made himself responsible for the statement that " the new President will have absolute independent control of the management of all the Government railways and that politics will be ruthlessly ruled out ".[2] The new management of the greatest single railway enterprise in the world, a

---

[1] See Order in Council, 20th January, 1923, entrusting to the Canadian National Railway Co. the management and operation of the Canadian Government Railways; and Order in Council, 30th January, 1923, amalgamating the Grand Trunk Railway of Canada with the Canadian National Railway Co. See also Canadian National Railways Act, 1919, by which unified control and operation were authorized.

[2] *Times*, 6th October, 1922.

system with 22,000 miles of line and employing 100,000 persons, became fully effective on 1st May, 1923, with the selection of Montreal as headquarters and the division of the immense territory covered by the system into separate regions for administrative purposes.

In order to get some idea how the new order of things is reflected in the financial results, the statistics for the year 1922 constitute the proper basis of comparison. Furthermore it has to be remembered that the Canadian National Railways include a considerable length of line in the United States and that the Central Vermont Railway was controlled by the system until it was purchased by the controlling systems in 1929.

For 1922 the results were as follows [1] :—

	$
Gross Operating Revenue.	
Canadian National Railway Lines in Canada . . .	203,062,345
Canadian National Railway Lines in United States . .	30,996,680
Total Canadian National Railways . . .	234,059,025
Central Vermont Railway	7,626,626
Total	$241,685,651

	$
Gross Operating Expenses.	
Canadian National Railway Lines in Canada . . .	205,572,978
Canadian National Railway Lines in United States . .	25,599,335
Total Canadian National Railways . . .	231,172,313
Central Vermont Railway	6,520,101
Total	$237,692,414

	$
Net Revenue or Deficit from Railway Operations.	
Deficit, Canadian National Railway Lines in Canada .	2,510,633
Revenue, Canadian National Railway Lines in United States	5,397,345
Total Revenue Canadian National Railways .	2,886,712
Central Vermont Railway Revenue . . .	1,106,525
Total Revenue . . .	$3,993,237

When non-operating income from rentals, mails, elevators and so forth have been added and certain necessary deductions, such as taxes, from gross income made, the total revenue was $1,499,782.

Fixed charges for all the lines were $60,196,694.

[1] Annual Statement by the Minister of Railways and Canals, *Dominion Debates*, 1924, vol. iii, p. 2,633.

The total deficit of $58,696,911 is apportioned thus :—

				$
Canadian National Railway Lines in Canada	.	.	.	55,194,974
Canadian National Railway Lines in United States	.	.		2,765,123
Total Canadian National Railways	.	.	.	57,960,097
Central Vermont Railway	.	.	.	736,814
1922 Total Deficit	.	.	.	$58,696,911

For 1923, the results for all the lines, the figures being compiled on the same basis as those quoted for 1922, were as follows :—

			$
Total Operating Revenue .	.	.	263,554,436
Total Operating Expenses	.	.	242,366,974
Net Revenue from Railway Operations			21,187,462
Total Income before Fixed Charges	.		13,364,875
Total Fixed Charges	.	.	66,144,226
1923 Total Deficit	.	.	$52,779,351

Of the total deficit for 1923, $48,978,595 is attributable to Canadian lines apportioned as follows :—

		$
Canadian National Railways, including Grand Trunk in Canada	.	985,016
Canadian Northern System	.	35,956,906
Canadian Government Railways	.	215,943
Grand Trunk Pacific Railway	.	11,820,729

The part of the deficit attributable to United States mileage was $3,800,754, distributed thus :—

		$
Grand Trunk, New England Lines	.	2,562,968
Grand Trunk Western Lines (Surplus).		36,153
Duluth, Winnipeg and Pacific Railway		192,264
Central Vermont Railway	.	1,081,675

The " operating ratio " for the Canadian National Railways, that is to say, the amount it takes to earn a dollar, otherwise the proportionate relationship of operating expenses to operating revenue, works out thus : In 1922, on the combined system, the operating ratio was 98·77 ; in 1923 it was 91·92. For the Canadian Pacific Railway the operating ratio in 1923 was 80·86.

Unified management and independent control accordingly exhibited immediately favourable results in that the operating ratio improved by over 7 per cent and the annual deficit was reduced by approximately $6,000,000. At most the hope was that this improvement would be sufficiently progressive to enable the railways not only to meet their operating charges, but also, within a few years, to meet all interest charges due to the public. There was, furthermore, testimony that with the new management better service had been inaugurated.[1]

If there is to be progressive improvement in the financial results of the Canadian National Railways viewed as a commercial undertaking, that improvement must be reflected in the relationship of operating expenses to operating revenue, and since any improvement in the operating ratio must be the result of improved economic conditions in Canada, it is on the lines operating in Canada that interest will be mainly concentrated. The prosperity of the railways owned by the Canadian Government in the United States must depend on economic conditions for which the Canadian Government or people are not responsible. It has been seen that in 1922 operating expenses of lines in Canada only exceeded operating revenue. In 1923, on these lines the position had so improved that revenue exceeded expenses by approximately 12 million dollars.

The Government ownership of railways on such a vast scale came about for the simple reason that it had become clear that Canadian Railways, with the exception of the Canadian Pacific, could not be run as a commercial proposition. Her railways could no longer be run as a commercial proposition because Canada was over-equipped.

As the Drayton-Acworth Report pointed out : " The growth of the mileage had far outstripped the growth of the population. In 1901, with a population of 5,371,315, Canada had 18,140 miles of railway in operation ; roughly, a mile of railway for every 300 inhabitants. In 1911, the population had increased by 34 per cent to 7,206,643, while the mileage had increased by 40 per cent to 25,400 miles— a mile of railway to every 284 inhabitants. Since 1911 the population has, it is understood, not much increased, but the

---

[1] In 1924 and 1925, taking Canadian National Railway lines in Canada only, results were as follows :—

	1924.		1925.
	$		$
Gross Operating Revenue .	201,224,493	.	208,218,920
Gross Operating Expenses	189,460,403	.	184,373,201
Net Revenue . .	$11,764,090	.	$23,845,719
Operating Ratio .	94 per cent.	.	88·5 per cent.

railway mileage open and under construction has grown to 40,584 miles. In other words, Canada has to-day, taking the present population as 7,500,000, only 185 inhabitants to support each mile of railway.[1] . . . The United States have 400 inhabitants per mile of line, the United Kingdom 2,000, Russia 4,000. Even Australia has 274 inhabitants to each mile of railway ; Argentine 238. And Canada has, what none of these other countries have to a comparable degree, a magnificent system of internal waterways which must always, so far as now can be foreseen, carry a very large proportion of the total traffic."

The over-building which these figures disclose would have been impossible had the railway builder been under the necessity of relying on private capital. It was the direct result of the stimulus of lavish Government aid in the shape of land grants, cash subsidies, loans and guarantees. The effect of indiscriminate public aid on railway enterprise is strikingly illustrated in the case of the Canadian Northern Railway.

The Drayton-Acworth Report expressed the opinion that "the mistakes that have been made by the Canadian Northern lie in unnecessary duplication of lines and in reaching out into territories offering but a poor traffic return, rather than in errors or extravagances in actual construction." On the same authority : " The Canadian Northern has a capital of $54,961 per mile ; the Grand Trunk of $127,340 [2] ; the Grand Trunk Pacific of $98,018 ". The errors of the Canadian Northern were clearly such as would follow from liberal State aid, especially when based on mileage constructed.

Hundreds of miles of unnecessary lines were constructed in competition with one another. Numerous unnecessary second stations were built in places where one station would be more convenient than two, where for example there is a station belonging to the old Canadian Northern and another belonging to the old Grand Trunk. Such duplication seriously increases overhead charges.

---

[1] These figures need adjustment in the light of the 1921 Canadian census, which disclosed a population of 8,788,483. In that year, according to the *Canada Year Book*, 39,192 mlies of railway were in operation, a mile of railway for every 222 inhabitants. The adjusted figures do not affect the general argument that railway mileage has grown at a faster rate than the population.

[2] The capitalization of the Grand Trunk, although apparently high, is not in fact excessive, inasmuch as it is a double track line.

It is not that State aid for railway development is inherently a vicious principle. As Sir Charles Tupper once pointed out : " It was a very proper and useful appropriation of public money to promote the construction of railways in various parts of the country, and where the commercial character of a road was not sufficient in itself to warrant obtaining capital for it the Government could come to its assistance, and by giving a certain amount of public aid it would not only promote the general trade and business of the country, but also would recoup, to a large extent, the expenditure then made, by the increased business that would be transacted and the increased revenue that would follow in its train." [1]

In Canada it has been the method of applying the principle of State aid that has been unsound, not the principle itself. Too often political rather than economic exigencies determined the construction of a line and decided its route. Often a line would be " bonused " when it duplicated an existing line or was otherwise unnecessary. Grants and subsidies were allowed promiscuously and uncritically.

In the early years of railway development in the United States, the State Governments granted lavish bonuses to railway corporations, being empowered so to do by their original constitution. " The scandal connected with railway bonuses in Illinois caused them in 1870 . . . to amend their constitution and they provided that neither the State nor the county, city, town or township or other municipality should issue bonds to pay for the stock of a railway or other private corporation or in any way aid such corporation. . . . The constitution was amended in this respect because of the absolute demoralization caused by the public bonusing of railways. . . . During the time of the early settlement of the western States when the States Government and municipalities granted bonuses to railways there existed such a state of corruption as absolutely to demoralize the electors. . . . The results were so serious that in every case, after 1865—the great wave of railway building swept over the United States from 1862 to 1868—almost every State amended its constitution and almost the first clause put in was a clause prohibiting aid to railways." [2]

It is remarkable how little Canada was able to profit by the lessons of economic history across the border.

[1] *Dominion Debates*, Session 1899, vol. iii, col. 9198.
[2] *Dominion Debates*, 1903, vol. iv, col. 9302.

The following was cited in the Canadian House of Commons as the official declaration of the Liberal Party during the General Election of 1896 : " The policy of bonusing railways by cash and land grants from the Dominion Government has become a fruitful source of jobbery, peculation and corruption. Under its operation favourites of the Governments have been enriched. Appropriations have been made for the sole purpose of purchasing the support of constituencies, and vast sums of money have been voted without regard to the public interest, while millions of acres of land that should have been held in trust by the Government for the future homes of hardy and deserving settlers have been handed over without consideration or justification to charter-hawkers." [1]

Sir Wilfred Laurier, Prime Minister, repudiated responsibility for the statement, but at the same time he added that " these charges of corruption and peculation were substantiated in more than one instance. . . . In the case of the Lake St. John Railway subsidy, the charge was brought home that the subsidy had been diverted to purposes of peculation and corruption.[2]

It is not, however, necessary to establish corruption and public demoralization in order to justify the removal of railway development from the political sphere. The Drayton-Acworth Commission explained their reasons for recommending that the management of the national railways should be entrusted to a body independent of politics in the following general terms : " The railway touches the life of the country at innumerable points. It can almost make one city and unmake another. It vitally affects the question whether an industry in one place is more or less profitable than in another. Every city wants to become a railway centre, to have railway works located within its limits. And the local member invariably wants it too. Every citizen wants the railway station placed where it best suits his own personal convenience, and wants that every express train shall stop at it. He naturally strives to secure these benefits for himself, and his local member naturally desires to help him in their attainment. The individual citizen, the local member, cannot be expected to see the railway situation as a whole ; to appreciate

---

[1] *Dominion Debates*, 1899, vol. iii, col. 9199.
[2] Ibid., col. 9205.

for instance, that an express which stops at every man's local station ceases to be an express at all. Even if he does appreciate it—human nature being what it is—he will be probably quite content if, by bringing political pressure to bear, he can gain an advantage in which his neighbour at the next station does not participate. It is too much to expect of the average merchant, the average manu-facturer, that if he finds that by pressure he can obtain for himself an exceptionally low rate, he will refrain from asking for it, because it gives him an unjustifiable advantage over a rival, or because he knows that the balance of net revenue must be made up by unreasonably higher rates paid by other people's traffic. . . . We believe that the history of railways all over the world, where the management is directly under a Minister responsible to a democratic Parliament, confirms our position that under such a system the public suffer because special interests obtain concessions at the expense of the community as a whole."

Assuming that it is the business of the government of a new country to attract population and that population will not come unless there are railways by which to market their produce, the policy of constructing railways in anticipation of settlement instead of waiting for settlement to justify railway construction must be accepted. That being accepted, State aid in some form or other for railway construction seems essential, although what form that State aid should take remains a subject of controversy.

In Canada, as in the neighbouring Republic, State subsidies to the earliest railways took the form of land grants. It has been seen how generously the first transcontinental line, the Canadian Pacific, was dealt with in this respect, " Up to the end of June, 1923, the Canadian Pacific Railway had disposed of 18,194,737 acres of agricultural lands, for which an average price of $7·87 per acre was received." [1] The allegation was that the system retarded the settlement of agricultural land. " Many years ago the system was adopted of surveying the country into odd-numbered and even-numbered sections and of holding the odd-numbered sections for railway purposes to be given to railways as government land grants. The even-numbered sections were kept as homesteads. We have had in the North-West

---

[1] *The Canadian Annual Review*, 1923, p. 360, quoting E. W. Beatty, K.C., President of the C.P. Railway.

Territory a state of affairs under which the great bulk of odd-numbered sections have been locked up by our obligations to furnish large quantities to railway companies. We have not been able to deal with the odd-numbered sections in the North-West or Manitoba because of the fact that we have large obligations outstanding to furnish land to railway companies." [1] It was also alleged that the railway companies held up tracts of land for speculative purposes. Furthermore there were cases where lines which had received State subsidies of land had been closed and become derelict,[2] and the question was not unnaturally asked : " Where are the subsidies and what has been the net result ? "

On the other hand it was argued that the land had become valuable only by reason of the construction of the railway. In the opinion of the Drayton-Acworth Commission : " Without railways the rich grain-growing provinces of the West would have remained a hunting and trapping district, or at best a grazing section, because it would have been impossible to get out the grain which constitutes the chief product of these provinces. . . . Great grants of land have been given to the two principal systems in the West. But without these railways the land would have been practically valueless."

There were also those who supported the proposal that land grants should be made to the railway companies that came after the Canadian Pacific, on the ground that those companies would do exactly what the Canadian Pacific had done for Canada and the American railway companies for the United States, that is to say, organize themselves into great immigration agencies in Europe and elsewhere. The President of the Canadian Pacific has stated that during the period up to 1923 " the Company had by direct efforts of its own secured the settlement of over 100,000 farmers in Western Canada." [3]

In the United States, the various States subsidized the railways with exemptions, cash bonuses and land grants. In return the railway corporations became emigration agents of a most aggressive type, organizing and advertising emigration schemes with the help of such means as " every principal railway station in Europe and even in the Dominion papered with their glowing advertisements ; floods of

---

[1] *Dominion Debates*, 1903, vol. iv, col. 8679.
[2] Ibid., col. 8715.
[3] *Canadian Annual Review*, 1923, p. 360.

pamphlets in every language ; arrangements perfected to
the minutest details for forwarding the ignorant and helpless
stranger from New York and Chicago to any point he
desires ; and perhaps a comfortable log shanty ready for
him when he gets there. . . . They make the doubter
believe that it is better to pay their company from five to
fifteen dollars an acre for " the best land in the world ",
" rich in minerals " with " no long winters ", accompanied
with free passes over the railway, and long credits, " one-
tenth down and the rest when it suits you ", than to take
up free grants elsewhere." [1]

The diary of Sandford Flemings' expedition through
Canada in 1872 [2] gives an amusing account of the efforts
of the American immigration agents of the time to divert
population from Manitoba across the border ; " Our
friends on Rat Creek gave us an inkling of them. On their
way from St. Pauls, Minnesota, with their teams and cattle, at
every post they heard those rumours in their most alarming
shapes, all of course duly authenticated. They were
repeatedly warned not to impoverish their families by going
to a cold, locust-devoured, barren land, where there was no
market and no freedom, but to settle in Minnesota. Agents
offered them " the best land in the world ", and when,
with British stupidity, they shut their ears to all tempta-
tions, obstacles were thrown in the way of their going on,
and costs and charges so multiplied that the threatened
impoverishment would have been a fact before they reached
Manitoba had they not been resolute and trusted entirely
to their own resources. Even when they reached Winnipeg
the gauntlet had still to be run. In that saloon-crowded
village is a knot of touters and indefatigable sympathizers
with American institutions, men who always calculated
that our North-West would drop like a ripe pear into the
lap of the Republic, who had been at the bottom of the
half-breed insurrection, and who were bitterly disappointed
to see their old dream never likely to be more than a dream.
These worthies told Grant's party quite confidentially
that they had been so many years in the country and had
not once seen a good crop. . . . Whatever their motives,
such are the facts. But the man who would indignantly
deny that there is any connexion between great schemes on
the other side of the boundary line and Winnipeg pothouse

[1] G. M. Grant, *Ocean to Ocean*, p. 91.
[2] Ibid., p. 85.

politicians has a very poor idea of the thoroughgoing activity of American railway directors and Minnesota land agents."

The consideration which brought about the final abandonment of land grants to railways was the desire to retain for the State the increment in land values produced by the presence of railways. The change of sentiment is reflected in the table showing the nature of the public aid accorded to the Canadian Northern. Land grants had not yet entirely disappeared, but in comparison with the Canadian Pacific they are relatively unimportant. In their place cash subsidies and loans appear at the top of the list. When later the Dominion Government had to determine the nature of the aid to be given to the Grand Trunk Pacific, it was announced that there would be no land grants, and such cash subsidies as were ultimately granted were small in amount and came entirely from Provincial Governments or municipalties. Instead the Government provided loans or purchased securities or guaranteed the companies' issues of bonds.

The policy of State aid by way of guarantee is criticized by the Drayton-Acworth Report in these terms : " We do not think the companies realized how serious the position would be if recourse had to be had to the guarantees. Whilst we are not prepared to say that in no circumstances should guarantees be given, we do feel that a policy of guarantees on a large scale is a dangerous policy. It is evident that guarantees had been given in the past without adequate appreciation of the fact that they might fall due and that if they did the burden would be grave. We recommend that in future no guarantees be given without being taken up into the books of the guarantor as a continuing liability and without some financial provision being made against the possibility of their falling due."

The Hudson Bay Railway was the subject of a further experiment in regard to the form which Government aid should take. A Statute of 1906 provided for a free land grant in aid of the railway, but under the Dominion Lands Act, 1908, "the right was given for a homesteader to purchase a pre-emption, and while nothing is said about the Hudson Bay Railway, the debates in the House would indicate that the Government had in mind at that time the idea of selling these pre-emptions and taking the money—or a portion of it at least—for the construction of the Hudson Bay

Railway, rather than granting . . . a free grant of land for that purpose. Consequently, the Act of 1908, as I understand it, repeals the Act of 1906, so far as the Hudson Bay Railway is concerned." [1] The understanding, which however was never expressed in statutory form was apparently that the money to be expended on the construction of the railway was to come from a special fund to be created by the sale of pre-emptions. [2]

The management of the Canadian National Railways is faced with its own peculiar problems, of which that of Canadian winter conditions and the competition of American routes and ports is one of the most difficult. Thus an undue proportion of the produce of the North-West which goes east passes along American routes, especially via Buffalo to New York, Boston or Portland, and the problem is to divert it over the canals and railroads which have been constructed in Canada at such enormous cost. The Canadian National Railways also have their share of the difficulties which face railway companies all over the world. Thus the difficulties of transportation companies in meeting competition by automobiles on account of road improvement have appeared in Canada as elsewhere. " The question will arise : should the railway companies of Canada forsake some of their steam lines and operate buses on short hauls or should they replace their steam roads on little longer hauls with gasoline or electric cars to take the place of the more expensive steam locomotives and regular trains." [3]

On the other hand, great increments of traffic are to be looked for with the exploitation of Canada's mineral wealth. The location of the great transcontinental lines enables transport to be provided for new mining areas with peculiar facility. To connect the Sullivan mine with the Canadian Pacific Railway Kootenay extension, a line of only 19 miles was necessary. A branch railway 44 miles in length connects with the Canadian National Railway's main line the rich gold and copper area being developed in the Rouyn district of north-west Quebec. [4]

Moreover, a railway company is quite capable of calling

---

[1] Hon. G. P. Graham (Acting Minister of Railways and Canals), *Dominion Debates*, 1923, vol. ii, p. 1068.

[2] See ibid., p. 1053.

[3] Annual Statement of Minister of Railways and Canals for 1924, *Dominion Debates*, 1925, vol. iii, p. 2898.

[4] *The Mineral Wealth of Canada*, issued by the Canadian Bank of Commerce, 1927.

into existence along its route new trades and industries, with mutual advantage to itself and the community. Thus already in 1916 the newly constructed Grand Trunk Pacific Railway was carrying two million pounds of fish a month, distributing it as far as Chicago, New York, and Montreal. " Fish as a commodity has not been largely used in the west until we opened up this industry . . . It is a very important industry as the high cost of meat is of great importance to Western people." [1]

The experiment of national ownership of railways on a vast scale combined with independent management will be watched with keen interest. It is capable of observation from different points of view : the national point of view and the shareholders' point of view. The shareholders have done badly, but the value of the railways as instruments in the development of Canada's resources is incalculable.

There are those who believe that in order to develop Western Canada by assisting in the movement of the surplus grain crop to the markets of the world, or to develop the coal or steel industry in eastern Canada, it would be a justifiable policy to carry that traffic at less than cost if necessary.

Looked at from the shareholders' and railway General Managers' point of view, the solution of the problem must be found along the line of greater density of traffic. It must be remembered that, so far as the Canadian National is concerned, there are several thousand miles of purely colonization railways. They are necessary to the development of the country, but they reduce the general good showing of the older established lines. Greater density of population will provide greater density of traffic where most needed, and when there are settled and prosperous communities contributing traffic to the colonization mileage, the lean sections of the national system will no longer absorb so much of the vitality of the lines belonging to the more settled parts of the Dominion.

[1] Dominions Royal Commission, *Minutes of Evidence*, 1916 [Cd. 8458] : Evidence of Mr. M. Donaldson, General Manager G.T.P. Railway, Q. 5415.

CHAPTER II

RAILWAY RATES

THE value of a farm or a mine depends not only on its productivity but also upon the cost of the transportation of its produce to market, and the power of a country to compete effectively in the markets of the world is largely dependent upon the amount which has to be added to the original cost of production on account of transport charges. Canada is a country of such vast distances that the cost of getting grain or pulpwood or asbestos to the ports of the Great Lakes or the St. Lawrence or the Pacific is bound to be a question of absorbing interest. And in Canada the question of railway rates is peculiarly complicated.

In the first place there is the competition of water transport. Comparative figures from the other side of the international boundary show how serious an influence on railway rates such competition can be : " On a common road the average cost of hauling a ton one mile is 25 cents : the average of the railroads is 0·72 cents or 7·2 mils per ton-mile : while the rate by canal of limited draught is but 2·4 mils : and by the lakes a small fraction of a mil only." [1]

The absence of water competition in the winter months is an even more potent factor in the increase of railway rates during that season as compared with summer rates than the increased operating expenses due to winter conditions. " The shippers complain that the winter rates

[1] Report by L. M. Haupt, *Bulletin* 21, U.S. Dept. of Agriculture.

are from 20 per cent to 25 per cent higher than the summer rates . . . The winter rates normally go into force about the 15th November and cease about 1st April. . . . The railway position is that the summer rates are based on St. Lawrence River, Lake Ontario and Lake Erie water competition, the direct boat line rates regulating the maximum which all rail lines can charge during the summer months. The rates so forced on the railways are frequently not remunerative, but they have to accept them for the time being, or go out of business." [1]

Another important factor in the intricate problem of Canadian railway rates has always been the competition of United States lines. Trade between eastern and western Canada did not develop so quickly as was expected when the transcontinental lines were built for the reason that United States railways brought manufacturing and commercial cities like Chicago, St. Paul and Spokane into closer touch with Western Canada than Canada's own industrial east. A glance at the map will show how much shorter is the haul from St. Paul and Chicago to the Canadian West than from Toronto and Montreal. In such circumstances it is not enough to give Canadian railways equal mileage rates with United States lines. Equal aggregate rates over longer distances or a tariff at the frontier will alone enable Canadian lines to compete successfully for traffic at many points near the international boundary. " North Alberta supplies grain, hay and vegetables and South Alberta cattle to the mining regions of British Columbia over the Canadian Pacific main line from Calgary and its branch lines and steamboat connexions. Our competitors who supply by far the largest part of the produce consumed in Kootenay are the farmers of eastern Washington and northern Idaho for whom the city of Spokane is the trade centre. Until February last their rate on grain was 25 cents per 100 to Nelson, which is a central point in Kootenay, while our rate was 50 cents per 100. Even with the duty in our favour we were not able to do business. In February last the Canadian Pacific cut the rate from Edmonton, which is the principal grain shipping point, to Nelson, to 35 cents per 100. With the duty in our favour this enabled us to compete with the Spokane 25 cent rate to certain Kootenay points. . . . But had it not been for the high duties we evidently would

[1] Report on Rate Grievances on Canadian Railways by Professor S. J. McLean, *Sessions Papers (Canada)*, 1902, No. 20*a*, pp. 65–6.

not have competed except at a very much lower price for produce." [1]

Nor have the people of the United States always been content merely to compete for traffic over lines on their own side of the boundary. They have shown themselves quite equal to competing in building construction on Canadian territory : " It is a fact which only requires to be known to make a grave impression . . . that the people of the United States belonging to the State of Washington, appreciating the advantages of the possession of British Columbia and of the valuable minerals which are there undeveloped, built a railway up into the Kootenay country and got possession of the business and the trade of that country and have built up the city of Spokane wholly out of the business which has originated in the Province of British Columbia." [2]

The means of inland communication, the development of which played so important a part in Canada's evolution subsequent to confederation, were the waterways and the railways. Roads can hardly be included in the same category ; hitherto they have been of local rather than national importance and at most have been feeders to the great waterways and railways. But the survey and establishment of the old trails as permanent highways, especially in the North-West, went steadily on, as also did the construction of new roads.

That road transport is an important factor in national development was brought out in one of the recommendations of the Drayton-Acworth Commission [3] : " We think the Government would do well to give serious consideration to the question of the cost of bringing grain from the farm

[1] *Dominion Debates*, 1897, vol. ii, col. 4560.

[2] Minister of Railways and Canals, *Dominion Debates*, 1897, vol. ii, col. 4519.

[3] Report of the Royal Commission to inquire into Railways and Transportation in Canada (20g.–1917). The substitution of motors for horses is helping substantially to solve the problem : " Thousands of Canadian farmers have not been slow to learn that it is possible to deliver perishable farm produce such as berries, fruit, garden truck, or dairy products from farm to market quickly and cheaply by motor, while return loads of supplies, empty crates or cans, can be handled by the same truck at low cost. In many cases vegetables are taken directly from the fields to the markets and even fat cattle are taken from the stables to slaughterhouses, farmers thereby reducing shrinkage costs. In one instance, which is typical, a farmer delivered 10,000 bushels of wheat a distance of 16 miles, making four round trips a day, with 252 bushels on each load. In the same time a four-horse team covered the route once and delivered only 125 bushels." *Times Supplement*, 20th March, 1928, p. xvii.

to the railway station. . . . We find that an average rate
per 100 lb. from Battleford . . . to Liverpool may be put
at not more than 50 cents by the all-rail route to Montreal.
By water from Port Arthur, which route carries the vast
proportion of the traffic, the through rate would not be
more than 40 cents per 100 lb. on the average. On the
other hand, typical examples of the cost of wagon haulage
have been brought to our notice. We find instances of a
cost of 33 cents per 100 lb. for a distance of 12 miles and of
54 cents per 100 lb. for 35 miles. And we are informed
that in some cases grain has to be hauled as much as
50 miles to a station. In other words, in cases such as these,
the cost of delivery at the station is as much as or even more
than the total through rate from the station to Liverpool."

But to be effective for the purpose indicated, the roads
must be such as will carry heavy motor traffic. Such roads
are costly, and in Canada, with its vast distances and its
sparse population, the development of such a system
of roads is a vast problem. Already " throughout the
Dominion there are but 25 persons to every mile of road,
and on an average there is one mile of road for every 10
square miles of land." [1] But of the 378,269 miles of roads
in the Dominion in 1926, no less than 323,629 miles were
earth roads. Only some 6,400 miles were macadam roads,
and of concrete roads there were about 1,000 miles.

Nevertheless, the increasingly important part played
in industrial and social life by motor transport even in the
present stage of road development has caused a certain
amount of perturbation in the minds of railway general
managers, especially in regard to passenger traffic. Sooner
or later such a form of competition must be met by lower
rates, or greater facilities, or both. In 1924 " the railways
in their passenger service alone were affected to the extent
of $24,000,000 by the automobile. The Canadian National
system's share of that sum in Canada was something over
$8,000,000 and if you add about $1\frac{3}{4}$ millions on our lines
in the United States you will find that the Canadian National
system sustained a loss in gross revenue in 1924 of nearly
$10,000,000 on passenger service alone on account of
the automobile.[2] Moreover " there can be no doubt that
motor vehicles are now carrying much of the short haul

---

[1] *Canada Year Book*, 1926, p. 616.
[2] Annual Statement of Minister of Railways and Canals for 1924,
Dominion Debates, 1925, vol. iii, p. 2898.

traffic formerly carried by steam and electric railways. In addition, a certain amount of traffic formerly carried over water routes has been diverted to these new modern carriers." [1] But since the greater part of this is short haul traffic, which is the least profitable of a railway company's business, the opinion is held by some that the motor vehicle creates as much business for the railway as it abstracts from them. Be that as it may, it seems clear that the freight motor car is destined to become an economic factor of increasing importance,[2] and a factor of which account must be taken in increasing measure in fixing railway rates.

The national aspect of road development in Canada has been recognized by the Dominion Government, and a policy of making grants to Provincial Governments in proportion to their own expenditure on highway development was instituted by the Canada Highways Act, 1919. Any highway for which such aid is granted must be constructed or improved in accordance with an agreement made between the Minister of Railways and Canals and the Provincial Government. The aid so given is 40 per cent of the cost of such construction or improvement.[3]

Any comparison between railway rates in Canada and the United States must be fallacious which does not take into consideration certain inherent differences of conditions. Climatic conditions in the winter are not so severe in the United States as in Canada. The low temperature and heavy fall of snow during the winter in many parts of Canada inevitably make the cost of transport during that season relatively high. Operation expenses are correspondingly less in the United States, and Canadian railways must of necessity impose a higher scale of rates.

The comparative density of population also has to be taken into account. In the United States, railway rates have been progressively reduced as population increased. So it is reasonable to assume it will be in Canada.

Furthermore, in order properly to appreciate the railway rate problem in Canada it is necessary to take into account the regional conflict of interests that exists.

The western Provinces, and in particular British Columbia, claim that rates from west to east should be no more than

---

[1] *Canada Year Book*, 1926.

[2] In 1923 the number of commercial cars or trucks registered in Canada was 56,219 ; in 1925 it was 76,267.

[3] Payments under this Act to 1926 amounted to $18,429,108.

those east to west. In effect this is a demand for the removal of the discrimination resulting from the existence of the mountain ranges of the west. The reply of the railways is that it costs nearly 60 per cent more to run trains through the Rocky Mountains than across the Prairies and that the mountain sections were enormously costly to build.

The Maritime Provinces' case for more favourable rates is based on their chronic grievances, diminishing or stationary population, diversion of traffic during the winter months from Canadian to United States ports, the lack of a market for their produce in the central Provinces, and the grant of more favourable rates to the Middle West. The claim is also made that lower rates are essential if the bargain made when the Maritime Provinces entered the Dominion is to be faithfully carried out.

This latter view, that " to the extent that commercial considerations were subordinate to national, imperial and strategic considerations, the cost should be borne by the Dominion and not by the traffic that might pass over the line " was accepted by the Royal Commission on Maritime Claims,[1] and that tribunal found that " the lower level of rates that prevailed on the Intercolonial Railway system prior to 1912 is rightly to be interpreted as the fulfilment by successive governments of the policy and pledges that surrounded the railway from its inception ". Since 1912, however, the freight rates had been increased by 92 per cent, while for the rest of Canada the increase had only been 55 per cent, a burden which was " responsible in very considerable measure for depressing abnormally in the Maritimes to-day business and enterprise ". The Commission felt called upon to apply an anomalous remedy to an anomalous position, in that it recommended an immediate reduction of 20 per cent on all rates on traffic in the Atlantic division of the Canadian National Railways, the cost of this relief to be borne by the Dominion Government. To this extent the Commission were prepared to withdraw the review of rates from the tribunal duly constituted to deal with such matters, the Railway Commission.

The railways of Canada never attained the same degree of " lawless independence " as the railways of the United States, probably because in Canada the railway era was later, and both the companies and the public were able to

---

[1] Appointed in 1926 under the chairmanship of Sir Andrew Duncan to inquire into the conditions and claims of the Maritime Provinces.

profit by the experience of the Republic. By that experience Canada was warned of the possible abuses against which provision had to be made and was also informed of the problems which were peculiarly incidental to a federal State.

By means of discrimination in rates the railway companies of the United States had shown themselves capable of becoming self-constituted arbiters of the fate of whole communities and entire towns ; rebates were granted to favoured consignors ; free passes were issued wholesale to persons in influential positions, on the one hand as a reward for services rendered and on the other to buy off inconvenient criticism. By the early 'seventies the demand for State control of railway companies was sufficiently insistent and weighty to induce the legislatures of several of the more important States to regulate railway rates. The " grangers " —the farmers of the Middle West who led the movement, would have none of the argument that a railroad had as much right to sell transportation at the highest price obtainable as the grocer or the hardware merchant their particular commodities. In 1876 the Supreme Court of the United States accepted the doctrine that railway companies were property " clothed with a public interest " and that a State had power to regulate charges made by common carriers. Thus far the principle of control was only secured for intra-State traffic. The Interstate Commerce Commission, asserting Federal control, and regulating interstate business, only came in 1887. The power of the Commission over rates went no further than to enable them to declare a rate unreasonable. Traders had to wait for President Roosevelt and the Hepburn Act of 1906 before they could ask the Commission not only to declare a rate unreasonable, but also to substitute rates that were just and reasonable. In 1910 the Commission was given power to investigate and alter railway rates of its own initiative and without waiting for specific complaints. The power given by the Transportation Act of 1920 to the Interstate Commerce Commission to pre-scribe minimum as well as maximum rates was a legacy of the Great War.

Attempts at regulation of rates are to be found in the charters of the earliest of the Canadian railway companies from 1851 onwards, but the methods of regulation differed widely. Some charters prescribed maximum rates and provision was made by which increased dividends should be counterbalanced by a reduction in rates. A tax on dividends in excess of a certain figure, a method which was a departure from existing precedents, was favoured until about 1850. The Railway Clauses Consolidation Act, 1851, provided for the fixing of tolls by the directors, " subject to the approval of the Governor in Council and that there were to be no preferences." [1]

When the Canadian Pacific Railway Company was incorporated in 1881 the Consolidated Railway Act, 1879, was in force. It vested the power to fix tolls in the directors, subject to the approval of the Governor in Council. Parliament was empowered to reduce the tolls so fixed only with the Company's consent and subject to the restriction that when so reduced they should produce not less than 15 per cent per annum (subsequently 10 per cent was fixed) profit on the capital expenditure on the railway.

In 1888 the regulation and control of railways in Canada, including the supervision of rates, was given to the Railway Committee of the Privy Council, sitting in Ottawa. Presumably the Royal Commission on whose recommendation this step was taken suggested the Railway Committee as a *pis aller*, for in their own words " the Commission admits that serious objection may be taken to the selection of the Railway Committee of the Privy Council as the general railway tribunal. The members cannot leave their duties at Ottawa and must therefore delegate to subordinates much very important work . . . They hold their office on a political tenure and are liable to sudden change whereby the value of their experience is lost. They can scarcely be regarded by the public as absolutely removed from personal or political bias as independent members of a permanent tribunal. They cannot possibly give their exclusive attention to their railway duties."[2]

In addition to the dual function, political and administrative, and the want of continuity of tenure in the Railway Committee, there were the further objections that the body had no place for members with technical training for the work, and that the lack of migratory organization and the concentration at Ottawa made it impossible to deal effectively with the smaller complaints, while for the rest the expense of travelling long distances to the tribunal was serious.

---

[1] See Reports upon Railway Rate Grievances, etc., by Professor S. J. McLean, *Sessional Papers, Canada* (No. 20a, 1902).
[2] Quoted in Report on Rate Grievances on Canadian Railways by Professor S. J. McLean, *Sessions Papers, Canada*, 1902, No. 20a, p. 75.

It was seen that, inasmuch as the work of railway regulation was administrative and not political, what was wanted was a body specially organized for the purpose and independent of political conditions. By 1903 Canada was able with advantage to draw upon the experience of England and the United States, where the problem of railway control had at last got beyond the transitory stage. England had settled down to the Railway and Canal Commission established by the Railway and Canal Traffic Act, 1888. In the United States the Interstate Commerce Commission had been established about the same time.

The Railway Committee of the Privy Council accordingly gave way to the Board of Railway Commissioners for Canada which was organized at the beginning of 1904.[1]

The constitution and powers of that controlling authority are now contained in the Railway Act, 1919.[2] A Board of Railway Commissioners for Canada is constituted consisting of six members appointed by the Governor in Council. The term of office is ten years. The Chief Commissioner must be a Judge of a Superior Court of Canada or one of its Provinces or a barrister or advocate of ten years' standing. The Commission is a Court of Record. There may be sittings in any part of Canada. The Board has the widest possible powers. It has " full jurisdiction to inquire into, hear and determine any application . . . complaining that any company or person has failed to do any act, matter or thing required to be done by this Act, or the Special Act, or by any regulation, order or direction made thereunder . . . or has done or is doing any act, matter or thing contrary to or in violation of this Act or the Special Act or any such regulation, order or direction ". And the Board may order the thing to be done or forbid the doing or continuing of it. The Board has power to act upon its own motion as well as upon complaint. There is an appeal on questions of law to the Supreme Court of Canada.

The Board has certain administrative as well as judicial functions. Thus no railway may be opened for traffic until inspected and certified to be safe by the Board. A picturesque sidelight on Canadian conditions is afforded

---

[1] Besides the Board of Railway Commissioners dealing with undertakings under the jurisdiction of the Dominion Government there are also in several of the Provinces bodies which have the supervision and control of local public utilities such as street railways under the jurisdiction of the Provinces and the regulation of their rates. One of the most important is the Ontario Railway and Municipal Board.

[2] *Revised Statutes of Canada*, 1927, chap. clxx.

by the provision which enables the Board to make orders and regulations " respecting the construction, use and maintenance, in connection with the railway, of fireguards or other works which may be deemed by the Board to be necessary . . . to prevent . . . fires from being started or occurring upon, along or near the right of way of the company " ; also " requiring the company to establish and maintain an efficient and competent staff of fire-rangers, equipped with appliances for fighting fires or preventing them from spreading ".[1] Repairs may be ordered and the use of any dangerous line forbidden by the Board, and it may impose speed limits. It may order the provision of adequate and suitable accommodation for the loading, unloading and carrying of traffic.

There are heavy penalties for neglect or refusal to obey any order of the Board.

The desirability of some body being in existence capable of mobilizing and co-ordinating the whole of the railways when the national interest demands it became apparent in Canada in 1915–16. The rule which is of general application in Great Britain and the United States, that a railway company is entitled to the traffic in that territory which its capital and enterprise have opened up, has been observed also in the Dominion. The 1915 grain crop of the Western Provinces was, however, so exceptionally heavy that it became apparent that the ordinary rules of traffic would have to be superseded if the harvest was to be saved and got to market. Accordingly in 1916 legislation was passed providing that where any railway company was unable or failed to provide adequately for the movement of grain from the Western Provinces to the elevators at the head of Lake Superior or to destinations further east, after the close of navigation on the Great Lakes, the Board could require any other railway company to transport such grain and to supply the necessary cars and engines. The Board were thus able to send other companies to the aid of those operating in the North-West and as a result " the whole crop was satisfactorily marketed and transported ".[2]

---

[1] By the use of oil instead of coal on 720 miles of its line from Prince Rupert to Jasper, the Grand Trunk Pacific Railway claimed to have avoided the risk of fire in that heavily wooded country and to have been able to dispense with the expensive fire-ranging staff which was necessary where coal was burned. *Dominions Royal Commission, Minutes of Evidence*, 1916 [*Cd.* 8458], Qs. 5402–3.

[2] *Dominions Royal Commission. Minutes of Evidence* [*Cd.* 8458]: Memorandum by the Board of Railway Commissioners, p. 403.

The experience gleaned in its own and other countries, notably in the neighbouring Republic, enabled a very comprehensive code of rules to be included in the Statutes for the regulation of railway rates, which it is the duty of the Board of Railway Commissioners to enforce. Equal tolls are to be charged for equal services. There is to be no discrimination, that is to say, " no reduction or advance in any such tolls. . . in favour of or against any particular person or company" using the railway, or as between different localities. As a consequence the public do not get the benefits of competition as between Canadian lines save as to services. The only possible competitive rates were those allowed to meet the competition of waterways or foreign railways. No undue preference may be given to any particular person or company or any particular description of traffic. No free passes are allowed except to Members of Parliament and members and officers of the Board itself.

All tolls must be authorized by the Board of Railway Commissioners and the Board has full power " to fix, determine and enforce just and reasonable rates ".

Freight tariffs are of three classes, namely, the standard freight tariff ; the special freight tariffs, which are lower than the standard tariff ; and competitive tariffs, which are the lowest of all.[1]

There are two classes of passenger tariffs, the standard tariff, and a lower special passenger tariff. Save for the Pullman rate and the sleeping rate there is practically only one passenger class all over the Dominion.

As is to be expected, the earliest railway tariff fights raged around the Canadian Pacific Company. During the first ten years of its existence that Railway had to face the constant hostility of the boards of trade and the farmers' associations, in particular in Manitoba and the North-West Territories. To them the Railway Company was simply a " giant monopoly " that used its strength tyrannously like a giant. " It cost one bushel of grain to send another to market over the lines of the Canadian Pacific Company." That the Railway Company had made settlement in those regions possible at all was a fact too easily forgotten.

---

[1] " The competitive tariffs deal with the tolls to or from specified points which the Board may consider, or may have declared, to be competitive points not subject to the long and short haul clause under the provisions of the Act." *Dominions Royal Commission. Minutes of Evidence*, 1916 [*Cd.* 8458], p. 398.

So persistent were the complaints of the North-West, that in 1894 the Canadian Government appointed a Commission to inquire into complaints of " exorbitant and unreasonable passenger and freight rates and of discrimination in both in the Province of Manitoba and the North-West territories ", which had been preferred primarily by the Legislative Assembly and the farmers' organizations.   The Commission reported in 1895,[1] and acquitted the Railway Companies on the charges brought against them.   A comparison of schedules covering the bulk of the traffic " does not bear out the charges that the rates in Manitoba and the North-West are either exorbitant or excessive ; on the contrary, they are exceedingly favourable as compared with the rates on American roads in contiguous territory ; and indeed your Commissioners believe that they are very little, if any, in excess of the average rates charged on corresponding traffic in the eastern provinces when it is considered that the great bulk of the traffic in grain, live-stock and coal in the west entails the hauling of about 75 per cent of the cars empty one way.   In connexion with the grain traffic it must also be borne in mind that it is practically confined to a short season of the year, and for that reason a much larger number of cars is required than if the shipments extended over a longer period ".   From the heavy freight handlers " there was an almost entire absence of complaints ".   As to alleged discrimination, " your Commissioners are of opinion that all shippers are on the same footing and that no discrimination exists."   Seeing that the Canadian Pacific Railway had some 18 million acres of unsold land and owned upwards of 3,000 miles of railway, " selfish motives alone would be ample and efficient safe-guards on the action of the company in regulating its general policy.   Any policy other than that favourable to settlers would be suicidal and ruinous to the Company."

An opportunity to drive a bargain with the Canadian Pacific Company occurred a year or two later when the railway approached the Government for a subsidy in aid of the projected Crow's Nest Pass Line in British Columbia.

The hands of Parliament were tied by the statutory provision for non-interference with the tolls of the Canadian Pacific Railway so long as the profit did not exceed 10 per cent, and when the Crow's Nest Pass project came before

---

[1] Report of the Railway Rates Commission. Canada. *Sessional Papers*. No. 39, 1895.

the House in 1897 the Government saw the opportunity to secure a greater measure of control over the tolls of this great company.

Accordingly by the Crow's Nest Pass Railway Act of 1897 the Canadian Pacific Railway was granted a subsidy for building the Crow's Nest Pass Line subject, however, to the condition that the Company entered into an agreement with the Government for a reduction in the freight rates on certain classes of merchandise, " westbound, from and including Fort William and all points east of Fort William . . . to all points west of Fort William." The agreement, which was duly entered into, provided for substantial reductions as from 1898. For the most part they were 10 per cent on such articles as cordage and binder twine, agricultural implements, iron, building materials, and livestock.. On green and fresh fruit the reduction was as much as $33\frac{1}{3}$ per cent. There was also to be a reduction of the existing rates on grain and flour from all points west of Fort William to Fort William and Port Arthur and all points east, of three cents per 100 pounds. No higher rates than the reduced rates were to be charged thereafter by the Company on traffic between the points named.

The revised rates were maintained without serious complaint until 1917, when war conditions made existing railway rates unremunerative, and higher rates were authorized. In 1924 preparations were made to return to pre-war conditions, when the Board of Railway Commissioners disallowed and directed the withdrawal of the tariffs re-establishing the Crow's Nest Pass rates.

The case went to the Supreme Court of Canada.[1] The two questions were (1) Were the Board entitled to authorize rates on the Canadian Pacific Railway in excess of those provided for in the Crow's Nest Pass Subsidy Act and Agreement ? and (2) If not, was the application of rates so provided for confined to traffic on the lines existing at the date of the Act to the exclusion of lines subsequently built ? [2]

---

[1] Governments of Alberta, etc. v. Canadian Pacific Railway Company (1925), *Supreme Court Reports (Canada)*, 155.

[2] The claim of the Canadian Pacific Railway Co. that the agreement applied only to lines in existence at the time of the agreement gave rise to allegations which illustrate the effects of discrimination in railway rates in Canada. It was claimed that as a consequence, " While rates to Winnipeg, Regina, and Calgary were reduced, those to Saskatoon and Edmonton remained as they had been. Rates from Hamilton were reduced, but those from Brantford not in 1897 on the C.P.R., remained at the higher level. The Canadian National Railway, which is not bound

The Supreme Court held that the rates provided for in the agreement were again in full force and vigour; that the Board had no power to authorize rates in excess of the Crow's Nest Pass rates, and that the Board's order was made without jurisdiction. It was further held that the application of the Crow's Nest Pass rates was confined to traffic between points existing on the railway in 1897.

The Crow's Nest Pass Agreement became a sort of battle cry in the North-West. It illustrates another difficulty which those who are struggling to place Canadian railways on an economically remunerative basis cannot ignore—the view held in some quarters that it would be economically sound to require the railways to carry Canadian produce even at a loss if thereby Canadian trade as a whole was stimulated. When the presentation of the Crow's Nest case to the Railway Commission was pending the matter was referred to in the Canadian Press in such terms as these : " Convinced that prosperity in the West is largely dependent on low freights the central western provinces will make a strong effort not only to have the Crow's Nest rates confirmed but to have competitive rates adjusted to this level on the basis that otherwise there is discrimination. The West is frankly not concerned with whether this would involve providing railway service at less than cost, with an increase in the deficits of the National system and a serious impairment of earnings of the C.P.R., and it is willing to try the experiment of starving the roads in order to get the benefits of the low rates and take a chance upon such rates resulting in impairment of efficiency of the transportation facilities upon which the prairies, probably more than any other section of the country, are dependent.

" Under the circumstances it is well that the rest of Canada should understand the case of the Prairie Provinces because taxpayers generally will be concerned with carrying the burden involved in providing these cheap rates.

---

in any way by the agreement, met the low rates of the C.P.R. at competitive points, but refrained from applying them to other points. Consequently, consumers on the whole network of lines north of the main line of the C.P.R. are paying higher freight rates on binder twine, implements, iron ware, fruit, and other commodities of the agreement than those in the south. They object, but discrimination is not fatal to consumers. The point of importance is that the discrimination, if continued, would destroy the wholesale trade of the northern cities in these commodities, to the benefit of Winnipeg. The farm implement business of Brantford would be destroyed in favour of that of Hamilton." *The Financial Post*, 12th September, 1924.

Technically and legally the West will be able to build up a strong case, and it is a question of holding to the letter of an unsound agreement, which originally affected only a small territory, or of adjusting rates on an equitable basis in accordance with prevailing costs of providing service." [1]

Nor is this " uneconomic " attitude to the railways confined to the North-West. In the Report of the Royal Commission on Maritime Claims [2] the Commissioners " were surprised to find, in the course of our investigation, business people who were prepared in some cases to press for a reduction in railway rates without regard to whether the rate was reasonable compensation to the railway or not ". And again, " Much of the evidence we heard in the Maritimes left the impression on our minds that witnesses thought the railways should be operated to the advantage of the trader irrespective of the financial results to the railway. In other words, what a railway administration might concede, in the exercise of its judgment on what was good business, or might ultimately be good business for itself, seemed to us to be demanded as a matter of right by the trader so that his own business might be profitably developed whether the operations of the railway were remunerative or not." The Commissioners' comment is that they " cannot conceive of a national system being efficiently administered on such a principle as that ".

[1] *The Financial Post*, 12th September, 1924.
[2] See note, p. 319.

CHAPTER 12

Shipping, Harbours and Ocean Highways

Introductory.

Inland Waterways.

    Canadian shipbuilding and its decline.
    Shipping on the Great Lakes.
    Effects of railway and United States competition.

The Atlantic Routes.

    Early history.
    The Atlantic Lines :—
        The Cunard Line.
        The Allan Line.
        The Canadian Pacific a competitor.
    Organization of ocean tracks.
    Rivalry of Canadian and United States ports.
    Canada's natural harbours.
        Harbour equipment.
    The All-Red route.
    The St. Lawrence passage and its difficulties.
        Effect on Insurance Rates.
    Halifax versus the St. Lawrence ports.

The Route to the West Indies.

    Canada's hereditary interest in the Islands.
    The benevolent big brother.
    Canada as the West Indian market.
    Subsidized shipping.
    The Canada-West Indian Agreement of 1925.

The Panama Canal Route.

    Canada's inland lake of grain and the outlets.
    The choking of the eastern channels.
    How the Canal was constructed.
    Its opening creates a new Gulf Stream of commerce.
    The new Economic Divide.
    The Canadian Pacific coast brought into relationship with Europe.
    Grain from the North-West *via* the Canal.
    Economic effects.

The Pacific.

    How Canada is in touch with the Orient.
    The Canadian Pacific Company's Steamers.
    The Rise of the Pacific ports.
        Victoria.
        Vancouver.
        Prince Rupert.
    The competition with United States Pacific ports.

The Native Canadian Steamship Lines.

    The early shipping trade of Quebec and the Maritime Provinces.
    Displaced by iron shipbuilding and railways.
    The Canadian Pacific Line.
        As extensions of railway routes.
        The " Empress " steamers on the Pacific.

THE consideration of Canadian shipping has to be approached from three different points. There is that aspect which is concerned with the system of inland waterways which is the unique possession of Canada save to the extent to which it is shared by the United States. There are the Atlantic routes, which connect the Dominion with the Mother country ; and on the Pacific side the Panama Canal has created a position of extraordinary interest. Inland water transport is a competitor with the railways. The ocean routes are really extensions of the great railway systems and without them the vast expenditure by the Dominion in railway and canal development would be largely in vain.

Inland Waterways

It is mainly in connexion with inland water transport that the building of ships as well as their movements has to be considered. Until the time of the Union an extensive wooden shipbuilding industry was carried on in Quebec and the Maritime Provinces. In 1865, Quebec-built ships to the number of 105, representing a total of 59,333 tons, were placed on the register.[1] Then iron and steel hulls became general and the shipbuilding industry of Eastern Canada languished and died, and since that time such shipbuilding as there is has been carried on at various of the ports of the Great Lakes and in British Columbia.

Geographical conditions enabled a certain amount of steel shipbuilding to develop on the Upper Lakes to meet

---

[1] *Canada Year Book*, 1921, p. 357.

the demand for freight carriers, especially grain, between points as far west as Fort William and Port Arthur on Lake Superior and as far east as Port Colborne at the Lake Erie end of the Welland Canal. These vessels had to be capable of carrying from 5,000 to 10,000 tons. Ships of this size could not pass the St. Lawrence canal system with its limit of 14 feet draught, and for this reason British shipbuilders were excluded from competition with the native shipbuilders for the construction of the larger type of vessel. The conditions described did not, however, exclude the British built vessel of smaller dimensions, and while the big freight carriers which cannot get beyond Port Colborne are Canadian built, the smaller vessels which pass through the canals and come down to Montreal were often built in a European shipyard.

The conditions protecting Canadian shipbuilders west of the St. Lawrence chain of canals in no way interfered with European competition in respect of vessels intended for ocean trade or the St. Lawrence trade as far up as Montreal, and in that competition the European shipyards were at an enormous advantage. " The cost of labour and material in Canada was so much higher than in the British Isles that it was estimated that up to the time of the outbreak of the war vessels could be built in Britain at a cost of about 40 per cent less than in Canada and in some years the difference was estimated as even greater than this."[1] Such a handicap practically ruled out Canadian shipbuilders in competition with shipyards in Great Britain and Scandinavia and other European countries, a handicap which led to a demand that the Government should subsidize shipbuilders.

The Lakes' shipbuilders were not without a precedent for their demand. A similar position had arisen on the Pacific coast and in that case the remedy by way of a government subsidy was applied. Vancouver shipbuilders were unable to compete with British shipbuilders for ships destined for the British Columbia trade. Labour in Britain was about 30 to 35 per cent cheaper than in the Province, and most of the machinery and equipment for the vessels had to come from Great Britain, all of which was subject to the $17\frac{1}{2}$ per cent duty.[2] By the British Columbia Shipping Act, 1916,[3]

---

[1] Dominions Royal Commission : Minutes of Evidence, 1916 [*Cd.* 8458], *Memorandum*, p. 241.
[2] Ibid, Q. 3050. [3] Chap. 51. The Act was repealed in 1922 (chap. 71).

provision was made for giving aid to the builder of ocean-going vessels primarily intended for handling the lumber trade of the Province. Loans were authorized up to 55 per cent of the value of ships built and registered in the Province, or a subsidy could be granted payable in ten annual instalments, each instalment up to 5 dollars a ton of cargo capacity. The subsidy provision was found the more acceptable. The ships contracted for under these provisions were wooden ships of 2,500 tons, the material used being Douglas fir.

The decline in shipping on the Great Lakes due to railway competition began about 1850. Passengers preferred railways to steamships and perishable goods requiring speedy transport naturally gravitated in the same direction. Finally the cargo boats on the Great Lakes had to depend for a living mainly on the transport of grain, pulpwood, coal and iron.

Moreover, of the traffic left by the railways for the steamships plying in the Great Lakes, the Americans captured and for a long time retained the major part. " For many years we had no Canadian bottoms on the Lakes, or at least very few, to move the grain from the west. The Americans had the business and they managed to keep it."[1] The consequence was of vast importance to Canada, for Canadian wheat carried in American bottoms found its way to American railways and American ports, so that it was said that " the Erie Canal and the New York Central Railway were the regulators of freight rates ".[2]   In later years conditions altered somewhat, so that the tonnage of Canadian shipping entering and clearing on the rivers and lakes between Canada and the United States has approached equality.[3]

The Atlantic Routes

Of the early voyagers to Canada, the names which live in history are Cabot, Cartier and Champlain. The story of the North Atlantic shipping routes begins in 1497 when

---

[1] *Dominion Debates, Session* 1903, vol. iv, col. 9178 : Speech by Mr. A. E. Kemp.

[2] Ibid.

[3] In 1914 the number of Canadian steamships arriving at River and Lake ports was 7,863, and the tonnage 5,830,926, as against 16,270 American steamships representing 9,378,264 tons. In 1927 the figures were 7,919 Canadian steamships entered, of 7,933,752 tons register and American steamships were 19,718 in number of 6,242,647 tons register. See *Canada Year Books*, 1916–17, p. 472, and 1927–8, p. 698.

Cabot navigated *The Matthew* with its crew of eighteen from Bristol to a land which has since been generally identified as the coast of what is now Nova Scotia.[1] The history of Canada begins in 1537 when Jacques Cartier, the French navigator, ascended the St. Lawrence. Champlain, the founder of Quebec, crossed the Atlantic a sufficient number of times in the early years of the seventeenth century to establish the passage as a normal undertaking and to remove it from the category of adventure.

The real revolution in ocean transport came with the application of steam to navigation, and it was a Canadian vessel that first accomplished the passage of the Atlantic entirely under steam power. The *Royal William*, a vessel of 1,370 tons, was constructed at Quebec and fitted with engines at Montreal. Leaving Pictou, Nova Scotia, in August, 1833, she reached London with her seven passengers and cargo of coal and miscellaneous goods after a voyage of twenty-five days.[2] The *Royal William* was the real parent of modern transatlantic travel, for it was her exploit that convinced Samuel Cunard, who already owned vessels sailing out of Halifax, that steam was the motive power of the future, and inspired him with the ambition to institute a line of steam vessels which should cross the Atlantic on regular dates. In the realization of that ambition the first of the Atlantic liners came into being, and the system of government subsidies to shipowners, by which payment is made for carrying the mails, inaugurated.

In 1838, on the strength of the first contract with the British Government for carrying the mails across the Atlantic by steamship, the mail service between Great Britain and North America was put on a regular basis and the great Cunard Line founded. The contract necessitated the construction of four vessels for service between Great Britain and Canadian and United States Atlantic ports. In 1840 the first of these four vessels, the *Britannia*,

---

[1] Columbus, it is true, reached the western continent in 1492, and his second voyage was in 1495, but there is no evidence that he ever sighted North America. His destinations on his four voyages were the West Indies and South America.

[2] The claim that the New York vessel *Savannah*, launched in 1818, was the first ocean steamship, seems now untenable. She appears to have been wind-propelled most of her time, but she had paddle wheels which could be lowered into the water in calm weather and driven by an engine placed on her deck. At other times the wheels were kept on deck folded up. See Sandford Fleming, "Canada and Ocean Highways," *Proceedings Royal Colonial Institute*, vol. 27, p. 403.

reached Halifax. She was a wooden paddle steamer of between 1,100 and 1,200 tons, capable of an average speed of 8½ knots. Her first voyage across the Atlantic took twelve and a half days. The success of the *Britannia* and her sister ships drove the sailing packets off the seas and for several years the Cunard Line was supreme on the Atlantic passage. In 1847 a new mail contract was entered into, providing for an annual subsidy of £173,000 for a fortnightly service from Queenstown to New York and once a fortnight from Queenstown *via* Halifax to Boston.[1]

Meanwhile there was coming about the change in steamship construction from paddle and simple engine to screw and compound engine which once more revolutionized transport by sea. "The first Cunard boats could only carry 225 tons cargo and 90 passengers and could only steam 8·7 knots per hour on an average, consuming 4·7 lb. of coal per i.h.p. per hour" while the first of their screw compound boats, the *Bothnia*, built in 1874, carried 3,000 tons of cargo and 340 saloon passengers besides steerage, and steamed on an average 13 knots, consuming only 2·2 lb. of coal per i.h.p. per hour.[2] The change synchronized with a challenge to the Cunard monopoly and with the determination of the Canadian Government to bring into being a line of steamers more definitely identified with the St. Lawrence traffic. While the original establishment of the line was acknowledged to have been a great benefit, the persistent renewal of the contract by the Imperial Government, a contract which was regarded as giving a bounty in favour of the American ports and to the detriment of the St. Lawrence route, when the necessity for it had ceased, had become an acute grievance in Canada.[3] Tenders were invited for a line of screw steamers and the contract went to the Allans, of Glasgow, a firm the head of which, Sir Hugh Allan, was a Scotsman settled in Montreal, whose name was afterwards to figure, not altogether fortunately, in Canadian railway enterprise. In 1856 the Allan Line commenced a fortnightly Canadian service, with four vessels, on the strength of an annual subsidy of $120,000. In 1858 the subsidy was increased to $208,000 in return for the undertaking of a weekly service.

---

[1] Report from Select Committee on Mail Contracts. *Minutes of Evidence*, 1868–9 (106), vi, 265, p. 76.

[2] Fry, H., *The History of North Atlantic Steam Navigation*, p. 49.

[3] See *Canada, 1849 to 1859*, by the Hon. A. T. Galt, London, 1860. Canada: Pamphlets. Vol. 1, No. 3, in Dominions Office and Colonial Office Library (hereafter referred to as D.O. & C.O. Library).

The Allan liners were the first to give passengers the comfort of covered decks. They were also the first to give Newfoundland a regular service. Before 1870 that Dominion maintained touch with Great Britain by forwarding and receiving mails by occasional steamers and by sailing packets. " All the merchants doing business at St. John's at that period utilized their own sailing vessels for the conveyance of letters between Newfoundland and the British Isles and took mail bags with general correspondence as well ; while the Allan Line sent ships occasionally. In 1872 an arrangement was made with the Allan Company for a regular service, the subsidy to be 60,000 dollars a year from the Colony and half that by the Imperial Government.[1]

More and more the Cunard line came to cultivate the American rather than the Canadian traffic, and in 1867 the Cunarders ceased to call at Halifax or any Canadian port.[2]

An important new chapter in the history of Canadian transport was opened when in 1903 the Canadian Pacific Company acquired from Elder Dempsters a large portion of the fleet of passenger and cargo vessels representing the old Beaver Line which had long competed with the Allan Line for Canadian traffic. Among them were four steamers with the twin screws which, with their two independent sets of engines and boilers, had recently been introduced as additional means of safety, inasmuch as a vessel so equipped could proceed on her course in spite of a broken

---

[1] *Dominions Royal Commission : Minutes of Evidence*, 1914 [*Cd*. 7711], p. 22. For the early history of the Allan Line, see *History of the Canadian Pacific Line*, by F. C. Bowen.

[2] Nevertheless, as the Dominions Royal Commission discovered, the Cunard Steamship Co. was in 1903 given special assistance by the British Government " in the shape of an advance of capital at low interest and a subsidy of £150,000 per annum for the construction of two vessels of 24–25 knots speed. These vessels were to be built specifically for the maintenance and development of the Company's line between Liverpool and New York or between other ports in Great Britain and the United States of America ", a state of things which drew from the Commission the caustic comment : " It is to us incredible that Your Majesty's Government should ever again contemplate the grant of assistance of the kind described simply to develop an ocean service with a foreign country." Dominions Royal Commission, *Fifth Interim Report*, 1917 [*Cd*. 8457], p. 22.

It was stated in evidence before the Dominions Royal Commission in 1914, that " the past few years had seen the White Star, Cunard, Hamburg-America and others . . . previously operating exclusively on the American routes establishing services to the St. Lawrence." [*Cd*. 7898], Evidence taken in Newfoundland, p. 24.

shaft or after the loss of a screw through a collision with say a whale or field ice.

During the thirty years preceding the outbreak of the Great War there was brought about a vast increase in the size of the vessels on the North Atlantic route, and a corresponding diminution in the length of the voyage. " Thirty years ago the largest vessel sailing between Liverpool and Canada was of 5,395 tons gross register : to-day the largest vessel in the trade is of 18,485 tons gross register. Thirty years ago the voyage between Liverpool and Canada occupied from nine to twelve days—it is now made in six days." [1] The risk of disaster has also been greatly reduced. The organization of the Atlantic shipping service has reached the degree where tracks varying with the seasons are prescribed in both directions. This system minimizes the possibility of a collision of ships going in opposite directions ; it also enables ships to follow courses where experience shows it to be unlikely that icebergs will be encountered. For Canadian traffic, tracks have been agreed for the periods February to April, April to May, and November to February.

We have seen something of the competition in the past between the Dominion and the Republic for population with which to fill their vacant spaces and we have followed the efforts of Canada to make herself independent of the railways of the United States. Another phase of the never-ending duel between the two nations now comes into view, that is to say, the rivalry between their respective ports, especially on the Atlantic, for traffic with which to feed their railways.

Shipbuilders and naval architects insist that the development of cheap and efficient transport by sea depends on the possibility of increasing the size and draught of vessels [2] and on the existence of harbours and waterways of a capacity

---

[1] Dominions Royal Commission, *Minutes of Evidence*, 1914 [*Cd.* 7710] Evidence of Sir Norman Hill, p. 24.

[2] " A vessel constructed of a depth sufficient to go to, say, 40 feet draught, does not cost so very much more than a vessel of a depth constructed to go to 29 feet draught . . . Supposing two ships are constructed, the one of 29 ft. draught and the other of 40 ft. draught, and in each case the draught necessary to float hull, machinery, etc., i.e. before paying cargo can be put in, is 23 ft. In one case there is only 6 ft. of draught available for paying cargo, whereas in the other case there is 17 ft." Memorandum presented to Dominions Royal Commission by Professor Sir J. H. Biles, and quoted in Final Report, 1917 [*Cd.* 8462], p. 108. On the same authority " increase of speed in the larger vessel would be much less costly ".

and depth adequate for the accommodation of such vessels. To no part of the British Empire has nature been more generous than to Canada in the supply of harbours both wide and deep. Halifax is an excellent natural harbour with a wide and unobstructed approach and a minimum depth at low water at the entrance of 36 feet. It is open all the year. St. John (New Brunswick), also a winter port, has a minimum depth of 26 feet. Quebec and Montreal each has a minimum depth of 30 feet. Instances of other harbours with great natural advantages but as yet only developed in a partial degree are Sydney (Nova Scotia) and St. Andrews (New Brunswick). Yet, in spite of the Dominion's natural advantages in the matter of harbours, a striking proportion of Canada's overseas trade passes through United States ports.

The peculiar problem which Canada has to face arises from the fact that her harbours are subject to the competition of Boston, Portland and other United States ports which are as readily accessible from the Canadian interior as Canada's own ports. According to the estimate put before the Dominion's Royal Commission, " in 1913 two-thirds of the Canadian export wheat was shipped through United States ports, and though quantities and proportions differ no doubt in different years, considerable diversion from Canadian ports appears to be a normal condition." [1] In 1927 and the two preceding years, of the total exports from Canada to overseas countries, 39 per cent went *via* the United States. On the other hand, as a result of propaganda in favour of the use of Canadian ports and tariff privileges to goods imported direct, imports into Canada *via* the United States were only 3·7 of the whole in 1927 and between 4 and 5 per cent in the preceding years.[2]

At the outset it has to be recognized that natural facilities are of themselves insufficient to attract traffic and that the engineer and the builder must come to the aid of nature if the organization for keeping Canadian traffic in Canadian hands is to be made effective. Unless the ocean ports of the Dominion have adequate equipment for accommodating vessels and handling traffic and in particular elevator accommodation for the storage of grain, the traffic must go elsewhere. In the period just before the Great

[1] Dominions Royal Commission, *Fifth Interim Report*, 1917 [*Cd*. 8457], p. 22.
[2] *Canada Year Book*, 1927–8, p. 481.

War, Quebec was complaining that quite early in the season when grain is moved, they had to refuse further consignments for want of storage accommodation. At that time the elevators on the Great Lakes had a capacity of 58 million bushels, whereas those at Canadian seaports could only store 13 million bushels.[1] The existence of such a disproportion in favour of the Lake ports was bound to render more difficult the diversion of the wheat traffic from United States to Canadian railways and seaports.

Again, the complaint of the Maritime Provinces has been that Canadian politicians have failed to make good their undertaking that Canadian trade should be developed through Canadian ports, and in particular Halifax and St. John. The Royal Commission on Maritime Claims (the Duncan Commission),[2] found it necessary to point out that something more than a slogan, " Canadian trade for Canadian ports," was necessary to solve the problem, and that was the development of facilities for handling traffic, and the Provinces were reminded that the difficulties that were experienced in connexion with the shipment of the million bushels of grain that went to Halifax in 1925 " arose from the inadequate loading accommodation provided for the elevator ". Delay and loss had also occurred at St. John through lack of accommodation for handling winter traffic.

The Commission expressed the opinion that " under existing conditions of proprietorship at these ports " the chances of development on an adequate scale were small, and they recommended the establishment of a statutory Harbour Commission in Halifax and St. John " whose business it would be to see that the port facilities are developed on such a scale as will gradually—but by no means slowly—create channels through which trade can expand both winter and summer ".

As to Montreal, the greatest grain port in the world, before 1910 its grain-handling equipment consisted of two elevators each of 1,000,000 bushel capacity, two obsolete wooden elevators belonging to the Canadian Pacific Railway Company, and a small fleet of floating transfer elevators. In 1916 there was an elevator of 4,000,000 bushels capacity,

[1] Dominions Royal Commission, *Minutes of Evidence*, 1916 [*Cd*. 8458], p. 307.
[2] Report of Royal Commission on Maritime Claims, Ottawa, 1926 (*Canada Pamphlets*, vol. 10, No. 263, in D.O. & C.O. Library).

another of 2,622,000 bushels, and the Grand Trunk elevator with a capacity of 2,150,000 bushels.[1]

All the time Canada's constant struggle with climatic conditions has to be borne in mind. The necessity for rushing the grain crop eastwards before winter conditions prevail means feverish activity for a few months during which the demands on the railways and lake steamers, and the labour connected with both, reach their peak. Moreover, elevator and harbour facilities have had to be constructed which enable over 200 million bushels of grain to be handled in a fraction of the year but which must stand idle for the rest of the time.

A further consideration which has to be borne in mind when considering the contest between Canadian and American ports and railways for traffic emerged when certain figures were placed before the Dominions Royal Commission.

Of 312,372,682 bushels of grain shipped from the Canadian " Head of the Lakes " for the year 1915–16, 180,844,019 bushels were diverted to the American routes and only 131,528,660 bushels shipped by the Canadian transportation lines.[2]

The diversion of two-thirds of the Canadian grain to the United States was ascribed to the lack of ships.

And not only had the Americans more ships, but they also had the faster ships. Although the distance between London and Montreal, *via* New York, is several hundred miles longer than by any Canadian route, yet the European mails could be delivered throughout Canada from one to two days earlier by way of New York than by Canadian ports. The consequence was that a large percentage of the Canadian mail as well as passengers reached their destination *via* United States ports. The reason was that the Canadian boats of 17 to 18 knots capacity had to compete with the United States ships doing 24 to 25 knots.[3]

The vision of an All-Red Route, by which is meant a highway for passenger and mail steamers between Great Britain and Australasia by way of Canada, all the calling places along which shall be on British territory or under

---

[1] Dominions Royal Commission, *Minutes of Evidence*, 1916 [*Cd.* 8458], p. 298.

[2] Ibid., p. 299.

[3] Dominions Royal Commission, *Minutes of Evidence*, 1914 [*Cd.* 7971], pp. 29–30.

British control, has long made an arresting appeal on sentimental and patriotic grounds to all the Dominions, but it is Canada that is most vitally interested in the scheme. The Canadian transcontinental railways would be vital links, and Canada would be enabled to compete with the United States upon better terms if Sir Wilfred Laurier's demand to the Colonial Conference of 1907 for a service equal to the best then in existence between New York and England were conceded.   One of the main considerations in favour of a direct fast line to Canada is that thereby the scandal, as Canadians have always regarded it, as well as the delay involved, in getting their passengers and mails through New York would be diminished.   The difference in distance in favour of the Liverpool to Halifax route as against Liverpool to New York, is in the neighbourhood of 1,000 miles, and Lord Strathcona expressed the opinion in 1908 that if a service could be established to Canada similar in speed to that given to New York by the *Lusitania* and *Mauretania*, nearly two days would be saved on the time then taken to convey mails and passengers to a Canadian port.[1]

It has been generally recognized that a scheme for an " All-Red Route " would require substantial Government aid, and that no such scheme could be self-supporting from the outset.   Recognizing this, the Colonial Conference of 1907 placed on record its recommendation that for the purpose of carrying the project into effect " such financial support as may be necessary should be contributed by Great Britain, Canada, Australia and New Zealand in equitable proportions ".[2]

But although harbours may be equipped and ships built it still remains to solve the problems which have been set by nature.

So far as the competition between the Canadian ports of the St. Lawrence and New York for traffic is a competition in speed, it has to be recognized that all the advantages are with the United States.   As ships become speedier, so the superior attractions of the United States ports become more and more apparent.   In the days of the timber ships Canada held her own, but in 1838 the introduction of steam power revolutionized travel by sea.   Hitherto

---

[1] Lord Strathcona, " The All-Red Route," *Proceedings, Royal Colonial Institute*, vol. 39, p. 256.
[2] Colonial Conference, 1907, *Minutes of Proceedings* [*Cd*. 3523], p. x.

thirty-four days westward and twenty days eastward had been regarded as a fair average time for crossing the Atlantic. In 1838 the voyage to the United States was accomplished in fifteen days. In 1856 the Cunard Line was doing it in nine days and in 1887 in a little over six days. In 1898 the North German liner *Kaiser Wilhelm der Grosse* made the run from New York to Southampton in five and three-quarter days. Each ten years during the latter part of the nineteenth century saw a reduction of approximately a day in the time of the passage to the United States. Not so, however, in the passage to the ports of the St. Lawrence. The fastest times made by the Allan Line between Liverpool and Quebec were nine and a half days in 1857, seven and three-quarter days in 1887, and eight days in 1897. The average time between Liverpool and Quebec in 1897 was nine and three-quarter days.[1]

The reason why Canada has failed to reap the same advantages from the increased speed of ships as the neighbouring Republic is to be found in the geographical and physical conditions of the St. Lawrence. In that region the twin bugbears of the navigator are icebergs, obstacles which drift with the currents so that their position cannot be shown on any chart, and the fog which pours in when the wind is in the south.

Two channels give entrance to the Gulf of St. Lawrence, the Strait of Belle Isle on the north of Newfoundland and Cabot Strait on the south. From Belle Isle the distance inland to Montreal is 900 miles. It provides a route to Europe shorter by 150 miles than that by way of Cabot Strait, but on the other hand " although the river and gulf may be sufficiently free from ice in May to admit of ships entering by Cabot Strait to ascend to Quebec and Montreal, Belle Isle remains practically closed until a later date. The more northern entrance is not generally available for ships until the last half of June and the regular mail steamers do not attempt to pass before July 1st. The explanation of the late opening of navigation by Belle Isle is well known. It is due to the fact that in the spring months the Arctic current descends from the north along the Labrador and Newfoundland coasts laden with innumerable icebergs which extend a long way to sea and drift into the Straits in the earlier months of summer so as to impede navigation. . . .

---

[1] Dobson, G. H., "Modern Transportation and Atlantic Express Tracks. Halifax, N.S., 1899" (*Canada Pamphlets*, No. 133. D.O. & C.O. Library.)

All winds from the southward bring up fog and during its prevalence the greatest caution has to be exercised in order to insure safety [1] . . . Icebergs are often very numerous in July. By September the conditions are generally improved both with respect to fog and icebergs. In October few icebergs are usually seen and sometimes none whatever. . . . Before the end of November, navigation by the waterway of the St. Lawrence is practically closed." [2]

The less direct route through Cabot Strait is available two months earlier, but " field ice may be looked for early in May on the approach to Cabot Strait and in some years in the Gulf. . . . In the Gulf as elsewhere southerly winds invariably bring up fog and ships for Quebec require to observe caution and reduce their speed according to the density of the fog." [3]

Save for Newfoundland sealing vessels or other specially constructed steamers, the two routes from the St. Lawrence to Europe are closed for five months of the year, and for a considerable proportion of the time when they are open the conditions of navigation for about one-third of the distance between Montreal and Great Britain make rapid steaming perilous and running to any schedule of time almost impossible. Records in the Post Office Department, Ottawa, show that in the case of one vessel in which the Department was interested there was a difference of ninety-eight hours between the fastest and the slowest trips in 1897 and a difference of 103 hours between the quickest trip in 1896 and the slowest in 1897. [4]

As a final item in the catalogue of difficulties along the whole length of the long run from Belle Isle to Rimouski, " the course of ships is confined between lines of rocky coasts on both sides. The currents are irregular, the waterways somewhat winding, and the channel narrow in places

---

[1] In 1894 the maximum duration of fogs for the five months when navigation was open were as follows :—

July	.	.	.	309 hours.
August	.	.		262 ,,
September	.	.		110 ,,
October	.	.		215 ,,
November	.	.		105 ,,

G. H. Dobson, op. cit.

[2] Sandford Fleming, " Steamship Service between Canada and Great Britain." Reprinted from *Queen's Quarterly*, Kingston, 1896 (*Canada Pamphlets*, No. 116, D.O. & C.O. Library).

[3] Sandford Fleming, op. cit.

[4] G. H. Dobson, op. cit.

the nearer the approach to Quebec. The waterways from Belle Isle to Quebec are so narrow that double lanes are impossible. The danger is increased by vessels of all kinds in the coasting and foreign trade." [1]

The dangers of the St. Lawrence route are reflected in the marine insurance rates and have led to complaints of discrimination against Canadian ports, in that vessels are charged higher rates of insurance to or from Canadian Atlantic ports than to or from the United States ports of New York, Boston or Portland. It is admitted that in the past there was some justification for the discrimination, but it is claimed that owing to improvements in the river channel this no longer exists. It is also pointed out that danger from the southern flow of Arctic ice is not confined to vessels for Canadian ports but has to be encountered by steamers to Boston and New York and that the only serious disaster due to ice for a period of many years was the loss of the *Titanic*, bound for New York. The underwriters admit the improvements in aids to navigation, but reply that the risks due to fog, ice and tidal currents in the outer approaches remain.[2]

As competitors with New York, Quebec and Montreal are handicapped by conditions which must survive so long as ice flows down from the north and fog up from the south. But in Halifax, its most easterly harbour, Canada has a port which is open all the year round and is without the special disadvantages of the ports of the St. Lawrence. " Nautical men are united in the opinion that Halifax is one of the best in the world, and that it is easier of access and egress than any other large harbour on the coast. From this harbour steamships of any class may leave at any condition of the tide to cross the ocean, every day of the year." [3] Moveover, the Canadian Atlantic ports have the advantage over those of the United States in the matter of distance to Europe   From Halifax to Liverpool

---

[1] Ibid. For purposes of marine insurance a distinction is drawn between the winter and summer seasons, a lower premium being paid during the latter. Thus in 1923 the figures for the insurance of grain were 20 cents per $100 during the summer normal, and 40 cents after 15th November (Imperial Shipping Committee, Second Report on Canadian Marine Insurance Rates, *Cmd*. 2447.) In 1924, the Joint Hull Committee agreed that the summer season should run from 16th May to 31st October (Imperial Shipping Committee, Interim Report, *Cmd*. 2249).

[2] Imperial Shipping Committee, Interim Report on Canadian Marine Insurance Rates, *Cmd*. 2249.

[3] Sandford Fleming, op. cit.

the distance is 2,485 miles and from St. John 2,747 miles, as compared with 3,010 miles from New York to Liverpool.

With St. John, Halifax is the terminus for Canadian Trans-Atlantic steamers when the St. Lawrence route is closed for the winter months. A comprehensive scheme of ocean terminals at Halifax for the transcontinental railways was approved by the Dominion Government in 1912 and the work was commenced in 1914.[1] A feature in the programme of improvements is a passenger landing quay 2,000 feet in length, a circumstance which suggests appreciation of Sandford Fleming's teaching that in steamship navigation, as on railways, in passenger traffic, speed and regularity are the primary considerations, while in the transport of freight economy comes first ; and that if a fast line of passenger steamships, equal in speed and power to any on the ocean, is to be established, it must be an " all year round line " from one of the splendid open harbours on the Atlantic seaboard, the St. Lawrence being left to its proper function of conveying Canada's staple products at the lowest rates.[2]

The Route to the West Indies.

Southwards the United States reaches out to the twenty-fifth degree of latitude, a point which is nearer the Equator than some of the Bahama Islands, and the northern boundary is the forty-ninth degree. Within the intervening twenty-four degrees are found the products of temperate, sub-tropical and tropical climes, and their possession of Alaska brings Americans into touch with the Arctic regions. Canada gets no further south than the temperate zone, and her traditional policy of cultivating close trade relations with the British West Indies and the suggestions which have been heard from time to time for closer political relations as well, are inspired by the desire of the Dominion to secure for herself the coffee, sugar, cocoa and other tropical and sub-tropical commodities which she cannot produce within her own borders and so, to some extent, to balance her economic disadvantage as compared with the neighbouring Republic.

The proposal for the admission of the British West Indies

[1] For details, see Dominions Royal Commission, Memoranda and Tables as to Chief Harbours, etc., 1917 [Cd. 8461].
[2] In December, 1928, it was announced that the White Star Line had closed its offices in Portland, Maine, and had inaugurated a schedule of East-bound sailings from Halifax.

to the Dominion has a basis of political precedent as well as economic expediency. When the Australian States accomplished federation, British New Guinea was incorporated as a dependency of the Commonwealth. Australia, New Zealand and South Africa took over responsibility for mandated territories as a result of their participation in the Great War. The United States have absorbed the Hawaiian Islands, Porto Rico, and the Danish West Indies. By bringing the British West Indies into her political system, Canada would bring within her own tariff walls tropical and sub-tropical products complementary to those produced north of the forty-ninth parallel. It is difficult, however, to imagine the West Indies as politically part of Canada so long as Newfoundland remains a separate Dominion. As a matter of practical politics, preferential trade and subsidized shipping have had to be relied on to bring Canada and the West Indies into the desired economic relationship.

In her trade relations with the British West Indies there has been on the part of Canada something of the attitude of the benevolent and long-suffering big brother. In 1890 Canadian proposals for commercial reciprocity came to nothing because the West Indian Colonies were afraid of offending the United States, then their best customers for sugar. In 1898, Canada extended the benefits of the British preferential tariff to all the British West Indian Colonies, no compensating advantages being either granted or asked. " Mr. Fielding claimed that Canada had some Imperial responsibilities in the matter, and he stated that, with a desire to assist Her Majesty's Government in dealing with these problems, the Canadian Government had decided to extend the preferential tariff to the West Indies without demanding any concessions in return." [1] A further opportunity for the display of benevolence came when, as a result of the Spanish-American war, Porto Rico and the Philippines were absorbed into the United States, and Cuba became its appendage. Their sugar was admitted into the United States on special terms, and the British West Indies found their natural market for sugar thereby practically annihilated. But " the policy of the Dominion has provided in Canada the market lost in the United States ", so averting

---

[1] Report of Royal Commission on Trade Relations between Canada and the West Indies, 1910 [*Cd*. 5369], p. 3.

the danger that sugar cultivation in the West Indies would be abandoned.[1]

But commercial preferences were of themselves insufficient to develop and maintain trade relations between Canada and the British West Indies. Adequate transport was the necessary corollary. Where the main products for export were other than sugar—the vegetables of Bermuda, the fruit of the Bahamas, the timber of British Honduras—adequate direct communication was the one essential for the promotion of trade relations. And always there is the length of the voyage between West Indian and Canadian ports and the geographical disadvantages of Canada as a market for the West Indies as compared with the United States.

Her import statistics suggest that the relative commercial importance of the West Indies to the Dominion has been steadily decreasing, but the policy of linking up more closely the different parts of the British Empire has been making a greater and greater appeal. To the solution of that larger problem the subsidized lines of shipping between Canada and the West Indies have made their contribution. Just as Canada is " an attempt to defy geography " (in the words of Goldwin Smith), so the linking up together of Canada and the British West Indies is another " attempt to defy geography ". By its very nearness and wealth, the United States tends to draw the British West Indies within its economic orbit. Canada, on the other hand, has to combat not only distance but also disparity of climate. While it is true that this very difference of climate makes for a sound basis of exchange, since the British West Indies produces sub-tropical fruit and commodities while Canada has wheat, fish and lumber to export, still the long haul, the awkwardness of the route either by the St. Lawrence or through St. John and Halifax, and the wintriness of Canada discourage trade and personal intercourse. After all, the problem of Canada and the British West Indies is only part of one of the great problems that the Mother Country has to meet, that is, the harmonizing of the interests of the two Empires within the British Empire, the tropical and sub-tropical Empire in Trust and the temperate Empire in Alliance.

Of the many shipping subsidy contracts entered into for

---

[1] Ibid., pp. 6–7. As illustrating the effect of the preference given by Canada : in 1896 Trinidad exported to Canada 329 tons of sugar, in 1908–9 the figures were 22,932 tons. For 1896 Barbados exported 855 tons to the Dominion : in 1908–9 exports were 12,774 tons (ibid., pp. 10–11).

the purpose of the British West Indies service, that of 1913 is interesting as embodying conditions in furtherance of the national policy.

In that year an agreement was entered into between the Government of Canada and the Royal Mail Steam Packet Company for a steamship service between Canada and the British West Indies every fourteen days. Four steamships were at an early date to be put upon the route between St. John and Halifax as ports of departure in Canada, and Georgetown, British Guiana, calling at certain of the West Indian Islands on the way. The purpose of the agreement being the encouragement of Canadian trade through Canadian channels, freight was to be delivered to the Intercolonial Railway at Halifax or St. John unless otherwise expressly routed. For this service a subsidy of £70,000 a year was to be paid.

The culmination of the long-sustained effort to bring together the Dominion and the islands in the Caribbean Sea was probably reached when, in July, 1925, the Canada-West Indies Trade Agreement was ratified. The main interest in the Treaty centred not in the mutual trade preferences but in the Articles in which provision was made for a subsidized fortnightly freight and passenger steamship service. To the heavy subsidies payable, the West Indies themselves agreed to contribute £45,000 : the Dominion agreed to find the balance. In the result the whole venture took on the aspect of a State enterprise, for under the Treaty five steamers were to be built with adequate cold storage accommodation, the whole enterprise to be controlled by the Canadian Government and managed by the Canadian National Railways.

The Panama Canal Route

The impression that one gets of conditions in the Prairie Provinces during the " fall " months is that of a vast yellow inland lake of grain seeking channels which will give it outlets to the sea. One sees the customary channels to the east open for part of the year only and then relentlessly closed by impenetrable barriers of ice until the return of spring once more releases the pent-up flood. Canadian nationalism has been seen struggling to keep Canadian traffic in Canadian hands, but in the end faced with the alternative of either using American transport and American Atlantic ports or seeing a substantial part of the national harvest perish. The dreaded passage round the Horn and the interminable trail across the Equator lay between possible Canadian outlets in the West and the European goal. Canada's difficulties have been her southern neighbours' opportunities, yet by a strange irony it is American enterprise that has provided Canada with a way out of a good many of her troubles. On August 15th, 1914, the Panama Canal was opened for traffic and at once it became possible to substitute ports on the Canadian Pacific coast for the ports on the Atlantic as the exits for the grain of the Prairie Provinces.

The tragic history of the Canal is well known. The idea of bisecting the continent of America by a canal is traceable back to the sixteenth century, but it was not until 1878 that the enterprise was seriously attempted. " The greatest liberty that man has ever taken with Nature," was the phrase in which Viscount Bryce summed up the completed enterprise. Certainly nature had shown her resentment. The career of the French corporation that acquired the concession in 1878 was marked by lively scandals and came to an inglorious end. The enterprise then passed into the hands of the United States whose Government, in 1904, concluded a treaty with the Republic of Panama whereby the United States was given sovereignty over a strip of land ten miles in width across the Isthmus. Through that strip the canal from the Pacific to the Atlantic was cut.

The utilization of lakes is an important feature of the canal and in particular Gatun Lake, a body of water covering an area of over 160 square miles, the surface of which is maintained at 85 feet above sea level by dams and locks. On both sides the Canal is approached from the sea by a dredged channel which enables vessels to reach the locks which lift vessels to the level of the inland lakes. The length of the Canal from Pacific to Atlantic is 44 nautical miles. The depth of water over the sills is 40 feet and vessels up to 1,000 feet in length can use the canal and find berthing accommodation at Cristobal, the port of entry on the Atlantic side, and Balboa on the Pacific. These terminal ports are under the control of the United States Government, and that Government is also responsible for the upkeep of the Canal as it was for its construction, and of course fixes the tolls.

With the opening of the Panama Canal a new sea route of vast importance came into existence, a new Gulf Stream of commerce which flowed south from the Canadian Pacific coast and then turned east through the Canal to Great Britain and the European continent. The effect on world transport of the elimination of the passage round Cape Horn is likely to have as revolutionary an effect on transport as the elimination of the passage round the Cape of Good Hope by the construction of the Suez Canal. The particular traffic most affected was that in Canadian wheat. The obstacles to the outflow from the Prairie Provinces to Europe by way of the Pacific ports disappeared. The all-sea route from British Columbia to Europe by way of Cape Horn is approximately 14,400 miles. By way of the Suez Canal it is 15,800 miles. The voyage by way of the Panama Canal is one of 8,400 miles, a saving of 6,000 miles. An all-sea route became possible. A great Economic Divide came into being in the centre of Saskatchewan, somewhere in the longitude of Moose Jaw; and whereas hitherto the rivers of wheat had all flowed eastwards, now they were to flow east and west. Montreal and Buffalo must henceforth see part of their grain traffic diverted to Vancouver and Prince Rupert.

At first doubts were expressed whether it would be possible to ship grain in bulk by a tropical route without deterioration consequent on the moisture content. However, " On February 25th, 1918, it was announced at Vancouver that the first bulk shipment from that port via the Panama Canal had arrived safely at a British port. A steamer loaded at the Government elevator in Vancouver, early in November, 1917, with 100,000 bushels of wheat from the Prairies, had made the journey to the United Kingdom via the Panama Canal." [1] And in the year 1920–1 twenty cargoes aggregating 138,435 tons were carried from British Columbia to the United Kingdom and Northern Europe.[2]

Provided it could be established, as was thus done, that wheat could be shipped by way of the Panama Canal in bulk, it was a reasonable expectation that during the open season of navigation grain shipments would be made at a less cost from points in Saskatchewan and Alberta west of Moose Jaw via the Pacific coast outlets and Panama than by the

---

[1] *Canadian Annual Review*, 1918, p. 534.
[2] F. C. Wade, Agent General for British Columbia, at the Royal Society of Arts (*Times*, 7th December, 1921).

eastern route, lake, and rail. After the close of navigation on the Great Lakes all things are in favour of the Pacific coast outlet, especially when the long rail haul is taken into consideration from Fort William to St. John, which means an additional rail haul of 1,376 miles.[1]

Again, the relief of the annual congestion of traffic in the east must favourably affect the cost of transport. The feverish rush to get the grain east in the short period that intervenes between the harvest and the setting-in of winter conditions is a most uneconomic method of marketing produce. The Dominions Royal Commission described this condition in the following terms : " Under present conditions there is a rush, immediately harvest is over, to get the grain down to the foot of the lakes before navigation closes. In October and November, 1913, the freight cars engaged in the wheat traffic to Fort William and Port Arthur were approximately three times the number required to handle the traffic if it had been equally distributed over the year. During the same two months the Canadian Pacific Railway Co. employed about twice as much labour in the Manitoba, Alberta, and Saskatchewan Divisions in connexion with the grain traffic as the number employed on the average throughout the year." [2]

The difficulty of passing the produce of the West through the gates of the East was bound to check the speed at which the still vast virgin territories of the Prairie Provinces could be brought under cultivation.

" I have estimated the arable land of Pacific Canada at easily 333,000,000 acres against 160,000,000 in Atlantic Canada. . . . A recent report of the British Board of Agriculture states that the entire wheat product of the world in 1908 was grown on about 240,000,000 acres of land. We are on the safe side in saying that the Pacific economic drainage basin of Canada possesses a combination of soil and climate with those conditions which are certain yet to be further modified with population and development, which will give Pacific Canada an agricultural area much larger than the world's total acreage in wheat." [3]   The service rendered to Europe by the Panama Canal in thus bringing

---

[1] See Dominions Royal Commission, *Minutes of Evidence*, 1917 [*Cd.* 8458], Q. 3028.

[2] Fifth Interim Report, 1917 [*Cd.* 8457], p. 25.

[3] F. B. Vrooman, " The Economic Effect of the Panama Canal on Western Canada." *United Empire Journal*, 1914, vol. v, p. 570.

the Continent into touch with such a vast potential food supply is obvious.

Moreover, the development of a large export traffic to the West must have an advantageous effect on the import trade to Western Canada. Ships calling at Canadian western ports had to leave for Europe with a large amount of empty space, whereas vessels bringing imports to Canadian eastern ports generally had the opportunity of leaving with an even heavier outward load.

No violent readjustment of traffic routes followed the opening of the Canal. The scarcity of shipping due to the Great War made that impossible, at any rate in the early years. With the decline in freight rates, however, a steady increase in the tonnage using the Canal became apparent,[1] and there gradually emerged the fact that a new trade route between Eastern and Western Canada had come into existence,[2] a fact of which the transcontinental railways had henceforth more and more to take account.

The Pacific

For an eleven knot vessel Yokohama is only fifteen days from Vancouver, and Shanghai eighteen days. Sydney is a voyage of a little more than three weeks. In a modern liner the voyage from Vancouver to Yokohama is a matter of only ten days. On the west, Canada is in touch with Asia by direct steam ship routes as she is on the east with Europe, and thus is she the " half-way house of the Empire ".

With the completion of the Canadian Pacific Railway, Canada's interest in the Pacific became apparent, and the new road for commerce to China and Japan, dreamed of by Cavelier de la Salle in his dangerous seigniory near Montreal more than two centuries previously, was to become an accomplished fact. The Government and the Company co-operated to bring the western terminus into touch with Asia and Australia. In 1889 a contract was concluded with the Railway Company by which there was to be a monthly

---

[1] The Annual Reports of the Governor of the Panama Canal show that the totals of commercial traffic through the Canal were as follows :—

1921	.	.	2,892 vessels and 11,599,214 cargo tonnage.
1927	.	.	5,475 ,, ,, 27,748,215 ,, ,,

[2] From the same source it appears that the tonnage passing through the Canal from the west coast of Canada was 125,638 long tons in 1921, and 1,548,783 in 1927. The traffic bound for the west coast of Canada passing through the Canal was strikingly less, being 126,414 long tons in 1921, and 248,009 in 1927, but nevertheless there has been the same gradual increase.

service of fast steamers between British Columbia and China and Japan. The annual subsidy of £60,000 was to be paid, as to £45,000 by the Imperial Government and as to £15,000 by the Government of Canada.[1]

Canada's increasing importance as a Pacific Power is manifested by the rise and growth of her Pacific ports, Victoria, Vancouver and Prince Rupert.

The origin of Victoria (B.C.) as a port goes back to the days of Fort Victoria, established by the Hudson's Bay Company in the first half of the nineteenth century. The gold discoveries in the Cariboo and Fraser River districts in the 'sixties caused a rush to British Columbia and a consequent increase in the traffic of the port. Afterwards development was slow until the beginning of the twentieth century, when accommodation had to be provided for the Canadian Pacific Railway steamships which sailed to China, Japan and Australia and later for those of the Grand Trunk Pacific Company.

Seeing that Vancouver is the terminus of two of Canada's transcontinental railways, that three lines join it from the United States, and that it is the port in America which is nearest the markets of the East, the growth of the city is easily comprehensible. In the early 'eighties Vancouver was little more than a sawmill clearing in the forest. Then the Canadian Pacific Railway decided to make the place its western terminus. By 1901 it had a population of 27,000, and was a port whence great steamers passed through the narrow entrance from the deep and spacious harbour to China, Japan and Australia, and also to Alaska. " There is here no maze of projecting wharves and docks to keep all these great steamers at arm's length. They float right up to the back gardens of the houses. As you sit at the club window . . . the masts and hull of an Australian liner seem about to touch the garden fence." [2] At the 1921 census Vancouver returned a population of 117,000.

Situated as she is on one of the finest harbours in the world, Vancouver is eminently fitted to be Canada's great gateway of the west. Just as the western ports of the United States, San Francisco, Tacoma and Portland (Oregon) load grain from the interior for Europe and Japan, so a substantial proportion of the trade of the great wheat and cattle country of the North-West has been going to the

---

[1] *Annual Register*, 1889, pp. 439–40.
[2] A. G. Bradley, *Canada in the Twentieth Century*, p. 382, London, 1905.

Pacific Coast rather than to Montreal or St. John. By 1923 the trend of traffic from Alberta and Saskatchewan towards the ports of British Columbia had become noticeable, especially of course the grain traffic. By way of the Panama Canal and to the Orient there were shipped in that year 17,829,687 bushels, an increase of approximately 10,000,000 bushels over the previous year. Of the total, 10,500,000 bushels went to Great Britain.[1] In 1921 the first shipment of chilled meat to leave Vancouver for Europe was sent across the Atlantic. It consisted of some 5,400 carcases of mutton.

In 1926 a new grain port on the Canadian Pacific coast came into existence when a Japanese vessel was loaded up by the Alberta Wheat Pool from the new Government elevator at Prince Rupert, and for the first time a ship left that port carrying grain to the markets of the world. By the end of the year some 2,000,000 bushels had been exported and shipments from Prince Rupert continued steadily thereafter.[2]

In the competition of the British Columbia ports with Seattle, Portland, San Francisco and other United States Pacific ports, the Canadian ports are in the happy position of belonging to a Province which provides the best bunker coal on the Pacific coast.

The Native Canadian Steamship Lines

Before the days of steam power and iron hulls, fleets of wooden ships were turned out of the shipbuilding yards of Quebec and the Maritime Provinces and sailed from the harbours of those Provinces. Quebec did a great lumber trade. Nova Scotia placed on the Atlantic some of the finest clippers that ever crossed the seas. The transition from wooden to iron hulls killed the Canadian shipbuilding industry, and the coming of the railways had far-reaching effects on Canadian shipping on the St. Lawrence as well as the Great Lakes. " Prior to the construction of the Canadian Pacific Railway the shipping trade of the port of Quebec consisted almost entirely of the shipping of square timber staves and deals to Great Britain and, to a limited extent, to France, Spain, South America, South Africa and Australia. These goods were shipped principally in sailing vessels of

---

[1] *Canadian Annual Review*, 1923, p. 338.
[2] *Canadian Annual Review*, 1926-7, p. 239.

from 700 to 1,500 tons register which did not draw much water. . . . Owing to the cutting out of the timber and the removal of saw-mills to the interior to points along the lines of new railways, the lumber trade of Quebec has diminished from year to year, and the sailing ships have almost disappeared and have been replaced by steamships, some of them with a capacity ten times as great as the average sailing ship of former days." [1] By 1914 the berths on the St. Lawrence front had become almost entirely occupied by the mail steamers of the Allan, Canadian Pacific, and Canadian Northern Lines, most of which were too large to get to Montreal.

Beginning with the advent of iron ships and steam railways, there was an almost blank interval in Canada's maritime history. But while railways had helped to destroy the old order, it became the destiny of railways to reconstitute Canada as a nation with a merchant marine of her own.

The Canadian Pacific Line

In Great Britain, competition for traffic was the sufficient reason why so many of the railway companies started steamship lines of their own from the coast termini as feeders to their own undertakings. The Canadian Pacific Railway Company, the first of the transcontinental lines, had laid its plans for reaching out across the Pacific before the rails reached the coast. In their case the spur of competition was not necessary. With the same faith and far-sighted vision that had enabled the builders of the line to carry on to the end, they proceeded at once to carry out plans for bringing the Orient into commercial relationship with the Dominion and to lay the foundation of a new Pacific Power.

At first the Canadian Pacific Company depended on chartered vessels on the Pacific side and on the Allan and other competing liners for the service they were creating to fit in with their railway organization on the Atlantic side. By boldly building for the Pacific routes and by taking over the ships of the Beaver and Allan Lines on the Atlantic side, by 1916 the Canadian Pacific Line had a fleet of over thirty steamers of its own sailing the Pacific and Atlantic Oceans.[2]

---

[1] Dominions Royal Commission, *Minutes of Evidence*, in 1916, of Mr. J. G. Scott, President, Quebec Board of Trade [*Cd.* 8458], p. 305.

[2] In 1928 a contract was placed on the Clyde by the C.P. Rly for a " monster liner" of 40,000 tons gross, for the Canadian Atlantic route. Hitherto vessels of this class had been confined to the New York service.

The vessels built by the Canadian Pacific Line for the route to the Orient were the well-known "Empress" steamers. The first of them, the *Empress of Japan*, was launched in 1890. She was capable of an average speed of 19 knots and her time from Yokohama to Vancouver was under ten days. Truly the "Empress" steamers played many parts. As well as fulfilling the normal functions of a liner, the "Empress" vessel was an auxiliary cruiser, built in accordance with Admiralty requirements. She was a subsidized mail boat, and she cultivated a tourist traffic.

The purchase of the Beaver Line steamers from Elder Dempsters and the consequent appearance of the Canadian Pacific Company in the Atlantic as a competitor for Canadian traffic inaugurated one of those exciting contests between rival transport agencies which used to provide the public with a good deal of gratuitous excitement. The Allan Line accepted the challenge and built the first turbine liners, ships of 11,000 tons gross and with a speed of 19 knots. The Canadian Pacific reply was to build the *Empress of Britain* and a sister ship, ships faster and bigger than the Allan Line's turbine steamers. The ships were over 14,000 tons and the notorious slogan "Twenty knots to Canada" was at last translated into deeds. In 1906 the *Virginian* accomplished the passage from Liverpool to Rimouski in five days twenty hours. Then the *Empress of Britain* did the voyage from Liverpool to Halifax in five days eighteen hours. Improvements were effected in provision for the comfort of passengers. By improvements in such matters as refrigerating arrangements the value of the ships as cargo carriers was augmented. The Allan liner *Corsican* was able to proceed safely to the end of her voyage after striking an iceberg off Belle Isle. The Canadian Pacific equally vindicated the reputation of their Line for safety when the *Mount Temple* stranded in a gale but got her 600 passengers ashore without a single casualty. Whereas in the 'fifties all that the Allan packets provided for emigrants from Liverpool to Quebec was "accommodation, water and firing, the water being very strictly limited", and the emigrants being "expected to bring their own provisions on board", in 1912, in the Allan liner *Scandinavian*, "even a piano was provided for the amusement of the passengers" in the steerage.[1]

[1] See F. C. Bowen, *History of the Canadian Pacific Line*.

At last the two Lines came to the conclusion that the public had benefited sufficiently from their expensive rivalry. In the years just before the Great War they co-operated in plans for reducing the expenditure inevitable from competition. In 1915 the Canadian Pacific Line took over the whole Allan Line fleet and so a great chapter in the history of Atlantic shipping was closed.

The Canadian Pacific Company was now in a better position to carry out its two objects : namely, " to provide for its rapidly increasing immigration business, and to ensure the immigrant proper care and attention from the time he left the shores of the Old Country until he stepped off the train at his prairie destination. It also gave the Company complete control from shipping point to destination, both as to carriage and rates on Canadian products seeking a European market." [1]

The disappearance of a formidable rival in no way diminished the enterprise of the Canadian Pacific management, and in 1922 the Company was able to boast that " C.P.R. ships sailed on every ocean and had their eye on every port of the globe ".

The union of a railway company and a shipping line in sentiment and in pecuniary interest is a mutually advantageous arrangement. Also to find the train waiting for the boat to come alongside is an attractive prospect for the passengers. But such a powerful combination of interests is not without its dangers. To take an instance from the United States : " The recent combination of the American lines and the purchase of the ocean transport reveals the fact . . . that the land lines practically control the situation and that the ocean lines are merely adjuncts. . . . The American combination by means of through bills of lading from the producing and shipping ports in the interior such as Chicago, St. Louis, Minneapolis, and so forth can practically control the freight, or almost entirely so, and a large proportion of the passengers, so as to make any competing ocean line with them unprofitable." [2]

It has accordingly been urged that it is not in the best interests of Canadian trade that dockage facilities at the ports should be owned by a railway company, as at

[1] See Dominions Royal Commission, *Minutes of Evidence*, 1916 [*Cd.* 8458], Q. 5674.
[2] Report from Select Committee on Steamship Subsidies 1902, 385. Evidence of Senator G. Drummond, Vice-President, Bank of Montreal, Q. 2986.

Vancouver, where the docks are Canadian Pacific Railway property and ocean traffic controlled by railway owned vessels, and the demand has been made that the Government should make effective provision for competition by the tramp steamers. One method of preventing the danger of such a shipping monopoly is legislation on the lines of the United States, where provision was made to the effect that no railway in the United States shall own steamships engaged in coastwise traffic through the Panama Canal. The alternative is the provision of Government owned and controlled terminals. The Canadian Government preferred the latter course, and undertook the erection of extensive dock and terminal facilities at Vancouver and at Halifax.

Meanwhile the Canadian Government found to hand an even more potent instrument for controlling ocean rates in the interests of her people.

The Canadian Government Merchant Marine

In 1920 a fleet of vessels built for the Dominion Government in Canadian shipyards with names, the adjectival part of which was *Canadian*, for instance, *Canadian Pioneer* and *Canadian Voyageur*, became active competitors for ocean traffic in the Atlantic and the Pacific. Although owned by the Government, just as the greater part of the railways were owned by the Government, it was early decided to put the Canadian Government Merchant Marine outside politics just as the Government railways were put out of politics. The Canadian Government Merchant Marine was accordingly organized as a subsidiary company of the Canadian National Railways and Sir Henry Thornton became responsible for the national ships as he was for the national railways.

The policy to be pursued in regard to the National fleet was thus declared at an early stage in its career by the responsible Minister : " As Minister of Marine I have never attempted to dictate in any way at all, neither has any member of the Government. The responsibility for success rests entirely on the shoulders of Mr. Hanna and his Board ; they determine what rates shall be laid down and what cargo shall be carried. As a business proposition we know that the ships will be better managed and operated if left entirely free of political influence." [1]

[1] Hon. C. C. Ballantyne at Montreal, 9 Jan., 1920. (Quoted in *Canadian Annual Review*, 1920, p. 360.)

The motives for the foundation of the Government fleet of merchant vessels were various. At the outset it was a war measure. The Imperial Government urged Canada to undertake the construction of a number of ships to replace some of those which had been sunk by German submarines. The desire to provide employment made the Canadian Government the less reluctant to carry out the request. At the same time Canada realized that she had spent very large sums on the development of internal transport. Canada felt that she was entitled to take such steps as would ensure the development of ocean transport from her ports in a manner that would supplement and fit into her railway system and in particular that freight rates should be fair and reasonable. It was alleged before the Dominions Royal Commission that the advantages gained by cheap internal transport had been offset by an excessive advance in ocean rates, and that the advance was the work of the Shipping Conference with its monopolistic tendencies.

To the Canadian exporter especially it is essential that freight rates should be kept as low as possible, seeing that nearly all Canadian exports have a low value in proportion to the space occupied and in relation to the cost of transportation.

Seeing then that although Canada had spent such great sums in improving methods of transport internally, but was largely dependent on the steamships of other countries to carry her produce across the ocean, it was but a short step to the demand that the Dominion Government should complete its work by carrying Dominion traffic in the Dominion's own steamers at reasonable rates of freight. Other reasons urged for the creation of the Canadian Government Merchant Marine during the closing years of the Great War were that inasmuch as the Government had taken over the railway intended to be operated by the Grand Trunk Pacific it had also inherited its obligations of materially reducing the cost of moving the grain of the North-Western farmer, of bringing the business to Canadian ports, and of providing ocean tonnage at these ports to handle it.

The original contracts were for sixty-three steel cargo vessels of six different types. In 1922 the five steamers and various smaller vessels of the Grand Trunk Pacific Railway service were taken over. At the end of 1924 the total fleet consisted of fifty-seven vessels of a total tonnage of 353,450. By sale or loss the fleet had been reduced to forty-six vessels at the end of 1926. These vessels went from Montreal, Quebec, St. John and Halifax to the West Indies, the United Kingdom, France and India. On the Pacific side they went from Vancouver and Victoria to Japan, China, Australia and New Zealand. A service through the Panama Canal linked up the Atlantic with the Pacific services. There was also a coastal service and freighters were sent to help the grain movement on the Great Lakes during the period of seasonal pressure. Some of the vessels were fitted out to convey cattle to the United Kingdom and several of the smaller vessels were used for the carriage of pulpwood from the Maritime Provinces to Quebec and Ontario ports.

The difficulties in the way of making the national fleet a financially remunerative asset were formidable. While full cargoes could generally be obtained on the outward trips, satisfactory cargoes were not usually found for the homeward voyage, and this circumstance increased operating expenses out of all proportion to operating revenues. This is in accordance with shipping experience in general in the Canadian trade. " Montreal has no large return cargoes in comparison with the amount shipped out. Canada ships out four tons for every one brought this way across the Atlantic." [1] There was also the competition of the older Lines to be faced, and in particular the other native Line, the Canadian Pacific. Quite early in its career the Canadian Government Merchant Marine vessels had to reduce their passenger rates between Halifax and Jamaica in order to meet competition from Boston and New York. The claim was made that at the outset the operations of the national fleet resulted in a profit. So new an organization could not, however, hope to prosper when the world-wide depression in the shipping industry set in, and from 1921 onwards a series of deficits were shown in the accounts. [2]

However, Canadians always have in mind their hereditary rival south of the frontier line, and a consideration which is bound to make some appeal is that if discrimination against Canada were attempted, the national fleet gave her the means of regulating rates of freight on the products of the farm, the manufactures of the country and the raw products of the nation.

[1] Dominion Debates, 1923, vol. ii. p. 1059.
[2] It hardly seems worth while to discuss the amount of the deficit inasmuch as it has been alleged that in the accounts insufficient amounts are shown for depreciation, with the result that the value of the fleet is seriously over-stated on the assets side.

Control of Freight Rates and of Movements of Ships

" It has not been adequately realized that the rates of
freight which may be charged on goods to and from the
Dominions are, in many cases, a more important factor in
the question of the development of inter-Imperial trade
than tariffs and tariff privileges on the present scale ",
so that " improvement in the cost of sea-transport is amongst
the most important problems which confront the statesmen
of the Empire to-day ".[1]

The indictment against shipping interests presented by
the Canadian Government in 1914 to the Dominions Royal
Commission, by whom the above quoted dictum was placed
on record, included various counts, the principal of which
was that shipping Companies using Canadian ports had
formed associations for fixing rates and generally advancing
their own interests ; that North Atlantic rates were practically fixed by a Shipping Conference ; and that in the
period 1907–13 the freight rates in grain and flour from
Montreal to London had practically doubled.[2]   This the
shipping companies had been able to do because the individual
shipowner had gradually been replaced by steamship
companies who were in a much stronger position when
bargaining for rates than the widely-scattered and largely
unorganized individual owner.

The names of nine of the principal Atlantic lines were
included in the North Atlantic Shipping Conference.   These
lines " issue a tariff for the different seasons, the tariff
being drawn to include general minimum rates on practically all, or at least on the chief commodities moving ",
but only for the movement westwards.   There was no
scarcity of room on the western movement, but on the eastern
movement such a scarcity was frequent.[3]

The question of shipping rates is one which affects all
countries to a greater or less degeee, but particular countries
are affected in particular ways.   Canada is particularly
affected by the competition of the ports and railways
of the United States.   Unduly high freight rates on Canadian
traffic may have the effect of drawing much of the export

[1] Dominions Royal Commission, *Final Report*, 1917 [*Cd.* 8462], pp.
127–8.

[2] The case against the Atlantic Combine is stated at length and in
somewhat emphatic terms in Mr. W. T. R. Preston's report re North
Atlantic Steamship Combine, 1925, *Canada Sessional Papers*, No. 45.

[3] See *Dominions Royal Commission* [*Cd.* 7710], Memorandum presented
by H. L. Drayton, K.C., p. 131.

trade and a certain amount of the import traffic to United States ports. Also it is particularly and profoundly affected by the freight rates for grain and flour, and " the export freight rate on flour from Montreal to London in the period 1907 to 1913 has gradually increased 91 per cent and that on grain between the same ports 102 per cent." [1]

The rise in freight cannot be gainsaid, but it has to be remembered that the depression in shipping that was so acute in the period 1903–7 was reflected in the North Atlantic rates. It was a time when " freights generally did not cover working expenses even without taking depreciation into account. The financial position of the British ship-owners generally was causing the gravest anxiety ; dividends were being passed by shipping companies of the highest standing and in many instances accumulations of loss were being written off by the reduction of share capitals. It was almost impossible to find new capital for shipbuilding, and ships and shares in the shipping companies could only be realized at a heavy loss." [2] As a result the shipping trade was starved for many years, inasmuch as it was impossible for shipowners to make provision for the replace-ment of worn-out vessels or to build the new ships necessary for an expanding trade when more prosperous times arrived.

In addition to the general complaint as to rates there is the particular complaint as to differentiation between commodities.

Since the 'nineties there have been complaints that the ocean steamship lines were charging excessive freight rates on flour as compared with wheat. Tramp steamers did not carry flour, so that while the rates for grain were open to competition, the rates on flour were fixed by the steamship combine.

The reply of the steamship companies was that the handling of grain in its loading, stowage, dunnaging and discharging, costs less than the handling of flour ; it occupies less space than flour ; it takes less time to deal with than flour ; and the risks of its sustaining damage are less, and accordingly the shipowner quotes a lower freight rate for grain than for flour.

[1] Ibid. *Minutes of Evidence* [*Cd.* 8458], Evidence of President of Quebec Board of Trade, p. 361.

[2] Ibid. [*Cd.* 7710], *Evidence of Sir Norman Hill*, p. 25.

The issue has the important characteristic that it involves a direct conflict of interest between the milling industry in the United Kingdom and that in Canada. " The former is interested in the highest possible, the latter in the lowest possible rates for flour as compared with grain." [1] And the United Kingdom is Canada's greatest market both for flour and grain.

The difference in ocean freight charges on grain and flour respectively, the " arbitrary " or " spread " as it is termed, which would give the shipowner an equal rate of freight on the different commodities he carries, seems a matter of arithmetical calculation and one capable of and suitable for ascertainment by a body having a controlling authority in ocean rates as already such a body controls railway rates.

No dependence could be placed on the competition of tramps as a check on the freight rates of the liners for reasons thus stated :—

Up to 1914 the greater part of Canada's grain was carried by liners from Montreal as freight for their lower holds, and at a lower rate than that at which a tramp steamer could be chartered for the service. This comparatively low rate was made possible by the higher priced freight carried in the other holds and by the carriage of passengers. " The prevailing rate for a number of years might be stated, from Liverpool to Montreal, 3s. to 3s. 6d. per quarter, which will run from 3 to 3½ cents per bushel. No tramp boat had been chartered to carry it at a lower rate than 5, 5½ and 6 shillings." [2] As a result tramp steamers seldom came to Montreal looking for cargo.

It also has to be remembered that freight rates are not entirely uninfluenced by general political questions ; " Before the adoption of its Tariff, Canada was a large importer of the heavy iron and steel manufactures of the United Kingdom, and these cargoes, besides paying a fair outward freight, provided the shipowner with the dead weight he required. On the homeward voyage the dead weight required was provided by the grain shipped in Canadian ports, which was often carried at merely nominal rates. When Canada ceased to import the heavy iron and steel manufactures of this country, it became a necessity to

---

[1] Dominions Royal Commission, Fifth Interim Report [Cd. 8457], p. 26.
[2] Dominions Royal Commission, Minutes of Evidence, 1916, [Cd. 8458], Q. 3347.

build vessels that could be sailed without dead weight cargoes, and in consequence the shipowner has now no necessity to carry grain as ballast." [1] One result of this restriction of Canadian cargoes, of Canada's desire to export freely but to import as little as possible except immigrants, was that the only boats that could live in the Canadian trade were boats which carried both cargo and passengers. The liner displaced the tramp save in the timber trade.

Basing their conclusions on their finding that " in normal times the combination of shipowners is strong enough to limit the freedom of shippers ", and that " in some cases shipowners have used this power to grant more favourable freight rates on foreign than on British goods," an instance of which was the lower rates on Canadian asbestos to foreign than to British ports [2], the Dominions Royal Commission arrived at the definite recommendation that " the operations of the steamship companies should not remain longer without some measure of Government control ".[3]

Direct control by a body resembling the United States Shipping Board [4] was contemplated. There are, however, indirect as well as direct means at the disposal of Governments by which freight rates may be to a greater or less degree controlled.

An instance showing how control of railway rates can influence the choice of the port of shipment as well as enable through arrangements for land and sea to be made is provided by the manner in which the Canadian Government attempted to give effect to the purposes for which that important section of the Canadian National Railways, the Grand Trunk Pacific Railway, was constructed, namely, to reduce the cost of moving the grain grown in the North-West and to bring the business to Canadian ports. " A freight rate of 6 cents per bushel, equivalent to 10 cents from Winnipeg, has been made upon export wheat from Armstrong to

---

[1] Dominions Royal Commission [*Cd.* 7710], *Evidence of Sir Norman Hill*, p. 27.

[2] " Shipments to Rotterdam and Antwerp, for western Continental consumption, involving a longer ocean haul, could be made at a lower rate than to English ports. Continental manufacturers were consequently enjoying an advantage over their British competitors." Dominions Royal Commission, *Minutes of Evidence*, 1916 [*Cd.* 8459], p. 289.

[3] Dominions Royal Commission. *Final Report*, 1917 [*Cd.* 8462], p. 167.

[4] Public Act, No. 260—64th Congress (H.R. 15455), and see [*Cd.* 8462], p. 129, where the *Final Report* summarizes the powers of the Board with regard to the control of ocean freights.

Quebec. As the normal rail and lake rate [1] from Winnipeg to Montreal is about 13 cents, this means a saving to the farmer of the North-West. . . . and it also means the beginning of a fulfilment of the promise made to Canadian ports, because it has already had the effect of loading six large ocean steamers at Quebec with grain from the North-West." [2]

In the Dominions the control of harbours is seldom left to local authorities, as it often is in the United Kingdom. So in Canada the Dominion Government undertook the necessary new construction at Halifax, St. John and Victoria, while it maintains control over the harbours of Quebec, Montreal and Vancouver through the Harbour Commissioners.

The Canadian Government has now come into possession of a substantial fleet of cargo steamers of its own, so completing the series of factors which enable it to quote competing rates on Canadian produce from its place of origin to its destination.

The method by which the Canadian Government can control shipping as the adjunct to the railways is accordingly by arranging railway rates so as to direct export traffic to particular ports and particular vessels. Another method is by means of the subsidy. The Dominion Government in 1913 granted an annual subsidy of $1,000,000 to various North Atlantic Lines for a tri-weekly mail service between Canada and Britain in summer and a semi-weekly service in winter. In addition to the million dollars thus voted by the Canadian Parliament for mail subsidies and steamship subventions to Canada and Great Britain Lines, $229,500 was voted for the Canada and West Indies route, $146,000 for the Canada to South Africa route, $300,000 for the Canada to Australia route, $200,000 for Canada and France and $121,000 for a line to China and Japan. [3]

It appears, however, that foreign governments have had a livelier appreciation of the shipping subsidy as an instrument of control than Great Britain and the Dominions. Thus in the beginning of the twentieth century: "In Germany the rates of freight and fares on subsidized liners are fixed with, and cannot be changed without, the consent of the

---

[1] i.e. transferring at Fort William into the Lake boats and thence to Montreal.[1]

[2] Dominions Royal Commission, *Evidence of Mr. J. G. Scott*, President, Quebec Board of Trade, 1916 [*Cd.* 8458], p. 306.

[3] *Canadian Annual Review*, 1913, p. 687.

Imperial Chancellor. In Austria the Austrian Lloyd may not alter its rates while the subsidy contract is in force without the consent of the Ministry of Commerce." [1]

The subsidy as a means of attracting traffic to Canadian ports was realized even before it became possible, in the manner already described, by the use of the power to control railway rates. Thus in 1897 it was made a condition of the subsidy that the liners should make St. John and Halifax their western winter termini, the subsidy hitherto paid to Lines making Portland, Maine, their terminal port being withdrawn. [2] The obvious purpose was to divert to the Canadian ports which were open all the year Canadian winter transatlantic traffic which had hitherto passed through the port in the United States.

---

[1] Report of Select Committee on Shipping Subsidies, 1902, 385, p. xiii.
[2] M. J. Patton, " Ocean Shipping." *Canada and its Provinces*, vol. 10, p. 621.

CHAPTER 13

TRADE RELATIONS

The contending " Pulls " towards England, towards the United States, and towards Canadian Nationalism.
The Old Colonial System and its demise in 1846. " Pull " towards England.
England's attempt to force Free Trade on North American Colonies, and the achievement of fiscal autonomy.
" Pull " towards the United States. Reciprocity Treaty.
" Incidental Protection." Cayley and Galt Tariffs.
" Exodus to Lamentations " : the pilgrimages to Washington to plead for Reciprocity after 1866.
" National Policy " of 1878 : real beginnings of Protectionism.
The Imperial Preference of 1897 : the " Pull " towards England revived.
Continuation of Protectionism during Liberal régime. Bounties on Iron and Steel.
Extension of Imperial Preferences throughout the Empire. Rejection of Reciprocity in 1911 by Canada.
High Protection versus Low Protection. Cleavage between the Free Trade Agricultural West and the Protectionist Industrial East.

THE commercial history of Canada has been dominated by two facts, its membership of the British Empire and its proximity to the United States.[1] Accordingly, there have been throughout the history of Canada the alternate pulls towards the Mother Country and towards the United States.

Before 1846 the pull towards the Mother Country prevailed as a result of both policy and natural tendencies. Policy was summarized in the Old Colonial System, or as much of it as remained, before 1846. Under the Old Colonial System heavier duties were laid on foreign goods entering the Colonies than on English goods, certain Colonial exports had always to be brought first to England, and disabilities were imposed on foreign shipping to prevent them sharing in the trade of the Empire. As a result the trade and shipping of Canada tended to run completely in Imperial channels. Moreover, policy was reinforced by natural tendencies. Before 1846 Canada was quite naturally focussed on the English market and not on the market in the United States. Canada and the United States were separated, not so much by distance as by lack of communications, and it was almost

[1] The United States is frequently spoken of as " Canada's only neighbour ".

easier and cheaper to send wheat, lumber and potash by canal, river and ocean to Old England than to send them overland to New England, with the exception of the Erie Canal route. What was true of exports was also true of imports, especially at a time when England was the undisputed workshop of the world and could manufacture textiles and metal goods more cheaply and efficiently than any other country. It is not surprising, then, that before 1846 the pull to the Mother Country prevailed.

After 1846 the situation changed, and the pull towards the United States became the stronger. Here, again, policy reflected natural tendencies. Between 1846 and 1849 the Old Colonial System was demolished, and Canada, obtaining its fiscal freedom and shaping its own policy, aimed at a reciprocal fiscal agreement with the United States. At the same time natural tendencies were binding Canada and the United States more closely together. Settlement was filling up the area round the Great Lakes on the American side and making the Republic a very close neighbour to Canada. Further, the building of railways brought Canada and New England into close touch. This made the Mother Country seem further away than ever, as it could be reached only by sailing ships, whose progress was slow on account of contrary winds, the winter freeze, and a long ocean voyage. Moreover, the United States was advancing rapidly as a manufacturing country, and was becoming more able to compete with England, especially with the advantages of cheaper and speedier transportation. The pull towards the United States resulted in the Reciprocity Treaty of 1854–66 between the United States and Canada, but the pull persisted long after the abrogation of the Treaty in 1866. Time and again Canada endeavoured to renew some sort of agreement for reciprocal trade with the United States, and Canada's endurance of many rebuffs only proved the strength of the pull towards the United States.

Not long after 1846 and even while the Reciprocity Treaty was in operation, a third pull or influence became discernible, the pull towards Canadian Nationalism and the development of Canadian resources and industries by means of Protection. Its advent was tentatively signalized by the " Incidental Protection " of the Cayley and Galt Tariffs of 1858–9, but after Federation in 1867 the way was completely paved for the National Policy of 1878 onwards. The National Policy was the economic expression of Canadian

Nationalism, just as Federation was its political expression. The National Policy was initiated, partly in retaliation for, partly in imitation of the Protectionist tariffs of the United States. Canada retaliated in response to the many rebuffs from the Republic. At the same time Canada was losing population by the drift south of the younger generation to the industries of the United States, and to prevent this drift industries in Canada were to be extended by Protection.[1] In addition it was alleged that the United States used Canada as a " slaughter market " for its surplus stock during the depression in trade in the 'seventies, wrecking or threatening to wreck such Canadian industries as did exist, and it was argued that " a higher tariff would open the factories and close the soup kitchens ". The pull towards Canadian Nationalism, once recognized, soon became the most powerful factor in shaping Canada's fiscal policy. The strength of this pull was emphasized when the Liberal Party, after denouncing the National Policy of Protection as "legalized robbery", came into power in 1896 and endorsed their opponents' policy, carrying it even further in certain particulars. To-day Protection is supported by the two traditional parties and is opposed with resolution only by the Prairie Provinces. This sectional cleavage between Industrial East and Agricultural West has created serious problems which will be discussed later in the chapter.

In the 'nineties the pull towards the Mother Country revived. Here again policy and natural tendencies were at work. In 1897 the Dominion granted the Mother Country preference in the Canadian market, a policy that has been maintained ever since. Even before the 'nineties, however, natural tendencies were drawing Canada and England together again. The triumph of the steamer in the 'seventies and 'eighties and the cutting down of the Atlantic voyage from two or three months to two or three weeks brought the English market within ready reach of the Canadian farmers. The steamers could also carry live cattle, and they built up an important live stock trade with the Mother Country. On the other hand, the American market was being ringed round with higher and higher tariffs, especially the MacKinley Tariff of 1890 and the Dingley Tariff of 1897, which shut out Canadian surplus produce and focussed

[1] This policy of latter years has been strongly supported in Quebec province, traditionally Liberal and low tariff in opinion, to prevent the young French Canadians going to the Protestant Republic.

Canada more and more on England. The United States had still a large wheat surplus to dispose of in foreign markets, and it had no intention of allowing Canada's natural products to invade the American market. In the 'nineties there was also a revival of Imperial sentiment, due again largely to economic factors. Railways, steamers, the telegraph and the cable were bringing even the most distant parts of the Empire into touch with each other, and were unlocking the natural resources of the Tropical Empire for the benefit of the rest of the Empire. Membership of the Empire meant free access to the tropical colonies, and in addition, the opportunity of reciprocal trade agreements. Further, the growing demand for capital throughout the Empire was met in the London money market, and this made the Dominions especially realize the importance of close contact with the Mother Country. Thus for many reasons the pull towards England revived in strength.

By way of summing up it can be said that since 1846 the three pulls have swayed backwards and forwards, usually with two in the ascendant and the third in the decline. Over the years three periods can be distinguished. First of all, between 1846 and 1867, there is the period of American ascendancy (witness the Reciprocity Treaty), together with a slight pull towards national development (witness the Cayley and Galt Tariffs and the policy of " Incidental Protection "), while the pull to the Mother Country is distinctly in the background. Secondly, between 1867 and 1897 national development (witness the National policy of 1878) and the American pull (witness the Pilgrimages to Washington) are jointly in the ascendant, while the pull towards England is still in the background. Thirdly comes the period after 1897, with the National Policy clearly in the saddle (witness the Liberal Party's maintenance of Protectionism), with the pull towards England of growing importance (witness the Imperial Preferences of 1897), and the pull towards the United States sinking into a decline (witness the rejection of Reciprocity in 1911).

Canada had no fiscal history of its own before 1846, its fiscal policy being determined by the Mother Country. It has been said : " The Empire was one, and the United Kingdom was that one." Thus the fiscal history of Canada before 1846, such as it is, forms part of the wider story of the Commercial Relations of the Empire, which had already been dealt with.

The situation in British North America in 1846 can be sketched in a few words. Till that date, despite many assaults, the Old Colonial System as a whole still held good. On the fiscal side that implied two things : a moderate Preference, the normal *ad valorem* rate of difference being 7 per cent, a few articles showing 10, 15 and 20 per cent discrimination,[1] in favour of imports from the Mother Country as against foreign imports, and, secondly, the absence of Protectionism as a device to build up industries in the Colonies or to secure the local market for local products. A slight exception must be made to the second feature of the Old Colonial System as it affected British North America. In 1825 Nova Scotia appropriated £500 as a bonus to a forge for making bar iron. In the years that followed, the two Maritime Provinces pursued this policy of aiding local industries further by such bounties and also by drawbacks on machinery or raw material imported.[2] Apart from such slight departures the characteristics of the fiscal system of British North America before 1846 were Imperial Preference and no Colonial Protection.

Then came 1846 with its revolution in Imperial commercial relations. The Old Colonial System was demolished, and a universal policy of Free Trade was substituted. The first feature of the Old System in the tariff of British North America, Imperial Preference, was abolished, or allowance was made for its abolition, by the Enabling Act of 1846,[3] which enabled the Colonies to abolish the compulsory preference on English goods imposed by England. This meant that the Colonies were no longer compelled to discriminate between English goods and foreign goods, but were to pursue an open door policy towards each and all. In retaliation for the Mother Country's withdrawal of favours to Colonial goods in the English market, the Colonies in British North America made haste to withdraw theirs, and by 1855 they had all gone. The second feature of the Old System as it applied to the Colonies, lack or absence of Protectionism, was thoroughly in accord with the new prevailing dogma of Free Trade, although for different reasons. All that required to be done was to stop such

---

[1] Correspondence with the Colonies respecting differential duties, etc. in *Parly. Papers*, 1847, xxxvii, p. 15.
[2] E. Porritt: " Fiscal and Diplomatic Freedom of British Overseas Dominions," p. 87.
[3] 9 and 10 Vic., c. 94.

transgressions of the rule as the bonuses and bounties voted in Nova Scotia and New Brunswick.

While the Mother Country had jettisoned the Old System and its positive control over Colonial tariffs, it had no intention of abandoning its negative control over the commercial relations of the Empire. This is clear from the witness of a contemporary Colonial Secretary. When the Imperial Government adopted Free Trade, said Earl Grey, " it did not abdicate the duty and the power of regulating the commercial policy, not only of the United Kingdom, but of the British Empire. The common interest of all parts of that extended Empire requires that its commercial policy should be the same throughout its numerous dependencies, nor is this less important than before because our policy is now directed to the removal instead of as formerly to the maintenance of artificial restriction on trade." [1] On account of the Imperial Government's determination to enforce Free Trade throughout the Empire, the imposition of differential duties and the adoption of Protectionism by the Colonies led to intense friction with the Imperial Government, and it was with reluctance that the Imperial Government, knowing what it would mean, conceded to the Colonies fiscal autonomy, or the right to frame their own tariffs freely.

Differential duties were essential to any scheme of Reciprocity or Imperial Preference. Differential duties had been forbidden in a Circular Dispatch of 1843, but that referred to inter-Imperial retaliation, for some of the Colonies had taken to penalizing each other.[2] In 1850 Canada imposed differential duties, and Earl Grey could only protest against them unavailingly as Canada had received self-government in 1848. At the same time a Bill imposing differential duties in a Maritime Province was refused the Royal Assent because it had not achieved complete self-government like Canada. However, Canada's precedent paved the way, and ere long the Imperial Government had withdrawn its opposition, though not without protest.[3]

---

[1] *Colonial Policy of Lord John Russell's Administration*, vol. 1, p. 281, cited by H. E. Egerton : *Short History of British Colonial Policy*, p. 333.

[2] Sir W. Colebrooke's Report on the Blue Book of New Brunswick, 1845, *Parly. Papers*, 1846, xxix, p. 580.

[3] Canada (meaning the present Provinces of Ontario and Quebec) had laws reserved as late as 1862, but the last law refused was in 1845. Nova Scotia had laws reserved till 1863 and refused till 1847, while New Brunswick had laws reserved till 1863 and refused as late as 1852 and 1856. *Parly. Papers*, 1864, xl, p. 709.

As for Protectionism, New Brunswick passed an Act granting a bounty on hemp. Earl Grey allowed the measure to pass provisionally, because it was for a limited time, but threatened to veto any similar measure.[1] In 1858 the Cayley Tariff of Canada, which had a protectionist tinge, was allowed to pass unnoticed, but in 1859 the Galt Tariff which had a stronger protectionist tinge, elicited in England a storm of disapproval, of which the Colonial Office had to take cognizance. Sir Edmund Head, in his despatch covering a copy of the Tariff, wrote to the Secretary of State for the Colonies : " It is to be regretted that the necessity which exists for meeting the financial engagements of the Province, and the depression of last year, have compelled the Government to propose rates of duty so high as those imposed by the present Act," but he went on to say : " There is nothing in the system adopted which professes to impose differential duties, or to fetter the freedom of trade."[2] Despite the professions or lack of professions in the tariff, English manufacturers were alarmed, fearing that the higher rates of duties would penalize their goods on entering the Canadian market. The Sheffield Chamber of Commerce and Manufactures sent up a strongly-worded Memorial of protest to the Duke of Newcastle, who was then the Secretary of State for the Colonies. The Memorial declared : " It cannot, be regarded as less than indecent, and a reproach, that while for fifteen years the Government, the greatest statesmen, and the Press of this country have been not only advocating, but practising the principles of free trade, the Government of one of her most important Colonies should have been advocating monopoly and protection." The argument that the tariff was dictated by the need of revenue was swept aside : " We are aware that the fiscal necessities of the Canadian Government are urged as the chief cause for passing the late Tariff Bill. This is not the whole truth ; no one can read the papers of the provinces and the speeches of the Members of both Houses, and be deceived for an instant, but even if that were the cause we conceive that Her Majesty's Government has a right to demand that what revenue is needed shall be raised in some other way than that which is opposed to the acknowledged

---

[1] Egerton, op. cit., p. 334.
[2] Correspondence on the Removal or Reduction of the Duties charged on British Goods entering Canada, in *Parly. Papers*, 1864, xli, p. 79.

commercial policy of the Imperial Government and destructive of the interests of those manufacturing towns in Great Britain which trade with Canada." [1] The Duke of Newcastle added some words of his own : " Practically, this heavy duty operates differentially in favour of the United States, in consequence of the facility for smuggling which so long a line of frontier affords, and the temptation to embark in it which a duty of 20 per cent offers," and concluded by saying : " I consider it my duty no less to the Colony than to the Mother Country, to express my regret that the experience of England, which has fully proved the injurious effect of the protective system, and the advantage of low duties upon manufactures, both as regards trade and revenue, should be lost sight of, and that such an Act as the present should have been passed." [2] The Canadian Government felt that the situation was so serious that they specially deputed Mr. (afterwards Sir) A. T. Galt, the Finance Minister, to answer the Duke's despatch. The Finance Minister thereupon drew up his reply : " Respect to the Imperial Government must always dictate the desire to satisfy them that the policy of this country is neither hastily nor unwisely formed ; and that due regard is had to the interests of the Mother Country as well as of the Province. But the Government of Canada acting for its Legislature and people cannot, through those feelings of deference which they owe to the Imperial authorities, in any manner waive or diminish the right of the people of Canada to decide for themselves both as to the mode and extent to which taxation shall be imposed. The Provincial Ministry are at all times ready to afford explanations in regard to the acts of the Legislature to which they are party : but subject to their duty and allegiance to Her Majesty, their responsibility in all general questions of policy must be to the Provincial Parliament, by whose confidence they administer the affairs of the country ; and in the imposition of taxation it is so plainly necessary that the Administration and people should be in accord, that the former cannot admit responsibility or require approval beyond that of the local Legislature. Self-government would be utterly annihilated if the views of the Imperial Government were to be preferred to those of the people of Canada. It is therefore the duty of the present Government distinctly to affirm the right of the Canadian

[1] Ibid., pp. 84, 85.   [2] Ibid., p. 83.

Legislature to adjust the taxation of the people in the way they deem best, even if it should unfortunately happen to meet the disapproval of the Imperial Ministry. Her Majesty cannot be advised to disallow such acts, unless Her advisers are prepared to assume the administration of the affairs of the Colony irrespective of the views of its inhabitants." [1] In his despatch the Duke of Newcastle had hinted that, however much he was opposed to the Tariff Act, he would not advise its refusal : " Whenever the authenticated Act of the Canadian Parliament on this subject arrives, I may probably feel that I can take no other course than signify to you the Queen's assent to it notwithstanding the objections raised against the law in this country." [2] On the receipt of the Finance Minister s reply, the Duke of Newcastle acted on his own hint and accepted the situation. The Tariff Act was ratified and the great battle for the fiscal freedom of the Colonies had been won, and Canada was fully embarked on a fiscal policy of its own devising.

The outstanding features in the first period of Canada's own fiscal history, from 1846 to 1867, were the pull towards the United States and the endeavour to arrange Reciprocity between Canada and the Republic. In May, 1846, Canada appealed to the Queen, in the event of the Corn Laws being repealed, to endeavour to secure for Canada free entrance of its products into the United States. Sir Richard Pakenham at Washington laid the matter before Secretary Walker, who, being a Free Trader, was well disposed towards the proposal. Nothing came of it, but Canada as a gesture of good will equalized the duties on American and English imports,[3] thus abolishing the long-standing Imperial Preference. In 1847 the Inspector-General of Canada spoke of meeting " on terms of friendly reciprocity any advance which the neighbouring Republic may be disposed to make for the mutual encouragement of industry and trade ".[4] The situation was serious for British North America, since the repeal of the preferences in the English market had reduced the prices of all Canadian products 20 per cent below the prices ruling in the United States. It meant that Canadian prices were fixed by American market conditions and the 20 per cent disparity was accounted for by the 20

---

[1] Ibid., p. 87–8.   [2] Ibid., p. 83.
[3] *Report on Reciprocity and Commercial Treaties*, drawn up for the United States Tariff Commission (" *R.C.T.*" hereafter), p. 67.
[4] " Mirror of Parliament ", March 24, 1847, quoted in *R.C.T.*, p. 65.

per cent duty on all Canadian products entering the Republic. However, the United States turned a deaf ear to all blandishments, and, despite Canada's importunity, Congress " did nothing, said nothing, thought nothing on the subject ".[1] The fact of the matter was that the United States saw that it stood to gain little by any Treaty of Reciprocity in mere natural products. So bitter was the disappointment in Canada that the cry of annexation to the United States was raised in 1849. If Canada could not obtain access to the American market as an outside Power, then the only thing for Canada to do was to become an integral part of the United States. Lord Elgin, the Governor-General, saw clearly that the most effective means of scotching annexation was to secure Reciprocity, and to that end he bent all his energies. Meanwhile, in 1850, the United States passed the Bonding Act which permitted goods bound for Canada to pass through the United States in bond without duty, and this Act greatly facilitated trade.

At last in 1854 Lord Elgin succeeded in negotiating a Reciprocity Treaty with the United States, which was to run from 1855 for ten years and was then terminable by either party on a year's notice. It had three chief provisions. It allowed American fishermen to fish north of the thirty-sixth parallel on equal terms with the fishermen of British North America. It threw open navigation on Lake Michigan, the St. Lawrence and the Canadian canals. It permitted reciprocal free trade in natural products between the United States and British North America.[2]

The effects of the Reciprocity Treaty on the trade of the United States and British North America are mixed up with the reactions of the American Civil War. The result of all the upheaval was that the Reciprocity agreement allowed British North America to gain much more than the United States expected or desired. British North America started off with a heavy adverse balance of trade with the United States in 1855, but by 1866 this had been transformed into a substantial balance in its favour. British North America flourished as it had never flourished before, with the magnificent market opened up to its wheat and lumber. That factor alone was sufficient to make the Americans want a revision of the terms of the Treaty. Other and

---

[1] Senator Seward, quoted in *R.C.T.*, p. 69.
[2] *R.C.T.*, p. 76.

stronger forces, however, worked for the total abrogation of the Treaty. The Federalists, who controlled the government after the Civil War, were considerably incensed with the alleged sympathy shown by British North America to the Confederates during the struggle. The fishery provision had not yielded the gain that the United States had expected, and besides the United States had made up its mind to poach in British waters. Canada had altered its canal tolls and dues somewhat to the detriment of the United States, and further the United States had decided that the use of Canadian waterways by American goods meant as much, if not more, to Canada as to the United States. Then, the United States, with its tremendous load of debt, wished to raise its tariff, and the Reciprocity Treaty stood in the way of that. Above all, Canada had adopted high tariffs on manufactures, which penalized imports from the United States, and this was declared to be an infringement of the spirit of the Treaty. Of course, Canada was quite entitled to alter its tariff on manufactures as it pleased, for that formed no part of the Reciprocity bargain. At the same time Canada had deliberately lowered its tariff to American manufactures as a gesture of good will, and then, having achieved its aim of Reciprocity, it raised its tariff on manufactures and thus deceived American expectations. So strong was the antagonism of the United States to Canada for the reasons given, that immediately the ten years had elapsed the United States gave notice of the termination of the Treaty, and in 1866 Reciprocity came to an end.

The second strand in the tangled skein of events between 1846 and 1867 is the rise of Protectionism in Canada. In the case of Canada, without any system of direct taxation, the tariff was the chief source of revenue. This rendered the situation rather complex, for a rise in the tariff might mean a move towards Protectionism or it might mean simply a need for more revenue. On the other hand, the very complexity formed a useful screen behind which Inspectors-General and, later, Finance Ministers could operate. After the Repeal of the Corn Laws and the passing of the Enabling Act, the uniform rate of duty was fixed at $7\frac{1}{2}$ per cent. In the years that followed the rate was progressively raised to 10 per cent, to $12\frac{1}{2}$ per cent, and in 1856 to 15 per cent. Then came the Cayley Tariff of 1858, which imposed 20 per cent on many important manufactures and

15 per cent on other goods. Finally, in 1859, Galt raised the rate to 25 per cent in certain cases, and to 20 per cent on the bulk of imports.[1]

When Galt was attacked in Canada for imposing a Protectionist tariff, he defended himself on the ground that rates hitherto adequate were now inadequate, on account of the depression in trade following 1857, to meet Canada's financial needs, and that his action was dictated by requirement for revenue and not by Protectionist leanings. Some seven years later he outlined his policy in retrospect in the course of a Budget speech : " The policy of this country has been to make every article of natural production imported into the province free, and for revenue purposes to impose duties on all those manufactured articles which it was thought were able to bear the burden, affording at the same time an incidental amount of protection to our manufacturers." [2] This argument of the need for revenue and of incidental protection met the demands of the day, and thereafter the problem of Protectionism slumbered. The Maritime Provinces, whose prosperity was based on extractive industries and who had no manufactures to speak of, were staunchly free trade, and undoubtedly influenced Dominion fiscal policy in that direction for ten years after Federation. In fact, latterly Galt seems to have espoused the idea of making Canada a low tariff country, with cheap food, cheap raw materials, and cheap labour supply, and thus inducing industrial development. All this was forgotten after 1878.

The abrogation of the Reciprocity Treaty in 1865–6 did not put an end to the pull towards the United States, since the further development of railways and of the West was binding the United States and Canada still more closely together. In fact, the abrogation almost seemed to intensify the pull, and the period between 1867 and 1897 was characterized by those unavailing and unending "Pilgrimages to Washington ", which were pithily summarized as " Exodus to Lamentations ". Canada had come to appreciate the tremendous boon of open access to the market just across the border, and eleven times between 1865 and 1898 did Canada endeavour to re-establish Reciprocity.[3]

---

[1] O. D. Skelton, *Life and Times of Sir A. T. Galt*, p. 268.

[2] *C.P.*, vol. 9, p. 133, and see *Canada*, 1849 *to* 1859, by the Hon. A. T. Galt, London, 1860. (Canada : Pamphlets, vol. 1, No. 3. in D.O. & C.O. Library.) *Cf.* " Canada and the British Preference," in *The Times*, 24/5/09.

[3] *C.P.*, vol. 9, table opposite p. 126.

Every time the United States refused. The reason for the different attitudes of the two countries is fairly apparent. The United States market meant much more to Canadian producers than the Canadian market meant to American producers. Even with hostile tariffs, between 1873 and 1894 the lowest percentage which the American trade formed in the total trade of Canada was 38·15, while the highest percentage which the Canadian trade formed in the total trade of the United States was 6·59.[1] Further, the United States was self-occupied on account of the settlement of the West. It was very slowly and reluctantly that Canada turned to its policy of national development as a dubious second best to reciprocal free trade with the Republic. An American Report testifies that " for years the thought of ultimate self-sufficiency was less attractive than that of immediate free trade with the United States, and the policy gained in strength only in proportion as the hope of reciprocity waned." [2]

Viewed in this light, the National Policy is seen as a species of retaliation for the United States' refusal of Reciprocity. In 1869 the Hon. John Rose, the Canadian Finance Minister, had gone to Washington on the usual pilgrimage to seek to arrange Reciprocity, and had been rebuffed. In retaliation he imposed duties in 1870 on coal, salt, grain, flour and hops coming from the United States. As the Republican elephant took no notice of the Canadian gnat, those duties were repealed in the following year. In the case of the Hon. George Brown's pilgrimage to Washington in 1874 on a further endeavour to arrange Reciprocity, great concessions were offered to the United States, even to admitting a long list of American manufactures into Canada free, such as agricultural implements, boots, shoes, furniture, vehicles, print paper, woollen tweeds, and cotton, iron, steel and leather manufactures. Even then the United States refused to nibble at Reciprocity, and Canada was in despair. The way now lay open for the National Policy.

In 1878 Sir John Macdonald swept into power on the National Policy programme, and in 1879 Mr. (afterwards Sir (Leonard Tilley, the Finance Minister, began to put that

---

[1] *R.C.T.*, p. 89. In a compendious work, in two volumes, on the Tariff History of the United States, Canada is only mentioned twice and then almost incidentally.

[2] Ibid., p. 92.

policy into practice. The two aims, of Protection to Canadian industries and of Retaliation against the United States, can be distinctly seen. Coal, flour and pig-iron were taken off the free list, and the general rates on American imports were raised by amounts varying from 20 to 100 per cent. Mr. Tilley himself stated that " a special effort had been made to adjust the duties so that the heaviest burden would fall upon American goods ".[1] On the other hand, the general tariff rates on manufactures, whether they came from the United States or from England, were raised from $17\frac{1}{2}$ per cent to 20, 25, 30 and 35 per cent. Thus the duty on agricultural implements was raised from $17\frac{1}{2}$ per cent to 25 per cent, brass manufactures from $17\frac{1}{2}$ per cent to 30 per cent, coal from being free to 50 cents per ton, cotton manufactures from $17\frac{1}{2}$ per cent to 20 per cent, house furniture from $17\frac{1}{2}$ per cent to 35 per cent, glass from $17\frac{1}{2}$ per cent to 30 per cent, pig-iron from being free to 2 dollars per ton, iron bars from 5 per cent to $17\frac{1}{2}$ per cent, sugar by 10 per cent, and woollen manfactures from $17\frac{1}{2}$ per cent to $7\frac{1}{2}$ cents per lb., and 20 per cent.[2] Behind this tariff wall Canada hoped to build up thriving industries in iron, wool and other lines.

Even with the adoption of a National Policy, Canada did not abandon all hope of a Reciprocity deal with the United States. The Tilley Tariff of 1879 contained definite provision for lowering the rates on American imports should a Reciprocity agreement be reached. The expectation of realizing Reciprocity, however, gradually faded, and, when in 1891 the United States proposed a Reciprocity agreement which entailed discrimination by Canada against the Mother Country, Canada indignantly turned the offer down. Of course, the American argument was thoroughly logical. If the United States and Canada were going to enter into a tariff alliance, there had to be tariff uniformity between the two countries, otherwise English goods would flow into the United States by the Canadian back door. Tariff uniformity necessarily meant discrimination against England. Accordingly, Reciprocity was never renewed in the period between 1867 and 1897.

Another departure connected with the same period was also designed to further the National Policy. This measure was

---

[1] *R.C.T.*, p. 96.
[2] Despatch respecting the New Customs Tariff of Canada, in *Parly. Papers*, 1878–9, li, pp. 20–3.

the bounty of $1\frac{1}{2}$ dollars per ton on pig-iron, which was first given in 1883, in addition to the existing tariff on imported iron, in order to foster the iron industry in Canada. The industry then consisted of three small furnaces, two in Quebec at Radnor and Drummondsville, and the third in Nova Scotia at Londonderry. By 1894 the bounty rate was 2 dollars a ton, and not only on pig-iron but also on bars and billets. This led to an expansion in the industry. In 1884 the Canadian output of pig-iron was 29,593 tons, and imports were 52,184 tons, whereas by 1895-6 the figures were respectively 52,871 and 36,010.[1] The chief development, however, took place after 1897, and will be treated later in the third period which runs from 1897 onwards.

The third and final period of Canadian fiscal history, in which the emphasis has been placed on Canadian Nationalism and the Imperial connexion, was ushered in by the grant of Preference to England in 1897 and by the waning of the desire for Reciprocity. The Hon. W. S. Fielding, the Finance Minister, speaking in 1899, said : " Whatever our American friends may have intended by their trade policy, there is one thing they certainly have done ; they have made Canadians more independent and self-reliant and have caused them to look more steadily than before to their home market and to their markets over the sea, where there is an open door. . . Therefore the market of our friends to the south of us is much less important to us than it was a few years ago, and we are better able to do without reciprocity than we have been at any previous time in the history of Canada."[2]

The leading feature of this period of Canadian Nationalism and of Imperialism is the further development of the policy of Protection. The grip of Protection on Canada was clearly shown when the Liberal Party was returned to power in 1896 on an avowedly anti-Protection platform. Nevertheless, the logic of the situation, together with resentment at the very high Dingley Tariff of 1897, was too strong for the Liberal Party, and it simply carried on the policy of its predecessor in office, although as late as 1904 the Hon. W. S. Fielding was still pleading " Incidental Protection ". Tariff rates were even raised on certain items, and the bounties on iron and steel were made much more generous. Moveover, the Liberal Government introduced the Anti-Dumping

[1] Sir R. Cartwright, *Canadian Debates*, 1897, i, p. 98.
[2] *R.C.T.*, p. 100.

Clause in 1904, which aimed at preventing the American manufacturers from using Canada as a slaughter-market for their surplus stock. Evidently Protection was well entrenched.

During the period from 1897 onwards the bounty system in connexion with the iron and steel industry reached its acme and then moved on to its demise. The bounties up to 1897 were small, never more than £25,000 in any one year.[1] In 1897 the system of bounties was greatly extended by the increase of the bonus on pig-iron made of Canadian ore from 2 to 3 dollars a ton, the payment of a bounty of 3 dollars a ton on bars and ingots, and of 2 dollars a ton on pig-iron made of foreign ores. In 1903 a bounty of 6 dollars a ton on steel rods to be used in the manufacture of wire was instituted. In 1907 the bounties were still further increased, so as to encourage smelting by electricity. By 1909 the output of iron had risen to 609,431 tons from 52,871 tons in 1896.[2] In 1910 it was found that the total amount paid out in bounties over the previous ten years was £3,600,000, which the Finance Minister defended on the ground that the bounties had been more than paid for by the yield of the duties on iron and steel imported into Canada.[3] In 1910 the bounties came to an end, but the tariff on imported iron and steel was continued. The output of furnaces and mills increased year by year, and during the war there was a great boom supplying the demand for munitions. In 1913 the output of steel was 1,168,993 tons, in 1918 it was 1,873,708 tons. Then came the post-war slump, and in 1926 the output was down to 737,000 tons.[4] Another factor in the decline was the lightening of the tariff on agricultural implements and motor car material. Thus imports of iron rose from $138,000,000 in 1922 to $219,000,000 in 1926.[5] The Duncan Commission, which was appointed to inquire into the grievances of the Maritime Provinces, recommended changes in the tariff and bounties to aid the Nova Scotian iron industry, but the Liberal Government refused to act in the matter.[6]

In 1897 Canada gave the Mother Country Preference

---

[1] E. Porritt, " Iron and Steel Bounties in Canada," in the *Political Science Quarterly*, 1907, vol. 22, p. 196.

[2] E. Porritt, *Revolt in Canada against the New Feudalism*, pp. 76-7.

[3] *C.P.*, vol. 9, pp. 201-3.

[4] T. Cantley, *Canadian Debates*, 24th February, 1927, pp. 658-9.

[5] H. H. Stevens, *Canadian Debates*, 25th February, 1927, p. 696.

[6] *The Times*, 19th March, 1927.

without asking for anything in return, showing the renewal of the pull to England and the revival of Imperial sentiment. The grant of Preference by the Liberals in 1897 was a very astute move. It lowered tariffs (which they had promised to do) in certain directions and thus was popular with farmers and free traders. It lowered tariffs on British goods and thus was popular with British manufacturers and Imperialists generally. It preserved the high tariffs against the Americans, the Canadian manufacturers' most deadly rivals in many respects, and thus was not unpopular even with Canadian manufacturers.

The Preference at first consisted of a reduction of one-eighth, then a year later of one-quarter of the duties imposed on imports. So pleased were the Free Traders that the Cobden Club presented its medal of honour to Sir Wilfrid Laurier. In 1900 the quarter reduction was increased to one-third, so that in the case of a 30 per cent duty the amount paid by British imports was lowered from $22\frac{1}{2}$ per cent to 20 per cent. While Canada asked for nothing in return, it apparently relied on " gratitude effecting more than importunity ".[1] In 1902 the Imperial Government imposed a duty on corn of 1s. a quarter as a revenue measure to help to defray the expenses of the South African War. Canada promptly asked that Canadian wheat should be exempted from this duty, in other words, that Canadian wheat should receive a slight preference in the Mother Country. This hope of reciprocal preference was disappointed by the abolition of the duty in the following year.[2] In the revision of 1906–7 the preference to the Mother Country of one-third was replaced by a particular tariff where the preference varied in amount from item to item. On the whole, this meant a diminution of the one-third reduction. It was due to the clamour of the Canadian industrialists, especially the woollen manufacturers, who complained that the Imperial Preference was stripping them of adequate protection and exposing them to blasts of competition that they could not withstand. This is an instance of the difficulty of reconciling the twin and rather contradictory policies of Protectionism and Imperial Preference. Nevertheless, Canada could claim that the result of the preference had been to revive the British

[1] C.P., vol. 9, p. 206.
[2] J. Lewis, " British Preference," in Economic and Social Conditions of the Dominion of Canada, 1923, edited by W. P. M. Kennedy, pp. 200–1.

import trade, as the following figures, giving the value of British imports for the respective years, demonstrate :—

1890   43,000,000 dollars
1896   29,000,000 dollars
1905   69,000,000 dollars.[1]

Meanwhile Canada was granting Preference to, or negotiating Preference with, other parts of the Empire. In 1898, following the original grant of Preference to the Mother Country, Canada had extended similar favours to the British West Indies, to India, Ceylon, Straits Settlements and New South Wales, all of those Colonies being on a Free Trade basis like the Mother Country. Negotiated Preference followed with New Zealand and South Africa in 1904, and with Australia in 1925. Further favours were extended to the British West Indies after negotiation in 1912–13, 1920 and 1925.

As with South Africa and the south-west area, Australia and Papua, New Zealand and Samoa, so with Canada and the British West Indies, the Dominions are throwing their ægis over tropical or sub-tropical lands which are yet in a state of economic dependency and need mothering. South Africa, Australia and New Zealand have received mandates for the administration of those dependent regions, but the link in the case of Canada and the British West Indies is not political but commercial and arranged on a Treaty basis. Canada gives a 50 per cent Preference on West Indian imports, excluding tobacco, cigars and alcohol, and the British West Indies in return give a varying amount of preference on Canadian imports (generally about 30 per cent) such as wheat, dairy produce and lumber. In addition, Canada promises to supply the Islands with a fortnightly steamer service, coming and going, for freight and passenger purposes. This last provision accentuates the importance of sea communications in a sea-girt Empire.

In 1907 Canada, the fiscal pioneer of the Empire, introduced the type of Tariff known as the Three-Decker, which with minor reservations still holds good in the Dominion and has even spread throughout part of the Empire. The Three-Decker Tariff has three scales of duties : (1) The General Scale which applies to countries generally which have no special privileges in the Canadian market ; (2) the

---

[1] J. Lewis, p. 207. See also " The Canadian Preferential Tariff," in *The Times Financial and Commercial Supplement*," 10th July, 1905.

Intermediate Scale, which applies to countries which have obtained Favoured Nation treatment in the Canadian market, and (3) the British Empire Scale, which applies to the Mother Country and such other parts of the Empire as have negotiated or received Preference in the Canadian market. Such is the fiscal system of Canada.

One reaction from the grant of preference to the Mother Country in 1897 proved the reality of Canada's national status. The proof was the Tariff War with Germany which raged between 1898 and 1910 and ended in " peace without victory " for Germany.[1] When Canada granted preference to the Mother Country in 1897, that favour was automatically enjoyed by Germany under the Favoured Nation Treaty which Germany had made with England. To prevent that, England denounced the treaty, and in resentment Germany placed the maximum tariff on Canadian imports in 1898. Canada remonstrated, but in vain, and in 1903 as a retaliatory measure the Hon. W. S. Fielding, the Finance Minister, imposed a special surtax of one-third on German imports over and above the general rate. This meant in some cases, where the general duties were 30 per cent, that German imports had to pay an impost of 40 per cent, while English goods were entering on payment of only 20 per cent. German imports fell off severely, much more severely than Canadian imports into Germany,[2] and in February, 1910, Germany made overtures of peace to Canada, which led to a termination of the hostilities. The German failure revealed the strength of Canada. " It failed," commented an American Report, " largely because the great degree of dependence of German trade and industry on the markets and raw materials of the British Empire placed in British hands a powerful weapon of counter-retaliation." [3]

Though the pull of the United States receded into the background after 1897, it yet remained, and remains, a considerable factor in Canadian politics and economics. The very size, wealth, kinship of blood and geographical proximity of the United States make this inevitable. It has been said that Canadians " have adopted the cabinet system of Britain and the party methods of the Republic ;

---

[1] E. Porritt, *Evolution of the Dominion of Canada*, pp. 444–6.

[2] W. S. Fielding, *Canadian Debates*, 1904, iii, c. 4350. The German imports fell off 38 per cent within a year.

[3] *Report on Colonial Tariff Policies* drawn up by the United States Tariff Commission, 1922, p. 651.

' God save the King ' is sung with more fervour than in England, but Broadway slang is on the free list, and baseball has ousted cricket " [1]. What is new about the period since 1897 is that for the first time in history the overture for Reciprocity came from the Republic. Up to 1898 the tide flowed towards Washington, but after 1898 the tide turned, and in 1911 took place the first Pilgrimage to Ottawa, when the United States passed an Act endorsing Reciprocity. There followed the dramatic election of 1911, in which Canada declared emphatically that it did not want Reciprocity. For thirty or forty years Canada had bargained for, had begged for, had bewailed the lack of, Reciprocity, and now, when it could have had it, Canada turned from it disdainfully. The reasons for Canada's refusal of Reciprocity were various. Canada was then in the full tide of prosperity : immigrants were flowing in, lands were being settled, the output of wheat was increasing quickly, and commerce and wealth and transportation were expanding marvellously : Canada felt it could do without the aid of the United States and be sufficient to itself. Again, Reciprocity was opposed not only by the manufacturers but also by the railway interests in Canada. Their lines ran east and west, and they wanted traffic to run east and west, that is, between Canada and England, and not to run north and south, that is, between Canada and the United States. Thus the very powerful interests of the railways opposed Reciprocity. There was also resentment at former rebuffs on the part of the United States, and now had come the golden opportunity of settling old scores. Further, there was the dark dread in Canada that Reciprocity was the first step on the road to annexation, that the American aim was for the " stars and stripes to float from Panama to the Pole ". Finally, Canadians argued that the American readiness to grant Reciprocity was due to their realization of the wealth of Canada's natural resources, which were all the more important as their own were being used up. " They have squandered their own resources," said the Canadians, "and now they want to come and plunder ours." For many and mingled motives Canada rejected Reciprocity with the United States in 1911, and this rejection marks the end of the overpowering pull towards the United States and the full dawn of Canadian Nationalism.

[1] *C.P.*, vol. 9, p. 101.

Protection, it has already been said, is now firmly entrenched in Canada, and has become the policy of the two traditional parties. During the War the policy of Protection marked time, but the Sales Tax which was imposed by a Liberal Government after the War was really a Protectionist device of a concealed nature. Not only the Dominion Government but the Provincial Governments and even the Municipalities also dabble with policies of industrial development nowadays. Provisions of Provincial Legislatures and Municipalities encouraging industries within their respective areas by granting sites rent-free and rate-free and by giving cheap loans are also Protectionist devices of a concealed nature. The whole of Canadian political life is pervaded by Protection.

So strong is the feeling against Protection amongst the farmers of the Prairie Provinces that a new political party, called the Progressives, came into being in 1919 to represent the farmers' interests and to combat High Tariffism. This represents the cleavage of interests between the industrial East and the agricultural West, a cleavage that has grown up since the 'nineties. Before the 'nineties the agricultural West scarcely existed as an economic factor. At that time both agriculture and industry were combined in Ontario, and the real cleavage then was between the agricultural and industrial West of Ontario, and the fishing, farming and lumbering East of the Maritime Provinces. Nowadays the situation is altogether changed. The East, which means Ontario, Quebec, and the Maritime Provinces, wants to monopolize the home market and to supply the West, which means the Prairie Provinces, with agricultural machinery, clothes, furniture, boots and shoes. The West, with an abundant surplus of wheat for export, sees no advantage in Protection, which simply raises the prices of the things it has to purchase over what it would pay if it could buy freely from the United States. The West even preaches the purchase of American goods as a patriotic duty, for thereby the Dominion finances are helped,[1] and, doubtless, the manufacturers of the East are spited. What the West would appreciate would be open access to the great market over the border. Thus the West desires full-blooded Reciprocity with the United States as ardently as the East now hates it.

[1] J. A. Stevenson, "Agrarian Movement in Canada," in *Edinburgh Review*, 1920, vol. 232, p. 98.

The Progessives, with their new National Policy of extending the free list, of reducing duties generally, and of establishing free trade with England,[1] have not achieved much success so far. Outwardly they have been allied with the Liberal Party, which has in deference to them reduced the tariff somewhat. The Liberal Party, however, contains a hard core of Protectionist opinion in the French-Canadian bloc of Quebec, which has put a stop to the lowering of the tariff.[2] Even the last Pilgrimage to Washington by the Hon. W. S. Fielding in 1922 did not have the cordial support of the Liberals, who feared that Reciprocity would entail a reduction of the Protection afforded to Canadian industries and were rather relieved to discover that the United States Government was hostile to the Canadian proposal of Reciprocity.[3] The issue, therefore, still seems to lie between the Liberals and Conservatives, in other words, between the two competing policies of a low tariff and a high tariff. It is apparent that Protection has come to stay in Canada, " and it will stay as long as it stays in the United States ". The only question is whether it will be high Protection or low Protection.

[1] J. A. Stevenson, " The Canadian Tariff," in *Social and Economic Conditions in the Dominion of Canada*, 1923, by W. P. M. Kennedy, p. 194.
[2] J. A. Stevenson, " Political and Economic Situation in Canada," in *Edinburgh Review*, 1925, vol. 241, p. 216.
[3] J. A. Stevenson, " Fiscal Politics in Canada," in *Edinburgh Review*, 1922, vol. 236, pp. 179–82.

CHAPTER 14

The Settlement of the Great Plains

Physical characteristics of region.

Early days in the North-West.
  The First Explorers.
  Difficulties from bad communications, want of markets, grass-hoppers and climate.
  Hudson's Bay Company surrenders rights of government.
  Spread of settlement outwards from Winnipeg.
  Manitoba a Province, 1870.
  Nature and growth of population.
  Alberta and Saskatchewan made Provinces, 1905.
  Features and population.
  Troubles from rebellions and land booms.
  Slow growth of towns.
  Winnipeg.

The Coming of the Settlers.
  Conditions from the first settlement in 1812 down to 1870.
  The settlers of the 'seventies:
    The settlers from Ontario.
    The Mennonites and their communal system.
    The Icelanders.
  The settlers of the 'eighties:
    Scottish crofter settlements.
    Colonization Companies.
  The foreign settlers of the 'nineties:
    The Central European element.
    Clifford Sifton's inauguration of the immigration campaign and the American invasion.
    The Ruthenians.
    The Doukhobors.
  Later settlements:
    The Barr Colony as an example of wrong methods.
    The advantage enjoyed by the self-sufficing settler (e.g. the Doukhobors) over the settler depending on the outside world for necessaries (e.g. the British).
  Settlers wanted rather than mere immigrants.
  British and American immigration compared.
  The foreign element.
  Post-war Schemes for British settlement.

The Reception of the Immigrant:
  Discomforts of the early immigrants.
  Recruiting methods.
  How the modern immigrant is shepherded.

The Dividing-up of the Land:
  The rectangular system of survey.
  Conditions on which land acquired.
    Homesteads.
    Pre-emption.

Changed conditions.
Tenancy and purchase take the place of free land.
The Canadian Pacific Railway Company's ready-made farms.
The treaties with the Indians.
Provincial and Dominion ownership of land.

Exploitation of the Soil:
The new type of settler.
Difficulties from climate, wolves and locusts.
Ranch versus homestead.
The change from dependence on cereals to mixed farming.

Irrigation in the semi-arid region:
Possibilities of crop regulation.
Alfalfa.
Government control of water resources.
The North-West Irrigation Act, 1894.
Irrigation enterprises of Canadian Pacific Railway Company and others.

THE story has now been told how the Dominion was equipped with the transcontinental railways which are the indispensable instruments of economic development on national lines and we have seen how shipping lines and trade routes have brought those internal means of communication into touch with the uttermost parts of the earth. The political organization of the Dominion on national lines has also been completed so that a chain of neighbouring Provinces, each with its own Legislature, extends from sea to sea. It now has to be shown how in post-1867 Canada the new territories thus brought into touch with one another and with the outer world have been opened up to settlement ; in particular, how the Prairie Provinces have been peopled and so transformed that the vast lands which only half a century ago were the haunt of the Indian and the buffalo have become the granary of the world and the pastures of horses, cattle and sheep ; how the expansive effort of the Dominion has expressed itself on the Pacific side in aspects so diverse as fruit farming in the south, and away in the inhospitable Yukon in the north a wild gold rush ; and how the Laurentian Plateau has been penetrated, and what was regarded as a forbidding waste found to be a veritable treasure-house of mineral deposits. A new people, the Canadian people, is seen being gradually evolved from diverse elements of the white races in which the British stock predominates, but with accretions from Continental Europe and with a strong admixture coming from the region south of the forty-ninth degree of latitude.

The vast territories of the Dominion which in 1867 were

not only unsettled, but unexplored, fall into three main divisions, each a type with marked characteristics and each with a record of settlement and progress along its own lines.

The Great Plains occupy the region extending westwards for about 1,000 miles from Winnipeg to the foothills of the Rocky Mountains and narrowing northwards along the valley of the Mackenzie River to a width of about 220 miles between the Laurentian Plateau and the mountains of the west.

The rough, rocky and heavily wooded surface of the Laurentian Plateau covers nearly the whole of the Labrador peninsula and occupies the region north of Lake Superior and between Hudson Bay and a line joining Winnipeg and Athabaska, Great Slave and Great Bear Lakes and extending to the Arctic coast.

The Cordilleran region is the mountainous area between the Pacific and the Great Plains which extends northwards from the United States through Canada into Alaska and includes nearly all British Columbia and the Yukon Territory.

The total area of Canada, excluding the islands in the Arctic Ocean, is reckoned at 3,209,000 square miles. At the period of the Great War some 28 per cent of this area, say 901,000 square miles, still remained unexplored. Of this unexplored territory about 110,000 square miles belong to the region of the Great Plains, for the most part the region in the Mackenzie Basin north of Peace River and Athabaska Lake. In the Cordilleran region some 130,000 miles belonged to the unknown, and the remaining unexplored territory, amounting to two-thirds of the whole, belonged to the Laurentian Plateau.[1]

The lands fitted for agricultural development, that is to say, in the region of the Great Plains, have filled up most quickly. The Peace River and the Athabaska River regions contain the largest area of unoccupied agricultural lands now remaining in the Dominion. It is in the northern region of the Great Plains and along the Clay Belt in Ontario that any further agricultural settlement must take place. The prospector has a much wider field. Thus so recently as 1916 it was computed that not much more than 5 per cent of the

---

[1] These are the figures given to the Dominions Royal Commission in 1916. See *Minutes of Evidence* [Cd. 8459], Memorandum by Mr. C. Camsell, *Geological Survey of Canada*, p. 273.

700,000 square miles that make up the Province of Quebec had been explored [1]; and the northern half of Ontario similarly awaited investigation.

Primarily Western Canada is an agricultural country, but a settler's holding can be regarded as something of a lucky-bag out of which he may at any time draw an unexpected prize. Thus, " while boring for water, coal has been found at Otterburne and St. Malo, on the east side of the Red River ; natural gas was reached right in the town of Melita at a depth of 381 feet ; brine of great strength has been found near Dauphin ; and near Miami a bed of natural cement has been discovered which a company is now manufacturing by mixing it with gypsum from Lake Manitoba, and of this material they are now turning out 75 barrels a day." [2] At first the territory was exploited mainly by cattlemen, Lethbridge being the centre of the ranching industry. Later came grain growing and mixed farming. The country is known to be rich in minerals, but so far mining has been merely a side line. The surrounding fields of natural gas may make of Medicine Hat an important industrial city.[3] The fur trade is still carried on in the Mackenzie district.

Early Days in the North-West

The first recorded penetration of the North-West by a white man took place while the French still had the ascendancy in Canada. La Vérendrye, pushing westward from Lake Superior, reached Lake Winnipeg and built a fort in 1738 at the junction of the Red and Assiniboine Rivers, where the city of Winnipeg now stands. His two sons, continuing their explorations by way of the Missouri, first saw the Rocky Mountains in 1743 from the Prairies at some point in what is now Montana and later discovered the Saskatchewan River. Succeeding expeditions were generally affairs of rival fur traders, among whom Anthony Hendry deserves mention as having ascended the Saskatchewan in 1754, and as being the first Englishman to penetrate

---

[1] Ibid : *Memorandum* by Department of Colonization, Quebec, at p. 285.

[2] *Report of Department of the Interior for* 1900–1, part ii, Immigration, p. 139 ; *Sessional Papers*, 1902, vol. 36. Similarly, to go further east : " While blasting with dynamite at Matheson, Ontario, to make a post-hole, a farmer discovered a deposit of free gold. He has sold his claim for $60,000 (£12,000), with a substantial share in the company developing the find." (*Times*, 24th April, 1929).

[3] For some account of the minerals of the North-West, see chapter 19.

thus far ; and Alexander Mackenzie who, after eight years
at the newly established Fort Chipewyan on Lake Athabaska, set out thence in the summer of 1789 to explore
the great river that bears his name, as being the first of the
great line of Scots whose names are writ so large in the
history of British North America. The story of the penetration of the North-West by the fur traders has been told in a
previous chapter. The next phase to be described is the
manner in which agriculture superseded the fur trade as the
white man's primary interest and the real settlement of the
Great Plains began.

In the 'seventies, the early years of the National Period in
Canada's economic history, the region which was to become
the Prairie Provinces had remarkable characteristics,
politically, physically and socially. Politically, the Hudson's
Bay Company held sway over a territory nearly as large as
the United States, for by their Charter they were " the true
and absolute Lords and Proprietors of the same Territory,
Limits and Places aforesaid." The settlers on the Red River
had as currency " a little gold and silver, but chiefly the
notes of the Hudson's Bay Company." [1] The Company
levied taxes and licence duties and administered justice.
Their purpose was to maintain a monopoly of the fur trade.
It was no part of the Company's business to encourage
agricultural settlements : " It was well understood among
both officers and servants of the Company that they were
employed solely in the interests of the fur trade and not as
agricultural agents or mining experts, and when we observed
fine vegetables raised on a few spots by the missionaries
we knew they were to be regarded simply as small oases in a
vast desert in which, by great care and a wonderful dispensa-
tion of Providence, such cultivation was made possible.
The rest of the country was to be considered as fit only for
furs, Indians and buffalo." [2] And there is plenty of evidence
that they actively discouraged the entrance into their
territory of any not directly or indirectly concerned with the
collection of the furs of the beaver and the musk-rat, the
marten and the ermine, the skunk and the mink, the
wolverine and the silver fox, the lynx and the bear, and their
transport to Montreal. A traveller in the late 'sixties testified

---

[1] Report of Select Committee on Red River and North-West Territory :
Ottawa, 1870. (*Canada : Pamphlets*, vol. 2, No. 62, in D.O. & C.O.
Library.)

[2] H. J. Moberly and W. B. Cameron, *When Fur was King*, 1929,
pp. 56–7.

that privately he was "treated with great courtesy and hospitality by several of the chief traders or factors, but there was an evident tendency on the part of the Company's servants generally to discourage my journeys. No active opposition was in any case offered to me, but discouraging reports were the invariable rule." [1] The only contact of the Company with the enterprise of settlement had been the part they had played in 1811 in connexion with Lord Selkirk's colony. It was no small part, as has already been described, inasmuch as it involved the grant of 116,000 square miles of the Company's territory for the establishment of the Scottish Colony on the Red River with its centre at what to-day is Winnipeg. The Company had also assumed direct control of Vancouver Island which in 1849 was granted to them for a term of years and they gave it an able administrator in the person of their chief factor, James Douglas. The early settlers in both regions had frequent occasion to be grateful to the Hudson's Bay Company for assistance in hard times.

The difficulties imposed by Nature on the regions of the North-West were thus summarized by a Committee of Inquiry in 1870 : " The principal drawbacks would seem to be distance from navigation and railway communications ; absence of markets for agricultural products ; occasional visits from grasshoppers and the cold of winter." [2] The " roads " were merely the tracks of buffalo hunters and the employees of the Hudson's Bay Company—two ruts in the prairie sod with a pathway between. The trains of Red River carts that traversed these tracks in single file were often a hundred in number. In the Saskatchewan country wolves might be seen dodging among the thickets and following the train as it passed along. Communication with the outer world was mainly maintained through St. Paul, a United States town which was really a distributing centre for the remote North-West, to which access was by means of carts over the unsettled prairies of Minnesota and then by small steamers on the Red River to Fort Garry, the present Winnipeg, a journey which took several weeks. The grasshopper was capable of being something more than a nuisance : the pest was wont to make a clean sweep of the crops, so reducing the settlers to a state of famine. One witness, a schoolmaster, told the Committee of Inquiry

[1] Paul Fountain, *The Great North-West*. London, 1904, pp. 91–2.
[2] Report of Select Committee on Red River, etc. (*supra*).

already referred to, how at one time he had as many as seventy-six pupils at Portage La Prairie, but " the grass-hopper famine broke up the school ". The heat was as high as 90° in the summer, and in winter the thermometer would be 30° to 40° below zero, but the rigours of the cold were mitigated by the dryness of the atmosphere. In a mixed population which has been variously calculated as numbering from 10,000 to 13,000 souls—traders and settlers connected with the Hudson's Bay Company, Lord Selkirk's settlers, who were mostly Scottish Highlanders, half-breeds and Indians—the only centre of population being Fort Garry, a mere village, there would be but little scope for markets or commerce of any kind. Clearly the North-West was an anomaly at hopeless variance with the newly awakened national conception of which confederation had been the expression. Equally clearly the anomaly would persist unless the region was brought into relationship with the other Canadian Provinces by adequate means of communication and unless it became one with British Columbia and the Eastern Provinces under a single govern-ment. For the fulfilment of the first condition the country had to wait until 1886 when the Canadian Pacific Railway was completed. The second was accomplished when in 1869 the Hudson's Bay Company, while retaining their trading privileges, agreed " to surrender to Her Majesty all the rights of government, property, etc., in Rupert's Land, and also all similar rights in any other part . . . of British North America not comprised in Rupert's Land, Canada or British Columbia ".

The change was accepted by the Company as inevitable. During their two hundred years of rule in the North-West they had enjoyed great privileges, but they secured that vast region for the British Empire. Henry Kelsey, who in 1691 was the first among white men to see the great plains, and Samuel Hearne, who in 1771 reached the Athabaska country and the mouth of the Coppermine River, were the first of a long line of Hudson's Bay Company agents who penetrated the country in all directions. The Company's forts and the trails and waterways connecting them were the frail net-work that constituted government and represented civiliza-tion. Upper Fort Garry, built by the Company in 1835, was the foundation of Winnipeg, and many of their trading posts elsewhere constituted the nucleus of what are now flourishing towns in the Prairie Provinces. Peaceable and indeed for the most part friendly relations had been maintained with the Indians, a condition of things which was in striking and creditable contrast with the more or less continuous warfare which went on between the settlers and the Indians on the American side of the international boundary. They had enemies, as monopolists must, and they had been ruthless in the steps they took to prevent any trading in furs without their authorization,[1] but the fact remains that for two centuries they controlled the country with no force at their disposal with which to enforce the law had it been necessary, a state of things which could only have been maintained by the goodwill of the people themselves. For two centuries the Hudson's Bay Company had been the faithful caretakers of Canada's great undeveloped estate in the North-West, and when the first Parliament of the new Dominion declared settlement, commerce and the development of the resources of the country to be dependent upon the establishment of a stable government, the Company acquiesced and handed over their trust to the beneficiaries, the Canadian people.

Organized settlement spread northwards and westwards from the Winnipeg region. The new phase in Canada's development which there began was described by Lord Dufferin, Governor-General of Canada, in his own picturesque manner, in a speech at Winnipeg in 1877 : " From its geographical position, and its peculiar characteristics, Manitoba may be regarded as the keystone of that mighty arch of sister Provinces which spans the continent from the Atlantic to the Pacific. It was here that Canada, emerging from her woods and forests, first gazed upon her rolling prairies and unexplored North-West, and learnt, as by an unexpected revelation, that her historical territories of the Canadas, her eastern seaboards of New Brunswick, Labrador, and Nova Scotia, her Laurentian lakes and valleys, corn lands and pastures, though themselves more extensive than half a dozen European Kingdoms, were but the vestibules and antechambers to that till then undreamt of Dominion,

---

[1] There is an interesting record of the trial in 1849 of a French half-breed named Sayre and three other Metis. The charge was that contrary to the rules of the Company's charter, the accused had accepted furs from the Indians in exchange for goods. Armed Metis surrounded the Court-house with the declared intention of resisting the infliction of any punishment on the accused. Sayre was acquitted on the plea that one of the Hudson's Bay Company's officers had given him permission to traffic. John Macoun, *Manitoba and the Great North West*, 1883, pp. 450–1.

whose illimitable dimensions alike confound the arithmetic of the surveyor and verification of the explorer. It was here that, counting her past achievements as but the preface and prelude to her future exertions and expanding destinies, she took a fresh departure, received the afflatus of a more imperial inspiration, and felt herself no longer a mere settler along the banks of a single river, but the owner of half a continent and in the magnitude of her possessions, in the wealth of her resources, in the sinews of her material might, the peer of any power on the earth." [1]

" The Red River," as it was commonly called, was formed into the Province of Manitoba and admitted into the Confederation in 1870. The new legislature soon got to work, and in 1871, as the fruits of its first Session, forty-three Bills were passed dealing not only with such essentials as highways, wills, taxation, and the establishment of a Supreme Court, but also such legislative sidelines as the better observance of the Sabbath and the destruction of Canadian thistles.

The measure of the growth of settlement in a new country is the increase of population ; the manner of its development must depend on the nature of the population. The diary of Sandford Fléming's expedition across Canada in 1872, describing conditions in that year, says of Manitoba, the population of which in the preceding year was about 25,000, that " not more than 2,000 are pure whites. One-fifth of the number are Indians, either living in houses or wanderers, one-third English or Scotch half-breeds, and rather more than a third French half-breeds." [2] It was a community with a precarious hold on life. Thus we are told : " In the autumn of 1867 the whole country was invaded by swarms of locusts, and these having deposited their eggs, the young insects in the following spring devoured every green thing on the face of the land. The result was that actual starvation stared the settlers in the face. . . . It was the darkest season for the settlement in many years, for not only were the crops destroyed, but the buffalo hunt and the fisheries proved to be complete failures, and even the rabbits and pheasants in the country had disappeared. There was, therefore, no food for the people except what could be obtained from the liberal donations of outside funds ". [3]

[1] Quoted by J. Macoun in *Manitoba and the Great North-West*, p. 509.
[2] G. M. Grant, *Ocean to Ocean*, p. 66.
[3] A. Begg, *History of the North-West*. Toronto, 1894, vol. ii, pp. 364–5.

The habits of life of the half-breeds was little suited to the new order of things. " Trading was out of the question to those who had neither goods nor money, nor credit to procure them . . . the buffalo had been driven to the extreme west and were getting scarcer ; freighting, which formerly gave employment to a large number of men with their horses, oxen and carts, was now done by steamers, flat boats and barges, on the Red River during the season of navigation, and in the winter by improved wagons, ' prairie schooners,' which replaced the ' cayuse ' and ox-cart ; as for farming, it had always been carried on in a desultory way by the native population, who regarded it as of secondary importance compared with the more congenial tasks which we have enumerated." [1]

A native population which could only carry on what was destined to be the staple industry of the country " in a desultory way " had to make way for a people for whom the pursuit of agriculture was the main purpose in life. " At the close of 1879, farm houses and cultivated fields were in sight all along the main road for 250 miles west of Winnipeg." [2] In 1926, Manitoba had a population of 639,000 and Winnipeg, which in 1870 consisted of " about thirty buildings outside the Fort, embracing eight stores, two saloons, two hotels, a mill and a church, the total population being 215 souls ",[3] was a capital city with 192,000 inhabitants.

In the remoter prairie regions the changes in half a century have been still more remarkable. In its early days Alberta was the home of the most powerful of the Indian nations in the whole of the North-West. On its plains roamed vast herds of buffalo, antelopes, and deer. Its mountains and lake regions were exploited by the fur company. When in 1869, as part of Rupert's Land and the North-Western territory, it passed from the control of the Hudson's Bay Company to that of the Canadian Government, the white population consisted of the Hudson's Bay Company's traders and a few missionaries. When, in 1905, the provinces of Alberta and Saskatchewan were carved out of the North-West Territories, their populations were respectively 185,412 and 257,763. By 1911 the figures were 374,205 and 492,432 and in 1921 they had further increased to 588,454 and 757,510

---

[1] A. Begg, *History of the North-West*, vol. ii, p. 86.
[2] Ibid., p. 388.
[3] J. Macoun, *Manitoba and the Great North-West*, 1883, p. 490.

respectively. But so vast is the territory that at that time caribou and moose still roamed the region around Lake Athabaska and in the same part of the province were to be found the last of the buffalo.

In Alberta through railway communication east and west now extends as far north as Edmonton in Alberta and Prince Albert in Saskatchewan. In 1872 the house of the missionary was the only habitation outside Fort Edmonton, the place 900 miles by cart trail north-west from Winnipeg, which was to become the capital of Alberta. By 1881, Edmonton was a town of some importance, with stores, grist and sawmills, an abundance of coal and an organized society from which had passed away the fear of hostile Indians that only ten years before beset the few settlers in the region,[1] but at the beginning of the twentieth century it was a place where the old and the new still met. At the store of the Hudson's Bay Company " well-dressed towns people, in the season's latest fashion, mixed with the bedecked and painted Indians, while squaws, placidly smoking, huddled on the floor." [2]

Prince Albert was originally a Presbyterian mission established about 1868. " For some years after its location, it was thought that besides Christianizing the Indians they could be taught farming, but buffalo being plenty they would not settle." In 1875, " Captain Moore, an Irish gentleman of means, brought machinery for a steam sawmill on wagons from Winnipeg, a distance of fully 700 miles." Then a grist mill was erected " and flour at once fell to Winnipeg prices ". In 1877 there were about 500 people in the settlement, and about 1,200 acres under cultivation. Four years later the district contained a white and half-breed population of about 3,000, and there were about 10,000 acres under crop, while the population of Prince Albert proper was about 800. To supply the needs of settlers, enterprising firms brought into the district portable flour mills.[3]

The young community had its periods of trial and trouble. There was the political fever of the Red River Rebellion under Riel in 1870, and the rising of the half-breeds in the Saskatchewan country in 1885, under the same leader, which brought him to the scaffold. Then the North-West

---

[1] J. Macoun, Manitoba and the Great North-West, 1883, pp. 112–13.
[2] Sir Wm. Schooling, The Hudson's Bay Company, 1670–1920, published by the Company, London, 1920, p. 109.
[3] J. Macoun, Manitoba and the Great North-West, 1883, p. 96.

has been afflicted with periodical visitations of two plagues, grasshoppers and real estate booms, and, of the two, the latter put back economic progress the more seriously. One such visitation was brought to its disastrous end in 1914 by the outbreak of the Great War. The period of convalescence from the land boom in the North-West which culminated in 1881-2, was prolonged. Towns were founded in all directions, but only a few have become more than shadows of their promised greatness. Thus, " in 1877, settlement reached the ' Big Plain ' beyond Pine Creek, and the next year Rapid City, on the Little Saskatchewan, was founded. The summer of 1878 saw a large immigration to the country around Rapid City," and by 1879 it was " without a rival in the estimation of Western people " [1] ; but it belied its name, for the population of 738 shown in 1906 had in 1916 sunk to 658.[2] Then in the spring of 1880 a rush took place to two embryo " cities " on opposite sides of the same river, and " the boats on the Assiniboine River were loaded with freight and crowded with passengers bound for Odanah and Minnedosa." "Owing to the certainty of the Portage la Prairie and Westbourne Railwa ypassing through these villages their future prosperity is secured," said a contemporary writer of no little authority.[3] The first city is not to be found in a modern map ; the second maintained a struggling existence, and in 1921 had attained a population of 1,505. The building of the Canadian Pacific Railway raised land speculation to fever heat and towns were born daily, many of them only to be stifled at their birth, but some survive as unexciting little towns of slow growth, whose early years are remembered as dreadful warnings to those who aspire to get rich quickly by speculating in Canadian town lots. Some few, having sown their wild oats, have achieved a certain degree of prosperity, but a degree in no way approaching what was promised in the days when the steel rails of the railway were gradually creeping towards them. The Syndicate constructing the line announced their intention of changing the location of a station to a place a mile and a half from the spot it first indicated, " and in a few days the new city of Brandon, 145 miles west of Winnipeg, was in the market . . . . Stores,

---

[1] J. Macoun, *Manitoba and the Great North-West*, p. 469.
[2] The population figures are from the *Canada Year Book* of 1916-17, p. 96.
[3] J. Macoun, op. cit., p. 484.

hotels, dwelling houses, and other buildings were run up
as if by magic, and where nothing but prairie was seen in
the spring the nucleus of a thriving city with all civilized
appliances appeared before the short summer was passed." [1]
In 1891 its population was only 3,778, but by 1921, it had
grown to 15,397. Emerson was a city of which great things
were prophesied. A contemporary writer looked forward
to the time when an impending railway extension would
" lay the whole country open commercially to the merchants
of Emerson, and lay the coals of the Souris Valley down in
the city to assist in building up her manufactures. In short,
it will make the Gate City a main point of distribution in
the work of settling up and developing the great North-
West ". [2] In 1916 the population of the Gate City had
struggled up to a little over a thousand. Portage la Prairie,
which was " next in importance to Emerson " in those
early days, was a " city " where in 1881 the same writer
found " business institutions of every class multiplying with
magic rapidity ", so that " landed property of every
description in and around the city has since the spring
of 1881 risen rapidly in price, and many old settlers, who
had for many years struggled along at farming, suddenly
found their lands becoming of great value and themselves
lifted from comparative poverty to opulence." [3] It is true
that Portage la Prairie has passed Emerson in the race,
but nevertheless in 1921 it could only show a population
of 6,766.

In Winnipeg " the excitement during the fall of 1881
amongst real estate owners was intense. . . . Thousands
of dollars were made by operators in a few minutes. Vast
fortunes were secured in a day. The excitement spread
like wildfire all over the country. Cool-headed professional
and business men, clerical as well as lay, left their callings
in other parts of the country for the scene of the modern
Canadian El Dorado. Real estate agents became as
numerous as the sands on the sea-shore. The educated and
the refined, as well as the illiterate, took part in land transactions. No regard was paid to whether the vendor had a
right to sell or not. Everything was taken for granted ". [4]
Fortunately the foundations of Winnipeg's great future

[1] J. Macoun, *Manitoba and the Great North-West*, pp. 472–3.
[2] Quoted by J. Macoun, ibid., p. 477.
[3] Ibid., at p. 480.
[4] J. Macoun, op. cit., pp. 495–6.

had already been laid. Until in recent years traffic began to be deflected to Pacific ports, the history of the North-West was the history of Winnipeg, and when in 1878–9, Selkirk, north of Winnipeg, was joined to St. Vincent on the frontier south of the Manitoba capital by a line running through that city, and a junction effected with St. Paul and Minneapolis, Winnipeg and through Winnipeg the North-West were brought into railway connexion with the outer world. Lord Dufferin once referred to the city as " the half-way house of the continent ", and the "umbilicus" of the Dominion. Since that time the transcontinental railways have made the capital of Manitoba the half-way house between East and West as well as North and South, and as the direct result there was in the Prairie Provinces in 1926 a population of 2,067,378, and, besides Winnipeg with its 192,000 people, there were the cities of Calgary and Edmonton, each with a population of over 65,000, and Regina and Saskatoon, each with over 30,000 inhabitants.

Whence came all these people into the region of the Great Plains ; how was the land divided among them ; and what did they do with it ? These are the questions to which answers next have to be attempted.

The Coming of the Settlers

The first settlement in the Prairie region, as has already been related, was that of the Scotch contingent under Lord Selkirk in 1812. Few in numbers at the commencement, they had multiplied but slowly by means of natural increase. Latterly they were being more and more swamped by French Canadians and Indian half-breeds, who settled there after retiring from the service of the Hudson's Bay Company. While the French and the Indians led a kind of vagabond hunting life, the Scotch settlers had become firmly attached to the soil and were not unprosperous : " Rich in food and clothing, all of them have likewise saved more or less money. No want of blankets here on the beds : the children well clothed, and the houses warm and comfortable. The barns teeming with grain, the stables with cattle, and all classes wearing more or less of their own manufacture. . . . The flail and the spinning-wheel are ever at work. . . . The people of the Red River possess singular advantages and incitements to self-support. Their salt, their soap, their sugar, their leather is supplied by the colony. Their

D d

lands, if not free, are almost so ; for they have no land-tax, no landlord, no rent days nor dues of any kind, either to Church or State. Every shilling they earn is their own. With the exception of iron, all their essentials are within their grasp every day in the year ; and as for luxuries, they are easily procured by labour at their very door. No farmers in the world, on a small scale, no settlement or colony of agriculturalists, can be pronounced so happy, independent, and comfortable as those in Red River. Their tea, their coffee, beef, pork, and mutton, and their wheaten loaf, may be seen on the table all the year round." [1] In 1870, the farms of the settlers stretched along the banks of the Red and the Assiniboine Rivers and scarcely trenched on the 800 miles of prairie lying beyond. The first Riel Rebellion, in 1869, marked the end of the old régime, and heralded the advent of a new period which was to be distinguished by an ever-increasing inflow of immigrants and settlers into the Canadian North-West.

The first settlers in the North-West in the 'seventies were Canadians from Ontario. " On 26th April, 1871, the first batch of immigrants arrived in Winnipeg. They left their homes in Ontario four weeks previously, travelling by rail to St. Cloud, Minnesota, from thence by wagons to Fort Abercrombie, on the Red River, and thence by flat boat to Winnipeg. The party consisted of eight men, and they came to Manitoba with the intention of taking up homesteads." [2] They and the old Selkirk settlers were the agricultural pioneers of the North-West. Throughout the 'seventies and 'eighties, Ontario supplied an increasing quota to swell the tide of colonization, and it was only after the 'nineties, when the foundations had been laid, that Ontario was outstripped by the United States, Austria, and England as the chief source of settlers for the North-West. The Ontario settlers were attracted to the North-West after 1871 by the Homestead policy of free grants of 160 acres and by the fertility of the soil and its ease of cultivation. Many of them, having sold out their farms in the Eastern Provinces of the Dominion, arrived with capital and with experience of Canadian farming which made them invaluable settlers. At the same time, and for much the same motives, farmers began to trickle out from England. In pre-railway days especially, the settlers had to have private means to

[1] A. Ross, *The Red River Colony*, 1856, pp. 207, 361.
[2] A. Begg, *History of the North-West*, vol. ii, p. 87.

meet the onerous expenses of settlement. "So far the settling on the lands has been attended with serious expense to the newcomer ; the time actually occupied in travelling, the amount of money requisite to pay fares and living by the way, and the high prices of labour, lumber, and supplies of every kind in the province, having proved a great obstacle in the way of its development." [1]

The foreign settlers of the 'seventies consisted of two distinct groups, Mennonites and Icelanders, of whom the Mennonites were much the more numerous and important. The Mennonites were German Quakers settled in Russia, who came in large numbers to the New World to seek religious liberty. The first contingent of Mennonites arrived in the North-West in the summer of 1874, and they were allotted townships to the west of the Red River. Their manner of settlement was in dorfs, " each consisting of from eight to eighteen large well-built and well-furnished houses."[2] The Mennonite settlers of 1874 had been well supplied with money, and did not need any outside assistance, but those of 1875 were so poor as to be unable to come of themselves. It was not the policy of the Dominion Government to give monetary assistance to settlers, and the solution of the difficulty was ultimately found in a Government loan, the repayment of which was guaranteed by their co-religionists established in Ontario. The Waterloo Society was formed of " about 150 well-to-do Canadian farmers of German extraction in the county of Waterloo, Ontario ", who pledged their farms as security for the loan, which amounted to 96,400 dollars. By 1892 the debt was finally and fully paid : 96,400 dollars of principal, 33,986·53 dollars of interest.[3] Under the Mennonite " Dorf " settlement, " the plan is, for a certain number, say twenty, to join together under the direction of their leaders, for the purpose of starting a ' Dorf '. The land being selected, comprising say 160 acres for each one entitled to enter an homestead, a site for the village or buildings is chosen as near the centre of the ' Dorf ' as possible, without regard to the question of who may be the individual owner of the land,

[1] Report of Surveyor-General on Dominion Lands for 1873–4, in Annual Report of the Department of the Interior, 1873–4, in *Sessional Papers*, 1875, vol. vii, p. 7.

[2] Annual Report of the Department of the Interior, 1874–5, Part I, Dominion Lands, p. 20, in *Sessional Papers*, 1876, vol. vii.

[3] Annual Report of the Department of the Interior, 1892, p. xxxi in *Sessional Papers*, 1893, vol. viii.

and about two acres in the village is allotted to each person on which to erect houses and stables and make a garden. The balance of the tract is then divided into three portions— land for cultivation, land for hay cutting, and land for grazing . . . the land for ploughing and hay cutting is sub-divided into long narrow strips, and the ' Schulz ' or headman of the village gives to each villager the strip of land he is to cultivate, and the strip upon which he is to cut hay, with both of which he has to be satisfied. The cattle of the village are herded in common." [1] This system of communal tenure and communal control of the land lasted until 1890, after which it began to break up. By 1900 it had disappeared, and the Mennonites were holding their lands on an individual tenure.[2] It appears that though communal methods were an initial advantage to settlement, yet ultimately the system became a drag on progress. " The fact that they are all bound to submit to the direction of the ' Schulz ', that they are compelled to accept the strips of land apportioned to them, whether their neighbours on either side are poor farmers who allow their ploughed lands to grow up in weeds or the reverse, and that the quantity of land is limited to this strip, without regard to the means, the industry, or the economy of the village, more than counterbalances the advantages referred to." [3] The Mennonite settlers in the North-West numbered 6,000,[4] and they have always been welcome. One member of the Dominion Legislature " knew from experience there is no class of settlers more desirable than those very Mennonites. They were a most industrious, thrifty, and honest people, and made the very best settlers ". It had been objected that they had been exempted from bearing arms. " It was because they wished for such an exemption that they had emigrated from Europe, and they had a special agreement with our Government securing to them that privilege ".[5]

---

[1] Report on the Dufferin Mennonite Reserve, 14th December, 1883, by Geo. Newcomb, in Annual Report of the Department of the Interior, 1883, Part I, Dominion Lands, p. 13, in *Sessional Papers*, 1884, vol. vii, Sec. 32 of 46 Vic. cap. 17, provided that homestead settlers embracing not less than twenty families might be permitted to settle together in a hamlet or village.

[2] *C.P.*, vol. xx, p. 296.

[3] Report on the Dufferin Mennonite Reserve, 14th December, 1883, by Geo. Newcomb, in Annual Report of the Department of the Interior, 1883, Part I, Dominion Lands, p. 14, in *Sessional Papers*, 1884, vol. 7.

[4] *C.P.*, vol. xx, p. 295.

[5] *Dominion Debates*, 1876, p. 1173.

This being so, it is not surprising to find it recorded in 1876 that there had not been a single case of disorder among them since they came to the country.[1] As to their industry and competency, Lord Dufferin, when Governor General, described how when visiting the Mennonite settlement which had been founded only two years previously he " passed village after village, homestead after homestead, furnished with all the conveniences and incidents of European comfort and a scientific agriculture, while on either side of the road cornfields already ripe for harvest and pastures populous with herds of cattle stretched away to the horizon ".[2]

In 1875 commenced the Icelandic immigration into the North-West. They did not come in companies as did the Mennonites, but continued to arrive in Canada in varying volume over a long series of years. In the case of the Icelanders, the community bond was not so much religious as national and lingual. They had left Iceland on account of the economic pinch, not on account of religious persecution. They had less capital than the Mennonites, and were less progressive settlers. Being half-fishermen, they generally settled near some lake where they could pursue their twin avocations. The first 300 established themselves on the west shore of Lake Winnipeg. The plan of settlement was that of long narrow villages close to and parallel with the shore for the purpose of fishing, while their farming and pasture lands were to lie behind the villages. A report of 1883 related that preoccupation with fishing had hindered the clearing of the land. In 1883 there were one hundred families spread along fifty miles of shore.[3] Ten years later it was reported that there were 10,000 Icelanders in the North-West, but of that number 4,000 were reckoned as living in towns.[4] The influx from Iceland in 1893 numbered 730, and some financial assistance had been given by the Manitoba Government to some of the immigrants who could not pay their own passages.[5] By 1898, Icelanders

---

[1] *Dominion Debates*, 1876, p. 1174.
[2] Speech at Winnipeg, August, 1877, quoted J. Macoun, *Manitoba and the Great North-West*, p.514.
[3] Report on the Icelandic Reserve, 8th December, 1883, by Geo. Newcomb, in Annual Report of the Department of the Interior, 1883, Part I, Dominion Lands, pp. 14–16, in *Sessional Papers*, 1884, vol. vii.
[4] Annual Report of the Department of the Interior, 1893, Part I, Dominion Lands, p. 8, in *Sessional Papers*, 1894, vol. x.
[5] Annual Report of the Department of the Interior, 1893, p. xlii, in *Sessional Papers*, 1894, vol. x.

were finding it still more difficult to muster the sufficient funds for emigration. This was due to two facts. Icelandic farmers had lost their market in England for their sheep by an English Act of Parliament, and money was scarce in Iceland. In addition, the steamship fares had been raised from 26 to 42 dollars as the result of the formation of a conference amongst the shipping lines.[1] The Icelanders acquired the English tongue with ease, and readily harmonized with Canadian institutions, but the Icelandic settlements were not so successful as some others, chiefly because of the poverty and inexperience of the settlers. As Lord Dufferin, the Governor-General, pointed out, " In Iceland there are neither trees, nor cornfields, nor highways. You cannot, therefore, expect an Icelander to exhibit an inspired proficiency in felling timber, ploughing land, or making roads, yet these are the three accomplishments most necessary to a colonist in Canada." [2]

Immigration had perceptibly quickened during the later 'seventies, a circumstance largely due to the fact that the railway from Eastern Canada had reached Winnipeg in 1879, and the journey which formerly took three weeks now lasted only fourteen hours. The isolation of the North-West was at an end. By 1879 settlement had spread 250 miles into the prairies west of Winnipeg.[3] In the 'eighties the tide of immigration into the North-West broadened and deepened. Scottish crofters and English paupers helped to swell the numbers, and after 1882, when the first efforts were made by the Dominion Government and the Canadian Pacific Railway Company to advertise the North-West in eastern Europe, the number of European settlers rapidly increased.

The Scottish crofters who emigrated were really paupers, and all were assisted to emigrate and to settle. They left Scotland because they were threatened with destitution as a consequence of the depression in the herring fishing industry and the collapse of cattle prices.[4] The money was generally found by philanthropic gentry, though in one case important aid was rendered by a grant from the

---

[1] Annual Report of the Department of the Interior, 1898, p. 236, Part II, Immigration, in *Sessional Papers*, 1899, vol. ii.

[2] Speech at Winnipeg, August, 1877, quoted J. Macoun, *Manitoba and the Great North-West*, p. 516.

[3] A. Begg, cited *C.P.*, vol. xix, p. 110.

[4] Report on the condition of the Cottar Population in the Lews, *Parly. Papers*, 1888, vol. lxxx, pp. 644–5.

Imperial Government. Sir James Rankin launched his colonization scheme in 1882. He bought 19,200 acres from the Canadian Pacific Railway Company and prepared farms for his colonists. Each farm had " a good frame house, a stable, and rough shed, horses or oxen, necessary agricultural implements, a well, and some twenty acres of ploughing done to start with and seed corn ". He sent out 130 emigrants in 1882–3, and some of them became his tenants on the half-crop system, but the bulk preferred to work for wages. The emigrants received over £770 by way of aid, but repaid only £59, although they had agreed to repay the full sum. Some went beyond the reach of his agent, and Sir James sadly confessed that " a distance of 5,000 miles somewhat dims the acuteness of conscience as far as debts are concerned ". Gradually his tenants bought their farms on the ten years' payment by instalments system, and the payment of crop rents, which had fluctuated widely, ceased. Summing up, Sir James said that the emigrants sent out "seem to have done fairly well for themselves, but not as farmers ".[1] In 1883, Lady Gordon Cathcart sent out to the North-West a few crofters at her own charges.[2] Later on this colony, known as the Benbecula Settlement, was reported to be doing well,[3] but as in the other case, they repaid nothing of the loans that had been advanced them. Twenty years afterwards a visitor to the settlement reported that " one man I saw rather resented the idea that he ought to pay it ; he thought he had quite done his duty in going out—that he was, in fact, more a creditor than a debtor ".[4] In 1887 Sir John Lister-Kaye initiated a colonization scheme which was, however, more akin to a plain emigration scheme than the others. He took over the property of the Canadian Agricultural Coal and Colonization Company, purchasing 105,000 acres and leasing 85,000 acres for grazing, the property being " completely equipped with farm buildings and agricultural implements " and stocked with 20,000 sheep, 8,000 cattle, and 500 mares. The emigrants selected were " engaged for one year's labour in Canada ", and their passage to the North-West was defrayed by Sir John in

[1] Memorandum by Sir James Rankin on his Colonization Scheme initiated in 1882, in *Cd*. 2979, p. 324.
[2] Report of Commission on Highland Crofters, 1884, in *Parly. Papers*, 1884, vol. xxxii, p. 105.
[3] Ronald Macdonald, Evidence before the Crofter Commission, in *Parly. Papers*, vol. xxxiii, 1884, pp. 770–1.
[4] W. Paton, Q. 1080, *Cd*., 2979.

return. No numbers are given and the subsequent history of the settlement is unchronicled.[1] The quasi-Governmental scheme of crofter settlement was controlled by a body of Commissioners under the Marquis of Lothian, who reported annually to Parliament. £13,120 was voted by Parliament, and £2,000 was raised by private subscription.[2] Two settlements were planted, one at Killarney in 1888, and a second at Saltcoats in 1889. While the settlement at Killarney was fairly successful, 24 crofters out of 30 repaying the Board of Commissioners in full, the Saltcoats settlement was an unmitigated failure, 71 out of the original 72 crofters abandoning their holdings. Most of the Saltcoats crofters went off to work for wages at the lumber mills.[3] One reason for the success of the Killarney settlement was that the crofters were not planted in a solid block, but were scattered amongst seasoned farmers, whereby "they could get advice and assistance and counsel when they required it."[4] They had also been able to earn good wages, working for the neighbouring farmers during their first year. Each crofter settler, according to the Memorandum of Arrangements, was to receive 160 acres of land free and in addition an advance of £120, which was to bear no interest for the first four years and was then to be redeemed in the succeeding eight years by an annuity of £20 17s. 8d., the interest averaging out at 4·6 per cent per annum over the twelve

[1] Memorandum by Sir John Lister-Kaye on his Colonization Scheme nitiated in 1887, in *Cd*. 2979, p. 322.

[2] Fifteenth Report on Crofter Colonization, 1906, *Cd*. 3145, p. 2. Also: "That the Board constituted as above will undertake by means of their agents, to settle the emigrants on the Government land, to provide temporarily for their wants, and to collect the instalments of capital and interest from them in the manner hereinafter mentioned, they having the benefit of the knowledge and experience both of the Canadian Government Land Agents and of the gratuitous co-operation of the officers of the Canadian Pacific Railway, the Hudson's Bay Company, and the Canadian North-West Land Company. That the Canadian Government will give free grant lands of 160 acres to each family. . . . That the foregoing Board will take by way of security for the sum of £120, or lesser sum so advanced, a mortgage on the 160 acres of free grant lands of the Dominion Government, including a lien on the chattels, the mortgage being secured in favour of the Board by legal agreement."—Crofter and Cottar Colonization Scheme ; Memorandum of Arrangements in *Parly. Papers*, 1888, vol. lxxx, p. 296. The Imperial Government was chary of direct State colonization. The Report of the Departmental Committee on agricultural settlements in British Colonies of 1906 said : "Thus, whether we turn to Canada, South Africa, or Australia, we fail to find an instance of a thoroughly successful effort at Colonization " [*Cd*. 2978], p. 5.

[3] J. G. Colmer, ibid., *Minutes of Evidence* [*Cd*. 2979], Q. 5369.

[4] J. G. Colmer, ibid., Q. 5340.

years.[1] The sum of £120 was found to be insufficient for
the Saltcoats settlers, and in 1890 it was increased to
£148 12s.[2] Further aid was rendered to the Killarney
settlers by the Canada North-West Land Company to the
extent of several hundred dollars.[3] All these advances were
covered by mortgages and liens on the farms, stock, and
implements possessed by the settlers. One reason for the
failure of the Saltcoats settlers was that they purchased
expensive machinery from private agents. They could
neither use the machinery nor pay for it, and so became
more and more financially involved.[4] In 1906 it was
reported that repayments made or prospective amounted
to £16,713, but unfortunately a good deal of the money
had been recovered by the selling up of the farms of
insolvent or absconding settlers, especially at Saltcoats,
where the crofters had been " led away by bad advice "
and " preferred to work for other people at weekly wages
rather than to persevere in their new life ".[5]

An effort by the Canadian Pacific Railway Company to
induce the Imperial Government to make an advance of
£1,000,000 for the emigration of 50,000 Irish paupers to a
colony in the North-West having failed, the Company
turned for emigrants to Eastern Europe.[6] However, other
paupers were brought out from England by private charities.
One example of many such was the London Colonization
Aid Society, which about 1880 sent out settlers from the
East End to Moosamin, also called the Baroness Burdett
Coutts Colony. There was scarcely any repayment of
advances, the emigrants preferring to leave the land and
slip into town occupations after having received a free
passage to Canada.[7] More important were the settlements
in the North-West of eastern Europeans during the 'eighties.
The Dominion Government and the railway and shipping
companies were the prime movers in advertising the country.
No advances were made to emigrants, but sometimes cheap

---

[1] Crofter and Cottar Colonization Scheme : Memorandum of Arrangements, in *Parly. Papers*, 1888, vol. lxxx, p. 296.
[2] Report of Commissioners of Colonization in Canada of Crofters and
Cottars, 1890, in *Parly. Papers*, 1890, vol. xxvii, p. 244.
[3] Ibid., p. 248.
[4] Report on Immigration by Professor James Mavor, p. 234, in Annual
Report of the Department of the Interior, 1899, in *Sessional Papers*,
1900, vol. x.
[5] Fifteenth Report on Crofter Colonization, 1906, *Cd.* 3145, p. 3.
[6] *C.P.*, vol. xx, p. 302.
[7] W. Paton, Q. 1080 ; also Qq. 252–6, *Cd.* 2979.

rates were given on the steamers and railways and the Government would sometimes make advances of seed grain, repayment of which was expected.

A new factor in the settlement of the prairies in the 'eighties was the rise of colonization companies resembling the old Canada Land Company and the British American Land Company. During the land boom twenty-six Colonization Companies came into being, controlling 2,973,978 acres of land. Those Colonization Companies spent considerable money in the North-West, and helped to open it up to settlement. " With the view of making their colonies as attractive as possible, most of the Companies are, at their own expense, furnishing their settlers with many necessary conveniences, such as saw and grist mills, stores, blacksmith and carpenters' shops, stage communication, and postal facilities where the regular departmental mail service has not already been established. They are also introducing superior qualities of seed grain, thoroughbred and well-graded live stock, and the most improved implements of husbandry, which it is said they offer at fair prices." [1] By 1886, most of the colonization companies had fallen into financial straits, and " by Order in Council of the 30th June, 1886, the machinery was provided by which the contracts of the various colonization companies with the Government might be terminated and their agreements returned to the Department of the Interior for cancellation ".[2]

By the efforts of the Dominion Government, the Colonization Companies, the Canadian Pacific Railway Company, which was one of the largest landowners in the country and a most successful recruiter of immigrants, by individual initiative and co-operative enterprise, the stream of immigration into Canada was more and more directed towards the North-West, so much so that in 1892 the immigration service was placed under the Department of the Interior which had to do with the settlement of the North-West, since " the tendency of immigration has of recent years been so largely in the direction of the immense agricultural areas of Manitoba and the North-West Territories." [3] In 1892 a large number of foreign colonies were there, forming more or less

---

[1] Annual Report of the Department of the Interior, 1883, p. xiii, in *Sessional Papers*, 1884, vol. 7.

[2] Annual Report of the Department of the Interior, 1886, p. xxxvi, *Sessional Papers*, 1887, vol. 6.

[3] Annual Report of the Department of the Interior, 1892, p. x, *Sessional Papers*, 1893, vol. 8.

homogeneous units. The most numerous were German, Icelandic, Norwegian, Swedish, and Danish, but there were also French, Belgian, Mennonite, and Austrian colonies. There was also a Mormon settlement in Alberta numbering 1,000, the members of which were described as " singularly economical, ingenious and progressive ". According to the Winnipeg Commissioner of Dominion Lands,[1] the Mormons, who had settled in Alberta in 1887, were " a very industrious, enterprising, and apparently well-to-do class of settler, who seem to be content to submit to the laws of the country and in nowise disposed to attempt the practice of polygamy ". It was also felt that since they had been able to live within their resources economically and to develop a condition of high cultivation from the uninviting and arid soil of Utah, their success in the Canadian North-West should be assured; while their experience of irrigation in the barren country whence they came was considered to promise considerable benefit to the other settlers along the foothills of the Rocky Mountains. This was all the work of ten years, since " in 1882 there were, outside the Mennonites and Icelanders, scarcely a hundred foreign settlers throughout the North-West ".[2] By 1898, some 5,000 Scandinavians and 15,360 Germans were there.[3]

Down to 1887 the statistics of homestead entries in the Canadian North-West are not particularly impressive. In 1874 there were 1,376 homestead entries ; in 1882 the number was 7,383 ; in 1887 it had dropped to 2,036. Moreover, a heavy percentage of such entries were afterwards cancelled, some because they had been merely speculative entries at the outset, others because the settlers had become dispirited by a series of misfortunes, among which the frosts of 1883 and 1884, and the rebellion of 1885, were prominent. Prairie fires were a constant anxiety, especially in the vicinity of railways. Of the 1788 homestead entries in 1878, no less than 1,193 had been cancelled by 1887.[4] Canada was but repeating the experience of the United

[1] Annual Report of the Department of the Interior, 1887, *Sessional Papers*, 1888, vol. 12.

[2] Annual Report of the Department of the Interior, 1893, Part III, Immigration, p. 39, in *Sessional Papers*, 1894, vol. 10.

[3] Annual Report of the Department of the Interior, 1899, Part II, Immigration, pp. 113–14, in *Sessional Papers*, 1900, vol. 10.

[4] Annual Report of Department of the Interior for 1887, *Sessional Papers*, Canada, 1888, vol. 12, p. xii.

States. Thus in Nebraska and Kansas, of the homestead entries during the years 1885, 1886, and 1887, only 40 per cent were perfected by actual residence and cultivation.[1] In the 'nineties, however, large new sources of immigrant settlers were tapped. These were principally the Americans, the Ruthenians and the Doukhobors.

The genesis of American immigration is usually dated 1897, as a result of the vigorous immigration propaganda then inaugurated by Clifford Sifton, Minister of the Interior, but before then Americans had begun to cross the boundary line on the prairies. As early as 1883 it was reported that many Americans and ex-Canadians from Dakota, Nebraska, Montana, Idaho, and Washington had settled in the North-West.[2] After 1840, the opening up of the prairie States of the American Union began to deflect the flow of immigration from British North America to the Republic. By 1880, however, the best available lands of Ohio, Illinois, Indiana, Missouri and Wisconsin had become largely taken up : Iowa and Minnesota were also rapidly filling ; and it became apparent that for area, fertility and availability the Canadian North-West must be the next great territory to attract population.[3] Moreover, as their holdings in Iowa, Nebraska, Minnesota, and the Dakotas became valuable, Americans began to sell them and to move to the cheap or free lands which the Canadian North-West offered them.

Nevertheless, the story of Canadian immigration continues to chronicle the arrival of foreigners rather than British for the sufficient reason that between 1891 and 1900 British emigrants were attracted to the United States, where the conditions of life approximated to the life to which they had become accustomed, rather than to Canada where they were offered the life of the pioneer with its primitive conditions. " Between 1891 and 1900, 726,000 persons emigrated from the United Kingdom, of which 520,000 (or 72 per cent) went to the United States ; 90,000 (or

---

[1] Ibid., p. xiii.

[2] Annual Report of the Department of the Interior, 1883, Part I, Dominion Lands, p. 5, in *Sessional Papers*, 1884, vol. 7.

[3] If emigration from the United Kingdom alone is considered, of 983,227 emigrants who left Great Britain and Ireland in the period 1815–40, rather more than half, namely 499,899 went to British North America. In the same period 417,765 went to the United States. Afterwards far larger numbers went annually to the United States than to Canada. (See S. C. Johnson, *Emigration from the United Kingdom to North America*, p. 16 and appendix I).

13 per cent) to British North America. . . ." [1] British emigrants, educated largely at the public expense, and trained in British technical schools and factories, transferred their allegiance and their industrial knowledge and ability to Canada's great rival, and Canada herself had to look to alien races for that increment to her population which was necessary if her great vacant spaces were to be filled.

The methods of the emigration agents of the High Commissioner for Canada during the 'nineties will be recalled by many still alive in Great Britain. There were the lantern lectures in the village hall describing the glories of the Dominion. Insidious and plausible persons got into conversation with farmers and farmer's sons and farm workers at country fairs and markets. Advertisements about Canada were a fruitful source of income to provincial newspapers. Pamphlets were circulated broadcast. The Steamship Companies were encouraged to advertise ; and the Post Offices were decorated with pictures of palatial liners traversing the wavelets of a turquoise and emerald Atlantic.

It all had a strikingly small effect on the English countryman. The farming class in the United Kingdom was comparatively small, and it was conservative in its habits and disinclined to move. Farmers did not care for it to be known that they were considering or even talking about emigration, and the emigration agent's company was accordingly rather shunned. And as often as not those who did decide on emigration fell victims to the superior attractions of the American as compared with the St. Lawrence route, and it could be taken for granted that the agents of the New York lines did not go out of their way to encourage the emigrant to go to the Canadian North-West or British Columbia.

But for the attraction of the virgin lands to the American agriculturalist, the drift from the United States across the northern border would be of quite minor importance. During the period 1903–4 to 1909–10, of 403,401 immigrants into Canada from the United States, 261,409 or 65 per cent were farmers or farm labourers. During the same period,

---

[1] Hon. G. W. Ross, Premier of Ontario, in letter to *The Times*, 9th September, 1901, quoted in Annual Report, Department of the Interior for 1900–1, Immigration, p. 12, *Sessional Papers*, 1902, The Canadian Emigration Agent in Ireland gave " the prepaid passages to the United States and the free and assisted passages to Queensland " as one of the difficulties (ibid., p. 38).

805,387 immigrants entered Canada through her ocean ports, mainly from Europe, and of this total those classed as farmers and farm labourers numbered 225,168 or 28 per cent. To the American mechanic, or even general labourer, Canada has little to offer, and for domestic assistance the Canadian housewife must rely almost entirely on immigration from Europe.[1]

In 1887–8 Canadians who had emigrated to the American west began to show a tendency to repatriate themselves. In particular, Dakota was found inhospitable. It suffered from frequent and fatal blizzards in winter, and was subject to visits from cyclones in summer. Moreover, timber was so scarce there that systematic stealing from the public lands on the Canadian side of the boundary was resorted to until, in the end, finding that " the destruction of timber by Dakota settlers had been enormous, in addition to which there was extensive smuggling and other evasions of our laws ", the Canadian authorities had to intervene, and a detachment of the North-West Mounted Police was " detailed to round up timber thieves and smugglers and generally to maintain law and order on the frontier ".[2] By 1893, Canadian emigration to the American prairies was showing signs of cessation.[3]

In the five years, 1897–1901, of the total immigration into Canada, the British Isles and the United States each contributed 29 per cent.[4] If the number of Homestead

---

[1] The Department of the Interior supplies the following figures in respect of the period referred to. (See *Canada : Pamphlets*, vol. 7, No. 198, in D.O & C.O. Library.)

	From United States.	Via Ocean Ports.
Farmers and farm labourers	261,409	225,168
General labourers	35,762	201,518
Mechanics	22,900	195,708
Clerks, traders, etc.	12,457	53,490
Miners	5,940	22,463
Domestics	1,242	45,199

[2] Annual Report of the Department of the Interior, 1888, *Sessional Papers*, 1889, p. xxv.

[3] Annual Report of the Department of the Interior, 1893, p. xi, in *Sessional Papers*, 1894, vol. 10. During the year 1913, there left Western Canada, declaring themselves Canadian settlers by birth or naturalization, and intending to reside permanently in the United States, 6,110 persons. During the same period there arrived in Western Canada, through the same places, from the United States, 59,559 persons declaring their intention to become citizens of the Dominion of Canada. Dominions Royal Commission, 1916 : Evidence of J. B. Walker, Commissioner of Immigration [*Cd.* 8458], p. 51.

[4] Annual Report of the Department of the Interior, 1900–1, p. xix, in *Sessional Papers*, 1902, vol. 10.

Entries be taken as the basis of comparison, in 1901 for the first time Americans headed the list by contributing 25 per cent of the North-West settlers, Ontario affording 20 per cent, and England only 8 per cent, and ever since then the United States has headed the list of nationalities making Homestead Entries.[1] It was also well known that American settlers were the chief purchasers of the large areas of land sold by the Canadian Pacific Railway and other companies. After 1901 the "American Invasion" continued and intensified, and before the War the Prairie Provinces contained 100,000 families of the best type.[2] These settlers, many of them "professional homesteaders" moving from State to State, generally had capital and experience of prairie farming. The statement has been placed on record by the Canadian Minister of the Interior that the arrivals from the United States who made homestead entry in the Western Provinces brought with them in one year alone, namely, the fiscal year 1907–8, more than $52,000,000 in cash and settlers' effects.[3] They therefore needed no Government assistance as to settlement or as to farming methods. Instead they were of assistance to poor and inexperienced settlers by giving them work on their farms, some of which were from 2,000 to 4,000 acres, and thus, by teaching them farming practice, helped to people the prairies successfully.

A curious incident in the outward flow of population occurred in 1896, when a number of residents of the province of Quebec were induced to emigrate to Brazil. The Brazilian agents who promoted the movement worked so energetically and yet so secretly that nearly a thousand people had been involved before the Canadian Government

---

[1] Statistics of Homestead Entries in the Western Provinces according to Nationalities are given from 1892 onwards in the Annual Reports of the Department of the Interior. The following figures are from that source, but they do not take into account the thousands of farmers, farm labourers, and domestic servants who settled in other parts of the Dominion. The average number of persons for each entry is 2·5.

	Ontario.	U.S.	England.	Total.
1900 .	. 1,887	1,307	639	7,426
1901 .	. 1,606	2,026	659	8,167
1902 .	. 2,583	4,761	1,096	14,673
1903 .	. 4,033	10,942	2,816	31,383
1904 .	. 3,692	7,730	3,486	26,073
1905 .	. 4,885	8,532	4,284	30,819

[2] C.P., vol. xx, p. 309.

[3] Immigration Facts and Figures, Ministry of the Interior, Ottawa, 1911 (Canada : Pamphlets, vol. 7, No. 198, in D.O. & C.O. Library).

could take any steps to arrest the outward movement. In the end more than half were successfully turned aside from their purpose, but of the four hundred or so who actually embarked for Brazil, " all were disappointed in their expectations and many of them had to be brought back in a dire state of poverty and distress at the expense of the government of Canada." [1] A few years later South America also became a competitor with Canada for the emigrants from Central Europe, in particular from Germany and Austria. Whereas formerly the European continental governments put every obstacle in the way of the emigration of their subjects, they now, in some measure, reversed that policy, permitting emigration to countries in which they were commercially interested.[2]

The Ruthenians, also called Galicians, began to enter the North-West in 1895, and they flowed in so steadily year after year that in 1901 they numbered no less than 26,000.[3] They were induced to leave their own country by pressure of economic circumstances. "The congestion of population on the Galician plain resulted in depression of wages for agricultural labour and in the rise of rents for the peasants' holdings. An active propaganda carried on by the railways and steamship companies informed the Galician peasants of the existence of no-rent lands in the Canadian West, and the offer of extremely low rates for transport to these lands induced them to embark for them." [4] In all the Galician settlers numbered 40,000. Their manner of life was very simple, their demands were few, they could work hard, and thus they tided over the difficulties inseparable from the lot of penniless settlers. A contemporary reported that the Ruthenians " dig a hole in the ground and roof it over and live there for a year and save everything ", and that they " get flour and live upon the flour and tea ".[5] Any seed lent by the Dominion Government was secured by a lien on the settler's farm, and the interest charged was 6 per cent.[6] The Ruthenians also worked on the railway, laboured for wealthier settlers,

[1] Annual Report of Department of the Interior for 1896 (*Sessional Papers*, Canada, 1897), p. xxxviii.
[2] Ditto, for 1900–1 (*Sessions Papers*, Canada, 1902), Immigration, p. 14.
[3] *C.P.*, vol. xx, pp. 304–5.
[4] J. Mavor, *My Windows on the Streets of the World*, vol. i, p. 366.
[5] J. Mavor, Q. 717, *Cd.* 2979.
[6] Annual Report of the Department of the Interior, 1899, p. xxi, in *Sessional Papers*, 1900, vol. 10.

toiled at lumber camps and timber mills, and thereby earned the money to plant themselves upon the land. In addition, the Ruthenians succeeded in establishing a system of co-operative credit. This system was made possible by the absolute trustworthiness of the Ruthenians or Galicians. " The system of co-operative credit organized by the Galicians was very simple. When a Galician was ready to begin work upon his homestead, he obtained the signature of forty or fifty of his friends who were already established. These signatures on a folio sheet of paper were appended to a note for one or two hundred dollars, drawn at three or four months. Such notes were readily accepted by the banks. They were discounted and the produce employed for the purchase of seed. . . . The implement makers also accepted these joint notes for machinery, and the merchants for supplies, and thus by means of frugality and punctuality on the one hand, and credit on the other hand, Galicians immigrating without means quickly established them-selves. I was told by bankers that the notes of the Galicians were always met." [1] By the 'nineties, private credit organiza-tions were established in the North-West, superseding the only former givers of credit, the Dominion Government, and land settlement companies like the Hudson's Bay Company. In other words, the credit resources of old settled lands had been organized and put at the disposal of trustworthy borrowers. This cheap capital, and the fact that the Ruthenians were both industrious and thrifty, needed to buy little, combined to conduct the Ruthenians to early and permanent success. If all other settlers in the North-West had been similarly trustworthy and thrifty, and if they had evolved such a system of credit, the settle-ment of the North-West would have proceeded much more rapidly and successfully than actually was the case. The Ruthenians were at first very unpopular. They were accused of being paupers and of being turbulent. In the end they proved themselves to be very valuable settlers. " They were placed largely on second-class land, scrubby in character, which the homesteaders from the United States or Eastern Canada passed by, and they at once proceeded to make comfortable homes for themselves." [2]

---

[1] J. Mavor, *My Windows on the Streets of the World*, vol. i pp. 366–7.

[2] *C.P.*, vol. xx, p. 305. See also Aylmer Maude, *A Peculiar People : The Doukhobors*, p. 51.

In 1899, a ready made system of communism was introduced with the great immigration of Doukhobors into the North-West, where, by the end of 1899, their total number was 7,400.[1] Their name means " Spirit-Wrestlers ", and in many ways they resembled the Mennonites. They left Russia in order to escape persecution at the hands of the Russian Government for their refusal to bear arms. Their expenses of migration and settlement were met partly by themselves and partly by means of loans and aid from other sources. At the commencement they raised an immigration fund of 29,000 dollars, and the first two parties that left for Canada, to the number of 4,000, possessed private means amounting to 45,000 dollars.[2] In addition, they were helped by the Society of Friends in the United States, who spent considerable time and money in assisting them to settle down. Still more important was the bonus money paid to the Doukhobors by the Dominion Government. This bonus per head of immigrants had been customarily paid to immigration agents, and to shipping companies and to others who organized immigration. " Since the committee by which the Doukhobor immigration was managed refused to accept any remuneration, this capitation commission, amounting to about 50,000 dollars (£10,000), was available for the expenses of settlement in addition to the resources of the Doukhobors themselves." [3] In addition to such subsidies and aids, the Doukhobors worked as manual labourers after their arrival, and earned extra money to help tide them over the first winter. Many worked on the railways which were then in course of construction in the North-West. Others scattered themselves over Canada and worked on farms. So great was this drain of men away from the Doukhobor settlements that the women were left to do the primary work of settlement. "Almost all the villages were built by the Doukhobor women. Lacking horses, the women also ploughed the land by harnessing themselves, twelve pairs of women to a plough,

---

[1] Annual Report of the Department of the Interior, 1899, p. xvii, in Sessional Papers, 1900, vol. 10.
[2] Annual Report of the Department of the Interior, 1898, p. xi, in Sessional Papers, 1899, vol. ii.
[3] J. Mavor, My Windows on the Streets of the World, vol. 2, p. 4. Aylmer Maude, A Peculiar People : The Doukhobors, p. 48. Annual Report of the Department of the Interior, 1898, p. xi, in Sessional Papers, 1899, vol. ii. Mavor says the bonus was 7 dollars 50 cents per head; Maude and the Report say it was £1 per head.

with one ploughman to drive them."[1] Finally, their settlement was facilitated by the fact that the Doukhobors lived a very self-sufficing life, bought little from the outside world, and therefore did not require much cash before they could make a living. Instead of importing bricks, they made them of clay in the neighbourhood, and instead of buying spades they made them themselves from iron bars, using charcoal of their own manufacture.[2] Shortly afterwards it was further reported : " The Doukhobors . . . are now building windmills to make their own flour. The domestic arts survive amongst them, such as weaving, for which they made their own looms. The villages are all now self-supporting, and will have grain and cattle to sell this fall."[3] That was two years after first settlement in the North-West. By 1902 they had begun to repay their debts.[4]

The Doukhobors held their land on a communal basis, a system which did not fit into the Canadian settlement system conveniently. The Dominion Government wished the grants to be the usual homesteads of 160 acres, but the Doukhobors refused to accept individual holdings and finally obtained their desire, the land being transferred to them in bulk.[5] During the first few years, however, there was a constant drift towards individualism, which was only stemmed with the arrival in 1903 of Peter Veregin, the Doukhobor's leader. Before then the Prince Albert Colony of Doukhobors was said to be rather individualistic, not holding their land in common, and only co-operating to a small degree with their fellow-countrymen in the north and south colonies.[6] Veregin, dominating the whole with his own remarkable personality, not only intensified the communalism of the Doukhobor settlers but rendered it much more efficient. " He gave their business affairs a legal status by forming the Doukhobor Trading Company, arranged credits, made large purchases of horses, cattle, and agricultural machinery, even introduced steam-engines, and generally infused intelligent activity into the whole

---

[1] A. Maude, pp. 180–1.
[2] Report on Immigration by Professor James Mavor, p. 233, footnote, in Annual Report of the Department of the Interior, 1899, in *Sessional Papers*, 1900, vol. 10.
[3] Annual Report of the Department of the Interior, 1900, part ii, Immigration, p. 120, in *Sessional Papers*, 1901, vol. 10.
[4] A. Maude, p. 181.   [5] *C.P.*, vol. xx, p. 305.
[6] J. Mavor, cited by A. Maude, p. 257.

enterprise."[1] Professor Mavor, on his visit, found that the practice of communism within the country was very simple. " All produce went into the common stock. The Doukhobor wheat all went to the Doukhobor elevators, the Doukhobor cattle were sold and the proceeds were deposited to the account of the Doukhobor Trading Company. Purchases of leather, textiles, tea, sugar, etc., were made wholesale, and these commodities were placed in the Doukhobor stores for delivery as demanded by the households requiring them. So far as I am aware, the spirit of the people was in general such that everyone worked as hard as he could and made no effort to dispose fraudulently of goods which he might obtain or demand from the Doukhobor stores. Yet by some means the people had small sums of money in their possession. I am not aware how they obtained these sums, probably it was found to be wise not to be too meticulous in demanding of the men working outside of the community the whole of the balance of their wages in excess of their own subsistence."[2] So far as the system of communalism was concerned, Professor Mavor estimated that about 20 per cent of the Doukhobors had become individualized, while 80 per cent were still living on a communal basis.[3] The internal organization of the Doukhobors was that of the village, each under its head man, while all the village heads again were under the supreme control of Veregin. So wealthy did the Doukhobors become that Veregin purchased on their behalf a large tract of land near Nelson in British Columbia, and thither half of the Doukhobors migrated. They became very successful fruit-farmers in the mild climate of the Pacific Coast, and during the War presented a great deal of jam to the troops.

The next group settlement after the Doukhobors was in methods and results in strong contrast with its predecessor. This settlement, the Barr Colony, was purely English, lacked almost all experience of farming and especially of prairie farming, possessed capital, had a very hard up-hill fight, and was at first, at any rate, rather a failure. It was organized in the first instance by a clergyman, named Barr, of the Church of England, who had some experience of Canadian conditions round about the year 1902. Barr

---

[1] J. Mavor, vol. 2, p. 24.
[2] Ibid., p. 31.   [3] Ibid.

advertised for settlers in England to form an " all-British colony ", which was to be " away from Canadian and foreign influences ".[1] So ignorant were the Barr colonists that they lost £4,000 to £5,000 worth of animals in the winter of 1903–4 due to " sheer ignorance " and " pre-occupation in social affairs ".[2] They simply starved these horses and cattle to death.[3] The settlers were at first too occupied with " the lawn tennis, the rifle range, the arsenal, the operatic societies, etc." ;[4] but afterwards, as their money disappeared, they settled down to the hard life of pioneers. So great were the hardships and so virulent were the complaints, that in May, 1903, Barr resigned, and was succeeded by another clergyman, named Lloyd, who united " the functions of spiritual guide, political administrator, and commercial agent, which Mr. Barr had exercised ".[5] Out of 2,100 expected homesteaders, only 299 effective home-steaders were settled in the colony by June, 1904, while others settled outside on homesteads to the number of 274.[6] The settlement was not compact, as Barr had planned, but was scattered, partly as a result of the Canadian Pacific Railway Company and the Hudson's Bay Company claims to sections of the land, and partly of the Dominion Government's policy which aimed at providing that experienced farmers should be at hand to render help to inexperienced settlers. Finally, on account of this very mixing, the aim of forming an " all-British Colony " was defeated, and Lloydminster, as the chief town was called, soon became penetrated through and through with the dreaded Canadian influences.[7]

The early failure of the Barr Colony may be ascribed largely to inexperience, lack of adaptability, thriftlessness, and individualism of the settlers. Another important factor was the isolation of the settlement in the early years. It was at first 100 miles from the nearest settlement and 200 miles from the railway. In August, 1905, the Canadian Northern Railway reached Lloydminster and by the autumn it had been carried on another 200 miles to Edmonton. Railway construction caused demand for oats to feed the horses, and for wheat to feed the men, and also caused a

---

[1] Memorandum on Barr Colony by Professor James Mavor, 8th December, 1905, in *Cd.* 2979, p. 283.

[2] Ibid., p. 288.   [3] J. Mavor, Q. 446, *Cd.* 2979.

[4] *Mavor Memorandum*, p. 291.   [5] *Mavor Memorandum*, p. 287.

[6] Ibid., p. 288.   [7] Ibid., p. 290.

demand for labourers. The Barr Colonists thereupon obtained good prices for their crops, but proved themselves inefficient labourers.[1] More important still was the fact that the railway gave the settlers access to the world market with their products. "When the first locomotive came within sight of Lloydminster the Barr Colonists 'sang and wept for joy'".[2] Many far-out settlers refused to believe that the railway had actually arrived, and they had to travel in with their slow-moving oxen and touch the rails for themselves before they would believe the good news.[3] In a few days land within a certain radius had advanced 20 dollars an acre, the nominal price before being 3 to 4 dollars per acre. By 1908–10 the wheat crops were yielding large returns, and prosperity had become general, and with increasing resources and skill the Barr colonists took to purchasing additional land [4] In 1905, Professor Mavor summarized the reasons for the early failure of the Barr colony as follows : " It had not been maturely conceived and was attempted on too large a scale, considering the conditions attending the foundation of a colony remote from railway facilities, by large numbers of settlers unfamiliar with agricultural methods existing in a new country." [5]

It will be seen that in the North-West there are two distinct classes of settlers. First of all there was that class which had reached such an advanced economic state that they were dependent on the outside world for many of their necessaries. This meant that they had very quickly to produce something that was in demand elsewhere, and something that would also pay the cost of transport to the market, and over and above yield a sufficient profit to the settlers. In many cases, of course, settlers of this class had capital of their own, out of which they were able to purchase necessaries until they got returns from their crops. In the bulk of cases, however, the settlers had not sufficient money to do this, and then very often hardship resulted. To tide themselves over the first years those settlers often hired themselves out as farm labourers, or as other kinds of workers. This procedure had two dangers, unless the settlers were very industrious and extremely attached

---

[1] Ibid., p. 290.
[2] C.P., vol. xix, p. 185.
[3] J. H. McCormick, Lloydminster, 1924, p. 198.
[4] Ibid., p. 225.
[5] Mavor Memorandum, p. 286.

to the land. There was always the tendency for such settler-labourers to lose heart at the slow progress made on their holdings or else to be attracted away by the comparatively high wages paid to labourers, and the result then was the same, for the holdings were abandoned and the work of settlement was retarded. The crofters from Scotland and the paupers from London are examples of this. On the other hand, the Americans and Eastern Canadians are examples of those who had capital, who tided over the bad period and remained firmly entrenched on the land.

Secondly, there was the class that had been used to simple living and had only reached a more or less self-sufficing economic state. The Slavs, for instance, lived mostly on vegetables, soup, and bread, using very little meat. Such settlers could supply practically all their own requirements, were only to a small degree dependent on the outside market, and were happily situated so long as they grew enough crops to feed themselves and their stock. In cases debts were incurred on account of immigration expenses, or the purchase of machinery, or the buying of food when the crops failed, but generally they were not overwhelmed with their lack of cash. After they had begun to produce a surplus and could get it to market, such a class prospered exceedingly, and almost everything they sold was clear addition to capital. A good example of this is the Doukhobors, who very speedily accumulated sufficient capital to buy enormous tracts of land elsewhere and settle down there as farmers of quite an advanced type. In some cases, as in that of the Doukhobors, the settlements were communistic in basis and organization, and though this may have hindered subsequent progress, still it certainly made for more stable well-being at the commencement than was enjoyed by the sternly individualistic English and Scotch settlements. Even where foreign settlers were not communistic in practice, a form of co-operation prevailed which did much to guarantee prosperity to the settlement at large. It was noticed that even the foreigners who had settled on individual lands helped each other considerably.[1] Another condition that favoured foreigners, especially eastern Europeans, was their inurement to the Continental type of climate found in Canada, whereas those from England were more used to the climate of the insular type. The fact remains, however,

[1] W. T. R. Preston, Qq. 85-6, Cd. 2979.

that the most important factor was the practical self-sufficiency of the European settlers. " It may be pointed out that while the British emigrant has developed a capacity for producing certain special commodities for sale, the continental emigrant has as a rule retained the capacity of producing everything that he requires for his own maintenance." [1] Thus it was said of the Scandinavians : " Much dependence is placed upon their cattle ; and they overcame the early difficulties incident to pioneer life by producing almost everything that they consume, being thus to a great extent relieved of the necessity of paying out cash." [2]   The women spun, wove cloth and made garments, while the men made their implements and utensils of wood, clay, or iron. The English and Scotch settlers with their dependence on an outside market required railways as a primary necessity for life, while the others could push ahead into the wilds and settle down in comfort. The mere rumour that a railway was going to be built caused the production of wheat to go up three-hundredfold in one district in the course of a single year.[3] With the coming of the railroad came prosperity. Professor Mavor summed up the whole situation thus : " When it comes to pioneer farming for years for a bare living, people with less craving for the society of cities and with fewer and less complicated wants have a great advantage over the British, Irish, or American settler. . . . It is the universal experience of every European people that the basis of a prosperous peasant population has been the self-contained village, at least until it has established itself as a special producer," and further, " those succeeded best who were most skilful in dealing with primitive conditions in a primitive way, and in choosing the moment when improvements could be introduced with effect." [4]

European settlers, brought up in the hard medieval school of unremitting toil, formed their own cultural groups, their own little worlds, where they could lead their own lives, and were content. Some of them introduced a welcome note of culture into a yet crude, young land. Icelandic, with

---

[1] Report on Immigration by Professor James Mavor, in Annual Report of the Department of the Interior, 1899, in *Sessional Papers*, 1900, vol. 10, p. 233.

[2] Annual Report of the Department of the Interior, 1893, Part I, Dominion Lands, p. 6, in *Sessional Papers*, 1894, vol. 10.

[3] *C.P*, vol. xix, p. 171.

[4] Report on Immigration by Professor James Mavor, pp. 234–5, in Annual Report of the Department of the Interior, 1899, in *Sessional Papers*, 1900, vol. 10.

its wealth of sagas, is taught in Manitoba University. The Ukranians petitioned for the establishment of a chair of Ukranian literature in a Western university, so that its folklore and poetry might become naturalized in their new home. In some of the Doukhobor villages it has been noticed that the tin water-spouts had been rudely shaped into grotesque figures in imitation of those to be seen on the medieval buildings of Europe. English settlers always looked over the heads of their neighbours to the great world outside.

The main purpose of the Dominion and Provincial Governments being not merely to bring people into the country but also to get them to settle on and develop the land, the success of their immigration policy is not measured so much by the number of immigrants arriving as by the number who have taken up homesteads ; by the number of new settlers rather than by the number of immigrants.

It has been seen that settlers from America have been most numerous, year by year outnumbering those from the British Isles. It does not follow that the total volume of immigration from the United Kingdom has been less than that from the United States. Thus of the 26,073 homestead entries on Crown lands in the Prairie Provinces and parts of British Columbia in 1903–4, Americans numbered 7,730, and English, Scotch, and Irish together only 4,664. But of the total of 130,330 immigrants into Canada the same year, the United Kingdom supplied 50,374 and the United States a less number, namely 45,171.[1] The Dominions Royal Commission found that during the period 1907–8 to 1914–15, " the immigrants from the United Kingdom, whilst forming 37 per cent of the whole number of arrivals . . . contributed only 27 per cent of the number of those who took up homesteads. On the other hand, those from the United States, whilst providing 36 per cent of the immigrants, formed more than 39 per cent of the home-steaders, whilst in the case of the 27 per cent who immigrated from other countries, they formed 33 per cent of the homesteaders."[2]

Nor were foreign elements unwelcome in the Dominion provided they made good settlers. The policy in the first

[1] Annual Report, Department of the Interior for 1903–4, *Sessional Papers*, 1905, vol. 39, No. 10, pp. xxv and xxxii. The nationality of the immigrants into the various Provinces is not stated.
[2] D.R.C. Fifth Interim Report [*Cd*. 8457], p. 13.

years of the twentieth century was primarily to fill up the
vacant lands, and if an American or a Belgian arrived
equipped with a knowledge of agriculture and the desire
to make good, he was more welcome than the young man
from Great Britain who went out but had to learn his
job after arrival. So the Canadian immigration agents
were as active in foreign countries as in the Motherland.
" As a result of the active propaganda undertaken by the
Department in these two countries, it will be observed that
there has been a marked improvement in the results achieved
. . . The French and Belgian agriculturalists are amongst
the best class that can be secured for the vacant lands of
Canada, and it is proposed to continue on somewhat similar
lines the work which is now being carried out in this
relation." And speaking of the United States and the
Department's " active measures which have been rewarded
with such unquestioned success ", the expectation was
recorded that " with the opening of two or three active
agencies in the Eastern States and a limited expenditure in
judicious advertising, the Department may look for and will
undoubtedly be rewarded with greater success than ever
in the past two or three years ".[1]

Another circumstance pointed to the growth of the foreign
element among the homesteaders of the North-West at a
greater rate than elsewhere in the Dominion. In 1903–4,
in order to relieve the dearth of labour in Ontario, steps
were taken to divert to that province as much as possible
the farm labouring class of immigrants, and some thousands
who would probably have gone on to the North-West were
induced to remain in Ontario. But it was found " almost
impracticable to divert much of the foreign population,
even of the farm labouring classes, to eastern provinces,
many of these people coming through to meet friends, and,
moreover, nearly all of the farm labourers from the Continent
appear to be desirous of securing lands for themselves first,
after which they go out to service and work, if they require
to do so, to equip themselves properly for carrying on their
farming operations." [2]

One of the reactions following on the Great War was a
renewed effort to stimulate British emigration to Canada
and the other Dominions. The new effort was definitely

[1] Annual Report, Department of the Interior for 1903–4, *Sessional Papers*, 1905, vol. 39, No. 10, p. xxxvi.
[2] Ibid., p. xxxiv.

directed towards the attraction of possible emigrants from the United Kingdom to the Dominions, instead of to foreign countries, and the Empire Settlement Act, 1922, which is the basis of the current policy of State-aided Empire settlement, is " An Act to make better provision for furthering British settlement in His Majesty's Oversea Dominions ". It provides for co-operation between the Imperial Government and the Governments of the Dominions in agreed schemes for jointly assisting the emigration of suitable persons from the United Kingdom to the Dominions. Such assistance may take the form of development or land settlement schemes, or assistance with passages, or allowances, or training. The Imperial Government may contribute half the cost of any scheme, but the aggregate contributions are limited under the Act to £3,000,000. While it was expected that the policy of the Act would minimise unemployment in the future, its primary purpose was that defined by Lord Milner at the conference of Prime Ministers of 1921, from which the Act resulted, namely to distribute the white population of the Empire in the manner most conducive to the development, stability and strength of the whole. It was not intended as a mere temporary expedient for dealing with depressed industrial conditions.

In the six years following the passing of the Act a number of schemes had come into existence in which Canada was specially interested.[1]

The high cost of trans-Atlantic fares had been found to check immigration just as a high tariff keeps out imports. In 1928 the normal ocean passage rate for third class passengers from the United Kingdom to Canada was £18 15s. In 1928 an agreement between the Government and the trans-Atlantic lines was announced by which the rate was reduced to £10 for British subjects emigrating from Great Britain for permanent residence in Canada. Later, emigrants to Canada under the Empire Settlement Act were enabled to go for the small sum of £2.

The settlement of families is regarded as the ideal form of oversea settlement, but at the same time openings for families in Canada are limited. There are plenty of openings for married men prepared to work on the land, but the wife must also be used to life on a farm, while in a new

---

[1] The numbers assisted to Canada under the Act were 27,113 in 1927, and 27,521 in 1928. (Report of Oversea Settlement Committee for 1928 [*Cmd*. 3308], p. 15.)

country children are an obvious difficulty. An attempt to solve the difficulty was made under the agreement entered into between the Imperial and Canadian Governments for the settlement of 3,000 families from the United Kingdom on farms in the various Provinces of Canada. " Under the agreement the Dominion Government undertakes to provide farms in settled and established districts, such farms to be provided with houses, and a portion of the farm lands to be fit for immediate cultivation." [1] Advances for stock and equipment may be made,[2] and when the male adult members of the family have gained adequate experience of Canadian farming practice, if necessary by working on farms in the neighbourhood, the family is given the choice of a farm, and thereafter they are supervised in their operations by Government experts.

Other agreements have been entered into with the Canadian Pacific Railway Company and the Hudson's Bay Company and with the Canadian Pacific Railway Company and the Scottish Immigrant Aid Society for the settlement of families on farms in the Prairie Provinces.

Schemes for training boys for farm work and women for farm household work have also been launched under the provisions of the Statute.[3] It is appreciated that farming is a calling which cannot be entered upon too young. The scheme is rounded and complete in that provision is made by which boys can go to Canada, receive preliminary training in agricultural institutions there, be then placed out to gain practical experience as farm-workers, and then, as the crown of all, be set up with farms of their own.

The Reception of the Immigrant

So recently as the decade subsequent to confederation, immigrants into Manitoba had to put up with all the discomfort inseparable from transport by wagon road with frequent changes to waterways. There was, for example, the Dawson route from Thunder Bay to Fort Garry, a distance of 477 miles, which was opened by the Canadian Government in 1871 as a channel to the North-West Territory, which had just become a portion of the Dominion.

---

[1] Report of Oversea Settlement Committee for 1928 [*Cdm.* 3308], p. 36.

[2] " The average cost to the settler of the farm and its equipment is estimated to amount to between £800 and £1,000, this sum being repayable by instalments over 25 years with interest of 5 per cent." (ibid., p. 36.)

[3] For particulars, see Appendix to the annual Reports of Oversea Settlement Committee.

Hitherto the only route had been through the United States, so that now the intending settler had the choice of two routes. The question seems to have been which of the two was the least uncomfortable. In the report of the Emigration Department, the agent at Winnipeg, referring to the Dawson route, said : " From the 1st of July up to the close of navigation (1874) the emigrant sheds were overflowed, which was principally owing to the inferior management of the Dawson route contractor, causing at the time very great loss to the new settlers, who were in many cases obliged to wait three to five weeks for their baggage after enduring a most trying voyage which lasted twenty-two days." [1] Also people who had travelled over the Dawson route " complained bitterly of the insolent treatment they had received from pups of officials ".[2] As to the experiences of the early immigrants when passing through the United States, Sir John A. Macdonald described them thus : " In the first place they came from Europe, they had not finally made up their minds in what part of the West to make their homes, and accordingly they were seduced by the runners and officers of the rival land companies of the Western States from their first intention to go to Manitoba or other portions of the British North-West. Those who took furniture or goods with them to be forwarded in bond, met with every possible obstruction ; they were also overcharged and the customs officers put them to every trouble." [3]

Not only was pre-railway transport uncomfortable for the immigrants ; it was also expensive to the Government. The average cost of carrying emigrants over the Dawson route was $25 per head, the fare charged to the emigrants themselves for the whole distance being $15 per head in 1872, and this was reduced to $10 per head in 1873.[4]

The difficulties of the route were of course reflected in the slowness with which population trickled through to the new territories. Passengers conveyed from 1871 to the end of 1873 numbered 2,739 persons, of whom only 805 were emigrants remaining permanently as settlers in Manitoba.[5] In 1875 the number was 1,877.[6]

[1] Quoted, *Dominion Debates*, 1876, p. 450.
[2] Ibid., p. 455.   [3] *Dominion Debates*, 1876, p. 453.
[4] *Sessional Papers*, Canada (No. 37), 1875, vol. viii.
[5] Ibid.
[6] *Sessional Papers*, Canada (No. 62), 1876, vol. ix. Meals were furnished at the various stations at 30 cents each. " Spirituous or fermented liquors

It has already been pointed out [1] that in new countries like the Dominion the recruitment of immigrants is essentially a matter for Government action and control, inasmuch as steps must be taken to exclude the unwanted ; schemes must be conceived and launched to attract and assist the eligible ; and the immigrant must be shepherded on his arrival in the new country.

At the time of the outbreak of the Great War, the immigration policy of the Canadian Government was certainly not open to any charge of indefiniteness. Only farmers, farm labourers, and domestic servants were wanted. No immigrant was brought to Canada at the expense of the Dominion Government ; only charitable or philanthropic organizations provided free or assisted passages. The Government made no loans of either money, stock, or implements. The means and provision necessary to start farming in Canada had to be found by the immigrant himself or with such private aid as he could command. Nevertheless, from 1907–8 onwards, the Government in fact spent approximately a million dollars a year in the attempt to acquire immigrants of the character they desired. Most of it was paid away in the form of bonuses to agents abroad for persons induced by them to settle in Western Canada. A bonus of $3 on a man, $2 on a woman, and $1 on a child was paid to agents in the United States who were instrumental in sending settlers. Steamship booking agents in Great Britain and Ireland and in France, Belgium, Holland, Denmark, Norway, Sweden, and Finland were paid a bonus of £1 a person of 18 years of age and over, and 10s. on persons below that age coming to Canada as farm workers or domestic servants.

Much of the trouble and expense incurred in procuring the acceptable immigrant would be wasted if steps were not taken to see that he fulfils his destiny on arrival. By the exercise of a degree of solicitude for immigrants, which seems almost paternal, a solicitude which by no means ceases at the port of entry, the Dominion and Provincial Governments are able to maintain control of the incoming stream of population. The result to the twentieth century immigrant is that he begins his life in Canada in much more comfortable circumstances than his predecessors.

are not allowed on the road, and any person having the same in their possession make themselves liable to fine and imprisonment." (Ibid.)

[1] See Chap. 12.

Arriving in a steamer of which the steerage accommodation is superior to the cabin accommodation furnished thirty years ago [1] : " he is at once taken in charge by the uniformed officials and two examinations take place, one of which is the medical examination, and the other the civil examination. As soon as the examinations are finished the immigrant is released and we have large buildings in which there is a restaurant and all conveniences of that kind. The train comes right into that building. If there is a large body of immigrants there is a special train, and the immigrant steps on to the train and starts on his journey. If it is where we have an agent, our agent places him and he is advised to go to where we have agents." [2] Then at Winnipeg, the gateway of the North-West : " At the depôt we have immigration halls with accommodation for over 2,000 people for day or night, bedrooms and dining-room accommodation, and all other necessary accommodation. When the trains arrive at the depôt they are met by uniformed officers conversant with the language of all countries from which we are receiving immigrants. When the immigrant steps from the train he is met by somebody who can speak to him ; he is brought to the Immigration Hall and registered, which registration consists of his age, his name, his nationality, the date of his arrival in Canada, the steamer he came on, and any destination that he may have in view. He is then given a bedroom or such other accommodation as he requires. The next day, or during the same day, as the case may be, he visits the office to discuss with the officer there as to his future. Most of our immigrants have no decided destination ; those who have rarely trouble us, they go to their destinations, to their friends, or to those who are either inviting them or under-taking to take care of them. Those who have no destination discuss with us their future prospects. Some, we find, are only looking for labour, skilled or unskilled, clerical or otherwise. Some again, we find, are looking for employment on the land, and some are looking for land. To deal with the land division first : We discuss with them the various parts of the country where there are homesteads, and we deal only with homestead lands. The Government,

---

[1] See Chap. 12 for an account of the conditions of the early Canadian passage.

[2] Dominions Royal Commission, *Minutes of Evidence* [Cd. 8458], Q. 1259. Compare the account given in chap. 9 of the conditions of transport into the interior in the middle of the nineteenth century.

or Government officers, have nothing whatever to do with settlement on the lands of land companies or other corporations owning land. We confine ourselves exclusively to settlement on homesteads in the three Prairie Provinces— Manitoba, Saskatchewan, and Alberta. We discuss with the prospective farmer the various localities, endeavour to find out what his past experience has been, what kind of farming he has done, what kind of land he has occupied, the country he came from, and so forth, and after discussing the conditions of homesteads in various sections we decide to advise him to go to a certain land district. He is provided with a cheap rate from Winnipeg to the centre of the land district to which he purposes to go. Armed with an introduction from our office he goes to the land agent in the land district, and is there provided with a plan of vacant lands, getting some description of the nature of the lands, whether they are bush land or clear land, and the kind of soil—in general terms only, of course—the distance from railroad stations, and other information of that kind. When he has decided that he will look for land in that district the Government provides a land guide, free of expense to the prospective settler. This man is familiar with the neighbourhood, having lived there for years. The prospective settler undertakes to pay for the hire and food of the vehicle that takes him to the prospective land, but the services of the land guide are provided by the Government. They go out to look for land, perhaps for two or three days, in some sections of the country possibly six or seven days. When they have decided if any land is suitable to the inclinations and experience of the settler, if he has seen something that suits him, the stake markings are taken from the survey, identified and brought back to the land office, where the prospective settler pays his entry fee of 10 dollars, and if it is found that no other entry has been made for those lands and that they are properly available for settlement, he makes his entry and receives his receipt therefor, which is a temporary title to enter upon them and occupy them. That is the process of settling the homesteader on the homestead. There is the other class who seek only employment on farms at farm work. . . . If the settler has any preference for any particular part of the country, and he frequently has, particularly if he has friends, we send him to that part of the country, providing him with a card of introduction to the farmer, giving the farmer's name, his land description, his post office, and his nearest station, so that when the immigrant takes his place on the train the conductor knows at what point to tell him to get off, and the farmer having been advised is expected to be at the station to receive him and take him out to the farm. We continually take an interest in such a settler, in the shape of hearing complaints from him and inquiring into them if anything goes wrong as to his keep, as to his food, as to his treatment, we continually take an interest in him. . . . The homesteader on the unpatented lands is the constant care of the Department, and we provide him with food, medicine, clothing, seed, and in fact everything he needs except his stock and implements, when we are satisfied he needs such assistance, taking a mortgage on the homestead for the amount advanced at a very low rate of interest." [1]

The Dividing-up of the Land

When the country had settled down after the Riel insurrection, and when bodies of immigrants from the older Provinces and from Great Britain began to arrive, it became apparent that a survey and division of the lands which had been taken over by the Government from the Hudson's Bay Company was essential and that laws regulating the acquisition of lands and the record of the title thereto must be adopted. The rectangular system of survey which had been adopted for Manitoba, the survey of which had been carried through during the period 1871–3, was followed throughout the North-West. In the result a map or plan of surveyed territory in the Canadian North-West suggests a huge chess board. The main division is into rectangular townships (which have nothing necessarily to do with urban settlement) each of 36 square miles. Each township is divided into thirty-six sections, each one mile square. There is a further sub-division into quarter sections of 160 acres each. Allowances for roads are made between township and sections.

The conditions on which settlers could acquire land were liberal, but at the same time were designed to prevent land being used as a mere speculative counter and to assure its development for agricultural purposes. The general form of Canadian land legislation for the purpose of

---

[1] Dominions Royal Commission, *Minutes of Evidence* [*Cd.* 8458]. Evidence of Mr. J. Bruce Walker, Commissioner of Immigration for Western Canada, pp. 47–8.

territory in process of settlement was borrowed from the United States. Land could be the subject of homestead rights or pre-emption rights. Any British subject, the head of a family or 21 years of age (later 18), was entitled to take up a quarter section of 160 acres of unappropriated public lands as a homestead and a quarter section as a pre-emption. The only payment required was a fee of $10 at the time of application, but cultivation and five years' (afterwards three years') residence were conditions which had to be fulfilled before a patent giving the settler the absolute property in the land could be issued. Meanwhile the title to the land remained in the Crown. Later it was provided that six months' residence out of each twelve would suffice. The pre-emption was purchasable at one dollar an acre. Certain lands were reserves for special purposes. These were the lands allotted to the Hudson's Bay Company under their agreement with the Government, school lands set apart as an endowment for purposes of education, timber lands set aside to ensure a supply of fuel and building material, and mineral lands.

The land system thus instituted worked well, save, perhaps, for one or two features, such as that which allowed scrip of the face value of 160 acres, which could be located on any quarter section of Dominion land open for sale or settlement, to be given to the half-breeds as compensation for their original interest in the lands taken over by the Government. The scrip, being freely transferable, gave rise to a vast amount of speculation, "Some of the wealthiest men of Winnipeg can trace their first start in life to successful trading in Half-Breed and Volunteer scrip." [1]

Then again, reference has been made to the school lands and the land reserved to the Hudson's Bay Company. The method of allocating such lands was to reserve two sections with the same number in each township for educational endowment purposes and similarly two sections in each township were handed over to the Hudson's Bay Company. This land was accordingly not available for settlement by homestead entry. The effect of this allocation of areas of land in the same township to different purposes was to retard close settlement.

The difficulty with which many settlers had to wrestle was want of capital, for often instead of devoting himsel to his own farm he had to seek employment part of the year in order to be able to live. The conditions of homestead entry, by which the ownership of the land remained in the Dominion Government for three years after the settler's entry thereon, made it impossible to find a remedy by raising money on mortgage. The settler had no title enabling him to use the land as security for the loan.

The right of pre-emption early fell into disuse and about 1890 it ceased. Referring to the decrease in the area taken up as pre-emptions in 1887, the Deputy Minister of the Interior regarded the tendency with little regret for " the opinion begins to gain favour with those who have paid close attention to the affairs of Manitoba and the North-West that, so far as relates to the grain growing portions of the country at least, 160 acres is the limit of the area which the average farmer can profitably work. The number of homesteaders who lately have not availed themselves of the privilege of pre-emption is an indication that this conviction is growing among the settlers themselves." [1]

From 1830 onwards the " Wakefield system " attracted the attention of all who were interested in colonial settlement. Edward Gibbon Wakefield's purpose was to discover means by which capital and labour could be introduced into a colony in such a manner as to lead to its more stable development. He disapproved not only of contemporary forms of emigration, but also of the system of free grants of colonial lands. His proposal was that such lands should be sold for " a sufficient price " and the purchase money applied to the promotion of emigration and the improvement of means of communication in the colony. [2] Force of circumstances brought about conditions which effected observance of Wakefield's principles, for only for a short time were free homesteads available as the principal means of attracting settlers to the North-West. At first the Canadian Pacific Railway Company devoted their attention almost entirely to promoting the settlement of the free Government lands within the railway belt and south of it to the International boundary, meantime making

---

[1] Annual Report of the Department of the Interior for 1887, *Sessional Papers*, 1888, vol. 12, p. x.

The number of pre-emption entries in 1874 was 643 ; in 1882 it was 5,654 ; in 1887 the number had sunk to 585. A large proportion of the pre-emption entries of the earlier years had been cancelled. Of the entries in 1874, no less than 92 per cent were cancelled (ibid., p. xii).

[2] See Wakefield's *Art of Colonization* for a complete statement of his views and theories.

little effort to effect sale of their own lands, assuming that until the free homesteads had been pretty well occupied there would be little opportunity for sale to settlers. By 1886 the free homestead lands in the railway belt and south of it as far west as Moosejaw had already largely been taken up.[1]

In the early years of the twentieth century tenancy was existing side by side with ownership and the North-West was no longer a country where every farmer was his own landlord.[2] The settler of very limited means might still become a homesteader, but he must be " willing to settle on a farm in a district where there is no schoolmaster and no doctor and no railway ", and a man who " has resolved to accept the rigours of a Canadian winter and all the hardships and loneliness that go to make up a pioneer's life ".[3] Purchase was taking the place of free grant. " For the ordinary man who does not care to be on the frontiers of civilization fighting nature at every step for a foothold, it seems to us better that he should remain a hired hand or a tenant farmer until he has made £400 or £500. With this money he could purchase a farm not very far from a railway station in a partially settled district. . . . Many can be got in good districts at from ten to fifteen dollars an acre." [4]

The conditions which brought the great influx of immigrants into the North–West in the first decade of the twentieth century ceased to exist during the next decade. The best of the free homestead lands had by then all been taken up, nor were other lands any longer to be purchased on cheap terms. In Saskatchewan, by the year 1915 over 26,500,000 acres had been granted on homestead terms and 8,000,000 acres of the surveyed area remained available for homestead entry,[5] but these 8,000,000 acres were not land of the same class or character as the 26,500,000 acres previously granted. Some of the lands remaining available

---

[1] Canadian Pacific Railway Annual Report for 1885.

[2] " Most of the abandoned farms are being taken up by renters. . . . There is quite a demand for farms to rent, a great many people want to rent rather than buy." (*D.R.C. Minutes of Evidence*, [*Cd.* 8459], Qs. 511–12.)

[3] *Canada : An Account of a trip across the Dominion by the Scottish Agricultural Commission in* 1908, p. 37. (Canada : Pamphlets, No. 217, in D.O. & C.O. Library.)

[4] Ibid.

[5] *Annual Report of Department of the Interior*, 1915.

were those which had been abandoned by former homesteaders ; most of the remainder was remote from transport
facilities and was bush and of poor value for arable purposes.
Otherwise the land available for settlement was held as
an investment, from which it was expected to realize a profit,
by the Canadian Pacific Railway Company, the Hudson's
Bay Company, and land investment companies. The settler
on such land required a certain amount of capital or he
had to face the burden of the payment of interest.

When we get to the year 1928, the Dominion Minister
of Immigration had to declare that " practically all the area
of land within easy reach of the railways was now held by
private individuals or companies, and was only available
to immigrants with ample funds." [1]

In its efforts to attract settlers from Great Britain, the
Canadian Pacific Railway Company held out remarkable
inducements. The settler from Dakota, or Iowa, or
Minnesota was prepared to live in tents or sod-built huts
until he had broken up the land and produced a crop,
whereas the British settler was not, and so to enable the
Briton to start fair with his American competitor the
Railway Company offered him a ready-made farm. The
colonist took possession of a going concern. The year
before he arrived his benevolent landlords had erected a
farm house and farm buildings ; they had fenced the land ;
sunk a well and brought fifty acres under cultivation. At
first the Canadian Pacific Company's ready-made farms
were available exclusively for British settlers. " Our effort
and desire was to obtain the British tenant farmer, but we
were only able to obtain a small proportion of the tenant
farmers, and so we took a certain number of people from
the cities and a certain number of ex-Army officers and ex-
soldiers of the old army, and for that reason a very considerable portion of them failed." [2] Thereupon the campaign
in Great Britain was closed down and the Company's
750 ready-made farms were thrown open to all nationalities. [3]

Realizing the financial weakness of new immigrants as a
class, the Canadian Pacific Railway in 1914 inaugurated

[1] *The Times*, 7th February, 1928.
[2] *D.R.C. Minutes of Evidence* [*Cd.* 8458], Evidence of J. S. Dennis,
C.P.Rly. Co., 1916, Q. 2738.
[3] As its share in the post-war attempt to encourage British settlement the C.P.Rly. Co. entered into an arrangement with the Hudson's
Bay Co. for the settlement of 200 families on improved farms before
1930, under the Empire Settlement Act, 1922. (See *ante*.)

a new land policy designed to surmount that discouraging difficulty. " Under our new policy a man . . . must carry a certain amount of live stock in addition to growing grain, and in order to induce him to become a sane farmer instead of what we call a grain minèr, and a settler instead of a speculator, we give him 20 years to pay for the land . . . we make provision that where a man buys our land under the settlement and colonizing contract we will advance him . . . up to $2,000, which will be used in building a house and barn, putting down a well . . . and in fencing. . . . Then for the purpose of inducing him to do what we call sane agriculture, mixed farming, we make him an advance of live stock, cattle, sheep and hogs, to the extent of $1,000." [1] Hitherto the Company had been content to sell their land with no questions asked. Under the new policy land was only sold subject to an obligation to occupy and improve it.

One of the questions which emerged for settlement when, in 1870, the territory between the Height of Land and the Rocky Mountains and extending from the United States boundary to the Arctic Ocean was transferred to the Dominion by the Hudson's Bay Company, was the manner in which the Indians were to be dealt with. It has been from early times the settled policy of the Dominion Government itself to assume responsibility for the charge of the Indians and to allow none but its own representatives to enter into transactions with them respecting land. All sales or surrender of land by Indians to others than the Crown are invalid. In regard to such portions of the transferred territory as were required for settlement or industrial development treaties were entered into. While the ultimate right to the soil was held to be in the Crown, it was recognized that the Indians should not be deprived of their occupation rights without their formal consent and compensation in the form of reserves.

Eight different treaties were entered into with the Indians of the North-West—with the Ojibways, the Crees, the Chipewyans, the Blackfoot Indians and other tribes with names the glamour of which has since largely departed.

---

[1] *D.R.C.* [*Cd.* 8458], Q. 2739. The Ontario Government also instituted in 1916 a scheme for advancing loans to settlers, the maximum for any one borrower being $500. The Dominion Government never entered upon a policy of financial loans to settlers.

The Federal and Provincial Legislatures have concurrent powers of legislation. Both can pass laws on the subject of immigration, but in the event of collision, federal law prevails.

" In general, the terms granted under these treaties were a present of twelve dollars and an annuity of five dollars for each man, woman and child as soon as the Chiefs signed the Treaty. Twenty-five dollars was given each Chief and fifteen dollars to each Headman, and a uniform of clothing befitting these two ranks every three years. Reserves of 640 acres for a family of five, or at the rate of 128 acres for every man, woman and child. An annual allowance of ammunition and twine was also granted ; and where farming and grazing operations are practicable and engaged in, a supply of agricultural implements, seed grain, cattle and carpenters' tools was to be provided. Schools were also to be established on the reserves. They were likewise permitted to pursue their avocations of hunting, trapping, and fishing throughout the territory surrendered." [1]

The total number of Indians within the limits of these Treaties was stated to be 27,124, and the annual sum expended in respect of Indians in the Territory, for annuities and for rationing and educating them during their years of helplessness and tutelage, over $750,000.[2] The purpose of the Government is to enable the Indian to become self-supporting. That their efforts in this direction have not been altogether in vain is apparent from the case of a tribe who, when they entered into the Treaty in 1874, were wild, painted Indians having buffalo-robes or blankets around their shoulders. " In 1903-4, just thirty years afterwards, the Indians within the Treaty, 4,482 in number, raised 90,979 bushels of wheat and 58,000 bushels of oats ; and the total value of their farm produce, including hay, was $138,798. They had also 5,075 head of horned cattle, their live stock of all kinds being valued at $226,888." [3]

In the Maritime Provinces, Quebec, Ontario and British Columbia, the public lands are in the hands of the Provincial Governments. The revenue derivable from such lands not being forthcoming in the case of the Prairie Provinces, where the public lands belonged to the Dominion, compensation had to be made in the form of grants from the central government. The difference in the two systems of land ownership had important reactions on the political life of the

---

[1] Hon. David Laird, *Our Indian Treaties*, Winnipeg, 1905 (Canada : Pamphlets, D.O. & C.O. Library, vol. 5, No. 163). The distribution of the money and goods in the " Treaty time " season is made the occasion for a festival of which an amusing account is given by Mrs. Louise Rourke in *The Land of the Frozen Tide*, chap. 18.
[2] Ibid.   [3] Ibid.

new Provinces. The reliance of the new Provinces on financial support from the Dominion Government was not conducive to economy. In 1875 the total resources of Manitoba derivable from the Dominion were $71,172. The Province had no other resources worth mentioning, nor was it possible to impose direct taxation on early settlers who needed all their resources for the initial expenses of settlement. " The additional revenue of the Province has been insignificant, the only important item having been that of licences for the sale of liquor which at one time reached about $10,000, but which by the combined operation of a stringent licence law and of the transfer to the City of Winnipeg of the fund derivable from licences within that corporation, has been reduced to a trifling sum. The only other sources of public revenue, the Province having no Crown lands, are Marriage licences and Law fees, from neither of which can any considerable sum be expected." The estimated annual deficit in 1875 was $43,000, and the sub-Committee of the central government which examined the matter [1] came to the conclusion that for a Province which still had a population of only about 36,000 a " simpler and more rudimentary form of self-government " would be more suitable, at any rate during the early years of settlement. It was not advisable to allow the expense of the machinery of government to absorb the great bulk of their available income to the exclusion of the maintenance and advancement of the material interests of the Province. For instance, a second Chamber seemed a luxury that might be dispensed with in the then existing circumstances.[2]

The Exploitation of the Soil

In the older Provinces of Canada, whether on the Atlantic side or the Pacific, the settler encountered a common enemy in the forest. In all these Provinces the clearance of his holding absorbed a good deal of his time and energy and inevitably postponed the day when the farm should come into full production. While such conditions had to be encountered, settlement could proceed but slowly, but such an experience tended to make settlement permanent ; the settler was a homemaker rather than a mere sojourner.

---

[1] *Sessional Papers*, Canada (No. 36), 1876, vol. ix.
[2] The Upper House was accordingly abolished (*Dominion Debates*, 1876, p. 707).

What the mass of intending emigrants wanted was prairie soil, land that they could plough at once without the tedious and exhausting years of labour required in woodland farming, chopping, rolling, burning, grubbing, stumping and levelling. Such land the Dominion was able to offer when the trans-continental railways open up the great plains of the North-West, but the settler who was attracted was on the whole less securely anchored to the soil than his predecessors. " Too often new settlement took on a speculative character, and instead of the good stockmen of the older Provinces, whose aim was to build a home even if it took a lifetime, a genera-tion grew up, many of whom had before them the aim of getting as much as possible out of their holdings in a few years and moving off to make their homes elsewhere when that was done." [1]

But although the pioneer in the North-West was spared the forest, conditions of climate and animals and insects provided for him a variety of troubles and anxieties. The variability of the climate was found to be a drawback. Some years rain was excessive. At other times there was drought. The melting of the snow might raise the rivers to disastrous flood levels. Insurance against hailstorms has been one of the most important branches of insurance business in the Dominion. Down to 1925, " the total premiums for the 16 years during which the business has been carried on in Canada amount to $40,398,368 and the total losses paid to $24,578,544." [2]

The losses of stock in the North-West due to winter conditions were sometimes calamitous. They were particu-larly heavy in the winter of 1886-7, when the only consolation the stock-owners on the Canadian side could find for the loss of from twelve to fifteen per cent of their animals was that in the grazing States and Territories on the other side of the international boundary the losses were three times as heavy. In explanation of those heavy casualties it was pointed out that " little or no preparation had, as a rule, been made for feeding or sheltering the stock ; and the abnormally low temperature, combined with strong winds and unusually heavy snow storms, was naturally very destructive to cattle on ranges which furnished no natural shelter in the localities to which the animals

[1] E. J. Ashton, " Western Canada To-day," *United Empire Journal*, Feb. 1926, vol. 17, p. 65.
[2] *Canada Year Book*, 1926, p. 859.

drifted".[1] Horses proved themselves better able to withstand the severe winters.

Wolves, otherwise coyotes, were another source of trial to the stock owner, and the pest was only kept under by the importation of what were described in an official report as " powerful and ferocious-looking wolf and staghounds ". In Alberta, in the 'nineties, wolves were still one of the afflictions of the stock-grazing districts. The Government paid a bounty of 5 dollars for each wolf killed. " Many hundred wolves were destroyed and a large proportion of the bounty was paid out to Indians. . . . It is possible that each wolf killed means about two calves or colts saved." [2]

Then again, smaller game can make life as unbearable in the far north of Canada during the short summer season as in the Tropics. Thus on the shores of Lake Athabasca : " Besides the mosquitoes we have the hated bulldog fly who pesters both man and beast and whose bite is so treacherous that it has sometimes been responsible for the deaths of the hard-worked horses on the portages that connect the various waterways. . . . Added to the bulldog fly and the mosquitoes we have also the biting sandflies, myriads of bluebottles and ordinary houseflies and grasshoppers which arrive in shoals almost as soon as the snow is gone, and completely destroy every blade of green within sight." [3] The vast areas of muskeg provide the mosquito with an ideal breeding ground. " But as the draining of the land round the settlements is gradually effected, the problem is slowly but surely being overcome. My husband remembers when the summer was a torment at Edmonton because of this plague, but nowadays it is rare to be bitten by a mosquito within the city and its surroundings." [4]

A more serious Canadian insect pest is the locust, or, as the North American species is sometimes called, the grasshopper, an insect which was capable in early days of reducing the settlers to the verge of starvation. Such a visitation was recorded in 1869. In that year, while negotiations were proceeding for the transfer to Canada of the jurisdiction and territorial rights of the Hudson's Bay Company, the Company had occasion to complain

---

[1] Annual Report of Department of the Interior for 1887. *Sessional Papers* (Canada), 1888, vol. 12, p. xix.
[2] Annual Report, Department of the Interior, for 1896, *Sessional Papers*, 1897, Dominion Lands, p. 31.
[3] Louise Rourke, *The Land of the Frozen Tide*, p. 300, London, 1928.
[4] Ibid., p. 302.

of a " trespass " on the soil of the Company by the Government, inasmuch as the latter had intimated their intention of constructing a road from Fort Garry to the Lake of the Woods. The reply of the Canadian Government was that information had been received that in consequence of the complete destruction of their crops by locusts, the people of the Red River settlement, some 12,000 to 15,000 in number, were in imminent danger of starvation during the coming winter ; that as no steps seemed to have been taken by the Company to provide the necessary supplies, the Government had appropriated $20,000 towards the construction of a road, some 90 miles in length, from Lake of the Woods to Fort Garry, and that the sum was to be spent in provisions to be given to the settlers in exchange for their labour on the road. The immediate object of the Government was declared to be " to supply food to a starving community about to be imprisoned for six months in the heart of a great wilderness, without roads or means of communication with their fellow subjects." [1]

Before the days of transcontinental railways, agriculture was carried on in the North-West on a very small scale. Missions of different denominations—Church of England, Roman Catholic, Presbyterian and Canada Methodists— were scattered up and down the country. Around these population clustered, and there and on the Police farms agriculture in the North-West had its beginnings.

---

[1] Report of Delegates appointed to negotiate for the acquisition of Rupert's Land and the North-West Territory : Ottawa, 1869 (*Canada : Pamphlets*, vol. 2, No. 56 in D.O. & C.O. Library).

The first appearance of locusts in formidable numbers in the Red River Valley appears to have been in 1818, six years after the foundation of Lord Selkirk's colony, " They then arrived on the wing in the last week of July and destroyed nearly everything but the wheat crop, which partly escaped, being nearly ripe. Eggs were deposited, and in the following spring the wheat and all other crops were destroyed as fast as they appeared above ground." There was a serious plague again in 1857, when " the crops are said to have been so far advanced as to escape great damage, but eggs were deposited, and in 1858 all the young grain was devoured." They appeared at intervals between 1864 and 1874. (J. Macoun, *Manitoba and the Great North-West*).

The control of locusts is one of the problems with which farmers in the Eastern Provinces have to contend. There, poisoned bran baits have been used on the land and with a certain amount of success. In Quebec Province, in 1915, a mixture of bran, paris green, molasses, and lemon, was distributed over a large area during June, " at which time the locusts were from one-quarter to one-half an inch in length." A few days afterwards, counts in various fields " ranged from 80 to 120 dead locusts to the square foot " (" Locust Control Work in Eastern Canada in 1915," by A. Gibson, in *46th Annual Report of Entomological Society of Ontario*, 1915).

The agricultural history of the North-West begins with the story of the establishment of great cattle ranches, which only survive until such time as the land is wanted for the homesteader. Then comes the time when the land has been transformed into a sea of grain ; and finally the stage is reached when the disposition is to turn to mixed farming as after all the safest.

The ranching system was inaugurated in the western plains of Canada about 1884, when there was little settlement, and the land between the Canadian Pacific Railway and the Manitoba boundary was still unenclosed so that cattle could range over an immense area, much as did the immense buffalo herds that preceded them. The Montana system was adopted by which the rancher agreed with the Government for the payment of a certain sum for grazing rights over a definite area. Grazing leases were issued for a term of 21 years at an annual rental of two cents an acre, subject, however, to the stipulation that lands included in a grazing lease could be withdrawn for homestead entry or sale.[1]

In the opening years of the twentieth century, the Canadian West was officially referred to as " maintaining its position as a stockbreeder's paradise ", while the breeding of horses was rapidly increasing, there being over 20,000 in 1901 on the ranges in southern Alberta alone. The raising of hogs was also making headway.[2] The tendency was, however, towards smaller ranches. The manner in which the conflict of interest between the rancher and the small man arose has been thus described. " The rancher wishes to have the whole country open so that his cattle may range at will everywhere, and objects to the presence of the small man with perhaps a couple of hundred head, several of whom usually locate near one another in some valley. These erect buildings and fence off pieces of country for winter pasture and thus offer considerable obstruction to the free passage of the range cattle along such occupied valley. The difference between the methods used in cattle raising by these two classes of cattle men is very marked and both in the matter of humanity and of utility is . . . largely in favour of the small man. The rancher trusts largely to Providence to preserve his cattle alive through winter

---

[1] Annual Report of Department of the Interior for 1900–1, Part I. Dominion Lands, p. 60, *Sessional Papers*, 1902.

[2] Ibid., part ii, *Immigration*, pp. 124–5.

storms, cuts a little hay sometimes, and argues that the cost of putting up hay is as great as the loss he is likely to suffer by his cattle dying during the winter. . . . The settler or small man on the other hand cuts or provides plenty of hay for every hoof he has, and as a consequence never loses any cattle by bad weather, and off the same amount of territory produces more than twice as many cattle." [1]

As early as 1896 some of the largest leaseholders relinquished their leases in compliance with the Government's request in order that the land might be opened for homestead entry and scheduled to railway companies as part of their land subsidies. " The total number of ranches is increasing, but the areas leased have been much smaller during the last few years, none of the tracts exceeding 6,000 acres. As a rule the lessees are settlers who acquire limited tracts adjoining or in the neighbourhood of their homesteads. The total number of leases now in force is 236, covering an area of 257,983 acres." [2] The leasing system which displaced the earlier free-ranging system had the advantage that it enabled the quantity of stock placed upon the ranges to be controlled, so preventing the grass from being eaten out.

Of all the natural assets with which the North-West has been so generously endowed, that to which the phenomenal development of this region is primarily due is the special suitability of the soil for the cultivation of all kinds of grain, and in particular wheat. The best part of the prairie lands of Manitoba and Saskatchewan are very rich in the constituents of plant food. Alberta, with a rather milder winter climate, carries a greater number of cattle and horses, but the southern region of the former home of the cowboy and the cattle-king, in spite of a low rainfall, has been found eminently suitable for wheat growing. At first development was retarded by the general adoption of the one crop system. Successive crops of grain must sooner or later ruin the best land, but soon the advantages of a diversity of crops were recognized. A still greater step forward was taken when the desirability of mixed farming rather than entire dependence on cereals was understood.

---

[1] Annual Report Department of Interior for 1896, Dominion Lands Surveys, p. 30, *Sessional Papers*, 1897.

[2] Annual Report, Department of Interior, 1896, *Sessional Papers*, 1897, vol. 31, p. xxx.

To this better understanding a contributory cause was the possibility of early frost in the North-West. In 1888, for example, about 20 per cent of the wheat crop of Manitoba was lost as the consequence of a frost which appeared in the middle of August. Damage to the wheat crop is not so crippling to the farmer who raises cattle, horses and sheep, for not only is the damage confined to a part only of farming operations rather than the whole, but even if the frost destroys the value of his grain for milling purposes it may still be good enough for the purpose of feeding his hogs and cattle.

The new policy received official approval in the early years of the century. Said the Minister for Agriculture in 1903 : " The people of Eastern Canada know the live stock interest is the basis of their prosperity. They know also that those who have gone to the North-West and Manitoba, while for a few years they do without live stock by reason of the virgin fertility of the soil and the ease with which they can raise great crops of wheat on the fertile prairies, in the near future they will have to adopt what is known as mixed husbandry and establish a live-stock interest. . . . We are going to have in Canada the same condition of affairs in the development of our North-West that the United States Republic has had. When the people from the east went into that country and began to spread out over the Mississippi plains and further west, they began to raise wheat and corn. They afterwards took to raising cattle to such an extent that to-day Chicago is the centre of a far greater trade in animal products than it is of a wheat and flour trade." [1]

But mixed farming in the Prairie Provinces is not without its difficulties save in certain favoured districts. As to North Saskatchewan : " That country is very bad for flies. Its grasses are water grasses, many of them sedges, which are not good for feed." [2] The difficulties of water supply over large areas of the prairies make the keeping of cattle a very hard problem in the winter season. Horses were a less difficult problem, " because if water is scarce the horses will feed on the snow." [3] Then again, the British large farm worked by a staff of wage labourers between whom and their employer there existed the traditional

---

[1] Dominion Debates, 1903, vol. iv, Col. 9520.
[2] D.R.C. Minutes of Evidence, 1916 [Cd. 8458], Q. 2239.
[3] Ibid., Q. 2356.

relation of master and man never took root in the Prairie Provinces, but there is a body of migratory labour for the purposes of the harvest resembling the body of Irish agricultural labourers who migrate to England during the harvest months. In Canada the harvest is earlier in the East than in the West, a circumstance which enables many sons of eastern farmers to migrate temporarily to the Prairies to help in the harvest there after the eastern harvest has been completed. The rather miscellaneous body constituted by the harvesters also includes railway workers who are tempted by the larger wages temporarily to exchange the railway for the fields, but when the winter season begins there is an all-round discharge of such temporary agricultural workers, and as they cannot return to the railway until the spring they contribute to the winter unemployment which is one of Canada's specially difficult problems. Migratory workers of this characters are not very helpful in the management of live stock. The division of the land into quarter sections produced a community of 160 acre farms, and the holder of one quarter section who wanted to extend the area of his farm might find the surrounding quarter sections taken up and himself shut in within his own 160 acres. This again made mixed farming difficult. " For the settler to proceed on a mixed farming basis economically he should have at least a half-section of land." [1]

The experience of the years immediately preceding the Great War, constituting as they did the black period in the economic history of the Prairie Provinces, had its share in encouraging the disposition to turn to mixed farming in spite of all the difficulties, as against reliance on cereals. Up to 1910 there had been prosperity and money from the banks was readily forthcoming. In 1910 there was a check. There was drought ; crops were light and prices low. The year following was very wet. " There was a heavy growth of straw, but poor, frost-bitten grain, and no market for it. Much grain was threshed from under the snow and went out of condition." [2] About this time there came a sudden rise in beef prices, but wheat crops continued poor and wheat prices unsatisfactory through 1912 and 1913. In 1914, during the summer months when the demand for labour in an agricultural country is at its maximum, " there were no less than 100,000 men

---

[1] D.R.C. *Minutes of Evidence*, 1916 [*Cd*. 8458], Q. 1971.
[2] D.R.C. *Minutes of Evidence* [*Cd*. 8459], Q. 458.

out of employment in Canada ".[1] The disaster to grain farming and the sudden increase in cattle values convinced farmers that where conditions made it possible their business should be, in part at any rate, stock raising.

The total land area of the three Prairie Provinces is estimated at 466,000,000 acres. Of this it is estimated that the possible farm land amounts to 215,000,000 acres. The census of 1921 showed that the area actually occupied as farm land was 88,000,000 acres or less than 19 per cent of the whole land area of Manitoba, Saskatchewan and Alberta. [2]

Irrigation in the Semi-arid Region

To the semi-arid area of the Prairie Provinces belong southern Alberta and the south-western corner of Saskatchewan, the whole containing about 80,000 square miles.[3] The soil of the greater part of this region is rich and it produces every year a good crop of grass, but it lacks moisture. Of the 49,000,000 acres in Alberta suitable for settlement, 20,000,000 are bare prairie, and of this about 60 per cent has too little rainfall. In addition the " Chinook " winds have to be reckoned with. Arriving from the west, while they temper the winter season and bring about the speedy disappearance of snow and ice, they are dreaded by the farmer when they arrive in the summer, for then these hot dry winds are apt to dry up his crops and sap their vitality at their critical stages of growth. Irrigation to a greater or less extent is accordingly necessary if this area is to be utilized for crops.[4] Moreover, " Experience alike in the arid region of the United States and in the semi-arid region of Canada, has shown the necessity of providing for a series of dry years. South-Western Nebraska was settled three times, the two first groups of settlers having abandoned their holdings because of continued drought. In Eastern Assiniboia the first settlers also abandoned their holdings, to be followed by a second group when the series of moist seasons came. In 1894 the Government of the North-West Territories expended $40,000 in relief of settlers ruined by the failure of crops in consequence of drought." [5]

---

[1] *D.R.C.* [*Cd.* 8459] Q. 1021. [2] *Canada Year Book*, 1926, p. 257.
[3] J. S. Dennis, *General Report on Irrigation*, Ottawa, 1895, p. 4.
[4] *D.R.C. Minutes of Evidence* [*Cd.* 8458], Evidence of William Pearce, 1916, p. 127.
[5] James Mavor, Report on the North-West of Canada [*Cd.* 2628], p. 51.

In addition to providing insurance against loss by drought, the benefits derivable from skilful irrigation in Southern Alberta are the production of larger yields of grain, and the encouragement of the live stock industry by the growth of alfalfa, timothy, and other fodder crops and the general adoption of mixed farming. " By applying the exact degree of moisture . . . the irrigation farmer can keep his crops growing until they have attained their maximum development. He then shuts off the water and ripens them quickly. He can make the wheat berries fill by watering when the grain is ' in milk '. He can ' clear ' the barley grain and produce the world's finest malting barley. The onion raiser keeps his bulbs growing until ripening time. He then dries them off, thus ensuring the most perfect keeping qualities." [1] Records taken by the Dominion Government Experimental Farm at Lethbridge from 1908 to 1914 showed that Red Fife wheat under dry farming averaged 26 bushels and under irrigation 46 bushels per acre. The dry-farmed crop of oats was 59 bushels per acre ; the irrigation crop was 42 bushels per acre more. The barley crop was doubled by irrigation, as also was the potato crop.[2]

" Probably the greatest boon that irrigation has conferred on mankind is the practical demonstration of the profitableness of the small farm, acre for acre, as compared with the large farm. Southern Alberta contains many striking proofs of this assertion. The day was when anything less than a section of land (640 acres) was looked upon as being too small, and from that area up to several thousand acres was considered none too large for a farm. But that day is now past, and farms have gradually decreased in size until to-day 40 acres under irrigation, well cultivated, will produce greater returns than four times that area under the old system. The increased prosperity that will certainly accrue to a country from the multiplication of small farms, as compared with the holding of large tracts of land by individuals, is apparent." [3]

Furthermore, irrigation has simplified the forage problem for the farmer in the drier parts of the Prairie Provinces who owns live stock. After the disappearance of open

---

[1] C. W. Peterson, " Irrigation in its Relation to Agriculture and Colonization," *United Empire Journal*, vol. i, 1910, p. 90.

[2] *D.R.C. Minutes of Evidence*, 1916. Evidence of Mr. F. H. Peters, of the Irrigation Branch of the Department of the Interior, Qs. 2095–6. See also ibid., Evidence of Mr. E. F. Drake, p. 171.

[3] C. W. Peterson, op. cit., p. 92.

ranging, provision had to be made not only for summer pasturage but also for winter feeding. For this purpose alfalfa has been found to be the most satisfactory crop, and without irrigation that crop cannot be grown successfully. Indeed, it was for the furnishing of this forage that irrigation was first advocated.[1]

Alfalfa is proving of immense advantage to the farmers of Alberta and Saskatchewan. It has been described as "the greatest forage plant the world has ever known", and under irrigation is one of the most remunerative crops a farmer can grow. One desirable characteristic is that it is a soil renovator as well as a regular forage crop, for instead of depleting the soil its roots replenish the soil with the nitrogenous fertilizing elements of the atmosphere and as soon as a crop has been cut and gathered the ground can be at once irrigated for the next growth.

Water storage was not necessary in the Prairie Provinces for the same purpose as in India, to mitigate the danger of famine. Rather was its purpose to raise a more valuable crop in a country where there was only sufficient rainfall to raise an inferior one. Nor has Canada so far been faced with the difficult engineering problems that make the great irrigation schemes carried out in India and Egypt such a romantic story,[2] although if ever the irrigation of the eastern portion of the semi-arid region is undertaken, where there is only a single river of any size, the Qu'Appelle River, problems of the greatest difficulty will have to be solved.

The principle of irrigation had been applied in Alberta and Saskatchewan from the days of the ranchers who were the earliest settlers, although their works were of the home-made variety, consisting usually of a primitive dam and headgate and a ditch or two for the irrigation of a few acres of hay for the purpose of the cattle-raising which in those days was almost the sole occupation in the district.

By reason of the conditions found in Alberta and Saskatchewan, the method of irrigation most suitable and common is that of flowing the water over the land from the ditches. Openings are made in the ditch and the water is allowed to run out over the land requiring irrigation. As the water spreads further and further afield a point is at last reached where its influence is exhausted. At this point a lateral

---

[1] *D.R.C. Minutes of Evidence*, 1916 [Cd, 8458.] Q. 2191, and pp. 170–1.
[2] See vol. i of the present work, pp. 366 ff.

ditch becomes necessary to carry a fresh supply to a lower belt of land. Another method, irrigation by submersion or flooding, is best suitable for flat or nearly flat lands. Tracts of land are covered with water which is allowed to remain until the soil has reached the required degree of saturation. It is necessary to raise earth ridges for the purpose of confining the water where wanted, and these ridges are the more numerous and close together according as the slope of the ground is more acute. When the ground is thus prepared the water is led on to the ground through the ditches.

In the early days of settlement, the use of water for irrigation was quite unregulated, but as settlement developed the necessity for an irrigation code became obvious in order to avoid disputes as to water rights, to protect those who had expended money in irrigation works, and to conserve supplies. Accordingly the North-West Irrigation Act was passed in 1894.[1] Its broad principles are capable of concise statement. All streams, lakes, springs or other surface sources of water supply are declared the property of the Dominion Government. Riparian rights no longer exist. The right to use such water may be granted to companies or to individuals, but subject to prescribed conditions, for irrigation, agricultural, domestic, industrial and other purposes. The Act is in fact a general water law governing the diversion and use of water for all purposes. The grantee of a water right possesses that right so long as he applies it to beneficial use and may forfeit it by abandonment or nonuse. A necessary corollary of the assumption of the general control of the water supply was the ascertainment by measurement and gauging of the supply of water actually available from each source, and grants of water rights are governed by this information.

Irrigation enterprise in this region was undertaken by the Canadian Pacific Railway Company on a substantial scale. The Bow River was selected as the source of supply. For the purpose of the scheme, 3,000,000 acres of land along the main line of the railway eastwards from Calgary were withdrawn from homestead entry by the Dominion Government and transferred to the Company. That amount of land was due to the Company, but it was now handed over

---

[1] The Act has been amended from time to time, but its essential features have remained unaltered. See now Revised Statues, Canada, 1906, c. 61, and amendments thereto.

in a solid block instead of the alternate sections. By taking over this area of three million acres in the semi-arid belt for the purpose of an irrigation scheme the Company can claim to have rendered productive a tract of land 125 miles in extent east and west, by some 50 miles north and south, which had been thought incapable of use for agricultural purposes. Furthermore the Canadian Pacific Railway Company took over and operated as their Lethbridge section an earlier undertaking, that of the Alberta Irrigation Company, which was begun in 1899 and was the first of these projects on any substantial scale.

The total area capable of irrigation by the Company's projects with their 4,200 miles of canals is approximately 750,000 acres, of which about 172,000 acres were actually irrigated in 1926.

Other public irrigation projects are that of the Canada Land and Irrigation Company, also in the Bow River basin, and schemes under the Irrigation Districts Act of Alberta.[1] These cover a further irrigable area of 364,000 acres, served by 1,215 miles of canals, 95,000 acres being actually under irrigation in 1926. In addition there are some 700 privately owned projects making possible the irrigation of an area estimated at 110,000 acres in the same year.[2]

To encourage settlement and the practice of irrigated farming in southern Alberta and South-Western Saskatchewan, where the average annual rainfall seldom exceeds 16 inches and is often below that figure, the Government undertook to sell land in the drier portions of the region at three dollars an acre, subject to conditions for ensuring irrigation which were designed to be as little onerous as possible upon settlers who in good faith construct and maintain the necessary works and irrigate the land. Later the terms were revised and the sale price of land became five dollars an acre subject however to a deduction of the cost of irrigation works up to a maximum of two dollars an acre.

In an irrigated arid region the system of scattered settlement by which each settler must occupy his own quarter section is manifestly unsuitable. The group or village system of settlement has been successful in Colorado, Utah, Idaho and other places all situated in the arid region of the United States, and immigrants from these places, who were

[1] *Revised Statutes*, Alberta, 1922, c. 114.
[2] These figures are from the *Canada Year Book*, 1927-8, pp. 285-6.

accustomed to the cultivation of dry soils and the use of irrigation, were the earliest settlers in the irrigated regions of Alberta. The desirability of encouraging the village system of settlement was recognized when the Canadian Government allowed the Canadian Pacific Railway Company to take the land wanted for their irrigation scheme in a solid block instead of in alternate sections.

CHAPTER 15

THE PENETRATION OF THE LAURENTIAN PLATEAU

Prospectors and mineral discoveries.
    Gold.
    Silver.
    Copper.
    Iron.
The agricultural possibilities of the Clay Belt.

THE penetration of the Laurentian Plateau, the name given to the southern area of the Canadian Shield, has resulted from the discovery of the Sudbury nickel-copper field, the Cobalt silver-cobalt mines, the Porcupine and Kirkland Lake gold mines and other rich metalliferous areas. This pre-Cambrian area of northern Ontario, abounding as it does in lakes and rivers, is accessible to prospectors during the period of the year from April to November, when the ground is clear of snow, and is accordingly one of the regions where a definite line of penetration can be observed. At the same time these same innumerable lakes and rivers, the results of arrested drainage and the liberal rainfall of the region, have so stimulated the growth of timber and vegetation over the whole of the Ontario part of the Canadian Shield as to put great difficulties in the way of the prospector in many regions where undoubtedly enormous mineral wealth lies buried.

At the close of the nineteenth century little was known of Ontario outside the region in the neighbourhood of the Great Lakes. The hinterland extending northwards to James Bay from Lake Nipissing was left to the Indian tribes and the only signs of penetration were the scattered trading posts of the Hudson's Bay Company. The vast trackless forests of spruce and jackpine made the region almost inaccessible save in canoes by way of lake and stream. In 1916 the Dominions Royal Commission were told that the region near the Manitoba boundary known as Patricia, covering 94,000,000 acres, was still unexplored and still a region about which practically nothing was known. The Canadian Pacific Railway had already opened up the territory north of Georgian Bay. The Temiskaming and

Northern Ontario Railway went north in the direction of James Bay, and just as the earlier line led to the discovery of the vast nickel-copper deposits of the Sudbury region in 1883, so the construction of the Temiskaming and Northern Ontario Railway was followed by the discovery of the rich silver deposits of Cobalt in 1903, and the Porcupine gold mines in 1909. The Kirkland Lake gold deposits were discovered further east towards Quebec in 1912.

Gold was found in Ontario so far back as 1866. The story of the discovery has been placed on record by the geologist who had then begun the work of geological exploration in the south-east of the Province. " In the early part of August, 1866, . . . I was informed that a metal, suspected to be gold, had just been taken from an opening . . . on the property of Mr. J. Richardson. A visit was at once made to the locality and the lot was found to be the same as that on which openings had previously been made for copper ore. . . . Mr. Richardson informed me that a person named Powell and an old Dutch miner had lately found flakes of yellow metal resembling copper, which he could beat out into thin leaves. At my request he showed me the specimens which he had collected, and I at once informed him that the metal was gold." [1] An important discovery of gold, this time in north-west Ontario, followed in 1871. A boom in this region reached its climax in 1897 ; the usual slump followed, and " inefficient management and stock jobbing operators caused the loss of much capital." [2] The great period in gold discovery in Ontario came in 1905–18 when literally an important gold area was found every year. Porcupine, the largest producer (the principal mine, the Hollinger, being one of the great gold mines of the world,) was discovered in 1909. Kirkland Lake, next in importance, dates from 1912. Up to 1911 the total output of gold in Ontario was relatively small and in the result unprofitable, the greatest output for any one year being something less than $500,000. In 1913 the value of the gold produced was over $4,500,000 and by 1923 Ontario was first in gold production among all the Canadian Provinces and American States with an output for the year valued at over 20 million dollars.

---

[1] H. G. Vennor, in report of the Geological Survey of Canada, 1866–9, quoted P. E. Hopkins, "Ontario Gold Deposits," 30*th Annual Report*, *Ontario Department of Mines*, Toronto, 1924, p. 1.

[2] Ibid., p. 3.

The gold deposits that have proved to be capable of profitable working in this region have all been lode gold deposits. No known placer deposits have yet been proved to be of commercial importance in the Province.[1]

There was an indication of Ontario's wealth in silver so long ago as 1868, when on an islet in Lake Superior, near Port Arthur, a settler " found a vein containing galena and silver from which ten labourers in fourteen days, working with tongs and long-handled shovels, took 28,073 pounds of ore that, after being smelted, sold for $23,115. On the rock was opened the Silver Islet mine, which was worked for fifteen years or more and yielded about 3,000,000 fine ounces of silver worth $3,500,000." [2]   It was, however, not until 1903, when the railway era had begun in the interior of Canada, that the real wealth of Ontario in, among other minerals, silver was appreciated. In that year two woodsmen, standing on the edge of a railway cutting, were amusing themselves by throwing small bits of rock into the lake, when they notices something which looked like lead. It turned out to be silver. Further examination disclosed " a profusion of blackened, tarnished silver in lumps, plates and nuggets up to ten pounds in weight.[3] Further discoveries made it clear that here, among the oldest rocks in the world, one of the greatest silver deposits ever known had come to light, and the fabulously rich Cobalt camp came into existence.

The economic advance of northern Ontario as a result of the discovery was rapid. In 1905 and 1906 an entirely new population had taken possession of what was a wilderness, and capital was attracted to the country in large amounts, especially from America.

The output of silver from Cobalt Camp was 206,000 ounces in 1904. In 1911 the peak was reached, the output being 31,507,000 ounces valued at $16,000,000 dollars. Then a gradual decline began. Nevertheless it could be said in 1924 that " an average of 2·1 tons of pure silver have been won from the mines of Cobalt for every 24 hours since they began to yield ".[4]   Certainly there was no reason

---

[1] H. G. Venner, in report of the Geological Survey of Canada, 1866–9, quoted P. E. Hopkins, *Ontario Gold Deposits*, 30th Annual Report, Ontario Department of Mines, Toronto, 1924, p. 8.

[2] *Ontario : Mines and Mineral Resources*, Toronto, 1924 (Canada : Pamphlets. No. 248 in D.O. & C.O. Library), p. 29.

[3] *Ontario : Mines and Mineral Resources.* Toronto, 1924, p. 31.

[4] Ibid.

to doubt that Canada would be easily able to retain its position as a silver-producing territory even though the yield of Cobalt Camp dwindled until it became quite unremunerative. The Gowganda area, 55 miles north-west of Cobalt, has an abundance of silver, but its productiveness has been hampered by distance from the railway and its general lack of transport facilities. The South Lorrain camp is about 18 miles to the south-east of Cobalt. Prematurely closed down as being worked out, the Keeley mine was bought for $100,000. " The manager of the English company which bought it diagnosed the geology of the property as indicating a strong probability of ore a short distance away from the old workings. A shaft was sunk and the hopes entertained were more than realized. A veritable treasure chamber of ore was struck. . . . Keeley is now producing at the rate of 135,000 ounces or more of silver a month, and is continuing to encounter good ore as the shaft descends." [1] The Frontier mine adjoining the Keeley has yielded ore consisting of large plates or masses of solid silver.

Copper seems to be everywhere in the Canadian Shield. From the Sudbury centre in Ontario the copper-producing region was ever widening until westwards it included Manitoba, where the development of the Flin Flon district was commenced in the last years of the War ; and eastwards, north-western Quebec, in the Rouyn district of which province one of the most notable discoveries in recent times of rich copper-gold ore was made. The Canadian National Railway is available ; there is abundant hydro-electric power ; and Quebec seems destined soon not only to recover but to surpass her former importance as a copper-producing area. Again, right away in the north-west " the copper-bearing rocks would seem to extend along the Arctic coast both east and west of the Coppermine River for about 500 miles in all, and probably many of the smaller islands off the coast are also of the same rocks, and the total area of these rocks undoubtedly amounts to many thousands of square miles." [2]

Some reference to the inhospitable nature of the country occupied by the southern part of the Canadian Shield where it skirts the northern side of Lake Superior and of the

[1] *Mining and Mineral Resources of Ontario*, Toronto, 1924.
[2] An Engineering Report quoted in *The Mineral Wealth of Canada* published by the Canadian Bank of Commerce, 1927, p. 27.

serious obstacle it presented to the railway builders has already been given.[1] Such penetration as has taken place in this region has been due to mining enterprise and in particular to that Cinderella of Canadian mining, the iron mining industry. For iron mining as a factor in Canadian economic history belongs to the past rather than the present. " Ontario has produced slightly over 5,000,000 short tons of ore and iron ore concentrates since the year 1869. The largest production was recorded in 1915, when 394,054 short tons was produced."[2] In 1924, the Province had no producing mines in operation.[3]

The discovery of a great stretch of excellent agricultural land within the confines of the Canadian Shield was one of those surprises that sometimes await the explorer. In 1900 the Government of Ontario organized an expedition for the purpose of reporting on the more northerly part of the province. They found that the great " Clay Belt ", running from the Quebec boundary west through Nipissing and into the district of Thunder Bay, an area of some 24,500 square miles and larger than the States of Massachusetts, Connecticut, Rhode Island, New Jersey, and Delaware combined, was a well-watered and " almost unbroken stretch of good farming land ", with a climate which " presents no obstacle to successful agricultural settlement ". It was also found to possess vast forests of spruce, jackpine, and poplar, and infinite resources in water power. The impression that the winters of this region were of Arctic severity and its summers too short to enable crops to mature was erroneous.[4]

The " Clay Belt ", according to geologists, " occupies a part of the basin that during the glacial period was submerged and covered with a coating of clay which smoothed over its inequalities and concealed most of the underlying rocks. Since its emergence the surface has been but slightly altered by drainage channels cut across it."[5] As to the quality of the soil, " A skilled eye could see that here was some of the finest soil for which a farmer could wish. . . .

---

[1] See Chapter 9.

[2] *Mines and Mineral Resources of Ontario*, Toronto, 1924, p. 55.

[3] Ibid., p. 48. Iron ore shipments from Canadian mines were 268,043 short tons in 1909 ; 307,634 in 1913 ; 398,112 (the highest) in 1915 ; 30,752 in 1923, and 200 in 1926 (*Canada Year Book*, 1927–8, p. 380).

[4] Report of Survey and Exploration of Northern Ontario, 1900, quoted *Dominion Debates*, 1903, vol. iv, col. 7684.

[5] *Canada Year Book*, 1927–8, p. 5.

Nature had endowed the land with all the nourishment it required for the propagation of a variety of crops, for the top soil was nothing but a thick layer of decayed vegetation—leaves, branches, and thick trunks which had bowed to the blast, or the ravages of time, and had disappeared into dust. . . . The so-called Clay Belt is clay only in regard to its subsoil. The top-soil . . . is a loam for the most part of a sandy nature." [1]

In addition to the natural quality of its soil, the Clay Belt of Ontario possesses other features that would *prima facie* suggest speedy settlement. The Grand Trunk Pacific Railway was located thus far north in order to open up the country. The great mining camps provide profitable markets for all forms of agricultural produce. The advantage to the agricultural industry of the close proximity of mining settlements was early recognized. "A few years ago the population were dependent upon the lumbering firms, who took the produce of the farmers at what price they chose without consulting the producer, who was invariably in debt to them. Money was very little used, and the whole country bore an air of poverty and hardship. Go now through the same section, and a very different prospect is presented. Produce of all descriptions commands a high price in cash; teams which had to be sent far up the rivers for lumbering in the winter are now in demand for drawing ore from the mine; the farmers rapidly accumulating, if not wealth, at least a sufficiency of means to which they have hitherto been strangers, the influx of strangers connected with the various workings is swelling out the population of the villages, and the additional revenue received in the form of taxes from the increased value of the land add to the municipal wealth, while the lands surrounding the district are rapidly rising in value." [2]

Here, then, in Ontario, in the Clay Belt, millions of acres of Crown lands await settlement. [3] It is good agricultural land, but unlike the prairie lands it is bush land that requires clearance before it can be brought into use, [4] and while such

---

[1] F. A. Talbot, *The Making of a Great Canadian Railway*, pp. 86–9.

[2] *The Resources of the Ottawa District*, Ottawa, 1872, p. 20. (Canada: Pamphlets, vol. 3, No. 69, in D.O. & C.O. Library.)

[3] The Dominions Royal Commission were told by the Director of Colonization for Ontario in 1916, that this land was to be had for 50 cents an acre. (*D.R.C. Minutes of Evidence* [Cd. 8458], Q. 2601).

[4] The cost of clearance was put at $25 an acre (*D.R.C Minutes of Evidence* [Cd. 8458], Q. 2610).

clearance is being effected the settler, unless he is a man of means, has to keep going by finding work with a neighbouring farmer, or in some mill.

Accordingly, the district does not attract settlers, although all the good and accessible agricultural land in Ontario has long been filled up. Agricultural settlement in the Province has made little advance geographically since the lands of the North-West became available. The Prairie Provinces or heavily timbered lands of second rate quality near home had long been the alternatives offered to the Ontario farmers' sons who wanted farms on their own account, and it is not surprising that the land which could be made into a farm without the preliminary heavy work of clearance was preferred. Similarly the signs are that the settlement of the Clay Belt, where also much clearance of timber has to be undertaken, will proceed but slowly while land in the Prairie Provinces remains available.

CHAPTER 16

THE DEVELOPMENT OF THE CORDILLERAN REGION

IT has been seen that agricultural settlement has been the characteristic of the Great Plains and that the pursuit of its mineral wealth has been the purpose of the penetration of the Canadian Shield. No single line of development has characterized the exploitation of the Cordilleran region save that part of it which is occupied by the Yukon territory, where the invasion of the 'nineties was entirely consequent on the gold discoveries. British Columbia has at different times attracted settlers and immigrants of every sort and condition, so that its economic development is a microcosm of the economic development of the Dominion. Fur traders, prospectors and miners, lumbermen, fishermen, ranchers, farmers and fruit growers have in turn helped to open up and settle the Pacific Province and to raise its population from 36,247, the figure at which it stood in 1871, the year when it entered the Confederation, to 524,582 in 1921.

British Columbia is the province of vast potentialities rather than present accomplishment. Thus it possesses the best coal on the Pacific Coast. The Vancouver Island coalfields, which are regarded as practically inexhaustible, provide the foundation of a possible great industrial region. The forest wealth of the province has been but slightly encroached upon, whereas on the Pacific coast of the United States the timber is disappearing right up to the snow line. A glance at the map suffices to make manifest the commanding position of the British Columbian ports in relation to the trade routes of the Pacific.

Exploitation of British Columbia's Natural Resources

The penetration of the country by the early fur traders has already been described.[1]

The mining history of British Columbia is a record of periods of hectic excitement separated by long stretches of stagnation and lethargy. The gold discoveries which have been such prominent features of the province attracted a class of immigrant whose desire was for sudden wealth rather than the pursuit of the more enduring branches of industry. The first gold rush commenced with the discovery in 1858 of placer gold in the Fraser River region, and was continued as a consequence of the further discovery two years later in the Cariboo district. It had all the attributes of squalor and lawlessness which seemed inseparable from such events in the early days of mining adventure. " The gold fever was at its height ; new mines were being discovered almost daily. Thousands of prospectors were coming in, hundreds returning ' dead broke '. They came from all parts of the world, and were of all conditions ; military officers, soldiers, sailors, lawyers, parsons, merchants, sons of bishops, men from Cornwall, from Australia, California, Mexico, Texas, gamblers, deserters— in fact, men of every race and kind imaginable. They besieged us with requests for work to enable them to progress a little further on the way to fortune, or to help them on their backward journey stranded and disheartened. All along the sixty miles of road were graves, chiefly of murdered men, but some of men who had died of hardships. Such was mining in 1864 in the Cariboo." [2]

---

[1] See Chapter 5.
[2] Moberly and Cameron, *When Fur was King*, London, 1929.

The prosperity which resulted from the discoveries was purely artificial, and the system of trade and industry which came into existence had the stability of an inverted cone. The whole colony was still dependent on California and Oregon for its cereals, its meat, and its farm produce. Reaction soon came. " Overtrading and excessive speculation . . . took place ; large stocks of goods were imported in the belief that population would rapidly increase. A huge system of credit was allowed to rule the market and trade generally was established on an insecure and false basis. Advances were made by the banks to the merchants, not only for the purchase of goods, but also to defray their carriage to the mines, and the market being overstocked, the banks were obliged to seize and sell at a ruinous sacrifice. . . . The natural result ensued, and at the close of 1865 it was evident that a financial crisis was imminent. Traders and merchants on all sides became bankrupt, the value of land decreased by one-half its former price, and the population steadily diminished." [1]

In British Columbia, as elsewhere in Canada, so far as the progress of the mining industry is a factor in the progress of settlement, serious development only began in the twentieth century. The value of mineral production in the province during the ten years 1906–15 was $267,000,000, while for the whole preceding fifty-five years the value was only $248,000,000.[2] All but about 5 per cent. of this value is represented by lead, copper, coal, zinc, silver, and gold.

Lead-zinc mining is largely centred in the Kootenay district. For many years the mines were operated under great difficulties owing to restricted markets and low prices, but improved metallurgical methods and extended uses brought about great activity. The vast ore reserves of the famous Sullivan mine illustrate both the mineral wealth of the country, and the metallurgical problems their variety and combination involve. " This immense body of ore, averaging about $16\frac{1}{2}$ per cent. lead, 7 oz. of silver to the ton, 14 per cent. zinc, 20 per cent. iron, and 10 per cent. silica, permits large-scale operations at almost any conceivable price level." [3]

[1] E. Graham Alston, *Colonial Handbook to British Columbia*, London, 1870 (Canada: Pamphlets, vol. 3, No. 66, in D.O. & C.O. Library).
[2] *D.R.C. Minutes of Evidence*, 1916 [*Cd.* 8459], Memorandum at p. 264.
[3] *The Mineral Wealth of Canada:* The Canadian Bank of Commerce, 1927. (Canada : Pamphlets, No. 266 in D.O. & C.O. Library, p. 39.)

Copper has long been one of British Columbia's chief metal products. As has been the case for a long time, more than half the copper output of Canada has come from British Columbia, and the reserves seem fabulous. Thus in the Similakameen district south-east of Vancouver there is what has been described as " a mountain of ore ". It is a fortunate circumstance that rich copper bearing areas have been found along the coast and among the numerous islands between Vancouver and Alaska, which are readily accessible. It is in copper mining that development in recent years has been most striking. " For the ten years 1896 to 1905, the output was 199,137,000 lbs. while for the next ten years ending with 1915 the amount was 451,712,000 lbs." [1]

Coal mining is an ancient industry in the province. " In 1849, the development of the first coal mines in British Columbia had begun. . . . Fort Rupert was uncompleted when Michael Muir, a Scottish miner, with his wife, a family of sons and daughters, and a small party of miners, was sent by the company to establish workings on the deposits. Upon sinking a shaft ninety feet, however, Muir declared the seam too small to be workable, and complications with the Indians arising, the miners left for California. . . . Additional and better mining machinery arrived in 1851, but more promising deposits having been disclosed by the Indians at Nanaimo, the plant was removed thither . . . . The famous Douglas seam was located in 1852. In the same year, Fort Nanaimo was erected in the neighbourhood. Two thousand tons were shipped in the following year, bringing $11 per ton at Nanaimo, and $28 at San Francisco." [2]

Dilke in *Greater Britain* points out the importance of coal reserves as factors in the future distribution of the world's industrial centres. " The three countries of the Pacific which must for a time at least rise to manufacturing greatness are Japan, Vancouver Island, and New South Wales, but which of them will become wealthiest and most powerful depends mainly on the amount of coal they respectively possess so situated as to be cheaply raised." In Vancouver Island the coal industry goes back to early times. Thence coal is exported to the United States of America, and there coal is supplied to ships on the Pacific routes. Elsewhere

---

[1] *D.R.C. Minutes of Evidence*, 1916 [*Cd.* 8459], Memorandum at p. 262.
[2] Coats and Gosnell, *Sir James Douglas*, pp. 190–1.

in the Province billions of tons of anthracite and bituminous coal, to say nothing of lignite, merely await transport connections to become vast sources of wealth.

Gold is more important in the Province's early than in its later history. Of the early gold rush something has already been said. In recent history the precious metals have had to yield precedence in relative importance to lead, copper, coal, and zinc. [1]

As a gold-producing Province British Columbia held the lead until 1897, but it was then passed by the Yukon and later by Ontario. The western Province, however, turned the tables on its rival when in 1926 its output of silver exceeded 10,500,000 ounces, a total which gave it first place among the silver-producing provinces of Canada.

In other natural products besides minerals, nature in British Columbia has been equally prolific and has built on an equally grand scale. As to the fish : " Salmon is so abundant that in the season they are commonly sold by the Indians for 6d. apiece, and of excellent quality. Sturgeon of enormous size are found in the sand banks at the mouths of the rivers, also a fine species of cod. The waters abound with halibut, smelt, herring, dog fish, flounders, whiting, and oysters. Herring and smelt are so abundant that they are absolutely raked into buckets by the Indians. The eulachon is a very valuable fish from its extremely oily nature ; the Indians press the oil from them. . . . Whaling has been pursued with great success . . . in the Gulf of Georgia." [2] Small wonder that British Columbia is easily first in a comparison of the value of the fisheries of the various provinces.[3] More has to be said about the industry hereafter when the subject of Oriental immigration comes to be considered.

The timber of the Province, again, is phenomenal. The forests and woodlands in British Columbia cover 182 million

---

[1] In 1926 the respective values of these minerals produced in British Columbia were :—

Lead . .	$18,012,509
Copper .	$12,292,450
Coal . .	$10,612,915
Zinc .	$10,154,214
Silver . .	$6,599,376
Gold . .	$4,669,065

[2] E. G. Alston, Colonial Handbooks, *British Columbia*, London, 1870.
[3] In 1926, the total value of the fisheries for all Canada was $56,360,633. Of this British Columbia contributed nearly half, namely $27,367,109, Nova Scotia was next highest.

acres. The giant Douglas fir and the great girth of the red cedar are notorious. Trees 300 ft. in height are common. The most valuable and widely distributed tree is the Douglas fir which grows up to 55°, where it is supplanted by cypress, red cedar, hemlock, and spruce. " Firs, the staple of commerce owing to their durability and strength, are widely distributed . . . the best average trees are 150 ft. high, and measure 5 to 6 ft. in diameter." [1]

The lumbering industry belongs to the earlier economic history of Canada. Lumbering was flourishing by the end of the 'sixties and in 1871 British Columbia exported timber to the value of $182,490, mostly to Chili, Peru, Australasia and China. From the Atlantic provinces the lumberman has been moving westwards to Lake Superior and northwards to the Hudson Bay slope. " New tree species and our largest stand of timber have been added to the Dominion by British Columbia." [2]

The Douglas fir, the " all utility " wood, as it is called, is largely exported to Great Britain and elsewhere. It is used by railways for sleepers, and by ship builders for decking. Among the miscellaneous uses to which it is put are the manufacture of doors, parquet blocks, and ply-wood, which is proof against warping. British Columbia's pulp woods, in particular the spruce, constitute the largest stand of pulp-wood in the world. The growth of the pulp and paper industry is one of the most notable developments of recent Canadian economic history, and it is in connection with that industry that the exploitation of the Dominion's forest wealth is most appropriately considered.

" We have seen timothy 6 feet high and clover more than knee deep. We have seen apple trees which grew 5 feet in a single year laden with fruit until they had to be bolted together with iron bolts to keep them from splitting." [3] In such a farmer's paradise one would expect eager settlement, but as a matter of fact, agricultural settlement in British Columbia has been tardy.

[1] A. S. White, " The Dominion of Canada, a Study in Regional Geography," Scottish Geographical Magazine, vol. 29 (1913).
[2] Canada Year Book, 1925, p. 323.
[3] Account of visit to Canada by the Scottish Agricultural Commission in 1908 (Canada : Pamphlets, vol. 8, No. 217, in D.O. & C.O. Library).

Agricultural Development : Cattle Ranch to Fruit Farm

Before the country was opened up by the Canadian Pacific Railway, and before the Government took active control of land administration, farmers were an insignificant proportion of the population as compared with miners, lumbermen, and fishermen. Such agricultural industry as there was took the form of cattle ranching, for there was a very profitable market for beef among the miners, and the men who took pack-horses up the Cariboo road during the gold rush of 1859 turned more readily to ranching than to small farming. " In this way many of the most fertile valleys were monopolised by a few individuals owning 1,000 to 30,000 acres—many more than they could possibly cultivate or utilize to the advantage of the community." [1] The coming of the railway, however, broke down the local monopoly of cattle grazing for beef, and from this and other causes " these big estates are now being sub-divided and sold in smaller parcels, with the result that small farms and orchards are becoming numerous on ground which was for years held as pasture only, or merely for purposes of speculation." [2]

Then again, British Columbia has a more benign climate than the Prairie Provinces. Nevertheless agricultural settlement was slow, for the country is mountainous and suitable land limited in quantity. It is mostly heavily timbered, and the settler who takes up land in British Columbia, especially in the lower Fraser Valley and the coast districts and the part of the province west of the Cascade Mountains, must generally be prepared to undertake the preliminary work of clearing away the fir, pine, cedar, and other timber as well as the undergrowth in order that a patch of forest may become a field. This preliminary work means chopping during the early summer months, and a great burn-up in August, while it may be several years before the final process in clearing operations is reached, that is to say, " stumping ", by which is meant burning or blasting out the bigger fir and cedar stumps or extracting them with a stumping machine.

---

[1] J. S. Redmayne, *Fruit Farming on the Dry Belt of British Columbia*, B.C. Development Association, Ltd., London, 1909, p. 20 (North America : Pamphlets No. 10, in D.O. & C.O. Library).
[2] Ibid.

Another reason why settlement in British Columbia languished in its early stages was that it took the form of isolated settlement over large areas. Settlers took up areas of 150 acres widely separated from one another. There was no local employment available to enable them to tide over the early stages while clearing their lands and it was difficult to market any produce they might have for disposal. Nor could they bulk consignments to get the advantage of the cheaper rates allowed on such consignments by the railways. The later tendency accordingly was to encourage closer settlement.

Perhaps the strongest reason of all why its industries remained so long dormant, and its great resources so little developed after the Province joined the Confederation, was the high rate of interest which capital commanded. The statement was made in 1870 that " money readily commands from 12 to 15 per cent per annum." [1]

On the Pacific side of the Dominion it was in Vancouver that agriculture and fruit culture first became comparatively important industries, but it was the discovery of the possibilities of the " Dry Belt " of British Columbia—the area which extends north and south between the parallel mountain ranges—for fruit culture that enabled the Province to develop its most notable agricultural pursuit.

Fruit cultivation in the Dry Belt of British Columbia was an importation from Washington and Oregon, where the industry had its origin and where systematic irrigation enabled it to reach so high a degree of development. Finding in British Columbia conditions of soil, climate, and rainfall similar to those of the Dry Belt in his own country, the American fruit-grower began to turn his attention northwards when the supply of suitable land on his own side of the international boundary approached exhaustion.

The story of the origin of the fruit-growing industry in this part of the world has been thus recorded :—

" The first fruit-trees grown on the Columbia sprang from the seed of an apple eaten at a dinner-party in London. The dinner had been given to Captain Simpson, of the Company's coast service. One of the ladies present, more in jest than in earnest, took from the apples brought on with the dessert, the seeds ; and dropping them into Simpson's pocket, told him to plant them when he should

[1] E. Graham Alston, *Colonial Handbooks, British Columbia*, London, 1870.

reach his North-West wilderness. The Captain had forgotten the circumstance until reminded of it while dining at Fort Vancouver in 1827 by finding in the pocket of the waistcoat, which he had worn last in London, the seeds playfully put there by his lady friend. Taking them out he gave them to Bruce, the gardener, who carefully planted them ; and thence within the territory of Oregon began the growth of apple-trees." [1]

The agricultural advantages of the Dry Belt consist in its peculiar productive soil and its climate. The moist vapours from the Pacific, which condense in the form of rain as they meet the mountains near the coast, pass upwards over the country intervening between the parallel ranges to fall again as rain when the inner mountain chains are encountered. Thus the Dry Belt escapes the excessive rainfall of spring and summer, and the snow of winter.

The Dry Belt is also advantageously situated for the purpose of marketing the produce its favourable natural circumstances enable it to grow. On the east it has the vast Prairie Provinces with their ever-increasing population. On the west are the populous coast districts. Moreover, in recent years the boxed apples of British Columbia have found their way in increasing quantities to the markets of Great Britain and continental Europe.

The conditions of fruit-farming in this region, holdings of five to ten acres each, grouped by circumstances of soil and irrigation, conduce to co-operative effort, and the co-operative principle has taken firm root, with the result that the grading and packing of the fruit have been much improved and advice as to markets and transport is available from the various Fruit Growers' Associations.

Apples are the principal crop. Pears are also grown. Peaches are produced, many of them for canning purposes, and the plums and apricots are dried. Intermediate crops of vegetables are grown between the fruit trees, and poultry raising and bee-keeping are also part of the varied occupations of the British Columbia farmer.

British Columbia has no monopoly of fruit production in Canada. Nova Scotia has grown apples from the time it was Acadia, and Great Britain now takes the bulk of its crop. In Ontario fruit culture for commercial purposes goes back for more than half a century and it is there that the industry has reached its highest degree of development.

[1] H. H. Bancroft, *History of the North-West Coast*, vol. 2, p. 441.

In British Columbia, fruit growing as a commercial undertaking only became possible when the Canadian Pacific Railway was built. Once started, however, the development of the industry has been rapid. In 1891 the area devoted to fruit culture was 6,500 acres. The census of 1921 shows a total area of 43,569 acres devoted to fruit culture in the Province.

Oriental Immigration

British Columbia has an immigration problem all her own. The other provinces may regret their inability to attract a larger proportion of immigrants of British stock and the high proportion of Central Europeans whom they have to accept if the country is to be developed with any reasonable degree of speed. But at least they are white races, and not incapable of assimilation into the body politic of the Dominion. Into British Columbia, however, there came immigrants whose absorption into the political system of Canada is regarded as out of the question ; immigrants, moreover, whose presence has a disturbing effect on the economic life of the Province.

Till the middle of the nineteenth century, the Northwest Coast of America remained the haunt of a handful of fur-traders and of a cluster of farmers who grew crops near the forts for the supply of the traders. Then came the great gold discoveries of California and the notorious Gold Rush. Europeans poured into the diggings from all parts of the world, crossing the continent in bullock-wagons and rounding Cape Horn in wind-jammers. Very shortly after the beginning of this rush the Chinese commenced to cross the Pacific, being driven out of their own country by overpopulation and the low standard of living and attracted to America by the high rate of remuneration offered there. Some entered into labour contracts with the Spanish in Mexico, but the bulk became labourers in the gold mining industry of California. About 1858, it became known that gold had been struck in what is now known as British Columbia. Immediately a mad stampede took place from California northwards. The Chinese followed and in the early 'sixties they were established in the placer mines of Cariboo. This was the first Oriental immigration into British territory in North America ; but once the stream of immigration had begun it continued to flow. Most of the Chinese located themselves in British Columbia, and even to-day the proportion found in Canada but outside of British Columbia is relatively small. In 1862, the Chinese numbered 2,500 as against a white population of 7,000 in summer, and 3,000 in winter.[1] Their increase of numbers was rapid, and it kept pace with the growth in population of the whites and Indians combined between the years 1880 and 1900.[2]

This increase was viewed with deepening alarm by the European section of the community, who feared the under-cutting of wage-rates or the assimilation of the white standard of living to the Chinese level. In 1885 the first Poll Tax was imposed, with the specific aim if checking the inflow on all Chinese entering the Dominion. The tax, which at first was $50 per head, was raised to $100 in 1901, and to $500 in 1903.[3] This effort to check Oriental immigration failed in its object. The chief effect of the tax was to lengthen the period of contract service which was necessary in order to enable the Chinese to repay the wealthy merchants and emigration companies who advanced them the necessary money for their fares as well as to pay the tax.[4]

In the opening years of the twentieth century, attention for a time was diverted from the Chinese to the Indians and the Japanese, whose immigration figures had begun to rival those of the Chinese.[5]

[1] R. C. L. Brown, *Essay on British Columbia* (1862), p. 52.

[2] Report of the Royal Commission on Chinese and Japanese Immigration, Session 1902, *Canadian Sessional Papers*, No. 54 (cited hereafter as "R.C.J.I.").

The relative increase in the population of British Columbia will be seen from the following table :—

	Whites and Indians.	Chinese.	Japanese.
1881 . . .	49,459	4,350	—
1891 . . .	89,263	8,910	—
1901 . . .	157,815	14,376*	4,578

* Incomplete, estimated at 16,000 (p. 8).

[3] Chinese Immigration Act, 1903, *Statutes of Canada*, 3 Edw. vii, chap. 8.

[4] J. Mavor, *My Windows on the Street of the World*, vol. i, p. 351. Professor Mavor expressed the view that "during the period of the debt-dependance, the Chinese are in fact peons or slaves of the company".

[5] The number of Japanese in Canada, according to the Census of 1901, was 4,674. In 1900 the Japanese Government prohibited the emigration of its subjects to America, and emigration figures fell off. From 1902 to 1904 the estimated annual number of immigrants into Canada was 250. In 1904–5 there were 354 Japanese immigrants. In 1905–6 the number was 1922, and in 1906–7 (nine months) it was 2,042. Then came the great influx of 1907, which led to anti-Oriental rioting. Japanese Immigration into Canada :—

Fiscal year 1907–8 . .	7,601
,, ,, 1908–9 . .	495
,, ,, 1909–10 . .	271
Seven months of 1910–11 .	295

According to the Census of 1921 there were 15,868 Japanese in Canada.

The Indian immigration figures never became serious, and the problem solved itself. With the rising tide of feeling in India against the emigration of Indian coolies to other parts of the Empire, the stream of Indian immigrants into Canada gradually dried up.

In the case of the Japanese, a solution was found in an agreement with the Japanese Government, whereby under machinery set up by the Japanese Government, immigrants from Japan were limited to small numbers.

In the proceedings which led up to this solution, the Japanese Government acted with great self-restraint. Under the Anglo-Japanese Treaty of 1894, which Canada accepted in 1906, after a full Parliamentary discussion, a treaty which dealt with trade matters as well as immigration questions, Japanese enjoyed the right to enter Canada as freely as British subjects. Opposition to Oriental immigration into the Province culminated in 1907 in riots and a demand for the abrogation of the Treaty. This demand the Canadian Government refused, pointing out that under the Treaty Canadian trade with Japan had substantially increased. Japan did not insist on the enforcement of her full rights under the Treaty, and, recognizing the existence of special circumstances in Canada's Pacific Provinces, decided to take effective steps to restrict emigration to the Dominion.[1]

With the Indians and Japanese fading out of the picture the Chinese once more came to the front. Their continued increase was viewed with the utmost repugnance by the European population, and pressure was brought to bear on the Government. The final upshot was that, in 1923, an Act was passed which abolished the Poll Tax on Chinese entering Canada, and confined the entry of Chinese to certain classes, such as merchants and students, who are not regarded as residents,[2] so that labour from China was completely excluded and the only increase possible in the case of the Chinese in Canada was by the natural means of the surplus of births over deaths among those already there and allowed to remain.

[1] See *Annual Register*, 1907, p. 457, and 1908, p. 448. See also Report of Commission appointed to investigate the riots, presented in 1908 (*Canada: Sessional Papers*, 1907–8, No. 74g) ; and Report of W. L. Mackenzie King on Methods by which Oriental Labourers have been induced to come to Canada, 1908 (Canada: Pamphlets No. 168, in D.O. and C.O. Library).

[2] Chinese Immigration Act, 1923, Chap. 38 (Revised Statutes, 1927, chap. 95).

The Oriental element in the population is widely dispersed in the industries of the Province. They form from one-third to one-half the labouring strength of the lumber mills, the saw-mills, the shingle mills, the fishing and the pulp and paper industry.[1] At the time of the Dominions Royal Commission, about 90 per cent. of the agricultural produce in Vancouver was coming from the Chinese, who had also secured the monopoly of market-gardening in Victoria.[2] The Oriental element at the beginning of the twentieth century were, however, chiefly found in connexion with the canning industry.[3] In the fishing industry there was a national division of labour, for while the Japanese supplied the bulk of the labour for the actual fishing operations, the Chinese manned the canning factories, which deal with both fish and fruit. The canning industry has been the real *raison d'être* of the Chinese immigration, and the battle over the question of immigration or non-immigration of Orientals has been fought out between the cannery owners on the one hand and the general public and the organizations of white labour on the other hand. The Chinese labourers were managed under the " boss " system, whereby a contract was entered into between the cannery owner and the boss, who guaranteed, paid and controlled the requisite number of labourers, thus relieving the owner of all worry, besides affording an economic and efficient labour force.[4] The cannery owners alleged that the industry

[1] *Canadian Annual Review*, 1923. From the figures given by Hon. A. M. Manson, Attorney-General of British Columbia, the proportion of Asiatics employed in various industries, aside from agriculture, was : logging camps, $7\frac{1}{2}$ per cent ; lumber mills, 41 per cent ; saw mills, 39 per cent ; shingle mills, 54 per cent ; baking establishments, 16 per cent ; fishing, 39 per cent ; fruit canning, 15 per cent ; coal mining, 15 per cent ; and pulp and paper, 37 per cent (p. 271).

[2] E. E. Braithwaite, "Canada and the Orient," *Canadian Magazine*, 1922, vol. lx, p. 16.

[3] *R.C.J.I.* (speaking of conditions about 1902) : " The canning industry : The great numbers of Japanese and Chinese engaged in it greatly exceeds the number of them employed in any other industry. . . . Of the twenty thousand employees engaged in the Fisheries, it is estimated that ten thousand are employed in and about the canneries and of these about six thousand are Chinese " (pp. 134–5).

[4] " The process of canning (making cans, filling, cooking, soldering, and boxing) is almost exclusively done by contract. The contracts are made with boss Chinamen who hire their own help in their own way. . . . The contractor makes an advance of from 30 dollars to 40 dollars to each Chinaman at the opening of the season to induce him to come. The contractor furnishes the provisions, where chiefly his profits are made. At the end of each month what he has supplied is made up and charged *pro rata* to the men in his employ " (ibid., p. 135).

could not thrive apart from the cheap docile labour of the Orient.[1] Their antagonists declared that the industry would have risen any way, even although the employers had been confined to white labour. The question of policy was settled in favour of non-immigration, but since the beginning of the century many factors have developed in favour of the white labourers, and the canning industry is flourishing to-day, despite non-immigration. Whether the industry would have flourished so greatly at the beginning is indeed doubtful in view of the circumstances of the time. It is at least possible that by reason of the dearness and scarcity and poor quality of early white labour on the Pacific, without Chinese labour the initiation of the industry would have been delayed and its development retarded.

The canning industry commenced about 1870, and grew steadily. Prosperity continued until the end of the century, when some degree of depression ensued on account of over-capitalization. At the same time complaints were made as to the shortage of Chinese labourers. This shortage was partly met by the installation of machinery for making the cans, which was run by whites. In this way machinery enabled white labourers to displace Chinese labourers, and in a way which was neither demoralising to the whites nor bad business from the employers' point of view. Employers, however, did not want to lose the Chinese labourers altogether, for although they might be excluded from one branch of the industry, they were still useful in another branch. The Chinese were still wanted for the packing of the cans—an operation performed by hand. What, in fact, happened, was that the Chinese no longer monopolised the industry. Instead, they were scattered over a variety of employments ranging from petty-shop-keeping to small farming. And however unpopular the Chinese may be in some sections of the industrial life of British Columbia, there is at any rate one aspect of the life of the community where they are sure of a welcome. " I believe that in the whole Province of British Columbia . . . there are not to be found six households which boast

[1] " The Chinese are steady in their habits, reliable in their work, and reliable to make contracts with. They won't strike while you have a big pile of fish on your dock. They are less trouble and less expense than whites. They are content with rough accommodation at the canneries. . . . I look upon them as steam engines or any other machine, the introduction of which deprives men of some particular employment, but in the long run it enormously increases the employment . . ." (R.C.J.I., H. O. Bell-Irving (Evidence), p. 145).

two English female domestic servants. But the Chinaman makes a most efficient substitute, and if his wages amount to £6 or £8 a month, he does the work of three ordinary British domestics, and does not stick on the order of his going, as he will cook, wash, mind the baby, and assist in the fruit farm in turn, besides being clean, honest, and trustworthy." [1]

Although the Japanese have entered the canning and other industries, they are for the most part identified with the pursuit of fishing. The reason for this was that many of the Japanese immigrants were fishermen in their own country. Before 1896 few Japanese engaged in fishing, but after that year the number of fishing licences issued to Japanese grew apace. In competition with the white fishermen they had the advantage of low costs and were able to undercut their rivals and to monopolize the occupation. This aroused intense jealousy among the whites, which in some cases led to riots. However, the limitation agreement between the Canadian and Japanese Governments helped to relieve the pressure, although it left the Japanese immigrants virtual masters of the fishing grounds to the extent permitted by their numbers. [2]

On the whole it does not appear that the Oriental races are destined to play a permanently important part in the economic development and social life of British Columbia. They rendered vital services to the Province in its early days. They have, in fact, done much the same work as was accomplished by the Chinese in the South African mines

[1] J. S. Redmayne, *Fruit Farming in the Dry Belt of British Columbia*, B.C. Development Association, Ltd., 1909, pp. 70-1.

[2] " It is in connexion with the fisheries that the presence of the Japanese has been most keenly felt as competitors with the whites. The following statement shows the total number of licences issued in British Columbia during the last five years, and to what extent the Japanese have encroached upon this business :—

Total number of Licences in British Columbia :—

Year.			Total.	To Japanese.
1896	.	.	3,533	452
1897	.	.	4,500	787
1898	.	.	4,435	876
1899	.	.	4,197	930
1900	.	.	4,892	1,892
1901	.	.	4,732	1,958 (p. 140)

Prior to 1896 comparatively few Japanese engaged in fishing, and a record of licences issued to them was not kept. . . . For each boat there is at least one additional puller, making over four thousand Japanese directly engaged in the fishing business, and many more indirectly connected therewith. The Japanese are expert fishermen, having followed that calling in their own land." (*R.C.J.I.*, at p. 355.)

after the South African War, that is to say, they helped to span a transitional period. The immigration of Chinese into tropical countries, for instance, Malaya, is on quite a different footing, for there white labourers are impossible, and so in Malaya the Chinese have come to stay. The very fact that British Columbia is a temperate region sounds the death-knell of Oriental colonization in that province.

The Englishness of British Columbia.

British Columbia more than any other of the Canadian Provinces has attracted the English settler. In striking contrast with Saskatchewan and Alberta, where the foreign-born element reaches its maximum percentage, British Columbia is the province where the British born element bears the greatest proportion to the total population.[1] The city and neighbourhood of Victoria have been described as " more English than any other of the whole of the great Dominion . . . the voice and tone is almost literally that of the old country." [2] To visitors, the orchards and home-steads of Vancouver suggest Devon and Kent. " The climate has no extremes. Few Englishmen like a quite equable all the year round climate, however good, but prefer a spring, summer, autumn and winter, and it better suits their constitutions. Here they get the four English seasons in many respects improved upon. . . . There are no mosquitoes." [3] The climate, the occupation offered and social conditions, all have their share in attracting the British immigrant, but the Englishness of British Columbia is deeply rooted in the history of the province.

The pioneers in the region, as has been already described,[4] were the Hudson's Bay Company. Their main pursuit was the fur trade, but they also brought a few settlers from England and established the English tradition. The corn and meat needed for the employees of the Company were at first imported overland from Canada or overseas from England. The fertility of the region, however, was obvious, and the practice grew up for each trading area and station

[1] According to the Census of 1921, the British-born element in British Columbia was 30·6 per cent of the total population. Approximately 50 per cent was Canadian-born : 30 per cent British born: and 20 per cent foreign-born (*Canada Year Book*, 1927–8, p. 124).

[2] A. G. Bradley, *Canada in the Twentieth Century*, London, 1905, p. 402.

[3] Ibid., p. 414.   [4] See Chapter 5.

to become self-sufficing, under the rule of McLoughlin.[1] Gradually supply outstripped demand and a modest export trade developed, and commercial connexions were established with the Russians in Alaska and with the Sandwich Islands.[2] This export trade was put on a definite footing by the agreement made in 1839–40 between the Company and the Russians, whereby the Company promised to supply the latter with an adequate supply of provisions at reasonable rates.[3] This agreement led virtually to the establishment of the Puget Sound Agricultural Company in 1840.[4]

Hitherto the necessary farming had been done almost exclusively by retired officials and servants of the Company. Now, with an increased and regularized demand, the Company commenced a moderate policy of immigration from England and Scotland. A later contribution to the directed stream of immigration may be mentioned now, as it partakes of the same nature as that of the Puget Sound Agricultural Company in that it was the deliberate policy of the great Company. That was the number of settlers introduced to work the colliery at Fort Rupert and Nanaimo on Vancouver Island in 1849 onwards. In that case, as in the case of the Puget Sound Company, the settlers were employees of the Company and under its control.

The Hudson's Bay Company controlled British Columbia

---

[1] " From the first, McLoughlin had recognized the agricultural possibilities of Oregon. . . . In the open spaces about Fort Vancouver axe and plough were set to work and corn and livestock reared. Sheep were brought from California, hogs from the Sandwich Islands, and cattle from Ross. Soon a flour mill worked by oxen was set up. Grist and saw mills followed on the Willamette. Horse-breeding for the brigades became extensive. In 1835, some thirty-five hundred feet of lumber were being sawn daily ; while the yield of grain was annually several thousands of bushels, and the number of animals constantly on hand several hundreds. By these activities the company was saved the expense of bringing supplies through the mountains or round Cape Horn ". (Coats and Gosnell : *Sir James Douglas*, p. 128.)

[2] Ibid., p. 78.

[3] Boam and Ashley, *British Columbia*, p. 34.

[4] " The grain which they (sc. the Company) produced, and the timber which they felled, they found a good market for in the South Sea Islands. . . . they had immense herds of cattle . . . and at last the undertaking exceeding their own means, they made an offset from the Hudson's Bay Company, called the Puget Sound Company . . . a good number of the gentlemen connected with the Hudson's Bay Company in association with others who are not connected with the Hudson's Bay Company formed the Paget Sound Company, who made very considerable agricultural establishments in that country." (*Report on the Hudson's Bay Company : Evidence of E. Ellice*, Q. 5849). Under the Oregon Boundary Treaty, 1846, the estates of the Puget Sound Company fell on the United States side of the new boundary line.

in a very real way throughout the 'forties and 'fifties. That they did so is a fact of vital importance, for they pursued a policy whereby they were able to dam back the oncoming flood of American settlers who were flowing into the Oregon region, so preserving British Columbia as a colony for British settlement at a later date. The Company's policy was dictated by the desire, firstly to keep out settlers of any sort except such as suited their convenience and so to preserve their monopoly of the fur trade ; and, secondly, to exclude, especially, American settlers who were turbulent and anti-English. The exclusion of American settlers, indeed of any settlers, was effected by the Company's twin measures of selling land dear and of preventing squatting. The high-scale price for land at £1 an acre had been determined on after conference with Earl Grey, and formed a virtual prohibition at a time when land on the American side of the border was to be had for little or nothing. This virtual prohibition might, however, have been circumvented by Americans squatting on the land, had the prohibition not been made effective by the influence of the company over the Indians, and the Indians' hatred of the Americans.[1]

[1] " In its dealings with the natives the Hudson's Bay Company, and the North-West Company before it, consistently displayed justice and moderation.   When crime was committed, the actual criminal was secured and punished, and the tribe from which he was taken was never made to suffer for the faults of one of its number.   The success of this policy was amply demonstrated on a hundred occasions, and the justice of the white man became in the course of time a quality to be respected, an attribute forbidding hostility.   Far different was the treatment meted to the Indians beyond the International boundary.   Men were invited in public prints to hunt them down, and mercy was denied alike to man, woman and child.   A price was placed upon their scalps : for that of every buck 100 dollars, for that of a squaw 50 dollars, and ' 25 dollars for everything in the shape of an Indian under ten years of age ' (Extract from the *Legislative Journals of Idaho Territory*).   There is a measure of iniquity which will goad the mildest peoples to acts of ferocious and inhuman retribution, and it is no matter for surprise that within the space of a few years no less a sum than 500,000,000 dollars was expended by the United States in Indian wars.   The Hudson's Bay Company had none of these troubles ".   (Boam and Ashley, op. cit., p. 34.)
" . . . . the number of persons engaged in the gold-digging is yet extremely limited, in consequence of the threatening attitude of the native tribes who, being hostile to the Americans, have uniformly opposed the entrance of American citizens into their country.   The people from American Oregon are therefore excluded from the gold district, except such as, resorting to the artifice of denying their country, succeed in passing for British subjects.   The persons at present engaged in the search of gold are chiefly of British origin and retired servants of the Hudson's Bay Company ".   (Correspondence relative to the Discovery of Gold in the Fraser River District in British North America, *Parliamentary Papers*, 1857–8, vol. xli, p. 250 ; Despatch from Governor Douglas to Henry Labouchere, M.P., 29th October, 1856.)

The period of the Gold Rush of 1858 onwards synchronized with the establishment of British Columbia as a colony and the Company's abdication of controlling power over its destinies. The Company's policy was still continued, for it held most of the best land in the colony, it controlled trade, and one of the Company's most experienced officials, Sir James Douglas, was head of the Administration. A few independent settlers had entered British Columbia in the 'fifties under the Company's policy of regulating immigration, since they could not choke it altogether. The Gold Rush put a different complexion on affairs. Immigrants flowed in, whether the Company liked it or not, but they were gold-diggers, and not agricultural settlers or squatters. After the eyes of the gold-diggings had been picked out, the miners went away. Moreover, the greater part were Americans. " John Nugent, special agent of the United States, estimated that in May, June, and July, twenty-three thousand persons went from San Francisco by sea, and about eight thousand more overland—safely thirty thousand or thirty-three thousand in all in the course of the season ; and that out of these there returned before February, 1859, all but three thousand." [1] By the end of the 'sixties the American tide of mining immigrants had ebbed away.[2] While the American immigrants had been the most numerous element in the Gold Rush, at the same time there were a goodly number of British from California, Australia, and England itself, and these tended to remain. In this way the scanty band of early settlers gained a distinct accretion.[3]

[1] *Nugent's Report*, 35th Cong. 2nd Sess. H. Ex. Doc. 3, p. 3, quoted H. H. Bancroft, *History of British Columbia* (1887). In 1862 " the American consul at Victoria estimated the mining population of the whole Colony at 15,000, three-fourths of the people being from California, Oregon and Washington ". (Gosnell, op. cit., pt. i, p. 171.)

[2] " A local census, in 1870, taken by the Colonial Government, did not return more than 9,100 white inhabitants, the majority of whom were resident in Victoria, New Westminster, and Nanaimo districts, whereas it is estimated that there was at least 25,000, some say 35,000 gold-seekers in the two colonies in 1858, although these were mainly transients. a large number of whom left almost as suddenly as they came. The second rush attracted by the Cariboo gold excitements brought a more permanent element ; probably two-thirds of these later comers remained ". (Gosnell, op. cit., pt. ii, p. 1.)

[3] " A series of letters written in the autumn and winter of 1861–2 by Donald Fraser, correspondent of the London *Times*, pictured the discoveries and excitements in Cariboo in somewhat roseate colours. . . . Bancroft, continuing, says that, in all, several thousand British subjects from England, Canada, Australia and New Zealand were induced by these letters to undertake the journey to British Columbia in the spring of 1862 ". (Gosnell, op. cit., pt. ii, p. 172.)

In the 'sixties British Columbia regarded itself as English rather than Canadian, since its communications with England by the ocean route round the Horn was easier and cheaper than the long and laborious route overland to the eastern side of the continent. Contributing at that time to the Englishness of the population of British Columbia were the Royal Engineers who planned and built roads, streets, and public buildings and did much other pioneer work in the Colony in 1859–63, and also the naval element, which was stationed at Esquimalt. Many, both of the military and naval units, settled in British Columbia on the expiry of their term of service, and few though they might have seemed in a large and populous Colony, they formed an important addition to the sparce population of British Columbia.

In 1886 the Canadian Pacific Railway was completed, and a new era in the history of British Columbia began. British Columbia was now linked with Canada and through Canada with England, instead of as formerly with Oregon and California. In circumstances which have been described, the foundations were laid in the province of a predominantly British settlement. The railway now built the super-structure, for they brought settlers in ever-increasing numbers. The settlers they brought were English and Canadians rather than Americans, for the population demanded in British Columbia was one comprising clerks, fruit farmers, and lumberers, and not wheat farmers. Canada and England supplied the former classes with ease. The United States were prepared to send wheat farmers, and these in fact have been moving north over the International boundary line into the provinces east of the rockies. They could have swamped British Columbia if British Columbia had needed them for, after all, they have much the most ready access to the province. But British Columbia has not wanted wheat farmers, and so its Englishness has survived.

The Yukon

Beginning with the gold discoveries in British Columbia in 1858, the gold-producing region in western Canada has gradually extended northwards, following the line of the vast mountain ranges which run throughout the whole length of the continent. The discoveries of the Fraser River were followed by those at Cariboo and Kootenay, which remained the most important placer mining regions in the world until the discoveries were made in the Klondike region in 1896. In each region placer mining was followed by the discovery of gold quartz veins, and the degree of development achieved of quartz mining depended on the degree of facility of access for the necessary machinery. No great degree of economic development can be attained in any region simply on the strength of placer mining. Placer mining is generally individual work. Quartz mining can only be exploited by aggregations of capital, the organization of labour and the purchase, transport, and installation of machinery.

The Yukon Territory has, for administrative purposes, been carved out of that vast vague region extending to the Arctic Circle, known as the North-West Territories. The Yukon is the western portion of that region, and lies between Alaska and the Mackenzie basin and north of British Columbia. It has an area of 207,000 square miles, and so is nearly as large as France. Three-fourths of its area is in the watershed of the Yukon River.

Here, as elsewhere, in these remote regions, the Hudson's Bay Company were the earliest pioneers of civilization. They established Fort Yukon as a trading post in 1847. The agents of the Hudson's Bay Company, however, practically withdrew from the region on the transfer of Alaska from Russia to the United States and its trade was left to the Americans and in particular the Alaska Commercial Company. The exploitation of Canadian territory by an American trading monopoly, however, seemed hardly compatible with the new conception of Canadian nationalism, and in 1887 the Canadian Government entrusted to Dr. Dawson and Mr. W. Ogilvie the organization of an expedition to explore the region drained by the Yukon.

The earliest records of gold in the Yukon go back to 1878, and from that time onwards new discoveries were made along the course of the various rivers. In 1887, Dr. Dawson and Mr. Ogilvie reported : " The general result so far has been to prove that six large and long rivers . . . yield ' fine gold ' along hundreds of miles of their lower courses." [1]

In 1896, G. W. Cormack made his memorable discovery

---

[1] Quoted in *The Yukon District of Canada*, a Pamphlet issued by the High Commissioner for Canada, 1897 (Canada . Pamphlets, vol. 4, No. 118, in D.O. & C.O. Library).

of gold on Bonanza Creek, an affluent of the river, the correct name of which was the Thron Duick, but which has come down to fame as the Klondike, and thither, and to Eldorado Creek and Skookum Gulch the mining population at once made their way. At the same time a capital town was founded, and appropriately enough named Dawson. According to Mr. Ogilvie's report to the Canadian Government at the beginning of 1897, " men cannot be got to work for love or money. One and a half dollars per hour is the wage paid the few men who hire for work. Some of the claims are so rich that every night a few pans of dirt suffice to pay the hired help when there is any. . . . It is beyond doubt that three pans on different claims in Eldorado Creek turned out $204, $212, and $216 . . . there were many running from $10 to $50." [1]

So far only placer mining [2] had been developed, but the search had been begun for the matrix from which the gold found in the river courses had come. The first notable discovery of gold quartz was reported in 1896.

About the same time coal was discovered in sufficient quantities to remove anxiety on a question of no little importance in such a climate as that of the Yukon region, namely, the question of fuel. But at best the lives of the miners were far from enviable. The men represented many nationalities and came from all climes. " The regulation ' miner's cabin ' is 12 feet by 14 feet, with walls 6 feet, and gables 8 feet in height. The roof is heavily earthed, and the cabin is generally very warm. Two, and sometimes three or four men will occupy a house of this size. The ventilation is usually bad. Those miners who do not work their claims during the winter confine themselves in these small huts most of the time. Very often they become indolent and careless, only eating those things which are most easily cooked or prepared." [3]

Nor was the route to the Klondike without hardship and danger. The normal route was by steamer from Vancouver and other Pacific coast towns to Skagway by the Chilcoot or White Passes and down the Yukon in canoes or boats to Dawson at the mouth of the Klondike River. By 1900, however, the pack-trail across the White Pass had been

---

[1] Ibid.

[2] In a placer mine the earth is taken out and sluiced, gold being found in particles in the alluvial detritus or deposits.

[3] Report of Assistant Surgeon A. E. Wills, of the Mounted Police Force, quoted in *Canada Pamphlets*, vol. iv, No. 118 (*supra*).

replaced by a railway and the canoes and small boats by a fleet of steamers, so that the journey from Vancouver to Dawson could be made in seven or eight days and in comfort.

By the beginning of the century the evolution of the Yukon Territory from an unstable and turbulent mining camp to a steady and permanent community was well advanced. Gold was still the chief product of the country, but there had also been extensive discoveries of copper, and hopes were entertained that copper smelting would become an important industry. Fuel had become an anxiety. The enormous amount of wood required for heating during the long winter, as well as for thawing ground and furnishing power for the purpose of mining operations, was threatening the exhaustion of the somewhat meagre supply of timber. At this critical stage coal was discovered of a sufficiently good quality to remove to a great extent the anxiety arising out of the threatened shortage of wood for purposes of fuel. The same cause was responsible for the more general use of the hydraulic method of mining by which steam replaced burning wood as the agent for thawing the ground.

Transport facilities remained the great requirement. The expense of getting necessary supplies into the country and of moving them from place to place when there was enormous. " Many instances can be furnished when three, four, five, and even ten times the cost paid for an article at Vancouver or Victoria has been paid for getting that article into position on some mining claim twenty or thirty miles from Dawson.''[1]

Amenities were making their appearance to supplement those which nature was discovered to have provided. Dawson was giving signs of permanency. In the first year of the century it had a total assessment of over $14,000,000, and it had qualified for its charter of incorporation and the grant of the privilege of managing its own municipal affairs. As to the rural districts, " The flowers of Dawson and the country are simply superb. Many vegetables grow to as great perfection as in any other part of Canada." As to the climate, the Commissioner for the Yukon after six months' experience (which, however, did not include the winter) was of opinion that " a more charming climate could not be found than has been enjoyed here for most of that time ".

[1] Annual Report of the Department of the Interior for 1900–1 in *Sessional Paper*, 1902 : *Yukon Territory*, pp. 3 and 4.

Moreover, the North-West Mounted Police had seen to it that the rough and criminal element that too frequently dominated mining camps had never been allowed to get control in Yukon, with the result that the territory was singularly free from crime. " To-day, as for several years past, men travel the loneliest trails, burdened themselves with gold or with horses and mules similarly burdened, without guard and without even being armed." [1]

After its hectic early years the Yukon Territory settled down to the career of a partially settled country where the arts of civilization are pursued in rather a small way. Thus we read that in the year 1925–6, patents for land were issued involving an area of 473 acres ; 92 permits to cut wood and timber were issued : " as in previous years coal was shipped to Dawson by the Five Fingers Coal Company for their mine at Tantalus Butte " ; the agricultural season resulted in " well-matured crops of excellent quality " ; the hospitals at Dawson, Whitehouse, and Mayo " maintained their reputation for excellent service ", but " the number of old people of both sexes given assistance is increasing year by year, and continues to be a serious drain on the finances of this Territory " ; public schools were maintained at the same three towns and assisted schools were opened at Selkirk and Keno City ; wolves and coyotes were reputed to be increasing ; and " an ordinance was passed to come into force on the affirmative vote of the people, to regulate the sale of beer ".[2]   The Takudah, Stick, and Tlingit tribes of Indianso ccupied themselves as usual with hunting, trapping, and fishing. They carried on no farming " owing to climatic conditions ", but they cultivated patches of potatoes and other vegetables.[3]

---

[1] Annual Report of the Department of the Interior for 1900–1 in *Sessional Paper*, 1902 : *Yukon Territory*, p. 5.

[2] Annual Report of Department of the Interior for 1925–6, p. 135 (*Annual Departmental Reports*, 1925–6, vol. ii).

[3] *Annual Report of Department of Indian Affairs for* 1925–6, p. 29 (ibid.).

CHAPTER 17

Food Production and Farming

WE have seen the Dominion equipped with means of communication, and population attracted to the areas thus opened up. It remains to see how the people of the new Canada were employed, and what were the products the railways carried.

Fur and fish have to give way to grain and minerals as the primary products of the country. Timber remains an important economic asset, both as lumber and as the foundation of a new industry, the manufacture of wood pulp. The manner in which the quick-growing varieties of wheat have been evolved so that the line of its limit of cultivation has been pushed further and further north is a story as interesting as that of the organization of the grain trade and the manner in which nature's impediments in the way of placing Canada's grain on the markets of the world have been overcome.

The North-West Mounted Police deprived the early mining camps of a good deal of that picturesqueness which comes from lawlessness, but otherwise the story of the Cariboo gold rush in British Columbia and of the later Klondike rush in the Yukon Territory are exciting enough, though from the economic point of view less important than the development of the asbestos deposits of Quebec and the nickel mines of Ontario, both of them minerals in the production of which Canada has a predominating position. Finally the stage is arrived at where, thanks to the infinite resources of her eastern Provinces in " white coal ", otherwise water power, Canada enters upon her career as an industrial State based on hydro-electric energy. Whether an industrial community is destined to grow up around the vast coalfields of Alberta is for the present an interesting speculation, as is also the possibility that the presence of vast iron and coal deposits, excellent harbours, infinite water power and the Panama Canal, may make British Columbia a great centre for shipbuilding and the iron and steel industries.

Lines of Development in Farming

By 1870 the lot of the settlers in the older Provinces had become much more tolerable than that of the early pioneers ; but success can still only be achieved by unremitting toil. It is possible from contemporary accounts to build up a picture of the life of the farmer in, for instance, Ottawa about 1870 and so to get some conception of agricultural conditions in early days.

He has accepted the general view that a farm of 100 to 120 acres, is large enough for one man. If he is without any capital at all he will have had no difficulty in getting employment at wages varying between 14 and 24 dollars a month with board and lodging, for in all new countries labour is scarce. Potatoes and wheat are the first crops generally raised on new land, and oats follow wheat. " In the newer townships the taxes rarely exceed a very few pence in the pound upon the assessed value, but all who

are on the assessment roll are compelled to do a few days'
statute labour annually upon the roads." [1]   The snow is off
the ground at the end of April.   Crops, though put in later,
mature earlier than in England, and reaping begins at the
beginning of August.   Early in October the harvest is in
and potash is now made, and the sleighs put in order for
winter work.   Besides wheat, barley and maize may be
grown, and potatoes and the other English garden vegetables
as well as pumpkins and melons can be raised.   Clearing,
threshing, and milling are winter occupations, and the
snow has provided a surface where travel by sleigh is made
possible over districts quite unpassable in summer.   If the
settler is in the vicinity of a lumber camp so much the
better, for the farmer gets the use of roads and bridges made
for the transport of the timber, and also finds in the
lumber shanties a sure and profitable market for his surplus
produce as well as companionship.

The necessity for scientific agriculture has not yet
appeared :   " Subsoil draining is unknown here ; a proper
rotation of crops scarcely ever adopted and yet the fertile
soil produces most abundant crops.   The complaint with
some of the farmers is that their land is too rich—no
necessity for manure.   A farmer at Fitzroy Harbour . . .
states that he has taken in succession fourteen crops of
wheat and oats without any manure and the last crop
was the best." [2]

By 1923 conditions have changed.   Ontario has a highly
developed and scientific system of mixed farming, and its
aggregate of agricultural production is the greatest of all
the provinces :   " Here, as in Quebec, dairying is the main
industry, except in the south of the province where fruit
farming prevails.   In studying the practical work on the
average Canadian homestead, the English visitor is struck
by the extraordinary amount of hard work that is accomplished by the Canadian farmer almost single-handed.
The farmers of a district, it is true, give each other much
mutual assistance, but on the whole Canadian farming is
to a large extent a one-man proposition.   A farmer with wife
and family can, of course, do better than when he is single,
but the difference is frequently to be found in the fact that

---

[1] The Resources of the Ottawa District, Ottawa, 1872. (*Canada :
Pamphlets*, vol. iii, No. 69 in D.O. & C.O. Library).
   [2] Ibid.

the farmer with a family occupies a larger farm and conducts operations on a larger scale than a single farmer can. . . . The farms range in size from about 60 to 100 acres, and the cows are milked in herds of about 12 to 16 head. . . . It is a common practice for farmers to have a young farm helper who is boarded in the house as one of the family. There is a great demand for juvenile helpers who are brought over by charitable organizations from Great Britain. . . . The eldest child was a girl of 14. . . . In this case the milking, after tea on Sunday, of some 12 cows, was all done in about half-an-hour by the farmer, the farm help, and the daughter referred to. On another farm the lady of the house, who had presided at the tea-table on Sunday in a silk dress, changed into working costume and helped her husband with the evening's milking. The milk, carefully strained, was placed in cool cement-lined pits ready for haulage to the dairy factory early in the following morning." [1]

Westward the course of wheat-growing in Canada has taken its way. " In 1880 all the wheat except 3·2 per cent., which was grown in Manitoba, and all the oats and barley were grown in the eastern provinces. In 1921, however, 93 per cent. of the total wheat of Canada, 67 per cent. of the oats and 74 per cent. of the barley were grown in the provinces of Manitoba, Saskatchewan, and Alberta." [2] For the eastern province the change was from wheat to cattle raising, dairying, fruit and vegetable growing, and bee culture. The competition of the North-West was doubtless the main, but it was not the sole cause of the adoption of mixed farming by the farmers of Ontario, Nova Scotia, and New Brunswick.

Throughout the 'seventies the annual Reports of the Commissioners of Agriculture for Ontario are one long wail as to the poor crops of wheat, owing to an unprecedented succession of years with bad weather and on account of the arrival of the Hessian fly and other noxious insects. In addition to the small quantity of the wheat output, there was the prevailing industrial depression in Europe and America, which formed a considerable part of Canada's grain market. The diminished multiplier and the diminished

---

[1] E. H. Godfrey, Canadian Farming (*North America : Pamphlets*, No. 28 in D.O. & C.O. Library).

[2] W. C. Hopper, Agriculture in Eastern Canada, in *The Annals of the American Academy of Political and Social Science*, vol. cvii, No. 196 (May, 1923), p. 67.

multiplicand during the 'seventies meant a diminished product. Accordingly, mixed farming was encouraged both by events and the counsel of the Commissioner of Agriculture in Ontario. Already in the 'sixties fruit-farming and dairy-farming were beginning, but after 1870 progress was rapid. To take perhaps the most important dairy export of after years, cheese, we find that in the 'sixties Canada actually imported the commodity in quite large quantities, but that in the 'seventies the Dominion was exporting it in ever increasing bulk. Similarly it was the 'seventies that saw the genesis of the export of live stock. By the beginning of the twentieth century Manitoba was overtaking Ontario in wheat production. Ten years later Ontario had fallen far into the rear.[1]

Canada is a country where the horses and cattle, sheep and pigs, poultry and bees have been included in the census since 1871. These statistics, save for poultry, disclose much less impressive progress than the figures showing the yearly increase in cereal production.[2]

Some account has already been given of the extensive horse and cattle ranches of Alberta [3] and British Columbia [4] and of the manner in which they had to make way for farms of smaller dimensions. The increasing use of mechanical traction must inevitably affect horse-breeding as a remunerative branch of business. On the other hand :

---

[1] The Canadian Census discloses the following figures :—

		1891	1901	1910
		(bushels)	(bushels)	(bushels)
Ontario :	Wheat	21,314,582	28,418,907	17,805,000
	Barley	13,419,354	16,087,962	20,727,000
	Oats	47,160,246	88,138,974	128,917,000
Manitoba :	Wheat	16,092,220	18,353,013*	41,159,000
	Barley	1,452,433	2,666,803*	13,826,000
	Oats	8,370,212	10,592,660*	41,742,000

* Figures reduced to almost one-half by drought.

(*Commission of Conservation*, 1911, *Lands, Fisheries and Game, and Minerals*, pp. 24, 27.)

[2] Statistics of the numbers of live stock and poultry in Canada for 1891 and 1921 are as follows :—

	1891	1921
Horses	1,470,572	3,624,262
Cattle	4,120,586	8,519,484
Sheep	2,563,781	3,203,966
Swine	1,733,850	3,404,730
Poultry of all kinds.	14,105,102	50,325,248
Hives of Bees,	199,288	185,530

(*Canada Year Book*, 1927–8, p. 252).

[3] See Chapter 14.   [4] See Chapter 16.

" Economic conditions are forcing people to use the cheapest form of power whether it be on the farm, in the lumber woods, or in the city, and this is supplied by horses," so that about 1923 horse-breeding was in process of revival.[1] Cattle are in a different category, and their increase in numbers is to a large extent an index to the growth of dairying rather than of beef production.

Cattle raising has had to face difficulties due to climate, to transport, and to politics, and meat production in Canada is on a much smaller scale than either wheat-growing or dairying. " Owing to the hard winters, the Dominion raises more cattle than can be finished. The practice frequently is to bring the animals through the winter on maintenance rations and then finish them off on grass during the summer. Cattle marketed off the grass are not well finished, and they are therefore sold at low prices during the late summer or fall." [2]

Exports of live cattle were practically entirely to the United States, for any sent to Great Britain were required to conform to the conditions applicable to all imported cattle since 1892, that they should be slaughtered at the port of entry, a measure meant as a safeguard against the introduction of contagious diseases into this country. The trade of Canada with Great Britain in store cattle had before 1892 been of some importance, but it was stopped by this embargo. The Canadian farmer chafed under the prohibition and in particular resented the implied imputation upon the health of Canadian cattle, although the freedom of Canadian cattle from serious disease was admitted on this side. The embargo on Canadian store cattle was removed in 1923. " No appreciable harm has been done to British agriculture, no benefit has accrued to the British consumer, and no substantial advantage has yet been gained by Canadian cattle-breeders." [3]

---

[1] Report of Minister of Agriculture for the Dominion for 1923–4, p. 33, in *Sessional Papers*, 1925, vol. 61.

[2] E. H. Godfrey, Canadian Farming (1924) (*North America : Pamphlets*, No. 28 in D.O. & C.O. Library.)

[3] Sir Henry Rew, K.C.B., *Economic Resources of Canada*, Ministry of Agriculture and Fisheries, 1925, p. 97. Live stock imported from Canada to the United Kingdom were :—

1922	19,960
1923	45,417
1924	76,978

(Accounts relating to Trade and Navigation of the United Kingdom, December, 1924).

The disappointment as to the effect of the removal of
the British embargo was in part traceable to high freight
rates. " Whilst during the years 1909 to 1913 the ocean
freight rate was $6 or 25s. per head, the present rate from
Montreal to Liverpool is $20 or 89s." Adding charges and
expenses en route, " the cost of conveyance from Calgary to
Liverpool for an animal of 1,200 lb. weight amounts to
$49·14 or £10 18s." [1] It is true that the United States is a
possible market where transport charges need not be a
serious impediment. But here the trouble is the tariff.
" When there was no duty, as was the case between the
years 1913 to 1921, the average annual exports across the
border were 260,000. In 1920 the number reached 500,216.
In 1922, the number was 217,480, but this fell to 96,873
in 1923, as a consequence of the tariff imposed in the
autumn of 1923 of 2 cents per lb. for animals over 1,050 lbs.,
and 1½ cents per lb. for animals under 1,050 lbs." [2]

The severity of the winter climate is an even greater
difficulty in the way of successful sheep breeding. The sheep
must be housed in winter ; the large flock which is possible
in milder climates is out of the question, and their numbers
are limited by the housing accommodation available.

In 1919 the Dominion Government gave official patronage
to Mr. V. Stefansson's idea that Canada's meat producing
resources might be increased by the semi-domestication of
reindeer and musk-sheep, by appointing a Commission to
inquire into the project. These animals roamed the north,
and would at least be capable of weathering winter conditions
without trouble. The Commission reported in 1920. They
suggested that the North American reindeer, the caribou,
should be crossed with the European reindeer, and were of
opinion that the yak and the musk-sheep might be profitably
domesticated. A large strip of Baffin Land was granted to
Mr. Stefansson for his experiment.

Among the newer forms of industry to which Canada is
turning, the development of fur farming, that is to say, the
raising of various kinds of fur-bearing animals in captivity,
has been contemporary with a decrease in the supply of the
more valuable furs from the wilds. The wild creatures have
been promoted to domesticity in the sense that they are
now the occupants of ranches, and in 1923–4 there were
" some thirty mink, seventeen racoon, twelve skunk, and

[1] E. H. Godfrey, *Canadian Farming (supra).*   [2] Ibid.

eight musk rat ranches in various parts of Canada ".[1] The silver fox industry has become firmly established throughout Canada, with Prince Edward Island as its headquarters. The pelt of the silver fox, " The Golden Pelt of the Fur Industry," is the highest priced fur on the market, and, since it cannot be successfully imitated, the silver fox may well be a source of considerable wealth to his breeder. To ensure his being bred true to type, silver foxes are inspected and registered by the Canadian National Records exactly as though they were British prize terriers.[2] At first the United States took most of the thousands of foxes exported, but about 1925 a European market was established, and Germany, France, Norway, and Great Britain went to Canada for foundation stock. " Russia gave some of her famous sable in exchange for silver foxes ".[3]

As fruit farming has developed into the characteristic industry of the Pacific Provinces, so co-operative dairying has been the most striking recent development in the eastern Provinces, especially Quebec and Ontario, where the first cheese factory was established so long ago as 1864. In these Provinces cheese is manufactured in factories, to each of which milk from 50 to 200 farms is brought daily. " The amount of cheese made on the farms apart from the factories is negligible, but the amount of home-made butter is almost equal to that of the creameries. . . . The tendency is towards replacement of dairy butter by that of the creamery."[4] Co-operative dairying, moreover, is spreading to the Prairie Provinces, and in Saskatchewan receives active assistance from the Provincial Government. Co-operative associations for the manufacture of butter and cheese may receive Government aid in the form of a loan, and also expert assistance in management, grading of butter and collective marketing. The dairy products of the Prairie Provinces have found a ready market on the Pacific coast, where previously New Zealand butter was conspicuous.[5] So powerful has the dairying interest proved

---

[1] Report of Dominion Minister of Agriculture for 1923–4, p. 36, in *Sessional Papers*, 1925, vol. lxi.

[2] In 1925 there were sold from Canadian fur farms 9,343 young silver foxes worth over $2,000,000 and 8,988 silver fox pelts worth $736,289 (*Canada Year Book*, 1927–8, p. 261).

[3] Report of Dominion Minister of Agriculture for 1925–6, p. 44, in *Annual Departmental Reports*, 1925–6, vol. ii.

[4] E. H. Godfrey, "Canadian Farming," a paper read in 1924 (*North America : Pamphlets*, No. 28, in D.O. & C.O. Library).

[5] *D.R.C. Minutes of Evidence* [*Cd.* 8459], Qs. 932a, 970.

itself that it has been able to protect its butter-making industry by securing the exclusion of butter substitutes, so that " it is at present a criminal offence to make, import, and sell margarine within the Dominion of Canada ".[1]

The importance of the products of dairy-farming in the economic history of Canada is often overlooked. During the slump in wheat during the 'seventies, 'eighties, and 'nineties, it was the export of cheese and butter and bacon and ham that enabled Canada to pay its way. Even during the 'nineties the value of the exported cheese, butter, bacon, and ham exceeded that of the exported wheat and flour, and in most years of that decade the value of the cheese alone exceeded that of the wheat. By the end of the first decade of the present century, wheat accounted for about 20 per cent. of the value of the Canadian exports, while cheese and bacon and ham accounted for over 10 per cent.

Canadian dairy farmers are favourably situated in that they have at their doors the largest consuming country in the world. Until quite recent times the United Kingdom was expected to take Canada's surplus dairy products. Now it is going to the United States in increasing quantities.[2]

State Aid to Agriculture

In a new country, agriculture must of necessity be in a large measure a State-aided industry. In Canada the attitude of the Government to its principal industry has been strictly paternal. Its earliest function in that character was the relief of distressed settlers. Thus, in 1876, the Dominion Government had to come to the rescue of distressed settlers in Manitoba whose crops had been destroyed by an insect plague which the Prime Minister described as " Locusts ", but which the Lieutenant-Governor, in asking that the loan of $60,000 to the sufferers might be increased to $85,000, preferred to describe as " grasshoppers ". Then again in 1887, as a result of drought and prairie fires, the crops of Assiniboia and in the Saskatchewan River settlements and other regions in the North-West were a failure,

[1] E. H. Godfrey, op. cit.
[2] Value of exports of butter, cheese, condensed milk, milk powder, and other milk products :—

	1924	1925	1926	1927
	$	$	$	$
To United Kingdom	24,945,162	29,733,328	38,983,256	25,097,806
To United States	9,577,155	8,475,151	9,507,530	12,304,425

and the Government felt called upon to make seed grain advances to the settlers. Over 100,000 bushels of wheat, oats, and barley were distributed, the stipulation being that the settlers should return it to the Government bushel for bushel. The year 1914 was another famine year in parts of Saskatchewan and Alberta. The crop was an absolute failure. Land that had been seeded in May remained a desert. Nothing was left for either feed or seed, so that in the spring of 1915 the Dominion Government had to go to the rescue and supply the necessary seed. In many instances, too, they had to supply food for stock and even groceries for the farmers' families.

But the most fruitful form of aid which the Dominion Government extends to the country's principal industry is through the varied administrative activities of its Department of Agriculture—the work of its experimental farms, the maintenance of a pedigree register, the control of agricultural diseases, the provision of dairying instruction, assistance to agricultural societies by, for example, the loaning of pure-bred bulls, the investigation of soils, the constant warfare waged on the wheat-stem sawfly, the European corn-borer and other insect pests, and the provision of cold storage in transport.

In 1884, farming was in " a most depressed " condition, and a Committee was appointed by the Dominion Government to inquire into the cause of the depression. " Careful investigation led to the conclusion that the lack of success was not due to any fault in the climate or soil of the country, nor to a lack of industry among the farmers, but to defective farming, to want of skill and knowledge in all departments. There was a lack of information as to proper preparation of the soil, the maintenance of its fertility, to a suitable rotation of crops, and 'as to selection of the best varieties of farm crops for sowing. There was a great want of a fuller knowledge regarding stock-breeding, and the adaptability of breeds to particular conditions. . . . There was a deplorable lack of knowledge as to the insects and diseases from which the farmer suffers large losses in crops. Also in regard to common weeds which sometimes over-run his fields and rob him of a large proportion of the fruits of his toil." [1]

[1] Dr. William Saunders, Evidence before Select Committee on Agriculture and Colonization, 1903, Appendix No. 2, pp. 97–8, quoted J. Mavor, *Report on the North-West of Canada*, 1904, [*Cd.* 2628], pp. 35–6.

The disease being diagnosed in these terms, the remedy applied was the establishment by the Dominion Government of a series of experimental farms.

The central experimental farm is at Ottawa. There and at the branch farms field observations are submitted to scientific tests. Illustrative results of the research work there done are the discovery of the virtues of early sowing, for in Canada the growing season is short and growth rapid, and the value of summer fallowing. Summer fallowing in Canada consists in tilling the land through the summer, leaving it unseeded until the autumn or next spring. The practice " through conservation of moisture in the ground and destruction of weeds enables the crops to resist drought and results in better yields ". [1]

Then cattle diseases have to be controlled. " The more malignant diseases of animals such as cattle plague, pleuropneumonia and foot-and-mouth disease are happily unknown," [2] but to prevent their introduction there are quarantine stations and inspection posts along the long international boundary, and animals may not be admitted elsewhere.

The dairying and fruit industries have been the subject of special Government solicitude. Thus, under the guidance of the Department, the " cow-testing movement " was inaugurated. Associations were formed the purpose of which was to organize over wide areas the collection of milk samples and the recording of their qualities. It was found that by weeding out unprofitable animals the milk yield could be substantially improved. Much attention has been given to the transport of perishable commodities to the end, for instance, that butter and fruit shall not be exposed to heat and dust on platforms and wharves, or cheese become over-heated in transit.

It is in connexion with the work carried on for the improvement of wheat varieties that the Experimental Farms have achieved their greatest triumph.

If His Majesty of Brobdingnag expressed a sound opinion when he declared that " whoever could make two ears of corn, or two blades of grass to grow upon a spot of ground where only one grew before, would deserve better of mankind, and do more essential service to his country than the whole

---

[1] E. H. Godfrey, "State Aid to Agriculture in Canada," *Journal of the Royal Agricultural Society of England*, vol. lxxi (1910).
[2] Ibid.

race of politicians put together," [1] then Dr. Charles Saunders, of the Central Experimental Farm at Ottawa, deserves to rank as one of the great benefactors of Canada and the human race.

In the early years of the North-West the wheat usually grown was the variety known as the hard Red Fife. Red Fife was originally a Galician wheat. Exported from Dantzig to Glasgow, a quantity of it was sent on, about 1842, to a Scotch farmer at Otonabee, Ontario, whose name, David Fife, thus became immortalized. This wheat was sown by Fife, and it prospered when all the grain in the neighbourhood was smitten with rust. Thereupon its popularity spread throughout the district. From Ontario it spread unto the United States and Manitoba, and by the 'eighties it had become the standard crop of Western Canada.

The celebrated variety of wheat known as " Marquis " was produced by Dr. Charles Saunders from a cross between Red Fife and an early ripening Indian wheat called Hard Red Calcutta, after a series of experiments, involving infinite patience, in the course of which hundreds of cross-bred strains were evolved, each having to be tested for the different desirable characteristics, that is to say, early ripening, freedom from rust, and good baking qualities. In 1903 there was a single head with a few grains. In 1904 there were twelve plants in a tiny plot in the experimental garden, and the resultant harvest was stored away in " a paper packet no larger than an envelope ". In 1906, two-thirds of a bushel had been obtained, and milling and baking tests fully confirmed Dr. Saunders' chewing test of the high milling and baking qualities of Marquis wheat. In 1907 about a quarter of an acre was sown with Marquis, and in that year and the following year, both bad crop years, Marquis did better than Red Fife. In 1909 some 400 samples were distributed among farmers in Western Canada, and since then Marquis has become the chief wheat crop grower and has entirely superseded Red Fife. [2] Among the virtues of Marquis wheat are abundance of yield, length of straw, and plumpness of grain, while the flour it yields is of good colour and has fine milling and baking qualities. The quality, however, which has made it such an important factor in the economic progress of the Canadian North-West,

---

[1] Dean Swift, *Gulliver's Travels*, pt. ii, chap. 7.
[2] See A. H. R. Buller, *Essays on Wheat*, pp. 206–18.

is its early ripening habit. Marquis ripens earlier than Red Fife by from three to five days, its period of growth being 110 days. "One of the difficulties incidental to grain growing on virgin soils is the appearance of early frosts, which, if they catch the grain in the dough stage, do irreparable damage, rendering the grain unfit either for milling or for seed. Any variety of grain, therefore, that has an early ripening habit—even if the ripening be earlier by only a few days—becomes of immense importance." [1] It is estimated that 90 per cent. of the wheat now grown in Western Canada is of the Marquis variety,[2] and the increment of gain to the Dominion and to Canadian farmers is many million dollars a year.

It is the ambition of the Central Farm at Ottawa to push the wheat-growing boundary further and further north by the production of a high quality wheat which will mature earlier even than Marquis and at the same time will resist rust, the arch enemy of the Manitoba wheat grower in particular. In the year 1925–6 several thousand bushels of a new variety of wheat called Garnet, of which great things were expected, were placed on the market by the Dominion Experimental Farms. Garnet matures from 5 to 10 days earlier than Marquis, and its yield is heavy. But Garnet is not so fine a milling wheat ; its resulting flour is creamy-yellow rather than the much-prized Marquis creamy-white.[3]

The effort to find a fine white milling wheat which is rust resistant has so far been unsuccessful, although the Dominion Rust Research Laboratory has isolated twelve varieties of the fungus. It appears to travel northwards from the United States where it is propagated by the barberry bush. Given favourable weather conditions, it will settle on the wheat stems and render it worthless. In Alberta rust is less serious, but in Manitoba it is responsible for a loss amounting to millions of dollars a year.[4]

The Provinces have their own Departments of Agriculture, which co-operate quite readily with the Dominion Government's institutions. At the farm connected with the Ontario Agricultural College at Guelph, conspicuously valuable work has been done. Something has already been

---

[1] E. H. Godfrey, "Canadian Farming" (*North America : Pamphlets*, No. 28, in D.O. & C.O. Library).
[2] Ibid.
[3] *The Times*, 1st July, 1927, p. xix.
[4] Ibid.

said about the work of the Dominion Central Experimental Farm at Ottawa in connexion with the discovery of new varieties of wheat. Valuable work has been done along similar lines at Guelph on behalf of growers of barley. " In 1899 a small sample of barley was imported to the College from Mandscheuri, Russia. This showed a greater yield than the previous best barley in use at the time, and it was distributed for general use during the succeeding years. In the spring of 1903, selected grains of Mandsscheuri barley were planted by hand at equal distances apart on the experimental plots. Thirty-three of the most promising ones were selected, harvested, and threshed. This process of selection was followed during the succeeding years, and the row No. 21 showed the best results, being even superior to the Mandscheuri. In 1907 it was first distributed to the public, and the experimental success was confirmed by practical work throughout the province. The result is that at the present time it is estimated that 96 per cent. of all the barley grown in the province is of either the Mandscheuri or O.A.C. 21 strain, and practically all the prizes at seed fairs and other competitions are taken by this variety. . . . It is figured that this new variety alone in the past sixteen years over the previous sixteen years has added $35,000,000 to the agricultural wealth of the province. The barley crop covers in the neighbourhood of 600,000 acres." [1]

The varieties of oats have also been much improved by experimental work and the Banner variety has become first favourite.

Wheat

Many economic regions in the past grew up on the basis of a single staple. Newfoundland grew up on fish, the Southern States of the Union on cotton, Australia on wool, while the early prosperity of tobacco-planting Virginia was said to be " founded on smoke ". So to-day Western Canada has grown up on wheat farming, and its prosperity depends on England's wheaten dietary.

The wheat trade has been the subject of almost continuous debate, inquiry, and action on the part of the Dominion and Provincial Parliaments ever since 1900. So much is this so, that the grain trade of Canada is more the subject

[1] *D.R.C. Minutes of Evidence* [*Cd.* 8459], p. 41.

of regulation than the grain trade of any other country in the world.[1] The place of the wheat trade in the life of Western Canada is fully revealed by its value in relation to the total production of the three Prairie Provinces. There wheat growing is the chief form of farming. In the total production figures for 1925, farming accounted in Saskatchewan for 93 per cent. of the value produced, Alberta 76 per cent., and Manitoba 62 per cent.[2] Even these figures under-estimate the importance of wheat-growing, for most of the non-agricultural occupations are largely dependent on wheat-growing for their livelihood, such as shop-keeping and grain dealing, which come under the heading of commerce. If any disease or insect pest were to ravage Canadian wheat, or if England were to cease consuming wheaten bread, the Prairie Provinces would immediately go bankrupt. The wheat trade is the life blood of Western Canada.

The concentration of Western Canada on wheat-farming is due to a number of factors, some geographical and others economic. While there are signs of a change over to mixed farming, that change over is likely to be comparatively slow apart from a radical alteration in one or more of the governing factors. The prairies are not flat but " rolling, after the manner of our Wiltshire downs, and watered by slow-running, muddy rivers, fringed with woods, and sprinkled with shallow lakes and ponds of every size ".[3] The soil is a rich humus ideally suited for wheat-growing. Here there is no laborious clearing of dense forest as in Eastern Canada, but a ploughing of the virgin soil in the fall, another ploughing in the spring, a sowing of the seed, and an ample harvest in the late summer. Then the rainfall, while slight (generally 20 inches and under), comes at the right season of the year, between April and June, and even the parched region of southern Alberta has been largely conquered by irrigation and dry-farming. Little winter wheat is grown, except in Alberta, and therefore the period for growth is short. Spring frosts linger late and fall frosts often arrive early, but the days of summer are long and the sunshine is intense in those high latitudes, so that growth is rapid. With quick ripening wheat, such as the Red Fife,

---

[1] W. C. Clark, " Country Elevators in the Canadian West," in *Queen's Quarterly*, 1916–17, vol. xxiv, p. 67.
[2] *Canada Year Book*, 1927–8, pp. 212, 214.
A. G. Bradley, in *British America* (edited by John Buchan), p. 132.

and later the Marquis, large harvests are garnered in Western Canada, where with ordinary wheats the yield would be small and uncertain. The wheat of Western Canada is hard, producing a strong flour.[1] This would have been a disadvantage but for the introduction of the purifier and of chilled-iron rolling in the 'seventies of the last century. Canadian wheat now is amongst the best in the world, both for quality and cleanness, and English millers pay good prices for it with a view to mixing it with the soft English wheat.[2]

Wheat can be grown in Western Canada cheaply and in bulk, can be handled and transported cheaply, can be stored without deterioration (and without cost of feeding), commands a ready price in the market (is a " cash crop "), and commands also a price that tends to rise on account of world factors. Hence the place of the wheat trade in the life of Western Canada.

The wheat belt in Canada moved steadily westward. At first in Quebec and then in Ontario, it was only in the 'nineties of last century that the wheat belt began to be located principally in Manitoba. By then Ontario was going over distinctly to mixed and dairy farming, being attracted thereto by the market it could find at home and abroad for its fruit and cheese and livestock, and being driven out of wheat farming by the cheaper production of Western Canada. Nowadays a considerable amount of prairie wheat is consumed in Eastern Canada, and that amount will grow.

In the 'nineties Manitoba was the chief wheat-producing area of Western Canada. Saskatchewan did not grow wheat at all for export till 1892, nor Alberta till 1898. In the latter year Manitoba produced five-sixths of the total wheat grown in Western Canada.[3] The opening-up of the Saskatchewan valley by the new railways soon wrought a change. In 1905 the North-West Territories had developed sufficiently to be split into the two provinces of Saskatchewan and Alberta. In 1909 Saskatchewan definitely passed Manitoba as a wheat producer and now Manitoba lags behind

---

[1] Hardness and softness of wheat are the effects chiefly of less or more moisture. Strength of flour is connected with glutinous content.

[2] Recently English millers have complained of adulteration and false grading, *The Times*, 12th April, 1928.

[3] Based on figures in Report on the North-West of Canada, with special references to Agricultural Production, by J. Mavor, 1904 [*Cd.* 2628], pp. 61, 68.

even Alberta.   To-day, rather than westward,[1] northward
the course of wheat-growing takes it way, but this development is partly held up by the lack of railway communication.
Wheat has even been grown near Dawson City, 64° North.[2]
The Peace River district, north and west of Edmonton, is
spoken of as the " last Great West ".[3]

The most striking features, then, of the development of
the wheat trade of Western Canada are its lateness, its
suddenness, and its colossal growth.   The reasons lie on the
surface.   There had to be settlement and cultivation on a
large scale, since before the 'nineties population was small
and confined mostly to Manitoba.   Winnipeg, before its
rather premature boom in the early 'eighties, was little
more than an overgrown village where Indian tepees had
recently stood.   Buffalo still roamed on the banks of the
Saskatchewan as late as the 'seventies.[4]   Secondly, as a
condition precedent to settlement, there had to be railway
construction to bring in settlers and to carry out the settlers'
produce quickly and cheaply.   Then the sort of wheat had
to be discovered which would thrive under the peculiar
conditions of Western Canada.   Finally, there had to be an
adequate and growing demand for the increasing wheat
production of the region.   Such were the four conditioning
factors in the development of the wheat trade of Western
Canada.

Wheat had been grown to some extent round the Hudson's
Bay Company's forts on Western Canada before 1812, but
only casually as a hobby.   The establishment of the Red
River Colony in that year by Lord Selkirk meant that wheat
growing and farming generally had arrived in Western
Canada.   Even then it was subsistence farming mainly, with
a small surplus which was bought up by the Hudson's Bay
Company at fixed prices for the feeding of their staff.   Any
further surplus was useless, because there was no market
for it, transport charges constituting a prohibitive barrier
between the Red River and England.   In 1876, the first
outward consignment of Manitoba wheat was sent to Eastern
Canada via Minnesota.   In 1883 a further consignment
went east by the Canadian Pacific Railway, and thereafter

[1] See p. 488.
[2] W. P. Rutter, *Wheat Growing in Canada, the United States, and the
Argentine*, pp. 4–5.
[3] J. M. Imrie, Evidence, Special Committee on Agricultural Conditions,
Appendix, *H/C. Journals*, vol. lx, 1923, pt. 2, p. 1444.
[4] J. McDougall, *On Western Trails in the Early 'Seventies*, passim.

a steady outward stream developed. By the 'nineties the stream of wheat exports to England was fast increasing, but it was only after 1900 that the swollen stream of wheat became a torrent.

Year by year the wheat acreage and the wheat exportation expanded as the four conditioning factors came into play. In 1883–90 the production of wheat in Western Canada averaged 8·3 million bushels ; in 1891–7 it averaged 19·2 million bushels, in 1898–1904 it averaged 47·0 million bushels, and that was merely a beginning.[1] From 1898 onwards settlers poured into Western Canada, not only from Eastern Canada and overseas, but also from the United States, where the best wheat-lands were now occupied, and the spacious days of free homesteads were over. So great was the influx that the number of net homestead entries in Western Canada doubled between 1897 and 1898, doubled again in 1902, and more than trebled in the following year.[2]

Again, after 1896 the Canadian Pacific Railway was supplemented by the Canadian Northern, and after 1904 by the Grand Trunk Pacific. " Unfortunately," it had been complained, " the main line of the Canadian Pacific Railway does not run through the best farming district of the North-West. After you leave the boundaries of Manitoba, it goes into a district affected by the droughts and dry winds coming from the great American desert to the south, and where the artificial application of water is necessary to produce crops. The Saskatchewan valley does not suffer from these disadvantages." [3] This fact helps to explain the rather slow development of Western Canada after the opening óf the Canadian Pacific Railway. The new railways together with the new branches of the Canadian Pacific Railway tapped these fresh and fertile wheat lands on the north Saskatchewan River from the late 'nineties onwards.

In the matter of suitable wheats, Red Fife had been introduced into Manitoba in 1882, after several failures of the existing species of wheat. Red Fife in turn was replaced

---

[1] Based on figures in [Cd. 2628], pp. 61, 66.
[2] Following figures are based on statistics given in [Cd. 2628], op. cit., p. 25 :—

1897	1,776	1901	5,538
1898	3,649	1902	7,666
1899	4,852	1903	24,042
1900	5,195	1904	23,358

[3] G. E. Casey, *Dominion Debates*, 1900, vol. i, col. 498.

by the superior Marquis, discovered in 1904, which was quick-ripening, rust-escaping,[1] of heavy yield, and with excellent milling and baking properties.

While England and other European and even Asiatic, countries were importing more wheat, the United States, Canada's greatest rival producer, was gradually falling out of the race. The Chinese and the Japanese imported wheat to make good shortages in their rice harvests.[2] The increasing population, and sometimes the diminishing wheat acreage, in England, Germany, and Italy demanded increased wheat imports into those countries. The rapidly mounting population of the United States left an ever-lessening margin of wheat for exportation, and Canada became the chief granary of the world.[3] But for this rapidly expanding demand for wheat in the world market since 1900, the price of wheat would have slumped severely and the progress of Western Canada would have been stringently curtailed. On the other hand, the development of the wheat trade of Western Canada helped to steady prices in the world market in the face of an increasing demand, and eased the lot of all those in many lands to whom wheaten bread is the staff of life.

The concentration of the farmers of Western Canada

[1] Marquis is not rust-resisting, but on account of its early ripening it is rust-escaping to a large extent.

[2] J. M. Imrie, *Special Committee on Agricultural Conditions*, p. 1442.

[3] PRODUCTION OF WHEAT BY CANADA AND THE UNITED STATES.

Year.	Canada. (bushels.)	United States. (bushels.)
1919	193,260,000	933,891,000
1920	263,189,000	833,027,000
1921	300,858,000	814,905,000
1922	399,786,000	867,598,000
1923	474,199,000	785,741,000
1924	262,097,000	872,673,000
1925	411,376,000	676,429,000
1926	409,811,000	832,809,000

(Culled from respective *Canada Year Books*.)

EXPORTATION OF WHEAT AND FLOUR FROM CANADA, FROM THE UNITED STATES, AND THE TOTAL FROM ALL COUNTRIES :

Year.	Canada.		United States.	
	Wheat. (bushels.)	Flour. (barrels.)	Wheat. (bushels.)	Flour. (barrels.)
1925–6	275,463,000	10,897,000	74,250,000	9,570,000
1926–7	251,264,000	9,237,000	148,336,000	13,463,000

	All Countries.	
	Wheat. (bushels.)	Flour. (barrels.)
1925–6	559,619,000	33,584,000
1926–7	705,887,000	34,786,000

(*Canada Year Book*, 1927–8, p. 295.)

on wheat growing has led to a stronger sense of corporate unity than is usual amongst farmers, despite their diversity of races, creeds and tongues. This sense of corporate unity has been further strengthened by the isolation of the farmers of Western Canada from the rest of the world. The Prairie Provinces are really a landlocked island. On the east there is the thousand mile barrier of the Canadian Shield, on the north the Arctic regions, on the west the towering ramparts of the Rockies, and on the south there is the tariff-barred frontier of the United States.

The distance of Western Canada from its principal markets has raised problems which also have called into activity that same sense of corporate unity. Those problems have been concerned with the bridging of the gulf between producers and ultimate consumers, the transportation of the grain, its transhipment and storage, its grading, weighing and cleaning, and its marketing. They are problems which have induced the Western farmers to agitate and organize, to demand on the one hand State aid and to practise on the other self-help.

While the problems which have arisen in connection with the organization of the wheat trade tend in practice to overlap, nevertheless they are logically distinct and permit of separate treatment. In the main they are : (a) Transportation ; (b) Shipment and Storage ; (c) Grading, Weighing and Cleaning, and (d) Marketing.

To take the wheat trade out of the realms of abstractions, it is best to follow the wheat right from the farm in Western Canada to the ultimate consumer, whether he be in Eastern Canada or in England. In such an account the problems of organization will be implicit, not explicit. After the reaping and threshing of the wheat, the farmers transport their grain by cart or motor-car, it may be 20 or 50 miles, to the nearest railway point as soon as possible. Granaries are not common, and very few farmers store their grain on their farms over the winter, as they can rarely afford to be out of their money for so long a time. Arrived at the railway, the farmers, if they are in a big way and can command railway cars, may load up the cars directly from their vehicles over a loading platform, or they may load up indirectly through an elevator which collects and stores the grain until cars are available. The elevator scoops the wheat up in buckets attached to an endless rubber belt and carries it aloft into bins, whence it can be unloaded into railway cars by allowing it to pour through the spouts at the bottom of the bins.   Elevators are owned and operated either by private companies or by the farmers co-operatively. Further, the farmers may sell their grain there and then to the elevator companies, or they may rail it to Winnipeg to private dealers or to co-operative agencies for sale on commission.   After the cars have been loaded, the wheat is hauled, generally to Winnipeg, where it is inspected and graded, and then it is sent on to lakeside at Fort William or Port Arthur, where it is finally inspected and graded. Some wheat now goes out by the Pacific ports, Prince Rupert and Vancouver, especially from Alberta and Western Saskatchewan after the winter freeze has " put the cork in the bottleneck " of Winnipeg,[1] and from those ports it is shipped to Europe via Panama and to Asia. The bulk of the traffic still goes out by Winnipeg and the Atlantic ports,[2] and the results are chronic congestion in the fall at Winnipeg and lakeside, and a feverish rush to get the wheat out before the winter freeze locks the water exit eastward.   Water transport is so very much cheaper than rail transport that very little wheat goes out of Canada by the all-rail route after the winter freeze,[3] it being more economical to store it throughout the winter in the country elevators or in the large terminal elevators on the lakeside or inland.

On account of the winter hold-up of lake traffic, the price of wheat in the Winnipeg market drops steadily as the second week of December approaches, on account of the diminishing likelihood of being able to transport the wheat by lake to outside markets.   From September till December the giant terminals at Port Arthur and Fort William spout a golden stream of wheat into the lake carriers.   These ships have come up the lakes with cargoes of coal and have been scoured out with scalding water to make them fit to carry the grain. This upward freight of coal gives Buffalo a great advantage as a wheat port, for it is the great coal port.   Down the lakes the routes of the carriers diverge : some seek Buffalo directly and thereby New York overland, others by canal and rail shipment seek Montreal and tide-water.   While

---

[1] J. M. Imrie, *Special Committee on Agricultural Conditions*, p. 1432.
[2] See diagram in *Canada Year Book*, 1927–8, p. 614.
[3] A. E. Kemp, *Dominion Debates*, 1903, vol. iv, col. 9,180, and E. Porritt, "Canada's National Grain Route," in *Political Science Quarterly*, 1918, vol. xxxiii, p. 351.

St. John and Portland and some other ports ship wheat to Europe, the two great Atlantic ports for Canadian wheat are New York and Montreal. Of the two, New York has considerable advantages. It is an all the year round port, whereas Montreal is closed for four to five months in the year. Furthermore, insurance rates and freight rates are much less from New York than from Montreal, on account partly of the great traffic of New York which attracts shoals of tramps who go " gunning for charters ",[1] but are seldom seen at Montreal. On reaching tide-water, all that remains is for the wheat to cross the ocean to reach Liverpool or some other European port, and its journey is complete.[2]

Transportation. The actual transportation of wheat from Western Canada falls into four stages : by cart or motor-car from the farm to the railway, by rail to lakeside and in certain cases beyond the lakes to the seaports, by lake-carrier and sometimes canal boat over the inland waterways, and finally by ocean ship from tide-water. Of the four stages rail transportation is the most important and has caused the most heartburning. The first stage is a matter largely of good roads, and with the advent of the motor-car there has been an improvement in that direction. Motor-cars, by their economy in time and other ways, have widened the radius of profitable farming away from the railways. The water stage excited less controversy than the railways. The lakes, being a " made way ", were the scene of intense competition, and rates were remarkably low. Recently, however, there have been complaints of agreements and understandings amongst the lake carriers, and it is said that the Western farmers have lost in extra lake rates what they had gained in reduced rail rates with the restoration of the Crow's Nest Pass Agreement in 1922.[3] The fourth stage has only excited strife between Canadian and American ports. Montreal complains of freight-rate discrimination in favour of New York and against Montreal. The farmers,

[1] E. Porritt, *Canada's National Grain Route*, p. 360.

[2] An investigation made in 1923 revealed that the cost of transporting 1,000 bushels of No. 1 Northern wheat from a farm in Western Canada to Liverpool averaged 40 cents or about 1s. 9d. a bushel. This figure covers commissions, inspection fees, insurance, dealers' profits, loading and unloading charges, as well as actual transportation costs (F. J. Horning, Chief of the Internal Trade Division of the Dominion Bureau of Statistics, quoted by E. H. Godfrey," Canadian Farming," in *North America Pamphlets* in the D.O. & C.O. Library, No. 28).

[3] C. M. Hamilton, *Special Committee on Agricultural Conditions*, pt. i, p. 1037, and see chap. 11.

however, have little ground for complaint, since shipping out by New York they get the advantage of the low American freight rates. It is clear, therefore, that the problem of transportation hinges principally on the railways.

Farmers soon came to regard railway rates as a matter of life and death. " The rates are everything. We can wait for the railroad for a year or two years, but if we have no control of rates we are at the mercy of the railroad ; the railroad is our master for all time, and we are its servants." [1] A Western lawyer suggested that the principle of the penny postage should be applied to the transportation of wheat from the Prairies, that a flat rate should be charged from the different towns in order to " annihilate the disability that at present exists in the case of our farmers who grow grain in the centre of this continent." [2] Farmers steadily supported the idea of State Railways, not from Socialistic motives but for sternly individualistic reasons. They knew that private railways must be run to pay, but that State railways might be run at a loss and thereby give them lower rates and greater profits. " Government ownership (it was bluntly said) means lower freight rates for the producers, whether farmers, miners, lumbermen, stockmen, or fishermen ".[3]

At first the Canadian Pacific Railway had an absolute monopoly of rail transport in Western Canada. Nevertheless the Company did its utmost under the sagacious management of Van Horne to foster traffic. In 1886 the rail rate from an average place like Brandon to lake-side was 30 cents per hundred. In 1887, in answer to a plea from the Western representatives, Van Horne reduced the rate from 30 cents to 24 cents. At the same time N. F. Davin, who acted as secretary to the group, laid down two basic principles : " that a railway in that new country was bound to reduce its rates in the ratio of increase of freight and population, and that there should be a triennial revision until the rates represented the cost of hauling and a reasonable profit added thereto, under conditions of full employment for plant and men." Rate reductions continued : In 1890 from 24 cents to 22 cents ; in 1893 to 19 cents ; in 1898 to 17½ cents ; and in 1899 to 16 cents.[4] A further reduction

---

[1] F. Oliver, *Dominion Debates*, 1903, vol. iii, col. 3485.
[2] N. F. Davin, *Dominion Debates*, 1900, vol. iii, col. 3254.
[3] W. F. Maclean, *Dominion Debates*, 1901, vol. i, col. 1075.
[4] N. F. Davin, *Dominion Debates*, 1900, vol. iii, cols. 3249–54. See for the whole subject, Division II, Chap. 11 of present vol.

was secured in 1904 on account of the competition of the Canadian Northern,[1] and thereafter rail rates passed out of the region of direct negotiations between railways and farmers representatives and came within the jurisdiction of the newly established Board of Railway Commissioners. The fairness of the early rate policy of the Canadian Pacific Railway was confirmed by the Railway Rates Commission which reported in 1895. Canadian rates were found to be lower than the corresponding American rates, and while local rates were higher in Western Canada than in Eastern Canada, this was accounted for by the higher operating charges in the West, fuel being 110 per cent dearer, labour 45 per cent, and general supplies 60 per cent.[2]

Another thing that troubled the farmers was the question of railway facilities, such as the adequacy of rolling stock and the nearness of the railways to the settlements. The great increase in the wheat output of Western Canada in 1901 and 1902 took the railways by surprise. Rolling stock was quite inadequate, and " dead " locomotives, which had been worked to a standstill, were lying up and down the line. The congestion became chronic in Winnipeg and was known as the " Wheat Blockade ". The Winnipeg Board of Trade passed a resolution in 1902 which began : " Whereas in the autumn and early winter of 1901, the farmers and business classes of Manitoba and the North-West Territories suffered severe losses through the inability of the Canadian Pacific Railway Company to cope with the grain traffic . . . and whereas the conditions in regard to grain transportation during the present shipping season are as bad as, if not worse than, those which prevailed in 1901 . . ."[3] The inward traffic, as well as the outward traffic, was jammed, and during the winter of 1902–3 Manitoba and the North-West Territories were " on the ragged edge of a coal famine," so that, it was said, farmers were driven to burn their fences, and even their furniture.[4] The railways blamed the new Manitoba Grain Act for delaying matters by inspection of the wheat, but the farmers pointed out that carloads of wheat often stood two months after inspection waiting to be moved. During 1902 alone the Wheat Block adewas said to have cost the farmers $5,000,000.[5]

[1] Cd. 2628, p. 98.
[2] H. A. Innis, Canadian Pacific Railway, pp. 176, 183.
[3] Quoted by W. Scott, Dominion Debates, 1903, vol. i, col. 2426.
[4] Ibid., c. 2431.   [5] Ibid., c. 2444.

The Canadian Pacific Railway learnt the lesson, and while congestion is an annual occurrence, there was no recurrence of the Wheat Blockade.

In 1903 it was computed that if a farmer was 20 miles away from a railway line he was at the extreme distance which enabled him to make a satisfactory living.[1] At the same time homestead settlers had to go 75 miles and more for their grants, and thus an intensive policy of building railway lines through the wheat lands some 30 or 40 miles apart was advocated.[2] Since then this policy has been largely carried out, and to-day the fertile wheat lands are grid-ironed by the main lines and branches of the two great competing railway systems. In addition rates and facilities are now reasonably suited to the farmers' requirements.

Shipment and Storage. Elevators, both country and terminal, perform the two fundamental functions of shipment and storage. Country elevators are much smaller than terminals,[3] for the catchment area of a country elevator is much smaller than that of terminals. It has been calculated that country elevators require to handle four times their capacity in wheat in order to pay.[4] Terminals, situated as they are at the central points on the Prairies as well as on lakeside, carry a large part of the Western wheat throughout the winter until the lakes thaw and shipping is resumed. In 1927 there were in Western Canada 4,437 country elevators with a capacity of 146,584,200 bushels and 119 terminals with a capacity of 138,179,000 bushels.[5] Elevators take advantage of the pouring capacity of wheat, and thereby economize both time and money. Formerly, it required a day to load a car from a wagon or flat warehouse without machinery; now it is done in 15 minutes by an elevator.[6] Such a saving of time enables the farmers to send their wheat out before the winter freeze and to get a better price for it. It also enables them to return more quickly to their work on the farm before the frosts set in.

When the wheat trade of Western Canada was small, it was handled by means of sacks and shipped through flat warehouses, and almost everything was done by hand. From 1884 to 1890 flat warehouses were built at all the

---

[1] Ibid., c. 2428.
[2] F. Oliver, *Dominion Debates*, 1903, vol. ii, col. 3484.
[3] See *Canada Year Book*, 1927–8, p. 616.
[4] J. G. Scott, Evidence, *Dominions Royal Commission*, Cd. 8458, p. 307.
[5] *Canada Year Book*, 1927–8, p. 616.
[6] W. C. Clark, *Country Elevators in the Canadian West*, p. 47.

railway sidings near settlements. After 1890, as the wheat
trade expanded, the existing method was found to be both
cumbersome and costly. In its place bulk-handling through
elevators was adopted, and in the 'nineties the tall towers of
the country elevators became familiar features on the
prairie landscape. When wheat was consigned to the
market in sacks, each consignment retained its identity and
was sold by means of samples. With bulk-handling, each
consignment lost its identity, and accordingly a system of
standard grades was introduced to determine the value of
each consignment. On arriving at the market in bulk the
wheat was sold by means of the grades, although samples
were still used, for •grades varied within themselves
appreciably.

While the Canadian Pacific Railway had built the terminals
itself from 1883 onwards till 1902, when private interests
entered the field,[1] country elevators from the commencement were built by private companies, but under the active
encouragement of the railway company. Realizing that
elevators were for the good of the wheat trade, the Canadian
Pacific Railway offered free sites alongside their line and
promised a monopoly to such companies as built " standard
elevators " as against shipment through flat warehouses
or direct shipment over loading platforms. The plan
achieved its end, and by 1900 there were 447 elevators
within the Manitoba inspection district. Of these elevators
421 were owned by elevator companies, millers and grain-
dealers, and 26 by farmers' companies.[2] The farmers'
elevators were not very efficiently managed, and they fared
badly. " Where unfair competition killed two, bad management killed four." [3]

Thus private interests other than the Railway controlled
the elevators, and very soon complaints arose from the
farmers as to their tyranny and unjust practices. The
elevator companies were accused of deducting excessive
dockage, which was the allowance for dirt in the uncleaned
grain. They were also accused of false weights. Further,
they were charged with undergrading the wheat. Finally
they were charged with exploiting their monopoly of shipment to buy wheat from the farmers at prices lower than

    [1] E. Porritt, *Canada's National Grain Route*, p. 348.
    [2] Report of Royal Commission on Shipment and Transportation of
Grain, p. 9, *Sessional Papers*, 1900, No. 81a, vol. xxxiv.
    [3] W. C. Clark, *Country Elevators in the Canadian West*, p. 61.

the market rate. The reason was that farmers were in a hurry to realize cash for their crop and instead of waiting till the crop had been sold at Winnipeg on commission they elected to sell it on the spot, and there the only buyer very often was the local elevator. Elevators either became grain-dealers or worked in very close conjunction with them.

So great was the outcry, that the Royal Commission on the Shipment and Transportation of Grain was appointed in 1899. It reported in 1900 and made a series of remedial recommendations. Overdocking, underweighing and undergrading were to be checked by Government regulation and supervision.[1] The exploitation of the farmer by means of the elevator companies' monopoly of shipment was to be ended by statute, which would permit the construction of loading platforms and flat warehouses and would order the railways to provide the farmers with cars for shipment over the platform or through the flat warehouse, apart from the elevator. " Though the furnishing of cars to farmers has been given as a privilege, they should, with proper restrictions, enjoy it as a legal right." [2]

The recommendations of the Report were promptly embodied in the Manitoba Grain Act of 1900, Section 42 of which gave the farmers the legal right to cars in their proper rotation for shipment over loading platforms or through flat warehouses. Breaches of Section 42 gave rise in 1901 to the Territorial Grain Growers' Association covering present-day Saskatchewan and Alberta, which took action against the Canadian Pacific Railway. The Association's victory in the Sintaluta case compelled the Company to obey Section 42 and to furnish cars to farmers in their proper rotation. Even then the farmers were not much better off, for the stars in their courses fought against Section 42. The Royal Commission had hoped that the flat warehouses and loading platforms would compete with, and act as checks on the elevators, thus breaking their monopoly and securing fair treatment for the farmers. Instead, elevators continued to hold a virtual monopoly of shipment on account of their superior speed, convenience and economy. Few or no flat warehouses were built, and loading platforms were only used by large farmers who could fill a car and had no need of storage.[3] Some other action

---

[1] For treatment of this subject, see section " Grading and Cleaning " (*post*).　　　　　　　　　　　　　[2] Report, p. 10.
[3] W. C. Clark, *Country Elevators in the Canadian West*, p. 60.

was necessary if the elevators' monopoly was to be broken.

In 1906 another Royal Commission was appointed to investigate the Grain Trade. The chief complaint was still the exploitation of the farmers by the elevators' monopoly. A subsidiary grievance was the wide " spread " or difference between the " street " price of wheat, which was the price paid for wheat as delivered at the elevator, and the " track " price of wheat, which was the price paid for wheat when loaded on the car. Obviously the " spread " varied with the number of cars available and the possibility of speedy transportation, so the Royal Commission recommended a plentiful supply of cars [1]—a counsel of perfection. On the grand charge of monopoly and exploitation, the farmers alleged as proofs the absence of competitive bidding at local points and the uniformity of wheat prices. But also there was the North-West Grain Dealers' Association, which, originating for the purpose of buying elevator supplies cheaply in bulk, regulated the buying price of grain in the country. If any dealers did not abide by the Association's price list, they were brought to heel by the united action of the other dealers. Further, elevator companies had been pooling receipts where their elevators were in competition with each other.[2] In the face of all this the Royal Commission made no definite recommendation.

One more matter the Royal Commission touched on. Terminal elevators were now coming to the fore as a bone of contention. Since 1902 they had been falling into the hands of the elevator companies, which were now charged with fraudulently mixing the wheat, with undercleaning the wheat, and with exploiting their monopoly of storage and transhipment by underpaying and overcharging. After examining the charges, the Royal Commission expressed a pious hope of " obtaining a good service from these elevators under the present ownership by having a more thorough system of supervision and control ".[3]

Such tepid recommendations were not likely to lead to any very vigorous action on the part of the Government, and were even less likely to command the assent of the farmers, whose indignation was now great. Under the inspiration of their leader, Partridge of Sintaluta, the

---

[1] Report of the Royal Commission on the Grain Trade of Canada, pp. 7–9, *Sessional Papers*, 1907–8, No. 59, vol. xlii.
[2] W. C. Clark, p. 64.   [3] Report, p. 39.

farmers had come out with a full-blooded programme of Nationalization. The Provincial Governments were to own and administer the country elevators, the Dominion Government was to own and administer the terminal elevators. The agitation was soon under way.

In a conference in 1908 with the three Premiers of the Prairie Provinces the farmers presented their demand for the Provincial ownership and administration of the country elevators.[1] No definite step was taken in answer until 1910 when the Manitoba Government took over the bulk of the elevators in the Province. The result of Provincial ownership and administration was loss and disappointment. For one thing, the elevators were not permitted to deal in grain and they thereby lost the chief chance of profit.[2] In addition, the farmers attributed the loss to the inflated purchase price of the elevators and to political jobbery in their management.[3] The experiment having failed, the Manitoba Government in 1912 leased the elevators to the Grain Growers' Grain Company, a co-operative farmers' body formed for commercial purposes. The new plan of Provincial ownership and co-operative administration by the farmers proved a success. Saskatchewan took a leaf out of Manitoba's book and adopted the plan of co-operative management from the beginning. By the Saskatchewan Co-operative Elevator Act of 1911 the Saskatchewan Co-operative Elevator Company was empowered to borrow 85 per cent of the capital necessary for its operations from the Provincial Government and to repay the loan in instalments stretching over 20 years.[4] The result was again success. In 1913 the Alberta Co-operative Elevator Company was established by an Act similar to the Saskatchewan one. Then in 1917, the Grain Growers' Grain Company and the Alberta Co-operative Elevator Company amalgamated to form the United Grain Growers, Ltd., with joint co-operative management of the elevators in Manitoba and Alberta.[5] The Saskatchewan Co-operative Elevator Company stood aloof from this movement, but was ultimately absorbed, not horizontally but vertically, by the Saskatchewan Wheat Pool.[6]

---

[1] J. C. Hopkins, *Canadian Annual Review*, 1908, p. 452.
[2] W. C. Clark, *Country Elevators in the Canadian West*, p. 58.
[3] L. A. Wood, *Farmers' Movements in Western Canada*, pp. 212, 220.
[4] Ibid., pp. 213–14.
[5] H. S. Patton, *Grain Growers' Co-operation in Western Canada*, pp. 170–7.
[6] See section " Marketing " (*post*).

In pursuance of the second article of the Partridge Plan, the farmers proceeded from 1908 onwards to bombard the Dominion Government with demands for the Dominion ownership and administration of the terminal elevators. The bombardment reached its height during the " Siege of Ottawa " in 1910, when five hundred farmers from Western Canada appeared in the Dominion Legislature and demanded the federal acquisition of terminals.[1]

The demand was partially met by the Canada Grain Act of 1912, which tightened up the regulation of privately owned terminals and provided for the building and leasing of terminals by the Dominion Government. The Dominion Government built a terminal at Port Arthur in 1913, and opened terminals at Saskatoon, Moose Jaw, and Calgary in 1914–15. The Grain Growers' Grain Company entered the terminal business by leasing three Canadian Pacific Railway elevators at Fort William.[2] More elevators were acquired later. Thus there were private companies, co-operative bodies, and the Dominion Government, all running terminals and competing with each other. Recently there has been a fourth entrant into the field, the Wheat Pool, which owns and runs both country elevators and terminals.[3]

The intrusion of co-operation into the elevator business has strangely enough tended to keep alive the old spirit of competition between the private companies and the co-operative bodies. It has certainly been effectual in breaking the former monopoly of the elevator companies. Where private farmers' companies failed and State bodies but rarely succeeded, co-operative bodies of farmers were a great success in both country elevator and terminal business, on account of their loyalty, their keen scrutiny and their effectual control over procedure. At the same time, while on the one hand the farmers have had the advantages of alternative means of shipment and a choice of buyers which mean better prices and better service, on the other hand the unnecessary duplication of plants at points lead to higher running costs than are absolutely essential, and the very keenness of the competition is a temptation to adulteration and other malpractices in the effort to cut costs. Government regulation and inspection are certainly necessary.

---

[1] Report of Proceedings at Farmers' Delegation, 1910, *Sessional Papers*, No. 113, 1911.

[2] L. A. Wood, pp. 215–18, and H. S. Patton, pp. 147–9.

[3] See section " Marketing " (*post*).

Grading, Cleaning, and Weighing.—" Canadian grain is divided into five general classes, viz. ' No grade,' ' Condemned,' ' Rejected,' ' Commercial grade,' and ' Statutory grade.' ' No grade ' includes all good grain that has an excessive moisture, being tough, damp, or wet, or otherwise unfit for warehousing. ' Condemned grain ' means all grain that is in a heating condition or is badly bin-burnt, whatever grade it might otherwise be. ' Rejected grain ' means all grain that is unsound, musty, dirty, smutty, or sprouted, or that contains a large admixture of other kinds of grain, seeds, or wild oats, or that from any other cause is unfit to be classed under any of the recognized grades. ' Commercial grade ' means grain which, because of climatic or other conditions, cannot be included in the grades provided for in the Act . . . ' Statutory grades ' means grain of the highest grades as defined by Parliament in the Grain Act. . . . Thus the statutory definitions can only be changed by Parliament ; they do not vary with the crop, but are constant. The commercial grades, on the other hand, are fixed by the Standards Board, and may vary from year to year. The Act defines four grades of Western spring wheat, viz. No. 1 Hard, No. 1 Northern, No. 2 Northern, and No. 3 Northern, whilst the Standards Board has defined three additional grades, viz. No. 4 Northern, No. 5 Northern, and No. 6 Northern. . . . Grain, as inspected and graded at Winnipeg, is received into the terminal elevators, but is again finally inspected and graded in bulk as it is loaded into the lake steamers. For this final grading the grain is sampled at three places, viz. in the funnels as the grain flows from the storage bins to the working house, on the floor of the working house, and on the steamers as it pours from the shipping bin to the hold." [1]

Before 1900, the work of grading had been largely left to private agencies and inspection was not obligatory, although the grades had been determined by an Act of 1874 and by Amendments of 1889 and 1891.[2] Complaints about unfair grading on the part of the farmers led to the Royal Commission on Shipment and Transportation of Grain in 1899, whose recommendations in turn led to the Manitoba Grain Act of 1900. By this Act a Government inspector was appointed, who was to grade the wheat as

---

[1] *Canada Year Book*, 1922–3, pp. 582–3. Recently there have been bitter complaints by the farmers of undergrading (*The Times*, 17th April, 1929).   [2] W. C. Clark, p. 51.

it passed through Winnipeg and whose decision was binding, though subject to appeal. Its title of *Manitoba* Grain Act was significant of the extent of the Western wheat trade in 1900. In 1912 the Act and all its subsequent amendments were codified along with the General Inspection Act in the Canada Grain Act. This Act set up the Board of three Grain Commissioners who, forming a subdivision of the Department of Trade and Commerce, supervised the inspection, but appeal was to a Survey Board " nominated by various bodies and Provincial Ministers of Agriculture ". In 1925, following another Royal Commission, the Canada Grain Act was thoroughly overhauled, but the system of grading remains much as before. In 1917 it could be said : During the busy season about two thousand cars are inspected every twenty-four hours in Winnipeg. The work proceeds seven days of the week and twenty-four hours of the day. The samplers must always be ready to open cars as soon as they arrive, so as not to delay the movement. So expert do they become that they can sample an entire train of forty or forty-five cars in about an hour. As it takes this length of time to change engines and crews, there is no delay.[1]

Weighing, formerly such a contentious matter, is under the strict scrutiny of the Dominion Government, and complaints are a thing of the past. The scales " are always inspected at least once a year by the Department of Inland Weights and Revenue of the Dominion Government. The officials of this department are constantly travelling about the country testing all scales used commercially. Their routes are not known. They come and go as they please. They have keys to all country elevators. They keep the scales constantly adjusted. The first information received by any line elevator company that its scales have been inspected is the bill for expenses of the inspector." [2]

While dockage is estimated at the country elevators, cleaning generally takes place at the terminals. About 70 per cent. of the wheat has to be cleaned before being spouted on board the lake carriers. The screenings are recleaned to recover any good grain and the refuse is burnt in the boiler furnaces.[3] Hospital elevators are used at

---

[1] C. B. Piper, *Principles of the Grain Trade*, pp. 33–4.
[2] Ibid., p. 69.
[3] Ibid., pp. 97–8.

terminal points for the treatment and recovery of damaged wheat.

Marketing.—Marketing presents the greatest problem of all in connexion with the wheat trade. The paradox of the wheat trade is that the farmer may virtually starve in the midst of plenty and thrive in the midst of famine. A good crop may ruin the farmer on account of the disastrous slump in prices, whereas a poor crop may mean prosperity by reason of soaring prices. The farmer, again, is deeply affected by general movements of prices, such as the general rise during the war and the post-war boom, and the general fall during the post-war slump. Since wholesale prices, especially of raw materials like grain, fluctuate more violently than ordinary retail prices, farmers do well in a period of rising prices, for their selling prices rise more rapidly than their purchase prices. Conversely in a time of falling prices farmers do badly. These are the basic facts behind the attempts to arrange orderly marketing (such as the Wheat Pools) whereby it is hoped that by holding over the surplus of a good year into a bad year, supplies will be roughly equated to needs and prices will be steadied to the great benefit of consumers and producers alike.

Orderly marketing, to be effective, requires large-scale operations, and the control of a good proportion of the international wheat market. It is an ambitious plan, and it was only attempted after war-time experience and after the farmers had tried their 'prentice hand on ordinary commission marketing on a small scale. This experiment in commission marketing was undertaken under the inspiration of Partridge of Sintaluta in 1906, and was only designed to return to the farmers some of the heavy toll supposed to be levied on them by the middlemen and commission agents on the Winnipeg Grain Exchange. The aim was not to subvert or revolutionize the existing order, but to act through recognized channels within the system, the farmers becoming their own middlemen or commission agents. The design of the Wheat Pools, on the other hand, is to transcend the existing order by establishing above it a new directing body, who will act through the existing order, but will eliminate blind competitive marketing and bring order out of chaos for the advantage of farmers and society generally.

Partridge believed that the grain dealers on the Winnipeg Exchange prejudiced the farmers by their excessive commission and their speculation. To break the monopoly of the grain dealers and put an end to their machinations, Partridge formed in 1906 the Grain Growers' Grain Company to operate on the Winnipeg Grain Exchange on behalf of the farmers. The Exchange promptly replied by expelling the Company for alleged breach of the Exchange rules, and when the Company was reinstated, made a second attempt to embarrass it by suspending the Commission rule in 1909–10. This stratagem depended on the fact that many of the dealers held interests in the elevators and could do with only a small commission or no commission at all on the Exchange, recouping themselves on the elevator business. The Company could not follow in this policy since, having no interest in the elevators, it depended entirely on its commission for income and could not bear even a whittling down of the commission. However, the farmers remained loyal to the Company, and at the end of the year the Exchange restored the Commission rule.[1]

The Company remains to-day a very important grain dealer, but only among equals. Other grain dealers, representing private interests, operate alongside the Company, and flourish as it flourishes. One mark of the Exchange's onslaught remains. The Company is not an orthodox co-operative body. The surplus, or profit, is returned to the Company's shareholders by means of dividends on their shares, and not to the Company's customers by means of dividends on their patronage. No doubt the Company's customers are guaranteed considerate treatment by a Company consisting of their own class. Then it may be argued that in so far as patronage corresponds to share-holdership, so far the dividends approach the co-operative ideal. The fact remains that the Company is run on ordinary business lines, and the Winnipeg Wheat Exchange was sufficiently strong to secure this before permitting the reinstatement of the Company in 1907.[2] The Company continues to look forward to the payment of the patronage dividend as an ideal.

The first effort of collective marketing was made during the war, which revealed the importance of Canadian wheat supplies to England and also to France and Italy. During the latter part of 1916 and the whole of 1917 and 1918 a Board of Grain Supervisors fixed wheat prices and regulated supplies. Wheat marketing was done by another body,

---

[1] H. S. Patton, pp. 73–5.   [2] Ibid., pp. 43–61.

the Wheat Export Company, which bought on behalf of the Royal Commission of Wheat Supplies acting jointly for England, France and Italy.[1]

The Royal Commission was retained after the war and, as the 1919 harvest threatened to be a short one, the Canadian Government set up the Canadian Wheat Board to market the crop and prevent any ramps. This was a Parliamentary monopoly: "No open trading took place on the Winnipeg Grain Exchange, existing grain-handling agencies merely receiving and forwarding wheat at fixed margins to the Board's account."[2] Good prices were paid to the farmers on account of the short crops, and the " spread " going to the dealers was minimized. The Board suddenly became popular in Western Canada, but in 1920 it came to an end with the abolition of the Royal Commission of Wheat Supplies.

Western Canada at once clamoured for its restoration, and the agitation became shriller with the fall in wheat prices. The fall was due, not to the disestablishment of the Board, but to more plentiful harvests in Canada and elsewhere, which brought down world wheat prices at a run. Controversy raged over the proposals for a compulsory State Pool and a voluntary Contract Pool. At last, finding the Government adamantine against a State Pool, the farmers decided to act for themselves by setting up voluntary Contract Pools on a Provincial basis.[3]

The voluntary Contract Pool is based on the promise of the farmers to hand over their entire marketable crop to the Pool. In return the farmers immediately receive a certain cash payment on account, and the residue is paid when the crop has been marketed and the handling and marketing costs have been deducted from the final selling price. The capital required is small, and is supplied by the farmers. Loans for financing the handling of the crop are made by the banks. The prosperity of the Pool depends on the good management of the officials and the loyalty of the members, that is, it depends on the corporate spirit of the farmers.[4]

Alberta led the way in 1923-4, the Alberta Co-operative Wheat Producers, Ltd., marketing 26 per cent. of the Alberta crop of that season with satisfactory results.

---

[1] C. R. Fay, *Agricultural Co-operation in the Canadian West*, pp. 458-9.
[2] H. S. Patton, p. 196.
[3] C. R. Fay, pp. 459-60.   [4] H. S. Patton, pp. 244-54.

Saskatchewan and Manitoba followed in 1924, and immediately the Canadian Co-operative Wheat Producers, Ltd., a central sales agency, was set up, which handled 38 per cent. of the crop of Western Canada that year. Since then the percentage handled by the combined Wheat Pool has increased to over 50 per cent.[1]

Friction soon came between the Pool and the Co-operative Elevators. While both were co-operative bodies set up to serve the farmers, they were quite distinct, with distinct functions and distinct sets of officials. Non-Pool farmers had as much right to use the co-operative elevators as the Pool farmers. Moreover, the elevators refused to report Pool farmers who broke their contract and sold elsewhere. Amalgamation was first attempted. It succeeded in Saskatchewan in 1925, when the Saskatchewan Co-operative Elevator Company was swallowed up by the Saskatchewan Pool. Co-operation was also tried, but all that happened was that the United Grain Growers, Ltd., which controls the co-operative elevators in Manitoba and Alberta, sold twenty-seven of its Alberta elevators to the Alberta Pool. All that remained was competition, and the Pool and the United Grain Growers, Ltd., now compete at a hundred and eighteen points since the Pool has built its own elevators both country and terminal.

The experiment of the Wheat Pool is still too young for much to be said about it definitely. The management seems to be quite efficient according to commercial standards and the loyalty of the farmers is firm. Breach of contract is occasionally pursued, but a blind eye is turned to odd carloads of grain that Pool farmers sell for ready money to private dealers. So great has been the initial success of Western Canada that Eastern Canada has followed its example, and now Ontario has its Wheat Pool.[2] The problem of orderly marketing does not concern merely a single year or a couple of years, but really a cycle of years, hence the difficulty. It would not be difficult to spread the marketing of the Canadian wheat crop over the twelve months equally or according to need. Nor would it be difficult, if good and bad seasons came alternately, to equate demand and supply. The root of the problem lies

[1] Ibid., pp. 216–24.

[2] In July, 1928, the Ontario Wheat Pool distributed its cheques at the end of its first year's operations. " This is the first time for many years that Ontario wheat has sold at a price within a reasonable distance of that of Western wheat " (*The Times*, 25th July, 1928).

in this, that good and bad years come in spells of varying and unknown duration, and the holding up of surpluses over a series of good years intensifies the difficulty.   This is the situation facing the Wheat Pool at present, and the solution is by no means easy.[1] Apart from abnormal times, however, the operations of the Wheat Pool should lessen the margin between producer prices and consumer prices, and thus benefit both farmers and the general public.

The wheat trade of Western Canada has now been surveyed as a whole, and the four groups of problems connected with the organization of the trade have been considered.   Different policies have been adopted to meet these problems: Governmental supervision in connexion with grading, weighing and cleaning; state action in connexion with transportation, shipment, and storage ; and co-operation in connexion with shipment and storage and marketing. Of the three policies, co-operation is the outstanding feature of the organization of the Western wheat trade. Its strength does not spring from a single root.   Partly it is due to the circumstances of frontier life and the absence of hired labour.   This explains the Logging Bee [2] of both Eastern and Western Canada.   Partly it is due to the concentration of the farmers on wheat, so facilitating united action. Farmers of British Columbia, with their diverse interests in wheat, fruit and stock, would find united action difficult. Partly it is due to the isolation of the farmers on their great land-locked island of the prairies.   Partly it is due to the fact that they are so largely dependent on innumerable intermediaries for reaching their distant and almost unknown markets, and to the further fact that these intermediaries may take advantage of the farmers' ignorance and separation from the markets.   Partly it is due to the fact that the farmers themselves are small, occupying owners with slender resources and little individual strength. Co-operation in Western Canada has shown itself in many guises, in buying material, and selling stock, poultry and lumber, but its most striking success has been in connexion with the wheat trade.

Agricultural Credit

One of the most difficult of the problems encountered by Canadian agricultural interests is that of finance.   No

[1] *The Times*, 14th May, 1929.
[2] A " Bee " is defined as " a social gathering of persons to do a job of work gratuitously ".

Canadian farmers' congress is complete without resolutions calling for improved credit facilities. An instance illustrating the economic loss to the Dominion consequent on the want of adequate agricultural credit facilities occurred in 1915, when "some 70,000 head of stockers and feeders . . . were shipped from the three Prairie Provinces to the United States, while at the same time enormous quantities of fodder and grain were available in our own country. The prices paid for these exported animals averaged slightly over $50, and as they would have practically doubled in value before the following spring, it is evident that approximately $3,000,000 was lost to Canada. . . . When it is borne in mind that the export of these animals was . . . due to the fact that the man who had the cattle did not have the feed, and the man who had the feed did not have the cattle nor the money with which to purchase and handle them, it is evident that a better. . . system of finance would have prevented this very considerable economic loss ".[1]

In the United States, previously to the legislation presently to be described, an attempt was made to deal with the problem by means of livestock banks and livestock loan companies whose special business it was to lend money to farmers at reasonable interest for the purpose of handling and feeding cattle. These institutions obtained their money from the banks in the Eastern States at say 5 to 6 per cent. and loaned it to farmers at probably 2 per cent. more.[2] The Canadian banking system is based upon the three months' turnover. In Canada, as elsewhere, such a system is unsuitable for the special needs of agriculture. The business of the farmer does not usually yield a quick return. His investment is in land or livestock, and he has to wait on the slow processes of nature for his dividends. Nature may be kind one year, and the next visit him with disease or adverse climatic conditions over which he has no more control than he has over fluctuations in prices. Such a specially precarious industry necessitates special financial arrangements, nevertheless " the agriculturist of Canada, in certain parts at least, pays considerably more for long term credits secured by his property than many of his competitors in other lands, as well as more than is paid by many of his fellow citizens in other walks of life for similar

---

[1] *D.R.C. Minutes of Evidence*, 1916 [*Cd.* 8459], p. 172.
[2] Ibid.

accommodation ".[1]   In Alberta in 1922 the rate for short
term loans from the banks varied from 8 to 10 per cent.
" according to the condition of the district and the degree
of competition present ".   The rate of interest on mortgages
was estimated to be from 8 to 9 per cent.   These figures
were considered to hold good for Western Canada generally.
In Eastern Canada interest rates were lower.[2]

The need is for a short term credit system [3] which shall
so organize the security offered as to secure more reasonable
rates of interest and shall increase the period of the loan so
as to make it consistent with the seasonal requirements of
agriculture ; and for a long term or mortgage credit system [4]
which shall " free the landowner from the necessity of
borrowing directly from the individual creditor, regulate
the payment of interest and capital so as to free the borrower
from the danger and anxiety associated with demands for
repayment under circumstances which make payment
impossible, and get rid of usurious rates of interest, putting
agriculture in this regard on the same basis as other
businesses equally secure ".[5]

The aim has been to lighten the farmers' burden by fixing
interest rates at from 6 to 7 per cent.[6]

In the United States, " the operations of the Federal
Farm Loan Board system offer through the National Farm
Loan Associations, the Federal Land Banks and the Joint
Stock Land Banks facilities for long term credits to the
farmers of that country which, when prudently availed of,
are of immense advantage to them " ; and " the Federal
Farm Loan Board system operating through the Federal
Intermediate Credit Banks and the Agricultural Credit
Corporations in the United States is designed to supply

---

[1] Report of Special Committee on Agricultural Conditions, .quoted
H. M. Tory, Report on Agricultural Credit, Ottawa, 1924 (*Sessional
Papers*, 1924, vol. lx, No. 142), p. 7.

[2] H. M. Tory, Report on Agricultural Credit (*supra*), pp. 83-4.

[3] " The term ' Short Term Credit ' has a different meaning in Europe
from that which it has in the United States.   In Europe it means all forms
of credit in relation to agriculture other than mortgage credit and in which
the security is personal or easily negotiable collateral.   In the United
States the term is used generally in reference to ordinary banking transactions of from three to six months.   In Canada it is used in the same
sense " (ibid., p. 10).

[4] " The term ' Long Term Credit ' is everywhere used to mean mortgage
credit and, in relation to agriculture, farm mortgage credit for terms of
five years or over " (ibid.).

[5] Ibid., p. 11.

[6] Ibid., p. 84.

to a very large extent to agriculturists . . . credit running from nine months to three years." [1]

The National Farm Loan Associations in the one case, and the National Agricultural Credit Corporations in the other, provide the co-operative element which is an essential feature of both the long and short term credit system. " In each federal district, National Farm Loan Associations must be organized by persons desiring to borrow money on farm mortgage security. The persons so desiring must sign articles of association. . . . These National Farm Loan Associations thus become incorporated and are the only medium, excepting in very special cases, through which persons desiring to borrow money from the Federal Land Bank can do so. They are, in reality, local semi-co-operative associations, associations of borrowers who become responsible for initiating all loans in their district. A National Farm Loan Association must consist of ten or more farmers whose joint applications for loans are not less than $20,000. Each borrower must subscribe for stock equivalent to 5 per cent. of the desired loan, and assume a liability, in case of loss, for an additional 5 per cent. . . . For example, should a borrower desire to borrow $1,000, he must buy 50 dollars worth of stock in the local association, and become liable for an additional 50 dollars in case of failure of members of the local association to meet their obligations. . . . It will be seen that under the Federal Farm Loan Act loans are not made by the Federal Land Banks directly to individuals, but only to individuals applying through associations and recommended by them for loans. Every member of the association making the recommendation becomes responsible to the extent of 10 per cent. of his own borrowings for the total indebtedness of the Association." [2]

The National Agricultural Credit Corporations fulfil similar functions in the short term credit system : " The scheme of the Federal Intermediate Credit Banks with regard to the individual borrower is identical with that under the Federal Land Banks, that is to say, no individual can have direct access for borrowing purposes to the Bank.

[1] Report of Special Committee on Agricultural Conditions (supra).

[2] H. M. Tory, Report on Agricultural Credit (supra), pp. 44–5. In 1924, seven years after their inauguration, the accounts of the Federal Land Banks showed Farm Loan Bonds outstanding to the amount of $685, 206, 665 (ibid., p. 51).

All loans made must be rediscounted loans made to a responsible corporation which in itself assumes responsibility for the repayment of the loan, so that a borrower must find his way to the Federal Intermediate Credit Bank through other organized financial machinery," namely, the National Agricultural Credit Corporations.[1]

In Canada it is not that the Dominion and Provincial Governments have been indifferent to the problem of agricultural credit. Every Province has passed legislation on the subject, but with the exception of that of Quebec the Provincial schemes have so far failed to attract popularity. Thus British Columbia passed an Agricultural Credits Act in 1898. The Government took power to loan money to associations of farmers. " The Act was passed as a result of a good deal of agitation, but no loans were ever made under it for the simple reason that the farmers were not prepared to accept the co-operative principle involved in it." [2] Later legislation provided for both long and short term credits, but " most of the money loaned has been used in refunding accumulated debts. The Act has not produced satisfactory results ".[3]

Taken together, " the total loans made through the Provincial machinery is about $23,000,000." [4] In 1924, " most of the organizations . . . have for the moment ceased to function, because of the difficulty of obtaining money at sufficiently low rate of interest and because of the danger of embarrassing the Provinces by increasing too greatly their bonded indebtedness." [5] For the rest, long term credit is a matter of private enterprise in the hands of the mortgage companies and the insurance companies, while for short term credit recourse must in general be had to the banks. In spite of the devotion of much parliamentary time to the subject and the accumulation of an extensive volume of evidence, Canada has so far failed to evolve any satisfactory general system of agricultural credit either for long or short terms.

It is because the people of the Province of Quebec are still a people apart from those of the rest of the Dominion, that rural credit institutions on co-operative principles

---

[1] Ibid., p. 60. At the end of the first year after their organization in 1923 the direct loans and discounts made by the twelve Federal Intermediate Credit Banks amounted to $41,409,368 (ibid., p. 62).

[2] Ibid., p. 68. [3] Ibid., p. 69.

[4] Ibid., p. 83. [5] Ibid.

have taken firm root among them, while elsewhere in Canada they have been plants of sickly growth. Co-operative credit has made headway among the small farmers of Quebec Province because race and religion have given them the social unity which is the foundation of the system.

The system began with the establishment in 1900 by M. Desjardins of the first of *Les Caisses Populaires* at Lévis. It was modelled on the Peoples' Co-operative Banks of Italy which in their turn drew their inspiration from the Raiffeisen Banks or Credit Societies of Germany. For the most part these banks operate in agricultural districts where conditions are stable and all the members of the community know one another, it being the rule of these institutions only to lend money for approved purposes to borrowers of known integrity residing in a limited area. Loans are most frequently made for the purchase of agricultural requisites at cost prices, but the increase of stock, the improvement of farm holdings, and the discharge of a debt to a tradesman may be among the purposes for which loans are approved. The capital of the bank is raised by the sale of five dollar shares and by the receipt of deposits. Only shareholders may be borrowers. Each bank is administered by a Board of five, and a committee of three considers and allows or refuses applications for loans.[1]

---

[1] In 1926 there were in Quebec 154 Co-operative Peoples' Banks and the total value of loans granted in that year was $4,496,956. This sum was made up of 15,843 different loans and was distributed among 10,418 borrowers (*Canada Year Book*, 1927–8, p. 764). The banks are subject to statutory control (Quebec Syndicates Act, 1906, as amended by the Act of 1919).

CHAPTER 18

The Mineral Wealth of the Dominion and its Exploitation

Mineral areas and their content:—
    The Canadian Shield and its minerals.
Modern methods, technical and financial.
Water power as an aid to mining development.
Gold:—
    British Columbia, Yukon and Ontario.
    Prospects of Canada as compared with other gold-producing countries.
Silver:—
    An asset of diminishing value.
    Ontario's decline and British Columbia's advance in production.
    Arsenic as a product of the mines and its uses.
Platinum.
Cobalt:—
    Its uses and incidence.
Nickel:—
    Discoveries in the Sudbury area.
    Its industrial importance.
    Canada's predominating position.
    Early troubles and modern organization of the industry.
Asbestos:—
    Predominating position of Quebec as producer.
    Competition of Rhodesia.
    Its quality and uses.
Copper:—
    The world position.
    Association of copper and nickel.
    Increasing output.
Lead and zinc:—
    Danger of over-production.
Coal:—
    Abundant reserves but not in right place.
    Proximity of United States coalfields.
    Vast reserves of the Prairie Provinces and their quality.
    Transport and technical problems.
Iron:—
    Disappointment of early expectations.
    Poor quality frequent.
    Foreign competition.
Corundum, graphite, mica, felspar, and talc.
Gypsum:—
    Its uses.
    Nova Scotia deposits.
    Exports to United States for manufacture.
Natural Gas and Oil.
Progress of mineral development since 1886.
Canada's advantages in competition with other countries.
Dominion control of mineral rights.

Conditions and Regulations as to mining rights.
Minerals as a source of public revenue.
The Department of Mines and its functions.
    Assistance to prospectors.

THE extent to which the prospector has been instrumental
in opening up new territory has been indicated.   It
remains to consider the mining industry from another point
of view, namely, the exploitation of the mineral wealth of
the Dominion as a national asset.

The claim is made that somewhere or other in the
Dominion is found practically every sort of mineral in
demand to-day except aluminium, tin, and precious stones.[1]
The pre-Cambrian rocks of the vast region called the
Canadian Shield, covering an area of nearly 2,000,000
square miles, are known to contain mineral deposits of
amazing quantity and variety, but outside the Canadian
Shield there is the Acadian region with one of the great
bituminous coalfields of the world ; in south-eastern
Quebec are mines which yield about 90 per cent. of the
world's production of asbestos ; British Columbia saw the
Cariboo gold rush and Yukon the Klondyke ; and the
Prairie Provinces are known to contain vast reserves of coal
and petroleum.   So far, however, it is the Canadian Shield
that has played the spectacular part in mineral discovery,
and in particular that part of the region lying within
Ontario and extending into western Quebec.   Here within
the comparatively narrow belt already explored have been
found the richest gold and silver deposits in recent mining
history, ore assaying as much as 30 per cent. in copper
content, mines that supply nearly all the nickel used throughout the world, as well as vast lead, zinc, and iron mines,
and a miscellaneous list of the less-known minerals : galena
and mica, graphite and kaolin, molybdenite, arsenic and
talc—to name only a few.   And the expert opinion is that
the limited field that so far has come into production is
characteristic of the whole pre-Cambrian system ; a system
which is really a continent, for the Canadian Shield, the
name given to the region where that system comes to the
surface, includes most of the provinces of Quebec and
Ontario (the only areas not belonging to the pre-Cambrian

[1] Minute diamonds have, however, been discovered, associated with
chromite, in the Tulameen district of British Columbia.   In Ontario
also similar diamonds have been found and again too small to be of
commercial importance.

system are those north of Lakes Erie and Ontario, along the St. Lawrence and south of Hudson Bay) thence its southern line cuts through the centres of Manitoba and Saskatchewan, and, passing through the extreme north-east corner of Alberta, travels north to the Arctic regions. Roughly it takes the form of a broad " U "-shaped belt around Hudson Bay, stretching from Labrador to the Arctic regions near the Alaska border.[1]

For the effective exploitation of this fabulous mineral wealth it is obvious that the old haphazard methods of prospecting, fraught with romance as they were, must be superseded by organized and thorough research with the aid of the delicate instruments which science has placed in the modern prospector's hands. The magnetometer detects iron ores and also other ores with which iron is associated. The gravimetric method is based on the measurement of variations in the densities of different

---

[1] The Dominions Royal Commission found that in regard to the mineral resources of Newfoundland " though much is surmised, comparatively little is known ". The Commissioners were, however, impressed by the deposits of hematite ore on Bell Island, which has an area of 12 square miles and is situated in Conception Bay in the extreme east of the Dominion, and the phenomenal output of the Wabana mines which are there being worked. " Our enquiries in other Dominions have revealed nothing at all comparable to these deposits in extent, except perhaps those at Iron Knob and Iron Monarch in South Australia. Any estimate as to their probable amount must necessarily partake largely of hypothesis, as the workings are mainly under the sea, but we may mention that Mr. Howley has estimated the probable quantity of ore in the whole area at over 3,500,000,000 tons. Up to the end of 1913, 12,000,000 tons of ore had actually been extracted ". As to its quality, a German engineer is reported to have described it in his somewhat limited English as " peaceable and well beloved ", intending to convey that it was easily reduced and was in favour with the furnacemen. A large proportion of the ore has been consumed at the Cape Breton works of the two companies operating the deposits ; a considerable amount was going to foreign countries which devoted themselves to the production of basic steel ; but only a comparatively small tonnage had as yet reached the United Kingdom.

Newfoundland is the oldest Dominion geologically as well as politically, and that being so, abundant mineral wealth is to be expected, but its exploitation has for the most part been so far only tentative. Copper mining has been carried on in the Dominion in a more or less desultory manner since 1864 and rich copper deposits appear to await development. The island is known to possess several large deposits of chromite, and iron pyrites is an abundant mineral. Nickel, antimony, lead, manganese, gold and silver are also there and sporadic attempts to mine them have been made. The coal deposits were estimated by the Geological Congress held in Toronto in 1913 at 500,000,000 tons. Non-metallic minerals occur in great variety, of which only a few have been exploited and these only in a small way. An infinite variety of building and ornamental stone is also found. (Dominions Royal Commission : Fourth Interim Report [Cd. 7711] and Minutes of Evidence, 1914 [Cd. 7898], Memorandum by Mr. J. P. Howley, Director of the Colonial Geological Survey, at p. 81.)

substances. There are also delicate instruments which reveal subterranean sounds and vibrations which vary in the different forms of strata. Going, too, is the lonely prospector, cut off from civilization, whose desperate gamble with fate may end in death from starvation. The aeroplane can now reach the remotest districts in a fraction of the time taken by the slow toilsome marches of the old days.

Improvements in metallurgical processes have given value to low grade ores previously considered worthless. Thus the " flotation " process [1] makes it possible to recover particular metals from highly complex ores and it has reduced the cost of treating ores of all kinds. Nowhere have the new methods been more readily adopted than in Canada.

Molybdenum is an instance which illustrates the manner in which metallurgical research can add new processes to industry.

" The Geological Survey was enabled to point out to the metal industries in Great Britain that we had in our midst considerable deposits of molybdenum, and that this metal could be used largely in place of tungsten in the hardening of steels. But the information fell on deaf ears until the outbreak of hostilities when, with the supplies of tungsten largely diminished, a demand arose at once for the molybdenum. . . . The production of this metal has now become a very important and profitable industry in our country." [2]

And not only have the methods of discovering and extracting the various minerals changed ; the financial organization of the mining industry is a more secure, if more sober, affair than in the old days.

For many years after confederation the familiar pursuits of farming, lumbering, shipbuilding and fishing absorbed all there was to spare of accumulated wealth, and Canada was unwilling and indeed unable to find capital for speculative enterprises such as mining. " In ordinary commercial transactions here, 12 per cent. per annum is no uncommon rate for accommodation ; while for mining operations

---

[1] " The method is to pulverize the ore and to add water and vegetable oil. The mixture is then placed in a tank or vat and agitated . . . which causes a froth carrying the mineral constituents to form on the surface. It is then a simple matter to recover the minerals " (*The Mineral Wealth of Canada*, published by the Canadian Bank of Commerce, 1927, p. 13).

[2] Professor J. C. McLennan, *Industrial Research in Canada*, University of Toronto Press, 1916 (*Canada Pamphlets*, vol. x, No. 272, in D.O. and C.O Library).

$2\frac{1}{2}$ to 5 per cent. a month was often charged with money plentiful, and now it could not be obtained for the latter purpose on any terms." [1]

Now financial resources, technical skill, and experience gathered from a wide field are mobilized, so that mining has become a stable industry. Nor is a modern mining company the temporary affair it often used to be. Mines sooner or later become exhausted, but the modern mining company looks ahead and expends a certain proportion of its resources in the search for further reserves of minerals to which to turn when their earlier discoveries shall be worked out.

Furthermore, the mining industry is peculiarly liable to ruinous price-cutting as the result of over-production. The corrective has been found, notably in the South African diamond mining industry, in combination on a large enough scale to make the restriction of output possible. In Canada a notable instance of the successful application of this method of industrial organization is supplied by the asbestos industry. After the Great War, over-production in Canada and competition from Rhodesia made the profitable working of many of the asbestos mines impossible. Thereupon the Canadian Asbestos Corporation was formed, the purpose of which was to absorb such a number of the mines as would enable a measure of control over the industry to be exercised sufficient to make possible the regulation of output. An improvement in prices was thereby brought about.[2]

It is a fortunate combination of circumstances that hydro-electric energy should be available so abundantly in conjunction with the great mineral fields of Canada. Cheap power enables low-grade ores to be dealt with which otherwise could not be profitably used. It is especially fortunate that abundant hydro-electric energy is available in Ontario, Quebec and Manitoba, inasmuch as coal is lacking in those Provinces. The Canadian Shield is a vast watershed and the Cordilleran regions of British Columbia and the Yukon territory, one of the most richly mineralized regions of the world, is remarkable for its water power resources in the shape of streams, rapids, and waterfalls.

Gold has been produced in Canada since very early times, and it has been found in every province except Prince

---

[1] *The Gold Yield of Nova Scotia*, Halifax, N.S., 1876 (*Canada Pamphlets*, vol. iii, No. 86, in D.O. and C.O. Library).

[2] *The Times*, 1st July, 1927, Supplement, p. xx.

Edward Island. The first recorded discovery was in 1824, when alluvial gold was found in the valley of the Chaudière, some fifty miles from the city of Quebec, and placer mining has been carried on there more or less intermittently ever since. Lode mining is recorded as having been carried on in Nova Scotia in 1858, and, on the other side of the continent, the mineral history of British Columbia began in the same year when the first return of placer gold shows a yield for the year worth $705,000.[1] Up to the year 1897, British Columbia held the lead as gold producer, but, in that year it was overhauled and passed by Yukon. It was a race between the two areas for supremacy in gold production until 1914, when Ontario got into first place and has since increased its lead year by year. The output of British Columbia has been maintained with reasonable regularity, but the exhaustion of the creeks of the Yukon by hydraulic mining and dredging ; the impossibility of working profitably any but the highest grade deposits owing to the high cost of labour and transport ; and the failure to find quartz of such a character as to attract capital for development, brought about the rapid decline of the Yukon Territory as a gold-producing area which began in 1917.[2]

The rise of Canada as a gold-producing country has been coincident with the decline of such notable gold-mining centres as Australia and the United States. The output of gold in Australasia declined from nearly 2,000,000 fine ounces in 1916, to slightly over 600,000 ounces in 1926. No important discoveries, with perhaps one exception, have been made since the Coolgardie field was opened in 1892, and the Australian goldfields appear to be nearing exhaustion. The gold output of the United States was halved in the same period, and here again there have been no striking discoveries for some considerable time, so that the anticipation is that output will show a steady decline. The output of the Transvaal was approximately the same in 1926 as in 1916. The prospect seems to be that Canada is the one country where an increased output of gold may reasonably be expected. In view of the fears that are

---

[1] D.R.C. *Minutes of Evidence*, 1916 [*Cd.* 8459], Memorandum by W. Fleet Robertson, at p. 262.

[2] The output of gold in the three areas in 1914 and 1926 was as follows :—

1914	In Ontario 268,264 oz.	B.C. 252,730 oz.	Yukon 247,940 oz.
1926	,, 1,497,215 oz.	,, 225,866 oz.	,, 25,601 oz.

sometimes expressed of a possible shortage in the metal, which is the basis of modern business, the position of Canada in the economic organization of the world may well become one of commanding importance.

Down to 1926, Canada had retained her place as third among the silver producing countries of the world, although Peru had become a close competitor. Mexico, in 1919, took the lead as a silver producing country, and has since retained her place as easily first, the United States falling back to second place. Owing primarily to the gradual adoption of the gold standard by the trading nations throughout the world, and the consequent receding importance of silver for monetary purposes, the metal seems destined to be an asset of diminishing value, relative and absolute.[1] Canada can contemplate this prospect with greater equanimity than other silver producing countries which are without the Dominion's extraordinary variety of mineral deposits.

Furthermore, the decline in Ontario's output of silver which has been apparent since 1911 has been offset by the progressive increase in the output by British Columbia. In 1926, when Ontario fell below the ten million ounces mark, British Columbia for the first time passed it. In the latter Province the silver is largely found in combination with lead. Arsenic to the extent of millions of pounds weight a year is one of the several products of the Cobalt silver mines, and is recovered as white arsenic at the silver refining works. As an insecticide it is used, for instance, in a compound which is made for combatting the boll-weevil which threatens the cotton crop in the United States, and as an ingredient in a mixture for killing the Colorado potato beetle.

Metals of the platinum group have in past years been obtained principally from the placer gravels of British Columbia. In the Tulameen district " the proportion of platinum recovered was greater than that of gold, and nuggets of platinum which weighed from one-fourth to one-half an ounce each were often found." [2] Now, however, most platinum metals produced in Canada come from Ontario, where platinum and palladium are obtained as a

---

[1] In 1921 the average price of silver per standard ounce in the London market was 36·89 pence ; in 1923 it was 31·93 pence, and in 1925 there was a slight recovery to 32·09 pence.

[2] C. Camsell, Geology and Mineral Deposits of the Tulameen District, B.C. (*Geological Survey Memorandum*, No. 26).

by-product from the refining of nickel matte. " Canadian nickel ores could, in fact, supply more palladium than is obtained from all the other sources in the world." [1]

For twenty years the world depended almost entirely for its supply of cobalt on the ores of the Cobalt district, discovered in 1902, which carry silver, cobalt, nickel, and arsenic. The discovery of cobalt-yielding ores in Central Africa has, however, broken down this practical monopoly, so that in 1926 Canada produced little more than half the world's output of this metal. The demand for cobalt is not likely to diminish. Metallic cobalt is a constituent of certain stainless steels, and in combination with other metal forms the alloy called " Stellite ", which by reason of its resistance to wear is used for dental and surgical instruments and for high-speed cutting tools. Cobalt oxide is used by the manufacturers of ceramic wares.

" During the construction of the Canadian Pacific Railway in 1883, large outcroppings of chalcopyrite and pyrrhotite were found near what is now the town of Sudbury. Mines having been opened on some of these, unexpected difficulties were encountered in the treatment of the ores at the works in the United States to which they were exported. Investigation proved these difficulties to be due to the presence of nickel in paying quantities." [2]

It was not until late in the nineteenth century, when the virtues of an alloy of steel and nickel were discovered, that the industrial importance of the latter metal was recognized. The addition of nickel to steel, iron, copper, and aluminium increases the strength of those metals, provides them with a surface capable of a high polish and protects them from corrosion. The Great War gave an enormous impulse to the manufacture of nickel steel with its increased strength and lightness. It became indispensable for armour plate, guns, armour-piercing projectiles and the tools and machinery which produced them. After the War the experience gained was applied to the arts of peace, and nickel and its alloys are used to a vastly greater extent than before 1914. It had long been used for coinage and plating purposes. Its uses in war had also long been recognized. Nickel steel is now used for the parts of automobiles and aeroplanes, for machines and machine tools, and engineering work of all

---

[1] D.R.C. Minutes of Evidence, 1916 [Cd. 8459], p. 302.
[2] Ibid., p. 293.

kinds wherein weight and bulk have to be reduced so far as possible. Nickel cast iron is used for wire and other purposes. Nickel silver enters largely into the manufacture of modern jewellery, table-ware, hospital and restaurant equipment, and so forth. Nickel plating is well known.

Here then is a metal in great and constantly increasing demand for war purposes as well as for the purposes of peaceful industry. When it is realized that the world's production of nickel in the year 1925 was over 40,500 tons and that of this 90 per cent., representing a value of 16 million dollars, came from Canada, the importance of this metal as a factor in the economic development of the Dominion can hardly be over-emphasized.

And this great factor in Canada's economic history has emerged since about the year 1889, when the total output of the Dominion was only 830,477 pounds, valued at about $500,000. In 1926 the total Canadian output was 65,700,000 pounds, and its value over 14,300,000 dollars, nearly all of which came from the Sudbury area in Ontario. Seeing that the second largest nickel-producing area in the world, that is to say, the island of New Caledonia, produces only about one-ninth of Ontario's output, and that no other nickel-producing area is in sight, while the reserves in the Laurentian Plateau seem limitless, the prospects seem to be that Canada will maintain its position as easily the first nickel-producing country in the world.

Want of organization as well as lack of capital and the wasteful conflict of rival interests were responsible for the false start made by the industry. The first discovery in the Sudbury district in 1883 was exploited as the Murray mine. The use of nickel in steel was for long practically the only use found for the metal and over-production soon swamped the market. Capital for development was not readily forthcoming, and in 1894 the Murray mine closed down. The industry was saved by its consolidation in the hands of two great companies, the International Nickel Company, which grew out of the pioneer concern, the Canadian Copper Company, and the Mond Nickel Company, founded in 1900. To stimulate the further use of nickel the price was reduced by these two great concerns to limits which made it difficult for concerns with smaller resources to live; but by the consolidation of interests, by the discovery of further uses for the metal and better methods of treating the ores, the nickel industry was safely brought through the speculative and experiment stage and placed on a solid financial basis.[1]

It has been seen that the Dominion has a predominating position in the world production of one of the metallic minerals, namely, nickel.   It occupies a similarly enviable position in regard to one of the non-metallic minerals, that is to say, asbestos.

The most notable asbestos producing region has been south-eastern Quebec on the edge of the eastern spur of the Canadian Shield.   There, in certain of the eastern townships, asbestos of the best variety, the chrysolite type, is found in serpentine rock.   Asbestos of varying quality has been found in Ontario from time to time, but so far the only region other than Quebec whose output of the superior type of asbestos is substantial is Rhodesia.   In 1909 Canada's output of asbestos was 87,300 tons.   In 1926 it had grown to 280,000 tons, or three-fourths of the world's production, Rhodesia coming next with 9 per cent.   One circumstance that enables Canada to regard with equanimity the rising output of Africa, as also the attempts of the Soviet authorities to restore Russia to the important place she once occupied in the industry by reason of the large deposits in the Urals and in Siberia, is her proximity to the country which, herself producing very little, is the greatest market for the product in the world, the United States.   Moreover new uses for the mineral are constantly being found, for the quality which renders asbestos valuable in industry is its power to withstand fire and heat.   It is accordingly extensively used as a fireproof and heat-resisting material [2] in buildings and for packing steam plants.   It is also widely used as an insulating material in the electrical industry.

In the Sudbury ores copper and nickel are usually associated, but Ontario does not occupy the predominating position in copper that the province enjoys in nickel.[3]   Until 1894, when it was displaced by Ontario, Quebec was the

---

[1] See "The Mineral Resources of Ontario," by W. A. Parks, Professor of Geology, Toronto University, in *Journal of the Royal Society of Arts*, 21st August, 1925, vol. 73, p. 898.

[2] " We may mention, as a matter of special interest, that crude asbestos is now being used in the manufacture of gloves for men handling the quick-firing guns at the front.   The heat generated is such that, without such gloves, it would be impossible to change the position of the guns in an emergency, except at the risk of severe burning " (*D.R.C. Fifth Interim Report*, 1917 [*Cd.* 8457], p. 47).

[3] In 1926 Canada's output of copper was approximately 4 per cent of the world's total.

chief copper-producing province of Canada.   For many
years it was the chief metal mined in British Columbia.
The United States remains by far the largest copper-
producing country in the world, and South America easily
retains the second place.   Development is being energetically
pushed forward in Rhodesia and the Belgian Congo and,
when difficulties of transport have been overcome, Africa
must take a high place among copper-producing countries.

The increase in the output of copper all over the world
is one of the most striking of post-war industrial phenomena.
In 1926 the world's production was 1,628,000 short tons,
a figure never before attained even in the year of crisis of
the Great War.[1]   When the development of copper-producing
areas which is being undertaken all over the world becomes
fruitful the possibilities of over-production become apparent.
In the competition for markets Canada seems likely to play
a leading part.   Although the existence of the Sudbury
deposits had long been known, it was not until 1883–4,
when the Canadian Pacific Railway was under construction,
that their development began to be seriously undertaken,
and at first the deposits were exploited for their copper
content only.   When in 1886 the association of nickel
with the copper was realized, the production of the two metals
increased rapidly.   In 1886 copper production in Canada
was $3\frac{1}{2}$ million pounds.   In 1913 it had increased to 77
million pounds.   In 1918, when the demand for copper
for munitions was at its height, Canada contributed over
118 million pounds.   Then came the post-war slump and
the necessity to liquidate the enormous surplus stocks of
copper for which some purpose other than the manufacture
of implements of war had to be found.   It was not until
1924 that Canada's output again exceeded 100 million
pounds.   In 1926 it had risen to over 133 million pounds or
about 65,000 short tons.

In addition to the vastness of the area coming into production, account has to be taken of the improved methods
in the mining, smelting, and refining of copper, which are
utilized by the wealthy and efficient organizations which
control Canadian mining.   Up to about 1910 vast bodies of
low-grade ore had to be rejected as unprofitable under the
methods of working then in existence.   Now these can be
worked with profit and production is increased accordingly.

---

[1] See *Canada Year Book*, 1927–8, p. 373.   A short ton is 2,000 lb.

For finding outlets for her copper Canada is not unfavourably situated in competition with other copper-producing countries. The United States doubled its consumption of copper between 1913 and 1926, and this great market is at Canada's doors. The conditions under which mining is conducted are highly favourable, and even if it becomes unprofitable to work the lower grade ores, vast fields of high grade ores are coming into production.

Lead and zinc are very frequently associated in ores. In 1887 lead produced from Canadian ores amounted to 204,800 pounds. In the year before the outbreak of the Great War the total was 37,662,000 pounds. In 1926 production had reached 283,800,000 pounds, worth over 19 million dollars, representing about 8 per cent. of the world's production of the metal. British Columbia has long been the headquarters of Canadian lead-mining in conjunction with zinc, but latterly the Canadian Shield has come into prominence as a potential lead-zinc mining area, especially in the region between the Ottawa River and Lake Ontario and westwards towards Georgian Bay. In the Sudbury district a deposit of complex zinc-copper-lead-silver ore has attracted attention. In 1923, Ontario's output of lead had reached over $4\frac{1}{2}$ million pounds.

As in the case of lead, zinc production in Canada has shown rapid increase, the less than 2 million pounds of 1911 having grown to 150 million pounds in 1926.

Both lead and zinc are a difficult market by reason of the occurrence of the metals in so many widely separated parts of the world and the possibility of over-production. Before the War the markets were frequently glutted for both metals. The war years compelled improved metallurgical methods, especially selective processes, for the separation of metals in complex ores, a factor of course still further increasing output. Canada in particular has to compete with a neighbour, the United States, which has long had the largest output of both metals, in 1926 producing over 40 per cent. of the world's output of lead and nearly one-half the total output of zinc.

The coal position in Canada is not without an aspect of irony. The Dominion has vast supplies of coal, anthracite (which has the greatest heating capacity), bituminous (the most used) and lignite. Her own coal deposits are distributed between all the Provinces with three exceptions, but those exceptions are the Provinces which are the most populous, Quebec, Ontario, and Manitoba.   And not only is the Dominion neighbour to the country which produces 40 per cent. of the world's output, but the great United States coalfields of Pennsylvania and Ohio are immediately south of and no great distance from those Provinces.

Most Canadian coal is lignite.   Nevertheless, Nova Scotia sends bituminous coal for domestic use and steam purposes to Quebec by way of the St. Lawrence as well as to the United States across the border.   In New Brunswick coal mining has been carried on for a century.   In Saskatchewan coal obtained locally was used in the blacksmith's forge forty years ago.   Alberta has many billions of tons of anthracite and bituminous coal, but its only market is the Prairie Provinces, so that its deposits are as yet scarcely scratched.   Whether freight rates will ever permit Alberta coal to compete with United States coal in Ontario and Quebec remains to be seen.   The bituminous deposits of Alberta extend into British Columbia, and in the Crow's Nest district in the east of that province is a coal-producing area of the first importance.   Most important of all is the Vancouver Island coal area.

The coal reserves in the Prairie Provinces are enormous. " In Saskatchewan the actual and probable reserves are estimated officially at over 59,000 million tons, but the same estimate for Alberta is twenty times as great, representing about one-seventh of the actual and possible reserves of the world." [1]   As the coal deposits extend east, however, they deteriorate.   " Thus at its western boundary the coal in Alberta is of good bituminous quality ; it gradually, as it extends eastwards, becomes lignitic or sub-bituminous, while in Saskatchewan it is wholly lignite." [2]   Lignite is of little use in its natural state, for " it contains . . . 18 to 28 per cent. of moisture, and when this is partially evaporated in a warm, dry, sunny atmosphere, the material crumbles away and tends to become little better than slack.   But there was no difference of opinion as to the practicability of so treating the lignite as to make it suitable for all fuel purposes at a price considerably less than that imported." [3] So lignite can be reduced to the form of briquettes and used in furnaces and for domestic purposes.

The problems are accordingly two : first, how to transport the bituminous coal so as to avoid the necessity of imports

[1] *D.R.C. Minutes of Evidence*, 1916 [*Cd.* 8459], at p. 277.
[2] Ibid.   [3] Ibid.

and make it a factor in the industrial development of the country ; and second, how not only to transport lignite, but also how to make it a useful and a usable substance.

It has been calculated that Canada possesses one-sixth of the world's coal reserves,[1] yet until the 'eighties the Dominion depended on the United States for the coal she wanted, and her imports have year by year since exceeded her own production, in some years by millions of tons.[2] Coal has been seen sold in Calgary " advertised on the street cars as Pennsylvania coal ".[3]

The position of Canada in regard to iron is somewhat similar to the position as to coal, and perhaps even more disappointing.

About 1870, when the vast potential wealth concealed below the surface was beginning to be suspected, although as yet little actual mining development had taken place, iron ore was known to exist all through the Laurentian chain of mountains, " but the only place where the mineral is as yet worked is in the township of Hull within a few miles of the capital, where a village called ' Ironsides ' has sprung into existence since the opening of the mine." It was thought at the time that in the coming rivalry between Canada and the United States in iron manufactures, Canada would have the advantage " not only because of the remarkably excellent quality of the Canadian metal, but on account of the low prices of labour and material employed here in its production ".[4] The surface gave an indication of what might be below. According to a contemporary observer, " The ground is strewn with large and small blocks of ore slightly oxidized by exposure to the atmosphere. . . . A small hill rises from slightly swampy ground to a height of about 100 feet, having a base of about 130 feet. The hill exposes a wall-like face from which, from top to bottom, there may be seen protruding immense blocks of ore." [5]

The reasons for the disappointment of early hopes are to be found in part in the nature of the iron itself and in part in economic conditions.

[1] *The Mineral Wealth of Canada*, The Canadian Bank of Commerce, 1927, p. 47.

[2] In 1926 Canada produced 16,500,000 short tons, exported 1,028,000 tons, imported from the United States 17,700,000 tons and from Great Britain 276,000 tons. Of the known world production Canada contributed a little over 1 per cent.

[3] *D.R.C. Minutes of Evidence*, 1916 [*Cd.* 8459], at p. 254.

[4] The " Resources of the Ontario District," Ottawa, 1872 (*Canada, Pamphlets*: vol. iii, No. 69, in D.O. and C.O. Library). [5] Ibid.

It is not that there is any lack of iron deposits in the Dominion. Iron deposits have been located all over the country. But some of the ores, for instance those of Quebec, contain titanium; others have a high sulphur content; much is of low grade—all conditions which make economical treatment difficult. Then in Ontario coal is a negligible quantity and iron without coal is apt to be a sterile asset. Above all there is the proximity of the vast deposits of hæmatite on the United States side of Lake Superior, where the iron mining industry has become largely centred and whence is imported the ore wanted for the blast furnaces of Ontario.

Numerous iron deposits again are known to exist in British Columbia, but production, owing to the lack of a great iron-smelting industry, has not reached important dimensions. Before it can reach important dimensions difficult technical problems have to be solved, for the greater part of British Columbia iron ores are magnetites and contain too high a percentage of sulphur to make them attractive. Moreover, on the Pacific coast of North America the competition of Chinese ores produced by cheap labour cannot be left out of account, and the competition of eastern iron would have to be met were the attempt made to cultivate the Prairie Provinces as possible markets.

In addition to the staple mineral products, other non-metallic minerals occur in the Dominion in great variety, and in particular in Ontario. Instances are corundum, a natural abrasive capable of withstanding a temperature of 3,600° F. and next to the diamond the hardest mineral known, which is used for the manufacture of wheels and other abrasive and polishing tools and agents; graphite, used in lubricants, stove polish, and in the manufacture of paints for iron and steel work; mica, the softness and flexibility of which, as it occurs in the basin of the Ottawa River, make it specially suitable for insulating electrical equipment; feldspar, which goes mostly to the United States for use in the pottery and allied industries; and talc, which is used in the manufacture of paper and in many other diverse ways, for it gives paper a glazed surface, its freedom from grit recommends it for toilet preparations, it strengthens pottery, it is a serviceable dressing for hides and fine leather, and it fulfils useful functions in the manufacture of textiles, rubber, paint, lubricants, and linoleum.

Then there is gypsum, used in an ever-increasing number of ways, from a building material in the form of plaster with fire-resisting qualities to the humble blackboard chalk ; which when calcined by heat to a fine powder becomes the familiar, centuries old, plaster of paris.

The development of native gypsum deposits in Manitoba enabled consumers to obtain cement at a saving of one-third of the cost of imported cement. This, in view of the diminishing supply and increasing cost of native lumber, was a highly important matter to the farmers, who thus got at a low cost materials for the construction of their buildings. Plaster of paris produced in Manitoba sold in Winnipeg at a price of $13 a ton as compared with $18 for imported plaster of paris.[1]

It is in Nova Scotia that the most important deposits of gypsum are to be found [2] and there the mineral has given rise to an economic situation of considerable interest. These practically inexhaustible deposits have been worked from the days of the earliest settlement of the country, and from the beginning the United States have controlled the industry, first as customers and later as owners of the quarries. In the early days the farmers would quarry out the rock and haul it to the coast for shipment in small coasting vessels to one of the ports on the Atlantic seaboard of the United States. Later the export to the United States millowners was more elaborately organized, and an attempt was also made to use the crude rock in Nova Scotia itself for manufacturing purposes, but the home demand was small, and the United States was the only market available. The inevitable result followed. The Canadian manufactured product was excluded from the United States by a prohibitive tariff and the Nova Scotia plaster mills closed down. The next step was consequent on the realization by the American manufacturers of the fact that their plaster mills entirely depended for their raw material on the crude rock obtained from the Maritime Provinces of Canada. Accordingly, they secured large tracts of gypsum lands so that " every quarry of importance operated in the Maritime

---

[1] Annual Report of Department of the Interior for 1900–1, Dominion Lands, p. 32 (*Sessional Papers*, 1902, vol xxxvi).

[2] The shipments from 1900 to 1912 inclusive were 3,164,213 tons, valued at $3,480,634, or $1·10 per ton (*D.R.C.*, Evidence taken in Maritime Provinces, 1914 [*Cd.* 7971], p. 151). In 1926, of a total Canadian production of 883,728 tons of gypsum, Nova Scotia produced 678,107 tons, valued at $1,187,918 (*Canada Year Book*, 1927–8, p. 354).

Provinces to-day is controlled by American capital ".[1]
The gypsum trade of the Maritime Provinces is an export
business, almost all Canadian production going to the United
States in a crude condition, where it is manufactured and in
part returns to Canada as wall-board, partition blocks,
wall-plaster, plaster cement or imitation marble, all of
which articles have gypsum as a base.

The stones available in the Dominion vary from lime-
stone, with its variety of uses, to the rare and beautiful
blue sodalite, capable of a fine polish and highly suitable
for decorative purposes in buildings.

Natural gas is exchanged into dollars in Ontario and in
Alberta, in the regions near Medicine Hat and Calgary. In
1910 the value of the natural gas used was $1,346,000.
In 1927 the figures had increased to $7,741,000, of which
total about 52 per cent. belonged to Ontario.

The first discoveries of natural gas in Ontario were made
at the respective ends of Lake Erie. In 1888 a field was
found near Windsor, on the extreme west, opposite Detroit,
and in the following year a field was opened up at the eastern
end, about 25 miles west of Niagara Falls. In both cases
the discoveries were rendered remunerative by the proximity
of American cities. Detroit and Toledo took the produce
of the western field and Buffalo and the Niagara Peninsula
that of the eastern. Later, producing wells made their
appearance at intervening points along the north shore of
Lake Erie. Here natural gas is used for the same purpose
as manufactured gas, and especially for domestic heating.

In Alberta, while some of the natural gas wells have been
exploited on a commercial basis, as those at Medicine Hat,
in the south of the Province, where a promising industrial
centre has arisen, others have to wait until settlement gives
them a value in dollars.

The main problem connected with the use of natural gas
is the prevention of its wasteful use. There is much to be said
for confining its use in industry to the production of power
through gas engines, its utilization for the production of
power through steam being quite uneconomical.

Associated with natural gas is usually found oil. The
first oil well on the American Continent was dug at Oil
Springs, Lambton County, in the south-west peninsula of
Ontario, as long ago as 1858, and that part of the Province

[1] D.R.C. *Minutes of Evidence* taken in 1914 [*Cd.* 7971], Memorandum
by Mr. W. F. Jennison, at p. 151.

is still an important oil producer, but the main centres of production have been moving westwards, so that now Alberta produces more oil than all the rest of Canada.[1] After about 1907 there was a steady decline in the production of oil, and in 1916 the time seemed at hand when the industry would have to be abandoned unless revived by new discoveries. The indications of the existence of crude oil in commercial quantities were felt to justify a systematic programme of prospecting and development. Success in Alberta saved the situation. The competition of the enormous output of the United States is bound to be a difficult factor for some time, but the indications are that western Canada is capable of becoming one of the greatest oil producing regions of the world.

The progress made by Canada in the exploitation of her mineral resources during the forty years beginning with 1886, the first year for which official statistics are available, is capable of expression in terms of total value of output which are impressive. In 1886 the total value of the mineral production of the Dominion was $10,221,255. In 1913 the total had grown to $145,634,812 and in 1926 had reached $240,437,123.[2] The first obvious effects of the exploitation of all this mineral wealth are the attraction of immigrants and capital,[3] and also the indirect effects on other aspects

---

[1] The production of crude petroleum in Canada during 1927 was 479,503 barrels, of which 321,154 barrels came from Alberta, 140,105 from Ontario, and 18,244 from New Brunswick (*Canada Year Book*, 1927–8, p. 386).

[2] The progress of mineral development in Canada as expressed in terms of value is exhibited in the following table, which is compiled from statistics in the respective *Canada Year Books* :—

Mineral.	Total Value in first year of comparison.		Total Value, 1913.	Total Value, 1926.
	Year.	Value.		
		$	$	$
Gold	1886	1,463,196	16,598,923	36,263,110
Copper	1886	385,550	11,753,606	17,490,300
Silver	1887	347,271	19,040,924	13,894,531
Nickel	1889	498,286	14,903,032	14,374,163
Lead	1908	1,814,221	1,754,705	19,240,661
Zinc	1908	3,215	186,827	11,110,413
Pig Iron	1909	9,581,864	16,540,012	16,660,974
Coal	1909	24,781,236	37,334,940	59,875,094
Asbestos	1909	2,284,587	3,830,909	10,099,423

[3] In 1926 the number of employees in the mining industries in Canada was 77,931, and the capital employed $688,000,000.

of economic progress: the construction of means of transport, the stimulus to agriculture to meet the needs of new mining communities, the development of water power and the erection of saw mills for the same purpose.

Only a fraction of Canada's mineral wealth has yet been explored, much less exploited, and the extent and variety of her minerals, metallic and non-metallic, are such that her output is likely to be limited only by the demand of the markets. In those markets she has to meet in increasing measure the competition of Rhodesia, Mexico, Australia, India and other countries where new mineral wealth is constantly being opened up. In that competition Canada has apparent advantages. At her door she has the United States, whose demand for minerals seems unlimited, but whose own mineral resources have been used up so rapidly that resort must soon be had to deposits which are costly to work and to low grade ores which can be made profitable only by costly processes. No other mining country has such great resources of timber and hydro-electric energy. The transport system whether by rail or waterway is capable of easy adaptation to meet new needs. It is a country where life and property are safe.

The Dominion Government retains control over mineral rights in Dominion lands, that is to say, in Manitoba, Saskatchewan, Alberta and the North-West and Yukon Territories. The Dominion Lands Act authorizes the Governor-General in Council to enact mining regulations. There are different regulations governing the leasing of coal-mining rights, petroleum and natural gas rights, the leasing of lands containing non-metallic minerals, the grant of entries for placer-mining claims and quartz-mining locations and of leases to dredge for gold in river beds. In British Columbia, by an arrangement between the federal and provincial Governments entered into in 1890, the precious metals within the railway belt are the property of the Province and the base metals are owned by the Government of Canada. The mining laws of the Province, however, cover all minerals. The obstacles which these laws and regulations place in the way of the exploitation of Canada's mineral wealth are certainly not formidable. Thus an Order in Council in 1901 declared all unappropriated Dominion lands in Manitoba, the North-West Territories and Yukon to be open for prospecting for petroleum by any individual or company so desiring, and that should oil be found in paying quantities an area of 640 acres would be sold to the discoverers at $1 an acre, subject to the prescribed royalty. Again, the holder of a free miner's certificate, which certificate is obtainable for a fee of $10 by an individual and from $50 to $100 by a company, is entitled to locate a claim 1,500 feet square on which he has discovered gold quartz. An expenditure of $100 a year must be made upon the claim and when $500 has been so expended the locator may purchase the land for $1 per acre.[1]

From early days the policy has been, while maintaining control, to put the fewest possible obstacles in the way of the exploitation of the mineral wealth of the country. Thus in British Columbia, the earliest of the gold-producing districts, the position so far back as 1870 was thus described : " The gold mining regulations are very simple. Any person may mine where he pleases, on unoccupied ground, on payment of an annual sum of £1 for a ' Free Miner's Certificate ', which is not transferable and must be recorded and a fee of 10s. paid therefor. The size of each claim is according to the nature and character of the ground. . . . Mining leases are granted on deposit of £25, but the lease cannot be assigned without the leave of the Gold Commissioner and is not in general to be for a term of more than 10 years ", and the area is limited.[2]

Again, under the Mining Acts of Ontario, any person over eighteen years of age is entitled, on payment of five dollars a year, to the miner's licence without which no person may prospect for minerals or stake out a mining claim.

In a newly settled country, where, for the most part, the land is in public ownership from the beginning, the minerals are capable of exploitation so as to become a valuable source of public revenue. Thus Nova Scotia has enormous coal deposits all of which are owned by the Province and leased to operators who work it on a royalty basis. The Dominion Royal Commission were informed in 1914 that approximately two-thirds of the revenue collected within the Province was from coal royalties.[3]

The Government of Ontario derives a revenue from the

[1] For further information, see Annual Report of Department of Interior for 1900–01 ; Dominion Lands, pp. 55–61, in *Sessional Papers*, 1902 ; and *D.R.C. Minutes of Evidence*, 1916 [*Cd*. 8459], pp. 260–314.

[2] E. Graham Alston, Colonial Handbook to British Columbia (*Canada : Pamphlets*, vol. iii, No. 66, in D.O. and C.O. Library).

[3] *D.R.C. Minutes of Evidence*, 1914 [*Cd*. 7971], Memorandum by Mr. T. Cantley, at p. 155.

mining industry in various ways. In addition to the sale and lease of Crown lands for mining purposes and fees for miners' licences, there is a mining tax, and royalties are levied. The tax is only in part for revenue purposes. The tax on lands granted under the mining regulations induces proprietors to prove their lands for minerals ; and a tax on natural gas per thousand cubic feet was primarily designed to prevent waste, which was considerable before the Act authorizing the tax was passed in 1907. Royalties from Cobalt silver mines alone aggregated nearly two million dollars up to 1915.[1]

Quebec gets a certain amount of revenue from miners' certificates and licences and. there is power to collect royalties on the produce of the mines, but, since the purpose of the Provincial Government has been rather to encourage mining than to regard it as a revenue-producing agency, royalties have not been enforced.[2]

In Quebec the principle has been observed since 1880 that in mining law the mineral rights should be separated from the surface rights, and should be capable of separate disposition. To acquire mining rights a miner's certificate must be obtained, the bearer of which is allowed to stake five claims of 40 acres each. The arrangements allow him to prospect the mining land thoroughly before buying it at the price of $5 per acre for gold, silver, copper and iron and $3 an acre for other metals. An expenditure of $500 for each 100 acres must be made within two years of sale, and until this condition is fulfilled the title to the land is not issued.

The Government of Ontario owns all the unalienated public or Crown lands within the Province and disposes of such lands for mining purposes in fee simple (at $2·50 to $3 an acre) or by lease.

The Dominion Government has never taken advantage of its possession of the public lands to impede in any way the development of the mining industry by private enterprise. Accordingly the duty of the Department of Mines at Ottawa, which was organized in 1907, taking over the duties of the Geological Survey which has been at work since 1842 and other allied branches of public work, " is not considered to be to discover valuable mineral or to assist the private

---

[1] D.R.C. *Minutes of Evidence*, 1917 [*Cd.* 8459], Memorandum on Mineral Resources of Ontario, at p. 297.
[2] Ibid., p. 287.

operator to work his property, but to provide the fundamental data and the solution of geological and other general problems, which it is then the duty of the prospector or mining engineer to turn to practical account. The work of the Government engineer, geologist or chemist is planned to avoid competing with that of the mining engineer or the assayer in private practice, and to be of such a character as to assist these professional men as well as the prospector and mine owner. The Department does not aim to do what the individual can or should do for himself, but tries to do what the individual cannot do. . . . Prospecting is not its business. . . . The geological explorer maps areas that are worth prospecting and brings them to the attention of prospectors who make the actual discovery of deposits." [1] By working out the geological structure the Department often determines the presence of deposits. In this way hundreds of square miles of coal lands are constantly being added to the known reserves. The clay industry lacked information of the occurrence of suitable raw materials. The Department has for years investigated clays and shales and has located deposits on which new industries are being built. Industries in want of a particular material are generally able to get the necessary information from the records of the Department.

[1] D.R.C. *Minutes of Evidence*, 1916 [*Cd.* 8459], Memorandum at p. 308.

CHAPTER 19

INDUSTRIAL EVOLUTION

A LTHOUGH undoubtedly a country of vast industrial
potentialities, Canada can hardly as yet be regarded
as an industrial country in being. Rather it is a country

with an industrial Province. British Columbia has all the ingredients of an industrial region ; she has untold mineral wealth, the coal which is so lacking in other parts of the Dominion, abundant water power, and a seaboard giving her access to the markets of Asia. The natural gas wells and the coalfields of Alberta may well be the foundation of an industrial centre spreading outward from Medicine Hat where the beginnings of an industrial region are already visible. The Maritime Provinces have long regarded themselves as the Cinderella of the Canadian family of Provinces, but it seems probable that the vast coalfields of Nova Scotia will become the basis of a great industrial region in eastern Canada. Many industries have already taken firm root in Quebec, particularly around Montreal. It is true that the transport of the coal mined in the Maritime Provinces must be by water, which means that for many months each year there would be but a small outlet for the produce of the mine were it not for local consumption, but the Dominion Iron and Steel Company affords an outlet for the coal industry during the season of closed navigation so that the industry can be kept alive all the year round. But, while these Provinces may claim legitimate expectation of future industrial greatness, so far Canada has only one Province, namely, Ontario, that can reasonably call itself an industrial region. In 1924, in all Canada 508,000 people were classified as employed in manufactures. Of these, 252,000, almost exactly half, belonged to Ontario, a proportion which it has approximately maintained since 1870, when statistics were first available.

The trade depression of the early 'seventies was acutely felt in Canada where trade and manufactures were still in the early stages of development, and there was a ready disposition on the part of Canadians to ascribe their troubles to the enmity of the United States and to look for a remedy in a tariff against American goods higher than the then existing $17\frac{1}{2}$ per cent. The slogan of the times was that Canada had become " the slaughter market of the Americans ". The sort of allegation was that " the Americans are sending furniture into Hamilton and the Canadian cities and having it auctioned for what it will bring, and this is not confined to furniture ".[1]

Other causes suggested by Canadians who hesitated to

---

[1] *Dominion Debates*, 1876, p. 79.

sacrifice their Free Trade principles were over-importation and over-production, and the injudicious use of credit, and especially the cheapness of credit obtainable in Great Britain. Then it has to be remembered that the Canadian tariff was not on a gold basis and the difference in value between American and Canadian money reduced the nominal $17\frac{1}{2}$ per cent to a very much lower figure.

Canadians were, not unnaturally, mainly concerned about the threatened destruction of their own nascent industries, but it seems apparent that it was the British market in Canada that the Americans were out to destroy. Between 1872 and 1875 " imports from Great Britain have decreased three millions while the imports from the United States have increased fifteen millions ".[1] A Montreal merchant told the Canadian House of Commons [2] how he had been invited to become the agent for a Pennsylvania firm for a certain description of goods hitherto procured from England and had received a communication in which he had been told, " We will send you a quantity of our goods ; we don't care what price you realize for them. If the English goods are selling for 15 cents sell ours for 14 cents, if at 12 cents sell ours for 11 cents. We are determined to get the Canadian market." The goods were sent, and " the prices were so reduced that the English articles was driven out of the market ".

Whatever the cause of the depression and whatever the purpose of American manufacturers, the " National Policy " was inaugurated with a great flourish in 1878, but nothing very impressive happened as the result of the protective duties that were then imposed, and it was not until the later 'nineties that Canadian industry got its real start. Thus, in the textile industry, " small mills were started, but, partly owing to difficult labour conditions they were not successful, and they were afterwards acquired by strong holders, who are now working them successfully. Several such mills were abandoned and all the mills now owned by the leading textile company in Canada are practically new within the last ten years." [3] Again, " a very large number of small mills formerly bought wool from neighbouring farmers, and instead of paying cash for it, returned

---

[1] *Dominion Debates*, 1876, p. 84.
[2] Ibid., p. 115.
[3] *Report on Conditions and Prospects of British Trade in Canada*, by R. Grigg, 1907 [*Cd.* 3868], p. 65.

so many yards of cloth or of ' rollcards ' which the farmers' wives would spin into yarn for hosiery, mitts, etc. Many of these were carding mills, and did not even weave their own cloth," and as late as 1907 it was recorded that " such mills under modern conditions are disappearing ".[1] In 1892 the process of industrializing Ontario had not progressed very far and " the life of the Province was still predominantly an agricultural and rural life ".[2]

Meanwhile the West was slowly but surely being settled by a purely agricultural population whose interests by no means ran on parallel lines with those of the eastern Provinces with their industrial ambitions. " When the Canadian Government acquired the North-West country and inaugurated the National Policy, the inducement was held out to Ontario, Quebec and the Maritime Provinces that this new country would fill up rapidly with a farming population and would assist to build up the industries of the eastern Provinces . . . and yet what do we find the representatives for the western Provinces doing ? We find them fighting against every industry in existence in the eastern Provinces. They look to the eastern Provinces for money to build their railways and develop their country, but they want their own money to flow over into the United States. They want agricultural implements placed on the free list so that they may buy them in the United States."[3]

Some of the bigger of the American industrial concerns did not wait for Canadians to come to them, they went to the Canadians. As would be expected in an agricultural country, the manufacture of agricultural implements and machinery was one of the earliest industries. The import was also large and practically entirely from the United States. But " the imports of agricultural implements into Canada fell from $2,655,000 in 1902 to $1,615,000 in 1906." [4] On the other hand, in the Dominion itself the output had increased from $9,600,000 in 1900 to $12,800,000 in 1905. Did this mean, as the statistics suggested, that Canadian manufacturers were fighting a winning battle against their invaders ? Not necessarily. " The rise in the Canadian production and the decline in imports is to some extend due to the transplanting of the manufactures from

[1] Ibid., p. 59.
[2] J. Mavor, *My Windows on the Street of the World*, vol. ii, pp. 322–3.
[3] *Dominion Debates*, 1897, vol. ii, cols. 4593–4.
[4] *Report on Conditions and Prospects of British Trade in Canada*, by R. Grigg, 1907 [*Cd.* 3868], p. 82.

the United States to the Dominion by American firms and notably by the Harvester Trust." [1]

The penetration of Canada by United States capital in the early years of the twentieth century and accordingly during the early years of Canada's industrial development is a factor the importance of which cannot be over-emphasized. Among the United States firms that had established branch factories in Ontario in 1907 were many of the most prominent. They represented manufacturers of agricultural implements and machinery, electrical machinery, malleable castings, foods, paints, pottery and cordage ; and " the largest portion of the enormous capital of over $30,000,000 invested by the Lake Superior Corporation at Sault Ste Marie, Ontario, in steel plants, pulp mills, saw mills, mineral reduction plant, and railways, is American." [2] The Canadian consumer would be the last to complain, and to the Canadian farmer the introduction of industrial concerns employing hundreds of hands meant a wider market for his produce ; while Canadian manufacturers learned the ways of large scale industry. But it was a defeat for the British manufacturer.

The normal line of advance for a country that desires to make the most of its natural assets is to organize manufacturing processes for the consumption of its own raw materials. The manufacture of Portland cement is one of the many instances where the process has been successful in Canada. The raw materials of Portland cement are found throughout the St. Lawrence lowlands. The Canadian output of 317,066 barrels of Portland cement in 1901 was increased to 2,152,562 in 1906.[3] In 1925 production was over 8,000,000 barrels and, whereas in pre-war years the Dominion had to import Portland cement to meet her domestic requirements, she has now become an exporter of this commodity.

A merely superficial consideration of Canada's natural resources reveals three as outstanding and characteristic assets for industrial exploitation. They are her mineral wealth, her forests, and her water power.

Mineral Manufacturing Processes

In 1887 there was not a single smelting works in Canada and any ore requiring treatment other than that by an

---

[1] Ibid., p. 82.　　　[2] Ibid., pp. 54, 111.　　　[3] Ibid., p. 99.

ordinary stamp mill had to be sent to the United States, Great Britain or Germany.[1]   Soon, however, the Dominion began to look forward to the time when she would be a great industrial country manufacturing within her own borders the mineral raw materials in which she is so rich. At the period of the investigations by the Dominions Royal Commission (1914–17) the process had not gone very far. A copper refinery, " the first in Canada," [2] was started in British Columbia in 1916, but at that time the general practice was to smelt the copper ore in the Province and to send the crude pig copper so produced to New York for refining and the separation of the precious metals.   Zinc ores were at that time all exported, mostly to the United States, there being no zinc smelting plant in the Province. The abundant and cheap hydro-electric power of the Province would enable refineries to operate under advantageous conditions, but the growth of the refining of metals locally must depend on the growth of a local market for the refined products.

The situation is similar with regard to the asbestos which is found so abundantly in Quebec.   The crude fibre is spun and woven into textiles and packings, but not on the spot. " The limited quantity consumed at home together with our inability for obvious reasons to meet the American and European competition . . . have not so far warranted the installation of the necessary machinery to manufacture these articles in Canada." [3]   The asbestos produced was accordingly exported as crude fibre.   When, however, the Commission came to report, they were able to say that the increasing price of lumber, which suggested a growing demand for asbestos boards and shingles in the near future, had encouraged certain enterprising firms to instal manufacturing machinery in the Province.[4]   By 1927 there had been established near the mines several manufacturing plants at which the fibre is worked up into different articles of commerce.[5]

Similarly with the nickel of Ontario, the matte, after smelting locally, was being exported by the Canadian Copper Company for refinement to New Jersey and by the

[1] *Annual Report of Department of Interior for* 1887, p. 51.
[2] *D.R.C. Minutes of Evidence* [*Cd.* 8459], p. 271.
[3] Ibid., p. 289.
[4] *D.R.C. Fifth Interim Report*, 1917 [*Cd.* 8457], p. 47.
[5] *Times Supplement*, 1st July, 1927, p. xx.

Mond Nickel Company to Wales. The Dominions Royal Commission, reporting in 1917, after expressing the opinion that it was " obviously desirable that the final process should be effected in Canada in so far as it is not conducted elsewhere in the British Empire " were able to say that the American Company " is at present erecting a refinery at Port Colborne at the foot of Lake Erie, while the British America Nickel Corporation which is in preparation for beginning work will, by arrangement, produce marketable nickel wholly in Canada", and the Commission looked forward to the time when there would be established in Canada a great metallurgical industry.[1]

As to silver : " At first the ore was all shipped out of the country, mostly to the United States, there being no facilities for refining it in Canada. . . . Refineries were established in South Ontario at Deloro in Hastings County and at Thorold and Welland on the Welland Canal where electrical power was cheap. Here and later in the camp itself silver bullion was produced, and now comparatively little ore goes out of the country." [2]

The iron industry, in spite of the shortage of iron deposits in the Province, had reached a high stage of development in Ontario at the time of the outbreak of the Great War. The blast furnaces there had, for some time, outstripped the iron mines and had been dependent upon the importation of ore from the United States. " In 1915, 916,399 tons of ore were smelted into 493,400 tons of pig iron in Ontario, of which quantity only 293,305 tons of ore, or 32 per cent, was of domestic origin. . . . There are now 11 furnaces, two having been added in 1913. Two use charcoal as fuel, all the rest coke either imported direct from the United States or made from imported coal." [3]

Seeing how great is the interest of United States industry in the produce of Canadian mines, it is not surprising to find how large is the amount of capital America is contributing to the development of mining in the Dominion. The Canadian Copper Company, in 1917, at any rate, the largest nickel producing Company, was employing almost exclusively American capital, and the British Columbia Copper Company

---

[1] [Cd. 8457], p. 45.

[2] Ontario : Mines and Mineral Resources, 1924, p. 40 (Canada : Pamphlets, No. 248 in D.O. and C.O. Library).

[3] D.R.C. Minutes of Evidence, 1916 [Cd. 8459], p. 294. For an account of early iron and steel plants in the Dominion see Canada Year Book, 1922–3, p. 452 ff.

is also American-owned. In the gold-mining district of
Ontario, the capital of the McIntyre Porcupine Mines, in
1917, $3,000,000, was mostly in American hands. The gold,
copper, lead and zinc deposits which have been found in
Manitoba have also attracted American capital for development purposes.

Timber ·and Wood-Pulp

As has already been seen, the exploitation of her timber
resources was, with fishing and the fur trade, the earliest
phase in Canada's economic development.[1] The forest wealth
of Eastern Canada enabled the Maritime Provinces, Upper
and Lower Canada, and Prince Edward Island, to develop
a commercial staple for exchange against manufactures
and other necessary imports. Through her timber trade
Eastern Canada was fated to attain the height of commercial
prosperity as the consequence of the preference given to
colonial timber in the British market during the Napoleonic
wars and to experience the inevitable reaction and the descent
into depression when the preference was withdrawn. We have
made the acquaintance of the lumberman of those early
days, roving, careless, improvident and undisciplined, by
his example demoralizing the young colonists who otherwise
might be content with the less eventful life of a farmer.
Then, as settlement penetrated further inland, so also did the
lumber industry, and the opening of the railway era created
a demand for lumber in Ontario and also provided the means
for its transport where river routes were not available.[2]
Ontario had a long career as the chief of the lumber provinces
until, in the twentieth century, British Columbia took
the lead.

Since confederation the salient facts in the exploitation
of Canada's timber wealth have been the creation of the
wood-pulp industry, the depletion of the United States'
supplies of soft wood and its reaction on the Dominion,
and the emergence of British Columbia as a great timber-
producing province. The main problem that has emerged
is how to avoid the exhaustion, within the lifetime of
the present generation, of the Dominion's merchantable
timber.

Most of the timber trade of the Dominion is with the

[1] See Division II, Chap. 3.
See Chapter 6.

United States.[1]   The great diversion from the British market
to that of America came when the railways were built.
Before the railway era all the lumber cut near the upper
waters of the St. John River were floated some 450 miles
down the river for shipment at St. John.   When railways
were built, lumber mills were built at strategic points on the
lines and the lumber that hitherto went to the port of St.
John for shipment to Great Britain was carried overland to
the United States.   Once the lumber had arrived at St. John
there was much in favour of the British market.   The steamers
that sailed from Montreal in the summer sailed from St. John
in the winter.   Cargo was wanted and was carried at a very
low freight.[2]   Moreover, " the British market is a very
steady market, and is not subject to great fluctuations.
The lengths they ask for are moderate . . .   The United
States markets seem to be affected by every little wind that
blows or every political sound there is in the air." [3]   But
the loss of trade by St. John was inevitable, for the cost of
transport by rail from the headwaters of the St. John to
the New York market was practically the same as the cost
of getting it to St. John, where the freight had to be added
as an additional charge before the British market was
reached.[4]   And now that the lumber manufacturer of the
eastern Provinces, who has for generations carried on the
business of converting logs into deals, boards and battens,
is finding himself embarrassed by the disappearance of the
larger pine and spruce and by the competition of the Pacific
coast where the mills can draw unlimited timber from the
virgin forest, it has been found that the new supply can be
got to the New York market with ease by way of the
Panama Canal.

It has long been the settled practice in the Dominion
not to alienate in fee simple timber lands but to retain their
ultimate title in the State.   Such timber lands as are private
property were in most cases originally the subject of grants
to railways or to settlement companies or to early individual
settlers, and the older the province the greater the degree

[1] " The total value of exported sawn lumber and other unmanufactured
or partially manufactured forest products in the fiscal year ended 31st
March, 1926, was over $115,000,000, of which about $96,000,000 worth
went to the United States and $12,000,000 to the United Kingdom "
(*Canada Year Book*, 1926, p. 282).
[2] *D.R.C. Minutes of Evidence*, 1914 [*Cd*. 7971], Q. 3095.
[3] *D.R.C. Minutes of Evidence*, 1914 [*Cd*. 7971], Q. 3102.
[4] Ibid, Q's. 3107–11.

of alienation that has taken place. In Nova Scotia the great bulk of the forest area has been alienated absolutely. The reason is to be found in the history of the province. The Maritime Provinces were early in touch with foreign markets by reason of their geographical position ; timber was readily available for sea-borne traffic ; and the process of denudation had proceeded very far indeed before it was realized that an asset which might be a source of revenue to the province was being given away, and that the power of control over timber areas which was necessary if they were to be conserved as farms rather than exhausted as mines was being entirely lost. On the other hand the forest wealth of British Columbia only began to be exploited within the lifetime of many still living, by which time the experience of the older provinces was available and the great bulk of the timber lands of the province are as a consequence the property of the province for all time. The system which has been evolved is one by which the Government sells the timber but keeps the land. Those wishing to exploit the timber become licensees. They are given a right of property in the timber they cut. The title to the land remains in the Crown. In the older provinces the Crown for this purpose is the Provincial Government. In the Prairie Provinces and the two areas in British Columbia known as the Railway Belt and the Peace River District, Crown lands are owned by the Federal Government.

In Nova Scotia " the practice of disposing of timber lands in fee simple . . . continued until 1899, the object apparently having been to settle the country, no matter whether farm or forest land was taken. In the latter year a lease system in connexion with timber lands was introduced, and lessees secured tenure for a twenty-years period (renewable for a further twenty years) at the fixed price of 40 cents per acre. . . . In 1904 the Act was amended, increasing the rate to 80 cents per acre, for which lessees were entitled to the privilege of cutting all timber to a diameter limit of ten inches. This practice continued until 1910 [1] when . . . provision was made for the disposal of timber on a stumpage basis.[2] The old provision for leasing, however, remained . . .

---

[1] *Crown Lands Act*, 1910. Revised Statutes of Nova Scotia, 1923, chap. 25, s. 43.

[2] Stumpage is the price paid for standing timber before it is chopped. It is the price paid to the owner of the land for the right to enter and cut timber.

and in actual practice it turned out that comparatively little timber was sold on the stumpage basis ". Legislation came too late, and 83 per cent. of the total forest area in Nova Scotia has been alienated in fee simple, and has passed out of the control of the province.[1]

In New Brunswick, although permanent alienation has not taken place to the same degree as in Nova Scotia, the great bulk of the forest area has been either alienated in fee simple or the timber cutting rights disposed of under long term licence or lease to lumbermen, pulp companies and others. Of the total forest area, 49·7 per cent. is in the former category, and 42·5 per cent. in the latter, so that only 7·8 per cent. remains under the control of the Province. In 1913 legislation was passed [2] authorizing the issue of a saw mill licence which was renewable from year to year for a period of twenty years, such renewal being conditional on the observance of the accompanying regulations. Stumpage was payable.

A relatively small proportion of the timber lands of Quebec have been alienated in fee simple. When this has taken place the forests of Quebec are in different forms of ownership. There are some six million acres of private forests which were sold to settlers or granted to railway companies as part of their land subsidies, or have come down from the old French seigniories. The Crown forests include the forests called " timber limits ", now mostly confined to the remoter upper river basins, which have been leased from time to time ; the township forest reserves for the use of the neighbouring communities ; and the virgin forests in which the only depredations have been those wrought by fire, storms, fungi, and insect invasions such as that of the spruce budworm. The forest lots sold to settlers under the special contract called " location ticket ", which imposes obligations as to residence and clearings, sooner or later revert to one or other of the above groups according as the settler does or does not fulfil the conditions of his location ticket. The sawmills draw most of their supplies from the private forest owners or the leased timber limits. The licence system, under which large areas of the more accessible timber have been disposed of, imposes regulations

---

[1] *Report of Royal Commission on Pulpwood, Canada* (Ottawa, 1924), p. 15.

[2] *Crown Lands Act.* Revised Statutes of New Brunswick, 1927, chap. 30, s. 9.

which have to be observed, but subject to this the licences. under which the timber is held, although in terms for a year, are virtually perpetual.[1]

In Ontario only between 3 and 4 per cent. of the total forest area has been alienated in fee simple.[2] Such alienation took the form of railway subsidies, grants to early settlement companies and scrip lands disposed of to veterans for services rendered. Here again, licenses may be granted to cut timber on ungranted public lands. The licences are for twelve months ; entitle the licensee to have exclusive possession of the land for the time being, and vest in him all rights of property in the timber cut. Returns as to the trees cut must be made to the proper officer, and Crown dues are levied.[3]

In the Prairie Provinces, the disposal of timber by the Federal Government has been confined to the licensing of timber berths to supply sawmill operations and to supply tie and other construction timber for railways and under a system of permits to provide settlers with timber for buildings and other structures.[4] Under the license system, the Crown retains title to the soil as well as the right of control over cutting operations, so that the title to the great bulk of the timber lands in these provinces remains with the Federal Government. The annual license system prevails.[5]

The lumber trade of British Columbia was called into existence by the Canadian Pacific Railway. Before that time the illimitable forest was looked upon as rather worse than useless, for land wanted for settlement had to be painfully cleared. If land was sold the trees were thrown in " along with the deer, the berry bushes, and the scenery ". Not until 1888 was it determined that timber as such had a value and that it might be made a source of public revenue. In that year timber ceased to be a free gift in British Columbia, and a royalty of 50 cents. a thousand feet, board measure, was charged on all timber cut on lands thereafter.[6] Timber lands could, however, still be acquired in fee simple.

---

[1] *Department of Lands and Forests Act.* Revised Statutes of Quebec, 1925, chap. 43, ss. 68–104.
[2] *Report of Royal Commission on Pulpwood*, p. 52.
[3] *Crown Timber Act.* Ontario Statutes : Revised edn. 1927, chap. 38.
[4] See *Dominion Lands Act, 1908.* Revised Statutes of Canada, 1927, chap. 113, s. 57.
[5] See ibid., ss. 49–50.
[6] A thousand feet of lumber, board measure, is a thousand square feet, one inch thick.

A revolutionary step was taken in 1896, when Crown timber lands were permanently withdrawn from the possibility of purchase and the public ownership of such lands proclaimed as a governing principle. All that could be alienated was the timber itself. There were to be no new freeholders of timber lands, only lessees or licensees. In 1905 the legislature made the boldest stroke of all by the institution of its system of " special timber licences ". The system has been described in the following terms :—
" In this year, 1905, the Government . . . invited private individuals to join it in a partnership in each and every square mile of the Crown forests. There was no sale, no auction, even no lease. The incoming partners were asked to sink no capital. The investor was merely asked to register a formal application to become a partner with the Government in the timber on such-and-such a square mile of the province—and the partnership was his. Stated in these attractive terms, the procedure sounds like some wild story of a commercial fairyland, where timber lands and wealth are given for the asking ; but the truth is that a number of sound and useful ' strings ' were attached to these British Columbian gifts—that, in fact, the gift idea was entirely absent from the mind of the Provincial Government. The Government freely admitted investors to partnership in Crown timber, it is true ; but it did so on its own terms absolutely, and it frankly admitted that only the future rise in stumpage and lumber values would enable it to say what those terms should be." [1]

During the two years for which the system was in force over 15,000 licences were issued. If anything, the scheme had been too successful. In 1907 the issue of licences was stopped, and the remaining lands reserved, pending a reconsideration of the policy to be pursued, the Government meanwhile drawing some £400,000 a year as its share of the partnership in the 15,000 licences. The ultimate system adopted provided for the sale of licences to cut and remove timber on Crown lands.[2] Thanks to its prolonged inaccessibility, almost 90 per cent. of the forest area of British Columbia remains unalienated.[3]

The Provinces which kept tight hold of their timber lands

---

[1] Hon. A. C. Flumerfelt, quoted in *The Times,* 24th May, 1911, p. 51.
[2] *Forest Act, 1923.* Revised Statutes of British Columbia, 1924, chap. 93, Part III.
[3] *Report of Royal Commission on Wood Pulp,* 1924, p. 80.

enjoy revenues therefrom which, in some cases, form a substantial proportion of the total annual revenues of the Province. In 1926 the province of Quebec received approximately $5,250,000 under the head of woods, forests, and timber, about one-fifth of its total income, the expenditure under the same head being just over $900,000. New Brunswick derived the same proportion of its income from a similar source. In British Columbia about one-sixth of the total income of the province comes from its forests. Having alienated most of the timber lands before the value as a revenue producing asset was realized, Nova Scotia only received some $15,000 under this head.[1]

The securing of many millions of dollars of revenue to the State is only one aspect of the policy which has now been generally adopted by the Federal and Provincial Governments under which timber areas are not disposed of in fee simple, but are exploited under a system of lease or licence. There are also purely economic aspects of first-class importance. The survey and segregation of forest lands are essentially matters for the State. In private ownership the temptation is to exploit timber as a mine. To attempt to cultivate a new crop of timber is to lay up treasure for posterity. That is more likely to be done by the State than by the individual owner. The influence of forests on the water supply is well recognized, and the maintenance of forests for irrigation purposes is again an affair of the State, as also is the organization of protection against fire and against insect and fungus enemies. These are matters which concern Canadian Governments in common with all governments of countries which possess large forest areas. Furthermore, in the case of Canada the policy of public ownership has had the supremely important result that it has enabled the Dominion to build up a great wood pulp industry within its own borders.

The depletion of their forests constitutes a problem which is causing Canadians a good deal of concern. The problem arises directly from the spread of the reading habit and the craze for silk stockings, for Canadian timber is the raw material of the wood pulp out of which much of the paper now used for newspapers and books is manufactured and, to a less but perhaps growing degree, of the artificial silk which has become such a favourite material for modern articles of clothing.

[1] See *Canada Year Book*, 1927–8, pp. 836–41.

Of the Canadian soft wood trees, the variety which is mainly used for the manufacture of wood pulp is spruce, constituting nearly three-fourths of the whole. The finest species, the Sitka spruce, much prized for the production of high-grade pulp and certain special lines of manufacture, belongs to British Columbia. Next come balsam fir and, in British Columbia, hemlock. Jackpine also enters appreciably into pulp manufacture, and its use for this purpose is expected to increase.

The manufacture of wood pulp on any substantial scale is a modern phase of Canadian industrial activity. Paper has been made in Canada since the first half of the nineteenth century but, since rag was the chief raw material used, the output was small and the product was dear. Experiments in the use of wood for paper manufacture led to the discovery that spruce, balsam and hemlock were suitable for the manufacture of at any rate the cheaper papers, a discovery which ensured for Canada pre-eminence in the production of a manufactured product in ever increasing demand.

There are different claimants for the honour of founding the first mill in Canada for the conversion of wood into pulp for the manufacture of paper, but in any case by 1870 the new industry had been founded. Its early career was obscure. " In the census of 1871 pulp-mills are not mentioned, but in 1881 five mills were reported with a total capital of $92,000, sixty-eight employees, and an output valued at $63,300. In 1891 there were twenty-four pulp mills," [1] while, " at the end of 1926, there were in operation in Canada 44 pulp-mills, 36 combined pulp and paper mills, and 35 mills making paper only, and since then the number has increased." [2] In these mills 30,000 persons were then employed, and they represented a capital investment of over $500,000,000.[3] In 1922 " Pulp and Paper products " showed the highest gross value in the list of Canadian manufacturing industries, thus displacing " flour and grist mill products " which had hitherto headed the list, and it has since increased its lead.

The process of reconstituting the branch of a tree into a sheet of paper is, in effect, the process of separating the

[1] *The Pulp and Paper Industry*, 1923 (Dominion Bureau of Statistics), p. 5.
[2] *Canada Year Book*, 1927-8, p. 312.
[3] Ibid., p. 319.

fibres composing the tree from each other, this mass of disintegrated fibres, otherwise pulp, being then reconstituted into a flat sheet.

Wood pulp is broadly classified under two heads, namely, " mechanical pulp " and " chemical pulp ", the basis of the classification being the manufacturing process used. To produce wood-pulp by the mechanical process, the wood having had its bark removed in a " barking " or " rossing " mill is pressed by hydraulic power against the face of a rapidly revolving grindstone. The wood is disintegrated into fibres which are carried away in a stream of water for further treatment. Chemical pulp is produced by one of three processes, in each of which the non-fibrous or non-cellulose components are dissolved and eliminated from the wood-substance The oldest of the chemical methods is the soda process. The most important and most frequently used is the sulphite process. Sulphite pulp is used in the manufacture not only of paper, but also of artificial silk. The first sulphite mill was established in 1887 in Ontario by the firm of Riordon, and, in 1916, as the managing director of the Riordon Pulp and Paper Company told the Dominions Royal Commission, the firm was producing, at its two mills, 225 tons a day of sulphite fibre for the manufacture of the higher grades of paper.[1] The sulphate process is a modification of the soda process introduced in 1907. The process produces pulp which is used for the manufacture of kraft paper for wrapping, bags, and other purposes where strength rather than whiteness is wanted.

Mechanical, otherwise groundwood pulp, is the cheapest variety and is the main constituent, that is to say 80 per cent., of newsprint. The other 20 per cent. is sulphite pulp. Its inferiority to chemical pulp is due to the non-elimination of the unenduring elements in the wood. In bulk, though not in value, the output of mechanical wood pulp has always exceeded that of chemical pulp of all forms combined.[2] For the better qualities of white paper, pulp produced by the sulphite or soda processes is the main constituent.

The great wood pulp manufacturing provinces are first Quebec, and second Ontario. British Columbia and New Brunswick have a substantial but much smaller

---

[1] D.R.C. Minutes of Evidence, 1916 [Cd. 8459], Qs. 2671–4.
[2] In 1926 the total output of mechanical pulp was 1,901,268 tons, valued at approximately $45,000,000, and of chemical pulp 1,251,178 tons, worth over $69,000,000.

output, and Nova Scotia has the smallest recorded output of all.[1]

The pulpwood mills have large timber holdings of their own. In the Eastern Provinces pulpwood is also purchased from the farmers, and new settlers in those Provinces look to their timber as a source of revenue until they are able to get returns from their crops. In British Columbia, however, the contribution of the farmers is negligible. " The reason is readily found in the absolutely different character which pulpwood operations assume in British Columbia as compared to those in Eastern Canada. Firstly, the few existing mills are not so situated as to permit of farmers participating in the supply, timber usually being available at closer range ; secondly, the class of timber used is of such large size, and consequently so difficult to operate, that the business of logging entails capital expenditure and logging experience far beyond the possibilities of the average farmer ; finally, the farming population within reach of the mills is so limited that the mills could not depend upon them as an essential or regular source of supply. In Eastern Canada, a farmer, with the help of his team and a few ordinary tools, may without difficulty get out a considerable quantity of wood ; on the Coast, for the class of pulpwood used, many thousands of dollars must be invested in equipment before a timber area may be successfully logged." [2] In this Province pulp mills either acquire their own timber lands or purchase a supply from the loggers who here constitute a separate industry.

Pulpwood has provided one most interesting episode in the industrial war between the Dominion and the Republic which waxes and wanes but never completely dies down. The results of past improvidence in the United States in

[1] Pulp production by these Provinces in 1926 was as follows :—

Quebec	.	.	1,672,339 tons of 2,000 lb. valued at				$59,218,576
Ontario	.	.	1,095,987	„	„	„	„	„	$38,008,752
British Columbia	260,188	„	„	„	„	„	$8,233,085
NewBrunswick	.	153,669	„	„	„	„	„	$8,424,327
Nova Scotia	.	47,608	„	„	„	„	„	$1,269,459

According to evidence presented to the Dominions Royal Commission in 1914 [Cd. 7898] there was in Newfoundland an area of 10,000 square miles of wooded land, pine, spruce and balsam fir predominating. " Newfoundland has never been a lumber exporting country to any extent and is never likely to be " (p. 55), but with the commencement of operations by the " Harmsworth " mills in 1909 a use for the timber resources of the Island was found in the manufacture of wood pulp on a large scale.

[2] *Report of Royal Commission on Pulpwood*, Ottawa, 1924, p. 89.

the use of softwood timber have been fully revealed. The
United States consumes about half the world's lumber,
and its softwood resources will soon be limited to the Western
States.   " The original forest area of 822 million acres
has been reduced to 463 million acres, of which only 137
million acres carry virgin timber.   This last mentioned
area is being cleared at the rate of 5½ million acres per annum,
so that . . . there appears to be only about 25 years'
supply apart from the produce of second-growth areas." [1]
New England and the Eastern States, the original headquarters of the lumbering industry in America, have long
ceased to supply their own needs.   In the Lake States
the denudation of the forests has been rapid and what
remains is threatened with extinction in less than ten years.
In the Gulf States, forest depletion is proceeding at the rate
of 3 million acres a year.   Only the Pacific Coast remains,
and thither lumbermen have been migrating.[2]   The measure
of the country's improvidence varies, but apparently the
annual consumption of the United States has been from
four to eight times the annual growth.[3]   Furthermore,
in the United States poplar has for some years been
extensively used for the manufacture of wood pulp, although
the quality of its fibre makes it an unsatisfactory raw
material as compared with the species mainly used
in Canada.

The demand of the United States for newsprint and other
forms of paper is insatiable.   When their own sources of
pulpwood supply began to show signs of exhaustion in the
near future the Republic began to draw upon the resources
of the forests of Canada.   " Since 1902 the exports of raw
pulpwood have gone exclusively to the United States and
have amounted annually to about 1,000,000 cords." [4]   It
was felt that to the extent to which Canadian forests were
to be depleted in order to provide manufacturers with raw
material, Canadians, and not their competitors in the United
States, should enjoy the profits derivable from the industry.
Conservation of resources was the reason alleged for

---

[1] Imperial Conference, 1926, *Appendices to Summary of Proceedings*
[*Cmd.* 2769], p. 326.

[2] *Canada in relation to the World's Timber Supply*. Department of
the Interior, Canada, 1924, p. 6.

[3] These were the extreme estimates at the 1927 meeting of the British
Association as reported in *The Times* of 8th and 12th September, 1927.

[4] *Canada Year Book*, 1927–8, p. 313. A " cord " is a cubic measure,
4 ft. × 4 ft. × 8 ft.

restricting exports, but also it was argued that the restriction of the export of unmanufactured pulpwood would stimulate the pulpwood industry in Canada, that American manufacturers who depended on Canadian timber would be induced to bring their works across the border, capital would be attracted, employment would be provided for workmen in Canada, and generally Canadians would enjoy in greater measure all the advantages flowing from the presence of a prosperous industry in their midst. Moreover, that Americans, having dissipated their own estate, should be allowed to appropriate Canada's was an intolerable thought to Canadians. The outcome was legislation by the forest Provinces, excepting only Nova Scotia, requiring the manufacture on Canadian soil before export of soft wood timber cut on Canadian Crown lands.[1]

Ontario began it : and its statutory provisions on the subject remains the most comprehensive of all the Provinces. By the Crown Timber Act [2] it is provided that : " All sales of timber limits which confer the right to cut and remove spruce or other softwood trees or timber, other than pine, suitable for manufacturing pulp or paper, and all licences or permits to cut the same on the limits so sold, and all agreements entered into or other authority conferred by the Minister by virtue of which such wood, trees or timber may be cut upon public lands " shall be subject to " the manufacturing condition ", that is to say, it must be " manufactured in Canada into merchantable pulp or paper, or into sawn lumber . . . utensils, or other articles of commerce or merchandise ".

There are similar provisions requiring birch, beech, maple, elm, ash or oak, and other hardwood trees cut on public lands, and also pine similarly cut, to be manufactured into sawn lumber in Canada.[3]

In 1910 Quebec imposed similar requirements as to the manufacture in Canada of all timber cut on Crown lands,[4]

---

[1] Newfoundland has similar legislation. By the Crown Lands, etc., Act (*Consolidated Statutes of Newfoundland*, 1916, ch. 129) " No holder of a timber or pulp licence shall take or carry away for exportation from the lands licensed any trees, logs or timber unless and until the same have been manufactured either into paper or paper pulp, sawn lumber, or other saleable products of timber."

[2] *Ontario Statutes*, Revised Edition, 1927, chap. 38, s. 5.

[3] Ibid., ss. 4 and 6.

[4] The procedure in this case was by Order in Council under the authority of the Lands and Forests Act (*Revised Statutes of Quebec*, 1925, chap. 44, s. 68).

and New Brunswick imposed the same restriction, but only on the soft woods, in 1911.[1]

British Columbia has adopted similar statutory restrictions, but somewhat different in form. It is there provided that " All timber cut on Crown lands, or on lands granted after 12th March, 1906, or on lands held under pre-emption record, shall be used in the Province, or be manufactured in the Province into boards, deal, joists, laths, shingles, or other sawn timber, or into wood pulp or paper," [2] but the export of piles, poles, railway ties and crib timber cut on Crown lands may be authorized,[3] as also " the export of unmanufactured timber from areas adjacent to the boundary of the Province in cases where it is proved . . . that such timber cannot, owing to topographical reasons, be profitably manufactured within the Province." [4] This dispensing power is exercised by the Government with the advice and assistance of the Log Export Committee, a body representative of the interests concerned.

Furthermore, a Timber Tax is levied on all timber (whether cut on public or private lands) cut within the Province: "Provided that a rebate of all the tax over 1 cent per 1,000 feet board measure shall be allowed when the timber upon which it is due or payable is manufactured or used in the Province."

In the Prairie Provinces and the Railway Belt, a strip 40 miles wide stretching from the summit of the Rockies westward, and the Peace River district, in British Columbia, the Federal authorities have control of natural resources. In those areas the Federal authorities have power to prohibit by Order in Council the exportation from Canada of pulpwood.[5]

Referring to the contention that restriction in exports of raw material would have a stimulating effect upon the pulpwood manufacturing industry in Canada, the Royal Commission on Pulpwood [6] points out that: "In addition to wood supplies, there are to be considered the questions of power and other economic factors. Under present

---

[1] Crown Lands Act, *Revised Statutes of New Brunswick*, 1927, chap. 30.
[2] The Forest Act, 1923, *Revised Statutes of British Columbia*, 1924, chap. 93, s. 86.
[3] Ibid., s. 89.
[4] Ibid., s. 90.
[5] The Export Act, *Revised Statutes of Canada*, 1927, chap. 63.
[6] Ottawa, 1924, at p. 221.

conditions at least, much of the wood exported is from areas or districts where mills are not within easy reach, and in some regions there is at least some doubt that the general wood supplies and other contributing factors would justify the erection of mills," but they add that " the experience already derived from provincial imposition of restrictions upon Crown land wood cannot be denied ". That experience is that since 1908 the percentage of the total pulpwood production of Canada exported in its unmanufactured state has progressively declined and the proportion used in Canadian pulp mills has correspondingly increased. In 1908 the proportion of pulpwood exported unmanufactured was 64 per cent, and the proportion used in Canadian pulp mills 36 per cent. By 1913 the proportions had become nearly equal. In 1926 only 25 per cent. of the total production was exported unmanufactured. It has also to be remembered that the gross output has increased enormously in the period, the total production of pulpwood in 1926 being more than four times that of 1908. In other words, whereas in 1908 the quantity of pulpwood used in Canadian mills was 482,000 cords, in 1926 it was 4,229,000 cords—or nine times as much. The export of unmanufactured pulpwood only increased in the same period from 842,000 cords to 1,391,000 cords—it had not doubled.

The position has accordingly been arrived at that timber owners enjoy unrestricted right of export only from private lands. The only exceptions to this rule are on the one hand Nova Scotia, where there are no restrictions on the export of timber, even though cut from Crown lands, and on the other, British Columbia, where the export of timber, even from private lands, is penalized by taxation. The absence of restriction in Nova Scotia is the result of her comparatively long history as a lumber province. Her geographical position gave the province ready access to foreign markets. This early lumber trade resulted in the alienation in fee simple of the great bulk of the forest area and the amount of timber land in the province to which restriction could apply is negligible. Elsewhere the restrictions are of very real moment. Thus in Quebec, when the Government early recognized the desirability of retaining in the Crown the title to forest lands, "governmental restrictions as to manufacture, calculated to prevent the export of raw wood, apply to over 87 per cent. of the available supplies."[1]

[1] *Report of Royal Commission on Pulpwood*, Canada (Ottawa, 1924), p. 42.

Taking Canada's resources in pulpwood as a whole, "almost 83 per cent. may be subjected to such restrictions if the respective Governments so desire ; most of it is already so restricted." [1]

Since 1902, as has already been seen, the exports of raw pulpwood from Canada have gone exclusively to the United States. Such exports must be drawn from Nova Scotia and in other provinces from privately owned timber lands. How relatively small those sources of supply are and how relatively soon they must become exhausted is apparent. A complete triumph appears to await the Canadian manufacturers.

An important aspect of legislative restriction, such as that under consideration, is to be seen in the resulting impotence of foreign control in the pulpwood timber trade, save in that small portion of it which enjoys unrestricted rights of export. In that minority of the timber trade the element of foreign control is conspicuous. In Nova Scotia, the province where the greatest proportion of timber lands have been alienated, of the 1,707 square miles of timber lands under foreign control "at least 1,331 square miles is held by three American pulp companies that do not manufacture pulp within the province ".[2] In New Brunswick, of the unrestricted area " 30 per cent or 1,270 square miles is controlled by foreign interests essentially American." [3] In Quebec, "so far as is known, approximately 60 per cent of the privately owned timber lands is controlled by foreign capital." [4] In British Columbia, " it is apparent from records of ownership, that at least 37 per cent. of Crown granted timber land is directly under foreign control, and undoubtedly a considerable additional area stands in the name of companies which, although operating under Canadian charter, are controlled by foreign capital." [5] As to Canada as a whole, " it has been determined that approximately 30 per cent. of private holdings is directly controlled by foreign companies, corporations and individuals." [6] The main interest of those controlling that 30 per cent. is to supply United States mills with Canadian spruce, balsam and popular. The demand

---

[1] *Report of Royal Commission on Pulpwood*, Canada, 1924, pp. 92-3.
[2] Ibid., p. 16.
[3] Ibid., p. 30.
[4] Ibid., p. 41.
[5] Ibid., p. 81.
[6] Ibid., p. 93.

that this leakage should be stopped and a complete embargo placed on the export of unmanufactured timber was the subject of enquiry in 1923-4 by the Canadian Royal Commission on Pulpwood. On this point the Commission preferred to make no recommendation. In the Canadian House of Commons the proposal had been consistently opposed by the representatives of the farmers, who were able to get better prices for their timber across the line than on the Canadian side and who feared being handed over to the tender mercies of a combine of Canadian pulp-mills.[1]

Canada has reached the position of being the second largest exporter of wood pulp in the world, her total being exceeded by Sweden only. Her competitors next in order are Norway, Finland and Germany. The depletion of the United States pulpwood resources, the vastness of the American demand for newsprint and the proximity of her market, are sufficient reasons why four-fifths of Canada's export of wood pulp should go to her southern neighbour to be mostly consumed in New York, Maine, Pennsylvania and New Hampshire.[2] " Over two-thirds of the newsprint paper consumed in the United States is either of Canadian manufacture or is made from pulpwood or woodpulp imported from Canada."[3] Great Britain's imports of wood pulp are mainly from Scandinavia. The haul is much shorter than from Canada and the Scandinavian trade has the advantage of a ballast rate.

It has been seen how the policy of the Dominion has been to retain its pulpwood for the manufacture within its own borders of wood pulp and what a phenomenal development of wood pulp manufacture has accompanied that policy. It is a natural next step to consume its own wood pulp and to produce the finished article in the various forms of paper products. Newsprint constitutes the great bulk of the output and Canada has become the largest producer of newsprint in the world. There has been a progressive increase in the production of wrapping paper and there has been considerable progress in the manufacture of paper boards.

[1] See *Dominion Debates*, 1923, pp. 4354 ff.

[2] In 1926, of a total Canadian export of 1,005,780 tons of wood pulp, 817,571 tons went to the United States, 112,537 tons to the United Kingdom, and 75,672 tons elsewhere.

[3] *Census of Industry : The Pulp and Paper Industry*, 1921 *and* 1922. Dominion Bureau of Statistics.

The manufacture of book and writing paper has developed more slowly.[1]

The pulp and paper industry is in Canada a highly organized body and the industry and the Government co-operate in research. The problems investigated by the Forest Products Laboratories of Canada for the benefit of the pulp and paper industry are highly technical, involving as they do problems in the chemistry of wood, timber, physics and wood preservation. Thus one section of the Laboratory undertook " to study the chemical composition of wood with a view to laying a sound foundation for chemical processes for the manufacture of paper pulp and other products ". Another branch attacked the problem of determining the causal fungus or fungi which gave Jack-pine its susceptibility to decay by so-called red stain and red rot.[2]

A scheme for co-operative research between the Government and the pulp and paper industry came into effect in 1925. Under this scheme the industry was to make a substantial annual contribution for a period of from two to five years, to be devoted to extending the investigations of the laboratories relative to pulp and paper. Control of the work was effected by means of a joint Committee on which the Government and the industry were to be represented. The committee was responsible to the Research section of the Canadian Pulp and Paper Association, which, in turn, was responsible to the Association and thence to the industry at large.[3]

It has to be realized that under hitherto existing conditions Canada's forest wealth is a wasting asset. Fire, insects, fungi and wind are the unrelenting enemies of the trees. " During the last five years, 723,250 acres of merchantable timber have been burned over annually." [4] The spruce budworm has done immense damage to the spruce and balsam fir forests in eastern Canada. " In timber it is estimated that 100 million cords of pulpwood have been destroyed by this insect and in New Brunswick the loss is

---

[1] Paper production in Canada in 1917 amounted to 853,689 tons, worth $58,750,341. Of this, newsprint amounted to 689,847 tons. In 1925 the total output of paper was 1,884,705 tons, worth $140,680,177, and newsprint was 1,536,523 tons.

[2] Annual Report of Department of Interior for 1925–6, pp. 84–5 (*Annual Departmental Reports*, 1925–6, vol. ii).

[3] Ibid., p. 82.

[4] *The Forests of Canada*, Department of the Interior, Ottawa, 1923, p. 35.

placed at 15 million cords . . . an average of nearly
1,350,000,000 cubic feet every year." [1] Among the fungi
enemies, the butt rot in balsam fir is specially prevalent.

The output of Canadian statistics is somewhat stunning
in its effect. Particularly is this so when timber is the
subject. The statement that, " With an annual utilization
of about 2,600,000,000 cubic feet, destruction by fire of
790,000,000 cubic feet, destruction by insects of
1,350,000,000 cubic feet, and an unknown loss due to the
fungus diseases, the forests have during the last five years
been depleted at the rate of upwards of 5,000,000,000
cubic feet per annum," [2] conveys a general sense of calamity ;
but the pity of it is probably better realized when one reads :
" The first thing that strikes the traveller traversing
the forest regions of this country on any of the transcontinental lines of railway is the prevalence of forest fires
that have occurred in the past. Monotonously, for mile after
mile, for hour after hour, the train passes through areas
which have been stripped of all forest growth by recurrent
fires. In many places the soil itself is largely gone and
nothing remains but bare rock which will be manifestly
incapable of supporting any growth for generations to
come." [3] Or there is the description of what happened in
Ontario so recently as July, 1916, when " a destructive
fire swept over the Matheson and Cochrane districts and
extended along the Porcupine branch of the T. and N.O.
burning almost everything along its course—settlers' homes
and crops, part of the Abitibi Pulp Mills plant, part of the
town of Iroquois Falls, with most of Matheson, Kelso,
Homer and Cochrane . . . The estimated loss of life had
been 250." [4]

Nevertheless the sheer waste of economic wealth that has
been permitted is made abundantly apparent by a concise
statement presented to the Imperial Conference of 1926.
" Originally Canada had probably nearly one thousand
billion [5] cubic feet of merchantable timber. Now there is
only about one quarter of that amount . . . Of the seven
hundred and odd billion cubic feet that has disappeared
from the once available supply, it must regretfully be

[1] *The Forests of Canada*, Department of the Interior, Ottawa, 1923.
[2] Ibid., p. 35.
[3] D. Roy Cameron, *Forest Fire Protection in Canada* (Address to the
British Association at Toronto, 1924).
[4] *Canadian Annual Review*, 1916, p. 485.
[5] In Canada a billion is a thousand millions.

admitted that only about one hundred and twenty billion feet has been used, while over half of the once almost inexhaustible (or at least so considered) forest wealth has been burnt." [1] Or, measuring the catastrophe another way : " According to the most recent statistics, the loss from fire, insects and fungi equals the amount of timber felled each year." [2] The statistical investigation that has been going on for years has arrived at a conclusion that is sufficiently startling. " The forest resources of Canada are being depleted at the rate of about 5 billion cubic feet annually through cutting, fire, insects and decay. If the reproduction and the young timber are not protected, the stand of merchantable timber accessible for exploitation will not withstand this drain for more than about 25 years." [3]

How to deal with insect pests and fungi is a problem for the scientist. Canadian entomologists have already done good work in directing operations how and when to clean up areas attacked by for instance the spruce budworm in the east and the Douglas fir bark beetle in the west, and mycologists have been of great value in disseminating information as to where and when to cut areas threatened with the fungi that attacks the roots of certain valuable conifers.

The prevention and control of forest fires are problems for the legislator and the administrator. The most frequent causes of forest fires have been found to be railways, camp fires, the burning of slash (forest débris) and lightning. Already the most serious waste, the severe loss caused by fires spreading from railways, has been greatly reduced through amendments to the Railway Act whereby the railways under the jurisdiction of the Dominion Board of Railway Commissioners have been made responsible for extinguishing fires due to railway agencies. Under the fire regulations of the Board the railways are required to take adequate preventive measures, such as the establishment of special patrols in forest sections, the construction of fire guards in the Prairie Provinces and the use of efficient spark arresters on locomotives. These measures have proved effective and the railways can no longer be regarded as the arch-offender in the causing of disastrous forest conflagrations.

[1] *Appendices to the Summary of Proceedings* [Cd. 2769], p. 342.
[2] Ibid., p. 326.
[3] Ibid., p. 343.

As to the other cause of forest fires through human agency, the method of education has apparently been effective in protecting the Canadian forests as it has in inculcating other social duties. "In the Province of Quebec, in the churches, where the people are nearly all Catholics and French, the priests talk continually about the fire, talk continually as to the care of the forests, and a generation is growing up now that really is trying to be careful of the forests. It is an educative age as to the care of the forests and there are not nearly as many fires or anything like the carelessness that there was a few years ago."[1]

The Dominion and Provincial Governments have evolved an elaborate fire-fighting organization into the service of which have been pressed the telephone, wireless, the motor-car, the weather prophet, who is now able to give "fire weather forecasts", and finally aircraft, by means of which fires can be detected in the early stages and fire-fighting men and appliances quickly rushed to the spot.

The real remedy, however, is to be found in regarding Canada's forests as crops to be renewed rather than as mines to be worked out once and for all and abandoned. Accordingly, "the policy of the Government is to extend . . . forest reserves so that eventually they shall include all non-agricultural lands capable of supporting tree growth and to provide for their maintenance in a forested condition by natural regeneration, except where entirely denuded areas demand artificial methods."[2]

The Harnessing of Water Power

In the early days of Canadian economic history, when the rivers were the highways and the birch-bark canoe the means of transport both for men and goods, the rapids were merely a danger that could only be surmounted by the exercise of nerve and skill, or an obstruction that had to be circumvented by laborious portages. It has now been realized that these same rapids are vast reservoirs of energy capable of supplying all the motive power needed to meet the demands of a modern industrial state.

Both in their bulk and in the manner of their distribution, Canada is generously endowed with primary power resources.

---

[1] D.R.C. Minutes of Evidence [Cd. 7971], Q. 3187.
[2] Canada Year Book, 1926–7, p. 304.

Except for part of the Middle West, either water-power or coal is present in abundance. Where there is no coal there is plenty of water-power. Notably this is the state of things in Quebec and Ontario. And where there is little water power there is abundant coal, as in Alberta. In the specially favoured Province of British Columbia both resources are available in largest measure and there are instances of coal mines being operated by hydro-electric energy.

The position as to primary motive power in the Dominion at the period about the end of the Great War was thus summarized: " We have steam and water-power in the Maritime Provinces with a predominance of the former. In Quebec, Ontario and eastern Manitoba water-power is the dominating source of power, every large centre and most of the smaller ones being supplied by electricity produced from water-power, either through the extensive network of transmission lines fed from large developments or by smaller local plants. In the Middle West large plants are steam operated, while the smaller ones use internal combustion engines. In British Columbia and western Alberta we again find water-power predominating, but the generous coal supply in certain districts also permits considerable steam operation." [1]

The growth of water-power development is largely the result of the solution of the problem of the long distance transmission of electricity during the last years of the nineteenth century. Whereas then approximately 170,000 h.p. had been installed in Canada, the installation had grown to 975,150 h.p. by the end of 1910 and 1,946,429 h.p. at the end of 1914. During the War years and the period of depression which followed, the rate of growth was slower, but the figures had grown to 2,508,454 h.p. at the end of 1920. Then an intensive period of development set in and at the end of 1927 the figure of 4,777,921 h.p. had been reached.

A survey of electric energy undertaken for the Canadian Commission of Conservation in 1918 disclosed in a striking manner the predominance of water-power as the primary motive power of electric generating plants. Of generating plants with an aggregate capacity of 2,107,743 h.p. hydro-electric plants represented 1,806,618 h.p. The balance were steam plants save for a number of small gas plants and oil

[1] Leo G. Denis, " Electric Generation and Distribution in Canada," *Commission of Conservation, Canada*, Ottawa, 1918, p. 3.

of gasoline plants.[1] The advantage of being able to rely on electricity generated from water-power became apparent when, during the latter year of the war, fuel became scarce and correspondingly costly. For central electric station use, especially, the percentage of hydraulic development over fuel increased from year to year, and in 1925 " over 98·3 per cent. of the total electrical output of Canada's central stations originated in the energy of falling water." [2]

Canada's resources in water-power are distributed throughout the Dominion, save in southern Alberta and Saskatchewan, and by a happy coincidence those resources are available in especially generous measure in the " Acute Fuel Area ", an official designation given to Ontario and Quebec by reason of their annual winter outcry about shortage of coal supplies, coal being the one mineral with which nature seems to have forgotten to provide these provinces.

At the end of 1925 the total available and developed water-power of the Dominion was over 4,250,000 h.p., which represented an average of 458 turbine horse-power installed per thousand of the population. Canada's *per capita* consumption of water-power was only exceeded by that of Norway.[3]

An analysis of Canada's hydraulic resources, conservatively estimated in 1928, led to the conclusion that the then existing recorded water-power resources of the Dominion would permit of a turbine installation of approximately 43,000,000 h.p.[4]

All this development has taken place since 1900, when about 150,000 represented the total installed horse-power.[5] Nevertheless at the beginning of 1928 the total installation

---

[1] Leo G. Denis, "Electric Generation and Distribution in Canada," *Commission of Conservation, Canada*, Ottawa, 1918.

[2] Water Power Resources of Canada : Department of the Interior, Dominion Water Power and Reclamation Service, Ottawa, 1927 (*North America : Pamphlets*, No. 48, in D.O. and C.O. Library).

[3]

						Turbine h.p. installed per 1,000 population.
Norway	.	.	.	.	.	740
Canada	.	.	.	.	.	458
Switzerland	.	.	.	.	.	437
Sweden	.	.	.	.	.	266
United States	.	.	.	.	.	106

[4] Water Power Resources of Canada. Department of the Interior. Dominion Water Power and Reclamation Service. Ottawa, 1928 (*North America : Pamphlets*, No. 48, in D.O. and C.O. Library).

[5] *Survey of Overseas Markets : Committee on Industry and Trade.* London, 1925, p. 308.

in water-wheels and turbines throughout the Dominion was only 4,777,921 h.p., that is to say, a little over 11 per cent. of the recorded water-power resources.

Relying on a natural phenomenon which is so wayward in its habits as a stream of water, hydro-electric installations have had to encounter the special difficulties incidental to that form of motive power. Low water may prevent the water-power plant from carrying its full load. To meet this emergency auxiliary steam plants are sometimes provided, but the conservation reservoir is a more economical method of providing for a shortage of power resulting from deficient flow. By a system of storage reservoirs from which water is released and carried over considerable distances to the power plant many of the early difficulties of hydro-electric installation due to low water have been overcome. Trouble from ice is to be expected. " Owing to temporary ice conditions we have had occasionally in recent years to use the supplementary steam plant in Toronto to help the manufacture of power for a few days or weeks." [1]

The public ownership of public utilities is universally accepted as a general principle in the Dominion. That the principle has been successfully applied has been ascribed to the character of the people. Being a young man's country, there is a spirit of optimism, and this, with the allied spirit of co-operation, provides a sound basis for ventures in public ownership. Moreover, a real and live interest is taken by the public in all utilities, so that equipment, operation and organization are seldom allowed to become out of date. [2]

Nevertheless the application of this principle is by no means uniform. In Ontario the Hydro-Electric Power Commission has greatly stimulated public ownership. In Quebec the great bulk of energy is distributed by private companies, but there are a number of municipal systems, some of which obtain their supply in block from the Shawinigan and other joint stock systems. [3] In the Prairie Provinces municipal control is the rule.

[1] William C. Noxon, "Hydro-Electric Development in Ontario, Canada." Paper read at meeting of Royal Colonial Institute, April, 1925, by Agent General for Ontario.

[2] A. G. Christie, in Proceedings, American Institute of Electrical Engineers, 1916, vol. xxxv, p. 33.

[3] At the beginning of 1927, while Ontario and Quebec had almost equal total installations, in Ontario the installation of commercial stations was only 28·4 per cent of the whole for the province, while in Quebec the commercial stations had an installation representing 98·8 per cent. of the total for the province (Water Power Resources of Canada, supra).

The view generally taken in the Dominion is that as a result of the remarkable advance in recent years in the development, transmission and use of electrical energy, water-power has assumed such an important bearing on domestic and industrial life that it can no longer be safely included in the category of private property and the problem is to secure the administration of water-power resources as a public utility, conserving for the community the increment in value which must accrue to water-powers of substantial capacity and favourable situation.

The Hydro-Electric Power Commission of Ontario has to its credit a great record of successful constructive effort on behalf of the industry of its Province.

The mines, the wood pulp and paper mills, the lumber mills, the factories, as also the municipal public services—all depend on the Commission for the motive power which is their life-blood.

The citizens of Ontario were quick to recognize the possibilities of hydro-electricity, and the history of the Commission is of special interest in that it is the story of a public organization which was able to build up from the very foundations one of the greatest edifices of its kind in the world.

The genesis of the Commission is to be found in a Resolution adopted by a Convention of Municipalities which met in June, 1902, at what was then Berlin and is now Kitchener, Ontario, urging " the advisability of the Government building and operating as a Government work lines for the transmission of electricity from Niagara Falls to the towns and cities of Ontario ". It was not, however, until 1906 that the principle of the Resolution was embodied in a statute. In that year an Act was passed creating the Hydro-Electric Power Commission of Ontario, and making provision " whereby all municipalities appeal to the Commission and make known their wants. The Commission is thus able to harmonize their various requirements and co-ordinate the municipalities into suitable groups or districts. The Hydro-Electric Power Commission is really a Department of the Government of Ontario, although independent of political changes and influence, and its function is to act as trustee for the people of Ontario and to supply hydro-electric light and power at cost to the municipalities. In 1908, bye-laws were passed by 13 municipalities authorizing their officials to make contracts with the

Commission for a supply of electrical power from Niagara Falls ".[1]

Beginning in a small way, the Commission at first bought power wholesale from the Ontario Power Company, which had taken over the first charter granted to a private company for exploiting Niagara, and sold it retail. The Commission also started construction on its own account, and in October 1910, the Premier of Ontario pressed a button in Kitchener which effected the connexion that produced the first current. In 1917 the Commission purchased outright the Ontario Power Company with a plant capacity which had then become one of 160,000 h.p. In 1920 it acquired the Toronto Power Company with its 125,000 h.p. capacity. By 1924 the total capacity administered by the Commission had grown to 864,690 h.p.[2] distributed between several " systems " in various parts of the province. The Niagara system, however, remains unchallenged as the largest, for it includes the Queenston-Chippewa Development, commenced in 1917, which constitutes the largest undertaking of its kind in the world.

The central conception of the scheme was to use to the maximum extent the total fall of 327 feet of the Niagara River between Lakes Erie and Ontario. The great Queenston power house now contains the greatest electric turbines in the world, each having a capacity of 60,000 h.p. and it was designed to accommodate ten of these monsters. Thence current is transmitted at 110,000 volts all over southwestern Ontario.[3]

In general the Commission supplies the power and the transmission, leaving to the municipalities the local distribution. Between them these public authorities were in 1925 serving a population of 2,250,000 of which over 400,000 were consumers. The area served is indicated by the fact that the transmission lines of the Commission have a total length of 3,500 miles. They serve villages where there are not thirty customers as well as Toronto.[4]

There is no form of industry in Canada which has not

---

[1] William C. Noxon, " Hydro-Electric Development in Ontario, Canada " (Paper read at a meeting of the Royal Colonial Institute, 7th April, 1925, by the Agent General for Ontario).

[2] Ibid.   [3] Ibid.

[4] The figures are for 1924–5. The average net charges to consumers for power service were e.g. $28·37 per horse-power per year in Toronto, 90 miles from Niagara Falls; $14·93 in Hamilton, 50 miles distant; $35·16 in Windsor, 250 miles from the point of generation (ibid.).

invoked the aid of hydro-electricity, but it is in mining and in the wood-pulp industry that its services have been so conspicuously valuable. In mining large power resources are necessary both in the extraction of the mineral and in crushing, smelting and refining. The availability of cheap power may make the profitable exploitation of a mine possible which otherwise would be left derelict. Also it makes available low grade deposits which would be of no commercial value if the necessary power were less cheap and abundant.

The remarkable state of things exists in Canada by which the Provinces which have the greatest mineral production have no coal. But by great good fortune those provinces have abundant water-power. Quebec and Ontario constitute the " Acute Fuel Area " of the Dominion. Were it not for their abundant hydro-electric resources these provinces would be almost totally dependent on coal imported from the United States. The cost of transporting coal from the Maritime Provinces and Alberta is prohibitive. In Alberta and Saskatchewan, it is true, they are not endowed with the same wealth of water-power, but then they have coal. " These coal deposits have in the past, as in Nova Scotia, been depended upon to provide power for their own exploitation, but upon the completion of the East Kootenay Power Company's transmission line into Alberta from British Columbia, a number of the Alberta mines contracted for supplies of hydro-electric power." [1] Also in the great coal-mining area of the Crow's Nest Pass and Elk River District in East Kootenay, hydro-electricity has to a great extent replaced coal as a source of power for mining.[2] In the Maritime Provinces, however, where almost 90 per cent of the mining carried on is coal mining, hydro-electric power has not yet been used to any substantial extent. The successful demonstration of its use for coal mining purposes further west will probably not be without its influence in the older provinces. In Quebec the vast amount of power used for the exploitation of its mineral wealth is almost entirely derived from hydraulic installations.

Taking Canada as a whole, 598,557 h.p. has been installed for the mineral industry in 1926, of which 72·8 per cent

---

[1] *Water Power in the Mineral Industries of Canada*, Department of the Interior, Ottawa, 1928 (*North America : Pamphlets*, No. 57, in D.O. & C.O Library).
[2] Ibid.

was water power, leaving 27·2 per cent for fuel-power, that is to say, steam, gas and oil.[1] How rapid has been the change to water-power from fuel is seen by the corresponding figures for 1st January, 1924, on which date " over half a million horse-power was used in the industry and of this 54 per cent was water-power, 44·6 per cent was steam-power, and 1·4 per cent was developed by internal combustion engines." [2] While a proportion of the whole was installed by the mines themselves, the greater proportion of the power was purchased from central electric stations.

It is appropriate that the first Canadian to accomplish the transmission of electric energy developed from water-power should have been the proprietor of an Ontario paper mill, John R. Barber, who in 1888 brought electricity to his mill over two miles of wire. Since then the Dominion's wood pulp and paper industry has acquired a predominating position which it owes to the fortunate proximity of enormous pulp-wood forests to correspondingly vast water-power resources capable of ready development.

On 1st January, 1928, all the provinces except Alberta, Saskatchewan, and Prince Edward Island appeared in the list of those using water-power for the purpose of the pulp and paper industry. Their combined total water-power turbine installation on that date represented 528,731 home-made horse-power actually developed by pulp and paper mills themselves. In addition to this total the pulp and paper industry purchased from hydro-electric central stations 774,241 h.p., so that the total water-power used in the pulp and paper industry was 1,302,972 h.p. Of this 1,016,961 was utilized by first converting it to hydro-electric energy for the more convenient electric motor drive, and only 286,011 was used to drive the mill equipment directly from turbines.[3]

The amount of power required to produce a given unit of product expressed in value is proportionately high in the pulp and paper industry. It takes about 100 h.p. to make a ton of paper per day. Canada's advantageous situation as manifested in her combination of cheap power with

---

[1] Ibid.

[2] *Water Power in the Mining Industry of Canada*, Department of the Interior, Ottawa, 1924 (*North America : Pamphlets*, No. 31, in D.O. and C.O. Library).

[3] *Water Power Resources of Canada*, Department of the Interior : Dominion Water Power and Reclamation Service (*North America : Pamphlets*, No. 48, in D.O. and C.O. Library).

abundant raw material sufficiently accounts for her commanding position in the industry.

In order fully to realize the importance of water-power as a factor in Canadian economic development it is necessary to remember that the absence of coal in Ontario and Quebec constituted a difficulty which had attained the dimensions of a national problem and stamped those provinces with the unenviable designation of the Acute Fuel Area. It was a national problem for the reason that Ontario and Quebec between them contain over 60 per cent of the total population of the Dominion and produce nearly 80 per cent of the total value of the manufacturing output. The region was designated the Acute Fuel Area because the two Provinces use over 55 per cent of the total coal consumed in the Dominion and 92 per cent of that consumption is of coal imported from the United States.[1]

Those concerned with the solution of the problem would have to consider three factors, that is to say, native coal, imported coal, and water-power. The first was out of the question. The cost of transport, especially to the industrial region of Ontario, made it prohibitive.[2] Vast quantities of coal have always been imported into Canada from the United States,[3] but it was not a desirable state of things and certainly not in harmony with a national policy that a coal strike in Pennsylvania and Ohio should be able to bring to a standstill most of the social, business and industrial life of the Dominion. In these circumstances it was small wonder that resort was had to the native water-power so abundantly available.

Comparative figures for 1910 and 1926 for Canada as a whole indicate that the country was justified in relying on water-power to solve its fuel difficulties.

In 1910 the total coal production in Canada was 12,909,152 tons. In 1926 it was 16,478,131 tons, an increase in the period of 28 per cent. Native coal accordingly did but little to meet the growing demands of industry and to solve the fuel problem.

In 1910 the hydraulic horse-power installed in all Canada was 975,150. In 1926 it was 4,556,266, an increase in the period of 367 per cent.

[1] These figures are in respect of 1925.

[2] In 1925 Ontario imported 11¼ million tons from the United States and received from other Canadian provinces only 32,700 tons.

[3] In 1925 the import of coal into Canada from the United States was 16¼ million tons.

To understand the significance of these figures in terms of coal alone, it is necessary to resort to a common denominator. The Water-Power Branch of the Department of the Interior has arrived at the conclusion that 1 h.p. of a hydro-electric installation is represented by an annual consumption of 9 tons of coal.[1] The coal equivalent of the installed hydraulic turbine horse-power for 1910 would accordingly have been 8,776,350 tons and for 1926 it would have been 41,006,394 tons. Purchased in the United States that quantity of coal would have cost many millions of dollars. Those millions of dollars have instead remained in the Dominion and may be regarded as the value to Canada of her own water-power. Had that water-power not been available, so that resort to imported coal would have been necessary, it is certain that industrial development in Ontario and Quebec would have been very considerably slower. Being abundantly available as the primary power for industrial purposes as well as cheap, water-power puts Canada in an obviously advantageous position as an industrial country.

[1] *The Utilization of Water Power in Canada in relation to Coal Production, Importation and Consumption*, Department of the Interior, Ottawa, 1924 (*North America : Pamphlets*, No. 29, in D.O. & C.O. Library).

EPILOGUE

MORE goes to the making of a nation than the construction of a political organization and a judiciary. These are but the skeleton of the organism of which agriculture is the flesh, trade the life-blood, railways and shipping routes the nerves, and minerals, forests and other natural products the nutriment. Much has been written about the political development of Canada. Our purpose has been to explore the less frequented but assuredly not less attractive paths of economic history; our task to discover which are the main routes and whither they lead.

It is a history that begins with a country almost empty of population, so that those who entered and took possession of the land were able to fashion it at will. We have seen the invading forces of civilization and economic development start from widely separated bases, from the Maritime Provinces and from Vancouver, from the St. Lawrence and from the Red River, each gradually radiating outwards until they coalesce and the country is a completely organized economic and political unit, the whole bound together by the steel rails of the transcontinental railways. We have seen how in the first thirty years of the nineteenth century the Maritime Provinces were the most important part of British North America with their fishing, their shipbuilding, their lumber industry, and their West Indian trade. Settlement moves inland and gradually Ontario dwarfs the importance of the Atlantic seaboard. It is a British plantation in an American sphere of influence. Isolated, self-contained, it is at first a Province of small farmers. Then it becomes the chief lumber province and later develops into the Dominion's first industrial region. From the different starting points, mere patches of civilization, where the population clung to the waterways which were the only means of communication for individuals, the only channels along which commerce could flow, we have seen the Canadian people pushing out into the Prairies of the North-West and transforming them into the granary of the Empire; penetrating the forbidding regions of the Canadian Shield and bringing to light their fabulous mineral wealth;

spreading, though thinly, over the region of the Cordilleras, some to grow fruit in the gentle climate of British Columbia, others to battle with the elements for gold amid the rigours of the Yukon.

Having seen the new territories opened up and population installed there, we have watched the new nation as it settled down to consolidate its gains by the exploitation of its resources and we have found the main streams of economic development to be agriculture, mining and the exploitation of the forests, and an industrial State, based on water-power, comes into view.

We have seen a great State starting on its career the possessor of the land, the minerals, the forests, the water-power and all the other natural resources of economic value. We have been able to see in what circumstances a Government alienated into private possession or retained as public property those different aspects of natural wealth. We have seen the Dominion become the possessor of the greatest State-owned railway system in the world, and a Province the possessor of the greatest electric undertaking, not in fulfilment of any programme of Socialistic reconstruction but by sheer force of circumstances. It has been our task to try to identify and to understand these circumstances.

Following the process of change since the picturesque days of the Indian and the buffalo, the *coureur de bois* and the lonely trapper, one cannot but be struck by the generally peaceful manner in which that change has been brought about. There was a little blood-letting on the Red River, but the struggle was as nothing when compared with the constant struggle with the forces of nature in which the early settlers were involved, a struggle which left them little time or energy for quarrels among themselves. Even the Indians have been induced to make way for their successors in the possession of the land without resort to violent methods and without the accompaniment of the horrors of Indian warfare such as characterized their dispossession south of the international boundary.

But conflicts of interests there were bound to be. There were collisions between the opposing political forces as represented by the Hudson's Bay Company and those who demanded representative government. But the company of traders recognized the inevitableness of the change and peacefully surrendered their political powers, satisfied to be allowed to develop the trading side of their organization in their own way. Then there were the colliding interests of the fur traders and the farmer, between the rover and the true settler, which had to be reconciled. The result was inevitable, and fur had to yield place to agriculture. The conflict of interests between East and West seems likely to occupy the attention of politicians for many a year.

More serious was the struggle against the forces of nature which has been constant but which had to be won before the economic conquest of the country was accomplished. The paralysis caused by the winter freezing of the waterways was circumvented by the building of the railways. In some instances the enemy was subdued and turned into an ally rather than destroyed. In the lives of the early settlers the forests and the rapids constituted a background of terror. Both have been tamed and subdued to the purposes of man. The forest was an obstacle in the way of agricultural settlement, an implacable enemy that had to be ruthlessly destroyed with fire and axe. Only in the lumber camps did the early farmer look a little less unkindly on the thick growth of spruce and balsam and poplar and jackpine, for there he found a market for his produce and a means of livelihood while waiting for his own crops to yield returns. Now, as the raw material of a great industry, the manufacture of woodpulp and paper, the forest is seen to be a great national asset and the main concern is how to preserve it from destruction. So with the rapids. They were the breaks in the chain of communications on which the country depended before the days of railways. Now they are envisaged as water-power, doing for Canada what coal did for the Mother Country.

The people who have survived the struggle cannot be a lotus-eating race. The Dominion has provided the opportunity for the exercise of the best of every aspect of human character and effort. The capitalist and the engineer were never allied in a better cause than when between them they accomplished the miracle of the Canadian Pacific Railway. The hydraulic engineer and the electrician came to grips with the rapids, subdued them, and made them the driving force of new industries. The agricultural scientist was able to devote himself to the cross-breeding of wheat so that it would flourish further and further north, every degree in its northward progress marking great accessions to the food supply of the world. The entomologist declared war on the insect pests that were the deadly enemies of the trees. The mineral ores of Ontario and Quebec and British Columbia provide problems for the metallurgist for many years to come. Nowhere else is there such scope for the working out of the conception of an organized agriculture based on science. Nor is the politician and the administrator denied his opportunity of sharing in the good work. In some directions the resources of the nation have been dissipated in spendthrift fashion. The practice of wheat " mining " has used up the fertility of great tracts of the finest soil in the world ; and how to substitute mixed farming and the rotation of crops is an urgent problem. We have seen how vast a toll is taken of the forests by fires, the result of human agency, and how frantic efforts have had to be made to conserve what remains.

Following the getting of the raw material, there naturally comes the desire to fashion it into the finished article. All the omens are that the Dominion is destined to become a great manufacturing nation. The raw materials, the means of transport to the coast, connexion with foreign markets are now all there, and just as the Mother Country built up her industrial supremacy on a basis of coal and steam, so Canada, as capital becomes available, is building up industries based on water-power and electricity, with the advantage over the Mother Country that her motive power, unlike coal, is inexhaustible and its exploitation infinitely cheaper.

The story of her economic development and the realization of the stage at which that development has arrived make manifest how fitting it is that Canada should be given a prominent place at the Conference table when the nations of the British Empire meet to discuss their domestic concerns, as also when the nations of the world assemble to consider the even larger issues of world politics. Elsewhere the margin of food and minerals available for export after the home demands have been satisfied is tending to diminish. Canada's exports of food products are an ever increasing quantity. Both for purposes of peace and war our civilization tends more and more to be based on minerals. The Dominion's infinite resources in metals and their great variety constitute a trust to be administered in the interests of the arts of peace throughout the world ; and her power of withholding them from those who would use them in the service of war make her one of the guarantors of lasting peace.

BIBLIOGRAPHY

CANADA

(1) General Description

Annual Reports of the Dominion Department of Agriculture.
Annual Reports of the Dominion Department of the Interior.
Annual Reports of the Dominion Department of Immigration and Colonization.
BRADLEY, A. G. *Canada* (Home University Library), 1912.
—— *Canada in the Twentieth Century*, 1903.
BUCHAN, J. (editor). *British America*, (Nations of To-day Series), 1923.
Canada Year Book (called Statistical Abstract and Record of Canada, 1886–8, *Statistical Year Book of Canada*, 1889–1904), 1905.—
Conservation Commission. Many reports on varied subjects. 1910.—
Dominions Royal Commission. Evidence taken in Maritime Canada, 1914–16. *Cd.* 7971.
—— Fifth Interim Report (Canada), 1917–18. *Cd.* 8457.
—— Evidence taken in Central and Western Canada, 1917–18. *Cd.* 8458. *Cd.* 8459.
GRAY, H. *Letters from Canada, showing the Present State of Canada, its Productions, Trade, Commercial Importance, and Political Relations,* 1809.
GRIFFITH, W. L. *The Dominion of Canada* (The All Red Series), 1911.
HAIGHT, C. *Life in Canada Fifty Years Ago*, 1885.
HERBERTSON, A. J., and HOWARTH, O. J. R. *Oxford Survey of the British Empire*, vol. iv. America, 1914.
HERIOT, G. *Travels through the Canadas, with an Account of the Productions Commerce and Inhabitants of those Provinces*, 1807.
JAMESON, MRS. *Sketches in Canada*, 1852.
—— *Winter Studies and Summer Rambles*, 2 vols.
KENNEDY, W. P. M. (editor). "Social and Economic Conditions in the Dominion of Canada," *Annals of American Academy of Political and Social Science*, vol. cvii, May, 1923.
LUCAS, SIR C. P. *Lord Durham's Report on the Affairs of British North America*, 3 vols., 1912.
MACTAGGART, J. *Three Years in Canada : An Account of the Actual State of the Country in 1826–8*, 1829.
MURRAY, H. *An Historical and Descriptive Account of British America*, 3 vols., 1839.
PARKIN, G. R. *The Great Dominion : Studies of Canada*, 1895.
SHIRREFF, P. *A Tour through North America, together with a Comprehensive View of the Canadas and United States, as adapted for Agricultural Emigration*, 1835.
SIEGFRIED, A. *The Race Question in Canada*, 1907.
STEVENSON, D. *Sketch of Civil Engineering of North America*, 1838.
WELD, I. *Travels through the States of North America and the Provinces of Upper and Lower Canada during the Years 1795, 1796 and 1797*, 2 vols., 1800.

(2) General History

DENT, J. C. *The Last Fifty Years : Canada since the Union of* 1841, 2 vols., 1881.
GALT, A. T. *Canada, 1849 to 1859*, 1860.

589

GODFREY, E. H. "Fifty Years of Canadian Progress, 1867–1917," in *Canada Year Book*, pp. 23–72, 1918.

HOPKINS, J. C. (editor). *Canadian Annual Review of Public Affairs*, 1902 *onwards*, 1903—

LUCAS, SIR C. P. *Historical Geography of the British Colonies*, vol. v : Canada (in 4 parts), 1908–16.

—— *History of Canada*, 1763–1812, 1909.

MORGAN, H. J. *Dominion Annual Register and Review*, 8 vols, 1878–86.

POPE, SIR J. *Memoirs of Sir John A. Macdonald*, 2 vols., 1894.

Proceedings and Transactions of the Royal Society of Canada, 1882—

SHORTT, A., and DOUGHTY, A. G. *Canada and its Provinces*, 23 vols., 1913–17 (with voluminous bibliography in vol. xxiii).

—— *Documents relating to the Constitutional History of Canada*, 1759–91, 1907.

SKELTON, O. D. *Life and Letters of Sir Wilfrid Laurier*, 1921.

—— *Life and Times of Sir A. T. Galt*, 1920.

SMITH, W. *History of the Post Office in British North America*, 1639–1870, 1920.

TROTTER, R. G. *Canadian Federation*, 1924.

TUPPER, SIR C. *Recollections of Sixty Years*, 1914.

WILLSON, B. *Life of Lord Strathcona*, 1915.

(3) THE PROVINCES

ALSTON, E. G. "Colonial Handbook to British Columbia," 1870, *Canada : Pamphlets*, at D.O. and C.O. Library, vol. iii, No. 66.

BANCROFT, H. H. *History of British Columbia*, 2 vols., 1890.

—— *History of the North-West Coast*, 2 vols., 1884.

—— *History of Oregon*, 2 vols., 1888.

BEGG, A. *History of British Columbia*, 1894.

—— *History of the North-West*, 3 vols., 1894–5.

BONNYCASTLE, SIR R. H. *The Canadas in 1841*, 2 vols., 1842.

—— *Canada and the Canadians in 1846*, 2 vols., 1846.

BRACQ, J. C. *Evolution of French Canada*, 1924.

BROWN, R. C. L. *Essay on British Columbia*, 1862.

CAMPBELL, D. *Nova Scotia in its Historical, Mercantile and Industrial Relations*, 1873.

CANNIFF, W. D. *History of the Settlement of Upper Canada*, 1869.

CLARKE, J. M. *The Heart of Gaspé*, 1913.

COONEY, —. *Compendious History of New Brunswick*, 1839.

GANONG, W. F. "Contributions to the History of New Brunswick," Nos. 1–6, *Transactions of the Royal Society of Canada*, 1895–1904.

GESNER, A. *New Brunswick, with Notes for Immigrants*, 1847.

HALIBURTON, T. C. *An Historical and Statistical Account of Nova Scotia*, 2 vols., 1829.

HARGRAVE, J. J. *Red River*, 1871.

HOWISON, J. *Sketches of Upper Canada, Domestic, Local and Characteristic, to which are added Practical Details for the Information of Emigrants of Every Class*, 1822.

JOHNSTON, J. F. W. *Report on the Agricultural Capabilities of the Province of New Brunswick*, 1850.

—— *Notes on North America, Agricultural, Economical and Social*, 2 vols., 1881.

LONGSTRETH, T. M. *The Silent Force*, 1927.

MACOUN, J. *Manitoba and the Great North-West*, 1883 (second edition).

McGREGOR, J. *Historical and Descriptive Sketches of the Maritime Colonies of British North America*, 1828.

MEARES, J. *Voyages made in the Years 1788 and 1789 from China to the North-West Coast of America*, 1790.

MONRO, A. *New Brunswick, with a brief Outline of Nova Scotia and Prince Edward Island, Their History, Civil Divisions, Geography and Productions*, 1855.

MOODIE, Mrs. S. *Roughing it in the Bush : or Life in Canada*, 2 vols., 1852.
MOORSOM, W. S. *Letters from Nova Scotia*, 1830.
MURDOCH, B. *History of Nova Scotia, or Acadie*, 3 vols., 1867.
Report of the Royal Commission on Maritime Claims, 1926.
ROSS, A. *Red River Settlement*, 1856.
" Yukon District of Canada, 1897," *Canada : Pamphlets*, at D.O. and C.O. Library, No. 118.

(4) THE TRADING COMPANIES

WILLSON, B. *The Great Company (a history of the Hudson Bay Company)*, 2 vols, 1900.
SELKIRK, LORD. *Sketch of the British Fur Trade in North America, with Observations relative to the North-West Company of Montreal*, 1816.
SCHOOLING, SIR W. *Hudson's Bay Company*, 1670–1920, 1920.
ROSS, A. *Fur Traders of the Far West*, 2 vols., 1855.
Report from the Committee appointed to inquire into the State and Condition of the Countries adjoining to Hudson's Bay, and of the Trade carried on there, 1749.
Report from the Select Committee on the Hudson's Bay Company, *Parliamentary Papers*, 1857 (Sess. 2), xv, 1.
On the Origin and Progress of the North-West Company of Canada, with a History of the Fur Trade as connected with that concern, 1811.
MASSON, L. F. R. *Les Bourgeois de la Compagnie du Nord-Ouest*, 2 vols., 1889–90.
MACKENZIE, SIR A. *General History of the Fur Trade from Canada to the North-West*, 1801.
DAVIDSON, G. C. *The North-West Company. University of California Publications in History*, vol. vii, 1918.
BRYCE, REV. GEO. *Remarkable History of the Hudson's Bay Company*, 1900.
MOBERLEY, H. J., and CAMERON, W.B. *When Fur was King*, 1929.

(5) TRANSPORT

BOWEN, F. C. *History of the Canadian Pacific Line*, 1928.
CROIL, J. *Steam Navigation and its Relation to the Commerce of Canada and the United States*, 1898.
DOBSON, G. H. *Modern Transportion and Atlantic Express Tracks*, 1899.
FLEMING, SANDFORD. *The Intercolonial : a Historical Sketch*, 1876.
FRY, H. *History of North Atlantic Steam Navigation*, 1896.
GRANT, G. M. *Ocean to Ocean*, 1925.
INNIS, H. A. *History of the Canadian Pacific Railway*, 1923.
KEEFER, T. C. *Canals of Canada : Their Prospects and Influence*, 1850.
MCLEAN, S. J. " Report on Rate Grievances on Canadian Railways," *Sess. Papers*, 1902, No. 20a.
PALMER, F. *Report on the Selection of a Terminal Port for the Hudson Bay Railway*, 1927.
Report of the Railway Rates Commission, *Sess. Papers*, 1895, No. 39.
Report of the Royal Commission to inquire into Railways and Transportation in Canada, 1917, *Sess. Papers, 20g*, vol. xii.
SKELTON, O. D. *The Railway-Builders*, 1916.
TALBOT, F. A. *The Making of a Great Canadian Railway : the Story of the Grand Trunk Pacific*, 1912.

(6) TRADE AND TARIFFS

ALLIN, C. D. and JONES, G. M. *Annexation, Preferential Trade and Reciprocity*, 1911.
ANDREWS, I. D. *Report on the Trade and Commerce of the British North American Colonies, and upon the Trade of the Great Lakes and Rivers*, 1854.
BEMIS, S. F. *Jay's Treaty*, 1923.
BLISS, H. *On Colonial Intercourse*, 1830.

BUCHANAN, I. *The Relations of the Industry of Canada with the Mother Country and the United States* (edited by H. J. Morgan), 1864.

Correspondence on the Removal or Reduction of the Duties charged on British Goods entering Canada, *Parly. Papers*, 1864, xli.

CORWIN, T. *Report on the Trade and Commerce of the British North American Colonies with the United States and other Countries* (Washington), 1851.

FIELD, F. W., and BEALE, L. B. *Report on the Trade of Canada and Newfoundland for the year* 1919 [*Cmd.* 720], 1920.

GOULD, N. *Sketches of the Trade of British America*, 1833.

PORRITT, E. *Sixty Years of Protection in Canada*, 1908.

Report of the Royal Commission on Trade Relations between Canada and the West Indies, 1910 [*Cd.* 5369].

SHEFFIELD, LORD. *Observations on the Commerce of the American States*, 1784.

SKELTON, O. D. "Canada and the Most Favoured Nation Treaties," *Queen's University Bulletin of the Departments of History and of Political and Economic Science*, No. 2, 1911.

(7) IMMIGRATION AND SETTLEMENT

A Statement of the Satisfactory Results which have attended Emigration to Upper Canada from the Establishment of the Canada Company until the Present Period, 1841. B.M., 8154, aaa, 50.

Advantages of Emigrating to the British Colonies of New Brunswick, Nova Scotia, etc., etc., by a Resident of St. John's, New Brunswick, 1832, B.M.: T, 1410 (6).

CARRUTHERS, W. A. *Emigration from the British Isles*, 1929.

CASSELL, J. *The Emigrant's Handbook*, 1852, B.M. 10002, c, 26.

Colonial Office: Papers and Despatches relative to Emigration to the North American Colonies, 1847–62.

COWAN, HELEN I. "British Emigration to British North America, 1783–1837," *University of Toronto Studies*, History and Economics, vol. iv, No. 2, 1928.

COYNE, J. H. *The Talbot Papers*, 1907.

ERMATINGER, C. O. *The Talbot Régime, or the First Half Century of the Talbot Settlement*, 1904.

GALT, J. *Autobiography*, 2 vols., 1833.

GOURLAY, R. F. *Statistical Account of Upper Canada. Compiled with a View to a Grand System of Emigration*, 2 vols., 1822.

Hints and Observations on the Disadvantages of Emigration to British America, by an Emigrant, 1833. B.M. 8275, aa, 1 (3).

JOHNSON, S. C. *History of Emigration from the United Kingdom to North America, 1763–1912*, 1913.

Lands in Canada West to be disposed of by the Canada Company, 1844. B.M. 1880, c, 1 (152).

MARTIN, CHESTER. *Lord Selkirk's Work in Canada*, 1916.

Remarks on the Earl of Selkirk's *On the Present State of the Highlands of Scotland*, etc., 1806.

Report of Royal Commission on Chinese and Japanese Immigration 1902, *Sessional Papers*, No. 54.

Report of the Royal Commission to Inquire into Methods by which Oriental labourers have been induced to come to Canada, 1908, *Sess. Papers*.

SELKIRK, LORD. *Observations on the Present State of the Highlands of Scotland with a View of the Causes and Probable Consequences of Emigration*, 1806.

SMITH, W. G. *Study in Canadian Immigration*, 1920.

STRICKLAND, S. *Twenty-Seven Years in Canada West, or the Experience of an Early Settler*, 2 vols, 1853.

WALLACE, W. S. *The United Empire Loyalists*, 1914.

(8) AGRICULTURE

BULLER, A. H. R. *Essays on Wheat*, 1919.
CLARK, W. C. " The County Elevator in the Canadian West," in the *Queen's Quarterly*, 1916–17, vol. xxiv, pp. 46–68.
EVANS, W. S. *The Canadian Wheat Pool*, 1926.
FAY, C. R. *Agricultural Co-operation in the Canadian West*, 1925.
HAMMATT, T. D. " Marketing Canadian Wheat," *United States Department of Commerce : Trade Information Bul.* 251, 1924.
MACGIBBON, D. A. *Traffic Routes for Canadian Grain*, 1926.
MACKINTOSH, W. A. " Agricultural Co-operation in Western Canada," *Queen's University Studies*, No. 2, 1924.
—— " The Canadian Wheat Pools," *Queen's University Department of History, etc., Bulletin* No. 51, 1925.
MAGILL, R. *International Grain Marketing*, 1926.
MAVOR, J. " Report to the Board of Trade on the North-West of Canada" [*Cd.* 2628], 1904.
—— *My Windows on the Street of the World*, 2 vols., 1923.
MORMAN, J. B., *Farm Credits in the United States and Canada*. 1924.
PATTON, H. S. " Grain-Growers' Co-opera ion in Western Canada," *Harvard Economic Studies*, No. 32, 1928 (with exhaustive bibliography).
PIPER, C. B. *Principles of the Grain Trade of Western Canada*, 1917 (second edition).
PORRITT, E. " Canada's National Grain Route," in the *Political Science Quarterly*, 1918, vol. xxxiii, pp. 344–77.
Report of the Royal Commission on Shipment and Transportation of Grain in Manitoba and the North-West Territories, 1899–1900, *Sess. Papers*, 1900, No. 81–81b.
Report of the Royal Commission on the Grain Trade, 1906–7, *Sess. Papers*, 1907, No. 59.
Report of the Royal Grain Inquiry Commission, 1923–4, *Sess. Papers*, 1925, No. 35.
Report on Agricultural Credit by H. M. Tory, 1924, *Sess. Papers*, 1924, No. 142.
Proceedings of the Special Committee to inquire into Agricultural Conditions, 1923, *Appendix to House of Commons Journals*, vol. lx, 1923, Parts 1 and 2.
REW, SIR R. H. " Economic Resources of Canada in relation to Britain's Food Supply," *Board of Agriculture and Fisheries Economic Series*, No. 3, 1924.
RUTTER, W. P. *Wheat Growing in Canada, the United States and the Argentine*, 1911.
WOOD, L. A. *Farmers' Movements in Canada*, 1924.

(9) OTHER INDUSTRIES

WALLACE, F. W. *Wooden Ships and Iron Men*, 1924.
Report of the Royal Commission on Pulpwood, 1924.
Reports on Timber Duties, *Parly. Papers*, 1820, iii, 381 ; 1821, vi, 1 ; 1835, xix.
REDMAYNE, J. S. " Fruit Farming on the Dry Belt of British Columbia," 1909, *North America Pamphlets*, at D.O. and C.O. Library, No. 10.
RANKIN, J. *A History of our Firm*, 1921.
" Mines and Mineral Resources of Ontario," 1924, *Canada Pamphlets* at D.O. and C.O. Library, No. 248.
Mineral Wealth of Canada, published by the Canadian Bank of Commerce, 1927.
MCLENNEN, J. C. " Industrial Research in Canada," 1916, *Canada Pamphlets*, at D.O. and C.O. Library, vol. x, No. 272.
KELLOGG, R. S. *Pulp Wood and Wood Pulp in North America*, 1923.
DONALD, W. J. A. *The Canadian Iron and Steel Industry*, 1915.

APPENDIX

BIBLIOGRAPHY OF VOLUME I

(The Empire as a Whole. The British Tropics).

EMPIRE

(1) GENERAL DESCRIPTION

Annual Colonial Reports for respective Colonies.
Dominions Office and Colonial Office List (Foreign Office List for " Sudan ").
Reports on Colonial Sections of the Colonial and India Exhibition, 1887.
Reports of the Colonial and (later) the Imperial Conferences, 1887, 1894, 1897, 1902, 1907, 1911, 1917, 1921, 1923, 1926, in *Parly. Papers*.
Statistical Abstract for the several British Colonies, Possessions and Protectorates, and Statistical Tables relating to British Colonies, Possessions and Protectorates, in *Parly. Papers*.
ASHLEY, W. J. (editor). *The British Dominions*, 1911.
GUNN, H. (editor). *The British Empire : A Survey*, 12 vols, 1924.
HERBERTSON, A. J., and HOWARTH, O. J. R. *Oxford Survey of the British Empire*, 6 vols., 1914.
MacCULLOCH, J. R. *Dictionary of Commerce*, 1832–9 (many later editions).
MARTIN, R. M. *Statistics of the Colonies of the British Empire*, 1839 and 1847.
—— *The British Colonies, their history, condition and resources*, 12 vols., ? 1850.
PORTER, G. R. *Progress of the Nation*, 1847, 1912 (new edition revised by F. W. Hirst).
Journal of the Royal Society of Arts (especially under the Colonial and Dominions Section).
Proceedings of the Royal Colonial Institute (now the Royal Empire Society), later called *The United Empire*, 1869—
The Round Table (a quarterly dealing with Imperial matters), 1910—

(2) HISTORY

Cambridge History of the British Empire (edited by Newton, A. P., Rose, J. H., and Benians, E. A.), 8 vols., 1929—
Cambridge Modern History, chapters dealing with the British Empire, 1902–11.
LUCAS, SIR C. P. *The British Empire*, 1915.
—— *Greater Rome and Greater Britain*, 1912.
—— *The Partition and Colonization of Africa*, 1922.
—— *Historical Geography of the British Colonies* (many vols., different editions).
OLDMIXON, J. *British Empire in America*, 2 vols., 1708.
JOHNSTON, SIR H. H. *The Opening Up of Africa*, 1911.
WOOLF, L. *Empire and Commerce in Africa*, 1920.

(3) IMPERIAL POLICY

BEER, G. L. *Origins of the British Colonial System*, 1908 and 1922.
—— *The Old Colonial System*, 1660–1754, 2 vols., 1913.
—— *British Colonial Policy*, 1754–65, 1922.
BOYD, C. W. *Speeches of Joseph Chamberlain*, 1914.

EGERTON, H. E. *Short History of British Colonial Policy*, 1910.
—— *British Colonial Policy in the Twentieth Century*, 1922.
KEITH, A. B. *Responsible Government in the Dominions*, 2 vols. (new edition), 1928.
LUGARD, SIR F. D. (now LORD). *Dual Mandate in British Tropical Africa*, 1922.
MILNER, LORD. *The Nation and the Empire*, 1913.
BRUCE, SIR C. *Broadstone of Empire*, 2 vols., 1910.
IRELAND, A. *Tropical Colonization*.
—— *The Far Eastern Tropics*.
—— *Colonial Administration in the Far East*.

(4) MIGRATION

Select Committee appointed to consider the subject of Emigration from the United Kingdom, Second Report, *Parly. Papers*, 1826–7, v, 2 : Third Report, *Parly. Papers*, 1826–7, v, 223.
Report on the Survey of the Coasts of Scotland, etc., relating to Emigration, *Parly. Papers*, 1802–3, iv.
Report of the Overseas Settlement Committee, 1919, *Cmd.* 573.
Report from the Select Committee appointed to inquire into the expediency of encouraging Emigration from the United Kingdom, *Parly. Papers*, 1826, iv, 1.
Reports from Select Committee appointed to inquire into the system of Transportation, its efficacy as a punishment, its influence on the moral state of society in the penal colonies, and how far it is susceptible of improvement, *Parly. Papers*, 1837, xix, 1 ; 1837–8, xxii, 1.
Reports on the Emigration of Artizans, *Parly. Papers*, 1824, v, 1, 49, 91, 183, 335, 589.
Report on Agricultural Settlements in British Colonies, 1906, *Cd.* 2978.
JOHNSTON, SIR H. H. *History of the Colonization of Africa by Alien Races*, 1899.
CAMPBELL, P. C. "Chinese Coolie Emigration within the Empire," *London School of Economics and Political Science Studies*, No. 72, 1923.

(5) TRADE AND TARIFFS

Interim Report of Balfour Committee, Survey of Overseas Markets, 1925.
Reports for the Department of Overseas Trade (usually called *D.O.T. Reports*), 1917.—
Dominions Royal Commission (on Migration, Natural Resources, Trade and Legislation), *Cd.* 6515–7, 7210, 7505, 7170–3, 7351, 7706–7, 7710–1, 7898, 7971, 8123, 8156, 8457–62 : 1912–18.
SARGENT, A. J. *Seaways of the Empire*, 1918.
NEWTON, A. P. (editor). *Staple Trades of the Empire*, 1918.
PAGE, W. *Commerce and Industry* (1815–1914), 2 vols., 1919.
Report of the Balfour of Burleigh Committee on Commercial and Industrial Policy after the War, *Cd.* 9035, 1918.
Return of the Differential Duties in favour of Colonies, 1823–60, *Cd.* 2394, 1905.
United States Tariff Commission, *Report on Colonial Tariff Policies*, 1922.
—— *Report on Reciprocity and Commercial Treaties*, 1919.
PORRITT, E. *Fiscal and Diplomatic Freedom of the British Overseas Dominions*, 1922.
TAZEWELL, L. W. *Review of the Negotiations between the United States of America and Great Britain respecting Commerce*, *1829*, B.M.: T, 1251 (9).
PAISH, G. "Great Britain's Capital Investments in Individual Colonial and Foreign Countries," *Journal of Royal Statistical Society*, vol. lxxiv, pp. 167–200.
JENKS, L. H. *Migration of British Capital to 1875*, 1927.
DRAGE, SIR G. *Imperial Organization of Trade*, 1911.
CHALMERS, R. *History of Currency in the British Colonies* (1894).

INDIA

(1) General Description

Statistical Abstract of British India over Decennial Periods, issued annually.
Report on the Moral and Material Progress and Condition of India, published
annually, 1862.—
HERBERTSON, A. J., and HOWARTH, O. J. R. *Oxford Survey of the British
Empire,* vol. ii, Asia, 1914.
LUCAS, SIR C. P. (editor). *Historical Geography of the British Colonies,*
vol. vii, India (in 2 parts), 1916–20.
Imperial Gazeteer of India, 26 vols. (especially vol. iii), 1907–8.
Indian Annual Register (edited by H. N. Mitra), Calcutta.
Indian Year Book (edited by S.r S. Reed), Bombay.
D.O.T. Report on India, 1919, *Cmd.* 442.
PILLAI, P. P. *Economic Conditions in India,* 1925.
LYALL, SIR A. C. *Asiatic Studies* (two series), 1882–9.
FULLER, SIR J. B. *Studies of Indian Life and Sentiment,* 1910.
HOLDERNESS, SIR T. W. *Peoples and Problems of India* (Home University
Library), 1912, 1920.
HUNTER, SIR W. W. *India of the Queen,* 1903.
HUNTER, SIR W. W. (editor). *Rulers of India,* 27 vols., 1890–9.
CURZON, LORD. *The Place of India in the Empire,* 1909.
CHIROL, SIR V. *India,* Modern World Series, 1926.
Cambridge History of India (edited by Rapson, E. J., Morison, Sir T., and
others), 6 vols., 1922.—
WATT, SIR G. *Dictionary of the Economic Products of India,* 6 vols, 1889–96.
ANSTEY, V. *Economic Development of India,* 1929.

(2) Administration

Montagu–Chelmsford Report on Indian Constitutional Reforms, *Cd.*
9109, 1918.
LOVETT, SIR H. V. *History of the Indian Nationalist Movement,* 1920.
AGA KHAN. *India in Transition,* 1918.
STRACHEY, SIR J. *India, its Administration and Progress,* 1911 (new
edition by Sir T. W. Holderness).
FRASER, LOVAT. *India under Curzon and After,* 1911.
RAGHAVAIYANGAR, S. S. *Memorandum on Forty Years' Progress in Madras
Presidency,* 1893.
ARNOLD, SIR E. *Marquis of Dalhousie's Administration of British India,*
2 vols., 1862–5.
DUTT, R. C. *Economic History of British India,* 1757–1837, 1906.
—— *Economic History of India in the Victorian Age,* 1906. ,
HUNTER, Sir W. W. *History of British India,* 2 vols., 1899–1900.
MESTON (LORD). *India at the Crossways,* Rede Lecture at Cambridge, 1920.
LYALL, SIR C. J. " Province of Assam," *Journal of the Royal Society of
Arts,* vol. 1, pp. 612–36, 1903.
MORELAND, W. H. *India at the Death of Akbar,* 1920.
—— *From Akbar to Aurangzeb,* 1923.
MORISON, SIR T. *India in Transition,* 1911.
—— *Economic Organization of an Indian Province,* 1906.
—— *Imperial Rule in India,* 1899.
ROBERTS, LORD. *Forty-One Years in India,* 2 vols., 1897.
RONALDSHAY, LORD (now Zetland, Marquis of). *Life of Lord Curzon,*
3 vols., 1928.
Memorandum on Results of Indian Administration during past 30 years
of British Rule, *C.* 5713, 1889.
Memorandum on the Results of Indian Administration in the past 50
Years, *Cd.* 4956 (continuation of *C.* 5713), 1909.
MILL, J. S. " Memorandum of the Improvements in the Administration
of India during the last 30 Years," 1858.

(3) ECONOMIC POLICY

LOVEDAY, A. *History and Economics of Indian Famines*, 1914.
LEES SMITH, H. B. *India and the Tariff Problem*, 1909.
Report of the Indian Fiscal Commission, 1922, *Cmd*. 1764.
BANERJEA, P. *Fiscal Policy in India*, 1923.
STRACHEY, J. and R. *Finance and Public Works of India*, 1882.
Report of Select Committee on Public Works, *Parly. Papers*, 1878, xii; 1878–9, ix.
Report of the Indian Irrigation Commission, 1901–3, 1904, *Cd*. 1851–4.
CONNELL, A. K. *Economic Revolution of India and the Public Works Policy*, 1883.
BUCKLEY, R. B. *Irrigation Works of India*, 1905.

(4) AGRICULTURE

Report of the Royal Commission on Agriculture in India, 1928 (Final Report), *Cmd*. 3132.
Papers regarding the Land Revenue System of British India, *Cd*. 1089, 1902.
KEATINGE, G. F. *Rural Economy in the Bombay Deccan*, 1912.
—— *Agricultural Progress in Western India*, 1921.
JACK, J. C. *Economic Life of a Bengal District*, 1916.
BADEN-POWELL, B. H. *Short Account of the Land Revenue and its Administration in British India, with a sketch of land tenures*, 1912 (revised by Holderness, Sir T. W.).
THORBURN, S. S. *Report on Peasant Indebtedness in Punjab*, 1896.
CALVERT, H. *Wealth and Welfare of Punjab*, 1922.
NICHOLSON, SIR, F. *Report on the Possibility of Introducing Land and Agricultural Banks in Madras Presidency*, 1895.
MORELAND, W. H. *Agriculture in the United Provinces*, 1912.
Report of the Committee on the Establishment of Co-operative Credit Societies in India, 1903, *Cd*. 1747.
CLAYTON, H. *Rural Development in Burma*, 1911.
DARLING, M. L. *Pubjab Peasantry in Prosperity and Debt*, 1928 (second edition).
WOLFF, H. W. *Co-operation in India*, 1919.
EWBANK, R. B. *Indian Co-operative Studies*, University of Bombay, Economic Series No. 2, 1920.

(5) INDUSTRY

Report of the Industrial Commission, 1916–18, *Cmd*. 51, 1919.
Report on Textile Factory Workers, 1907, *Cd*. 3617.
FOLEY, B. *Report on Labour in Bengal*, 1906.
CUMMING, SIR J. G. *Review of the Industrial Position and Prospects of Bengal in* 1908, 1908.
WACHA, SIR D. E. *Life of J. N. Tata*, 1915.
Report of the Indian Factory Labour Commission, 1908, *Cd*. 4292, *Cd*. 4519.
Report of the Indian Factory Commission, *Parly. Papers*, 1890–1, lix.
GUPTA, G. N. *Industries and Resources of Eastern Bengal and Assam*, 1908.
FRASER, LOVAT. *Iron and Steel in India*, 1919.
CHATTERTON, SIR A. *Industrial Evolution in India*, 1912.
KYDD, J. C. *History of Indian Factory Legislation*, 1920.
BURNETT-HURST, A. R. *Labour and Housing in Bombay*, 1925.
GADGIL, D. R. *Industrial Evolution of India in Recent Times*, 1924.
BROUGHTON, G. M. *Labour in Indian Industries*, 1924.

(6) TRANSPORT, TRADE AND CURRENCY

Report on Causes of Delay that has occurred in Railway Construction, *Parly. Papers*, 1857–8, xiv, 161.

Report of the Acworth Commission on Railways, *Cmd.* 1512, 1921.
Report of the Mackay Committee on Railways, *Cd.* 4111, 1908.
JAGTIANI, H. M. *The Rôle of the State in the Provision of Railways*, 1924.
HAMILTON, C. J. *Trade Relations between England and India*, 1600–1896, 1919.
Report of the Committee on Emigration from India, *Cd.* 5192, 1910.
KEYNES, J. M. *Indian Currency and Finance*, 1913.
Report of the Babington-Smith Committee appointed to inquire into Indian Exchange and Currency, 1920, *Cmd.* 527.
Report of the Chamberlain Commission on Finance and Currency, 1914, *Cd.* 7236–9.
DATTA, K. L. *Report of the Inquiry into the Rise of Prices in India*, 5 vols., 1914.

MALAYA

Annual Reports of the Federated Malay States.
Federated Malay States Information Agency Handbook.
HERBERTSON, A. J., and HOWARTH, O. J. R. *Oxford Survey of the British Empire*, vol. li, Asia, 1914.
MILLS, L. A. *British Malaya*, 1824–67, 1926.
SWETTENHAM, SIR F. *British Malaya, An Account of the Origin and Progress of British Influence in Malaya*, 1906.
SYDNEY, R. J. H. *Malay Land*, 1926.
WATSON, SIR M. " Prevention of Malaria in the Federated Malay States," in Ross, Sir R.: *Prevention of Malaria*, pp. 554–62. 1910.
WINSTEDT, R. O. *Malaya*, 1923.

NIGERIA

BURNS, A. C. *History of Nigeria*, 1929.
CLIFFORD, SIR H. *Addresses to the Nigerian Council*, 1920–5.
DUDGEON, G. C. *Agricultural Forest Products of British West Africa*, 1922.
GEARY, SIR W. N. M. *Nigeria under British Rule*, 1927.
HERBERTSON, A. J., and HOWARTH, O. J. R. *Oxford Survey of the British Empire*, vol. iii, Africa, 1914.
LUCAS, SIR C. P. *Historical Geography of the British Colonies*, vol. iii, West Africa (revised by A. B. Keith), 1913.
LUGARD, LADY (formerly Shaw, Flora). *A Tropical Dependency*, 1905.
LUGARD, SIR F. D. (now Lord). " Report on the Amalgamation of Northern and Southern Nigeria," *Cmd.* 468, 1920.
McPHEE, A. *Economic Revolution in British West Africa*, 1926.
Report on a visit to West Africa, by W. G. A. Ormsby-Gore, *Cmd.* 2744, 1926.

KENYA AND UGANDA

BUCHANAN, SIR G. *British East Africa*, 1922.
Correspondence and Further Correspondence relating to Zanzibar, 1886–90.
Reports on Zanzibar, 1893–4, 1894, *Parly. Papers*, 1886, xlvii ; 1887, lix ; 1888, lxxiv ; 1893–4, lxii ; 1895, lxxi.
Despatch relating to Native Labour, *Cmd.* 873, 1920.
ELIOT, SIR C. N. E. *The East African Protectorate*, 1905.
HERBERTSON, A. J., and HOWARTH, O. J. R., *Oxford Survey of the British Empire*, vol. iii, Africa, 1914.
INGRAMS, W. H. *Zanzibar, An Account of its People, Industries, and History*, 1924.
JOHNSTON, SIR H. H. *The Uganda Protectorate*, 2 vols., 1902.
LEYS, N. *Kenya*, 1924.
LUGARD, SIR F. D. *Rise of Our East African Empire*, 2 vols., 1893.
NORDEN, H. *White and Black in East Africa*, 1924.
Report of the East African Commission, *Cmd.* 2387, 1925.
ROSS, W. M. *Kenya from Within*, 1927.

INDEX

Agriculture, scientific, 45, 487.
Air transport, 80–1
All Red cable, 80.
All Red route, 340.
Annual industrial censuses, 6.
Australia, abolition of transportation,
9 ; agricultural machinery manufacture, 40 ; agriculture, importance
of rainfall, 28, 32 ; agriculture,
labour shortage, 28 ; pasture to
arable, 32 ; importance of
machinery, 33 ; arbitration, failure
of, 42 *nn.* ; artesian bores, 33 ;
Asiatics, fear of, 49 ; boots, 6 ;
closer settlement, 9, 31 ; cloth, 6,
39 ; coal, 40 ; cold storage, importance, 32 ; emigration difficulties,
86 ; Federation, 15, 16 ; fiscal
freedom, 61 ; gold, 6 ; at Ballarat,
12 ; attracts immigrants, 13, 94 ;
promotes railways, 13 ; spreads
settlement, 14 ; Coolgardie goldfield
532 ; Government aid, reasons, 45 ;
Imperial Preference, 68 ; with
Canada, 383 ; Indian trade, 24 ;
Industrial Revolution, 9–10 ; iron,
39–40 ; Labour movement, strength
of, 41–2 ; fear of immigration, 94,
96, 98 ; land disposal, 94 ; loan in
New York, 76 ; problem of convict
emancipation, 9 ; Protectionism,
48 ; railways, different gauges, 15,
22 ; built by States, 21 ; serve
existing traffic, 22 ; expensive to
construct, 22 ; heavy indebtedness,
22–3 ; State policies, 46 ; Sectional-
ism, 48 ; sheep farms, 43 ; shipping,
importance, 24 ; State Line, 24 ;
antipathy to Rings, 24 ; " Socialisme
sans doctrine," 42 ; squattocracy,
31 ; Syme, David, 63 ; tin in
Tasmania, 14 ; towns, growth
of, 41 ; Tropical Australia, development, 99–100 ; wheat, recent importance, 32 ; handled in bags, 35 ;
" White Australia " policy, 9, 13,
42 ; wool, 6, 23, 32 ; develops
capitalism, 13 ; great importance,
35 ; bounties on manufacture, 39.

Balfour Committee on Industry and
Trade, 72.

Balfour of Burleigh Committee, 70.
Barter, in human beings, 4 ; in rum, 5 ;
in Canada, 116, 121, 135, 157–60,
200, 202, 215, 246.
Beam wireless, 80.
Belgian Congo copper, 537.

CANADA :
Abitibi Pulp Mills, 573
Acadie, 142 ; Acadians deported, 143.
Agricultural machinery manufacture,
39, 552–3.
Agriculture (*see also under*
" Farming "), cheap credit, 27 ;
small men, 28 ; labour shortage, 28 ;
machinery importance, 33 ; develop-
ment, 485–93 ; State Aid, 493–8 ;
credit facilities, 521–6.
Aircraft, manifold uses, 81, 575.
Alaska, 477, 481.
Alaska Commercial Company, 481.
Alberta (*see also* " North West " and
" Prairie Provinces ") ; advantages
of alfalfa, 450 ; advantages of
irrigation, 449 ; encourages small-
holdings, 449 ; Alberta Co-operative
Elevator Company, 513 ; forms
United Grain Growers, Ltd.,
513 ; Alberta Co-operative Wheat
Producers, Ltd., 519, 520 ; Alberta
Irrigation Company, 452 ; area of
dry lands, 448 ; Bow River irrigation scheme, 451–2 ; Canada Land
and Irrigation Company, 452 ;
Canadian Pacific Railway's irrigation
area, 452 ; " Chinook " winds, 448 ;
close settlement, 452–3 ; coal, 486,
539 ; crop failures and Government
relief, 494 ; dry farming, 499 ;
farming importance, 499 ; formation
of Province, 397, 500 ; gas, natural,
543 ; growth of Province, 398 ; horse-
breeding, 444 ; irrigated land sales,
452 ; irrigation, 111, 448–53,
499 ; irrigation methods, 450–1 ;
Mormons, 411 ; North-West Irrigation Act, 451 ; oil, 544 ; primitive
irrigation, 450 ; rust losses, 497 ;
settlement (*see under* " North-West
settlement ") ; suited for stock,
445 ; Territorial Grain Growers'
Association, 511 ; wheat, 488 ;

601

Printed in Great Britain by Stephen Austin & Sons, Ltd., Hertford.

LIST OF STUDIES IN ECONOMICS AND POLITICAL SCIENCE

Series of Monographs by Lecturers and Students connected with the London School of Economics and Political Science

EDITED BY THE

DIRECTOR OF THE LONDON SCHOOL OF ECONOMICS AND POLITICAL SCIENCE

*Volumes marked thus * are out of print*

1. The History of Local Rates in England. The substance of five lectures given at the School in November and December, 1895. By EDWIN CANNAN, M.A., LL.D. 1896 ; second enlarged edition, 1912 ; reprinted 1927 ; xv, 215 pp., Crown 8vo, cloth. 6s. net.
P. S. King & Son.

2. Select Documents Illustrating the History of Trade Unionism. I.—THE TAILORING TRADE. By F. W. GALTON. With a Preface by SIDNEY WEBB, LL.B. 1896 ; 242 pp., Crown 8vo, cloth. 5s.
P. S. King & Son.

*3. German Social Democracy. Six lectures delivered at the School in February and March, 1896. By the HON. BERTRAND RUSSELL, B.A., late Fellow of Trinity College, Cambridge. With an Appendix on Social Democracy and the Woman Question in Germany. By ALYS RUSSELL, B.A. 1896 ; 204 pp., Crown 8vo, cloth. 3s. 6d.
P. S. King & Son.

4. The Referendum in Switzerland. By M. SIMON DEPLOIGE, University of Louvain. With a Letter on the Referendum in Belgium by M. J. VAN DEN HEUVEL, Professor of International Law in the University of Louvain. Translated by C. P. TREVELYAN, M.A., Trinity College, Cambridge, and edited with Notes, Introduction, Bibliography, and Appendices by LILIAN TOMN (Mrs. Knowles), of Girton College, Cambridge, Research Student at the School. 1898 : x, 334 pp., Crown 8vo, cloth. 7s. 6d. *P. S. King & Son.*

*5. The Economic Policy of Colbert. By A. J. SARGENT, M.A., Senior Hulme Exhibitioner, Brasenose College, Oxford ; and Whately Prizeman, 1897, Trinity College, Dublin. 1899 ; viii, 138 pp., Crown 8vo, cloth. 2s. 6d. *P. S. King & Son.*

*6. Local Variations in Wages. By F. W. LAWRENCE, M.A., Fellow of Trinity College, Cambridge. 1899 ; viii, 90 pp., with Index and 18 Maps and Diagrams. Quarto, 11 in. by 8½ in., cloth. 8s. 6d.
Longmans, Green & Co.

*7. The Receipt Roll of the Exchequer for Michaelmas Term of the Thirty-first Year of Henry II. (1185). A unique fragment transcribed and edited by the Class in Palæography and Diplomatic, under the supervision of the Lecturer, HUBERT HALL, F.S.A., of H.M. Public Record Office. With thirty-one Facsimile Plates in Collotype and Parallel readings from the contemporary Pipe Rill. 1899 ; vii, 37 pp., Folio.

LIST OF STUDIES

*17. India and the Tariff Problem. By H. B. LEES SMITH, M.A.
M.P. 1909 ; 120 pp., Crown 8vo, cloth. 3s. 6d. net.

Constable & Co.

*18. Practical Notes on the Management of Elections. Three
Lectures delivered at the School in November, 1909, by ELLIS T.
POWELL, LL.B., D.Sc. (Econ.), London. 52 pp., 8vo, paper. 1s. 6d. net.

P. S. King & Son.

*19. The Political Development of Japan. By G. E. UYEHARA,
B.A., Washington, D.Sc. (Econ.), London. xxiv, 296 pp., Demy
8vo, cloth. 1910. 8s. 6d. net. *Constable & Co.*

20. National and Local Finance. By J. WATSON GRICE, D.Sc.
(Econ.), London. Preface by SIDNEY WEBB, LL.B. 1910 ; 428 pp.,
Demy 8vo, cloth. 12s. net. *P. S. King & Son.*

*21. An Example of Communal Currency. Facts about the
Guernsey Market-house. By J. THEODORE HARRIS, B.A., with an
Introduction by SIDNEY WEBB, LL.B. 1911 ; xiv, 62 pp., Crown
8vo, cloth. 1s. 6d. net. *P. S. King & Son.*

22. Municipal Origins. History of Private Bill Legislation. By
F. H. SPENCER, LL.B., D.Sc. (Econ.), London ; with a Preface by
Sir EDWARD CLARKE, K.C. 1911 ; xi, 333 pp., Demy 8vo, cloth.
10s. 6d. net. *Constable & Co.*

23. Seasonal Trades. By VARIOUS AUTHORS. With an Introduction by SIDNEY WEBB. Edited by SIDNEY WEBB, LL.B., and
ARNOLD FREEMAN, M.A. 1912 ; xi, 410 pp., Demy 8vo, cloth. 7s. 6d net.

Constable & Co.

24. Grants in Aid. A Criticism and a Proposal. By SIDNEY
WEBB, LL.B. 1911 ; vii, 135 pp., Demy 8vo, cloth. 5s. net.

Longmans, Green & Co.

25. The Panama Canal : A Study in International Law. By H.
ARIAS, B.A., LL.D., 1911 ; xiv, 188 pp., 2 maps, bibliography. Demy
8vo, cloth. 10s. 6d. net. *P. S. King & Son.*

26. Combination Among Railway Companies. By W. A.
ROBERTSON, B.A. 1912 ; 105 pp., Demy 8vo, cloth. 1s. 6d. net ;
paper, 1s. net. *Constable & Co.*

*27. War and the Private Citizen : Studies in International Law.
By A. PEARCE HIGGINS, M.A., LL.D ; with Introductory Note by
the Rt. Hon. Arthur Cohen, K.C. 1912 ; xvi, 200 pp., Demy 8vo,
cloth. 5s. net. *P. S. King & Son.*

*28. Life in an English Village : An Economic and Historical
Survey of the Parish of Corsley, in Wiltshire. By M. F. DAVIES, 1909 ;
xiii, 319 pp., illustrations, bibliography, Demy 8vo, cloth, 10s. 6d. net.

T. Fisher Unwin.

*29. **English Apprenticeship and Child Labour :** A History. By O. JOCELYN DUNLOP, D.Sc. (Econ.), London ; with a Supplementary Section on the Modern Problem of Juvenile Labour, by the Author and R. D. DENMAN, M.P. 1912 ; 390 pp., bibliography, Demy 8vo, cloth. 10s. 6d. net. *T. Fisher Unwin.*

*30. **Origin of Property and the Formation of the Village Community.** By J. ST. LEWINSKI, D.Ec.Sc., Brussels. 1913 ; xi, 71 pp., Demy 8vo, cloth. 3s. 6d. net. *Constable & Co.*

*31. **The Tendency towards Industrial Combination (in some Spheres of British Industry).** By G. R. CARTER, M.A. 1913 ; xxiii. 391 pp., Demy 8vo, cloth. 6s. net. *Constable & Co.*

*32. **Tariffs at Work ;** An Outline of Practical Tariff Administration. By JOHN HEDLEY HIGGINSON, B.Sc. (Econ.), London, Mitchel-Student of the University of London ; Cobden Prizeman and Silver Medallist. 1913 ; 150 pp., Crown 8vo, cloth. 2s. 6d. net. *P. S. King & Son.*

*33. **English Taxation, 1640-1799.** An Essay on Policy and Opinion. By WILLIAM KENNEDY, M.A., D.Sc. (Econ.), London ; Shaw Research Student of the London School of Economics and Political Science. 1913 ; 200 pp., Demy 8vo. 7s. 6d. net. *G. Bell & Sons.*

34. **Emigration from the United Kingdom to North America, 1763-1912.** By STANLEY C. JOHNSON, M.A., Cambridge, D.Sc. (Econ.), London. 1913 ; xvi, 387 pp., Demy 8vo, cloth. 7s. 6d. net. *George Routledge & Sons.*

35. **The Financing of the Hundred Years' War, 1337-60.** By SCHUYLER B. TERRY. 1913 ; xvi, 199 pp., Demy 8vo, cloth. 6s. net. *Constable & Co.*

36. **Kinship and Social Organization.** By W. H. R. RIVERS, M.D., F.R.S., Fellow of St. John's College, Cambridge. 1914 ; 96 pp., Demy 8vo, cloth. 2s. 6d. net. *Constable & Co.*

37. **The Nature and First Principle of Taxation.** By ROBERT JONES, D.Sc. (Econ.), London ; with a Preface by SIDNEY WEBB, LL.B. 1914 ; xvii, 299 pp., Demy 8vo, cloth. 8s. 6d. net. *P. S. King & Son.*

*38. **The Export of Capital.** By C. K. HOBSON, M.A., D.Sc. (Econ.), London, F.S.S., Shaw Research Student of the London School of Economics and Political Science. 1914 ; xxv, 264 pp., Demy 8vo, cloth. 7s. 6d. net. *Constable & Co.*

39. **Industrial Training.** By NORMAN BURRELL DEARLE, M.A., D.Sc. (Econ.), London, Fellow of All Souls' College, Oxford ; Shaw Research Student of the London School of Economics and Political Science. 1914 ; 610 pp., Demy 8vo, cloth. 10s. 6d. net. *P S. King & Son.*

LIST OF STUDIES

*40. Theory of Rates and Fares. From the French of Charles Colson's " Transports et tarifs " (3rd edn., 1907), by L. R. CHRISTIE, G. LEEDHAM and C. TRAVIS. Edited and arranged by CHARLES TRAVIS, with an Introduction by W. M. ACWORTH, M.A. 1914 ; viii, 195 pp., Demy 8vo, cloth. 3s. 6d. net. *G. Bell & Sons Ltd.*

41. Advertising : A Study of a Modern Business Power. By G. W. GOODALL, B.Sc. (Econ.), London ; with an Introduction by SIDNEY WEBB, LL.B. 1914 ; xviii, 91 pp., Demy 8vo, cloth. 2s. 6d. net ; paper, 1s. 6d. net. *Constable & Co.*

42. English Railways : Their Development and their Relation to the State. By EDWARD CARNEGIE CLEVELAND-STEVENS, M.A., Christ Church, Oxford ; D.Sc. (Econ.), London ; Shaw Research Student of the London School of Economics and Political Science. 1915 ; xvi, 325 pp., Demy 8vo., cloth. 7s. 6d. net. *George Routledge & Sons.*

*43. The Lands of the Scottish Kings in England. By MARGARET F. MOORE, M.A., ; with an Introduction by P. HUME BROWN, M.A., LL.D., D.D., Professor of Ancient Scottish History and Palæography, University of Edinburgh. 1915 ; xii, 141 pp., Demy 8vo cloth. 5s. net. *George Allen & Unwin.*

44. The Colonization of Australia, 1829-42 ; The Wakefield Experiment in Empire Building. By RICHARD C. MILLS, LL.M., Melbourne ; D.Sc. (Econ.), London ; with an Introduction by GRAHAM WALLAS, M.A., Professor of Political Science in the University of London. 1915 ; xx, 363 pp., Demy 8vo, cloth. 10s. 6d. net. *Sidgwick & Jackson.*

45. The Philosophy of Nietzsche. By A. WOLF, M.A., D.Lit., Fellow of University College, London ; Reader in Logic and Ethics in the University of London. 1915 ; 114 pp., Demy 8vo, cloth, 3s. 6d. net. *Constable & Co.*

46. English Public Health Administration. By B. G. BANNINGTON with a Preface by GRAHAM WALLAS, M.A., Professor of Political Science in the University of London. 1915 ; second (revised) edition, 1929 ; xvi, 325 pp., Demy 8vo, cloth. 15s. net. *P. S. King & Son.*

47. British Incomes and Property : The Application of Official Statistics to Economic Problems. By SIR JOSIAH STAMP, K.B.E., D.Sc., Guy Medallist of the Royal Statistical Society, late of the Inland Revenue Department. With illustrative charts. 1916 ; second edition, 1920. xvi, 538 pp., Demy 8vo, cloth. 15s. net. *P. S. King & Son.*

*48. Village Government in British India. By JOHN MATTHAI. D.Sc. (Econ.), London ; with a Preface by SIDNEY WEBB, LL.B., Professor of Public Administration in the University of London, 1915 ; xix, 211 pp., Demy 8vo, cloth. 4s. 6d. net. *T. Fisher Unwin.*

49. Welfare Work : Employer's Experiments for Improving Working Conditions in Factories. By E. D. PROUD (Mrs. Gordon Pavy), B.A., Adelaide ; D.Sc. (Econ.), London ; with a Foreword by the Rt. Hon D. Lloyd George, M.P. Prime Minister. 1916 ; 3rd. edn. 1918 ; xx, 368 pp., Demy 8vo, cloth. 8s. 6d. net. *George Bell & Sons.*

50. The Development of Rates of Postage. By A. D. SMITH. D.Sc. (Econ.) London, F.S.S., of the Secretary's Office, General Post Office; with an Introduction by the Rt. Hon. HERBERT SAMUEL, M.P., Postmaster-General, 1910-16. 1917; xii, 431 pp. Demy 8vo, cloth. 16s. net. *George Allen & Unwin.*

51. Metaphysical Theory of the State. By L. T. HOBHOUSE, M.A., Martin White Professor of Sociology in the University of London. 1918; 156 pp., Demy 8vo, cloth. 7s. 6d. net.

George Allen & Unwin.

52. Outlines of Social Philosophy By J. S. MACKENZIE, M.A., Professor of Logic and Philosophy in the University College of South Wales. 1918; 280 pp., Demy 8vo, cloth. 10s. 6d. net.

George Allen & Unwin.

53. Economic Phenomena Before and After War. By SLAVKO SECEROV, Ph.D., M.Sc. (Econ.), London, F.S.S. 1919; viii., 226 pp., Demy 8vo, cloth. 10s. 6d. net. *George Routledge & Sons.*

*54. Gold, Prices, and the Witwaterstrand. By R. A. LEHFELDT, D.Sc., Professor of Economics at the South African School of Mines and Technology, Johannesburg (University of South Africa); Correspondent for South Africa of the Royal Economic Society. 1919; 130 pp., Crown 8vo, cloth. 5s. net. *P. S. King & Son.*

55. Exercises in Logic. By A. WOLF, M.A., D.Lit., Fellow of University College, London; Reader in Logic and Ethics in the University of London. 1919; 78 pp., Crown 8vo, paper. 3s. net.

George Allen & Unwin.

56. Working Life of English Women in the 17th Century. By ALICE CLARK, Shaw Research Student of the London School of Economics and Political Science. 1919; viii, 328 pp., Demy 8vo, cloth. 10s. 6d. net. *George Routledge & Sons.*

57. Animal Foodstuffs; their Production and Consumption with special reference to the British Empire. By E. W. SHANAHAN, M.A., New Zealand; D.Sc. (Econ.), London. 1920; viii, 331 pp., Demy 8vo, cloth. 10s. 6d. net. *George Routledge & Sons.*

58. Commercial Advertising. A course of lectures given at the School. By THOMAS RUSSELL, President of the Incorporated Society of Advertisement Consultants; sometime Advertisement Manager of the *Times*. 1919; x, 306 pp., Demy 8vo, cloth. 10s. 6d. net.

G. P. Putnam's Sons.

59. Some Aspects of The Inequality of Incomes in Modern Communities. By HUGH DALTON, M.A., D.Sc. (Econ.), 1920. Third edition 1929; 390 pp., Demy 8vo, cloth. 10s. 6d. net. *George Routledge & Sons.*

60. History of Social Development. From the German of F. Muller-Lyer's " Phasen der Kultur," 1908 by E. C. and H. A. LAKE.

George Allen & Unwin.

LIST OF STUDIES

61.—The Industrial and Commercial Revolutions in Great Britain during the Nineteenth Century.
By LILIAN C. A. KNOWLES, Litt.D., Dublin ; Hist. Tripos and Law Tripos, Girton College, Cambridge ; Reader in Economic History in the University of London. 1921 ; xii, 416 pp., Demy 8vo, cloth. Fifth Edition 1927 ; 7s. 6d. net. *George Routledge & Sons.*

62.—Tariffs : a Study in Method.
By T. E. G. GREGORY, B.Sc. (Econ.), London ; Sir Ernest Cassel, Reader in Commerce in the University of London. 1921 ; xv, 518 pp., Demy 8vo, cloth. 25s. net. *Charles Griffin & Co.*

63.—The Theory of Marginal Value.
Nine Lectures delivered at the School in Michaelmas Term, 1920. By L. V. BIRCK, M.A., D.Ec. Sc., Professor of Economics and Finance in the University of Copenhagen. 1922 ; viii, 351 pp., Demy 8vo, cloth. 14s. net. *George Routledge & Sons.*

64.—The Principle of Official Independence.
By R. McGREGOR DAWSON, M.Sc. (Econ.), London., M.A. 1922 ; xv, 268 pp. Demy 8vo, cloth. 10s. 6d. net. *P. S. King & Son.*

65.—Argonauts of the Western Pacific.
An account of Native Enterprise and Adventure in the Archipelagoes of Eastern New Guinea. By BRONISLAW MALINOWSKI, Ph.D., D.Sc., 1922 ; xxxii, 528 pp., with 5 Maps and 66 Plates. Royal 8vo. 21s. net. *George Routledge & Sons.*

66.—Principles of Public Finance.
By HUGH DALTON, M.A., D.Sc. (Econ.), M.P. Fifth Edition, 1929 ; xvi, 298 pp., Crown 8vo, cloth, 5s. net. *George Routledge & Sons.*

67.—Commercial Relations between India and England.
By BAL KRISHNA, Ph.D. (Econ.), London, M.A., F.S.S. ; Principal Rajaram College, Kolhapur, Bombay. 1924 ; xxii, 370 pp., Demy 8vo, cloth. 14s. net. *George Routledge & Sons.*

68.—Wages in the Coal Industry.
By J. W. F. ROWE, B.A., Cambridge. 1923 ; (viii) 174 pp., Demy 8vo, cloth. 10s. 6d. net. *P. S. King & Son.*

69.—The Co-operative Movement in Japan.
By KIYOSHI OGATA, B.Com., Tokyo. Preface by Professor SIDNEY WEBB, LL.B., M.P. 1923 ; xv, 362 pp., Demy 8vo, cloth. 12s.6d. net. *P. S. King & Son.*

70.—The British Trade Boards System.
By DOROTHY SELLS, M.A., Ph.D. 1923 ; vii, 293 pp., Demy 8vo, cloth. 12s. 6d. net. *P. S. King & Son.*

71.—Second chambers in Theory and Practice.
By H. B. LEES-SMITH, M.A. 1923 ; 256 pp., Demy 8vo. cloth. 7s. 6d. net. *George Allen & Unwin.*

72.—Chinese Coolie Emigration to Countries within the British Empire.
By PERSIA CRAWFORD CAMPBELL, M.A. (Sydney) ; M.Sc. (Econ.), London ; British Fellow of Bryn Mawr College, U.S.A. 1922-23. Preface by Hon. W. PEMBER REEVES, Ph.D. 1923 ; xxiii, 240 pp., Demy 8vo, cloth. 10s. 6d. net. *P. S. King & Son.*

73.—The rôle of the State in the provision of Railways.
By H. M. JAGTIANI, M.Sc. (Econ.), London, Barrister-at-Law ; B.A., LL.B., Bombay. Introduction by Sir WILLIAM ACWORTH, K.C.S.I. 1924 ; xi, 146 pp., Demy 8vo, cloth. 8s. 6d. net. *P. S. King & Son.*

74.—Dock Labour and Decasualisation.
By E. C. P. LASCELLES and S. S. BULLOCK, *Ratan Tata* Research Student, London School of Economics. 1924 ; xi, 201 pp., Demy 8vo, cloth. 10s. 6d. net. *P. S. King & Son.*

75.—Labour and Housing in Bombay.
By A. R. BURNETT-HURST, M.Sc. (Econ.), London ; Professor, and Dean of the Faculties of Commerce and Economics, University of Allahabad. 1925 ; xiv, 152 pp., Demy 8vo, cloth. 10s. 6d. *P. S. King & Son.*

76.—The Economic Development of the British Overseas Empire 1763-1914.
By L. C. A. KNOWLES, M.A., Litt.D., Trinity Coll., Dublin ; Lecturer at the London School of Economics. 1924 ; Revised Edn. 1928, xvi, 556 pp., Demy 8vo, cloth. 10s. 6d. net. *George Routledge & Sons.*

77.—Unemployment Relief in Great Britain : a study in State Socialism.
By FELIX MORLEY. 1924 ; xvii, 204 pp. Large Crown 8vo, cloth, 6s. net. *George Routledge & Sons.*

78.—Economic Conditions in India. By P. PADMANABHA PILLAI, B.A., B.L., Ph.D. (Econ.). With Introductory Note by GILBERT SLATER. M.A., D.Sc. (Econ.). 1925 ; xviii, 330 pp., Demy 8vo, cloth. 12s. 6d. net. *George Routledge & Sons.*

79.—The Law relating to Public Service Undertakings (excluding transport). By FRANK NOEL KEEN, LL.B., Barrister-at-Law. 1925 ; xii, 320 pp., Demy 8vo, cloth. 15s. net. *P. S. King & Son.*

80.—Social Aspects of the Business Cycle. By DOROTHY SWAINE THOMAS, A.B. (Columbia) ; Ph.D. (Econ.), London ; Hutchinson Research Medallist of the London School of Economics. 1925 ; xvi, 218 pp., Royal 8vo, cloth. 10s. 6d. net. *George Routledge & Sons.*

81.—Capitalist Enterprise and Social Progress. By MAURICE HERBERT DOBB, B.A. (Cambridge) ; Research Student of the London School of Economics. 1925 ; x, 410 pp., Demy 8vo, cloth, 12s. 6d. net. *George Routledge & Sons.*

82.—Has Poverty Diminished ? By ARTHUR LYON BOWLEY, D.Sc., F.B.A., Trinity College, Cambridge ; Professor of Statistics in the University of London, and MARGARET H. HOGG, M.A., Newnham College Cambridge, formerly Assistant in the Statistical Department, London School of Economics. 1925 ; viii, 236 pp. Demy 8vo, cloth. 10s. 6d. net. *P. S. King & Son.*

LIST OF STUDIES

83.—Some Problems of Wages and their Regulation. By ALLAN
G. B. FISHER, B.A., Melbourne ; Ph.D. (Econ.), London. 1926 ; xviii,
287 pp., Demy 8vo, cloth. 12s. 6d. net.   *P. S. King & Son.*

84.—Factory Legislation and its Administration. By HENRY A.
MESS, B.A., *Ratan Tata* Research Student, London School of Economics.
1926 ; xii, 228 pp., Demy 8vo, cloth. 12s. 6d. net.   *P. S. King & Son.*

85.—Economic Development of Russia. By MARGARET S. MILLER,
M.A., B.Com., Edinburgh; Ph.D. (Econ.), London. 1926 ; xviii, 311 pp.
Demy 8vo, cloth. 12s. 6d. net.   *P. S. King & Son.*

**86.—Wages and the State : a Comparative Study of the Problems
of State Wage Regulation.** By (Mrs.) EVELINE M. BURNS, D.Sc. (Econ.)
London Assistant in the Department of Economics, London School of
Economics. 1926. x, 443 pp., Demy 8vo., cloth. 16s. net.
                                        P. S. King & Son.

**87.—The Origin and Early History of Insurance including the
Contract of Bottomry.** By C. F. TRENERRY, B.A., D.Sc., A.I.A.
1926 ; xiv, 330 pp., Demy 8vo, cloth. 15s. net.   *P. S. King & Son.*

**88.—Social Progress and Educational Waste ; a study of the
"Free-Place" and Scholarship System.** By KENNETH LINDSAY, B.A.,
Oxon. With a Preface by Viscount HALDANE. 1926 ; viii, 216 pp.,
Demy 8vo, cloth. 7s. 6d. net.   *George Routledge & Sons.*

89.—The Economic Revolution in British West Africa. By
ALLAN MCPHEE, M.A., B.Com., Ph.D. 1926 ; xiv, 322 pp., Demy
8vo, cloth. 12s. 6d. net.   *George Routledge & Sons.*

90.—Indian Railways : Rates and Regulations. By N. B. MEHTA,
Ph.D. (Econ.), London. 1927 ; xi, 188 pp., Demy 8vo, cloth. 10s. 6d. net.
                                        P. S. King & Son.

91.—Income Tax in Great Britain and the U.S.A. By HARRISON
B. SPAULDING, B.A., (Toronto). 1927 ; 320 pp., Demy 8vo, cloth.
12s. net.   *P. S. King & Son.*

92.—London Essays in Economics. A Volume in Honour of
EDWIN CANNAN. Edited by Professor T. E. GREGORY and Dr. HUGH
DALTON, M.P. Introductory Note by Sir WILLIAM BEVERIDGE, K.C.B.
1927 ; xii, 376 pp., Demy 8vo, cloth. 10s. 6d. net.
                                        George Routledge & Sons.

93.—Foreign Diplomacy in China. By PHILIP JOSEPH, LL.B.
(McGill), Ph.D. (London). 1928 ; 458 pp., Demy 8vo, cloth, 16s. net.
                                        Allen & Unwin.

94.—Wages in Theory and Practice. By J. W. F. ROWE, M.A.,
M.Sc. 1928 ; x, 277 pp., Demy 8vo, cloth, 12s. 6d. net.
                                        George Routledge & Sons.

LIST OF STUDIES

95.—History of French Colonial Policy, 1870-1925. By STEPHEN H. ROBERTS, M.A., Professor of History, University of Sydney. 1929. 2 vols. xvi, 700 pp., Royal 8vo, cloth. 42s. net. *P. S. King & Son.*

96.—Clothing Workers of Great Britain. By S. P. DOBBS, B.A. 1928; xiv, 216 pp., Demy 8vo, cloth. 10s. 6d. net.
George Routledge & Sons.

97.—Allegiance in Church and State: the Problem of the Non-jurors in the English Revolution. By L. M. HAWKINS. 1928; viii, 200 pp., Crown 8vo, cloth. 6s. net. *George Routledge & Sons.*

98. Economics of Inheritance. By JOSIAH WEDGWOOD. 1929; xviii, 276 pp. Demy 8vo, cloth, 12s. 6d. net. *George Routledge & Sons.*

99. Economic Control, with special reference to Australia. By N. SKENE SMITH, B.Com. (London). 1929; 330 pp., Demy 8vo, cloth. 15s. net. *P. S. King & Son.*

100. The Chronicle of Melrose. A complete facsimile edition, in full-size collotype plates, of the original manuscript in the British Museum. Edited with an index and an introduction by W. C. DICKINSON, M.A., D.Litt., and A. O. ANDERSON, M.A. (In the press.)

101.—Nationality: its Nature and Problems. By BERNARD JOSEPH, B.A., B.C.L. (McGill), Ph.D. (London). 1929; xii, 380 pp., Demy 8vo, cloth. 10s. 6d. net. *Allen & Unwin.*

102. Evolution of the Indian Income Tax. By J. P. NIYOGI, M.A., B.L. (Cal.), 1929; viii, 326 pp. Demy 8vo, cloth, 12s. 6d. net.
P. S. King & Son.

103. Economic Development of the British Overseas Empire— Vol. II. By the late LILIAN C. A. KNOWLES, M.A., LL.M. (Cantab.) Litt. D., and C. M. KNOWLES, LL.B. 1930; xxiv, 616 pp. (In the press)
George Routledge & Sons.

104. Gabriel Bonnot de Mably. By E. A. WHITFIELD. (In the press). *George Routledge & Sons.*

LIST OF STUDIES

Monographs on Sociology

3. The Material Culture and Social Institutions of the Simpler Peoples. By L. T. HOBHOUSE, M.A., Martin White Professor of Sociology in the University of London, G. C. WHEELER, B.A., and M. GINSBERG, B.A. 1915. 300 pp., Demy 8vo, paper (reprinting).
Chapman & Hall.

4. Village and Town Life in China. By TAO LI KUNG, B.Sc. (Econ.), London, and LEONG YEW KOH, LL.B., B.Sc (Econ.), London. Edited by L. T. HOBHOUSE, M.A. 1915; repr. 1924; 170 pp., Demy 8vo, cloth. 6s. net.
George Allen & Unwin.

Series of Bibliographies

1. A Bibliography of Unemployment and the Unemployed. By F. ISABEL TAYLOR, B.Sc. (Econ.), London. Preface by SIDNEY WEBB, LL.B. 1909; xix, 71 pp., Demy 8vo, cloth, 2s. net; paper, 1s. 6d. net.
P. S. King & Son.

2. Two Select Bibliographies of Mediaeval Historical Study. By MARGARET F. MOORE, M.A.; with Preface and Appendix by HUBERT HALL, F.S.A. 1912; 185 pp., Demy 8vo, cloth. 5s. net.
Constable & Co.

3. Bibliography of Roadmaking and Roads in the United Kingdom. By DOROTHY BALLEN, B.Sc. (Econ.), London; an enlarged and revised edition of a similar work compiled by Mr. and Mrs. Sidney Webb in 1906. 1914; xviii, 281 pp., Demy 8vo, cloth. 15s. net.
P. S. King & Son.

4. A Select Bibliography for the Study, Sources, and Literature of English Mediaeval Economic History. Edited by HUBERT HALL, F.S.A. 1914; xiii, 350 pp., Demy 8vo, cloth. 5s. net.
P. S. King & Son.

5. A Guide to British Parliamentary and Official Publications. By H. B. LEES-SMITH, M.A., Queen's College, Oxford; Lecturer in Public administration in the London School of Economics. 1924; 23 pp., 4to, paper wrapper. 2s. net. *Oxford University Press.*

6. A Select Bibliography of Economic Theory, 1870-1928. Compiled by HAROLD E. BATSON, B.Sc. (Econ.) London; with an Introduction by DR. HUGH DALTON. (In the press).
George Routledge & Sons.

7. A Bibliography of the Monroe Doctrine, 1919-1929. By PHILLIPS BRADLEY. 1930; 40 pp., crown 8vo, paper, 2s. net.
Garden City Press.

Series of Geographical Studies

1. The Reigate Sheet of the One-Inch Ordnance Survey. A Study in the Geography of the Surrey Hills. By ELLEN SMITH. Introduction by H. J. MACKINDER, M.A., M.P. 1910; xix, 110 pp., 6 maps, 23 illustrations. Crown 8vo, cloth. 5s. net. *A. & C. Black.*

*2. The Highlands of South-West Surrey. A Geographical Study in Sand and Clay. By E. C. MATTHEWS. 1911; viii, 124 pp., 7 maps, 8 illustrations. 8vo, cloth. 5s. net. *A. & C. Black.*

LIST OF STUDIES

3. London on the Thames : a Geographical Study. By (Mrs.) HILDA ORMSBY, B.Sc. (Econ.), London. 1924 ; xiv, 190 pp., maps, ills., Demy 8vo, cloth. 8s. 6d. net. *Sifton, Praed & Co.*

Series of Contour Maps of Critical Areas

1. The Hudson-Mohawk Gap. Prepared by the Diagram Company from a map by B. B. DICKINSON. 1913 ; 1 sheet 18 in. by 22½ in. Scale 20 miles to 1 inch. 6d. net ; post free, folded 7d., rolled 9d.
Sifton, Praed & Co.

Studies in Commerce

1.—The True Basis of Efficiency. By LAWRENCE R. DICKSEE, M.Com., F.C.A., Sir Ernest Cassel Professor of Accountancy and Business Methods in the University of London. 1922 ; xi, 90 pp., Demy 8vo, cloth. 5s. net. *Gee & Co.*

2.—The Ship and her Work. By Sir WESTCOTT STILE ABELL, K.B.E., M.Eng., M.I.N.A., M.I.C.E. ; Chief Ship Surveyor, Lloyd's Register of Shipping. 1923 ; 114 pp., 3 diags., etc., 4 tabs., Demy 8vo, cloth. 7s. 6d. net. *Gee & Co.*

3.—Selections of French Handwriting. By E. L. LITTON. 1929 ; pp. (43). 2s. net. *Gee & Co.*

4.—Selections of German Handwriting. By WILLIAM ROSE, M.A., Ph.D. 1929. pp. (74). 3s. 6d. net. *Gee & Co.*

5.—Refrigeration as applied to the Transportation and Storage of Food Products. By E. W. SHANAHAN, M.A., D.Sc. (Econ.). 1929 ; pp. x, 96, Demy 8vo, cloth. 5s. net. *Gee & Co.*

A Tabular Guide to the Foreign Trade Statistics of Twenty-one Principal Countries. By FREDERICK BROWN, B.Sc. (Econ.), London ; Assistant in the Statistical Department, London School of Economics. 1926 ; 125, 33 pp., 4to, paper. 7s. 6d. net. *Students' Bookshops Ltd.*

Edward Fry Library of International Law. Catalogue of the books, pamphlets and other documents in the Library, together with other works bearing on the subject of international law contained in the library of the London School of Economics. Compiled and edited by B. M. HEADICAR, Librarian of the London School of Economics and Secretary to the Trustees of the Edward Fry Library. 1923 ; viii, 174 pp., Demy 8vo, cloth. 5s. net (*with new supplement to 31st May, 1925*). *London School of Economics.*